# Lamont's
# financial glossary

the definitive, plain english, money and
investment dictionary

Tenth edition

Barclay W. Lamont

www.lamontsglossary.com

**First Edition**
printed March 1985
reprinted July 1985
reprinted January 1986
© Lamont & Partners Limited 1985
All rights reserved

**Second Edition**
printed August 1986
reprinted February 1987
© Lamont & Partners Limited 1986
All rights reserved

**Third Edition**
printed January 1988
© Lamont & Partners Limited 1988
All rights reserved

**Fourth Edition**
printed April 1989
© Lamont & Partners Plc 1989
All rights reserved

**Fifth Edition**
printed September 1990
© IPS Lamont Plc 1990
All rights reserved

**Sixth Edition**
printed April 1993
© B.W. Lamont 1993
All rights reserved

**Seventh Edition**
printed October 1996
© B.W. Lamont 1996
All rights reserved

**Eighth Edition**
printed January 1997
© B.W. Lamont 1997
All rights reserved

**Ninth Edition**
printed March 2004
© B.W. Lamont 2004
All rights reserved

**Tenth Edition**
printed August 2009
©Taxbriefs 2009
All rights reserved

Taxbriefs Limited
2-5 Benjamin Street
London EC1M 5QL

Telephone 020 7250 0967
Facsimile 020 7251 8867
Email info@taxbriefs.co.uk
www.taxbriefs.co.uk

ISBN 978-1-905482-32-0

British Library Cataloguing-in-Publication Data. A catalogue record for this book is available from the British Library.

Printed in Great Britian by the MPG Books Group, Bodmin and Kings Lynn.

# Foreword

This new tenth edition marks a major milestone in the development of the glossary into the most comprehensive financial dictionary covering UK and European financial terminology.

Marked by the co-operation with Taxbriefs as the new publisher and the collapse of the western world's banking system, there has been a significant increase in the number of definitions and a marked upgrading of the scope of definitions and areas covered.

When the glossary was first published in 1985 professor Jim Gower, architect of the 1986 Financial Services Act, was kind enough to write the foreword to the first edition. In it he said he hoped: "...advances in automation and technology do not result in those offering financial services being allowed to forget that, directly or indirectly, it is the public that they serve."

Well, how completely the credit crunch has confirmed his fears. By the turn of the century the financial services and banking industry had become more and more preoccupied with esoteric and complex financial products far removed from the requirements of their customers. The zero sum game had become almost the only game in town; and the ability of even sophisticated investors to fully grasp the implications of many types of wholesale investment all but lost. Warren Buffett had earlier described derivatives as weapons of financial destruction – and also suggested that you shouldn't invest in something you don't understand.

A proper understanding is a key prerequisite to avoiding misfortune and whilst it does not guarantee riches, it offers the participant at least an informed choice. Investors big and small need to be better informed about their choices and the choices being made for them. Recent financial turmoil has highlighted the lack of transparency in a number of areas where a better understanding of the process by both the customer and the regulator might have resulted in a different outcome. This glossary may help draw the veil of misunderstanding back a fraction for some participants and, if so, perhaps we will be defining fewer terms like ponzi , toxic asset, TARP and quantitative easing in future editions.

Certainly the new generation of bankers and financiers will have learned the lessons of the credit crunch and be more conscious that investment management and investment banking are ultimately there to benefit shareholders and the public who invest their money to provide for their future and protect their savings. Part of this evolution is a greater understanding of the process, the products, the markets and the way they are regulated. The relationship between institutions and their customers must be characterised by mutual trust borne of transparency and understanding rather than concealed by jargon and complexity.

I hope you find the glossary and its website useful and trust it may help you become a little richer or, at least, a little less poor. The financial jungle is inhabited by some pretty fearsome creatures and we need all the help we can get when we deal with them.

## Barclay W. Lamont – 2009

# A

**A-Day** The start date of the *simplified regime* for pensions, 6 April 2006.

**a priori** Known to be true independently of experience of the real world. Economists and other scientists often take a set of assumptions and reach certain conclusions by use of logical deductive reasoning alone (ie without observation and testing empirical data).

**'A' shares** A *class* of *ordinary shares* with different rights, normally affecting voting. A *company* can issue *shares* classed as A and B etc., each of which can have restricted or no *voting rights* but which participate in *profits* and *dividends* in the ordinary way *pari passu* with *ordinary shares*.

**AAA** The triple-A grading is the highest *commercial paper* or *credit rating* applied by *Fitch* or *Standard & Poor's*. See: *credit rating*.

**abbreviated accounts** To alleviate the burden of accounting on small businesses the abbreviated accounts of a *small company* or *limited liability partnership (LLP)* do not have to include the full *balance sheet, profit & loss account* or *directors report* normally required by *Companies House,* but must include: abbreviated *balance sheet* and notes explaining in more detail the make-up of the figures in the *balance sheet* (and a special *auditor's report* – unless the *company* is exempt from an *audit,* i.e. *companies* with a *turnover* of not more than £6.5 million or a *balance sheet* total of not more than £3.26 million).

**ABI** See: *Association of British Insurers.*

**above the line** 1. In modern *UK* accounting practice, above the line refers to items in a *profit & loss account* that show the composition of *profits,* as opposed to how the *profits* are distributed. See: *below the line.* 2. In national *accounts,* such as *balance of payments,* above the line transactions are linked to revenue as opposed to *capital.* 3. In advertising, expenditure specific to the purchase of advertising media (as opposed to *below the line* which is public relations, mail shots, promotions etc.).

**absolute advantage** Term used in *trade theory.* Country A is said to have an absolute advantage in the production of a certain good over country B if A can produce more output of that good than B using the same resource inputs (ie A is more productive than B). Paradoxically, even if country A has an absolute advantage in the production of two goods, X and Y, over country B, there can still be beneficial trade for both countries if country B *exports* the good for which its disadvantage is least (where it has a '*comparative advantage*') and *imports* the good where the *productivity* advantage of A is greatest.

**absolute return** The percentage return that an *asset* or *portfolio* generates in terms of gain or loss made in relation only to the cost of the *asset* or *investment.* Absolute return is different to relative return since relative return is measured against a *benchmark* such as a *stock market index.* An absolute return product would target positive returns regardless of market environment and is a measure often used by *hedge funds.*

**absorption** Term used in *macroeconomics* referring to the total (aggregate) expenditure on final goods and services in an economy. Domestic absorption is thus the expenditure on domestic goods, and equals aggregate consumption plus *investment* plus government expenditure, and is identical to *national income* less *net exports.*

**ACA** Short for: Association of Consultin g Actuaries, Associate of the Institute of Chartered Accountants. See also: *chartered accountant.*

**1**

**ACCA** See: *Chartered Association of Certified Accountants.* See also: *certified accountant.*

**acceleration** In *technical analysis*, a term describing the increase or decrease in the *speed* or *momentum* of a price *trend.*

**accelerator** In macroeconomic theory, the accelerator (also: accelerator coefficient) refers to the amount of *investment* induced by a change in output. Investment and output are linked by the accelerator and the *multiplier* – together these effects are thought to produce a cyclical *pattern* of economic *growth.*

**acceptor** Someone who agrees to pay a *bill of exchange* by signing the face of the *bill* or accepting its *endorsement.*

**accommodation bill** A *bill* that has been signed by a person other than the *acceptor* who guarantees payment of the *bill of exchange* should the *acceptor default.* Accommodation bills are also known as *windbills* or *windmills.*

**accommodation endorser** A party that endorses a loan (ie transfers responsibility) to another party. Should the receiving party (the endorsee of the loan) *default*, the endorser becomes liable as the guarantor.

**account** Formerly a period of time on the *London Stock Exchange* during which dealings were settled. Settlement was generally made ten days after the end of the account, called the *account day* (or settlement day). Account days fell on Mondays, and clients received statements on preceding Thursdays, which allowed time for settlement. Rolling settlement has now been introduced where all account deals are settled within three days. See: *CREST, T+3.*

**account day** See: *account.*

**Accounts Modernisation Directive** On 28 November 2005 the Chancellor announced that the government would be abolishing the Operating and Financial Review (OFR) requirements for GB-listed businesses in line with the aim of reducing regulatory burden. *Directors* of *listed companies* no longer have to produce an OFR from April 2006 onwards, and are no longer required to report according to the detailed requirements specified by the OFR regulations. The *EU* Accounts Modernisation Directive was intended to increase the comparability between *companies* in the EU through a common reporting framework. To achieve this objective, the Union requires common financial reporting standards that are transparent, fully understood, properly audited and effectively enforced. The Directive brings European accounting requirements in line with modern accounting practice and increases the reporting remit to take account of the growing demand for non-financial comment and *analysis.*

**accountant** A person trained to keep *accounts* and records for individuals and businesses. Normally qualified people, they act as *auditors* and *administrators*, and arbiters in matters related to *tax*, finance and quantum. The *Financial Services Authority* allows accountants with membership of certain organisations (recognised professional bodies – *RPBs*) to give *investment* advice to their clients, as long as this advice does not constitute a major proportion of their business (see: *authorisation*). These *RPBs* are: *Institute of Chartered Accountants in England and Wales,* Institute of Chartered Accountants in Scotland, Institute of Chartered Accountants in Ireland and the *Chartered Association of Certified Accountants.*

**accounting concepts** The generally accepted framework of accounting rests on four assumptions (contained in the Companies Act 1985). The first two represent basic choices between possible alternative accounting systems, whereas the latter two spell out common-sense rules: 1. The *going concern* concept assumes that the business will continue in the foreseeable future; therefore *assets* are valued as such and not at *liquidation* prices or forced sale prices, which are usually lower. 2. The *accruals concept* records revenues (*income*) and costs (expenses) as the business earns or incurs (ie accrues) them. This approach is distinct from *cash accounting* (which preceded *accrual* accounting historically) where a business recorded receiving *money* as *income* and recorded costs as they were paid. Some non-commercial entities, such as the government, still use *cash accounting*. 3. The *consistency concept* calls for all commercial transactions to be accounted for in the same way over time. This is important for comparison purposes. 4. The *prudence concept* proposes a conservative approach to the credit of *income* or *profits* and a pessimistic approach to future liabilities.

**accounting period** See: *tax year*.

**accounting rate of return (ARR)** A term used in *investment appraisal*, the *ARR* is the expected *net profit* of an *investment* divided by the *net book value* of the *assets* invested, usually expressed as a percentage.

**Accounting Standards Board (ASB)** A subsidiary of the *Financial Reporting Council* (*FRC*), the *ASB* was formed following the Companies Act 1989. The *ASB* sets and issues guidelines (*Financial Reporting Standards*) which are designed to improve the standards for *UK* accounting practice, some of which are enforceable by law. See also: *Financial Reporting Review Panel* (*FRRP*), *Urgent Issues Task Force* (*UITF*).

**accounts** The financial reports all *limited liability companies* must prepare and, for larger *companies*, which must be audited. They include a *balance sheet* and a *profit & loss account*. See: *annual report, audit, report and accounts*.

**accounts payable** *US* term for *creditors* (ie suppliers of goods and services to the *company* not yet paid).

**accounts receivable** *US* term for *debtors* (ie parties owing *money* to the *company*).

**accrual** An expense incurred during an *accounting period* but not paid by the end of that period. Also called: accrued charge. See: *accounting concepts*.

**accruals concept** See: *accounting concepts*.

**accrued benefits** A term used to describe *pension* benefits to which a *member* is entitled for service up to a given point, whether the *member* continues in office or not.

**accrued income scheme** For the calculation of *income tax* in the *UK*, when an individual disposes of *fixed interest securities* the *interest* accrued between the last *interest* payment and the disposal date is regarded as *income* of the individual selling the *security*. The buyer need not pay *income tax* on this proportion of the amount received as the next *income* payment.

**accrued interest** 1. Interest due but not yet received or paid. 2. The seller of a *bond* must compensate the buyer for the accrued *interest* since the last *coupon* date. The *bond*'s *dirty price* equals the *clean price* plus accrued *interest*. See: *day count conventions*.

**accumulated contributions** The total contributions to a *pension* scheme for a particular *member*, enhanced where appropriate by *interest* or *growth*.

**accumulation trust** See: *discretionary trusts*.

**accumulation units** Normally applied to *unit trusts*, OEICs or *unit-linked life assurance* funds where *interest* and *dividends* are rolled up or automatically reinvested to increase the unit *value*. In the case of *unit trusts* and OEICs , *income tax* is still payable on the reinvested *income*. In the case of some long-term *unit-linked life assurance* policies, units may be divided between *initial units*, from which the *life assurance company* takes charges, and accumulation units, where only fund management and not *initial charges* are taken.

**acid test ratio**  See: *quick ratio*.

**ACII**  Short for: Associate of the *Chartered Insurance Institute*.

**acquisition**  One *company* taking a *controlling interest* in another. Often *companies* are willing to pay more than the market price of the *shares* if they hope to complete an acquisition. See: *controlling director, subsidiary company*.

**ACT**  See: *advance corporation tax*.

**activity rate**  Proportion of the population who are in work or available for work (ie in the *labour force*). Sometimes defined as the proportion of the population aged 16–65 who are in the *labour force*. Sometimes called the 'participation rate'.

**actuals**  Physical *commodities* or *shares*, as opposed to *futures contracts* and *options*. Also called '*physicals*'.

**actuarial assumptions**  A set of assumptions regarding *inflation*, mortality, *rates of return*, increases in *earnings* etc. used by an *actuary* in valuing pension *liabilities*.

**actuarial certificate**  Certification by an *actuary* most commonly used in *solvency* tests on contracted-out *pension* schemes and for deficit-reduction contributions.

**actuarial valuation**  An assessment of a *pension* scheme by an *actuary* to ascertain whether there are sufficient *assets* to meet liabilities, such as current and future *pension* payments.

**accretion/accretive**  Adding value. An *acquisition* or *target* is considered accretive if it improves the '*value*' of the overall business. If the profitability, *p/e, earnings,* etc. are improved then there is an element of accretion. The big advantage *quoted companies* have is that they can make *acquisitions* by buying private companies with better multiples than theirs by issuing new *shares* and exchanging them for the *target's shares.*

**actuary**  A member of a profession skilled in evaluating and assessing *risks*, particularly those of a long-term and financial nature. Actuaries monitor and advise on the *solvency* of *life assurance companies,* general insurance companies and *pension* funds and have statutory responsibilities in this connection; as a consequence they are usually closely concerned with the setting of *premium* rates and contribution levels. Members of the Institute of Actuaries and of the Faculty of Actuaries.

**ad valorem**  Literally translated from the Latin as 'according to *value*', it is the method of assessing duties or taxes on goods or property as a percentage of the price per item. An example is *value added tax*. Compare: *specific tax.*

**additional state pension**  The earnings-related element of the *state pension* over and above basic *state pension*. See also: *state earnings-related pension scheme.*

**additional voluntary contributions (AVCS)**  Employee members of occupational pension schemes can make additional voluntary contributions to an AVC pension arrangement to secure additional retirement benefits. Such payments will generally qualify for full income tax relief, subject to the employee's total contributions to all pension arrangements not being more than 100% of their UK relevant earnings. AVCs may be closely integrated with the employer's scheme, even if the underlying investments are managed by a third party. Freestanding AVC arrangements, which have no specific scheme link, were offered until A-Day, but have now been replaced by personal pensions.

**adjudication**  1. A court judgment or decision. 2. An *assessment* of the *stamp duty* due on a document made by HMRC.

**adjustable rate mortgage (ARM)**  See: *variable rate mortgage.*

**adjustable rate preferred stock (ARP)**  *US cumulative preference shares* or *stock* with *dividends* linked to the *yield* on *US Treasury bills.*

**adjustment mechanism** A statistical method of removing *balance of payments* surpluses or *deficits*.

**adjustment speed** A comparative measure of the time it takes for a particular market to respond to changes in economic conditions. Foreign exchange, *commodity*, *stock* and *bond* markets are generally quick in adjusting to changes in *supply and demand*. Product markets typically tend to respond more slowly because of the administrative effort involved in changing marked prices. Much slower still is adjustment of the labour market, since wages are usually only revised on an annual basis.

**administration** A court order under the *Insolvency Act 1986* (similar to a *Chapter 11* order in the *US*) where a *company* is protected from its *creditors* with a view to salvaging it as a *going concern*. The *company* is run by an *administrator* who acts much as a *receiver*. The purpose of such an order is to ensure that the business can continue to function, either to overcome short-term difficulties or to be sold or restructured to preserve aspects of the business that would be lost if it were to go into *liquidation*. Also an order effecting an *individual voluntary arrangement*.

**administration order** See: *administration*.

**administrator** An individual given the responsibility of managing someone else's property, particularly an *estate* of someone who was intestate (see: *intestacy*) or who has made an *individual voluntary arrangement* or whose *company* is in *administration* as a result of an *administration order* (see: *administration*).

**ADR** See: *American Depository Receipt*.

**ADST** See: *approved deferred share trust*.

**advance corporation tax (ACT)** Prior to 6 April 1999 *companies* had to pay advance corporation tax on their *dividends* and other qualifying *distributions*. The ACT paid could be set off against any subsequent corporation tax liability. Such *distributions* were then deemed to be *franked income*, which in turn, in the hands of *UK* taxpayers, was deemed to have had *basic rate tax* deducted. A reduced system of imputation remains with the *continuation* of a *tax credit*, which is currently (2009/10) 10%.

**advance decline line** See: *advance decline ratio*.

**advance decline ratio** A barometer of sentiment showing the *ratio* between declining and advancing *stocks* during a predetermined trading period.

**advise fate** Term applied when a *bank* receiving a cheque asks the paying *bank* directly (ie not through a *clearing house*) whether or not the cheque will be paid on receipt.

**AED** *currency code* for: Arab Emirates Dirham.

**AER** See: *Annual Effective Rate*.

**AFA** *currency code* for: *Afghanistan* Afghani.

**AFBD** See: *Association of Futures Brokers and Dealers*.

**affiliate** A *company* that is related to another *company* in some way, more specifically it is when a *company* holds a minority interest in another *company*, typically with 20% to 50% ownership.

**afghani** *Afghanistan*'s standard *currency*. 1 afghani = 100 *puls*.

**Afghanistan** Standard *currency*: afghani. 1 *afghani* = 100 *puls*.

**after hours deal** *Securities* on most markets can be traded after the main exchange has officially closed (on the *kerb*) and these are usually treated as *early bargains* and notified to the exchange when it commences trading the next day.

**AG** Short for German: Aktiengesellschaft. Equivalent to the British: *plc*.

**age allowance** An *allowance* made against *income* for the purposes of calculating *income tax* for a single person 65 years or over or a married couple or civil partnership with at least one member born before 6 April 1935, with an increased *allowance* over age 75. This *personal allowance* reduces by a proportion of total *income* over a certain level (£22,900 in 2009/10).

**agency broker** A *stockbroker* who provides dealing facilities for private clients and institutions but is not a principal *market maker*.

**aggregate demand** The total demand for goods and services from consumers, investors, governments and foreigners in an economy.

**agio** 1. Fee charged by a *bank* or a similar institution for changing foreign *currency*. 2. The difference (*turn*, *spread*) between a *bank*'s *interest rates* for lending and for *borrowing money*.

**AGM** See: *annual general meeting*.

**agora** *Currency* unit of *Israel*. 100 agora = 1 shekel.

**agreed takeover** A *takeover* where the majority of *shareholders* (normally 51%) and the *board* agree to a *bid* when it is launched. Such *bids* are therefore a mere formality. See: *recommended takeover*.

**Agricultural Bank** A *bank* that specialises in providing long-term loans for agricultural development. Also called '*Land Bank*'.

**AIBD** Short for: Association of International Bond Dealers.

**AIC** See: *Association of Investment Companies*.

**aid trade provision (ATP)** An arrangement whereby British aid in the form of subsidised loans is given to developing countries provided they purchase goods and services from *UK companies*. See: *soft loan*.

**AIM** See: *Alternative Investment Market*.

**AIMA** See: *Alternative Investment Management Association*.

**Aktb** Short for Swedish: Aktiebolaget. Equivalent to British: *plc*.

**Al-ajr** Islamic term which refers to *commission*, fees or wages charged for services.

**Al-rahn** Islamic term describing an arrangement whereby a valuable *asset* is placed as *collateral* for a debt. The *collateral* may be disposed of in the event of a *default*.

**Albania** Standard *currency*: lek. 1 lek = 100 qindarka.

**Algeria** Standard *currency*: Algerian *dinar*. 1 *dinar* = 100 *centimes*.

**ALL** *currency code* for: Albanian Lek.

**alligator spread** A *spread* in the *options* market that 'eats the investor alive' with high *commission* costs. The term is used when a *broker* arranges a combination of *puts* and *calls* that generate so much *commission* that the client is unlikely to turn much of a *profit*, even if the markets move as anticipated.

**allotment** Where there is a new *offer* of *shares*, either by new issue or otherwise, they are issued on the basis of a *prospectus* so that *shares* can be allocated at a fixed price (see: *flotation*). Where demand for *shares* exceeds the *shares* available, allotment is either made on a random or proportional basis. Allocation of these *shares* is made by means of a *letter of allotment*. This entitles the recipient to a certain number of *shares* as stated in this letter subject to payment. See: *ballot, renunciation, tender*.

**allotment letter** See: *allotment.*

**allowance** Charge against *income* for the purpose of calculating *income tax.* These are normally limited to *personal allowances* and effectively represent a level below which *income* is tax-free. They are currently index-linked.

**alpha coefficient** The alpha coefficient, usually referred to as alpha, is a risk-adjusted measure of the return on an investment. Alpha is widely used to assess investment managers.

**Alternative Investment Management Association (AIMA)** AIMA is the professional trade association representing the hedge fund industry with a worldwide membership of 1,280 corporate members. It was established in 1990 and is based in London.

**Alternative Investment Market (AIM)** Regulated by the *London Stock Exchange,* this is a market opened for trading on 19 June 1995. It was designed for small, young and growing *companies,* which are likely to be of higher *risk* and their *securities* less liquid than those admitted to the *London Stock Exchange*'s *Official List.* It replaced the *Unlisted Securities Market* in the *UK.* Regulations governing *shares* in this market are less stringent than those with a *full listing* and the *Stock Exchange* does not govern their activities directly but through *nominated advisors (nomads)* approved by the Exchange who take responsibility for the *companies'* actions and dealings. In January 2009 there were 1,530 companies listed on AIM with a total market value of £38bn. 20% of the companies were international. See also: *PLUS Markets.*

**amalgamation** The joining of two or more *companies* by *merger* or *acquisition.*

**ambulance stocks** Particularly popular in *Japan,* these are recommended *investments* selected especially for clients whose *portfolios* have performed poorly. The resulting excellent performance of the *stock* serves to renew good relations between the client and broker!

**AMD** *currency code* for: Armenian Dram.

**America** See: *United States.*

**American Depository Receipt (ADR)** A *certificate* issued by a *US bank* stating that a specific number of a foreign *company*'s *shares* have been deposited with them and that the *ADR* will reflect any movement in the *value* of the *shares.* Used where overseas investors cannot buy the *shares* directly, thus providing them with indirect but equivalent participation. See also: *participating certificates.*

**American option** See: *option.*

**American Samoa** Dependency of the *US.* Standard *currency*: *US dollar.*

**American Stock Exchange (AMEX)** The second largest (physical) *stock exchange* in *America,* called *AMEX,* located at 86 Trinity Place, Manhattan; formerly called the 'Curb Exchange'. Most of the *stocks* and *bonds* traded are of small- to medium-size *companies,* with a large number of oil and gas corporations. Some *over-the-counter stocks* are traded as well as a large number of foreign *stocks.* Increasingly offering *derivatives* for trading. Its main *index* is:

- *AMEX* Market Value Index. Contains 16 sub-indices. Base *values* were readjusted: 5 July 1983 = 50.

Compare: *New York Stock Exchange (NYSE), NASDAQ.* See also: *United States.*

**AMEX** See: *American Stock Exchange.*

**amortisation** 1. Repayments of the *capital* element of a loan as separate from the *interest.* 2. In *America,* the regular repayment of *interest* and principal to pay off a loan by maturity. 3. Reduction in *value* of an intangible *asset* or a *lease.* Means basically the same as *depreciation* (which is used in connection with *tangible assets*) but the accounting treatment of it varies, because of the difficulty in valuing *intangibles.*

**amortising mortgage** A type of *mortgage* agreement in which the principal and *interest* are paid off in regular payments of about the same size. Known in the *UK* as a *repayment mortgage*. Compare: *balloon mortgage*.

**amortization** See: *amortisation*.

**Amsterdam Stock Exchange** See under: *Netherlands*.

**analysis** 1. A general term meaning the investigation of all known facts pertaining to the item in question. 2. Observation and calculation of the relevant facts in connection with the market behaviour of a certain *investment* form, eg *share* price, *spot currency* rate. Technical analysis refers to the examination of historical price (and *volume*) movements of the *investment* form, especially to predict future movements. Fundamental analysis involves regarding the *investment* form in terms of more general issues, such as economic and political influences, internal organisation, *management* and liquidity. Quantitative analysis refers to a mathematical analysis of *investments* on the basis of their potential return and *risk*.

**Andean Pact** Group of South American countries that have combined as a free-trade area. Comprises *Bolivia*, *Argentina*, *Paraguay*, *Peru* and *Venezuela*.

**Andorra** Standard *currency*: *euro*.

**ANG** *currency code* for: Netherlands Antillean Guilder.

**angel** Also 'business angel'. An *equity* investor in a new/small/start-up business who subscribes for *shares* and, sometimes, participates in the business by providing advice, contacts or services for little or no fee. Made famous by the TV programme Dragon's Den, business angels have operated in the *UK* for many years and provide *equity* finance for entrepreneurs that is rarely available from any other source.

**Angola** Standard *currency*: *kwanza*. 1 *kwanza* = 100 *lwei*.

**Anguilla** Dependency of the *UK*. Standard *currency*: East Caribbean *dollar*.

**annual allowance** The maximum tax-efficient total pension contributions from all sources that may normally be made to an individual's pension arrangements during a single tax year. For 2009/10 the allowance is £245,000. It will rise to £255,000 in 2010/11 and stay at that level until at least 2015/16.

**annual allowance charge** The 40% income tax charge levied on an individual when the *annual allowance* is exceeded. The charge is on the excess over the *annual allowance* and waived in the tax year of death or in respect of contribution to a plan from which benefits are drawn in the same tax year.

**Annual Effective Rate (AER)** *AER* means the Annual Effective Rate of *interest*, which represents the *gross* rate of *interest* as if paid and compounded on an annual basis. For *investment* the Net *AER* is the amount payable after deduction of *basic rate income tax* at the time. The Gross *AER* is the amount of *interest* payable before the deduction of *income tax*.

**annual general meeting (AGM)** Every *public limited company* must hold a meeting of its *members* (*shareholders*) once every calendar year. This is normally to consider the *accounts* and reports of *directors* and *auditors*, the declaration of a *dividend* and the appointment or reappointment of *auditors* and/or *directors*. The *AGM* is often the only opportunity for *shareholders* to voice opinions to the *directors* of publicly quoted *companies*. For public *companies* 21 days' notice is required; for other *companies*, 14 days'. In the *UK* it became optional, with effect from 1 October 2007, for any private *company* to hold an *AGM*, unless its articles of association specifically require it to do so. See: *extraordinary general meeting*, *proxy*, *resolution*.

**Annual Investment Allowance (AIA)** Tax *allowance* given to *companies*, *partnerships* and individuals for acquiring *assets* in the *tax year*. The allowance is 100% of the pruchase cost of the plant and machinery, subject to a maximum of £50,000 per year. The *allowance* is given as a deduction against taxable *profits*. The AIA replaced a system of first year allowances, which were more generous for larger companies.

**annual percentage rate (APR)** Used as a *benchmark* for comparing *interest rates*, mainly for *borrowing* rates. Shows total *gross* annual *interest* charges on *capital* outstanding over the period of the loan or *investment*. For *interest* that is charged or paid more frequently than annually, the *APR* shows the equivalent annual rate. For example, 2% *interest* charged monthly *compounds* to an effective charge of 26.82% *APR*, though the stated *interest* would be 24% per year. All credit purchases must now show equivalent *APR*. See also: *AER*.

**annual report** In accordance with statutory obligations (the *Companies Acts*), the annual *accounts* and the *directors'* report of all *UK limited liability companies* must be issued to *members* and filed at *Companies House*, where they are deemed to be in the public domain. *Sole traders* and *partnerships* (but not limited liability partnerships) have no obligation to make *accounts* available to anyone but the HMRC. See: *report and accounts*.

**annual returns** Details of the *share capital* and holdings of *directors* as at 14 days after the *annual general meeting*. Each *financial year* all *limited companies* need to file their *annual reports* with *Companies House*.

**annuity** An *income* receivable for a specified period or for life of the annuitant (ie person receiving the annuity), secured by the payment of a *capital* sum. These annuities cannot strictly be encashed and usually cease on the death of the annuitant or on the earlier end of a fixed term. For non-pension annuities, the *income* provided is deemed to be split into *capital*, which is untaxable, and *interest*, which is taxable. Rates depend on those prevailing generally, with an additional amount paid to take account of the prospects for mortality during the payment period. Normally advisable only for older people and those without dependents or for use in conjunction with *pension* payments.

For calculation purposes, annuities are regarded as a sequence of payments made at equal time intervals. When the payments are made at the ends of the payment intervals, one refers to an 'ordinary annuity'. When the payments are made at the beginnings of the payment intervals, the annuity is called an 'annuity due'. For an ordinary annuity with a fixed term, the annuity is calculated by the following formula:

$$S = Rs_{n;i} = R\left(\frac{(1+i)^n - 1}{i}\right)$$

where P is the purchase price, R is the regular payment, n is the total number of payments (= number of periods) and i is the *interest rate* per period. See also: *compulsory purchase annuity*, *Hancock annuity*, *open market option*, *purchased life annuity*, *temporary annuity*.

**anomaly switching** See under: *arbitrage*, *gilt switches*.

**Antigua & Barbuda** Standard *currency*: East Caribbean *dollar*.

**ANZCER** See: *Australia New Zealand Closer Economic Relations*.

**AON** *currency code* for: Angolan New Kwanza.

**APACS** See: *Association for Payment Clearing Services*.

**APC** See: Auditing Practices Committee.

**apex** A term used in *technical analysis* in the following two senses: 1. The highest point of a price movement. 2. The tip (vertex) of a *triangle*. Compare: *cradle*.

**APL** Short for: Association of Pension Lawyers.

**appreciation** 1. The increase in *value* (or price). Often, appreciation is due to *inflation*. 2. Capital is referred to as *growth*. 3. An increase in a *currency's value* with respect to another *currency* or *currencies*. Usually used when referring to *floating exchange rates*. If *exchange rates* are fixed, one uses the term '*revaluation*'.

**appropriate personal pension scheme** A *personal pension* or *free-standing additional voluntary contribution* scheme granted an appropriate scheme certificate by HMRC, allowing it to be used for *contracting out*.

**appropriation** Where a *unit trust* is being favoured by investors and more units are being bought than sold, ie where the managers need to purchase *securities* from the surplus *cash* invested by unit holders. See also: *expropriation*.

**Approved Milage Allowance Payments** An HMRC scheme allowing individuals to be re-imbursed for using their own cars for business purposes paid at 40p per mile for the first 10,000 miles and 10p per mile thereafter in a tax year. Payments are *tax* free. Different levels of payment apply to motor cycles and cycles.

**APPS** See: *appropriate personal pension scheme*.

**APR** See: *annual percentage rate*.

**APSS** HMRC Audit and Pension Scheme Services (APSS) which deals with the tax treatment and registration of pension arrangements.

**ARB** See: *arbitrageur*.

**arbitrage** Simultaneously trading in *assets* or different forms of the same *assets*, *currency* or *bills of exchange* in different international markets for (nearly) riskless, guaranteed *profit*. See: *arbitrageur*.

**arbitrageur** 1. A market professional who takes positions in *currencies, stocks* or *bonds* by using *actuals, futures* and/or *options* to lock in a reasonably certain *profit* from the anomalous or inherent price advantages of one vehicle against another, normally in the same holding. 2. In *America* the expression is used more generally to describe someone who speculates in *securities* and financial *instruments* – particularly *derivatives*.

**Argentina** The main *stock market* is the Buenos Aires Stock Exchange, established in 1854.

The main *index* is:

• Buenos Aires Stock Exchange General Index. Base: 29 December 1977 = 100.

There are other stock exchanges in Córdoba, La Plata, Rosario, and Mendoza. There is an electronic exchange: Mercado Abierto Electrónico *SA*. Standard *currency*: peso. 1 *peso* = 100 centavos.

**arithmetic mean** See under: *mean*.

**ARM** See: *adjustable rate mortgage*. See under: *variable rate mortgage*.

**arm's length** Term used to describe the basis of a transaction between two unconnected parties on a purely commercial basis. Sometimes business done between connected or associated parties needs to done on an arm's length basis to ensure that one or other party is not being unfairly disadvantaged and this normally involves a degree of independent professional arbitration or *valuation*. Contrast: *associated operations*.

**Armenia** Standard *currency*: *dram*. 1 *dram* = 100 *luma*.

**ARP** See: *adjustable rate preferred stock.*

**ARR** See: *accounting rate of return.*

**arrangement** Instead of declaring bankruptcy, *debtors* with liquidity problems may enter into agreements with their *creditors* to partly pay off debts. A '*scheme of arrangement*' must be drawn up in which the *assets* of the *debtor* are proportionately divided up between *creditors*. Once this scheme has been agreed, a '*deed of arrangement*' must be registered with the *Department for Business, Innovation and Skills* within seven days. See: *bankrupt, individual voluntary arrangement.*

**ARS** *currency code* for: Argentine Peso.

**Articles of Association** One of the two constitutional documents of a *company*, the other being the *Memorandum of Association*. It deals with the internal relationship of a *company* with its *members* (*shareholders*). This relationship varies from *company* to *company*, but once established is binding and can only be changed by a *special resolution.*

**Aruba** Former dependency of the *Netherlands*. Standard *currency*: Aruba *florin*, closely linked to US dollar.

**ASB** See: *Accounting Standards Board.*

**ASEAN** See: *Association of South East Asian Nations.*

**assay** The test of a metal's purity to verify that it meets the standards for trading on a *commodities* exchange. For instance, a 100 troy ounce bar of refined *gold* must be assayed at a *fineness* of not less than 995 before it can be used in settlement of a *gold contract*. See: *bullion.*

**assented stock** During *takeover bids* in the *US*, different prices may be quoted for *stock* where the owner does (assented stock) or doesn't (*non-assented stock*) agree with the terms of the *takeover.*

**assessment** The *tax* authority's estimate of a party's *tax* bill. Under normal circumstances, the taxpayer will self-assess, but if HMRC issue an assessment, the taxpayer has the right to appeal against the assessment within a certain time frame. See: *General Commissioners, Special Commissioners, tax tribunal.*

**asset** 1. Anything owned that is of benefit. Assets can be tangible (such as property, machinery, *stock*, *debtors*, *cash* or *investments*) or intangible (such as *goodwill*, *patents*, R&D, *trade marks*, *copyrights* or brand names). 2. For personal taxation, an asset is any form of property (anything of *value* other than *income* or chattels) owned by an individual, either at home or abroad. See also: *capital gains tax.*

**asset backed** An asset-backed *security* is a debt *security* that is collateralised by a pool of *assets* or the *cash flows* from these *assets*. The pool of *assets* that has been securitised could be *mortgages*, credit card *receivables*, car loans, etc. In the credit crisis the high risk of many asset-backed *securities* has become apparent. The term can also apply to loans which are supported by specific assets.

**asset management** The management of *asset backed investments* for an individual or a group by a professional *investment* manager.

**asset stripping** A frowned-upon and now out of favour process by which a controlling shareholder sells off the *assets* of a *company* and pays the proceeds to the *shareholders* or sells the *assets* of the *company* leaving a *cash* shell. They will often then sell their holding and take no further interest in the *company*. The main objection to this practice is that it can undermine the financial stability of the business and disadvantage the employees. See also: *shell company.*

**asset value**  The *assets* of a *company* for *equity shareholders* are the total *assets* (property, *stock, cash* balances etc.) of the *company* minus all the liabilities in the *balance sheet* (loans, *creditors, bank overdrafts* etc.) minus all the prior *capital* (including *debentures, loan stocks* and *preference shares*). The *net asset value* is this sum divided by the number of *shares* to give a figure per *share*. See: *asset*.

**assignment**  The legal transfer of property from one party to another, normally by *deed*.

**associate**  Any relative, partner, *trustee, executor* (or personal representative of the deceased), *company* or corporate body with an interest in relevant transactions, *shares* or obligations.

**associate company**  A *company* that is partly owned but not controlled by another *company*. See: *subsidiary company*.

**associated operations**  One operation dependent on another, normally to effect a *transfer of value*. A term commonly used in matters of taxation to establish the relationship between two apparently unconnected events used as a device to generate artificial *profits* or losses. See: *arm's length, Ramsay, Furniss V Dowson*.

**Association for Payment Clearing Services (APACS)**  Set up in 1985, *APACS* manages *bank* payment and cheque clearing in the *UK*. See also: *Town Clearing*.

**Association of British Insurers**  Established in 1985, *ABI* is a trade association – its members constitute the vast majority of British *insurance companies*.

**Association of Futures Brokers and Dealers (AFBD)**  Formerly a *Self-Regulating Organisation*. Then, as part of the *Financial Services Act 1986*, was amalgamated with *TSA* (*The Securities Association*) to form the *SFA* (*Securities and Futures Authority*). Currently, part of the *Financial Services Authority* (*FSA*).

**Association of Investment Companies (AIC)**  Founded in 1932, the Association of Investment Companies (*AIC*) is the collective voice for *investment trust companies* both in the UK and in the Channel Islands. The *AIC*'s main purpose is the protection, promotion and advancement of the common interests of its member companies and their *shareholders*. Address: 3rd Floor, Durrant House, 8–13 Chiswell Street, London EC1Y 4YY. Telephone: 020-7282 5555.

**Association of South East Asian Nations (ASEAN)**  More a political than an economic group, promoting free trade among its members. Founding nations were *Indonesia, Malaysia*, the *Philippines, Singapore* and *Thailand*. In 1995 *Vietnam* joined. Has some trade agreements with other South East Asian countries. Effectively a free-trade area since 2000.

**assurance**  The business of providing for an event which will certainly happen, such as retirement and death, as opposed to *insurance*, which provides against things which may happen, such as fire and accident. Assurance *companies* therefore deal mainly in areas of *life assurance* and *pensions*.

**assured**  The named *beneficiary* of a *life assurance* policy in the event of maturity; or the death of the life who may be the same or different. Effectively the policyholder.

**AST**  See: *automated screen trading*.

**ASX**  Short for: Australian Stock Exchange. See under: *Australia*.

**at best**  In qualifying an instruction to a *broker*, 'at best' indicates that one wishes the *broker* to conduct the market transaction immediately at the *best price* possible.

**at call**  Cash *deposits* on the *money market* that are available for *value* at immediate notice. See: *call money*.

**at limit** In qualifying an instruction to a *broker*, 'at limit' indicates that one wishes the *broker* to perform the market transaction up to a specified limiting price (a price ceiling if one is buying, a price *floor* if one is selling), within a certain time frame.

**at par** Refers to the *nominal value* or *face value* of a *security*. For instance, *gilts* are always redeemed at par, ie at their *face value* of £100 per unit.

**at the money** An *option* whose *exercise price* is approximately the same as the current market price of the *underlying security*.

**Athens Stock Exchange** See under: *Greece*.

**ATM** See: *automated teller machine*.

**ATP** See: *aid trade provision*.

**att** *Currency* sub-unit of *Laos*. 100 atts = 1 *kip*.

**attachment** The procedure enabling a *creditor* to obtain payment from the *debtor*. The procedure entails obtaining a court order called a *garnishee* order so that *assets* due to the *debtor* from a third party (for instance, wages from the *debtor*'s employer) are frozen and paid directly to the *creditor*. The third party is referred to as the '*garnishee*'. See: *escrow*.

**ATX** Short for: Austrian Traded Index. See under: *Austria*.

**auction** Generally, a sale of goods where the price is determined by potential buyers declaring *bids* and with the highest declared price (above any reserve or minimum) securing purchase. Gilts and *Treasury bonds* are often sold by auction. See also: *Dutch auction*.

**AUD** *currency code* for: Australian Dollar.

**audit** 1. An external audit is a professional examination and *verification* by an independent qualified *accountant* of a *limited company*'s accounting documents and supporting data for the purpose of rendering an opinion as to their fairness, consistency and conformity with generally accepted accounting standards. All larger incorporated bodies in the *United Kingdom* are required to submit annual *accounts* prepared by an *auditor* on this basis. See also: *accounting concepts, auditor's report*. 2. An internal audit is an examination and report of a particular situation in a *company* at the discretion of the *company* by professionally trained employees of that *company*. This situation may not necessarily involve purely financial matters, eg an audit of the information systems of the *company* or an audit of the safety regulations.

**audit trail** Record of past transactions of an organisation. All financial transactions in a business must be traceable from beginning to end from any point in the accounting system. An *auditor* must be able to verify each and every transaction from the trail of the transaction through the *company*'s *accounts*.

**audited accounts** Accounts of a *limited company* signed off by a firm of external *auditors*.

**auditor** The *accountant* or accounting firm that performs an *audit* and provides an *auditor's report*. External auditors are usually *certified accountants* or *chartered accountants* appointed to perform an independent *audit* on a *company*. External auditors must have no connection with, own no *shares* in and have no executive involvement with the *company*, and are involved in preparing the statutory *report and accounts* on an annual basis by visiting the *company*. Internal auditors are appropriately trained employees of a *company* and perform a range of functions, not all accounting-specific, and cannot *audit* a *company*'s annual *accounts*. See 'internal audit' under: *audit*.

**auditor's report** Following an *audit*, the conclusions that the *auditors* reach on the annual *accounts* and directors' report on a *company*. If the *company* is a *limited company*, the *auditors* are required by the Companies Act 2006 to decide whether or not the *accounts* give a 'true and fair view' of the *company* and that they have been prepared in accordance with the Act. The *auditor*'s report must be filed together with the annual *accounts* with the *Registrar of Companies* at *Companies House*. See: *accounting concepts, report and accounts*.

**Australia** The Australian Stock Exchange (*ASX*) has state subsidiaries in Sydney, Melbourne, Brisbane, Perth, Adelaide and Hobart. The main *indices* are all *market capitalisation* weighted:

- *ASX 100* Index. Base: 31 December 1990 = 1000.
- *ASX* All Ordinaries Share Price Index. Base: 31 December 1990 = 1000.
- Twenty Leaders Index. Base: December 1979 = 250.
- All Ordinary Index. Shows *capital value* and change in *total return*. Contains approximately 490 *stocks* representing some 90% of the market, arithmetically weighted. Base: 1 January 1980 = 500.

The *Sydney Futures Exchange* is a *Recognised Investment Exchange* in the UK. Standard *currency*: Australian *dollar*. 1 *dollar* = 100 *cents*.

**Australia New Zealand Closer Economic Relations (ANZCER)** A free-trade area formed between *Australia* and *New Zealand*. It applies a *common external tariff* toward external countries.

**Austria** The main *stock market* is the Vienna Stock Exchange. The main *indices* are:

- Vienna Stock Exchange. Share Index – Contains all *stocks listed* on the official list. The constituent *companies* are weighted by *share value* using the *Paasche* method. Base: 31 December 1967 = 100.
- Austrian Traded Index – Contains 20 domestic *stocks*, weighted by *market capitalisation*. Base: 2 January 1991 = 1000.
- Credit Bank Aktien – Arithmetic weighting of 20 *stocks*. Base: 30 December 1984 = 100.

Standard *currency*: euro. 1 euro = 100 *cents*. Previous *currency* was the *Schilling*, until the introduction of the *euro* on 1 January 2002.

**autarky** Situation where a country does not engage in foreign trade.

**authorisation** Under section 19 of *The Financial Services and Markets Act 2000*, any person who carries on a regulated financial activity in the UK must be authorised by the *Financial Services Authority* (FSA) or be specifically exempt. The range of regulated activities includes accepting deposits, giving investment advice, lending for home purchase, dealing in investments and managing investments.

**authorised capital** The amount of *share capital* that a *limited company* is authorised to issue. This does not provide any indication of the worth of the *company* and simply allows it to issue further *shares* without altering its Memorandum and Articles. The real worth of a *company* relates to its *issued capital* and *reserves*, its *net asset value* and its profitability.

**automated screen trading (AST)** The computerised information systems used in *securities* and other forms of trading for the display of price information and transacting deals directly from the computer screen.

**automated teller machine (ATM)** Device that allows one to execute a number of banking transactions (especially *cash* withdrawals) by using a *bank* or credit card and personal identification number (PIN) without contact with a banking official. Especially useful as most of them operate 24 hours a day, every day. Also known as '*cash* dispensers'.

**aval** The guarantee on a *bill of exchange* or *promissory note*, usually made by a *bank*.

**AVCS** See: *additional voluntary contributions*.

**average** A statistical concept of a number that represents the 'middle' of a set of numbers. Formally called a measure of central locality (as distinct from dispersion which is measured by *standard deviation*). There are several different definitions of the average, the most important being the *mean*, the *median* and the *mode*. Usually, when speaking of the 'average', one is referring to the *mean*. See also: *moving average*.

**average earnings scheme** An occupational pension scheme where the benefit for each year of membership is related to that specific year's relevant *earnings* (as opposed to the salary on retirement).

**average rate of taxation** Simply, the total *tax* paid by a person divided by that person's total *income*. Contrast: *marginal tax rate*.

**averaging** Increasing one's holding in an *investment* when it falls in the hope of reducing the impact of short-term fluctuations and in order to decrease the *average* cost of that entire holding. This can be useful in the case of holdings where it is not possible to accurately determine short-term movements. If an investor wishes to build up a substantial holding over a period of time he/she will '*average* in' at certain price levels. Alternatively if the investor wishes to dispose of a large holding, he/she may '*average* out' by selling over a period at certain times. See: *pound cost averaging*.

**avo** *Currency* sub-unit of *Macau*. 100 avos = 1 *pataca*.

**AWG** *currency code* for: Aruban Guilder.

**Azerbaijan** Standard *currency*: manat. 1 *manat* = 100 *gopik*.

**AZM** *currency code* for: Azerbaijanian Manat.

**Aztech** A touch-sensitive screen-based financial information system used by financial institutions in the *UK*.

# B

**baby bond** A special *endowment* policy available for children under 18 years of age, offered by *Friendly Societies* and providing totally tax-free returns. The government currently limits the maximum *investment* to £18 per month or £200 per year.

**back to back credit** A credit agreement between two parties arranged by an intermediary who conceals their respective identities by acting as principal so that in future transactions there is no possibility of the intermediary being circumvented and the parties dealing directly with each other. Also called: *countervailing credit*.

**back to back loan** Loans in one country or *currency* backed by *security* in another. These can provide some protection for overseas or domestic investors against *exchange rate* fluctuations. Difficulties can arise, however, where there is too large a disparity between *interest rates* in the countries concerned.

**backward integration** See: *vertical integration*.

**back office** See: *cage*.

**backwardation** 1. Term used in *futures* markets where the price of a *stock* or *commodity* available for future *delivery* is lower than the *cash* or *spot price*. In most cases, especially with *commodities*, the price for future *delivery* is normally higher to allow for *insurance* and *warehousing*, and this is known as *contango*. 2. Sometimes backwardation occurs when a *market maker* quotes a buying price for a *share* lower than the selling price given by other *market makers*.

**BACS** See: *Bankers Automated Clearing System*.

**badges of trade** The six principles that HMRC applies to decide whether a transaction is Trade or Investment as set out in the Radcliffe Report in 1954. The categories are subject matter, period of ownership, frequency of transactions, supplementary work, circumstances responsible for sale, and motive.

**Bahamas** Standard *currency*: *dollar*. 1 *dollar* = 100 *cents*.

**Bahrain** Standard *currency*: *dinar*. 1 *dinar* = 1,000 *fils*.

**baht** *Thailand*'s standard *currency*. 1 baht = 100 *satang*.

**Bai al-dayn** An Islamic term describing the sale of debt. To enable the sale to take place, the debts arising out of *contract* of exchanges or aqad ai muawadhat, such as trade financing (based on the underlying *contracts* of *Murubaha*) or *asset* sale (based on the underlying *contract* of bai muajjal or *Bai bithaman ajil*) are securitised. These *securities*, being the certificates of debt or Shahadah al dayn, are evidence of the debt and the commitment of the *debtor* under the *contract* of exchanges entered into. These *securities* are traded in the *secondary market* under the concept of Aai al-dayn. Maturities of these *securities* range from as little as one month to longer term. Only *securities* evidencing bona fide commercial transactions can be traded.

**Bai al salam** Islamic term for the *contract* for the sale of goods, where the price is paid in advance and the goods are delivered in the future.

**Bai bithaman ajil** Islamic term. This *contract* refers to the sale of goods on a deferred payment basis. Equipment or goods (the *assets*) requested by the client are bought by the *bank*, which subsequently sells the goods to the client at an agreed price (the sale price), which includes the *bank*'s mark-up (*profit*). The client may be allowed to settle payment by instalments within a pre-agreed period, or in a lump sum. Similar to a *Murubaha contract*, this is also a credit sale.

**baiza** Currency unit of *Oman*. 1,000 baiza = 1 *rial*.

**balance of payments** A complete statistical record of a country's economic transactions with the rest of the world over a period of time, usually one year. Indicates the *value* of goods and services the country has been importing and exporting, whether the country has been borrowing from or lending *money* to the rest of the world and whether the *central bank* has increased or decreased its *reserves* of foreign *currency*. In the *UK*, the data is collected by National Statistics from a number of sources, but it is impossible to record every transaction, so some inaccuracy is inherent in the statistics. The sources include customs authorities, data on *capital* inflows and outflows, surveys of tourist numbers and expenditure, *banks*, multinationals, *investment* houses and *pension* funds. In the *US*, this task is performed by the *US* Department of Commerce. To make comparisons between countries' balance of payments figures easier, the *International Monetary Fund* (*IMF*) has issued guidelines for data collection and representation, in its 'Balance of Payments Manual'. The *IMF* also publishes the statistics of all its member countries in standard format in the 'Balance of Payments Statistics Yearbook' and 'International Financial Statistics'. The balance of payments account must, like all double-entry *accounts*, balance. Thus a surplus or *deficit* in the balance of payments refers to imbalances in the sub-accounts that comprise the balance of payments account. The main sub-accounts are the *current account*, the *capital account* and the source of official *funding*. The first comprises the *trade balance*, services, *income*, *profits*, *dividends* and unilateral transfers. The second consists of *capital* inflows/outflows as represented by *investment*, borrowing/lending and sale/purchase of *assets*. The sum of the current and *capital* balances (plus a statistical discrepancy) gives the total *currency* flow. Positive represents an inflow, and this is usually taken to mean a balance of payments surplus, whereas a negative total *currency* flow is interpreted as a *deficit*. This must balance the source of official *funding* account, which consists of *central bank* borrowing/lending from other *central banks*, an increase/decrease of foreign *reserves*, or borrowing/repaying the *IMF* (positive *values* indicate *net borrowing* or a fall of foreign *reserves*). See: *balance of trade*.

**balance of trade** The *net* difference over a period of time between the *value* of a country's *imports* and *exports* of merchantable goods. Excludes services such as tourism, *insurance* and banking (*invisibles*). See also: *balance of payments*, *current account*, *visibles*.

**balance sheet** A statement produced at regular intervals, normally at the end of a *limited company*'s *financial year*, showing a breakdown of *assets*, *capital* and *current liabilities*. Company *annual reports* are now issued in a standard form as a result of stipulations contained in the *Companies Acts*. The balance sheet gives some measure of the *value* of the organisation to which it relates and needs to show a *net* surplus for the *company* to be considered *solvent*.

**balanced budget** Occurs when government expenditure equals government revenues. See: *Public Sector Borrowing Requirement*, *Public Sector Debt Repayment*.

**balanced budget multiplier** The extent to which total domestic *income* in an economy (*gross domestic product*) changes as a result of an increase in government spending that is financed wholly from an increase in taxation. Government spending injects demand (and thus raises *income*) in an economy, but taxation causes a decrease in demand, though by a smaller amount, since some of the *income* lost would have been in the form of savings; thus in theory the *net* effect is a small increase in total domestic *income*. See: *multiplier* (sense 1.)

**balboa** *Panama*'s standard *currency*. 1 balboa = 100 centesimos.

**balloon** In repaying a loan or a *lease*, a balloon is a large payment (often at the end of the repayment period) of part of the loan.

**balloon mortgage** A *mortgage* in which some or all of the original principal or some *interest* is still outstanding at the end of the *mortgage* agreement period (also called a 'non-amortising *mortgage*'), which is normally repaid by a *sinking fund* that can be accumulated by a savings plan, *life assurance* or a *pension* lump sum. With a balloon mortgage a lump sum has to be repaid at the end of the term to cover the remaining debt, as opposed to a *repayment mortgage* where both *capital* and *interest* are repaid in regular amounts over the *mortgage* period. See: *amortising mortgage, interest only mortgage*.

**ballot** Where a new *share* issue is oversubscribed, some or all of the applications are 'put into a hat' and applications withdrawn at random to be granted part or all of those *shares* applied for. Applications not selected are unsuccessful and are returned. See also: *flotation, tender, oversubscription, weighted ballot*.

**Baltic Exchange** Founded in 1744 and severely damaged by an IRA bomb in 1992, the Baltic Exchange is the world's oldest and premier international shipping exchange. It provides the only regulated marketplace for shipbroking. Its members – predominantly ship owners, cargo interests and shipbrokers – are concerned with the matching of bulk ships, bulk cargoes and the sale and purchase of vessels. Specialist freight movements by air and *commodity* trading also take place at the Exchange. Membership is international, comprising over 550 *companies* and 2,000 individuals from over 40 nationalities, and is also open to non-trading maritime organisations including shipping *banks*, lawyers, insurers, P&I Clubs, classification services etc. Situated at St Mary Axe, London EC3A 8BH.

**BAM** *currency code* for: Bosnian Convertible Marka.

**band earnings** Earnings on which individuals and their employers have to pay full rate *National Insurance* contributions. Band *earnings* are *earnings* which fall between the lower and upper *earnings* limits. State second pension benefits no longer accrue in relation to all earnings within this band.

**Bangladesh** Standard *currency*: *taka*. 1 *taka* = 100 paisa.

**bani** Currency sub-unit of *Romania*. 100 bani = 1 *leu*.

**bank** An institution for handling other people's *money*. Historically depositories for *cash* and guarantees of loans, banks have become the providers of all financial services. *UK* banks are governed by statute, specifically the *Banking Acts 1979, 1987,* and *2009* and the *EC First Banking Directive*. *Clearing banks* deal mainly with the general public and small businesses, as opposed to *investment banks*, which deal in *corporate finance* and fund management. Complaints against any bank are arbitrated by the *Financial Ombudsman Service*.

**bank account** Normally a current account with a *clearing bank* that allows the account holder to write cheques against *cash* held in his or her account. Proof of identity is required for individuals (see: *money laundering* regulations) and a *certificate of incorporation* for a *company*. Cash can only be withdrawn equivalent to the *cash* in the account unless an *overdraft* has been agreed in writing.

**bank bill** A *bill of exchange* accepted, issued or guaranteed by a *bank*. Subject to the *credit rating* of the *bank*, it is considered less risky than a *trade bill*.

**bank charge** Amounts charged to customer *bank accounts* for (certain) transactions, such as issuing cheques, running an *overdraft*, agreeing a loan, writing a letter, advising a balance, stopping or bouncing a cheque, having a meeting or issuing a *draft*.

**bank draft** A cheque issued by a *bank* in its own name or in the name of a correspondent *bank* to the order of a client under which payment cannot be rescinded, and which is invariably honoured.

**Bank for International Settlements (BIS)** With headquarters in Basle, *Switzerland*, it was originally formed to coordinate First World War reparation payments. It is now the clearer for *central banks* and works closely with the *International Monetary Fund*.

**bank giro** Method of settling accounts using the banking rather than postal system. See also: *giro*.

**bank guarantee** An undertaking by a *bank* to cover a debt or a transaction. Can be used as an alternative to offering *security* for a debt, although *banks* usually require good *security* themselves.

**bank loan** A short-term personal loan from a *bank*, usually over three or four years, that is amortised by level monthly instalments of *capital* and *interest*. Can be secured or unsecured, with an *interest rate* linked to the *bank*'s own *base rate*.

**Bank of England** Founded by an Act of Parliament in 1694 to provide funds to William III to continue waging war against the French. It was nationalised as the state-owned *central bank* in 1946, given independence in 1998, and is the issuer of *bank* notes in England and Wales. Its major customers are the government and other domestic *banks*, as well as overseas *banks* and international organisations. It is a *lender of last resort* to its customers and it controls the amount of *money* in circulation in accordance with or by reference to government policy. It is also responsible, in consultation with the Treasury, for managing *money supply* by intervening in the *money markets*. It may also intervene in the *foreign exchange market* for the government. The Monetary Policy Committee (MPC) of the bank sets short term interest rates and is charged with keeping consumer price index inflation within 1% of a 2% target set by the Treasury. The *FSA* has taken over the Bank's regulatory role in the banking sector. The Debt Management Office now deals with gilt issuance and debt, which used to be a responsibility of the Bank. Sometimes known as the *Old Lady of Threadneedle Street*. See: *Monetary Policy Committee*.

**Bank of Japan (BOJ)** The *central bank* of *Japan*.

**bank rate** The lowest rate that the *Bank of England* uses to lend to other *banks*. It sets the basis for calculating *interest rates* on *deposits* etc. The bank rate used to be known as the *Minimum Lending Rate*. Now usually called: *base rate*.

**bank transfer** A transfer of funds between different accounts or different *banks* made without the use of cheques or *drafts*. Sometimes known as *telegraphic transfers*, these are used normally to transfer large amounts of *capital* without undue delay.

**bankers acceptance** A *time draft* or *promissory note* that has been guaranteed by a *bank* and which can be traded for *value*.

**Bankers Automated Clearing System (BACS)** The Bankers Automated Clearing System (*BACS*) is owned by 15 of the *UK*'s major *banks* and *building societies,* and is responsible for the automated processing of Direct Debits, Direct Credits, Standing Orders and other *inter-bank* payments. To use the *BACS* service, a *company* must hold an account with one of the sponsoring *banks* or *building socities*. Payments made under direct debit and direct credit totalled £3.7 trillion in 2007. Over 115,000 businesses are currently registered as users of the *BACS* system.

**bankers cheque**  See: *bank draft.*

**bankers order**  See: *standing order.*

**Banking Acts 1979 and 1987**  *UK* Acts of Parliament that defined the parameters within which *banks* should operate and did away with second line *banks* known as licensed *deposit* takers. The Acts gave supervisory powers to the Bank of England which have now largely passed to the *FSA.*

**Banking Act 2009**  This Act was passed in the wake of the problems with Northern Rock and gives the Bank of England, the Treasury and the Financial Services Authority power to intervene instantly to nationalise or sell off troubled banks.

**bankrupt**  Somebody who is unable to discharge their financial obligations and is subject to a bankruptcy order. Someone is declared bankrupt in a court by a *creditor* or *creditors* owed more than £750, and if such an order is made the court appoints a *receiver* or a *trustee in bankruptcy* who takes possession of the *debtor*'s property (with the exception of tools of their trade and some clothing) and then compiles a list of debts and *assets* which are dealt with under the terms of the *Insolvency Act 1986.* Once the debts have been paid or a *scheme of arrangement* has been reached, a *debtor* can apply to be discharged from bankruptcy and then be certified. Here the bankrupt person is given a certificate of misfortune, stating that the bankruptcy was not caused by any wrongful or dishonest act, and is referred to as a *certified bankrupt.* Undischarged bankrupts may not act as *directors* or take part in the management of a *company.* They may not sit or vote in the House of Lords or the House of Commons, they may not be appointed to act as a Justice of the Peace and may not hold the offices of Mayor, Alderman, Councillor or County Councillor. There are strict limits on the amount of credit an *undischarged bankrupt* may obtain and restrictions on entering into certain *contracts.* See also: *administration, individual voluntary arrangement, insolvency.*

**Bankruptcy Reform Act 1978**  American statute reforming bankruptcy law – particularly its *Chapter 11.*

**banque d'affair**  The French word for: *merchant bank.*

**Banque de France**  The *central bank* of *France.*

**bar**  Slang for one million.

**Barbados**  The *stock market* is called the Securities Exchange of Barbados. The number of *listed companies* in 1993 was 16. The main *index* is: Securities Exchange of Barbados Share Index. Base: 1 January 1988 = 100. Standard *currency: dollar.* 1 *dollar* = 100 *cents.*

**Barber Judgment**  As a result of the legal precedent resulting from the case of 'Barber v Guardian Royal Exchange Assurance Group (1983)' it has become a statutory requirement that men and women in the same *occupational pension scheme* will be able to take benefits at the same age without disadvantage.

**bargain**  A purchase or sale on the *stock exchange*, sometimes known as a *contract.*

**barometer stock**  A *bellwether* stock. See: *bellwether.*

**barter**  Exchanging goods or services for other goods or services instead of paying *money* for them. See also *counter trade, payment in kind.*

**base date**  The particular date taken to be the *base period* in an *index.*

**base period**  The time used as the reference point in calculating comparative *index values.* Normally, the base period is allocated the number 100 (as in: 1992 = 100), and all other periods' *values* are measured with reference to the *values* at that time.

**base rate** The rate commonly used as the minimum level at which institutions, particularly *banks*, will lend *money*. Most loans are expressed in terms of a certain percentage over base rate. The greater the *risk* or the smaller the client, the greater number of percentage points over the base rate will be charged.

**base weighted index** A type of *index* in which the *values* are compared to the *value* in the *base year* or *base date*, which is the reference point for all other *values*.

**base year** A specific year taken to be the *base period* in *indices*.

**basic component** The basic single person's *state pension* payable to anyone who has fulfilled the minimum *National Insurance* contribution requirements.

**basic rate** The rate of *income tax* between the 10% savings and higher rate bands – the most commonly paid *tax* rate. Tax deducted or relieved at source is normally at the basic rate. See: *tax*.

**basis** The difference in price between a *futures contract* and its *underlying asset*.

**basis point** 1. The unit of an *index*. The movement of an *index* will be described either by the change in basis points or by percentage movement, the two invariably being quite different. See: *tick*. 2. When speaking of *yield spread* or differential, a basis point (bp) is one percent of one percent (ie 0.01% or 0.0001). Sometimes referred to as "bips". Not to be confused with: *point*. Compare: *p.p.*

**basis point value (BPV)** A measure of the price change of a *portfolio* of *bonds* associated with a *basis point* change in *yield*. See: *yield, Macaulay's duration*.

$$BPV = \frac{\text{Macaulay's duration}}{[1 + (\text{gross redemption yield} / 2)]} \times \text{portfolio market value} \times 0.0001$$

**basis price** A *quotation* only designed to give a buyer or a seller a rough guide to the price of *shares*. The actual dealing price will vary in accordance with the size of the transaction and the availability of the *stock*. See also: *magenta, matched bargain*.

**basket of currencies** A selection of certain *currencies* which are weighted (see: *weighted average*) in a certain way for the purpose of comparison and calculation. Some countries will attempt to manage their exchange rates against a basket of currencies.

**Basle 2** Banking Directive governing *liquidity*, assets and practice that affects bankers, b*rokers, fund managers, custodians, market makers* and mid and *back office* managers, *dealers*, corporate financiers, etc. by establishing rigorous *risk* and capital management requirements designed to ensure that a *bank* holds *capital reserves* appropriate to the *risk* the *bank* exposes itself to through its lending and investment practices. Generally these rules mean that the greater the *risk* to which the *bank* is exposed, the greater the amount of *capital* the bank needs to hold to safeguard its *solvency* and overall economic stability. Basel II uses a 'three pillars' concept – (1) minimum *capital* requirements (addressing *risk*); (2) supervisory review; and (3) market discipline – to promote greater stability in the financial system. Introduced in 2004/05.

**BBD** *currency code* for: *Barbados* Dollar.

**BCEAO** Short for: Banque Centrale des Etats de l'Afrique de l'Ouest.

**BCG matrix** A business *analysis* scheme in matrix form developed by the Boston Consulting Group (BCG), a firm of business consultants. It is used to analyse product development within a firm where one axis of the matrix measures market *growth* rate and the other market share. The different product types are categorised within the matrix. The matrix can also be used to categorise businesses as to their market share and *growth* rate. Also called: *Boston matrix*.

**BDT** *currency code* for: Bangladeshi Taka.

**BEAC** Short for: Banque des Etats de l'Afrique Centrale.

**bear** A person who thinks that the prices or *values* of *investments* are going to go down for one reason or another. Either realists or pessimists. Contrast: *bull*.

**bear closing** See: *short covering*.

**bear hug** Notice to a *target's board* that a *tender offer* is imminent or under consideration. Variations include the 'strong bear hug', in which the *tender offer* is made public, intensifying pressure on the *target*. The 'teddy bear hug' is when the *target company* indicates that it is in favour of the *merger*, but only at a higher price than that offered.

**bear market** A market characterised by consistent falls in *share* prices as a result of deteriorating prospects for industrial profitability. One or more of a number of factors such as rising *interest rates*, *inflation* or *stagflation*, increases in raw material prices, poor trade performance, weakening *currencies*, *GDP* decline, tighter credit or overcapacity, may contribute. May be anticipated by an *analysis* of macroeconomic factors. See also: *crash*, *recession*, *top-down*. Compare: *bull market*.

**bear position** In a *bear market*, an investor or *dealer* may sell *shares* (or *currencies*, *commodities* etc., depending on the type of market) without actually having them, in the hope of buying them back later at a lower price and making a *profit*. This is known as *selling short* or creating a bear position. Closing or *covering* a bear position is buying back the *shares* sold to finish the transaction. Compare: *bull position*.

**bear squeeze** Occurs when prices go up (or are forced up) hurting anyone who still has a *bear position* to *cover*. See: *squeeze*.

**bear trap** See: *spike*.

**bearer security** A *bond* or *share* where no registration of ownership is required; it is represented by a *certificate* that has an intrinsic *cash value*. The investor or holder's name does not appear on the *stock*, and accordingly anyone who presents the *certificate* has the right to receive the *cash value*. Dividends are normally reclaimed by using *coupons*, which are detached from the *certificate*.

**bearish** Attitude of an investor who believes prices will fall.

**bed and breakfast** Selling a holding and buying it back again shortly afterwards to realise a *capital gain* or loss. The technique was used by individuals to minimise the effects of *capital gains tax* but is no longer effective.

**beggar my neighbour policy** A unilateral measure adopted by a country acting in self-interest that has an adverse effect on its trading partners. Such a policy may be the imposition of *trade tariffs*, *exchange controls* or *quotas* in order to protect domestic *companies*.

**Beige Book** 'Summary of Commentary on Current Economic Conditions' by Federal Reserve District (US). Commonly known as the Beige Book, this report is published eight times per year. Each *Federal Reserve Bank* gathers anecdotal information on current economic conditions in its district through reports from *bank* and branch *directors* and interviews with key business contacts, economists, market experts, and other sources. The Beige Book summarises this information by district and *sector*. An overall summary of the twelve district reports is prepared by a designated *Federal Reserve Bank* on a rotating basis. An important economic commentary that can have considerable influence on market sentiment in the *US*.

**Belarus** Standard *currency*: Belorussian *rouble*.

**BELFOX** Short for: Belgian Futures and Options Exchange. See under: *Belgium*.

**Belgium** The main *stock market* is the Brussels Stock Exchange. Its main *indices* are: Cash Market Return Index – Comprises all domestic *stocks* on the official list. Weighted by *market capitalisation* using *Paasche formula*. Adjusted for *capital* changes of *companies* and *dividend* payments. Base: 1 January 1980 = 1,000. BEL 20 Index – Comprises the 20 largest and most liquid *stocks*. Weighted by *market capitalisation* and liquidity. Base: 1 January 1991 = 1,000. There is also a *stock market* in Antwerp. *BELFOX* is the Belgium Futures and Options Exchange, established in January 1990. It trades in *futures contracts* (government *bond*, 3-month BIBOR *interest rate*, BEL 20 *index future*) and *options contracts* (*stock options*, government *bond options*, *exchange rate options*). Standard *currency*: *euro*. 1 *euro* = 100 *cents*. Currency was the Belgian *franc*, prior to the introduction of the *euro* on 1 January 2002.

**Belize** Standard *currency*: *dollar*. 1 *dollar* = 100 *cents*.

**bellwether** An acknowledged barometer of economic, market or corporate sentiment, a bellwether town, business or person is representative of the health of its peers generally.

**below the line** 1. In modern *UK* accounting practice, below the line refers to items in a *profit & loss account* that refer to how the *profit* is distributed, as opposed to how it is made up. More generally these items also appear in the *balance sheet*. 2. In national accounts, below the line transactions are linked to *capital* as opposed to revenue. 3. In marketing this refers to promotions, mail shots and public relations as opposed to media advertising. Contrast: *above the line*.

**benchmark** A performance comparator used to determine the relative rate of increase/decrease in a market or *security*. A benchmark is often a target against which *investment* performance is measured. See: *performance appraisal*.

**beneficial owner** The person or persons who have ultimate rights to the *value* of an *investment* or property, as distinct from the registered owner, who may be a *nominee*.

**beneficiary** An individual or corporation that stands to benefit financially from a will, *trust*, gift, *insurance* policy, *pension*, charity or bequest. **benchmark** – 2: Also a comparative review of similar businesses where elements such as sales per employee, GP, *margins*, and other financial data available from published *accounts* can be compared against a benchmark such as the industry *average* or against a more successful competitor. Contrast: *settlor*.

**benefit in kind** Benefits over and above salary, like the use of a car or house or other tangible benefits in addition to *cash* remuneration. Tax is normally charged on benefits in kind, and usually employer *National Insurance* charges are also levied. See: *perk*.

**Benelux** Together, the countries *Belgium*, the *Netherlands* and *Luxembourg*.

**Benin** Standard *currency*: African *franc*.

**Bermuda** Dependency of the *UK*. Standard *currency*: *dollar*.

**Berne Union** The International Union of Credit and Investment Insurers. A union of credit insurers from the main industrial nations (except *Japan*), whose objective is to exchange information on credit terms. The *Export Credits Guarantee Department* is a member.

**BERR** See: *Department for Business, Enterprise and Regulatory Reform*.

**best advice** The *Financial Services Act 1986* determined that clients should be advised by *Independent Financial Advisors* (*IFAs*) on the basis of demonstrable comparisons of alternative financial products. Advisors will need to be aware of their client's circumstances and show, where possible, that their recommendations are based on an unbiased assessment of what is best for each individual client.

**best price** An instruction to buy an *investment* in the market for the best price available at the time the instruction was made rather than at a specific price.

**bet** Slang for a short-term unhedged speculative *investment* position, normally in *derivatives*, for example, up-bet and down-bet for *long position* (*bull*) and *short position* (*bear*). More generally any type of *investment* designed to generate short-term gain. See: *zero-sum game*.

**beta coefficient** A factor used in *quantitative analysis* to describe the *volatility* of movements in the price (and thus returns) of a particular *investment*. Technically, it is the *covariance* of the *investment* in relation to the rest of the market, divided by the *variance* of the market. It is a relative measure of the *systematic risk* of the *investment*. An *investment* with a beta coefficient greater than that of the market is more volatile than the market, and vice versa. A beta of unity denotes a *volatility* equivalent to that of the market as a whole. A negative beta implies that the *investment* returns fall when the market rises, and vice versa. See: *alpha coefficient, capital asset pricing model*.

**BGL** *currency code* for: Bulgarian Lev.

**BHD** *currency code* for: Bahraini Dinar.

**Bhutan** Standard *currencies*: Indian *rupee, ngultrum*. 1 *ngultrum* = 100 *chetrum*.

**bid** 1. Price which an individual is prepared to pay in, say, an *auction*, to which costs and *commissions* are added. 2. The price at which a *market maker* or institution will buy back *shares* or units; ie the price at which the investor disposes of a holding of *shares* or units; it is lower than the *offer price*. See: *bid-offer spread*. 3. In a *takeover* attempt, an indication of the price which an individual or institution will pay for *shares* in a *company* where they wish to acquire a *controlling interest*. Very often the first round of negotiations is with the *board* and *shareholders*, and can result in the terms of the bid being improved.

**bid offer spread** See: *bid-offer spread*.

**bid-offer spread** The difference in the buying and selling price of most *investments* including *front end load* funds such as *unit trusts* and *unit-linked life assurance* funds; this can include the total cost of purchasing the holding, the *market maker's turn* (= *profit margin*) or *commission* and *stamp duty*. Normally there is no additional charge for selling *unit trusts* and life funds, as this is immediately reflected in the *bid price*. From the client's (investor's) point of view the cost of selling (at *bid*) and buying (at *offer*) any *investment* at any one moment in time is the *spread* between the two and this can vary, not only with the type of *investment* but with trading conditions and the size of the transaction. With collective *investments* the difference is normally fixed and can be between 0% and 8%. With *shares* it can be less than 1% and over 10%. See: *cancellation price*.

**bid price** See: *bid*.

**bid valuation** *Unit trusts* and *unit-linked life assurance* funds normally match buyers and sellers of units to keep costs down. In most cases the number of unit holders will increase but there are occasions where sales exceed purchases. If these *net* redemptions cause the managers to sell holdings the fund will be valued on a *bid* basis, where the bid price reflects the actual sale value of holdings within the fund, after allowing for all sale costs. This can be particularly severe in the case of property funds. See also: *expropriation*.

**bidder** The *company*, individual or group of individuals making an *offer* to control another *company*. See under: *controlling director*.

**BIF** *currency code* for: Burundi Franc.

**Big Bang** Colloquialism for the abandonment of *single capacity* in the *London Stock Exchange*, the ending of fixed *commissions* and the internationalisation of trading practices in *UK securities* on 27 October 1986, prior to which all *Stock Exchange* transactions needed to be made through a *jobber* via a *stockbroker*.

**Big Blue** Colloquialism for IBM (International Business Machines Inc.), whose *shares* are traded on *Wall Street*.

**Big Board** Colloquialism for the *New York Stock Exchange* (*Wall Street*), because of the large electronic price information board that dominates the Exchange.

**Big Four** The four largest public accountancy firms in the world: PricewaterhouseCoopers, Deloitte Touche Tohmatsu, Ernst & Young and KPMG.

**BIBA** Short for: British Insurance Brokers Association, a trade association.

**bilateral oligopoly** A market where there are not only very few sellers or manufacturers but very few buyers. Normally a highly specialised *oligopoly* dealing in rare, restricted or bespoke products or services.

**bill** See: *bill of exchange*.

**bill broker** Buyer and seller of *bills of exchange*, usually *Treasury bills*. Also: *discount broker*.

**bill of exchange** Strictly defined as 'an unconditional order in writing, addressed by one person to another, signed by the person giving it, requiring the person to whom it is addressed to pay on demand, or at a fixed or determinable future time, a sum in *money*, to, or to the order of, a specified person, or to the bearer'. Covered by the Bills of Exchange Act 1882. See also: *discount house* (which is now accepted to be a trillion).

**bill of lading** A document used in foreign trade similar to a delivery note and normally accompanied by a *bill of exchange* drawn upon the purchaser. A bill of lading is acceptable as a document of title, although it is not legally binding.

**bill rate** *Bills of exchange* are discounted in the *discount market* at bill rates depending on their perceived *quality*. A process that determines the *discount rate*.

**billion** Now accepted as one thousand million on both sides of the Atlantic. Used to be a million million in British English (which is now accepted to be a trillion).

**BIMBO** A form of a *buyout* that incorporates characteristics of both a *management buyout* and a *management buy-in*. A BIMBO occurs when existing *management* – along with outside managers – decide to buy out a *company*. The existing *management* represents the buyout portion while the outside managers represent the buy-in portion. See: MBO.

**birr** *Ethiopia*'s standard *currency*. 1 birr = 100 *cents*.

**BIS** See: *Bank for International Settlements*.

**BIS** See: *Department for Business, Innovation and Skills*.

**black book** A pre-planned strategic defence which can be activated in the event of a *hostile takeover* attempt.

**black economy** A term used to cover undeclared *cash* transactions made for the purposes of avoiding *tax* or *exchange controls*, or by way of criminal activity.

**Black Friday** The original Black Friday was 24 September 1869, when a group of investors attempted to corner the *gold* market. This caused a business panic and the resulting action caused a *depression*. See: *Kondratieff wave*. See also: *Black Monday, Black Tuesday, Black Wednesday*.

**black hole** The discrepancy in the global *balance of payments* figure, due to inaccuracies in statistical data collection and the influence of the *black economy*.

**black knight** A *company* attempting the *hostile takeover* of another *company*. See also: *grey knight, white knight*.

**Black Monday**  Black Monday occurred on 19 October 1987. On this day, £50.6bn was wiped off the *value* of the *London Stock Exchange*, at the time the largest fall in its history. More than five times as much was wiped off *shares* as in the previous biggest fall, on 6 August. The causes were fears about the *dollar* and the US *trade deficit* combined later with reaction to the American attack on an Iranian oil platform in the Gulf. The attack caused a worldwide sell-off in *stock markets*, from *Japan* to New York. At one stage the Financial Times Stock Exchange 100-share *index* was more than 300 *points* down, a greater percentage fall than the 12.8% on *Wall Street* on the day of the great *crash* in 1929. By the *close* in London, an only too brief lull in *Wall Street*'s headlong plunge had brought the *FTSE* 100 *index* back a little to *close* at 2,052.3, down 249.6 on the day and a fall of 10.8%. See also: *Black Tuesday, Black Wednesday, Black Friday*.

**Black–Scholes pricing model**  Used for valuing *call options*. The five inputs to the model are the underlying *stock price*, the *exercise price*, the time to expiry, the risk-free *interest rate* and the *volatility* or *standard deviation* of the *stock* price. The price of a *put option* can be derived from the price of a *call option*.

**Black Tuesday**  The first day of the Wall St *crash* – 29 October 1929. See also: *Black Monday, Black Wednesday, Black Friday*.

**Black Wednesday**  The day on which the British *pound Sterling* exited the *ERM* (*Exchange Rate Mechanism*) and subsequently collapsed: 16 September 1992. Originally 28 October 1929, when high winds whipped up dust storms in the dust bowl of central America, putting many farmers out of business and heralding the Great Depression. See also: *Black Monday, Black Tuesday, Black Friday*.

**blanket policy**  An *insurance* policy covering a number of articles or eventualities with an aggregate sum insured.

**Blind Trust**  A *trust* set up for a public figure, run on a discretionary basis by *trustees*, where the *investments* are kept secret from the investor to ensure no conflicts of interest or opportunities for *insider trading*.

**block order purchase system (BLOX)**  An automated system for the purchase (or sale) of large quantities of *securities* on the *London Stock Exchange*.

**block trade**  Large order to buy or sell *securities*. On the London Stock Exchange it refers to trades of at least 75 times the *Normal Market Size (NMS)* for a *security* with an *NMS* of 2,000 *shares* or of at least 50 times the *NMS* for a *security* with an *NMS* of 1,000 *shares*. On the *New York Stock Exchange* it is an order of at least 10,000 *shares* or a transaction valued at $200,000 or more.

**Bloomberg**  Founded by Michael R. Bloomberg in 1981, it is a financial information-services, news and media *company*. Based in New York, the *company* employs more than 10,000 people in over 126 offices around the world.

**BLOX**  See: *block order purchase system*.

**Blue Book**  1. Colloquial for the *UK National Accounts*. 2. Also called: *City Code*.

**blue button**  A now outmoded expression used to describe a trainee *stockbroker* who was allowed to collect prices but not to transact *investment* dealings on the *London Stock Exchange* floor pre-1986. See also: *dual capacity*.

**blue chip**  A term used for an *investment* that is essentially solid and substantial. Blue chip *company shares* are normally household names with a consistent *growth* and *dividend* record, stable *management* and very substantial *assets*. There are no strictly defined parameters for a blue chip *company*, but they are normally *companies* where *pension* funds and institutions invest a substantial proportion of their *equity capital*. Named after a high-denomination gambling chip. See also: *trustee investment*.

**blue chip out** A term used by venture capitalists (see: *venture capital*) for a *company* that does not wish to obtain a *quotation* in its own right, preferring instead to be taken over by a *blue chip company* with a *quotation* of its own. This allows the original venture capitalists to be repaid, while ensuring a continued source of *funding* for the *company*.

**BMD** *currency code* for: Bermudian Dollar.

**BND** *currency code* for: Brunei Dollar.

**board** The board of *directors* comprising a chairman and all the *directors* who control the day-to-day activities of a *limited liability company*. Decisions are made by a majority, each *director* having one vote with the exception of the chairman, who has one vote plus a casting vote. Members may also include a managing *director* or chief executive, who has overall executive responsibility, and a finance *director*, normally a qualified *accountant*, who is responsible for the *accounts* and ensuring that the *company* is financially viable. The power and constitution of the board may be determined specifically by the *Articles of Association*.

**BOB** *currency code* for: Bolivian Boliviano.

**BoE** See: *Bank of England*.

**boiler room** An operation where salesmen working for unlicensed firms sell unlisted or non-existent *securities*. Usually with a prestigious address but used only for telephone sales. See also: *bucket shop*.

**BOJ** See: *Bank of Japan*.

**bolivar** *Venezuela*'s standard *currency*. 1 bolivar = 100 centimos.

**Bolivia** The main *stock exchange* is the Bolivian Stock Exchange in La Paz. Standard *currency*: boliviano. 1 *boliviano* = 100 *centavos*.

**boliviano** *Bolivia*'s standard *currency*. 1 boliviano = 100 *centavos*.

**Bollinger bands** A somewhat esoteric term used in *technical analysis* to signify a *channel trend* in which the *channel* walls around a *moving average* line are considered elastic, so as to snugly fit around the price movements.

**Bombay Stock Exchange** See under: *India*.

**bona vacantia** A property or *asset* with no apparent owner or claimant. Could be property in, say, the hands of a liquidator, or *shares* whose original owners have died and whose heirs are untraceable. Such property ultimately reverts to the Crown. See also: *intestacy*.

**bond** Another name for a *fixed interest security* – particularly one issued by governments, *companies*, local authorities and *investment* institutions. In most cases repayment is guaranteed or underwritten by a government or corporation. Its general characteristics are that it is: negotiable (ie can be bought or sold); issued for a certain fixed period (until maturity), with the exemption of 'perpetual' (or 'undated') issues; carrying a *coupon* (ie a 'straight'), unless it is a *zero-coupon bond* (ie a 'zero'); paid regularly (usually semi-annually in the *UK* and *US*, annually in *Germany* and *France* and the *eurobond* market). In addition, some markets allow for the *coupons* to be detached from the bond when issued in bearer form (where the *coupons* are called the 'tint'; see: *bearer security*) and negotiated separately. Mostly, bonds are redeemed *at par*. See also: *debenture, income bond, investment bond, premium bonds*.

**bond washing** The practice of selling a *fixed interest security cum dividend* where any *accrued interest* is treated as a *capital gain* and buying *ex dividend* thus stripping out the *dividend* in exchange for *capital growth*. The rules regarding the taxation of accrued *income* in the *UK* were long ago changed to ensure that the practice is not a worthwhile dodge for higher rate *tax* payers. See also: *dividend stripping*.

**bonded goods** Imported merchandise retained in a bonded warehouse and subject to the payment of customs or excise duty.

**bonus** Discretionary amount provided to holders of *with-profits life assurance* policies dependent on the profitability of the *life assurance company* and its *investments*. In the past, *life assurance companies* endeavoured to increase their bonuses but since the early 1990s bonus rates have fallen to the point where some are 0%. A bonus once declared cannot be withdrawn. See also *reversionary bonus, terminal bonus.*

**bonus issue** Synonymous with: *scrip issue.*

**book** *Investments* held to the account of a *broker* or manager for resale. Also a *float* of units kept by the managers of a *unit trust* or *mutual fund* to balance sales with redemptions and to avoid creating or cashing units specifically for future purchases or sales. Sometimes called: *box.*

**book reserve scheme** A *pension* scheme where the employer is responsible for paying the benefits to pensioners and the scheme is financed by a *provision* in the employer's *accounts.*

**book value** 1. The *value* of an *asset* in a *balance sheet* after *depreciation*. May differ significantly from its *market value*. 2. The '*net asset value*' of a *company*'s *shares*. Calculated as total *assets* minus intangible *assets* minus *current liabilities* minus long-term liabilities and *equity* classes that have a prior claim, which gives a figure for the total *net asset* available for payment in case of *liquidation.*

**bootstrap** A *cash offer* in the *US* for a *controlling interest* followed by an *offer* at a lower price to acquire the remainder of the *company*'s *shares*. This can not only reduce the cost of the *bid* but ensure that the *controlling interest* is firmly established at outset. In the *UK* the same price must be paid for all the *shares* if the *offer* is successful.

**borrowing** This is a term used on a *futures* market describing the purchase of a *contract* for a near date and simultaneously selling forward a new date further ahead. See also: *carrying.*

**borsa** The Italian word for: *stock exchange.*

**Börse** The German word for: *stock exchange.*

**Boston matrix** See: *BCG matrix.*

**Botswana** The *stock exchange* was established in 1989, called the Botswana Stock Market (BSM). The number of *shares* quoted in 1995 was 12. The main *index* is: Share Market Index. Comprises 10 *shares*. Base: 19 June 1989 = 100. Standard *currency: pula.* 1 *pula* = 100 *thebe.*

**bottom fishing** Buying *shares* after a market decline in the expectation that it might be the low point of the market.

**bottom-up** Refers to the method of assessing an *investment* (normally in a *quoted company* – but also in a *sector* or even a country) based on particular factors relating to its profitability such as *assets, cash flow*, market share, *profit margins*, order book and the *management*'s performance. Technical considerations such as its *earnings per share* and *dividend yield* are also relevant. Such an assessment implies an intimate understanding of its trading position and a close relationship with its *management*. Such an *analysis* tends to discount macroeconomic and political factors. See also: *top-down.*

**bottomry** The *mortgage* of a ship. Where *money* is required to pay for temporary repairs and other expenses outside the ship's home port, the ship itself is used as *security* against such a loan.

**bought deal** Where a *market maker* or *broker* will purchase a substantial line of new or existing *stock* with the prospect of selling it on at better levels to their clients at a later date. This can be used in cases of a *vendor placing* where the *company* wants to raise *cash* for an *acquisition*. Also transactions in *securities* that do not generate a *turn* or a *commission* but are completed for a fee.

**bourse** Originally used to describe the French Stock Exchange. Derived from the French word meaning bursary or purse of *money* (which would presumably have been exchanged for an *equity* holding in a *company*). This term is now used to describe European *stock exchanges*.

**boutique** A term used for a small specialist investment management operation, independent of major banks or insurance companies.

**box** Another word for: *book*.

**BP curve** A curve used in macroeconomic *analysis* showing the combinations of *interest rates* and *real national income* for which the *balance of payments* is in *equilibrium* (ie the *reserves* are not changing). The slope of the BP curve shows the degree of 'capital' mobility' internationally. If *capital* is very mobile (ie international investors can quickly and easily invest their funds in different countries to take advantage of higher *interest rates*), then the BP curve will be relatively flat. The less mobile the *capital*, the steeper the BP curve. See: *IS curve, LM curve, Mundell-Fleming model*.

**BPV** See: *basis point value*.

**Brady bond** *US* dollar-denominated *bond* issued by an *emerging market*, particularly those in Latin America, and collateralised by US Treasury *zero-coupon bonds*. Brady bonds arose from an effort in the 1980s to reduce the debt held by less-developed countries that were frequently defaulting on loans. The *bonds* are named after Treasury Secretary Nicholas Brady, who helped international monetary organisations institute the program of debt-reduction. Defaulted loans were converted into *bonds* with *US zero-coupon* Treasury *bonds* as *collateral*. Because the Brady bonds were backed by *zero-coupon bonds*, repayment of principal was assured. The Brady bonds themselves are coupon-bearing *bonds* with a variety of rate options (fixed, variable, step, etc.) with maturities of between 10 and 30 years. Issued *at par* or at a discount, Brady bonds often include *warrants* for raw materials available in the country of origin or other *options*.

**Brazil** The main *stock exchange* is the Rio de Janeiro Stock Exchange, established in 1845. It is one of the most automated *stock exchanges* in the world. Its main *index* is:

- National Index (I-SENN Index). It covers the eight exchanges: Fortaleza, Recife, Salvador, Belo Horizonte, Rio de Janeiro, Santos, Curitiba, Porto Alegre. They are integrated by SENN, the national electronic trading system. The I-SENN comprises the 50 most traded (by *value*) *stocks* of these eight exchanges. It is a trade *value weighted index*. Base: 16 September 1991 = 1,000.

The second largest exchange is the São Paulo Stock Exchange (BOVESPA). Its main *index* is:

- BOVESPA Index (I-BOVESPA). It represents the current cruzeiro *real value* of a hypothetical *stock portfolio* purchased on 2 January 1968. Standard *currency*: real. 1 real = 100 *centavos*.

**break even point** 1. The *volume* of output a firm must produce or sell in order to just cover its costs. 2. The market price at which a transaction neither yields a *profit* nor a loss.

**break forward** A *money market instrument* combining the features of forward *foreign exchange contracts* and *currency options*. It is a *forward contract* which can be unwound at a rate previously agreed between a customer and the issuing *bank*. This enables the customer to lock in a rate but to break it if the market moves in his favour. Unlike *options* there is no *premium*, the cost being built into the fixed rate.

**break-up** *Companies* selling *assets* and/or *subsidiary companies*. *Conglomerates* or industrial *holding companies* often have a *share* price of less than the combined *value* of the businesses they own and a break-up can release this *profit*. See also: *break-up bid, asset stripping*.

**break-up bid** Some industrial *holding companies* and *conglomerates* can become large and unwieldy and their *share* price, as a result, reflects a *value* less than the sum total of the individual *companies* within the group. Break-up bids offer *shareholders* the prospect of crystallising the *value* of the underlying *companies* and achieving a higher *share* price by selling off most or all of the holdings as individual units.

**break-up value** Synonymous with: *private market value*.

**breakout** Movement of a price outside a certain *chart pattern*. A breakout can turn out to be a false alarm and return into the *chart pattern* (a *pullback* or *throwback*) or confirm itself as a longer-lasting phenomenon.

**Bretton Woods** The place in New Hampshire, *USA*, where a meeting was held on 1 July 1944 which led to the founding of the *International Monetary Fund* and the *World Bank*.

**bridge financing** Short-term *funding* for a venture *company* which is on the point of raising additional *equity capital* either from investors or by means of a *flotation*. See: *mezzanine finance*.

**bridging loan** Temporary loan to cover the position which will ultimately be covered by *long term* finance such as somebody moving house who temporarily owns two houses simultaneously.

**British Virgin Islands (BVI)** Dependency of *UK*. Standard *currency*: US dollar.

**BRL** *currency code* for: Brazilian Real.

**broad money** Another term for: *M4*.

**broadening top** A *reversal pattern* used in *technical analysis* which resembles an inverted symmetrical, inverted ascending or inverted descending triangle. The difference is, the tops and bottoms of these *patterns* do not necessarily stop at the envelope lines, and rather than diminishing *volume* as in the inverted triangles, the trading *volume* within any one of the three broadening tops tends to be unusually high and irregular throughout. The *breakout* direction is similar to the respective inverted triangle, but nothing can be said about the extent of the ensuing price movement. Also called: *megaphone*.

**broker** An intermediary for two parties, normally a member of a professional or regulated body, enabling them to enter into a *contract* to which the broker acts not as principal but as agent. A broker's remuneration consists of *commission* which is normally calculated as a percentage of the sum involved in the *contract* but may be fixed according to a tariff especially for small transactions. Brokers are used because they have specialised knowledge of the certain markets in addition to introducing buyers and sellers. See: *IFA, stockbroker*.

**broker fund** An *investment bond* or *unit-linked pension* fund managed by an *Independent Financial Advisor*, which contains life funds, *unit trusts*, OEICs and occasionally direct *equities*, underwritten by a *life assurance company* and managed by the *broker* at the *broker*'s discretion for a fee of normally 1%, payable in addition to the standard charges of the *life assurance company*. Broker funds have become relatively rare and are now often 'branded' funds run by external fund managers. See also: *unfettered discretion shell bond*.

**broker loan rate**  The rate at which American *brokers* borrow from *banks* to cover the *investment* positions taken by their clients. The rate is usually a percent point above short-term *interest rates* such as *Federal funds rate* and the *Treasury bill* rate.

**broker-dealer**  A *broker* who is involved in the marketing (market making) as well as the buying and selling of *securities* on the client's behalf. See: *inter-dealer broker*.

**brokerage**  The remuneration due to a *broker* on fulfilment of a *contract* – polite word for *commission*.

**Brunei**  Standard *currency*: *dollar*. 1 *dollar* = 100 *sen*.

**BSD**  *currency code* for: *Bahamian Dollar*.

**BTN**  *currency code* for: *Bhutan* Ngultrum.

**BTP**  Short for Italian: Buoni del Tesoro Poliennali. An Italian government *bond*.

**bubble**  An overbought market position. Inevitably about to burst, many market bubbles represent a situation that cannot last, characterised by historically unsustainable *valuations* created by enthusiastic investor demand, in turn driven by fad, fashion or media frenzy. See: *South Sea Bubble*.

**bucket shop**  Slang expression used to describe *brokers* dealing in *stocks*, *shares* or *commodities* who are not members of a recognised Exchange. See: *boiler room*.

**budget**  1. A target *profit & loss account* prepared by a *company* or individual as an estimate or prediction of their finances for a period in the future. 2. The Budget: the *UK*'s financial plan for the coming *tax year*, presented to Parliament normally in March by the Chancellor of the Exchequer. It reveals the Treasury's predictions for the economy, *money supply* and borrowing targets and any taxation changes.

**budget deficit**  The excess of domestic government expenditure over government *income*, in the form of duties, taxes, reserve *income* and extraordinary revenue such as *privatisation* proceeds. A *deficit* is normally financed by the issue of *government securities* and borrowing. Most economists argue that persistent budget deficits purely represent *deferred taxation* and governments should seek a *balanced budget* on average or in the longer term by regulating taxation and expenditure. Keynesians advocate that governments should run budget deficits during *recessions* in order to stimulate aggregate demand (see: *pump priming*) and *monetarists* and neo-classical macroeconomists argue that budget deficits simply stimulate *inflation* and crowd out (see: *crowding-out*) private *investment*. See also: *PSBR*.

**budget surplus**  The opposite to *budget deficit*, ie the excess of government receipts over government spending. Budget surpluses reduce the level of *national debt*. See: *Public Sector Debt Repayment*.

**buffer stock**  The accumulation of surplus raw materials in times of over-supply. The buffer stock will be used to purchase excess production to protect the producer's price and when there is a shortage the buffer stock will be reduced. See: *green currencies, mountain*.

**building society**  Originally mutual institutions providing loans (*mortgages*) to house purchasers with funds obtained from depositors and run on the differential between the amount paid and received in *interest*. The societies offered only loans for the purchase of residential property on a first-charge basis over periods between 10 and 25 years. *Mortgages* were either repayment or *balloon* (externally funded using an *endowment*, savings plan or *pension*). Many building societies converted to banks in the 1980s and 1990s. Those that remain can now offer a wide range of services and some look very similar to banks. They are regulated by the *FSA*.

**Bulgaria** Sofia is home to the First Bulgarian Stock Exchange (FBSE). The number of *listed shares* in 1994 was 13. Its main *index* is the FBSE Index, which comprises all domestic *stocks* on the official list. It is a *share price index* weighted by *market capitalisation*. Standard *currency*: lev. 1 *lev* = 100 *stotinki*.

**Bulis** From German: Bundesliquiditatsschatzwechsel. A German one-year government *bill*.

**bull** A term applied to an investor who feels that prices and *values* will increase. Either a realist or an optimist. Contrast: *bear*.

**bull market** Market where prices are on the rise and expected to rise further in the medium term. Some traders may establish a *bull position*. Compare: *bear market*.

**bull position** Also called: *long position*, buying *long*. In a *bull market*, a trader may buy and hold on to the *securities* in the hope of selling them at a higher price later or may take a *long position* in the *futures* market or buy a *put option* or *write* a *call option*. Compare: *bear position*.

**bulldog bond** A sterling-denominated *bond* issued in the *UK* by a foreign investor.

**bullet** A *fixed interest security* issued with a single fixed *maturity date*.

**bullion** A precious metal, such as *gold*, silver, platinum or palladium, in near pure form. Traded in bars or *ingots* and sometimes comes in the form of coin (bullion coin, as distinct from *numismatic coin*). See: *assay*.

**bumble bees** Job hoppers with excellent qualifications and CVs who change jobs frequently, benefiting from outstanding inducements and settlements. Quite common in financial circles.

**Bund** From German: *Bundesanleihe*. A long-term German government *bond*.

**Bundesanleihe** Also known as *Bund*. It is a long-term German government *bond*.

**Bundesbank** The *central bank* of *Germany*. It is by constitution independent of the German government. The bank is still very influential, although monetary policy is now in the hands of the ECB.

**Bundesobligation** A German federal *bond*.

**burden of dependency** Refers to the up-keep of the dependent population (unemployed, very young, very old, and disabled etc.) by the tax-paying employed and self-employed in the *labour force*.

**Burkina Faso** Standard *currency*: African *franc*.

**Burma** Subsequently: *Myanmar*. Standard *currency*: kyat. 1 *kyat* = 100 *pyas*.

**burn rate** The rate at which a newly-launched venture *company* utilises *equity capital* to fund fixed overheads. This normally occurs in the start-up period before trading cashflow turns positive.

**burn-out turnaround** The complete restructuring of a troubled *company* with a *refinancing* package which severely dilutes the percentage holdings of existing investors whilst saving the *company* from possible *liquidation*.

**Burundi** Standard *currency*: franc. 1 *franc* = 100 *centimes*.

**business cycle** Within the general (long-term) *trend* of *real GDP*, which for the *UK* has been upward, there are short-term fluctuations around the *trend*, referred to as 'cyclical' fluctuations. Business cycles are the cyclical fluctuations in business activity after seasonal adjustments (see: *seasonality*) have been made. The general descriptive (ie non-technical) characteristics of the business cycle are a 'trough' (high *unemployment*, low demand relative to supply capacity) followed by a recovery phase until eventually a 'peak' (capacity is highly utilised, low *unemployment*) is reached; thereafter there is a contraction in the economy (called a *recession*) until the next trough is reached. A prolonged *recession* is called a *depression*. The entire falling half of a business cycle is often termed a '*slump*'; and the rising half is called a 'boom'. During business cycles, many economic sectors are affected at about the same time but to generally different extents. Historically in the *UK*, the time period between successive peaks has varied within the range of five to ten years. Increasing awareness amongst governments and central bankers and the application of *monetarist* constraints without too much political *intervention* was thought to be softening the cycles until the *Credit Crunch* of 2007 onwards. See: *soft landing*.

**business judgement rule** A legal concept embodied in various state corporation laws in the *United States* that has provided *management* and *boards* of *directors* with virtual immunity from shareholder law suits. It permits *directors* great discretion in adopting *defensive tactics*. The rule is often invoked when *directors* and *management* are accused of acting out of self-interest during *takeover bids*. Recent court decisions have lessened the immunity provided by the rule.

**business model** A general term used to describe how an enterprise makes *money*. The basic concept of any non-governmental, non-charitable business is to make a *profit* or at least match its expenses, and how it intends to accomplish this defines its business model. Buying spanners and selling them to retailers at a *profit*, or selling digital databases to large corporations, are simplistic business models and a *business plan* will then go on to describe the detail. When a business goes into *liquidation* this can euphemistically be described as the failure of the business model. See: *Treasury model*.

**business plan** A detailed outline setting out the plans, objectives and financial *projections* of a business over a stated period, often three, five, or ten years. Most worthwhile *companies* have a business or corporate plan against which *directors* can regularly review their *company*'s progress – some Japanese *companies* have hundred-year corporate plans! For new businesses it is an essential document for raising *funding*. The plan should quantify and outline business objectives, *management* and staffing, products and marketing, the marketplace and the competition, *risk* and return for investors as well as providing monthly *cash flows* and production figures for at least the first year, with a projected *profit & loss account* for the first three years. It must also outline the strategy and tactics the *company* intends to use in achieving its objectives. Often this includes a *SWOT analysis*, looking at the strengths, weaknesses, opportunities and threats to the business.

**business risk (ERM)** Risk management as applied to business. Enterprise Risk Management has only recently become an acknowledged discipline and stems from *insurance risk management* where threats to *profits* or *assets* can be insured. It is also possible to either insure or protect business risk by identifying and proactively addressing *risks* and opportunities; in this way a *company* can protect the viability of the business. Whilst it is not always possible to insure against business risks, it is certainly possible to mitigate them through marketing, *acquisition* or organic development.

**busted bond** A *bond* on which the issuer has defaulted; older Russian, Chinese and South American busted bonds have become collectors items purely for their aesthetic *value*.

**butterfly** A complex *option* strategy designed primarily to collect *option premiums* in situations of low *volatility*; involving the purchase of a low strike put/call, the sale of two mid strike calls/puts and the purchase of a high strike call/put all in the same *security*.

**butut** *Currency* sub-unit of the *Gambia*. 100 butut = 1 *dalasi*.

**buy-back** A venture capitalist will at some point wish to see a return of *capital*. This is usually accomplished by the *company* obtaining a *quotation* or being taken over. A buy-back allows the *company* itself to buy back its own *shares* from the original investor thus retaining its independence and satisfying the venture capitalist. This also enhances the *value* of those *shares* not bought back though it can only be accomplished from accumulated *profit*.

**buying forward** Accomplished in the *futures* markets this involves buying *commodities*, *securities, foreign exchange*, etc., for *delivery* at a date in the future in order to establish a *bull position* or *cover* a *delivery* commitment. In the case of *foreign exchange* a forward purchase may be made to *cover* a future payment in a foreign *currency* and *hedge* any *currency* fluctuation in the *interim*.

**buyout** 1. A *member* of an *occupational pension scheme* has the choice to transfer, without loss, to another *pension* scheme. See: *Section 32, buyout policy*. 2. Term applied to a *listed company* buying back its *shares* from the public, either by making an offer to purchase or by buying in the market. 3. See: *leveraged buyout*. 4. See: *management buyout*.

**buyout policy** A *pension* policy where the *deferred pension* of an early leaver can be bought out of an occupational scheme. An employee can choose an *insurance company* with which to take out a *deferred annuity* policy. If the occupational scheme is contracted out, the *annuity* must match any *guaranteed minimum pension*. See: *Section 32*.

**BV** From Dutch: Besloten Vennootschap. Equivalent to the British: *private limited company (Ltd)*. See also: *NV*.

**BWP** *currency code* for: *Botswana* Pula.

**BYB** *currency code* for: Belarussian Ruble.

**BZD** *currency code* for: *Belize* Dollar.

# C

**CA** See: *chartered accountant.*

**cable** Slang for the dollar–sterling *spot exchange rate.*

**CAC** From the French: Cotation Assistée en Continue. The electronic trading system in the *Paris Bourse* from which the *CAC-40* Index is derived. See under: *France.*

**CAC-40** See under: *France.*

**CAD** 1. See: *Capital Adequacy Directive* and *cash against documents.* 2. *Currency code* for: Canadian Dollar.

**cage** *US* term for the part of the back office of a stockbroking or *portfolio* management firm which deals with the settlement of transactions undertaken by the firm and its clients.

**call** 1. A period in which trading is conducted on a particular *futures* market by a 'call chairman' inviting *bids* and *offers*, usually held at the beginning and end of a trading session, interspersed with trading by *open outcry.* 2. A term used in *company* law for demands made by a *company* that *members* (*shareholders*) should pay certain sums due on the *shares* they hold. A liquidator may make a call immediately irrespective of any agreement the *company* has made with the *shareholders.* The unpaid portion of a *partly paid share* can be called up under these circumstances. See: *call option.*

**call money** Deposits placed on the *money market* which are available at immediate notice.

**call option** A call option *contract* confers the right, though not the obligation, to buy a fixed number of *shares* at a specified price within a predetermined period of time. See also: *put.*

**call-over** A market in which traders in *commodities*, *physicals* and *futures* negotiate by *open outcry.* Usually, traders form *rings* to facilitate the communication, which gives rise to the term *ring trading.* For example, the *London Metal Exchange* trading floor ('the ring') opens at 11.40 when each of the eight metal *contracts* trades in turn for a five-minute period. This process is repeated at 12.30 after a ten-minute break. This second call-over gives rise to the settlement and official prices for the day, which are announced at, or near, 13.15, and then a period of trading called 'the *kerb*' begins. This period lasts until 14.45, during which time all eight *contracts* are traded simultaneously. The morning floor-trading session ends at the *close* of 'the *kerb*', and until the afternoon session at 14.55, inter-office trading takes place.

**called-up capital** The proportion of the issued *share capital* that has been subscribed (including the paid part of *partly paid shares*). See under: *share capital.*

**CalPERS** The California Public Employees' Retirement System (CalPERS) manages pension and health benefits for more than 1.6m California public employees, retirees and their families. As at 31 December 2008 CalPERS controlled the investments of the largest public pension fund in the United States, worth $183.3 billion. CalPERS is an activist shareholder and its size means that it is able to exercise considerable influence on the companies in which it invests.

**Cambodia** Standard *currency*: riel. 1 *riel* = 100 *sen.*

**Cameroon** Standard *currency*: African *franc*.

**Canada** The main *stock exchanges* are the Toronto Stock Exchange (TSE), the Montreal Stock Exchange and the Vancouver Stock Exchange. The TSE has the following main *indices*: TSE 60 Index. Comprises the largest and most liquid *stocks* in the Canadian market and covers about 75% of the market by capitalisation. It is a so-called *stock* 'float-quoted *market value*' ranking, ie it takes into account the total *capitalisation* of *stock* less control blocks of 15% or more. It uses a modified *Paasche formula*, TSX Composite, which is the Canadian equivalent of the USA S+P 500, but contains 300 shares. Standard *currency*: Canadian *Dollar*.

**Canary Wharf** Canary Wharf is a former docklands area, a couple of miles to the east of *the City*, which has been developed into a rival financial centre over the last 25 years. *The Financial Services Authority* has its headquarters in Canary Wharf Tower.

**cancellation price** A price determined by a formula laid down by the FSA, indicating the maximum *spread* between the *offer* and *bid* prices for *unit trusts*. This is the minimum permissible price at which the *value* of units can be quoted; though the *bid* price for units in a *collective investment scheme* is normally higher, it can be used at the manager's discretion to discourage substantial redemptions.

**canons of taxation** In 1776 Adam Smith set down four canons of taxation against which any *tax* can be judged. More recently, a fifth stipulation was added: 1. Certainty. The level, timing and type of *tax* should be made explicit by government authorities. 2. Convenience. Payment should be made as convenient as possible for the taxpayer. 3. Economy. Collection of taxes should be cost-effective. 4. Equity. The *tax* should be as fair as possible in terms of taxpayers sharing the burden. 5. Consistency. The *tax* system should be consistent with the objectives of economic policy. See: *principles of taxation*.

**cap** An *interest rate option* to protect borrowers from a rate of *interest* rising against them. See: *collar, floor*.

**cap and collar mortgage** A type of variable *mortgage* in which the *interest rate* levied on the borrower cannot rise above or drop below certain limits.

**Cape Verde Islands** Standard *currency*: escudo. 1 *escudo* = 100 *centavos*.

**capex** See: *capital expenditure*.

**capital** 1. The total *assets* of a person or organisation minus their total liabilities; if this figure is negative they are insolvent. 2. In economic theory, capital refers to *real* capital (physical capital), ie the equipment used to produce goods and services in an organisation, as opposed to financial capital. Capital is thus a *factor of production* whose cost is called rental cost (of capital). 3. Anything that can be considered as beneficial for *productivity* in an organisation, eg *human capital*. 4. Funds invested in a *company*, either in the form of *shares* (*share capital* or *equity*) or loans (*loan capital*).

**capital account** See under: *balance of payments*.

**capital adequacy** The extent to which a *bank* can meet the requirements of *creditors* and depositors, measured in terms of the total available funds of the *bank*. Also where a regulated *investment* firm has to conform to the European *Capital Adequacy Directive*.

**Capital Adequacy Directive (CAD)** From 1 January 1996 all regulated *investment* management firms doing business in the European Community have had to conform to the *CAD*, which dictates certain minimum liquidity levels for the *net* (*cash* or *near cash*) *capital* resources of such firms. The levels depend on the degree of discretion the firms have over clients' funds and on whether they handle clients' monies directly. The *CAD* is an integral part of the *Investment Services Directive*. An amendment to *CAD*, called *CAD*

II, provided amendments including previously omitted regulations for internal VaR measures. There is currently a *CAD* III in development.

**capital allowances** *Tax allowances* against the cost or *depreciation* of specific business *assets* such as plant and machinery (as opposed to property) to encourage or focus business *investment*.

**capital asset** Another term for: *fixed asset*.

**capital asset pricing model (CAPM)** Model used in quantitative analysis that relates risk and return of a diversified portfolio, ie a portfolio from which unsystematic risk has been fully eliminated and only the systematic risk component is faced. The model utilises a highly idealised market incorporating a number of simplifying assumptions. The investor spreads funds across the full market (diversification) with some investments in 'risk-free' *securities*. The terminology used for the model is that the funds invested in the market – and representative of it – are termed the 'market portfolio' and the remainder of funds invested in the risk-free investments are the 'risk- free portfolio', thus splitting the whole portfolio into two distinct parts. The return to the investor is measured by the return generated from the investor's whole portfolio (R) and the risk is measured by the proportion of funds available to the investor locked into risk-free investments (ß), which is equivalent to the beta coefficient of risk of an investment. Other factors within the model are the returns expected from investing in the risk-free portfolio (RF) and the return from the market portfolio (RM). The '*securities market line*' is derived as the risk-return profile the investor wishes to face:

$$R = R_F + \beta(R_M - R_F)$$

In other words, the investor can expect to achieve a risk-free return (RF) plus a proportion of market-risk *premium* (RM-RF) depending on the level of relative *risk* (ß) the investor is willing to take. The *CAPM* can theoretically be used as an instrument of *investment appraisal*, since *investments* lying above the *security market line* (SML) are *undervalued* and those lying below the SML are *overvalued*.

**capital commitments** An amount of *money* agreed by the *board* of *directors* to be spent on fixed (ie *capital*) *assets*. Must be noted on the *company*'s *balance sheet*. See: *provision*.

**capital consumption** Also called: total *depreciation*. An estimate of an economy's total *depreciation* of *capital* equipment. Due to the difficulty of valuing *depreciation* and problems involved in aggregating across an entire economy, the estimate is bound to be rather inaccurate. However, it is required in order to obtain *net national income* figures (ie *net national product, net domestic product*) from the *gross national income* estimates (ie *gross national product, gross domestic product*).

**capital conversion plan** A now little used concept used by *unit-linked life assurance companies* to pay the *premiums* to a qualifying *Maximum Investment Plan* by encashing a series of *investment bonds* or using a *temporary annuity*. The product was offered as a single package and when investment bods were used the maximum investment plan had variable premiums to accommodate the different values of each bond as it is cashed at the end of each successive year. The internal tax treatment of life companies now limits the tax benefits of such complex arrangements.

**capital employed** *Capital* involved in a transaction or business representing the original *net capital* used to fund the undertaking and equivalent to the *net assets* of a business. See: *return on capital employed*.

**capital expenditure** Spending on *fixed assets* (*capital assets*). For a *limited company* the *value* of the acquired *asset* is noted in the *balance sheet* and the purchase price is not deducted from the *profit & loss account*.

**capital gain** The increase in price (*capital value*) of an *asset* or *investment* above the purchase price realised on sale less expenses and ignoring any *income* from the *asset*. Also referred to as *net capital appreciation*. In the UK, the investor must pay *capital gains tax* at 18% on most *capital* gains above a certain level.

**capital gains tax (CGT)** Introduced in 1965 as a *tax* on the *net appreciation* in the *value* of an *asset*, this is now charged on *net* gains (ie realised *profits* offset against losses) above a certain annual level (£9,600 in 2008/09). The main exemptions are owner-occupied property and chattels. *Pension* funds and charities are exempt. No capital gains tax is payable on *assets* realised as a result of the death of the owner. *Fixed interest securities* issued by both the government and corporations in the *UK* are normally free of capital gains tax for individual investors, as are *National Savings* Certificates. See also: *doomsday price*.

**capital gearing** The ratio of the *equity capital* of a business against all *loan stock* and *preference shares* and other borrowings. If most of the *capital employed* by the business is in *shares* (*equity*) it has low *capital gearing*, and if most of it is *loan stock,* it is highly geared. Highly geared *companies* provide higher returns to *shareholders* when times are good, but they are more vulnerable to weak trading conditions.

**capital growth** The increase in *capital value* excluding all *income*. See: *capital gain*.

**capitalism** Characterised by the operation of a free *market economy* and determination of *value by profit*, and price by *supply and demand*. Capitalism as determined by Marx is the commercial opposite of Communism, which relies on a mode of production determined not by demand but by the social bureaucracy in a managed economy. Capitalism as an economic model has recently suffered a setback after the 2008 *Credit Crunch* and is often considered to be driven by greed. Generally, however, it is accepted that *market forces* are a more reliable determinant of price and *profit* than any political construct – particularly after the collapse of Communism exemplified by the Autumn of Nations in 1989.

**capital line** See under: *Markowitz model*.

**capital loss** Loss made by the sale of *assets* not bought for resale. Contrast: *capital profit*.

**capital market** A general term used to describe a recognised and regulated market where *long term capital* is raised for industry and government from private and corporate investors through *investment* vehicles structured by *banks* and *investment* institutions. Includes *stock* and *bond* markets in industrialised countries. See: *primary market, Recognised Investment Exchange, secondary market*.

**capital profit** Profit made by the sale of *assets* not bought for resale ignoring any *income*. Capital profits that occur in trading *companies* are treated simply as *trading profits* and taxed under *corporation tax* rules. See: *capital gain*.

**capital reserves** These are known under the Companies Act 1985 as *undistributable reserves* and are *reserves* not distributed to *shareholders* as *dividends*. They include *profits* from the *revaluation* of *assets* in the *revaluation* reserve account and *profits* made on the issue of *shares* above *par value* recorded in the *share premium account*. See: *reserves*.

**capital shares** See: *split trust, capital* (sense 4).

**capital subscribed** See: *issued capital*.

**Capital Taxes Office (CTO)** The branch of HMRC that used to deal with the evaluation of *capital* transfers, especially those which give rise to *inheritance tax*. Now HMRC Capital Taxes.

**capital transfer tax** Formerly the *tax* levied on gifts and inheritances replacing *estate duty*. Itself replaced in the *UK* in 1986 by *inheritance tax*.

**capital units** Units allocated to long-term *unit-linked life assurance* policy and *pension* plan holders from which the *insurance company* derived its charges. These units were normally allocated to planholders in the first two years, from then an amount of approximately 4% per year was withdrawn by the *insurance company* as a prior charge on the unit price, regardless of how the *investment* was performing. The performance of these units was significantly reduced as a result of the *gearing* that occurs when this charge is taken during a period when units are falling in *value*. Capital units fell out of favour in the late 1990s when the imminent arrival of stakeholder pensions forced down charges on UK pension plans. See also: *initial units*.

**capitalisation** The *value* of a *limited company* as determined by the *par value*, issue price or market price (whichever is greatest) of its *shares* and the total number of *shares* in issue. This can be used as a criterion for *investment* where any *companies* above or below a certain *market capitalisation* will be considered. The size of *stock markets* is often determined by the total aggregate of the capitalisation of all the *shares* quoted on that market. See: *Normal Market Size*.

**capitalisation issue** An issue creating additional *share capital* either by the issue of new *shares* for old as with a *scrip issue* or by *share* rationalisation. See: *capitalise*.

**capitalise** To introduce *capital* into a *limited company* by creating *shares* or *stock* which are exchanged by the *company* for *cash*. *Shares* are created to raise additional *capital*, though only redeemable *shares* or *stock* can effect a reversal of this process. Other *shares* (ordinary) can only be realised by being bought by a third party or bought back by the *company* from surplus *reserves*. If this is done for an existing *company* the *pre-emption rights* of existing *shareholders* need to be considered.

**capitalised value** 1. The *book value* of an *asset* as recorded in a *company*'s *balance sheet* after *depreciation* and unlikely to be an accurate estimate of the *asset*'s *market value*. If it is felt that the true *value* of an *asset* is appreciably different from the estimate of capitalised *value*, the *asset* should be revalued and its new *value* recorded in the *balance sheet*. 2. An approximation of the *value* of an *asset* in terms of the *income* it generates and the current *interest rate*:

$$\text{capitalised value} = \frac{\text{annual income}}{\text{prevailing } \textit{base} \text{ interest rate (\%)}} \times 100$$

3. The *value* of a *company* expressed as the total *value* of all its *shares* and *stock* at current market prices. See *capitalisation*.

**capitulation** The period at the bottom of a bear market (or crash) when *bulls* throw in the towel and which is supposed to mark the bottom of the market.

**CAPM** See: *capital asset pricing model*.

**captive fund** A *venture capital* fund owned and controlled by a larger financial services group. See: *Venture Capital Trust*.

**CAR** 1. Short for: *gross* equivalent *compound annual return*. A *benchmark* rate used to describe the *total return* available from a deposit *investment* where the *interest* credit is reinvested. Obviously, the more frequent the *interest* credits the better the rate on a compounded basis. See: *annual percentage rate*. 2. A *commodity futures contract*. A throwback to the days when *commodities* were transported in railway cars.

**carat** 1. The measure of actual *gold* in a *gold* alloy. Fine *gold* is 24 carats. 22 carats contains 11 parts of *gold* out of the total 12 parts. 2. Also used to measure the weight of precious stones. Equal to 3.17 troy grains or 200 milligrammes. See: *assay*.

**carpetbagging** The de-mutualisations of *building societies* in the *UK* in the 1980s and early 1990s saw carpetbagging become a popular way of making *money* by opening an account with a mutual society in the hope that it converted to a limited corporation, and offer a financial 'incentive' to encourage members to vote for the conversion. De-mutualisation had run its course by the mid-1990s and now new depositors with a building society often have to sign any possible windfall to charity. The fallout from the *credit crunch* has called into question the wisdom of the whole process, notably for what was once the largest building society – the Halifax.

**carrot equity** A *venture capital* term used to describe *options* either for investors or managers to subscribe for further *equity* in a newly formed *company* if that *company* delivers performance above or below predetermined target levels.

**carry trade** An investment strategy which involves borrowing low yielding currency and then reinvesting in a higher yielding currency or other assets. Until the *credit crunch*, the most popular currency to borrow was the Yen. This was often matched with investment in Australian or New Zealand dollars. The risk in this strategy is that the carry trader has to pay back more as a result of currency movements than they gain from the higher interest rate. Thus when carry trades unwind, conditions can be frenetic as everyone 'rushes for the exit'.

**carrying** The term given to either lending or borrowing operations when trading *futures*. Such transactions are referred to as 'carries'.

**carrying charge** The cost of taking actual delivery in a given month and storing, insuring, financing and redelivering against the next delivery month on the same *commodity market*.

**cartel** The banding together of *companies* in a related industry to set prices and avoid competition. Under certain circumstances and in certain countries operating a cartel can be illegal, as it hinders competition and impedes free trade. However, some institutions quite legitimately form cartels to fix prices and rates, for example the *Organisation of Petroleum Exporting Countries* (*OPEC*).

**cash** Immediately accessible or realisable *assets* that do not fluctuate in *value*. Normally notes and coin, credit balances in *current accounts* and instant access *deposit* accounts. See: *near money*.

**cash accounting** Cash accounting enables individuals and businesses to account for *VAT* on the basis of payments received and made, instead of on *tax* invoices issued and received. The *VAT* payable or repayable for each *accounting period* will be the difference between the total amount of *VAT* included in payments received from customers and the total amount of *VAT* included in payments made to suppliers. Also a method of business management based entirely on *cash flow*, ignoring *accruals, debtors, depreciation,* etc.

**cash against documents (CAD)** Where export and title documents are sent to an agent or *bank* in the importing country and are released to the importer only upon payment. Contrast: *documents against acceptance*.

**cash alternative** Shareholders of a *target company* will often be offered *shares* in the bidding *company* as an alternative to their existing *shares*. They may also be offered a *cash* alternative which may have a slightly lower *value* than the *shares* offered. In some cases *loan notes* are also offered to allow an element of rollover relief.

**cash and carry** This is an operation used in the *futures* markets where, in a *contango* market, the differential between the *cash* price and the three months price reflects the costs of *insurance*, storage and current *interest rates*. Should that differential be greater then a potential *profit* can be made: *cash* metal is bought and forward metal sold simultaneously, thus 'trapping' a return. *Capital* can only be invested in this manner when the *contango* reflects not only the normal storage and *insurance* costs but also a *yield* greater than that currently available on the *money markets*.

**cash cow** A cash generative business that reliably and regularly makes *profits* and which often has a large market share within a mature industry.

**cash equivalent transfer value (CETV)** The *transfer value* of a pension arrangement, calculated in accordance with DWP regulations.

**cash flow** Analysts usually use this term as shorthand for *profit* retention plus *depreciation*. In simple terms this represents the movement of funds through a business during a given trading period, thus indicating the amount by which the liquid resources have increased or decreased during that period. The movement of funds can be shown in the form of a *cash flow statement* or forecast which will provide information as to the sources and application of *capital* during the period, any change in the form in which *working capital* is held, and what finance will be available for running the business during the next trading period.

**cash flow statement** Accounting report of the source and use of funds during a given time period in a business. These must be issued by larger *companies* in accordance with *Financial Reporting Standard* 1 (*FRS* 1).

**cash option** See: *commutation*.

**cash ratio** The *cash* held by a *bank* against the amount owed to customers or depositors. This *money* earns no *interest* for the *bank* (as it cannot be lent out or deposited elsewhere) and accordingly it is kept as small as possible. The minimum cash ratio is determined by the FSA in the *UK* and the *Federal Reserve System* in the *US*. See: *multiplier*.

**cash settlement** Deals relating to *investments* purchased which are due to be paid immediately (normally within two days), as distinct from those for account settlement. Gilt-edged and new-issue transactions are normally paid for in this way. See: *T+3*.

**CAT standard** CAT standards were introduced by the government to encourage saving in the late 1990s. 'CAT' stood for Cost, Access and Term and the standards were intended to inform investors that the product matched certain *benchmarks*. CAT standards were voluntary and not a government endorsement of a product. CAT standards failed to achieve their goal and were abolished in 2005.

**catching bargain** A *contract* capable of being deemed invalid as a result of one party attempting to dupe the other. Also known as an *unconscionable bargain*.

**CATS** Short for: Computer assisted trading system. Such systems have been installed in a number of international brokerages to assist programme trading.

**cats** Discounted *zero-coupon bonds*. See: *deep discount bonds*, *zero-coupon bonds*.

**caveat emptor** Loosely translated from the Latin as 'buyer beware', this phrase denotes a now unpopular tradition where the onus for determining the quality of the product or *investment* is on the buyer. The *Consumer Credit Act 1974*, the Trade Descriptions Act 1968, the Unfair Contract Terms Act 1977, and indeed the regulation of the *investment* industry as a whole have switched the emphasis to the supplier, who must now provide an adequate description of his goods or services and, in some cases, ensure its suitability for the client.

**Cayman Islands** Dependency of the *UK*. Standard *currency*: Cayman Islands *dollar*.

**CBI** Short for: Confederation of British Industry.

**CBOE** See: *Chicago Board Options Exchange*.

**CBoT** See: *Chicago Board of Trade*.

**CCA** See: *current cost accounting*.

**CD** See: *certificate of deposit*.

**CDF** *currency code* for: Congolese Franc.

**CEDEL** See: *Centrale de Livraison de Valeurs Mobilières*.

**cedi** Standard *currency* of *Ghana*. 1 cedi = 100 *pesewas*.

**caution** Registering a 'caution' against a *Land Registry* title is a method of ensuring that the registered property cannot be sold without prior notice to the cautioner, who claims an interest of some kind in the property concerned. Any prospective purchaser of the property will require the *vendor* to get the caution removed from the title before the purchase proceeds. This is done by a process of 'warming off' the caution by means of a notice lodged with the *Land Registry* and sent to the cautioner who is then obliged either to make good his claim on the property or have the caution removed from the title.

**CDO** See: *Collaterised Debt Obligations*.

**CDS** See: *Credit Default Swaps*.

**cent** *Currency* sub-unit of the following countries and territories: *Antigua & Barbuda, Australia, Bahamas, Barbados, Belize, Bermuda, British Virgin Islands, Brunei, Cayman Islands, Dominica, Fiji, Grenada, Guam, Guyana, Hong Kong, Jamaica, Kiribati, Liberia, Micronesia, New Zealand, Puerto Rico, St Kitts and Nevis, Singapore, Solomon Islands, Taiwan, Tuvalu, Trinidad & Tobago, USA, Virgin Islands, Zimbabwe*: 100 cents = 1 *dollar; Ethiopia*: 100 cents = 1 *birr; Kenya, Somalia, Tanzania, Uganda,*: 100 cents = 1 *shilling; Namibia, South Africa*: 100 cents = 1 *rand; Mauritius, Seychelles, Sri Lanka*: 100 cents = 1 *rupee; Aruba*: 100 cents = 1 *florin; Swaziland*: 100 cents = 1 *lilangeni; Sierra Leone*: 100 cents = 1 *leone*. Eurozone: 100 cents = 1 euro.

**centavo** *Currency* sub-unit of the following countries and territories: *Nicaragua*: 100 centavos = 1 *córdoba; Cape Verde,* Madeira, *Portugal;* = 100 centavos = 1 *escudo; São Tomé e Príncipe:* 100 centavos = 1 *dobra; Peru*: 100 centavos = 1 nuevo *sol; Mozambique*: 100 centavos = 1 *metical; Honduras*: 100 centavos = 1 *lempira; Guatemala*: 100 centavos = 1 *quetzal; El Salvador*: 100 centavos = 1 *colón; Argentina, Chile, Colombia, Cuba, Dominican Republic, Guinea-Bissau, Mexico,* the *Philippines*: 100 centavos = 1 *peso; Bolivia*: 100 centavos = 1 *boliviano; Brazil*: 100 centavos = 1 *real; Ecuador*: 100 centavos = 1 *sucre*.

**centésimo** *Currency* sub-unit of the following countries: *Panama*: 100 centésimos = 1 *balboa; Uruguay*: 100 centésimos = 1 *peso*.

**centime** *Currency* sub-unit of the following countries: *Algeria*: 100 centimes = 1 *dinar*. *Benin, Burkina Faso, Burundi, Cameroon, Central African Republic*, Chad, *Comoros, Congo, Djibouti, Equatorial Guinea, Gabon, Guinea, Ivory Coast, Liechtenstein, Madagascar, Mali, Niger, Rwanda, Senegal, Switzerland*, Tahiti, *Togo*: 100 centimes = 1 *franc*; *Haiti*: 100 centimes = 1 *gourde*; *Morocco*: 100 centimes = 1 *dirham*.

**céntimo** *Currency* sub-unit of the following countries: *Costa Rica*: 100 céntimos = 1 *colón*; *Paraguay*: 100 céntimos = 1 *guaraní*; *Andorra, Spain*: 100 céntimos = 1 *peseta*; *Venezuela*: 100 céntimos = 1 *bolívar*.

**Central African Republic** Standard *currency*: African *franc*.

**central bank** Normally a government *bank* or the major *bank* in a country responsible for its primary debt market (see: *primary market*) and implementing national *monetary policy*. All major countries have a central *bank* to control the *money supply*, regulate the banking system, *underwrite* and print banknotes, lend to other *banks*, finance *budget* and *balance of payments deficits*, manage *gold* and *currency reserves*, set *interest rates*, maintain *exchange rates* and act as a *lender of last resort*. Most central *banks* are controlled by the government, but there are a few which operate largely independently of the government and where the chairman of the *bank* is a non-political appointee, most notably the *Bundesbank* (*Germany*) and the *Federal Reserve System* (*US*). See also: *Bank for International Settlements, Bank of England, International Monetary Fund*.

**Central Government Net Cash Requirement (CGNCR)** The Central Government Net Cash Requirement (CGNCR) is the amount of cash that the central government needs to borrow to finance that part of its total expenditure (including lending to public corporations and local authorities) not covered by taxation and other current and capital receipts.

**Central Registration Depository (CRD)** In the *US*, a large computerised database (created by *NASD*) of over 40,000 members of the *investment* industry who deal with the public. It contains information on their employment history and qualifications.

**certificate** The document traditionally issued by the *company secretary* or *registrar* satisfying ownership of *stocks*, *shares* or *unit trusts*. This document had no monetary *value* except in the case of *bearer securities* and simply confirms relevant registration details. The certificate was normally the instrument of transfer, where it could be passed on to the new owner, re-registered or renounced to the managers. While some trading is still based on certificates, nearly all trading today is paperless. See: *share certificate, CREST*.

**Certificate in Financial Planning (CertPFS)** The Certificate in Financial Planning is the Chartered Insurance Institute (CII) level 3 benchmark qualification for financial advisers. It covers regulatory issues, the mechanics and purpose of the main retail investment products and the mechanics of giving financial advice. The Certificate is the successor to the Financial Planning Certificate (FPC).

**certificate of deposit (CD)** Instruments (a securitised *bank deposit*) issued by *banks* and financial institutions confirming that a *deposit* has been taken over a certain period at a certain rate. Used in the *wholesale money* market, they can be bought and sold in their own right. In the *UK* the minimum size is £50,000, increasing in multiples of £10,000. *CDs* are traded purely on a *yield basis*.

**certificate of incorporation** A *certificate* issued by *Companies House* confirming that a *limited company* has been registered and giving its *registered number*.

**certificated stock** Stocks of a *commodity* that have been graded and appraised and passed as acceptable to be tendered on a particular *futures* market.

**certification** A note on the *transfer deed*, upon the sale of *shares*, to show that the *certificate* has been lodged with the *company's registrars* or with the *Stock Exchange*. This is necessary for any certificated trade when the seller is not parting with all of a holding or when the *shares* are bought by more than one person. New *certificates* are then issued to cover the exact redistribution of ownership. See: *share certificate*.

**certified accountant** Member of the *Chartered Association of Certified Accountants*. Members are recognised as qualified to *audit company accounts* by the *Department for Business, Enterprise and Regulatory Reform*. Similar to *chartered accountants*. Ranked within the Chartered Association as *associates* (*ACCA*) or fellows (*FCCA*). The *US* equivalent is a certified public *accountant* (*CPA*) who must have met the statutory licensing requirements of the state in which they operate. See: *accountant*.

**certified bankrupt** See under: *bankrupt*.

**CESR** See: *Committee of European Securities Regulators*.

**CET** See: *common external tariff*.

**CETV** See: *cash equivalent transfer value*.

**ceteris paribus** Latin term often used in economics to mean: 'other things remaining the same'. Used, for instance, to isolate the theoretical effect of the change of one variable in a model. For example, the increase of the price of petrol will, ceteris paribus, increase industry's costs and lower its *profits*.

**CFC** See: *United Nations Common Fund for Commodities*.

**CFD** See: *Contract for Difference*.

**CFTC** See: *Commodity Futures Trading Commission*.

**CGBR** See: *Central Government Borrowing Requirement*.

**CGT** See: *capital gains tax*.

**chain-linked** Refers to *indices*. When adjustments are made to the composition of *indices* (eg *capital* changes of constituent *companies* of the *index*), 'chain-linking' is a technique that ensures that the *index* is kept at the same level before and after the adjustment, thus making sure that there are no discontinuities in the *index* which would render it inaccurate.

**chamber of commerce** A voluntary organisation operating in most towns comprising of businessmen and women who represent their commercial interests to local and central government. The London Chamber of Commerce is the largest such organisation in the *UK* and also fulfils a training role, running several commercial courses for which it sets examinations. Most *UK* chambers of commerce are affiliated to the Association of British Chambers of Commerce.

**channel** Used in *technical analysis*. 1. Strictly, a channel occurs when the tops of *rallies* and the bottoms of *reactions* are enveloped by lines that are (approximately) parallel to each other – the area between them is called the channel. The lines can be directed upward (ascending *trend* channel), downward (descending *trend* channel) or to the side (horizontal *trend* channel). 2. Sometimes the successive peaks and troughs of the price *trend* do not fit into a smooth channel, but some computer programs calculate and display an average *channel trend*. 3. Furthermore, a channel is also used to describe the space between 'walls' that are calculated as a fixed percentage above and below a *moving average* line.

**channel trend** See: *channel*.

**CHAPS** Short for: Clearing House Automatic Payments System.

**Chapter 7** Chapter 7 of the United States Code (Bankruptcy Code) governs the process of *liquidation* under the bankruptcy laws of the *United States*. (In contrast, *Chapter 11* governs the process of reorganisation of a *debtor* in bankruptcy – similar to *administration* in the UK.) Chapter 7 is the most common form of bankruptcy in the *United States* and, like a *liquidation* in the UK, holds little prospect of the business surviving and deals primarily with the division and distribution of any *assets* to *creditors* and *shareholders*.

**Chapter 11** A section of the *US Bankruptcy Reform Act 1978* providing similar benefits for ailing or insolvent *companies* to *administration* in the UK. In *America* an insolvent *company* can file for Chapter 11 to protect it from *creditors* who would otherwise force it into *liquidation*. It gives a business in financial difficulties time to restructure its affairs and obtain additional finance or sell parts of the business that might be lost if it were to go into *liquidation*. Those managing the business continue to run it, but are under an obligation to produce a schedule of repayment for *creditors*.

**charge** 1. A *lien* over land or property to secure a loan. It gives the *creditor* in whose favour it is granted (the 'chargee') the right to payment from the proceeds of sale of the land charged. Land or property can have a series of charges ranked first, second, third etc., each being subsidiary to the other but all in priority to claims against the *debtor* by *unsecured creditors*. All charges on land and property in the *UK* have to be registered with HM *Land Registry*. 2. An interest in a *company asset* granted to a *creditor* (eg a *debenture*) to secure the amount owing. Formal charges must be registered with the *Registrar of Companies* at *Companies House*. A *fixed charge* (or specific charge) is attached to a specific item of property (eg land); a *floating charge* is granted in respect of general *assets* (eg *cash*, *stock in trade*), to which it will not attach until the *company* is wound up. A charge generally describes a formal agreement to transfer *assets* or the proceeds of the sale of *assets* to the charge holder in the event of a *default* on agreed payments to him/her.

**chargeable event** A transaction which potentially gives rise to a charge of either *income tax*, *capital gains tax* or *inheritance tax*.

**Charitable Covenant** An effective form of giving to charities giving the payer *tax* relief. Individuals and *companies* can take advantage of the provisions and charities receiving the covenant can generally reclaim the basic rate *tax* deducted on payments from individuals from HMRC. See also: *covenant*.

**charitable trusts** Trusts registered and approved by the Charity Commissioners exempt from most *tax* and designed to finance charitable projects.

**chart** See under: *chartism, technical analysis*.

**chart pattern** See: *pattern*.

**chartered accountant** A member of one of the three original accounting bodies (called Institute of Chartered Accountants) in England & Wales, Scotland, and Ireland, which were given a royal charter. Other accounting bodies have also received charters and are recognised (*Chartered Association of Certified Accountants, Chartered Institute of Management Accountants, Chartered Institute of Public Finance and Accountancy*) but are not called chartered accountants. See: *accountant, certified accountant*.

**Chartered Association of Certified Accountants** See under: *certified accountant*.

**Chartered Institute of Management Accountants** See under: *chartered accountant*.

**Chartered Institute of Public Finance and Accountancy** See under: *chartered accountant*.

**Chartered Insurance Institute (CII)** A body, with royal charter, that provides qualifications and sets ethical standards for the *insurance* industry. Offers the associateship diploma (*ACII*) and fellowship diploma (*FCII*).

**chartism** A *chart* normally plots the historical movement of an *investment*, showing the relationship between time and price; it is used in *technical analysis*. Essentially a record of movement in the *value* of an *investment* or the *turnover* in purchases or sales of that *investment*. A chartist or technical analyst, in *investment* terms, is normally a person who interprets *chart* data to anticipate future price movements. Chartists employ occasionally complex and often esoteric methods of trying to anticipate future movements and tend to rely on the fact that history repeats itself – the best guide to tomorrow being what happened yesterday. A chart point normally indicates a certain price above or below which a certain amount of buying or selling may occur. A *breakout* above or below a certain chart point may indicate a rise or fall in prices to a certain *support level* or *resistance level*. A number of *chart patterns* are illustrated and explained in the Glossary. See: *analysis*.

**checking account** American *bank* term for what is known as a *current account* in *UK banks*.

**chetrum** Currency unit of *Bhutan*. 100 chetrums = 1 *ngultrum*.

**CHF** *currency code* for: Swiss Franc.

**Chicago Board of Trade (CBoT)** World's largest and oldest *futures* exchange, established 1848.

**Chicago Board Options Exchange (CBOE)** Established in 1972 to deal exclusively in *calls*. *Puts* were also traded in 1977. Primary business is *index options* for S&P 100 and 500.

**Chicago Board Options Exchange Volatility Index (VIX)** A popular measure of the *implied volatility* of *S&P 500 index options* – otherwise known as a *fear index*. A high value corresponds to a more volatile market because of the higher cost of *risk* mitigating *options*; the *index* is designed to represent the measure of the market's expectation of *volatility* over a forthcoming 30-day period.

**Chicago Mercantile Exchange (CME)** A major *US* exchange for *futures* and *options*, established in 1919. It consists of three divisions: *CME International Monetary Market (IMM)*. Deals in *currencies*, coins, *Treasury bills*, Treasury notes, *CDs*, *eurodollar* time *deposits* Index & Options Market (IOM).

**Child Tax Credit** A tax credit generally paid to the main carer of a child aged under 16 (19 if the child is in full time education). The payment is means tested, but the threshold for the maximum basic child tax credit (worth £545 a year in 2009/10) is at least £50,000 a year total (joint) income.

**Child Trust Fund (CTF)** An initiative launched by the UK government in 2003 to encourage parents and children to save for the future. Most UK children born on or after 1 September 2002 qualify for a Child Trust Fund account into which the state initially places either £250 or £500 depending on circumstances. The state will make additional contributions of £250 or £500 to the account on the child's 7th birthday. Parents, relatives and even the child themselves may make additional contributions to the account up to a total value of £1,200 per year. The government has suggested there will also be payments at age 11 and 16, but no legislative provision has yet been made. The account may normally be accessed only when the child reaches 18 years old and benefits from the same *tax* and status treatment as an *ISA*. The *CTF* account is triggered when a parent applies for child benefit (given to all children) when a voucher is issued, which may be used to open a *CTF* account with a provider and type of the parent's choice. If the voucher is not used within one year then HMRC opens a stakeholder type account automatically. About a quarter of all accounts are opened by HMRC.

**Chile** The name of Chile's *stock market* is the Santiago Stock Exchange. The number of *securities* traded in 1994 was 272. Its main *indices* are: General Price Index (IGPA). Originally created in 1958. Comprises 119 *shares*. Base: 30 December 1980 = 100. Selective Price Index (IPSA). Contains the 40 most frequently traded *stocks*. Rebased annually on 30 December at 100. Also operates an electronic exchange: Bolsa Electrónica de Chile. Standard *currency*: *peso*. 1 *peso* = 100 *centavos*.

**China** The country opened its *securities* market in 1988. China operates the Securities Trading Automated Quotations System (STAQ system). It is a computerised national *securities OTC market* that connects users and *member firms* through satellite and cable lines in China's main cities. In June 1994, STAQ linked up to the Shanghai and Shenzhen Stock Exchanges. STAQ compiles the following *indices*: STAQ Treasury Bond Index. Base: 5 December 1990 = 100. STAQ Legal Person Share Index. Base: 8 July 1992 = 100. Both the Shenzhen and Shanghai Stock Exchanges opened in 1990. B-shares are open to foreign investors on the Shenzhen Stock Exchange. The 'China Index' comprises all *listed shares* on these two exchanges. Standard *currency*: *renminbi* denominated in *yuan*.

**Chinese wall** This is an arrangement whereby information known to persons involved in one part of a business is not available, directly or indirectly, to those involved in another part of the business and it is accepted that, in each of the parts of the business so divided, decisions will be taken without reference to any interest which any other such part or any person in any other such part of the business may have in the matter. Designed to protect investors advised by market-making institutions who have a direct interest in the *shares* or the trading of the *shares* of the *company* involved. Here *market makers* may alter the price on the basis of the information they have rather than the *supply and demand* for the *share* itself. See also: *insider dealing*.

**CHIPS** Short for: 'Clearing House Inter-Bank Payments System'. An electronic system for the payment of funds operated by *US banks*. Compare: *SWIFT*. See: *clearing house*.

**Chi-X** Chi-X was the first order-driven pan-European equities *multilateral trading facility (MTF)*. It is owned by Instinet Europe, part of Nomura Holdings.

**chon** *Currency* unit of both *South Korea* and *North Korea*. 100 chon = 1 *won*.

**Christmas Island** Dependency of *Australia*. Standard *currency*: Australian *dollar*.

**churning** Unjustified activity in an *investment portfolio* designed more to generate *commissions* than to alter the strategic disposition of *investments* to good effect.

**CID** Confidential invoice discounting. *Factoring* but without the supplier/customer being aware that they are paying a *bank* rather the firm itself. See: *factoring*.

**CII** See: *Chartered Insurance Institute*.

**CIMPS** Short for: contracted-in *money purchase* scheme. A *company pension* scheme funded by the employer which can accept employee contributions but not *National Insurance* rebates. See also: *money purchase*.

**CIP** See: *covered interest parity*.

**circular flow of national income** A simplified macroeconomic model that forms the basis for most *analysis*. The model summarises the *real* and monetary flows in the economy. The two basic components of the economy are households and firms. Households consume goods and services, produced by firms (consumption); firms pay households wages for the production of these goods and services (*income*). This is the basic circular flow. More components are added to represent the government sector, the *capital market* and the foreign sector. The *income* flow is thus extended. The model can be summarised as '*injections*' (consumption *C*, investment *I*, exports *X*) into the domestic *income* flow being matched by '*withdrawals*' (savings *S*, taxation *T*, imports *M*):

$$C + I + X = S + T + M.$$

**City Code on Takeovers and Mergers** Also called: *Blue Book*. The City Code is a rule book that regulates *takeover* and *merger* activity in the UK. The *Panel on Takeovers and Mergers* (*POTAM*) is a panel whose duty it is to make sure that organisations in the UK adhere to these rules. Central to the City Code are ten general principles and key rules of *takeovers*: 1. The pre-bid environment. Details of the *bid* should not be leaked to the public before it has been organised and announced. This is to prevent *volatility* in the market for the *company*'s *stock*. Before the *bid* is made public, the predatory *company* must inform the *target*'s *board*. 2. *Bid* timings. After the announcement of a *bid*, there is a fixed time frame for the subsequent events. 3. Announcement day. After the announcement, the predator has 28 days to inform the *target* of the details of the *bid*. 4. Posting day. This is the day on which the *target* (and the public) receive the details. This is the reference day (zero day) for subsequent dealings. The *target*'s *board* has 14 days to voice its opinion on the *bid*. 5. First *closing* day. The first day that the *bid* can *close* is day 21. On this day the predator *company* will review the number of acceptances of the *offer* from the *target*'s *shareholders*. (i) If the level of acceptances set in the *offer* document has been reached (the *offer* has gone 'unconditional', usually at a level over 50%), the acceptances are honoured by the predator. Shareholders resisting the *takeover* then have a further 14 days to take up the *offer*. (ii) If the *bid* has not been accepted by *shareholders*, the predator has the choice to increase the level of the *bid* and extend the *offer* period or abandon the *bid*. 6. Last defence documents. The *target* may issue its last defence documents on day 39. 7. Last *offer* amendment. The predator must make its last amendment to *bid* level on day 46. After this date it is not able to buy *shares* in the market at above this price. 8. Final *closing*. The *bid* can remain open for 60 days. By this date it must have gone unconditional or the *bid* will lapse. In the latter case the predator cannot make another *takeover offer* for 12 months. 9. Mandatory *bids*. Control of the *target* is achieved on gaining over 50% of the *shares*. POTAM, however, regards over 30% as effective control and requires *shareholders* with holdings above that level to make a mandatory *offer*. If a shareholder already has a *stake* of between 30% and 50%, the mandatory *offer* must be made if the shareholder subsequently buys more than 1% in any 12-month period. This mandatory *bid* must be at the *best price* paid by the shareholder within the last 12 months. 10. Post-bid environment. An *offer* that has gone unconditional must remain open for a further 14 days. If a predator reaches an acceptance level of 90% or more it can force the minority *shareholders* to sell their *shares* (compulsory purchase procedures within the Companies Act). See: *dawn raid, Substantial Acquisition Rules*.

**class** 1. All *options* of the same type pertaining to the same *underlying security*. 2. A *share* type: small, medium, large by *capitalisation*. 3. *Normal Market Size* categories.

**class action** An American expression generally describing a civil legal action brought by a number of plaintiffs (a class of plaintiff) against a single defendant that gives considerable cost savings and has a particularly threatening impact on the defendant. Groups of people affected by a dangerous drug or a defective product are an example of this. Theoretically those affected by *toxic assets* hitherto described as being of investment grade might consider a class action against a *rating agency*.

**clawback** The reclamation of *tax* relief granted under circumstances where a transaction qualified for relief but which as a result of subsequent events has become ineligible for such relief. There are normally a set of preconditions allowing *tax* relief in certain areas and these conditions will normally need to be met over a period of years during which *tax* relief is granted. A series of transactions may be disqualified by subsequent events and HMRC will often require the return of relief previously granted.

**clean bond** A *fixed interest security* whose price is calculated without taking into account any *accrued interest*.

**clean price** The price of a *fixed interest security* calculated without taking into account any *accrued interest*. This is usually the quoted price.

**clearing bank** A high street *bank* regulated by the *FSA* that deals with the general public and offers *current accounts* whose cheques are cleared through a *UK clearing house*. See: *Big Four, joint-stock bank*.

**clearing house** An organisation which sets off the amounts owing between *banks* as a result of various cheques drawn on their account so that only one sum needs to be paid from one *bank* to another. This avoids individual transactions for each cheque drawn by simply producing a *net* debit or credit after all the various cheques have been taken into account on each day. Also used by *futures* exchanges to settle *contracts* between member companies. See: *Town Clearing*.

**client account** A specific account set aside by a professional person or firm authorised (see: *authorisation*) to handle clients' *money*, which must have *trustee status*, to and from which clients' *capital* is paid and withdrawn. The account should not form part of the *company*'s trading activities, to ensure that clients' monies are kept completely separate from all day-to-day business transactions. Such an account is specifically designated to protect clients from *insolvency* or sharp practice. Such an account is compulsory for any *company* legally handling *investments* on behalf of clients.

**client agreement** See: *customer agreement*.

**close** 1. As in: the close. The *closing* period or *call* of a session. 2. As in: to close. A transaction to liquidate, balance or negate an existing position or to complete a transaction.

**close company** A *company* controlled only by the *directors* or by five or fewer participants. See: *limited company*.

**closed end fund** A type of fund that is *listed* on a *stock exchange* or offered by an *investment* institution and has a fixed number of *shares* or units, unlike *open-end funds* which issue and redeem *shares* and units on a frequent basis. In *America* a closed-end *investment company* is the equivalent of the traditional *UK investment trust*. Contrast: *open-ended investment company*.

**closed fund** *US* term for a *mutual fund* that has become too large and subsequently has stopped issuing *shares*. In the *UK* it refers to a *life assurance* fund that operates only for existing policy holders and is closed to new entrants.

**closing** Ending a commitment or transaction or neutralising an *open position*.

**closing deal** The trade comprising a *closing sale* or *closing purchase* to complete a transaction.

**closing prices** The last quoted buyers' and sellers' prices recorded at the end of the trading session for each day.

**closing purchase** A purchase of *securities* to close a *short position* or the purchase of a *future* identical to a *future* already sold – again to *cover* a *short position*. Also a transaction by which a *writer* buys an *option* having exactly the same terms as an *option* which he or she has previously sold, thus terminating the liability.

**closing sale** Opposite to *closing purchase*. A sale of *securities* or *futures* to close a *long position* or dispose of a *physical*. Also a transaction in which the holder of an *option* disposes of it.

**CLP** *currency code* for: Chilean Peso.

**CME** See: *Chicago Mercantile Exchange*.

**CMO** See: *collateralised mortgage obligation*.

**CNAR** See: *compound net annual return*. The *rate of return* on a *deposit* type *investment* allowing for the reinvestment of after-tax *interest* to be compounded at the various intervals that it is credited. A *benchmark* for establishing *annual returns* from various types of *deposits*. See also: *annual percentage rate, compound annual return*.

**CNMV** From Spanish: Comisión del Mercado de Valores. The Madrid Stock Exchange. See under: *Spain*.

**CNY** *currency code* for: Yuan Renminbi. See: *China*.

**COB** From French: Commissions des Operations de Bourse. The French *stock market* watchdog. Has statutory regulatory powers in line with British and American regulators.

**Cocos Islands** Dependency of *Australia*. Standard *currency*: Australian *dollar*.

**Code Number** A number allocated to an individual by the *Inland Revenue* to enable the correct *tax* to be deducted at source under *PAYE* (*pay-as-you-earn* scheme).

**Coffee Sugar and Cocoa Exchange (CSCE)** An important, independently incorporated exchange in New York, dealing in *futures* and *options* in cocoa, coffee, sugar, cheddar cheese and non-fat dry milk. Merged with New York Cotton Exchange in 1998 as a subsidiary of the New York Board of Trade.

**cold call** An unsolicited contact which results in the sale of a financial product or *investment*. The FSA restricts unsolicited canvassing of investors and allows them a *cooling-off period* during which they can change their minds if they have entered into a transaction as a result of a cold call.

**cold shouldering** See under: *Panel on Takeovers and Mergers*.

**collar** A combination of two *interest rate* options to provide protection against a rate of *interest* fluctuating too widely, ie a *straddle* of a *cap* and a *floor*.

**collateral** An American expression used to describe a *security* put up by a borrower in addition to this promise to repay. The precise English definition is a *security* put up by someone other than the borrower, either in support of the guarantee or as a third-party *security* in place of the guarantee. Where *security* is put up by the borrower to support the promise to pay, this is known as a direct *security*.

**collateralised debt obligation (CDO)** *CDOs* are packaged loans that have been securitised. Often constructed from a *portfolio* of fixed-income *assets* such as mortgages and fixed-term personal loans with *banks* and finance institutions, these *assets* are divided by *credit reference agencies* into different *tranches*: senior *tranches* (rated AAA), mezzanine *tranches* (AA to BB) and *equity tranches* (unrated) where the higher the *risk* the higher the *yield*. These are then mixed into *portfolios (sliced and diced)* and then securitised (turned into *shares* or *bonds*) and sold as *fixed interest securities* on the open market. It is generally accepted that the seeds of the 2008 *Credit Crunch* lay in the complexity of CDO products where it was difficult if not impossible to determine the content of the finished securitised product. This was further compounded by the inadequacy of *risk* models used by *credit reference agencies* to value these products. Furthermore many institutions buying *CDOs* were unable to monitor credit performance and/or estimate expected *cash flows* making these 'assets' very difficult to value accurately. As many CDO products are held on a *mark to market* basis paralysis in the credit markets and the collapse of *liquidity* in these products led to substantial write-downs in 2008 leading to much of this market being classified as toxic. See: *securitisation, sliced and diced, CMO, Credit Crunch, toxic asset, NINJA, TARP, sub-prime mortgage*.

**collateralised mortgage obligation (CMO)** An *investment* in a fund made up from *mortgages* structured as a *bond* backed by a pool of *mortgages* owned by various *mortgage* issuers. The principal *cash flows* of the pool are channelled sequentially into a series of *bonds* from which *interest* payments are made bi-annually. The securitisation of these funds can conceal the source and quality of the underlying *mortgages* and the expansion of this market has been identified as one of the causes of the 2008 *Credit Crunch*.

**collective investment scheme** Any *investments* which enable participants to benefit from *profits* or *income* arising from the *acquisition*, holding, management or disposal of some or all of the underlying *investments* in which they participate, such as *unit trusts*, OEICs, *investment trusts*, *managed funds* and *mutual funds*. Basically a fund run by an individual manager or institution made up of *investments* from a large number of small investors and divided into one *class* of units or *shares* that represent the amount invested. See: *Undertaking for Collective Investments in Transferable Securities, open-ended investment company*.

**Colombia** The Bogotá Stock Exchange was established in 1928. The number of *listed companies* in 1994 was 105. Its main *index* is: IBB Share Price Index. The other *stock markets* are: Medellín Stock Exchange, Occidente Stock Exchange (in Cali). Standard *currency*: peso. 1 *peso* = 100 *centavos*.

**colón** Standard *currency* of the following countries: *Costa Rica*: 1 colón = 100 *céntimos*; *El Salvador*: 1 colón = 100 *centavos*.

**COMEX** See: the *Commodity Exchange of New York*.

**comfort letter** An American term where a *bank* or *accountant* writes a letter as proof of their client's financial repute. This has no legal significance.

**commercial paper** Unsecured short-term debt traded in the *money market*. Issued by major creditworthy institutions such as *banks, insurance companies* and *trust companies*, it is simply a *promissory note* issued at a *discount* to its *face value* maturing within twelve months.

**commercial rate of interest** A term often used to assess the *value* of the use of *capital*. The rate can be determined by reference to the basis on which *banks* make *secured loans*, eg 2% to 3% above *base rate*. Confirmation of the rate applying to associated parties lending or borrowing on an *arm's length* basis needs to be obtained from an independent third party such as a *bank*.

**Commerzbank Index** See under: *Germany*.

**commission** Payment to an intermediary for services rendered often based on the *value* of the goods handled. Such commission or *brokerage* is often paid at a predetermined percentage rate.

**commission house** An organisation, normally a *stockbroker*, that specialises in buying and/or selling *investments* on behalf of clients and being paid *commission* as opposed to researching, trading or dealing in its own right.

**commitment fee** A fee charged by a *bank* or a *broker*, at outset, for the provision or continuance of a loan. See: *bank charge*.

**Committee of European Securities Regulators (CESR)** The CESR is an independent Committee of European Securities Regulators. The role of the CESR is to improve co-ordination among securities regulators, to act as an advisory group to assist the EU Commission and to work to ensure more consistent and timely day-to-day implementation of community legislation across the EU.

**commodity** Basically a tangible *asset* that has a *market value*. The term is normally applied to raw materials and foodstuffs traded on various exchanges throughout the world. Invariably these commodities are traded for future delivery, and the commodity exchanges offer suppliers and consumers a predetermined price for the supply and delivery of their goods. Here the speculators take the *risk* of short-term fluctuations and tend to smooth out price movements and correct anomalies. As a field of *investment*, this sector is notorious for high *risk* and high reward as the *futures contracts* can be traded on *margin*, allowing *gearing* of *profits* or losses. Owing to the *volatility* of price movements commodity *contracts* can prove to be a dangerous *investment* for the smaller private investor. See: *CAR, Commodity Exchange of New York, futures, London Metal Exchange, lot, physical, rings, softs, syndicate*.

**commodity broker** A regulated and accredited *broker* who deals in *commodities*, normally a member or *associate* of a *commodity* exchange, who trades on behalf of investors in a *commodity market*. The rules governing the procedure adopted in each market vary from *commodity* to *commodity*, as the functions of *brokers*. Most *commodities* are traded for producers and consumers by members of an exchange using *open outcry* and instructions are passed to members by *brokers*. Speculators in the market who do not produce or consume the *commodities* are clients of a *broker* who acts as intermediary.

**Commodity Exchange Center** The *Coffee Sugar and Cocoa Exchange* (*CSCE*), the *New York Cotton Exchange* (*NYCE*) and the *New York Mercantile Exchange* (*NYMEX*) and their divisions in New York are known collectively as the Commodity Exchange Center.

**Commodity Futures Trading Commission (CFTC)** Independent agency in the *US* created by Congress in 1974 responsible for regulating the *commodity futures* and *options* markets. The *CFTC* is responsible for ensuring market integrity and protecting market participants against manipulation, abusive trade practices and fraud.

**commodity market** A market in which *commodities* are traded. The main terminal markets in *commodities* are in London, Chicago and New York although there are many *primary markets* in the country of *origin*. Some *commodities* are dealt with at *auctions* (eg tea), each lot sold having been examined by dealers, but most deal with *commodities* that have been classified according to established quality standards (*certificated stock*). Both *actuals* and *futures* are traded on *commodity* exchanges, often by *open outcry* during a *call* session, in which *dealers* are represented by *commodity brokers* who are members of the exchange. Many *commodity* exchanges offer *option* dealing in *futures* and settlement of differences on *futures* through a *clearing house*. As *commodity* prices are volatile, *commodity* exchanges offer consumers and producers hedging facilities provided by speculators and investors who also help to create an active and liquid market. Many markets have *limits* (see: *trading curb*) within which prices can move in one *call* session to control price *volatility*. See: *commodity*.

**Common Budget** A *European Commission* fund deriving monies from all duties and levies on *imports* into the *European Union*.

**common external tariff (CET)** When a group of countries each agree to impose the same *tariff* rates for goods imported from countries outside the group. An example is the *European Union* which has a *CET* to non-Member States, duties from which fund the *Common Budget*.

**Common Market** An old term for the *European Union* (*EU*).

**common market** A *customs union* that allows the free movement of *factors of production*, such as labour. Originally the *EU* was known as a common market, upon the *UK*'s entry into the then *European Economic Community* (*EEC*) in 1972. The *EEC* was primarily a trading union, similar to *NAFTA*. However, the *EU* has steadily adopted a more federal structure. The development of a European Parliament, European law, and the single European *currency* (*euro*) with its blanket *monetary policy* shows that the *EU* has become far more than simply a common market.

**common stock** The *US* term for *ordinary shares* or *equities* usually issued as *bearer securities*.

**common trading platform (CTP)** A computerised system providing *IFAs* with information on *assurance* products for *quotation* and comparison purposes subscribed to by most major *life assurance companies*.

**commutation** An alternative available when taking a *pension* represented by the amount of *cash* available if a certain element of *pension income* is forsaken upon retirement. Usually the cash provided is less than the open market cost of the pension foregone. Called a *cash* lump sum or pension commencement lump sum, it is normally *tax* free.

**Comoros** Standard *currency*: African *franc*.

**Companies Act 2006** Received Royal Assent in November 2006 and updates previous *Companies Acts* – particularly in restating almost all the provisions contained in the 1985 Act and the Company Law provisions of the 1989 Act; it deals with electronic filing of documents in relation to formation, filing and secretarial requirements as well as reporting to *shareholders* and disclosure generally. It deals with the management and decision-making process within *limited companies*, and safeguards for officers and members, raising *capital* and *annual returns*, reconstructions, *mergers* and *takeovers*. It also deals with the regulation of *companies* outside the ambit of the *Companies Acts* and the disqualification of *directors*, officers and *auditors* in the *UK* and overseas.

**Companies Acts** The generic term covering the statutory rules governing the conduct, structure and performance of *limited companies* and their *directors* and treatment of their *shareholders* and employees. Includes Companies Acts of 1967, 1970, 1980, 1981, 1985, 1989, 2006 etc.

**Companies House** A place where a central register of all the *limited liability companies* in the *United Kingdom*, whether public or private, is kept and which issues *certificates of incorporation* and trading permissions. All the details of the *directors*, *Memorandum & Articles of Association*, name changes, *registered office*, *registered number*, *members*, *debentures*, *accounts* and *balance sheet* must be lodged (registered) here initially and in the form of *annual returns* and remain available for scrutiny by any member of the public. Known as the *Registrar of Companies*, it is based in Cardiff at Companies House, Crown Way, Cardiff CF4 3UZ.

**company** An economic unit that exists as a legal entity distinct from its owners and managers. The most common type of company is a registered company (or as is more common in the *US*: corporation) under the *Companies Acts*. A *limited company* is a company in which the liability of the owners for debts is limited (usually to the *net assets* of the company), as opposed to an *unlimited company* such as a *partnership* (in which the owners may have to use their personal *assets* to pay for the company's debts and which need not be registered). A registered company is either a *public limited company* (*plc*) or a *private limited company* (*Ltd*) or a company *limited by guarantee*, details of which can be freely obtained at *Companies House*.

**company director** See: *director*.

**company doctor**  A seasoned businessman or corporate *accountant*, acting normally as a *non-executive director*, who is experienced in correcting the ailments of troubled *companies*.

**company seal**  An impress mark for *companies* to certify documents, obtained from *Companies House*. See: *seal*.

**company secretary**  An officer of a *limited company* whose duties include the filing of statutory *annual returns* at *Companies House*, keeping a register of *shareholders* and filing all relevant statutory documents for the *company* including details of *directors*, name changes and *Memorandum & Articles of Association* as well as issuing notices of meetings and *resolutions*. See: *Section 212*.

**company voluntary arrangement**  See: *voluntary arrangement.*

**comparative advantage**  See: *absolute advantage.*

**comparative method**  See under: *valuation* (sense 2).

**Competition Commission (CC)**  A statutory commission to regulate *takeover, merger* and potential *monopoly* situations involving *UK companies*. Formerly the *Monopolies and Mergers Commission (MMC).*

**completion meeting**  The meeting at which all documents connected with a sale, *capital* injection, *takeover, merger* or *going public* are completed including the *placing* or *underwriting agreement* and, if appropriate, *funding* or payment provided by a banker's *draft*. See: *flotation.*

**compliance**  Self-policing by a financial firm or *Independent Financial Advisor* governed by the *Financial Services and Markets Act 2000* to ensure that financial regulations are being obeyed. The Act strengthened rules applied to firms involved in the business of managing, marketing and dealing in *investments*, and they must have their own compliance departments to ensure that the rules of the FSA are strictly adhered to.

**composite index**  *Index* used for tracking the changes in a number of items, as opposed to a single item. The best example is the *Retail Price Index (RPI)* which uses a basket of goods. The composite index may or not be weighted (see: *weighted index*). In addition to this, the method used for combining the constituent items in the *index* is either arithmetic or geometric. In the following the prices of different goods are used for illustrative purposes. There are assumed to be m different items (1, 2, 3, ..., m), with respective prices P1, P2, P3, ..., Pm, and quantities Q1, Q2, Q3, ..., Qm where i denotes the general item, Pi its *value* and Qi its quantity. The subscripts 0 and n refer respectively to *base period* and current period *values*. 1. Arithmetic *index*. The arithmetic *index* is calculated in a similar fashion to taking the *mean (average)* of the individual items' relative price *indices* (see: *index*). Now this *mean* is called the '*average* price relative *index*' and is as follows:

$$\text{unweighted arithmetic index} = \sum_{i=1}^{m} \frac{P_{i_n}}{P_{i_0}} \times \text{base index value}$$

The disadvantage of the '*average* price relative *index*' is that all items are considered of equal importance, ie each item is equally weighted. From this concept the unweighted arithmetic *index* is defined as:

$$\text{average price relative index} = \frac{1}{m} \sum_{i=1}^{m} \frac{P_{i_n}}{P_{i_0}} \times \text{base index value}$$

This method can be generalised to cover the case of weighted arithmetic *indices*, thus generally speaking:

weighted arithmetic index =

$$\frac{\text{sum of quantity weighted current period values}}{\text{sum of quantity weighted base period values}} \times \text{base index value}$$

But there are different methods of weighting the items in terms of using quantities calculated at different periods, ie base and current periods. If current period quantities only are used for weighting, the *index* is called a *Paasche index*; if *base period* quantities only are used, the *index* is a *Laspeyres index*; and if relevant quantities in relation to the period (ie base quantities in *base period*, current quantities in current period) are used, the *index* is termed a date-weighted *index*.

Paasche index $\qquad = \dfrac{\Sigma_{i=1}^{m} Pi_n Qi_n}{\Sigma_{i=1}^{m} Pi_0 Qi_n}$

Laspeyres index $\qquad = \dfrac{\Sigma_{i=1}^{m} Pi_n Qi_0}{\Sigma_{i=1}^{m} Pi_0 Qi_0}$

Date-weighted index $\qquad = \dfrac{\Sigma_{i=1}^{m} Pi_n Qi_n}{\Sigma_{i=1}^{m} Pi_0 Qi_0}$

These three *indices*, along with the *average* price relative *index*, which assigns equal weights to each item, constitute the weighted arithmetic *indices*. There is an equivalent, slightly easier, method of actually computing these *indices*: see under *weighting factor*. Points to note for the investor are: the *Paasche index* understates *inflation* or *growth* because it is based on the current quantities and thus places less weight on the items that experience higher price increases. It does not take into account that the holder of an *investment portfolio* will *switch* into *investments* that appreciate more quickly, and thus the *Paasche index* may understate *portfolio* performance. By similar reasoning, the *Laspeyres index* overstates *inflation* and understates *portfolio* performance. The date-weighted *index* is the best of the three for these purposes. Arithmetic *indices* are the most appropriate way of measuring *portfolio* performance. This is because the returns on *securities* constituting the *portfolio* are summed up within the formula to obtain the *total return* of the *portfolio*. This differs from the methodology employed in calculating the geometric *index*, which is described next. 2. Geometric *index*. The geometric *index* is one calculated along the same lines as the *geometric mean*. It is thus calculated as follows:

$$(\text{unweighted}) \text{ geometric index} = \sqrt[m]{\frac{\text{product of current period values}}{\text{product of base period values}}} \times \text{base index value}$$

If the items constituting the *index* are quantity-weighted, then the geometric *index* must take this into account. If an item appears a number of times, then it must be multiplied by itself that number of times. For example, if an item i (of price Pi) occurs Qi times, ie there is a quantity Qi of item i at price Pi, then the relevant product is PiQi using power notation. Thus the weighted geometric *index* can be expressed as follows:

$$\text{weighted geometric index} = \sqrt[Q]{\frac{(P1^{Q1})_n \times (P2^{Q2})_n \times \ldots \times (Pm^{Qm})_n}{(P1^{Q1})_0 \times (P2^{Q2})_0 \times \ldots \times (Pm^{Qm})_0}} \times \text{base index value}$$

where $Q = Q1 + Q2 + \ldots + Qm$, the total number of items. This is a date-weighted *index*. The Paasche and Laspeyres *indices* are not usually calculated for the geometric method of constructing *indices*. Furthermore, there are some important drawbacks of this method. The geometric *index* is not representative for the return on a *portfolio*, as stated earlier. It is also less sensitive to larger increases in price and more sensitive to large price declines, compared with the arithmetic method, so it will understate *portfolio* performance in *bull markets* or inflationary periods. Lastly, if any item's price is zero, the geometric *index* cannot be calculated (but the arithmetic *index* can). In addition, some market *indices* do not include the payment of *income* by a *security* (*dividends* in the case of *shares* and *interest* for bonds), such as the *Financial Times Share Indices*. In contrast some *bond indices*, such as the Citigroup World Government Bond *indices*, do include the *value* of *coupon* payments, and are thus *total return indices*. See also: *chain-linked, MSCI Indices*.

**compound** A general term for *values* that accumulate, where increments are calculated on accumulated rather than base *values*.

**Compound Annual Growth Rate (CAGR)** The equivalent to *CAR* when applied to economic and market factors such as consumer spending, market penetration, worldwide sales etc. as well as capital items.

**compound annual return (CAR)** The *total return* on an *investment* in which the *interest* payments are compounded with the principal invested. Usually quoted as a *gross* figure. See also: *compound net annual return, interest*.

**compound interest** See under: *interest*.

**compound net annual return (CNAR)** The *compound annual return* (*CAR*) in which deductions at *basic rate tax* have been made on *interest* payments.

**COMPS** See: *contracted-out money purchase scheme*.

**comptroller** A term used more in the *US* to refer to the (chief) financial officer (finance *director*) in some *companies* or groups of *companies*.

**compulsory purchase annuity** An *annuity* which usually, under the terms of a *pension*, must be purchased with the fund accumulated in the *member*'s *pension* fund by the *trustees* for the benefit of the individual *member* to pay his or her *pension income* in retirement. Such annuities can be written on a joint-life basis, (see: *joint-life and last survivor annuities*) which will provide the surviving partner with a reduced *income* for life. The resultant *pension income* is taxed as earned *income* and does not benefit from the '*capital* element' concession applicable to purchased life annuities.

**concert** Also: concert party. Apparently unconnected *shareholders* acting secretly and in unison to manipulate price, management or control of a *company*.

**conditional bid** A *bid* conditional on a predetermined percentage of the *shareholders* accepting the terms offered or on some other factor such as *board* acceptance or the sale of a *subsidiary company*.

**conditionality** The conditions under which the *International Monetary Fund* (*IMF*) provides *balance of payments* support to member states. Support will only be given provided it is accompanied by steps to solve the underlying fiscal problem. Programs of economic reform are agreed with the member (see: *three-D*) including the attainment of a sustainable *balance of payments*. The *IMF* issues general guidelines of conditionality principles, and these are used as the basis for most intergovernmental lending.

**Confederation of British Industry (CBI)** The *CBI* is the *UK's* leading employers organisation working with the UK government, international legislators and policy-makers to help *UK* businesses compete effectively.

**confirmation** When used in the context of *technical analysis* this refers to the precept requiring another *indicator* or *index* to move in a similarly important way to the price in question. Such a requirement is a major part of the *Dow Theory* (where the Industrials and Transportation Averages are compared), but the principle of confirmation is also used when price is compared with the movement of an *indicator* such as a *relative strength* line or a *momentum* line or even a *moving average*. An example would be a price breaking into new high ground; confidence could then be placed in the signal made by the price if the *indicator* has made a similar *breakout*.

**conflict of interest** A general term describing a conflict between self-interest and professional interest that might arise where a *director* acts for two competing *companies* but has *shares* in one and not the other. Professional firms sometimes find themselves acting for two parties to a dispute or *bid* and have to withdraw totally or from one party. *Auditors* cannot have any interest in *companies* whose *accounts* they *audit*. Many public *companies* have *non-executive directors* to balance control and ensure that such conflicts do not arise.

**conglomerate** A group composed of various *companies* in different businesses. Generally considered to be difficult to evaluate, such groups can supposedly bring the benefits of better management, sound financial backing and *economies of scale* to *companies* within their control. More recently, such *companies* have been susceptible to *break-up bids*. See: *break-up*.

**Congo** Standard *currency*: African *franc*.

**connected parties** In order to establish *material interests* of a *shareholder*, connected parties are defined as: 1. *shares* owned by a *connected person*. 2. *shares* owned by a connected or controlled *company* (under the Companies Act a controlled *company* is one in which the shareholder holds a *stake* of 33⅓%). 3. any *concert* parties.

**connected person** A person is 'connected' with an individual if the person is the wife, husband, relative or the spouse of a relative or is so connected with the spouse of that individual or has an interest in a *trust* or settlement or corporate body or *partnership* that relates to or has an interest in a relevant transaction. See: *associate*.

**consent letter** A letter required from any expert named in a *prospectus* which consents to the issue of the *prospectus* with the inclusion of their letters or reports and references to their name.

**consideration** If a *contract* other than a *contract* by *deed* is to be binding, the promise of the one party must be supported by the agreement of the other party to do or not to do some act, or to pay some *money*. The agreement by the other party is known as the consideration. In *investment* terms, the consideration is the monetary *value* of a *contract* for either the purchase or the sale of such an *investment*. The consideration is the *value* before *commissions*, charges, *stamp duty* and other transfer expenses are deducted, and thus not the full cost or proceeds, for *capital gains tax* purposes.

**consistency concept** See: *accounting concepts*.

**consolidated accounts** The *accounts* of a *company* together with all its *subsidiary companies*, presented in one set of figures.

**Consolidated Fund** The Exchequer Account held by the *Bank of England* and controlled by the Treasury, covering all government revenue and expenditure. It was formed in 1787 by the consolidation of several government funds.

**Consolidated Quotation Service (CQS)** A service offered by *NASDAQ* in the *US* providing *quotations* on *stocks listed* on the *New York Stock Exchange* and the *American Stock Exchange* and selected *securities* on regional *stock exchanges*.

**consolidation pattern** Another term for: *continuance pattern*.

**Consols** Government consolidated *stock*. This *stock* has no final *redemption date* and was issued at various times at various rates of *interest*. The price varies according to the rate of *interest* prevailing at the time. Consols were once a significant part of the gilt market, but are now 'rump' stocks with limited liquidity.

**consortium** A group of investors with common interests, or businesses with common *shareholders*, that form an association to benefit from *economies of scale* or gain market influence or to benefit generally from strength in numbers.

**constant dollar plan** The *US* name for *pound cost averaging*, ie the payment of a specified sum of *money* at regular intervals to purchase units or *shares* in an *asset backed investment* as part of a savings plan. Also called '*dollar cost averaging*'.

**consumer credit** Short-term loans to an individual for the purchase of goods. The most common forms are credit accounts at retail outlets, personal loans from *banks* and *finance houses*, *hire purchase* and credit cards. The *Consumer Credit Act 1974* has given the borrower greater protection, particularly with regard to regulations covering the description of the true rate of *interest* being charged. The Act also makes it necessary for anyone giving credit to obtain a consumer credit licence and be placed on the *consumer credit register*.

**Consumer Credit Act 2006** A *UK* Act of Parliament protecting the borrower in credit agreements, loans and *mortgages*. The Act requires full written details of the true *interest rate* (ie *annual percentage rate*) to be quoted, a *cooling-off period* to be given and all agreements to be confirmed in writing. The Act does not cover *bank overdrafts*. The Act replaced the Consumer Credit Act 1974 and came fully into effect on 1 October 2008.

**consumer credit register** The register kept by the Office of Fair Trading (OFT), as required by the *Consumer Credit Act 2006*, of all those who have applied for or been granted a *consumer credit* licence. The register contains details of undetermined applications and licences that are in force or have at any time been suspended or revoked, as well as details of decisions given by the OFT under the Acts and any appeals. The public is entitled to inspect the register on payment of a fee.

**consumer prices index (CPI)** The UK price index used for setting the Bank of England's inflation target. Originally called the Harmonial Index of Consumer Prices (HICP) until December 2003. Base: January 1996 = 100.

**contango** The difference (increase) in price between the *spot price* and the price quoted for forward delivery, reflecting storage, *insurance* and finance.

**contingent interest** An interest in a transaction or undertaking that is dependent on a specific predetermined event rather than a *vested interest* which applies regardless of circumstance.

**contingent liability** A liability in a *balance sheet* as a provision for an expense that will arise if a particular event occurs. Examples include a court case pending or loss of *earnings* as a result of a customer invoking a penalty clause in a *contract*. Under the Companies Act 2006, such liabilities must be explained by a note on the *company balance sheet*.

**contingent liability transaction** A transaction where the client can incur a loss in excess of the initial *investment* – many *derivative* transactions have this capacity. Firms in the *UK* are not permitted to carry out such a transaction on behalf of a private customer unless the transaction is made on a *Designated Investment Exchange* or a *Recognised Investment Exchange*, or unless the purpose of the transaction is to *hedge* against a *currency risk*.

**continuance pattern** A *chart pattern* which breaks out in the same direction as the preceding trend. Compare: reversal pattern.

**contra** A balancing entry made to correct, amend or cancel an entry from another account. See: *accounting concepts*.

**contract** 1. An agreement between two parties detailing the terms and conditions of their association. 2. The unit of weight laid down by the individual *commodity markets* as being the standard contract, ie cocoa in units of 5 *tons*, hence 5 contracts = 25 *tons*. 3. See: *contract note*. 4. See: *bargain*. 5. See: *Contract for Difference*.

**Contract for Difference (CFD)** Developed to allow the *capital* benefits of investing in a *stock* without having to physically own or pay for it. No *dividends* are available and the difference between the underlying price when the *contract* is bought and sold is the *profit* or loss. The *contract* is a *derivative* and can relate to a number of selected physical *stocks* and *bonds* individually or to their respective *indices*. Similar to an *option* but without a specific time *premium*. Normally based on a £1 per *point* movement up or down, *profit* or loss will depend on the difference when bought or sold — when *long*, a position is closed by selling the same number of open *CFDs*, and a *short position* is closed by buying them. See also: *synthetic asset*.

**contract note** Written confirmation of the purchase or sale of an *investment* issued immediately the *bargain* is struck, legally binding subject to genuine error. See: *E&OE*.

**contracted-out money purchase scheme (COMPS)** An employer *pension* funded by *National Insurance* rebates and, usually, employer contributions. Used to contract out of the *state second pension scheme*, where the ultimate benefits will depend on the *capital* invested and the performance of the underlying *investments*. This method of contracting out is set to be abolished from April 2012. See *contracting out*, *money purchase*.

**contracting out** The use of a statutory arrangement whereby employees (and employers) can opt out of the *second state pension scheme*. In final salary schemes and certain *money purchase pension* plans this will result in a reduction in *National Insurance* contributions for the employer and employee and in an amount at least equivalent to this reduction in the *National Insurance* contribution being diverted into the plan. See also: *contracted-out money purchase scheme*, *government incentive payment*, *guaranteed minimum pension*.

**contracting-out certificate** A certificate issued by *HMRC* for an *occupational pension scheme* which satisfies the relevant conditions, confirming that *members* named in the certificate are to be treated as being in contracted-out employment. (See: *contracting out*).

**contractors valuation** See under: *valuation* (sense 2).

**contractual scheme** A *pension* scheme where the payment of benefits to *members* is enforceable by law.

**contributory pension scheme** A *pension* scheme where *members* are required to contribute to the scheme as well as their employer.

**controlling director** By definition, a *director* who, either alone or together with his or her spouse, minor children and the *trustees* of any settlement in which he or she has an interest, owns *shares* carrying more than 20% of the *voting rights* in a *company* or a *company* controlling that *company*; or by virtue of rights conferred by the *Articles of Association* or *shareholders'* agreements etc. A controlling *shareholder* will, however, normally be considered to be someone owning more than 50% of a *company*, though controlling shareholdings can in practice be less than this if the remaining *shares* are owned by a number of diverse interests. In the day-to-day activities of a *limited company* the *board* of *directors* controls the *company* and accordingly control of the *board* is a vital aspect of control. *Directors* can only be removed by a majority of the *shareholders* at an *annual general meeting* or *extraordinary general meeting*. See: *associate, City Code on Takeovers and Mergers, subsidiary company.*

**controlling interest** See under: *controlling director.*

**convertibility** With respect to *currencies*, convertibility refers to the extent to which governments allow their *currencies* to be exchanged with others. Major trading nations must have freely *convertible currencies* to facilitate world trade. Governments often intervene to stabilise their *currencies* or those of others. The *pound Sterling* has been freely *convertible* since 1979. See: *exchange controls, foreign exchange, intervention, peg, reserve currency.*

**convertible** Loan *stock* with rights to convert to *ordinary shares* or *preference shares* at some stated time in the future. This also applies to *stock* issued by the government, which the holder has the right to convert to a new *stock* instead of, or rather than, obtaining repayment.

**Convertible Mark (KM)** Standard currency of Boznia-Herzegovina. 1 Convertible Mark = 100 pfennig

**convertible term insurance** Term *insurance* with a guarantee that the policy can be converted to a *whole of life policy* during or at the end of its term without additional medical evidence. See: *renewable term insurance.*

**convexity** The convexity is a measure of how a *bond*'s price varies as its *yield* varies. It is the speed at which the *bond*'s rate of price changes as the *yield* changes (mathematically: the second *derivative* of the price with respect to *yield*), divided by the *bond*'s price. See also: *duration, Macaulay's duration.*

**Cook Islands** Dependency of *New Zealand*. Standard *currency: New Zealand dollar.*

**Cooke ratio** This is a formula commonly used to measure *solvency*. Also known as the Risk-Asset *ratio*. It is given as: RAR(%) = ACB/TOWRA where ACB is adjusted *capital* base and TOWRA is total of weighted *risk assets*. The original *capital* regulations for western *banks* are outlined by the Basle Committee on Banking Supervision in the Basle Capital Accord of 1988, and state that the RAR has to be equal to at least 8% of total *assets*, after applying risk-weighting coefficients to the *assets*, on and off balance sheet.

**cooling-off period** A statutory period during which an individual can cancel an investment product, financial agreement (eg credit) or insurance contract and receive a refund of the monies paid. The period can be between 5 and 30 days depending upon the transaction involved.

**COP** *currency code* for: Colombian Peso.

**copyright** A property right which subsists in the following descriptions of work: original literary, dramatic, musical or artistic works, sound recordings, films, broadcasts or cable programmes and the typographical arrangement of published editions. The copyright is held by the person who has created the work, and varies in length based on the nature of the work. The copyright owner is given the following exclusive rights: to make copies of the copyright work; to issue copies of the work to the public; to rent or lend the work to the public; to perform, show or play the work in public; to broadcast the work or include it in a cable transmission; and to make an adaptation of the work or to do any of the above acts to an adaptation of the work. A person who is not the copyright owner must have the permission of the copyright owner to do any of the above. Commercial Copyright also applies to the design of goods though Patents and Trade Mark registration are normally used to strengthen the owner's title.

**cordoba** Standard *currency* unit of *Nicaragua*. 1 cordoba = 100 *centavos*.

**corporate by-laws** American equivalent of *Memorandum & Articles of Association* in the UK.

**corporate finance** A general term pertaining to matters relating to the funding of business. A venture capitalist is involved in the business of corporate finance as is an investor in *equity*. Most commonly used to refer to the raising and managing of *equity* and debt *capital* for *quoted companies* and for those that hope to be *listed* in the future.

**corporate governance** Corporate governance is commonly referred to as a system by which organisations are directed and controlled. It is the process by which *company* objectives are established, achieved and monitored. Corporate governance is concerned with the relationships and responsibilities between the *board, management, shareholders* and other relevant stakeholders within a legal and regulatory framework.

**corporate raider** See: *raider*.

**corporate venturing** A *large company* may take a *venture capital stake* in a new specialist *company* either directly or through a *venture capital* fund in order to obtain information on the business of that *company* or its markets, either for information purposes or to gain a foothold in a potential *acquisition*, without the expense and *management* expertise that would be required for the *company* to undertake the project on its own.

**corporation tax** An annual *tax* on the *profits* of all incorporated bodies and unincorporated associations (but not *partnerships*). Originally introduced in the 1965 Finance Act in place of *income tax* previously charged to such bodies. See: *accounts, advance corporation tax, profit & loss account*.

**correlation coefficient** A statistical measure, used in *quantitative analysis*, of the extent to which two variables (x and y, say) 'run' in the same direction, ie how they are related to each other. It is usually given the symbol: r and lies between the numbers −1 and +1. A coefficient of +1 means that the variables are perfectly positively related, ie one variable increases linearly as the other increases. A coefficient of −1 means that the variables have a perfectly negative relationship, ie one variable decreases linearly as the other increases. A coefficient of 0 indicates that there is no (linear) relationship between the two variables, ie they are independent. A coefficient close to zero means that there is only a

$$r = \frac{\text{cov}(x,y)}{\sigma_x \sigma_y}$$

weak relationship; the closer the coefficient is to unity (positive or negative) the stronger the relationship. The formula is:

where cov (x,y) is the *covariance* of the variables x and y, and $\sigma_x$ and $\sigma_y$ are their *standard deviations*.

**cost accounting** A branch of accounting concerned with providing the information that enables the *management* of a firm to evaluate production costs.

**cost benefit analysis** A method of evaluating a particular project by comparing the relevant economic costs and the potential benefits. Used for *investment* projects by calculating outlays and returns, and estimating the *net present value* (*NPV*) of the project: if this is positive the project would be profitable. Cost benefit analysis is also used by governments in an attempt to evaluate all the social costs and benefits of a public project (eg road building) particularly with reference to the *multiplier*.

**cost of capital** The *rate of return* that a business could earn if it chose another *investment* with equal *risk* – in other words, the *opportunity cost* of the funds employed as a result of an *investment* decision. Cost of capital is also calculated using a *weighted average* of a firm's costs of debt and classes of *equity*. Also called the 'composite cost of *capital*'.

**cost of sale** Business expenses, when classified by function, relating specifically to the manufacture, distribution and marketing of goods or services as distinct from salaries, *taxes*, research, *depreciation*, administration and *overheads*, etc. and may be fixed or *variable costs*. Disclosure of information about the cost of sales in conjunction with *revenue* from the sale of goods provides relevant information about the *gross margin, a benchmark* frequently used to judge performance.

**cost-push inflation** A term used to define a cause of *inflation* where the cost of labour and/or raw materials increases, causing an increase in the price of the finished product. See also: *demand-pull inflation*.

**Costa Rica** San José is home to the National Stock Exchange. In 1994, the number of *listed companies* was 113. Standard *currency: colón*. 1 *colón* = 100 *céntimos*.

**counter trade** Similar to *barter* but providing for the *cash* proceeds of goods accepted as trade, rather than the goods themselves. See also: *payment in kind*.

**counterparty** A party to a *contract*.

**counterparty risk** The risk that the other party to a transaction defaults by not meeting its obligations.

**countervailing credit** See: *back to back credit*.

**coupon** 1. A *warrant*, detachable from a *bond* or *share certificate,* which must be presented for payment of *interest* or *dividend* to the appointed agents of the issuing authority or *company*. 2. A term often used to describe the *gross* monetary *value* of *income* or *yield* from a *fixed interest security*. See also: *bearer security*.

**Court of Auditors** A body appointed by the Council of Ministers of the *European Union* (*EU*) to investigate and report on the *income* and expenditure of the Community. It has one representative of each of the 27 Member States. The Court has refused to sign off EU accounts for the last 14 years.

**covariance** A statistical measure of the relationship between two variables used in *quantitative analysis*. If the variables move in the same direction, the covariance is positive. If they run in opposite directions the covariance is negative. A zero covariance indicates that the variables are unrelated. However, if the 'strength' of the relationship is required,

$$\text{cov}(x, y) = \frac{1}{n} \sum_{i=1}^{i=n} x_i y_i - \bar{x}\,\bar{y}$$

then the related statistical measure called the *correlation coefficient* must be calculated. The formula for the covariance between variables, say, x and y, which each have n *values* is:

An important property of covariance is: the covariance of a variable with itself is the *variance* of that variable, ie cov(x,x) = var(x). See: *analysis*.

**covenant** A class of payment which provides for payments at annual or more frequent intervals. In the case of charities the *deeds* must be capable of exceeding three years. Individual payments under a charitable *deed of covenant* are usually eligible for *income tax* relief.

**cover** 1. Underlying *stock* pledged as *collateral* for a written *option*. 2. The number of times a *company*'s *dividend* is covered by its *net profit*. See: *dividend cover*. 3. Eliminating a *currency risk* by using a future or forward position that effectively cancels any fluctuation. See also: *hedge*.

**covered interest parity (CIP)** A condition that holds true due to the presence of

$$F = \left[ \frac{1 + r^*}{1 + r} \right] S$$

*arbitrageurs* in the *foreign exchange market*. It states that the forward *exchange rate* is related to the *spot exchange rate*, domestic and foreign *interest rates*, as follows:

where F is the one-year forward exchange quote (in terms of foreign *currency* per unit of domestic *currency*), S is the *spot exchange rate* (again in terms of foreign *currency* per unit of domestic *currency*), r is the one-year domestic *interest rate* and r* is the one-year foreign *interest rate*. If, say, the three-month forward *exchange rate* is to be calculated, then the *interest rates* must be divided by four. Similarly, the six-month forward *exchange rate* quotation is

$$\frac{F - S}{S} = r^* - r$$

computed by dividing both *interest rates* by two. The approximate formula for *CIP* is also very useful:

It shows that if the foreign *interest rate* is higher than the domestic *interest rate*, then the domestic *currency* will be at a *forward discount* by an equivalent percentage, while if the domestic *interest rate* is lower than the foreign *interest rate* the domestic *currency* will be at a *forward premium* by an equivalent percentage. Compare: *uncovered interest parity (UIP)*. See also: *Fisher Effect*.

**covering** A general term for neutralising an *investment* position by *closing* or hedging or buying or selling a *contract* with the opposite effect of the one to be neutralised. A covered position is also a *derivatives* position held by someone who also holds the *physical*.

**CPA** Short for: certified public *accountant* in *America*. See: *certified accountant*.

**CPI** See: *consumer prices index*.

**CPI Index** A *contract* on the New York *Coffee Sugar and Cocoa Exchange* (CSCE) which allows investors to *bet* on the level of the *US consumer price index* at fixed dates in the future.

**CPIC** Short for: Company Pensions Information Centre.

**cradle** The intersection point of the two converging envelope lines of a symmetrical *triangle*. Compare: *apex* (sense 2).

**crash** A sudden crisis of confidence in *investment* markets characterised by dramatic falls in the prices of *stocks* and *shares*. Normally brought about by the total evaporation of buying interest and evidence of panic selling. A crash is not to be confused with a *bear market*, where specific macroeconomic factors such as economic decline or increases in the price of raw materials or *interest rates* have a long-term impact on industries' profitability. In the *stock market* crashes of 1929 and 1987, economic and industrial health was generally considered excellent, while in the *bear markets* of 1974 and 2008 increased oil prices, *inflation* and severe monetary constraints or the availability of bank finance had a specific and predictable impact on industries' profitability. A crash tends to be more emotive, leaving markets temporarily over-sold. Knock-on effects to industry are limited in the shorter term, but the reaction of governments to such a crisis of confidence has a significant bearing on subsequent economic events. See: *Black Monday, dead cat bounce, Kondratieff wave, meltdown, Credit Crunch.*

**Crawling peg** A method of exchange rate control in which government authorities adjust a fixed exchange rate frequently in small amounts. It is a perhaps inadequate compromise between floating exchange rates and fixed exchange rates. Also known as: sliding peg. See: *intervention, peg*

**CRC** *currency code* for: Costa Rican Colón.

**CRD** See: *Central Registration Depository.*

**creation price** The cost of creating a unit, equal to the cost of the respective *securities* and associated expenses plus any accrued *income*, in a *unit trust.*

**Credit Crunch** October 2008 worldwide banking collapse resulting in *nationalisation* of bank *equity* and *assets* as well as governments and countries becoming *illiquid*. Substantial relief was offered by larger governments and the IMF and was followed by dramatic interest rate reductions. The process is believed to have started when suspect (sub-prime) *mortgages* which were securitised began to default when the US property market collapsed. The knock-on effect of this caused a devaluation of bank assets that comprised of these CMOs (and CDOs) and other suspect *mortgages*. This was followed by Lehman Brothers filing for *Chapter 11* bankruptcy protection on 15 September 2008. The collapse of Lehman Brothers was the largest bankruptcy filing in US history, with Lehman holding over $600 *billion* in assets. In the *UK* Northern Rock became *illiquid* and was nationalised, as was part of the Bradford & Bingley. Other major *banks* such as HBOS and RBS participated in a government *equity* purchase programme and interest rates were reduced to the lowest ever levels. The effects of this resulted in a protracted worldwide *recession*. See: *TARP, sub-prime mortgage.*

**Credit Default Swaps (CDS)** A credit default swap (CDS) is an unregulated credit *derivative contract*. Primarily an *insurance* policy against a *debtor* defaulting on their loan. The policy is then traded or swapped for another or bought by periodic *premiums*. A substantial market ($3 *trillion*) that had become vulnerable to the *Credit Crunch* of 2008 when difficult trading conditions put much of the market under the threat of claims against the policies.

**credit guarantee** See: *credit insurance.*

**credit insurance** A special *insurance* policy taken out with a factor to protect a lender or *creditor* against bad debts.

**credit rating** 1. Evaluation of how creditworthy an individual or a *company* is. There now exist a number of *credit reference agencies* that collect data on individuals' credit history and disclose the information to parties for a fee. 2. Credit rating also applies to corporations and their *loan capital*. A number of substantial *companies* provide data on corporations and *banks* and have established gradings which determine the *investment quality* of their *capital* from *investment* grade to 'junk' (see: *junk bond*). See: *Moody's, Standard & Poor's*.

**credit reference agency**  See under: *credit rating*.

**credit risk**  There are three components to credit risk. Commonly credit risk refers to *default risk*, the *risk* that a party does not receive a payment from another party when it is due. When looking at credit risk with respect to *bond investment*, credit risk refers not only to the *bond* issuer defaulting on *interest* or principal payments, but also to the *risk* that the *bond* is downgraded or the credit *spread* (the *yield* on the *bond* versus government *bonds*) widens.

**credit squeeze**  The term given to the effect of measures restricting the *money supply* on the economy. These measures include raising *interest rates* and imposing lending restrictions on *banks*.

**creditor**  A party to which one owes *money*. In a *company's balance sheet*, creditors appear as a separate heading (or: *accounts payable*) under *current liabilities*, differentiated as those due to be paid within and beyond one accounting year, ie short and *long term*.

**creditor turnover**  A performance *ratio* of a *company*. It is obtained by dividing the *turnover* by *creditors* due within one year.

**creeping takeover**  Americanism for the gradual accumulation of a *company's stock* through open-market purchases. Federal *US* law requires no public disclosure of *stock* ownership or *takeover* intentions until the *stake* reaches 5%. See: *Section (13d)*. In the UK a *stake* of 3% must be declared (see: *material interests*). See also: *dawn raid, Substantial Acquisition Rules*.

**CREST**  CREST (not an acronym) is the electronic *share* dealing settlement and registration system which gives investors the choice to settle in dematerialised (ie without the use of *share certificates*) or certificated form. It was developed by CRESTCo. and replaced the old paper stock transfer system called *Talisman* in 1997.

**critical illness insurance**  See: *dread diseases*.

**Croatia**  Standard *currency*: kuna. 1 kuna = 100 lipa.

**cross currency interest rate swap**  See: *interest rate swap*.

**crowding-out**  1. If government spending increases, this has the effect of reducing ('crowding-out') *private sector* spending (called consumption). 2. In addition, if the *money supply* is fixed, then increases in *CGNCR* due to increased government spending will tend to increase *interest rates*, which causes a fall in *private sector investment* (this is called 'financial crowding-out'. 3. The term is also used in a broad sense to suggest that government spending uses up national resources to the extent that private consumption, *investment* and *exports* decrease.

**crown jewels**  A general term for specific *assets* or *subsidiary companies* within a *conglomerate* that are particularly valuable and of particular interest to potential *bidders*.

**CRT**  See: *composite rate tax*.

**CSCE**  See: *Coffee Sugar and Cocoa Exchange of New York*.

**CTF**  See: *Child Trust Fund*.

**CTO**  See: *Capital Taxes Office*.

**CTP**  See: *common trading platform*.

**Cuba** Standard *currency*: *peso*. 1 *peso* = 100 *centavos*.

**cum** A Latin prefix meaning 'with'. Contrast: *ex*.

**cum dividend** A *share* quoted 'cum dividend' carries the right to a recently declared *dividend*. '*cum scrip*' and '*cum rights*' carry similar implications. The entitlement is normally there without the prefix being used. Compare: *ex dividend*.

**cum new** With respect to *shares*, 'cum new' denotes that the *share* is offered for sale with a *scrip issue* or *rights issue*. Contrast: *ex new*.

**cum rights** A *share* quoted 'cum rights' carries the right to a recently declared *rights issue*. Contrast: *ex rights*.

**cum scrip** A *share* quoted 'cum scrip' carries the right to a recently declared *scrip issue*. Contrast: *ex scrip*.

**cumulative** Usually used in connection with *preference shares*, where the *share* carries the right to receive *dividend* arrears before any other *dividends* are paid on lower ranking *stocks* such as *ordinary shares*.

**cumulative preferred** *Preference shares* where the *dividends* will accumulate if omitted as a result of insufficient *earnings* or *capital expenditure*. Dividends on *ordinary shares* cannot be paid until the obligation is met.

**CUP** *currency code* for: Cuban Peso.

**curb** A restriction or suspension of *volume* or programme trading when a market falls or rises by a certain number of *points*. On *Wall Street trading curbs* for the January 2009 quarter are effected when the market rises or falls by 50 *points* on the *Dow Jones*, at which point all trading is suspended for up to an hour. See also: *AMEX, circuit breaker*.

**currency** 1. A term covering any type of *money* used in an economy. 2. The legal tender of a particular nation. The Glossary contains information on all of the world's currencies. See country name or the particular currency for more information.

**currency code** In most cases, the currency code is composed of the country's two-character international country code plus an extra character to denote the *currency* unit. For example, the international country code for the *United Kingdom* is 'GB' plus a one-character *currency* designator for *pounds* 'P' gives a *UK* currency code of '*GBP*'. There are exceptions to this such as *XPT*, the designation for Platinum ounces. ISO 4217 is the standard for international currency codes and the codes in common use are usually (but not always) the same as the ISO standard.

**currency future** A *financial futures contract* in which a *currency* for forward delivery is bought or sold at a particular *exchange rate*. Corporations that sell products around the world can *hedge* their *currency risk* with these *futures*.

**currency interest rate swap** See: *interest rate swap*.

**currency mortgage** A *mortgage* taken out in a foreign *currency* with the potential advantage of lower *interest rates* and *currency* gains. Normally more appropriate for the financially aware, as they can result in *currency* losses which might give rise to increased repayments of *capital* and/or *interest*.

**currency option** An *option contract* giving the right, but not the obligation, either to buy or sell a specified *currency* at a *fixed exchange rate* within a given period. The rate agreed is called the exercise (or strike) rate. This is the *exchange rate* at which the buyer has the right to buy or sell the *currency*.

**currency swap** See under: *swap*.

**current account** 1. A *bank account* with a *clearing bank* or *building society* that provides only the ability to draw *cash* or cheques against a *cash* balance or *overdraft* and provides no or minimal *interest* on credit balances. 2. The total of visible balance (exported goods minus imported goods) plus invisible balance (services, *interest, dividends,* unilateral transfers). A sub-account of the *balance of payments.*

**current assets** Assets of a *company* receivable within one year, ie *debtors, cash* at *bank stock* etc.

**current cost accounting** The term used for the conversion of a *company*'s accounting figures to show the effects of *inflation.* A series of rules have been devised by the official accountancy bodies to try to show how *inflation* over the year has affected: (a) *fixed assets,* including extra *depreciation* needed to cover replacement at current costs; (b) the cost of replacing *stock* at current prices; (c) the balance of *money* owed and *money* owing, for goods and services. See also: *accounts, historic cost accounting, inflation accounting.*

**current liabilities** A *company*'s *creditors* due to be paid within one year.

**current ratio** A *ratio* of financial status of a *company* that measures its ability to deal with short-term liabilities, ie it measures a *company*'s liquidity. It is calculated as follows:

$$\text{current ratio} = \frac{\text{current assets}}{\text{current liabilities}}$$

For the average manufacturing *company,* a current *ratio* of between 1.5 to 2.0 would be expected. Suitable *ratio* figures will vary from industry to industry. If the current *ratio* is too high, then it means that too much *money* is tied up in *working capital;* too low a current *ratio* would imply liquidity problems. An indication of *gearing.*

**current yield** The *annual return,* before *tax,* on an *investment* at its current price represented by the *interest* or *dividend.* In the case of *gilt-edged securities* or other fixed-interest *stocks* repayable at a specific date, it is known also as the *flat yield.* In this case it represents the *annual return* from the *interest* only, not any increase in price on the maturity of the *stock.* See also: *yield.*

**custodian** A body, normally a *bank* or financial institution, entrusted with holding *stocks* or *investments* on behalf of third parties for safekeeping.

**custodian trustee** A *trustee,* often an officer of a *bank,* responsible for the *assets* of a *trust* or *pension* fund who not only holds these *assets* but who has responsibility for their ultimate delivery to the rightful beneficiaries. See also: *trust corporation.*

**customer agreement** From April 1988, *investment* and financial firms in the *UK* must have a written agreement with all their clients outlining the basis on which their account is to be managed.

**Customs and Excise** Merged with the *Inland Revenue* in April 2005 to form HM Revenue and Customs, The Board of Customs & Excise had the responsibility for collecting customs and excise duties and *VAT* and detecting evasion of *tax* and duty payment and the import of illegal goods through an investigative division. Also runs a statistical office that collects data on *imports* and *exports.*

**customs union** An agreement between a group of countries to have no *tariffs* between them (as in a *free trade area*) and a *common external tariff* (*CET*) towards countries outside the group. A further step towards economic integration would be to allow the free movement of *factors of production* (eg labour) which would then be termed: *common market.*

**CVE** *currency code* for: Cape Verde Escudo.

**cyclical unemployment** Also called: *demand deficient unemployment. Unemployment* occurring in an economy because the aggregate desired expenditure does not suffice to purchase the total output of a fully employed *labour force.* See: *business cycle, full employment.*

**cyclicality** The period over which a *commodity, stock, share* or *currency* (or any free-market price) completes a full cycle of price movement measured from one major low to the next. It can also refer to the shorter-term cycle which often occurs within a major *trend* and many times within a complete cycle. *Stocks* and *shares* tend to have a cyclicality similar in length to one another but the cyclicality of *commodities* can vary considerably, although metals tend to run in unison. See also: *business cycle.*

**Cyprus** Standard *currency: pound.* 1 *euro* = 100 *cents.*

**Czech Republic** The Prague Stock Exchange has the following main *index*: Stock Exchange Index PX50, which comprises the most frequently traded *shares* on the Prague Stock Exchange. It is weighted by *market capitalisation*. Base: 5 April 1994 = 1,000. Standard *currency: koruna.* 1 *koruna* = 100 *haleru.*

**CZK** *currency code* for: Czech Koruna.

# D

**Daily Official List (DOL)** See: *Official List*.

**daimyo bond** A *yen fixed interest security* issued in *bearer security* form on the Japanese markets and as a *eurobond* by the *World Bank*.

**daisy chain** Artificial *volume* created by market manipulators that gives the appearance of activity in *shares* so as to lure genuine investors. See: *ramping*.

**dalasi** Standard *currency* of the *Gambia*. 1 dalasi = 100 *butut*.

**Data Protection Act 1998** The Data Protection Act 1998 requires anyone who handles personal information (eg client details) to comply with a number of important principles. It also gives individuals rights over their personal information.

**Datastream** An information system providing *company* reports and analyses as well as historic price information.

**dated stock** A fixed-interest *stock* with a *redemption date*. See: *undated stock, bullet*.

**dawn raid** A term describing an acquisitive *company* buying a substantial number of another *company*'s *shares* before the market becomes aware of events, at a price higher than previously registered, usually giving the buyer a strategic *stake*. Under the rules of the *City Code on Takeovers and Mergers* a *bid* must be made public on achieving a holding of 30%. The practice of dawn raids is limited by *POTAM*'s *Substantial Acquisition Rules* (*SARs*). Under the *SARs*, a 'dawn raid' is defined as a raid of nearly 15%.

**Dawson** See: *Furniss v Dawson*.

**DAX** See: *Germany*.

**day count conventions** Different markets use different conventions for calculating *accrued interest* on *bonds*. *Accrued interest* accumulates linearly for the period from the last *coupon* date to the *settlement date*. Thus the proportion of time for that period in terms of one year is calculated and then multiplied by the annualised *coupon* rate.

- The 'actual/365' basis for calculating *accrued interest* is as follows: the actual number of days from the last *coupon* to the *settlement date* is counted and then divided by 365 days; this is then multiplied by the annualised *coupon* rate to obtain the *accrued interest*. This method is used for *UK gilts*.

- The *US* Treasury market uses the 'actual/actual' basis for calculating *accrued interest*: the actual number of days from the last *coupon* date to the *settlement date* is counted and divided by twice the actual number of days in the *coupon* period (one takes twice the *coupon* period because the *coupon* is paid semi-annually). The result is multiplied by the annualised *coupon* rate to obtain the *accrued interest*.

- The *eurobond* market pays an annual *coupon* and uses a '30/360' basis. This means that the number of days from the last *coupon* date to the *settlement date* are counted on the assumption that all months have 30 days. This figure is divided by 360. The result is multiplied by the annual *coupon* rate to obtain the *accrued interest*.

**day order** Orders given at a fixed or limited price which are valid for that day and, if not executed, are automatically cancelled at the end of the day.

**DBERR** Department for Business, Enterprise and Regulatory Reform. See: *Department for Business, Innovation and Skills*.

**DCF** See: *discounted cash flow*.

**dead cat bounce** An Americanism used to describe a temporary market recovery after a significant fall as opposed to the reversal of a *bear trend*. This is often a result of *short covering* rather than genuine buying. The analogy describes a temporary respite in a lifeless market which will inevitably keep falling. See: *bear trap, crash, spike*.

**dead cross** See under: *golden cross*.

**dealer** A *market maker* or an employee of an *investment* firm who executes market transactions for clients or the firm itself. Name for a *jobber*. See: *foreign exchange, inter-dealer broker*.

**death duties** See: *inheritance tax*.

**death valley curve** A *venture capital* term used to describe the period during which a start-up *company* will utilise *equity capital* to fund fixed overheads before *cash flow* turns positive. The early losses created will erode the *company's capital* base, with the result that the *company's* ability to raise further finance is reduced at its most critical point. See also: *maximum slippage*.

**debenture** A *bond, deed* or *fixed interest security* issued by a *company* or demanded by a *bank*, usually secured on *company assets* either specifically or in general. Debenture *stock* may be quoted on a *stock exchange*. A debenture ranks ahead of everything except the liquidator's fees in the event of a *liquidation*, and debenture *interest* must be paid before *dividends* are declared. The debenture *deed* is normally held by *trustees* on behalf of holders and the *company* is required to maintain a register of its debentures and notify *Companies House*. In the case where debenture *stock* is issued on the open market its *value* will depend on the *yield* and the issuer's *credit rating*. In all cases debentures are secured on actual or potential *assets* of the *company*. A *mortgage debenture* will be secured on a specific property, or a floating debenture will be backed by all the *company's assets*. Exceptions to this are naked or *unsecured debentures* which rely on the *company's* promise to pay. See: *loan stock*.

**debt bomb** Colloquialism for the potentially explosive repercussions of a *default* by a major international *debtor* on the Western financial system.

**debt discounting** Trading in the debt of *companies* or countries. The going rate for the debt of a distressed company may be only 25p in the *pound* because of the company's financial condition – ie the chances of it being repaid are 4:1 against or 25%. See: *forfaiting*.

**debt instrument** A *bond* or *deed* that certifies and defines the terms of a loan between two or more parties and can be assigned. See: *bill of exchange, fixed interest security, loan stock, mortgage, promissory note*.

**debt ratio** A financial status *ratio* for a *company*. Shows how *solvent* a *company* is. It is calculated as the total debt (long and short-term *creditors*) divided by total *capital employed* (which equals debt plus *equity*). Shows the extent to which *assets* have been financed from debt and is a good indication of a *company's gearing*. A low debt *ratio* means that the *company* has an 'equity cushion'. Compare: *debt-equity ratio*.

**debt service ratio (DSR)** The proportion of annual export *earnings* needed to service a country's external debts, including both *interest* payments and repayment of principal. The *DSR* is an important statistic indicating the depth of a country's *indebtedness*. The impact of debt *rescheduling* can be examined in comparing pre- and post-rescheduling *DSRs*.

**debt-equity ratio** 1. A financial status *ratio* for a *company*, showing its *solvency*. It is simply the total debt divided by *equity*. This shows the extent to which *equity* can cushion *creditors'* claims in the event of a *liquidation*. 2. Also the long-term debt divided by *shareholders' equity*. This is used as an indication for *gearing*. Compare: *debt ratio*.

**debtor** Someone who owes the *company money*. The *US* term that is being used increasingly in the *UK* is: *accounts receivable*.

**debtor turnover** A performance *ratio* of a *company*. It is given by dividing the *turnover* by the *debtor* figure.

**decimalisation** The change in *Sterling* on 15 February 1971 from *pounds, shillings* and pence (Lsd – 20 *shillings* to the *pound*, twelve pennies to the *shilling*) to decimal *currency* with one hundred new pence to the *pound*.

**declaration of solvency** A statutory declaration made by the *directors* of a *company* in *voluntary liquidation* confirming that the *company* will be able to pay its *creditors* in full within a specified period, not exceeding 12 months from the date of the declaration. It must contain a statement of the *company*'s *assets* and liabilities with a copy to the *Registrar of Companies*. A *director* who participates in a declaration of solvency without reasonable grounds will be liable to a fine or imprisonment on conviction. See: *insolvency*.

**declinature** The expression used by *insurance companies* when they officially decline to accept a proposal for *insurance* or *assurance*.

**decreasing returns** See: *diminishing returns*.

**decreasing term insurance** A form of *term insurance* with a reducing death benefit over a set period primarily to cover a reducing liability such as a debt that is being gradually repaid, or reducing *tax* liability, such as a lifetime gift under *inheritance tax*.

**deductions at source** Tax deducted from *income* before it is paid. Salaries and *pension income* via *pay-as-you-earn* and *deposit investments* in the *UK* have *tax* deducted.

**deed** A legally binding document that has been signed, sealed, witnessed and delivered and that sets out the terms of and confirms an agreement between two or more parties.

**deed of adherence** A legal document admitting an employer to a *pension* scheme containing the employer's undertaking to comply with provisions of the scheme.

**deed of appointment** A legal document appointing a new *trustee*.

**deed of arrangement** Also called: *deed* of *assignment*. The formal *arrangement* made by someone who owes *money* with those to whom the *money* is owed. This normally occurs when the individual has insufficient funds to settle his or her debts and agrees on either a reduced amount or a period over which the *money* can be paid. A *deed* of *assignment* will be where the individual assigns certain *assets* to cover these debts in the case of say, a bankruptcy (See: *bankrupt*) or *insolvency*. See: *individual voluntary arrangement*.

**deed of covenant** See: *covenant*.

**deed of trust** See: *trust deed*.

**deep discount bonds** A *fixed interest security* without a *coupon* issued at a substantial *discount* to its redemption *value*. Accordingly no (see: *zero*) *income* is payable by the *security* but the return is represented wholly by the discounted *value* at issue against the *par value* at redemption. The investor's entire return is therefore represented purely in terms of *capital gain* although in the *UK* the return is often taxed as *income*. See: *cats, STAGS, tigers, zebras, zero-coupon bond*.

**default** The failure of a client to settle an obligation when it is due. See also: *Stock Exchange Mutual Reference Library*.

**default risk** The *risk* that the holder of a *bond* will not receive *interest* payment or repayment of principal when it is due. See: *credit rating*.

**defeasance** Provision found in some debt agreements whereby the *contract* is nullified if specified acts are performed.

**defensive tactics**  Actions taken to resist an unwelcome *takeover*. See: *Jonestown defence, porcupine provisions*.

**deferred annuity**  An *annuity* which will commence *income* payments at a future date (ie a *pension* on retirement). The rate receivable will be higher than an immediate *annuity*. Originally a term used to describe certain *self-employed pensions* or *Section 226–226A pensions* which have since been replaced by *personal pensions*.

**deferred ordinary share**  1. A type of ordinary *share* issued to founder members of a *company* which only pays *dividends* after all other types of ordinary *share* have been paid. 2. A type of *share* which pays a reduced *dividend* for a number of years, after which it ranks *pari passu* with other *ordinary shares*.

**deferred pension**  An employee in a *pension* scheme who leaves before retirement is entitled to a deferred or preserved *pension*. This is calculated in the same way as a normal *pension* by multiplying the number of years of service by a fraction (usually 1/60th). The purchase *money* in a deferred *pension* should not normally be less than the *member*'s total contributions.

**deferred taxation**  A sum set aside for *tax* in the *accounts* of a corporation that will become payable in a period other than that under review. This arises because of the different periods determined by *tax* regulations and accounting convention.

**deficit**  Simply the amount by which revenue falls below expenditure. Deficit financing is where governments borrow *money* to supplement revenue. The *trade deficit* is where *imports* exceed the *value* of *exports* and a *budget deficit* is where taxes and government revenues fall below government spending. See: *balance of payments, balance of trade, Central Government Borrowing Requirement, Public Sector Borrowing Requirement*.

**deficit financing**  Government borrowing to make up for an *income* shortfall. This stimulates the economy in the shorter term; the longer-term effects of servicing this debt can however force up *interest rates* and be recessionary. See: *Public Sector Borrowing Requirement*.

**defined benefit scheme**  A *pension* scheme where the rules specify the benefits to be paid and the scheme financed to meet these specific benefits; rather than a *money purchase* scheme.

**defined contribution scheme**  A *pension* scheme such as a *money purchase* scheme where only the rate of contribution is specified in the rules.

**definitive trust deed**  The detailed *trust deed* for a *pension* scheme which follows an *interim trust deed*.

**deflation**  A fall in the absolute price of consumer goods and raw materials. Deflation is the opposite of *inflation*; it should not be confused with *disinflation*, which is a slowing down in the rate of price increases, ie a reduced rate of *inflation*. The only major period of deflation in this century occurred during the Great Depression in the 1920s and 1930s. Government policies to reduce the rate of *inflation* are often described as deflationary but they only attempt to introduce an element of *disinflation*. Economists, particularly Keynesians, (see: *Keynesian economics*), believe that an underlying rate of up to 4% *inflation* is essential for a growing and vigorous economy. See: *hyperinflation, disinflation*.

**deflator**  A factor used to obtain *real values* from inflated *values* (ie *values* influenced by *inflation*), eg *real GDP* figures from *money GDP* figures. See: *implicit deflator*.

**del credere agent**  An agent bearing the *risk* of non-payment by customers.

**delivery**  On the *London Stock Exchange*, the formal transfer of the *share certificate* to the new owner. See: *CREST*.

**delta** The factor by which an *option* price varies in relation to the price of the *investment* or *asset* into which it is convertible.

**demand deficient unemployment** If the aggregate desired level of spending in an economy is insufficient to purchase all the output produced by a fully employed *labour force*, the resulting *unemployment* is termed demand-deficient. Also called: *cyclical unemployment*.

**demand-pull inflation** A direct cause of *inflation* where demand for goods and services is not met by the supply and prices or wages are increased because of scarcity. See also: *cost-push inflation*.

**demerger** The splitting of a *company*, often originally formed as a result of a *merger*, into two (or more) separate *companies*. Unlike a *management buyout* (where a division of the *company* is sold to existing *management*) or a *divestment* (where a division is sold to other *shareholders*), a demerger gives the existing *shareholders shares* in both *companies*. See: *break-up*.

**demurrage** Monetary penalties for non-performance of a building or shipping *contract*. Financial penalties will be agreed for each day completion is delayed or ships are kept waiting.

**demutualisation** A process where a business, club or association (or *stock exchange*) changes from being run for its members or customers and becomes an incorporated business run for *profit*.

**Denmark** The Copenhagen Stock Exchange was granted the status of *Designated Investment Exchange* by the *UK SIB*. Its main *indices* are:

- KFX Index – Comprises the 20 most liquid *shares* selected annually. It doesn't take into account *dividend* payments. Base: 3 July 1989 = 100.

- Copenhagen Stock Exchange Total Share Index. Contains nearly all domestic *shares* on the Exchange. Rebased on 1 January 1983 at 100.

Standard *currency*: *krone*. 1 *krone* = 100 *øre*.

**denomination** 1. The *face value* of a *security*, ie the sum to be paid on its redemption or its *par value*. 2. Nominating the *currency* used by the parties to a *contract* See: *scout*.

**Department of Trade and Industry (DTI)** See: *Department for Business, Innovation and Skills (BIS)*.

**Department for Business, Enterprise and Regulatory Reform (BERR)** See: *Department for Business, Innovation and Skills (BIS)*.

**Department for Business, Innovation and Skills (BIS)** Responsible for domestic and international trade policy in the *UK* as well as the promotion of *exports*, industrial policy, competition policy and consumer protection. The department also determines policy on scientific research and development, *company* legislation and the *Registrar of Companies*, *patents* and the *Patent Office*. The government department maintains relations with the *Office of Fair Trading* and the *Competition Commission*, and will act jointly with them on major issues. *Formerly the Department for Business, Enterprise and Regulatory Reform (BERR)*.

**Department for Work and Pensions (DWP)** The government department responsible for the administration of social security benefits, including state pensions. Formerly the Department for Social Security (DSS).

**deposit** Account for *cash* where *interest* is paid. Sometimes certain conditions of withdrawal are stipulated. Capital sums are guaranteed and a rate of *interest*, dependent on general rates prevailing in the market place, is credited on a regular basis during the *term* of the deposit. Only *banks* and *building societies* can take deposits in the *UK*. See: *compound annual return, compound net annual return, current account, money market.*

**depreciation** 1. An amount charged to the *profit & loss account* of a *limited company* covering the ageing or diminution in *value* of a fixed *asset* over time. The amount charged is normally based on a percentage of the *value* of the *asset* and can reflect different views of depreciation. Two commonly used methods are: (i) *straight line depreciation* and (ii) *diminishing balance depreciation.* 2. A fall in the *value* of a *currency* with a *floating exchange rate.* Depreciation normally refers to long-term realignments in *value.* For *currencies* with a *fixed exchange rate* there can be no depreciation without a *devaluation.*

**depression** A severe economic condition combining oversupply, increasing *unemployment,* rising *stock* levels, *disinflation* and a general sustained slowdown in business activity. Characterised by the Great Depression of the 1920s in *America,* which was preceded by a *stock market crash.* See: *recession, stagflation.*

**deregulation** 1. The regulation of an industry by private bodies rather than by statute. This often increases the form of regulation but allows all the rules to be enforced by the industry's elected governing body rather than civil servants. The government can provide broad outlines within which the regulatory bodies can operate and supervise their effectiveness. See: *Financial Services Authority.* 2. Deregulation of an economy involves, for example, *privatisation* of public industry, making provisions for greater competition, removal of *exchange rate* controls, removal of state subsidies, and leaving *interest rates* to *market forces.*

**derivative** An *instrument* derived from a *security, currency* or *commodity,* or an *index* or *indicator* representing any of these, the price of which will move in a direct relationship to the price of the base *instrument* or *index.* This can apply, for instance, to a *futures contract* based on the prices of particular *fixed interest securities* or indeed an *index* of these *fixed interest securities.* It could also apply to an *option contract* based on the fluctuation in *interest rates,* the *index* of a world *stock market* or even *inflation.* Contrast: *actuals, physicals.* See: *zero-sum game.*

**Designated Professional Body (DPB)** A professional body designated by the Financial Services Authority whose members can carry out a limited range of regulated activities (classified as exempt regulated activities) without having to obtain direct authorisation from the Financial Services Authority. The activities must be incidental to the core business activities of the firm. The DPBs are the Law Society of England & Wales, the Law Society of Scotland, the Law Society of Northern Ireland, the Institute of Chartered Accountants in England and Wales, the Institute of Chartered Accountants of Scotland, the Institute of Chartered Accountants in Ireland, the Association of Chartered Certified Accountants, the Institute of Actuaries, the Council for Licensed Conveyancers and the Royal Institution of Chartered Surveyors.

**Designated Territories** Countries recognised by the *Financial Services Authority (FSA)* as being able to provide *assurance* and collective *investment* services in the *UK* since they provide equivalent investor protection to that available in the *UK.* These include *Guernsey,* Jersey, the Isle of Man and *Bermuda.* See: *Investment Services Directive.*

**Deutsche Terminbörse (DTB)** The German Futures and Options Exchange in Frankfurt. It was set up in 1990. The *DTB* uses a fully computerised system with integrated trading and clearing.

**Deutscher Aktienindex (DAX)** German *share index.* See under: *Germany.*

**Deutschmark**  Standard *currency* of *Germany*, before the introduction of the *euro* on 1 January 2002. 1 Deutschmark = 100 *Pfennigs*.

**devaluation**  The reduction in the *value* of a *currency* normally contrived by the domestic government to correct a trade imbalance or readjust *currency parity*. Compare: *depreciation, intervention, peg*.

**development capital**  Finance for more established *companies* which are profitable, or nearly profitable, offered by *merchant banks* and *venture capital companies* and used for *organic growth* or *acquisition* expansion. See: *equity injection*.

**diamond**  A *chart pattern* used in *technical analysis*. It is usually a *reversal pattern*. It resembles a geometric rhombus (a 'pushed-over' square) or a four-point diamond. It is best described as a *broadening top* which after two or three swings changes into a *triangle* (nearly always a symmetrical *triangle*). It should show diminishing *volume* in the part of the formation resembling the symmetrical *triangle*. It is expected to move, after *breakout*, at least as far as the greatest (vertical) width of the *pattern*.

**dilution of equity**  Occurs when there is an issue of additional *ordinary shares* or a maturing *share option* in a *company* without there being a corresponding increase in the *assets* or *productivity*. Consequently, the *share* price will fall to accommodate the *equity dilution*. See: *burn-out turnaround, equity injection, pre-emption rights, rights issue*.

**diminishing balance depreciation**  An 'accelerated' method of calculating *depreciation* of an *asset*. The remaining *value* (ie initial cost or *value* of the *asset* less accumulated *appreciation*) reduced by a constant percentage each *accounting period*. Thus the *depreciation* charge in *money* terms is large at first and subsequently reduces (hence the term: diminishing balance). This method is thought to assess an *asset's value* more realistically than, for instance, the straight-line method. Once the expected life and the residual *value* of the *asset* are estimated, the fixed percentage used for depreciating the *net value* after each *accounting period* is calculated using the following formula:

$$r = \left(1 - \sqrt[n]{\frac{R}{C}}\right) \times 100\%$$

where r is the required fixed percentage charge, R is the residual *value*, C is the original cost and n is the number of years of expected useful life of the *asset*. The constant percentage will depreciate the *asset* to (approximately) its residual *value* after the useful life has expired. For example, if equipment is bought at £60,000 and its residual *value* is estimated at £10,000 after a useful life of five years, then according to the formula the percentage charge is about 30%. Thus the *depreciation* charge after the first year is 30% of £60,000 = £18,000 and after the second year it is 30% of the remaining £42,000 = £12,600 and so on. A figure of 20% is commonly used in the *UK* for tax purposes. Also called: *reduced balance depreciation*. See: *straight line depreciation*.

**diminishing returns**  Also: *decreasing returns* (to scale). Situation in which output increases less than proportionately to inputs as the scale of production increases. Often called: diseconomies of scale. Contrast: *increasing returns*.

**dinar**  1. Standard *currency* unit of the following nations: *Algeria*: 1 dinar = 100 *centimes*; *Bahrain, Iraq, Jordan, Kuwait, Yemen*: 1 dinar = 1000 *fils*; *Tunisia*: 1 dinar = 1,000 *millimes*; *Croatia, Libya*: 1 dinar = 1,000 *dirhams*; 2. *Currency* sub-unit of *Iran*: 100 dinars = 1 *rial*.

**direct debit** An instruction to one's *bank* to pay on request a certain sum from one's *current account* at regular intervals to a third party. A direct debit can be for unspecified amounts or amounts within certain parameters. If the *beneficiary* of a direct debit fraudulently increases the amount the operating *bank* automatically accepts liability. Compare: *standing order*.

**directional strategy** A term applied to *hedge funds* that aims to add value by participating in the movement or direction of financial markets, including *stock markets, commodities* and *currencies*. They may also add *value* from *security* selection within markets. Non-directional strategies do not deliberately take on *market risk* and aim to add value by identifying mispricing of *securities* within markets. See: *momentum*.

**direct taxation** Tax directly levied on *income*, such as *income tax*, where the person who receives the *income* pays the *tax*, thereby suffering a reduction in *income*; as opposed to *indirect taxation*, where the *tax* is levied on goods purchased by the taxpayer and is thus a *tax* on consumption or spending.

**director** An individual appointed to the *board* of a *limited company* and registered as such with the *Registrar of Companies*, who has executive responsibility for the day-to-day duties of the *company* and responsibilities in the following order of priority: *shareholders*, staff, *creditors* and (some might add) self last. The director's designation (eg finance, operations, sales) will indicate the division of the *company* for which he or she has a specific remit, but they all have joint and several (collective) obligations. A director has statutory access to all the *company*'s books and records and cannot claim ignorance as a defence to a breach of his or her general obligations. The managing director or chief executive has primary responsibility for the conduct of the *company*'s business activities, the finance director for its liquidity and *accounts* and the chairman, who is also a director, for the conduct of the *board*. All *plcs* require at least two directors; other *limited companies* must have one director plus a *company secretary*. See: *wrongful trading*.

**directors report** An *annual report* by the *directors* of a *limited company* to its *shareholders* forming part of the *company*'s *accounts* filed with the *Registrar of Companies* under the Companies Act 2006. The information includes the principal activities of the *company*, a fair review of the circumstances of the business, likely future developments, details of research and development, significant issues on the sale, purchase or *valuation* of *assets*, *dividends*, transfers to *reserves*, names of the *directors* and their interests in the *company* during the period, employee statistics and any political or charitable gifts made during the period.

**dirham** 1. Standard *currency* unit of: *Morocco*: 1 dirham = 100 *centimes*; *United Arab Emirates*: 1 dirham = 100 *fils*; 2. *Currency* sub-unit of: *Qatar*: 100 dirhams = *riyal*; *Libya*: 1,000 dirhams = 1 *dinar*.

**dirty bond** A *fixed interest security* whose price reflects an allowance for *accrued interest*. Compare: *clean bond*.

**dirty float** Another term for: *managed float*.

**dirty price** The dirty price of a *bond* equals its *clean price* (which is usually the quoted price) plus the *accrued interest*.

**disbursement** A payment made by a professional person, such as a solicitor or banker, to a third party on behalf of a client. This is reclaimed under a specific heading when the client receives the account.

**disclosure regulations** Regulations issued under the Social Security Pensions Act 1975 requiring disclosure of information on *pension* and benefit schemes to interested parties.

**discount** A deduction made in the market price of a *security* for some reason. Government *stock* may be issued at a discount to its maturity *value*, so as to create an element of *capital gains* as an attraction. Short-term *Treasury bills* or *bills of exchange* are issued at a discount from their maturity *value* to create a return. *Shares* may be priced by investors at a discount to their theoretical *net asset value*. *Investment trust shares* are often judged by the extent of the discount on their *portfolio's net asset values*. Compare: *premium*. See: *discount house*.

**discount broker** Another term for: *bill broker*.

**discount house** City institutions whose business is *discounting bills of exchange, trade bills, bank bills* and *Treasury bills*. They provide a balancing and regulatory flow of short-term funds mainly to *clearing banks*.

**discount market** The element of the primary *money market* dominated by *banks, discount houses* and *bill brokers*. By borrowing *money* at short notice from commercial *banks* or *discount houses, bill brokers* can profitably *discount bills of exchange*, especially *Treasury bills*, and trade them in the discount market.

**discount rate** 1. The *base rate* that *US Federal Reserve Banks* charge member *banks* using *government securities* as *collateral*. This provides a base for rates generally, and these member *banks* will charge their customers a point or so above the *discount* rate. See: *prime rate*. 2. A measure of the annual return of a *discount instrument* (ie a short-term *security* that does not pay *interest*) that has n days to maturity, by comparing the gain with its *nominal value*:

$$\text{discount rate (\%)} = \frac{(\text{nominal value} - \text{purchase price})}{\text{nominal value}} \times \frac{365}{n} \times 100$$

Compare: *discount yield, money market yield*.

**discount yield** A measure of the annual return of a *discount instrument* (ie a *short term security* that does not pay *interest*) that has n days to maturity, by comparing the gain with its purchase price.

$$\text{discount yield (\%)} = \frac{(\text{nominal value} - \text{purchase price})}{\text{purchase price}} \times \frac{365}{n} \times 100$$

Compare: *discount rate, money market yield*

**discounted cash flow (DCF)** A technique used in *investment appraisal* to assess whether or not a particular *investment* is worthwhile or not. A certain *benchmark interest rate* is used for *discounting* (sense 2). This *benchmark* can be calculated in the following distinct ways: 1. The *interest rate* obtainable from a similar alternative *investment* with the same expected *risk* (along the lines of reasoning of *opportunity cost*) – often called the *cost of capital*. 2. The *interest rate* of a riskless *security* (best approximated by the *redemption yield* of a government *bond* of equivalent term) plus a 'risk premium' to account for the additional *risk* element of the *investment* under consideration. 3. Simply the investor's required *rate of return* determined by methods other than the two above examples of DCF techniques are *net present value* (NPV) and *internal rate of return* (IRR) calculations. The basic assumptions underlying *DCF* techniques are: The future *cash flows* are known with certainty. The *interest rate* used for *discounting* future *cash flows* is constant over the entire *term* of the *investment*. Except for calculating the *net present value* of receipts from the *investment*, the size and timing of receipts from the *investment* is irrelevant. *NPV* – one assumes that surplus funds generated can be reinvested at the *discount rate* (ie the *cost of capital* used in calculating the *NPV*). *IRR* – one assumes that surplus funds generated can be reinvested at a *rate of return* equal to *IRR*.

**discounting** 1. Discounting is the deduction made in the market price of a *security*, either by *market forces* or by an *issuing house* to increase the attractions of their *stocks*. See: *discount, zero*. 2. Using a certain *interest rate*, discounting is the calculation of present monetary *values* or *cash flows* from future values/cash flows. Discounting is used in *net present value* (*NPV*) and *internal rate of return* (*IRR*) techniques in order to take into account the time *value of money*. It is the opposite process to compounding. See: *compound*.

**discretionary service** In *investment* terms this refers to engaging the services of an *investment* adviser who has complete discretion (often within prescribed *limits*) as to where a client's *capital* may be invested without reference to the client other than at prior agreed reporting dates.

**discretionary trust** A *trust* where the *trustees* have absolute discretion during the *trust* period as to how much, if any, of the *income* or *capital* arising from the *trust* is distributed to its beneficiaries. At the end of the *trust* period, the *trustees* are responsible for distributing the balance into specified *shares*.

**disequilibrium** A state of imbalance, ie a particular situation is not in *equilibrium*.

**disinflation** A slowing-down in the rate of *inflation*, ie price levels are increasing, but at a decreased rate. An absolute decrease in price levels is termed *deflation*. Disinflation can also describe an economic or government policy designed to bring down the rate of *inflation*.

**displacement effect** The past observed tendency that governments have of raising their spending during periods when they are at war and maintaining a higher than pre-war spending after the war has ceased.

**disposable income** Net pay or *income* after all compulsory deductions, such as *income tax*, *pension* contributions and *National Insurance*.

**distributable profits** The *profits* or *reserves* of a *limited company* that are available for *distribution* as *dividends*. They consist of a *company*'s accumulated *realised profits* after deducting all realised losses, except for any of the *net realised profits* that have been previously capitalised. *Limited companies* may not distribute *profits* that would reduce *assets* to less than the sum of their *called-up capital* and their *undistributable reserves*, ie *shareholders*' funds.

**distribution** 1. A payment by a *limited company* from its *distributable profits* by means of a regular *dividend*. 2. A *dividend* on which *advance corporation tax* has been paid. For *UK tax* purposes a distribution includes, in addition to *dividends*, any payment, whether in *cash* or kind, out of the *assets* of a *company* in respect of *shares* of that *company*, except repayments of *capital*. 3. The distribution (marketing) of goods to consumers through wholesalers and retailers. 4. The legal division of property and *assets* eg of a *bankrupt* person or a deceased's *estate*.

**distributor funds** Distributor fund status is awarded by HMRC to offshore funds which generally distribute more than 85% of the accumulated *income* received by the funds annually and only on these funds can *growth* be taxed as *capital gains*.

**divergence indicator** A statistical measure of the amount by which individual national *currencies* of *EC* Member States are allowed to move away from the agreed *central parity* and the *EC* Unit.

**diversification** For *investment* this implies a greater *spread* of holdings and *sectors* primarily to reduce *volatility* and *risk* and prevent an unbalanced exposure to *investments* that do not perform as expected. For business this can be used to describe a broadening of products or services and most particularly involvement in a new aspect of the business.

**divestment** 1. Selling off (liquidating) the *assets* of a *company* (the opposite to: *investment*). 2. The splitting up of a *company*, ie the opposite of a *merger* or *acquisition*.

**dividend** The *distribution* to *shareholders* out of *company profits*. Company dividends are decided (declared) by the *directors* and announced at the *annual general meeting* and six-monthly at the *interim* results and expressed as a dividend per *share*. Dividends provide an *income* in addition to any *capital growth* and increase as the profitability of the *company* increases. *UK* dividends are declared with a non-reclaimable 10% *tax credit* to the holder which covers the basic rate taxpayer's liability. *Unit trusts* and OEIC's similarly pay dividends to their investors from the *income* received by the *fund*, which is usually paid in similar form to a *company* dividend. See: *franked income, scrip dividend*.

**dividend cover** A *stock market ratio*. The dividend cover is defined as:

$$\text{dividend cover} = \frac{\text{earnings per share}}{\text{dividend per share}}$$

Accordingly if the cover is high (where the *dividend* could be paid several times over from *profits*), *profits* are being retained for the business and are well protected; when cover is low the *company* can barely pay the *dividend* and will sometimes subsidise it from *reserves*. The reciprocal of dividend cover is the '*dividend payout ratio*'.

**dividend mandate** This is an authority provided by the shareholder to the *company* specifying to whom *dividends* are to be paid.

**dividend payout ratio** Reciprocal of *dividend cover*.

**dividend reinvestment plan (DRIP)** Many UK companies offer a dividend reinvestment plan (DRIP) which automatically reinvests shareholder dividends in further shares. The additional shares are acquired in the open market, incurring stamp duty and commission (usually charged at preferential rates) for the investor. Contrast: *scrip dividends*.

**dividend restraint** Often imposed as a matter of government policy, this is the restriction of *dividend* payments to *shareholders* without fixed *dividend* rights. See: *preference shares*.

**dividend stripping** The practice of purchasing a *security* just before it pays a *dividend* (while *x.d.*) and selling it afterwards. This can sometimes allow a loss in exchange for *income* and may prove tax-efficient for some investors. See: *bond washing*.

**dividend valuation model (DVM)** The hypothesis that the *market value* of a *security* at any time is determined by the *present value* of the expected *income* receipts (*cash flows*) discounted at the investor's required *rate of return*.

**dividend waiver** A decision not to take *dividends*, normally by a major shareholder, in order to maintain corporate *cash* balances.

**dividend warrant** This is the cheque for the *dividend* payment and is accompanied by a voucher giving details of the payment together with any *equalisation* and *tax credit*.

**dividend yield** A *stock market ratio*. Calculated as *dividend* per *share* divided by its current market price. One can take *dividend* as either a *gross* or a *net* figure, though it is normally quoted net in the UK and gross elsewhere. This represents only part of the return to the shareholder, since it does not take into account any *capital gain* or loss. See under: *yield*.

**DJF** *currency code* for: *Djibouti* Franc.

**Djibouti** Standard *currency*: *franc*. 1 *franc* = 100 *centimes*.

**DKK** *currency code* for: Danish Krone.

**dobra** Standard *currency* of *São Tomé e Príncipe*. 1 dobra = 100 *centavos*.

**documents against acceptance** A means of payment used in international trade where the seller sends the documents, including a *bill of exchange*, to a *bank*. The *bank* will only release title to the goods when the *bill* has been accepted. See: *cash against documents*.

**DOL** See: *Daily Official List*.

**dollar** A standard *currency* unit (1 dollar = 100 *cents*) in the following countries and territories; *Antigua & Barbuda, Australia, Bahamas, Barbados, Belize, Bermuda, British Virgin Islands, Brunei, Canada, Cayman Islands, Dominica, Fiji, Grenada, Guam, Guyana, Hong Kong, Jamaica, Kiribati, Liberia, Federated States of Micronesia, New Zealand, Puerto Rico, St Kitts and Nevis, Singapore, Solomon Islands, Taiwan, Trinidad & Tobago, Tuvalu, USA, Virgin Islands, Zimbabwe.*

**dollar cost averaging** Another term for: *constant dollar plan*.

**domestic bond** *Bond* that is denominated in domestic *currency* and issued in issuer's own country through a *syndicate* of *banks*. In contrast to *eurobonds*, which are issued globally and not in domestic *currency*. Compare: *foreign bond*.

**domicile** The country of a person's permanent home and not that person's nationality or temporary place of *residence*. Domicile is determined by both the physical fact of *residence* and the intention to reside there permanently. For example, a citizen of a foreign country who is resident in the *UK* is not necessarily domiciled there unless there is a clear intention to make the *UK* a permanent home. Under the common law, it is domicile and not *residence* or nationality that determines a person's civil status. Outside the UK many countries do not differentiate between residence and domicile for tax purposes. A corporation may also have a domicile, which is determined by the location of its *registered office*.

**Dominica** Standard *currency*: *dollar*. 1 *dollar* = 100 *cents*.

**Dominican Republic** Standard *currency*: *peso*. 1 *peso* = 100 *centavos*.

**dong** Standard *currency* of *Vietnam*. 1 dong = 10 *hao* = 100 *xu* = 1,000 *trinh*.

**donor** One who gives an *asset* to another party or, technically: one whose *estate* is made less by a gift. Normally associated with chargeable gifts and *inheritance tax*. See: *settlor*.

**doomsday price** The price of *shares* on 5 April 1965, when *capital gains tax* was introduced.

**DOP** *currency code* for: Dominican Peso.

**double bottom** See under: *double top*.

**double dipping** See: *two-timing*.

**double option** 1. An *option* to declare oneself either as a buyer or seller by a predetermined date for an agreed *premium*. 2. Also a prior agreement to sell *company* or *partnership shares* to the remaining *shareholders* from a deceased *member's estate*.

**double taxation agreement** An agreement between two countries allowing *tax* paid in one country to be offset against that due in the other on the same *income*.

**double taxation relief** This is the relief afforded a *company* or individual with income abroad, the *income* being taxed in that country. Relief can be given either by offsetting the foreign *tax* paid when calculating income at home or by averaging the overall *tax* payable at the rate applicable here.

**double top** A *reversal pattern* to an uptrend used in *technical analysis*. Similar to the *head and shoulders pattern*, except that the buyers are exhausted earlier. The first 'top' is formed on high *volume* after a small *reaction* in the *trend*. The top is followed by a larger *reaction* (at least 15%) on diminishing activity. Another *rally* (top) to the previous high (±3%) is made on a lower *volume* than the first top. The tops should be separated by at least one month. The *neckline* is drawn across the two preceding reversal troughs.

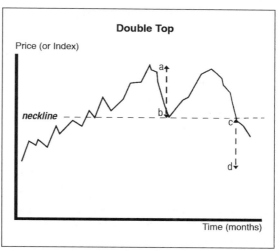

The breakthrough is confirmed when the price drops below that of the *neckline*. It is considered likely that the price will further drop to a distance (c to d) equal to the distance between the price peak and the *neckline* (a to b). Also called: M formation. The equivalent *reversal pattern* to a downtrend is called a '*double bottom*' (or a *W formation*).

**Dow** Charles Dow. The best known of technical analysts: famed for his development on the *Dow Jones* Stock Market Averages and the *Dow Theory*. See: *technical analysis*.

**Dow Jones (Index)** Another name for the Dow Jones Industrial Average. See under: *Dow Jones Stock Averages*.

**Dow Jones Stock Averages** A set of *indices* compiled daily from *New York Stock Exchange closing prices*. The *averages* are unweighted arithmetic *indices*, useful for showing general price movements:

- Industrial Average. Consists of 30 *stocks,* not all of which are industrial (eg four banks). Referred to as the '*Dow Jones*'. Probably the most widely quoted *US index.*

- Transportation Average. Consists of 20 transportation *stocks*.

- Utility Average. Consists of 15 utility *stocks*. Composite Average. Comprises all 65 *stocks* that constitute the above three averages.

**Dow Theory** Theory that a major *trend* in the *stock market* must be confirmed by a similar movement in the *Dow Jones* Industrial Average and the *Dow Jones* Transportation Average. According to Dow Theory, a significant *trend* is not confirmed until both *Dow Jones indices* reach the new highs or lows; if this does not occur the market will fall back to its former trading *range*. Dow Theory proponents often disagree on when a true *breakout* has occurred and, in any case, miss a major portion of the up or down move while waiting for their signals.

**down and dirty** An Americanism describing a practice where major investors in a troubled *company* arrange for *refinancing* at a rate that would significantly dilute remaining *shareholders' stakes* were they not to participate in the *refinancing*.

**down tick** See: *up tick*.

**downsizing** A colloquialism for making large numbers of staff redundant. When a *company* becomes unprofitable or inefficient as a result of macroeconomic factors (such as the increasing use of computers) it will adjust by using machines at the expense of human resources. Shedding staff can also provide a quick fix to improve short-term profitability.

**DPB** See: *Designated Professional Bodies*.

**DPS** Short for: *dividend* per *share* (in pence). See: *dividend*.

**drachma** Formerly the standard *currency* of Greece, until the introduction of the *euro* on 1 January 2002. 1 drachma = 100 *leptas*.

**draft** An American term for a signed order, which cannot be rescinded, by which one party (drawer) instructs another party (drawee) to pay a specified sum to a third party (*payee*). *Payee* and drawer are usually the same person. In foreign transactions, a draft is usually called a *bill of exchange*. When prepared without supporting papers, it is a clean draft. With papers or documents attached, it is a documentary draft. A sight draft is payable on demand. A *time draft* is payable either on a definite date or at a fixed time after sight or demand. See: *bank draft*.

**dragon markets** A colloquialism for *emerging markets* and economies of the Pacific basin, including *Indonesia, South Korea, Malaysia*, the *Philippines, Thailand* and *Vietnam*. They are characterised by above-average *GDP growth*, cheap labour and high *savings ratios*.

**dram** Standard *currency* of *Armenia*. 1 dram = 100 *luma*.

**drawdown** 1. The drawing of a pre-agreed line of credit by a borrower. 2. Shorthand for *income drawdown*.

**drawing rights** Amount used by members of the *International Monetary Fund* (*IMF*) to purchase foreign *currencies* in order to alleviate any undesirable short-term fluctuations. Extended in 1968 as the new International Reserve Currency System called *Special Drawing Rights* (*SDRs*).

**dread diseases** *Critical illness insurance*. A form of *insurance* policy that pays on the diagnosis of a specified serious or terminal illness rather than a death claim.

**DRIP** See: *dividend reinvestment plan*.

**drip-feed** A *venture capital* term used to describe the *funding* of a start-up *company* in gradual stages rather than by an initial injection of *capital*. The term is also used for other types of gradual investment.

**drop dead fee** A fee paid by *bidders* to lenders when a proposed *acquisition* fails and lines of credit established to finance the *acquisition* are not used. This arrangement allows *bidders* to commit themselves to large *acquisitions* without actually having to draw on the *money* or *risk* over-extending themselves in the financial markets.

**drop lock** An agreement which allows a variable rate loan package such as a *mortgage* to be turned into a fixed rate loan in the event of a prescribed decline in *interest rates*. See: *swap*.

**DSR** See: *debt service ratio*.

**DSS** Department for Social Security. See: *Department for Work and Pensions*.

**DTB** See: *Deutsche Terminbörse.*

**dual capacity** Investment institutions in the *UK* can act both as agent and principal whereas prior to October 1986 (the *Big Bang*) transactions on the *London Stock Exchange* had to be placed through a *jobber*, via a *stockbroker*, each in their *single capacity.*

**due diligence** A *corporate finance* term describing an independent investigation, normally by a team of *accountants,* into the accuracy of accounting information and the viability and prospects of a business that is the potential *target* of an *acquisition.* A due diligence report provides a third-party assessment of audited figures and can extend to additional research into management accounts, order books, staff morale etc. Generally used to test assertions by *management* about the *value* of their business.

**dumping** Selling goods in foreign markets at below domestic price for non-cost reasons, eg in order to gain market *share* or to reduce oversupply.

**duopoly** Market situation where there are many buyers and only two sellers. Compare: *duopsony, monopoly.*

**duopsony** Market situation where there are many sellers and only two buyers. Compare: *duopoly, monopsony.*

**duration** A measure in *quantitative analysis* of a *security*'s 'length' that takes into account the periodic *coupon* payments. Specifically, it is the *weighted average* maturity of all payments from a *security, coupon* plus principal, where the weights are the discounted *present values* of the payments. As such the duration is shorter than the stated term to maturity on all *securities* except for *zero-coupon bonds*, for which they are equal because the *zero-coupon bond* is a single-payment *security.* The term is useful because it is closely linked to 'modified duration', which is *volatility.* See: *convexity, Macaulay's duration.*

**Dutch auction** The method first used for selling tulips in *Holland*, where the price starts high and gradually reduces. The first *bidder* is the buyer. *US Treasury Bonds* are sold in this way.

**DVM** See: *dividend valuation model.*

**DWP** See: *Department for Work and Pensions.*

**DZD** *currency code* for: Algerian Dinar.

# E

**E&OE** Short for: 'Errors and Omissions Excepted'. Normally found on a *quotation* or *contract note*; absolves the writer from the legal obligation to abide by the figures if a genuine error has occurred.

**eagle** A *US* ten-*dollar gold* coin.

**EAR** See: *The Effective Annualised Rate (EAR)*.

**early bargain (EB)** These are *stock exchange* transactions made late in the day and deemed to have been transacted the following day. See also: *after hours deal*.

**earn-out** The purchase of a business where the price is predicated by the amount the business earns over a period subsequent to the sale. Designed to maintain the enthusiastic involvement of the former owners of the business and validate the accuracy of their forecasts for the business.

**earnings** The *profit* available for *equity* holders of the *company*. Normally expressed as *earnings per share*, it is the *net profit* after *tax*, after preference *dividends* and after any *minority interest*.

**earnings per share (eps)** A *ratio* expressing a *company*'s *earnings* (ie *profit* after *tax* and *extraordinary items*) over the total number of *ordinary shares* in issue.

$$\text{eps} = \frac{\text{profit after tax and extraordinary items}}{\text{total number of ordinary shares in issue}}$$

If the denominator includes *shares* that are going to be issued in the near future by the *company*, by the use of *convertibles* for instance, one refers to '*fully diluted earnings* per *share*'. Compare: *price earnings ratio*.

**earnings yield** 1. Used in reference to *stock exchange investments*, this is the *ratio* of *earnings* over total *equity capital* at the current *market value*. See: *profit earnings ratio*. 2. See under: *yield*.

**EASDAQ** Short for: European Association of Securities Dealers Automated Quotation System. The European equivalent of *NASDAQ*. Based in *Belgium*, EASDAQ was intended to replicate the success of *NASDAQ*, its US-based equivalent, as a pan-European screenbased electronic market for higher *risk*, high tech *stocks* and *shares*. In March 2001, *NASDAQ* acquired a majority *stake* in EASDAQ which it then closed in 2003.

**EB** A *stock exchange* term denoting an *early bargain*.

**EBDIT** *Earnings* before *depreciation, interest* and *tax*. *Gross profit* of a *company* before any deductions. Used to measure core profitability. See: *EBITDA*.

**EBITDA** Earnings before *interest, tax, depreciation* and *amortisation*. A popular measure of corporate profitability designed to give an impression of potential *cash* returns. See: *EBDIT*.

**EC** See: *European Community*.

**ECB** See: *European Central Bank*.

**ECGD** See: *Export Credits Guarantee Department*.

**e-commerce** Primarily trade over the internet. A growing element of retail sales is taking place over the web and many businesses now offer online shopping facilities for customers. Settlement is by credit or debit card and merchandise is delivered by post or courier. Statutory distance-selling regulations govern these transactions and provide considerable consumer protection including a no quibble returns entitlement.

**econometrics** A branch of economics using statistical models of historical information to interpret and predict future *trends*. See: *quantitative analysis*.

**economic indicators** Important statistics showing the state of the economy at a particular time. Much information can be gleaned from these *indicators* about the direction the economy is heading in. Examples of the *indicators* are: *unemployment* figures, *money supply*, *inflation*, *interest rates*, Gross Domestic Product and *balance of trade* etc. See also: *leading indicators*.

**economies of scale** Benefits of size where expenditure on systems, advertising, research etc. is a smaller proportion of total expenditure for a larger enterprise and is often cited as the main benefit of a *merger* or *takeover*. Also the cost savings of buying or selling, where *discounts* can be achieved or savings made on large-scale *distribution*. See: *increasing returns*.

**ECP** See: *euro commercial paper*.

**ECS** *currency code* for: *Ecuador* Sucre.

**ECU** A composite monetary unit consisting of a basket of *European Community currencies* that served as the predecessor to the *euro*.

**Ecuador** Ecuador has two exchanges, established by Presidential decree in 1969: the Quito Stock Exchange and the Guayaquil Stock Exchange. Standard *currency*: *sucre*. 1 *sucre* = 100 *centavos*.

**EDX London** EDX London is the equity derivatives market formed by the OMHEX and the *London Stock Exchange* in 2003. It is a *Recognised Investment Exchange* which provides its members with the ability to trade Scandinavian derivatives listed by Stockholmsbörsen, Copenhagen Stock Exchange and Oslo Børs.

**EEC** See: *European Economic Community*.

**EEK** *currency code* for: Estonian Kroon.

**Effective Annualised Rate (EAR)** EAR does not take into account any additional charges — for example, arrangement fees, securities charges, or monthly fees that may be due. A more appropriate measure is AER which includes all costs and is used as a *benchmark* rate.

**effective exchange rate** A *trade-weighted index* that shows the movement of the *exchange rate* of the country in question against a weighted basket of foreign *currencies* with which the country trades. See also: *nominal exchange rate, real exchange rate*.

**efficient frontier** The efficient frontier is a product of *modern portfolio theory* and is a line plotted on a risk-return graph which theoretically represents the most efficient portfolio for any given level of risk. Alternatively it can be used to show the lowest risk portfolio for any given level of return. The efficient frontier is the bedrock of many asset allocation systems.

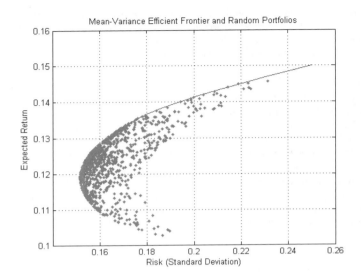

efficient market theory A prognosis that *investment* markets reflect the knowledge and expectation of all investors and that these prices and their *indices* give a totally accurate picture of the health of the underlying industries and economies they represent. The theory dictates that in the long run it is impossible to out-perform the market by *stock* selection. See also: *index fund.*

**EFG**  See: *Enterprise Finance Guarantee Scheme.*

**EFRBS**  See: *Employer Financed Retirement Benefits Scheme.*

**EFTPOS**  See: *Electronic Funds Transfer at Point of Sale.*

**EGM**  See: *extraordinary general meeting.*

**EGP**  *currency code* for: Egyptian Pound.

**Egypt**  Egypt has two exchanges, the Cairo Stock Exchange and the Alexandria Stock Exchange. Standard *currency*: Egyptian *pound.* 1 Egyptian *pound* = 100 *piastres* = 1,000 *millièmes.*

**EIB**  See: *European Investment Bank.*

**EIS**  See: *Enterprise Investment Scheme.*

**El Salvador**  Standard *currency*: colón. 1 *colón* = 100 *centavos.*

elasticity  A measure of the responsiveness of one variable to the change in another. It is expressed as the percentage change induced in the variable in question divided by the percentage change in another variable. For example, the (price) elasticity of demand for a particular good or service is the percentage change in quantity demanded divided by the percentage change in the price that brought about the change in demand. Important to estimate in order to see, for example, whether a firm's revenue will increase as a result of raising the price of its product.

**Electronic Funds Transfer at Point of Sale (EFTPOS)**  System that automatically debits a client's *bank account* from a retail outlet by the use of a plastic magnetic card.

**eligible paper** 1. In the *UK*, any first-class *security* (such as *Treasury bills*) that has been accepted by a British *bank* that the *Bank of England* thus deems eligible for rediscounting or as security for lending to a *discount house*. 2. In the *US*, those *securities* that the *Federal Reserve Bank* accepts for rediscounting.

**Elliott wave theory** A controversial *chart* theory which uses cyclical *chart patterns* ('waves') in order to predict future price movements, developed by Ralph Elliott. It uses a number of waves (ie *chart* cycles) of varying duration, their relative height fixed in proportions determined by the *Fibonacci numbers*. Elliott theory is intended to apply to *equity* market *indices* and not to individual *securities*. Even proponents of the theory agree that it works better in some situations than others – it is said to work well for *emerging markets*. See: *technical analysis*.

**EMA** See: *European Monetary Agreement*.

**embargo** Government order to restrict or prohibit *imports* from and *exports* to a certain country or region for political, or sometimes economic, reasons.

**embedded value** Normally applied to *life assurance companies* where the *value* of the *company* exceeds its *asset value* due to *reserves* allocated to policyholders that may not need to be distributed. In addition, the costs of servicing and distributing new business to policyholders is expensive and it can be several years before the *company* makes a *profit* on a policy.

**EMCOF** See: *European Monetary Co-operation Fund*. See under: *European Monetary System*.

**emerging market** A small *stock market* in a newly industrialised or Third World country that is becoming or is likely to become a player on the world economic stage. The emerging markets (according to the *MSCI Indices*) are: *Argentina, Brazil, Chile, China, Czech Republic, Egypt, Hungary, India, Indonesia, Israel, South Korea, Malaysia, Mexico, Peru*, the *Philippines, Poland, South Africa, Taiwan, Thailand* and *Turkey*. Also a market for emerging *companies* or for *companies* developing products such as electronic or biological technology. See: *Alternative Investment Market, Emerging Markets Free Index (EMF), Tequila Slammer*.

**Emerging Markets Free Index (EMF)** *Index* developed by Morgan Stanley Capital International. Indexes the *stock markets* of *Argentina, Chile, Jordan, Malaysia, Mexico*, the *Philippines* and *Thailand*; selected because of their accessibility to foreign investors. See: *MSCI Indices*.

**EMF** See: *Emerging Markets Free Index*.

**emoluments** A term meaning 'all salaries, fees, wages, perquisites, and *profits* whatsoever' being taxable, ie chargeable to *tax*.

**Employee Retirement Income Security Act 1974 (ERISA)** An American law governing the operation of *personal pension* plans, which established the *pension* benefit guarantee corporation and general guidelines for the management of *pension* funds. See: *401(k) Plan, Individual Retirement Account*.

**employee share ownership plan (ESOP)** An arrangement popular in *America* where a special *trust* is set up by the *company* to transfer its *shares* to employees over a period of years. In the *UK* the term is often used to describe a trust set up as part of an employee share ownership scheme.

**employee share ownership trust (ESOT)** *Companies* wishing to promote *share* ownership can use specially established trusts – often set up with offshore trustees – to hold shares for an employee share ownership plan. See also: *employee share ownership plan*.

**Employer Financed Retirement Benefits Scheme (EFRBS)** A pension scheme which is not registered with HMRC under the *simplified regime* provisions of the Finance Act 2004. The EFRBS replaced *funded unapproved retirement benefit schemes (FURBS)*. Employer contributions to EFRBS only receive tax relief when the member receives taxable benefits and the underlying fund is taxable. Contributions are not taxable on the member, but benefits are fully taxable. Funds within EFRBS are subject to normal trust taxation rules. EFRBS are normally only used to top up benefits where the *lifetime allowance* would otherwise be exceeded.

**EMS** See: *European Monetary System*. See: *snake, Exchange Rate Mechanism*.

**EMU** See: *European Monetary Union*.

**encumbered** See: *unencumbered*.

**endorsement** 1. A term originally used with reference to *bills of exchange*. It transfers the ownership of the *bill* to its new holder. This is achieved by the original holder signing the *bill* on the reverse making it payable to the new holder. There is no limit to the number of times a *bill* can be endorsed as long as the endorsement is always written on the *bill* itself. 2. An amendment to policy terms or conditions on a *life assurance* policy.

**endowment** A type of *life assurance* policy which pays a *sum assured* on the death of the life *assured* or at the end of an agreed term, whichever is the earlier date. Furthermore, a *with-profits policy* will provide sums over and above the *sum assured* by the addition of *bonuses*. This type of policy was often used in the repayment of a personal *mortgage* or as a form of saving. The attraction of the *contract* was diminished by the abolition of *life assurance premium* relief in the 1984 Finance Act and the subsequent launch of personal equity plans. See also: *qualifying policy, reversionary bonus, terminal bonus, low-cost endowment, low-cost mortgage*.

**enduring power of attorney (EPA)** A special *power of attorney* used to protect the *assets* of people who have been certified under the Mental Health Act 1983 or who for some other reason are incapable of managing their financial affairs, approved by the Court of Protection. Replaced by lasting power of attorney from 1 October 2007. EPAs created before this date continue to have effect.

**Engel expenditure curve** A curve used to show the relationship between an individual's expenditure on a certain type of *commodity* depending on his or her *income*. The diagram shows that a certain 'threshold' *income* must be earned before any expenditure on the *commodity* is made. Sub-sequently the expenditure rises, but at a decreasing rate, showing the *decreasing returns* derived from

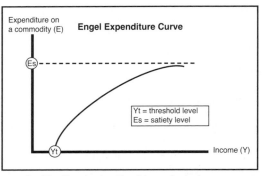

additional consumption of the *commodity*. Finally, a 'satiety' level is reached where no more of that *commodity* is desired, no matter how much *money* the individual earns.

**enhanced protection**  One of the two types of *transitional protection* for members of pension schemes whose total benefit value exceed the annual allowance. An election for enhanced protection, which had to be made by 6 April 2009, protects all of the benefits from a *lifetime allowance charge*, provided that after 5 April 2006 no contributions are made and no additional benefits accrued (other than in limited circumstances). Contrast: *Primary protection*.

**Enterprise Finance Guarantee Scheme (EFG)**  Launched in January 2009, as a result of the *Credit Crunch* and subsequent *recession*, to help smaller businesses get *bank* loans of up to £1 million. The *UK* government announced the launch of the Enterprise Finance Guarantee Scheme (*EFG*), as part of an effort to stimulate *bank* lending to businesses. The scheme aims to help credit-worthy *companies* with the government guaranteeing 75% of any loans made and the *bank* covering the remaining 25%. The scheme was initially designed to provide £1 billion of guarantees to support £1.3 *billion* of bank lending (originally only available to March 2010) available for loans of up to £1 *million* to be repaid over a period of up to 10 years. Initially available via: Barclays, Clydesdale/Yorkshire Bank, HBOS, HSBC, Lloyds TSB, RBS/Natwest and Northern Bank.

**Enterprise Investment Scheme (EIS)**  A scheme designed to encourage *investment* in small businesses replacing the *Business Expansion Scheme* in 1994. It allows *income tax* relief of 20% on an *investment* in the *shares* of a qualifying *company* of up to £500,000 each *tax year* to a maximum of 30% shareholding. No *capital gains tax* applies if the *shares* are held for three years, and any losses may be offset against *capital gains* or *income* for *tax* purposes. The *shares* must be paid in full; connected loans are not allowed and nor are preferential rights. Participation is limited to *companies* with *gross assets* of no more than £7 million and less than 50 equivalent full time employees. 80% of the money must be used within 12 months and the remaining 20% within 24 months. *Companies* must be unquoted (but can be listed on AIM) but cannot be primarily involved in property, finance, legal, accountancy, *leasing*, licensing or royalties. They cannot be *subsidiary companies* and must trade wholly or mainly in the *UK*.

**enterprise zone**  Areas (normally of high *unemployment*) selected by the government where *capital* and *tax* incentives were provided to encourage industry and building developments. The last enterprise zone ended its ten-year life in 2005.

**enterprise zone trust (EZT)**  A fund of investors participating in one or a number of qualifying *enterprise zone* property *investments*. Most EZTs are now in the process of being wound up.

**Entrepreneurs' relief**  Entrepreneurs' relief was introduced from 6 April 2008 as a limited replacement for capital gains tax business assets taper relief. The relief can be claimed by individuals against gains resulting from the disposal of qualifying business assets, which have been owned for at least one year. Qualifying business assets are:

• assets used in the business (such as commercial property and goodwill) that were part of the disposal of the whole or part of the business, whether carried on as a sole trader or partnership.

• assets that were in used for the business or a partnership of which the individual was a member, that were disposed of within the period of three years after the business ceased.

• shares in, or securities of, a 'personal company', ie one in which the individual has at least a 5% shareholding. The company (or, where the shares are in a holding company of a group, the group of companies) must either be a trading company or have been so within the previous three years.

• assets owned personally but used in a business carried on by either a partnership of which the individual is a member, or by their personal trading company (or by a company in a trading group, the holding company of which is their 'personal company'), provided that the disposal is associated with a disposal of the individual's interest in the partnership or shares or securities. In such cases relief is restricted where rent is charged for the asset.

The relief operates by reducing the capital gain by 4/9ths, so that the effective rate of tax becomes 10% (18% x 5/9), the same as the rate that generally applied under business assets taper relief. However, unlike the previous relief, there is a £1,000,000 lifetime limit to the amount of gains eligible for entrepreneurs' relief.

Disposals of business assets by trustees can also qualify for entrepreneurs' relief, but only where there is a beneficiary who owns sufficient shares personally for the company to qualify as their 'personal company' or who runs or has run a business that used the trust's assets.

**EOE** See: *European Options Exchange.*

**EPI** Short for: *euro commercial paper* issue. See: *euro commercial paper.*

**EPP** See: *executive pension plan.* See also: *pension.*

**eps** See: *earnings per share.*

**equal access** The Social Security Pensions Act 1975 requires identical entry conditions to any *pension* scheme for both sexes.

**equalisation** This applies particularly to *unit trusts.* Income from a *unit trust* or OEIC accrues during periods between *dividend distributions* and is added to the unit share price. New investors purchasing an *investment* at any time will be paying for some of their next *income* payment in the unit share price, effectively turning *capital* into *income* (which may be more severely taxed). Directed by this position, the fund groups introduced an equalisation factor into each *distribution* and this proportion of the total *distribution* is not subject to any *income tax* deductions. With reference to *hedge funds* with *high water marks,* it is the accounting method which ensures that all investors pay the correct *performance fee.*

**equalisation of estates** The former strategy of dividing family *assets* between husband and wife to ensure that maximum benefit is derived from the individual *inheritance tax* nil-rate *bands* on death. The advent of transferable nil rate bands has largely rendered the exercise unnecessary.

**equalisation of pension rights** See: *Barber Judgment.*

**equation of exchange** See under: *quantity theory of money.*

**Equatorial Guinea** Standard *currency:* African *franc.*

**equilibrium** A point or position at which the variable in question comes to rest and where the opposing forces on it cancel out. The equilibrium is said to be 'stable' if small variations in the forces do not tend to push the variable far from its equilibrium, and 'unstable' if a small imbalance in the forces causes the variable to move far and maybe continuously from the equilibrium position. An example of a

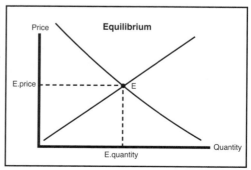

stable equilibrium is the price of a good or service normally established by *market forces*; the *supply and demand* intersect at a certain price and output quantity, called the equilibrium point.

**equities** The term given to *investments* in a *company listed* on a *stock exchange*, as opposed to fixed-*interest investments* and property. A general term for *ordinary shares* having an interest in *profits* of a *company*. See: *fixed interest security*.

**equity** 1. The residue of a holding in a *company* after all prior claims have been met. Equity holders are, therefore, entitled to the *earnings* and *assets* of a *company* or property after all prior *charges* on *capital* have been settled. 2. The *money* left over and paid to the borrower of an *asset* in a *mortgage* or *hire purchase* agreement, after that *asset* has been sold and the lender has been fully repaid. See also: *negative equity*. 3. A *company*'s *ordinary share capital*. See: *equities*. 4. In a brokerage account, the excess of *securities* over the debit balance in a *margin account*. 5. In the English legal system, equity was originally introduced to mitigate the harshness of common law. The division of common law and equity still exists; in the case where there is disagreement between the two, equity prevails.

**equity capital** Usually the ordinary *shareholders'* stake in the *share capital* (*equity*) of a *company*. On winding-up, they have a right to a *share* in the *company*'s *profits* and surplus after the other *creditors* have been paid. Other *shareholders*, such as holders of *pre-emption rights*, may also be classified as sharing in the *equity capital* for this purpose.

**equity dilution** See: *dilution of equity*.

**equity financing** Raising *money* for a *company* by issuing ordinary and/or *preference shares*. See: *capitalise*.

**equity gearing** See: *capital gearing*.

**equity injection** The infusion of new *capital* (*cash*) into a business by creating new or additional *shares* as opposed to loans. This will cause *dilution of equity* but improve the *company*'s *reserves* proportionally.

**equity kicker** In cases where a business has been financed by *venture capital* or loans, the rate of *interest* and the repayment terms of the loan can be improved by offering some *ordinary shares* to the lender. This can form part of an initial transaction or come into operation when the *company* is not as successful for either party as had been anticipated or, conversely, turns out to be much more successful when *shares* are offered as an incentive to the executives.

**equity release** Equity release is a means of using the *value* of an owner-occupied property to allow the owner to receive either a lump sum or regular monthly *income* by using the *unencumbered value* accumulated in the property. There are two types of equity release: a *mortgage* plan or a *home reversion plan*. In both instances, age is the primary factor in determining the percentage of the *value* that can be released. See also: *home income plan*.

**ERDF** See: *European Regional Development Fund*.

**ERISA** See: *Employee Retirement Income Security Act 1974*.

**Eritrea** Standard *currency*: Ethiopian *birr*.

**ERM** Enterprise *risk management*. See: *risk management*.

**ERM** See: *Exchange Rate Mechanism*.

**ERN** *currency code* for: Eritrean Nakfa.

**ERNIE** Short for: Electronic Random Number Indicator Equipment. The computer used by *National Savings and Investments* to select winning *premium bonds*.

**escalation** A term used to describe the method by which a *pension* benefit in payment or as a preserved benefit is automatically increased at regular intervals by a specific amount or rate or by linking it to an *index* such as the *Retail Price Index*.

**escrow** *Assets* in the form of *cash*, *near cash* or property held suspended by a third party against the performance of a *contract*. See also: *garnishee*.

**escudo** Standard *currency* of *Cape Verde Islands*. Formerly the standard *currency* of *Portugal*, until the introduction of the *euro* on 1 January 2002. 1 escudo = 100 *centavos*.

**ESOP** See: *employee share ownership plan*.

**ESOT** See: *employee share ownership trust*.

**estate** For *inheritance tax* purposes, an individual's estate is his/her total *assets* less total liabilities.

**estate duty** Sometimes known as *death duty*, this was a *tax* on the transfer of *assets* on death or within a certain period before death. It was repealed in the 1975 Finance Act and replaced by *capital transfer tax*, which itself has been superseded by *inheritance tax*.

**Estonia** Standard *currency*: *kroon*. 1 *kroon* = 100 senti.

**ETB** *currency code* for: Ethiopian Birr.

**ETC** See: *exchange traded commodity*.

**ETF** See: *exchange traded fund*.

**ETN** See: *exchange traded note*.

**ethical investment** *Investment* that aims to avoid *companies* that are involved in certain activities such as the manufacture of armaments, cigarettes, animal research or alcohol, or that are involved in trade with countries deemed to have infringed certain human rights. They can also be *investments* in *companies* where the emphasis is placed on the protection of the environment, charitable works, medical research or other benign activities. They are sometimes known as *green investments* or socially responsible investments.

**Ethical Investment Research Information Services (EIRIS)** An organisation providing information on *ethical investment*.

**Ethiopia** Standard *currency*: Ethiopian *birr*. 1 *birr* = 100 *cents*.

**EU** See: *European Union*.

**EUR** *currency code* for: Euro.

**EUREX** EUREX is a major derivatives exchange jointly operated by Deutsche Börse AG and SIX Swiss Exchange. In December 2007 EUREX acquired the International Securities Exchange, the world's largest equity options exchange based in the US.

**Euribor** Euro Interbank Offered Rate. A euro-denominated interest rate charged by large banks among themselves on euro-denominated loans. The euro equivalent of LIBOR for Sterling.

**euro** The euro is the single *currency* used across 16 *European Union* Member States. Introduced on 1 January 1999, legal tender first went into circulation on 1 January 2002 in 12 countries. Euro *monetary policy* is controlled by the *European Central Bank* (*ECB*). The introduction of the euro has created the world's second biggest economic unit narrowly behind the *US dollar*. See: *Eurozone, EU*. 1 euro = 100 *cents*.

**Euro-Top 100 Index** See under: the *Netherlands*.

**Euro Zone** The countries using the *euro* (launched 1 January 1999). *Greece* qualified in 2000 and was admitted on 1 January 2001. Physical coins and banknotes were introduced on 1 January 2002. *Slovenia* qualified in 2006 and was admitted on 1 January 2007. *Cyprus* and *Malta* qualified in 2007 and were admitted on 1 January 2008. *Slovakia* qualified in 2008 and joined on 1 January 2009 when there were 16 Member States in the Euro Zone. The *EU* has 27 Member States in total (2009).

**eurobond** This is an international *bond* (usually with a minimum maturity of 5 years and a maximum maturity of 20 years) issued in markets outside the domestic market of the issuer by a *syndicate* of international *banks*. They are unsecured *bearer securities*. Their *denomination* can be relatively low (for example, as little as $1,000), but the issue is to a large extent taken up by large institutions, such as the *World Bank*, the *EU* and multinationals. Interest payments from these *bonds* are free of any withholding taxes. It has become a popular market for raising *capital* since the anonymity of investors on the *secondary market* is assured. Most *new issues* take place in the substantial London market. The issues are sold on the *secondary market* on an *over-the-counter* basis by specialist *dealers*. The *bonds* exists as '*straights*' (ie with a fixed rate of *interest*, usually paying annually), as *floating rate notes* (ie with variable *interest rates*, based on the *London Inter-Bank Offered Rate*, usually the *interest rate* is adjusted and *interest* is paid every six months) and as 'perpetuals' (which have no *redemption date*). A variation on the '*straights*' is that they also may come as *convertibles* (into *shares* in the issuing *company*) or with *warrants* attached (giving the right to buy *shares* at a predetermined date at a predetermined time).

**Euroclear** Settlement house, based in Brussels, for clearing *eurobonds*.

**eurocurrency** Non-domestic *currency* held in a European country. For instance, *yen* deposited in *France* are termed 'euroyen', *dollars* held in an English *bank* are called '*eurodollars*'.

**eurocurrency market** Market in *eurocurrencies* for the financing of international trade and *investment*.

**eurodollar** *US dollars* held in *banks* outside the *USA*. The term used to refer only to *dollars* held in European *banks*, but now the term usage has extended to all non-US *banks*' *dollars* (thus the term 'Asiandollar', ie *dollars* held in Asian *banks*). The eurodollar market emerged in London in the late 1950s.

**eurodollar certificate of deposit** *Certificate of deposit* issued by *banks* not resident in the *US* (usually, but not necessarily, in Europe), denominated in *dollars*.

**Euroland** See: *Eurozone*.

**euromarket** The market that deals principally in *eurobonds*, *euro commercial papers* and *euronotes*, whose base is in London (smaller markets exist in Paris, Brussels and Frankfurt). It came about in the late 1950s to finance international trade and the main participants in the market are large institutions.

**European Central Bank (ECB)** The European System of Central Banks (ESCB) is composed of the European Central Bank (*ECB*) and the national *central banks* (NCBs) of all 27 *EU* Member States (2009). The 'Eurosystem' is the term used to refer to the *ECB* and the NCBs of the Member States which have adopted the *euro*. The NCBs of the Member States which do not participate in the *euro* area, however, are members of the ESCB with a special status – while they are allowed to conduct their respective national *monetary policies*, they do not take part in the decision-making with regard to the single *monetary policy* for the *euro* area and the implementation of such decisions. In accordance with the Treaty establishing the *European Community* (the 'Treaty') and the Statute of the European System of Central Banks and of the European Central Bank (the 'Statute of the ESCB') the primary objective of the Eurosystem is to maintain price stability (which the ECB measures as LPI inflation close to, but below, 2%) Without prejudice to this objective, the Eurosystem shall support the general economic policies in the Community and act in accordance with the principles of an open market economy. The basic tasks to be carried out by the Eurosystem are: to define and implement the *monetary policy* of the *euro* area; to conduct *foreign exchange* operations; to hold and manage the official foreign *reserves* of the Member States; and to promote the smooth operation of payment systems.

**European Commission** The executive body of the *European Union* comprising commissioners from Member States to arbitrate disputes and supervise development.

**European Community (EC)** Now (since 1 November 1993, the *Maastricht Treaty*) more commonly called: *European Union (EU)*. The *EC* was formed in 1967 through the merger of the *EEC*, Euratom (European Atomic Energy Community) and the ECSC (European Coal and Steel Community). The *EC* also comprises the *European Commission* (since 1987; it meets in Brussels), the European Parliament (it meets in Strasbourg; its committee is in Brussels) and the European Court of Justice (which meets in *Luxembourg*). Recently, the *EC* has adopted a group *currency*, the *euro*, for its member nations. From 1 January 1999, 12 countries within the *EC* dropped their own *currencies* and adopted the *euro*. By 2009 another four countries had done so. Only *Denmark*, *Sweden* and the *UK* opted out of joining initially. The *EC* has since expanded its borders to include 12 central, eastern and southern European countries.

**European Currency Unit** See: *ECU*.

**European Economic Community (EEC)** Formerly called: the *Common Market*. An economic association of western European countries established after the Treaty of Rome (1957). Its object was to abolish customs barriers and *cartels*, and to promote common agricultural and trade policies. Until 1987 the term *EEC* was generally used to signify the *European Community* (*EC*). In 1993, the *Maastricht Treaty* changed the name from the *EC* to *European Union*, and helped move the *EU* to a far more federal structure. Free trade between countries, a European parliament, European courts and a European single *currency* (*euro*) all show moves towards a federal Europe. The current shape of the *EU* is much changed from the original *EEC*.

**European Investment Bank (EIB)** The task of the European Investment Bank (*EIB*), the *European Union*'s financing institution, is to contribute towards the integration, balanced development and economic and social cohesion of the Member States. To this end, it raises on the markets substantial *volumes* of funds which it directs on the most favourable terms towards financing *capital* projects according with the objectives of the Union. Outside the Union the *EIB* implements the financial components of agreements concluded under European development aid and cooperation policies. It is non-profit-making and charges *interest* at a rate at which it borrows. Its headquarters are in *Luxembourg*.

**European Monetary Co-operation Fund (EMCOF)** See under: *European Monetary System*.

**European Monetary Fund** See under: *European Monetary System*.

**European Monetary System (EMS)** A monetary system set up by the *European Community* in 1979 with a view to stabilising member countries' *currencies* and eventually to create a common *currency*. The prelude to the *EMS* was the introduction of the *Exchange Rate Mechanism* (*ERM*) which used an artificial, weighted *currency* unit called the *European Currency Unit* (*ECU*) to which the *ERM* member countries must maintain a fixed *parity* (within limits). Also, a *European Monetary Co-operation Fund* (*EMCOF*) was set up which credited *ECUs* to countries that deposit 20% of their *gold* and foreign *reserves*. Thus *EMCOF* acted as a *clearing house* for member countries' *central bank intervention* in the foreign market in order to maintain *parity*. With *European Monetary Union, EMCOF* has been replaced with the *European Monetary Fund* and the *euro* established as the *currency* of participating members.

**European Monetary Union (EMU)** On 1 January 1999, 12 European countries entered into the '*euro*', the focal point of European Monetary Union. Four joined later. Entry to the euro means that monetary control is handed to the *European Central Bank*, and one blanket *interest rate* is used. *EMU* has been met with much scepticism in many *EU* countries, especially in the *UK*. This has, in part, led to the *UK* holding back from entry for the time being. The 16 member countries are (2009): *France, Germany, Luxembourg, Belgium, Spain, Cyprus, Malta, Slovakia, Slovinia, Portugal, Greece, Austria, Finland, Italy*, Ireland and the *Netherlands*. See: *European Union*.

**European option** See under: *option*.

**European Options Exchange (EOE)** A *traded options* market based in Amsterdam. It is affiliated to the *Amsterdam Stock Exchange*. It deals predominantly in *currency options*. See under: the *Netherlands*.

**European Regional Development Fund** A central fund for the development of underdeveloped areas in the *European Community* particularly with high levels of *unemployment* or poverty.

**European style option** See: *option*.

**European Union (EU)** The six original members of the *EU* (then called the *European Economic Community*), joining after the Treaty of Rome in 1957, were the *Benelux* countries, *France*, the former West *Germany* (now the unified *Germany* is a member) and *Italy*. After the Treaty of Accession (1972), *Denmark*, Ireland and the *UK* joined. *Greece* followed in 1981; *Spain* and *Portugal* in 1986; and *Austria, Finland* and *Sweden* in 1995, bringing the total to 15. Ten new members joined on 1 May 2004: *Cyprus, Czech Republic, Estonia, Hungary, Latvia, Lithuania, Malta, Poland, Slovakia, Slovenia. Bulgaria* and *Romania* then entered the EU in 2007. The *EU* has its own *currency*, the *euro*, to which 16 of the 27 current Member States have signed up.

**euroyen bond** A *bond* issued on the international markets not subject to *withholding tax* and denominated in *yen*. Some euroyen bond issues are designed to benefit from a fall or a rise in the Japanese *stock market*.

**event risk** The *risk*, for instance, that a *bond* will receive a lower *rating* because of *takeover* proceedings causing a decline in *bond quality*.

**evergreen** A loan facility set to run for a period of years, but reviewed on a more frequent basis. Say a loan is offered on a three-year basis and reviewed every year; if the loan is renewed it is for a further year and it will therefore run for a further three years. If the loan is not renewed at the review period it still has a further two years to run.

**evergreen fund** A *venture capital* fund which supports start-up *companies* with a continuing source of *capital*, thus sponsoring their development on an ongoing basis.

**ex** Latin for 'without'. Prefixes another term to denote that the benefit is not included with the purchase of the *security* when the details of the *security* are quoted. Contrast: *cum*.

**ex all (x.a.)** Denotes that the seller of the *security* keeps all benefits.

**ex bonus (x.b.)** When quoted alongside a *security*, it means that the *vendor* keeps the *bonus*.

**95**

**ex capitalisation (x.c. or x.cap.)** Means that the purchaser of the *security* is not entitled to the *capitalisation issue*.

**ex coupon (x.cp.)** The seller of the *security* keeps the *coupon*.

**ex dividend (x.d. or x.div.)** *Dividend distributions* are paid on a regular basis by *companies* to investors generally. To facilitate both smooth administration and orderly price movements prior to each *distribution*, there is a specially defined day when an *investment* is quoted *ex*, or without, the *dividend*. In theory the price will fall by the total amount of the proposed *net dividend* although in practice the reduction is often slightly less. The period during which *gilts* trade ex dividend is 7 business days (exception: 10 business days for 3½% War Loan).

**ex interest (x.in.)** Denotes that the *security* is priced without the most recent *interest* payment.

**ex new** Shares are quoted ex new when their price does not include the right to take new (*scrip issue*) *shares* being offered.

**ex rights** The buyer of the *security* is not entitled to the *rights issue*.

**ex scrip** Means that the *security* is priced without the right to the *scrip issue*.

**ex warrants** Denotes that the sale of the *security* is without *warrants*.

**ex-gratia** Often used for payments made where, although not legally bound, the payer feels a moral obligation to do so.

**ex-growth** This is a *stock exchange* term describing a *stock* from which the *earnings* for the shareholder are unlikely to increase in the foreseeable future and, at best, will remain level.

**exchange controls** Abolished in the *UK* in 1979, exchange controls restricted the movement of *capital* abroad. See also: *dollar premium*.

**exchange equalisation account** A government account managed by the *Bank of England*, containing the official *gold* and *foreign exchange reserves*, as well as *Special Drawing Rights*. It is used to conduct *foreign exchange* operations (FXOs) to influence the *exchange rate*.

**exchange of contracts** The point at which a *contract* is deemed to have been agreed, but prior to its completion. At exchange a non-refundable *deposit* can be provided as a gesture of good faith. In the property market it is often difficult to enforce an exchange of contracts, although the *vendor* will retain the *deposit* if the *contract* is not completed.

**exchange rate** The price of one nation's *currency* in terms of another nation's *currency*. It is usually expressed as the number of domestic *currency* units per foreign *currency* unit, but in some cases, as in the *UK*, the exchange rate is given in terms of how many foreign *currency* units can be exchanged for one domestic *currency* unit. One *quotation* is simply the reciprocal of the other. The exchange rate is given as two prices, the buying and selling rate. The *spread* between the two rates represents *commission* to the organisation conducting the exchange. Financial newspapers usually only quote one exchange rate between two *currencies*: this is the midpoint between the buying and selling rates for transactions in excess of £50,000. Others quote *tourist rates* which have a much larger *spread*.

**Exchange Rate Mechanism (ERM)** Used as a precursor to the introduction of the *euro* this was the system by which *parity* between European *currencies* was regulated. Member *currencies* were only allowed to diverge within certain parameters and European *banks* were supposed to act in *concert* to ensure that these *parities* are maintained. The *UK* withdrew, after nearly two years of turbulent membership, in October 1992. ERM II now exists for those EU countries which want to join the euro. See: *European Monetary System*.

**exchange traded commodity (ETC)** ETCs are investment vehicles (asset backed bonds), similar to *exchange traded funds*, that track the performance of an underlying commodity index or a single commodity. ETCs are traded and settled exactly like normal shares and provide a convenient and simple way of gaining commodity exposure with good liquidity.

**exchange traded fund (ETF)** A fund, common in *America* and increasingly so in Europe, that tracks an index (see: *index fund*) but can be traded like a *share*, allowing for *options* and *short selling*. Because ETFs are traded on *stock exchanges* their prices fluctuate throughout the day (unlike most *mutual funds*). ETFs can be more tax-efficient than normal mutual funds and since they track *indices* they have low operating and transaction costs and there are no sales loads or investment minimums. The first *ETF* created was the *Standard and Poor's* Deposit Receipt (*SPDR*, pronounced Spider) in 1993, which gave investors an easy way to track the S&P 500 without buying an *index fund*.

**exchange traded notes (ETNs)** Exchange traded notes are financial instruments, similar in many respects to *exchange traded funds*. However, ETNs are derivative based and do not operate as a fund holding underlying assets. As such they carry counterparty risk which a directly invested ETF does not. However, the ETN structure can have tax advantages.

**exchequer stock** A government *security* used to raise funds in the market to meet *long term* financial liabilities of the British government. The names of the *stocks* (eg Exchequer, Treasury), have no particular significance other than in those cases where a particular *stock* was issued to finance a nationalised industry. Eg 3% Transport 1978/88. See also: *fixed interest security, gilts*.

**excluded assets trust** A *trust* used to ensure the exclusion of *assets* of non-UK domiciled (see: *domicile*) persons resident in the *UK* from any taxation in the *UK* and protect them against future changes in legislation.

**execution only** The relationship between a client and an *investment broker* or *Independent Financial Advisor* where the *broker* purely acts on the client's instructions and not in an advisory capacity. See also: *management agreement*.

**executive pension plan (EPP)** Can be taken out by senior executives and *directors* of a *company* where the *company* provides tax-deductible contributions to enhance their *pension*. Such *pension* plans can be written on an individual basis with only one *member* if necessary. Such plans can be additional to any group *pension* that the *company* provides. Since the launch of the simplified regime new EPPs have become rare; self invested personal pension plans are preferred. See also: *capping, pension*.

**executor** A person appointed in a will to act in the administration of the deceased's *estate*.

**exempt** See under: *zero-rated*.

**exempt persons** Organisations that were exempt from *authorisation* under the Financial Services Act to carry out *investment* business and were: 1. *Recognised Investment Exchanges*. Exempt from dealing but require direct *authorisation* from the *FSA* to carry out the actual running of the exchange. 2. *Recognised Clearing Houses*. Same as above. 3. Listed *money market* institutions. Eg the *wholesale money* market is regulated by the *FSA*. 4. *Bank of England*.5. *Lloyds* and people authorised by *Lloyds* to carry out *investment* business.

**exempt trust** A *trust*, fund or *unit trust* that is tax-exempt, which can only be used by charities or *pension* funds.

**exercise notice** A formal notification that the holder of an *option* wishes to buy (in the case of a *call option*) or sell (in the case of a *put option*) the *underlying security* at the *exercise price*.

**exercise price** The price at which the buyer of an *option* may buy (in the case of a *call option*) or sell (in the case of a *put option*) the *underlying security*. Also called: *strike price*.

**exit** A *venture capital* term describing the ability of investors to see a return on the *equity* they have purchased. They will require an exit which normally takes the form of a *flotation* or a *takeover* of the *company* they have supported.

**exotics** Derivatives of various types with unusual features, usually *options* with non standard exercise or payment rights. A non-*vanilla derivative*.

**expiry date** The last day on which an *option* may be exercised.

**exponential smoothing** 1. A *moving average* weighted in such a way that successive prices in the *average* are weighted exponentially, ie by a power (usually greater than unity). The greater weight is given to more recent periods. 2. The use of this exponentially weighted *moving average* to forecast future prices on the basis of past prices.

**Export Credits Guarantee Department (ECGD)** *UK* government agency that was to a large extent privatised in 1991. Its aim is to make available *insurance* to exporters and to insure overseas *investment*.

**exports** Goods and services produced domestically and sold abroad. See: *balance of payments*.

**expression of wish** A term used to describe a *nomination* of *beneficiaries* which is advisory rather than obligatory to the *trustees* of a *pension* or *trust*.

**expropriation** The process of reducing a *unit trust* fund by cancelling units. Payments are made to the unit holder by the *trustees* from the sale of the equivalent amount of *underlying securities*, ie when more units are being encashed than are being bought by unit holders and the *trust* is on a *net* redemption basis. See also: *appropriation, bid valuation*.

**external balance** An economic position of a nation where the supply of the domestic *currency* equals its demand. Thus there is *equilibrium* in the nation's *balance of payments*. See also: *internal balance*.

**extraordinary general meeting (EGM)** Any meeting other than the *annual general meeting* called during the year is termed *EGM*. 14 days' notice is required for an *EGM* unless matters require a '*special resolution*' (requiring a 75% approval, instead of the simple majority needed for an ordinary *resolution*), in which case 21 days' notice is required. Notice periods can be waived if 95% of *shareholders* agree. If 10% or more *shareholders* request an *EGM*, the *company* must comply, and notice of the *EGM* must be sent within 21 days. See also: *resolution, annual general meeting*.

**extraordinary item/loss/profit** A non-recurring item whose occurrence must be explained in a *company*'s *report and accounts*. Examples are: large *write offs*, *acquisition* of another *company*, large-scale damage that was not insured (eg by earthquake), and *windfall profits*.

**extraordinary resolution** See: *resolution*.

**eyrir** Standard *currency* unit of *Iceland*. The plural of eyrir is aurar. 100 aurar = 1 *króna*.

**EZT** Short for: *enterprise zone trust*.

# F

**face value**  The *value* stated on a *certificate* relating to a holding, ie one thousand *ordinary shares* of 25 pence each. This rarely has any significance with regard to the true *value* of that holding and is often determined by the price at which the *company* was originally capitalised. In the case of *fixed interest securities* the face value is the *par value*. Otherwise known as *nominal value*.

**fact-find**  See: *know your customer*.

**factor**  An individual or organisation that engages in *factoring*.

**factor markets**  Term used in economics denoting markets on which *factors of production* are bought and sold.

**factor of production**  Economic resources employed in the production of goods and services of an economy. Most commonly, the three factors of production are land, labour and *capital*. The rewards (payments) due to each factor of production are: land earns rents, labour receives wages and *capital* obtains *interest*. Sometimes entrepreneurship is taken to be a fourth factor, earning *profits*, and sometimes it is included in the labour category.

**factoring**  Factoring is similar to *invoice discounting*, which is the practice of obtaining *money* on the *security* of book debts. A *factor*, however, normally accepts responsibility for credit control, debt collection and credit *risk*. There are two principal types of factoring: 'with service' is the collection of debts and the assumption of credit *risk*. Invoices are handed to the *factor* who pays monies to the customer at stated intervals. The other 'with service plus finance' is where the *factor* pays the customer up to 90% of the invoice *value* at once. Due to the obvious *risks* involved a *factor* chooses his *debtors* and customers carefully and will normally charge a requisite fee for their services.

**Faeroe Islands**  Dependency of *Denmark*. Standard *currency*: Danish *krone*.

**fair price provisions**  Corporate charter or bylaw provisions in *America* whereby a *bidder* must pay the same price and form of consideration for all *shares* purchased. The intention is to prevent two-tier *takeover bids* in which one price is offered from some *stock* (usually enough to gain control) and a lower price for the remainder. In the *UK* transactions are governed by the City Code.

**fair value**  The amount for which an *asset* could be sold or a *liability* settled between knowledgeable, willing parties in an *arm's length* transaction.

**Falkland Islands**  Dependency of *UK*. Standard *currency*: Falkland Islands *pound*.

**fallen angel**  A fallen angel is fixed interest security which originally had an investment grade credit rating, but has since been down-rated to sub-investment grade (ie below BBB- or Baa3). As many investors can only hold investment grade securities, a high turnover of the stock can result when the fall occurs.

**Fannie Mae**  Nickname for the Federal National Mortgage Association in *America*.

**FAR**  See: *free asset ratio*.

**farthing**  One quarter of a pre-decimalisation *penny*. The very last date a farthing was issued was 1956, and the farthing was demonetised shortly after, at the end of 1960.

**FCA**  Short for: Fellow of the Institute of Chartered Accountants. See: *chartered accountant*.

**FCCA** Short for: Fellow of the *Chartered Association of Certified Accountants*. See: *certified accountant*.

**FCIA** See: *Foreign Credit Insurance Association*.

**FCII** Short for: Fellow of the *Chartered Insurance Institute*.

**FDIC** See: *Federal Deposit Insurance Corporation*.

**fear index** See: *Chicago Board Options Exchange Volatility Index (VIX)*.

**Fed** See: the *Federal Reserve System*.

**Fed funds** Funds that are immediately available in the *US Federal Reserve Banks*, for use overnight or sometimes longer (when they are known as 'Term *Fed* Funds') by another *Federal Reserve Bank*. Rates fluctuate continuously and the prevailing rate is called the '*Federal funds rate*'.

**Federal Deposit Insurance Corporation (FDIC)** An American federal agency set up in 1933 that provides *deposit insurance* for *US banks* and *thrift institutions*. The *FDIC* is organised into two funds that provide the *insurance*: the Bank Insurance Fund (BIF) deals with the banking institutions and the Savings Association Insurance Fund (SAIF) insures *thrift institutions*.

**Federal funding rate** The rate at which the *US Federal Reserve Bank* lends *money* to the banking system.

**Federal funds rate** *Interest rate* charged by *banks* with excess liquidity or *reserves* via a Federal Reserve District Bank to *banks* needing short-term liquidity. The most sensitive *indicator* of *interest rate* movements in *America*, as it is subject to daily market fluctuations. See: *Federal Reserve System*.

**Federal Home Loan Mortgage Corporation (FHLMC)** See: *Freddie Mac*.

**Federal Open Market Committee (FOMC)** The committee that determines *interest rates* and credit policies for the *Federal Reserve System* in *America*. The *FOMC* has 12 members, 7 of whom are members of the *Federal Reserve Board*, 4 are presidents of the regional *Federal Reserve Banks* (picked from 5 in rotation) and the last is president of the *Federal Reserve Bank* of New York. The Committee decides on the level of *interest rates* through *open market operations* of buying *Treasury bonds* and meets once a month.

**Federal Reserve Bank** In *America* there are 12 of these *banks*, located in various states, whose duty it is to monitor the commercial and savings *banks* in their region and ensure that they observe the *Federal Reserve Board*'s policy and regulations. They are governed by the *Federal Reserve Board* and make up the *Federal Reserve System*. See also: *Federal Open Market Committee*.

**Federal Reserve Board** The governing body of the American banking system. It comprises seven members, appointed by the President subject to Senate confirmation, who serve 14-year terms and govern the *Federal Reserve System*.

**Federal Reserve System** Established by the Federal Reserve Act 1913 it is effectively the *US central bank*. The Federal Reserve System (the *Fed*) comprises 12 regional *banks* (*Federal Reserve Banks*), their 24 branches and other national and state *banks* within the Federal Reserve System and is governed by the *Federal Reserve Board*. The *Fed* controls the supply of *money* and the level of *interest rates* as well as regulating and coordinating the affairs of all other American *banks*. It also supervises the minting of *money* and acts as a central *clearing house*. The chairman of the Federal Reserve holds a non-political appointment and the *Fed* is independent of the *US* government. See: *Federal Open Market Committee*.

**Federated States of Micronesia**   Standard *currency*: *US dollar*.

**fen**   *Currency* sub-unit used in *China*. 100 fen = 1 *yuan*.

**fiat money**   Money that has been accepted as a medium of exchange by government decree, not backed by *gold reserves* ('the *gold standard*') nor having *intrinsic value*. Nearly all paper *money* used in the world today is fiat money. Instead of backing the *currency* by *gold*, governments now usually issue new *money* by buying *securities*, in what is called a '*fiduciary issue*'.

**Fibonacci numbers**   Fibonacci numbers are found to have varied applications in nature. Classical architects used these numbers as a basis for building proportions. They are also used in some controversial theories of *technical analysis*. The sequence of Fibonacci numbers starts with 0 followed by 1. Each consecutive number in the series is found by adding the preceding two numbers together – thus the third number in the sequence is (0+1) = 1; the fourth is (1+1) = 2; the fifth is (1+2) = 3; and so on. Thus the first 15 numbers in the Fibonacci sequence are: 0, 1, 1, 2, 3, 5, 8, 13, 21, 34, 55, 89, 144, 233, 377. A mathematical oddity of the sequence is that in the higher numbers (after about the 13th number), it is found that the ratio between successive numbers (higher upon lower) settles at around 1.618 and the ratio between alternate numbers is 2.618. These are the Fibonacci ratios. See: *Elliott wave theory*.

**fidelity insurance**   An *insurance* policy providing protection against dishonesty, fraud and/or breach of *contract* by an employee.

**fiduciary**   A general term to describe an account or instrument of *value* not directly backed by *assets*.

**fiduciary issue**   See under: *fiat money*.

**FIFO**   See: *first in first out*.

**Fiji**   Standard *currency*: Fiji *dollar*. 1 Fiji *dollar* = 100 *cents*.

**fill or kill**   Colloquialism used by *futures dealers* for an order to offer a trade to a *futures pit* for either immediate fulfilment or abandonment. Also applied to other order driven markets.

**fillér**   *Currency* sub-unit of *Hungary*. 100 fillér = 1 *forint*.

**fils**   *Currency* sub-unit : *United Arab Emirates*: 100 fils = 1 *dirham*; *Bahrain, Iraq, Jordan, Kuwait*: 1,000 fils = 1 *dinar*; *Yemen*: 1,000 fils = 10 *riyal* = 1 *dinar*.

**FIMBRA**   See: *Financial Intermediaries Managers & Brokers Regulatory Association*.

**final earnings scheme**   A *pension* where the benefit is calculated by reference to the *member*'s *pensionable earnings* over a period before *pension* date or termination of service.

**final pensionable earnings**   The *earnings* on which a *pension* is based, which can be on or prior to retirement or termination of service.

**final remuneration**   The maximum *earnings* on which approved *pension* benefits can be based.

**final salary pension**   Term used to describe an occupational *pension* scheme that offers predetermined levels of *pension* benefit, usually expressed as a fraction of final salary. A typical scheme would, for example, offer a *pension* of one-sixtieth of the final salary for each year of service within the *company* or as a *member* of the scheme. Although the ultimate level of *pension* benefits in retirement is determined, the cost of provision is not and accordingly contributions are indeterminate and need to be reviewed on a regular basis. See: *pension fraction*.

**finance company** See: *finance house*.

**finance house** A *company* whose business is the lending of *money*, generally of a more speculative nature. Involved with *hire purchase* or loans not acceptable to *clearing banks*, they tend to charge an appropriately higher rate of *interest*.

**financial advisor** A firm, sometimes a *merchant bank* or independent *broker* who will provide advice on monetary matters. These can relate to corporate financial advice regarding *mergers* and *acquisitions* or personal financial advice regarding savings, *pensions* and *investments*. Such firms are now regulated by the *Financial Services Authority*. See: *Independent Financial Advisor*.

**financial futures** Investments based on the future (forward) price of financial *indices*, *instruments*, *currencies* or individual *securities*. See: *futures*, *derivatives*.

**Financial Industry Regulatory Authority (FINRA)** The Financial Industry Regulatory Authority (FINRA) is the largest non-governmental regulator for all securities firms operating in the United States. FINRA oversees nearly 5,000 brokerage firms and approximately 663,000 registered securities representatives. It was created in July 2007 through the consolidation of the National Association of Securities Dealers (NASD) and the member regulation, enforcement and arbitration functions of the New York Stock Exchange (NYSE).

**Financial Intermediaries Managers & Brokers Regulatory Assoc (FIMBRA)** A former self-regulatory body which merged with LAUTRO in 1994 under the Financial Services Act 1986.

**financial model** The financial representation of a business (usually in terms of a set of projected financial statements and/or key performance indicators) through the identification, logical expression and manipulation of the key drivers upon that business. The financial model allows business managers to explore the impact of different operational and financial options or scenarios for the business including for example: new *investment appraisal; mergers* and *acquisitions; divestments; macroeconomic* shocks, etc.

**Financial Ombudsman Service (FOS)** With the introduction of the *Financial Services and Markets Act 2000*, the *Financial Ombudsman Service* (*FOS*) replaced the existing ombudsmen and legally became the statutory ombudsman scheme covering most areas of personal finance. The *FOS* aims to satisfy the *Financial Services Authority* (*FSA*) objective to maintain market confidence by providing a dispute resolution procedure.

**Financial Planning Certificate (FPC)** Was granted after a series of examinations, set by the *CII*, allowing a person to practice as a *financial advisor*. Replaced in 2004/05 by the *Certificate in Financial Planning*.

**financial ratio** See: *ratio*.

**Financial Reporting Council (FRC)** A *UK company*, established in 1989 and *limited by guarantee*, to oversee and support the work of the *Accounting Standards Board* and the *Financial Reporting Review Panel* to review and improve reporting and accounting standards. Its *board* is appointed jointly by the Secretary of State for Trade and Industry and the Governor of the *Bank of England*.

**Financial Reporting Review Panel (FRRP)** A subsidiary of the *Financial Reporting Council*, it investigates breaches of the accounting requirements of the Companies Act 1985 by public *companies* and large private *companies* and is empowered to take legal remedial action. All other *companies* are subject to scrutiny by the *Department for Business, Innovation and Skills*.

**Financial Reporting Standard (FRS)** A statement by the *Accounting Standards Board* (*ASB*), on standards of accounting practice. See also: *Statement of Standard Accounting Practice* (*SSAP*)

**Financial Services Act 1986** The Act which had established a framework for the protection of investors and which required the registration and monitoring (see: *authorisation*) of *investment* businesses under the control of the Secretary of State for Trade and Industry and replaced the Prevention of Fraud (Investments) Act 1958. The Financial Services Act resulted from the *Gower Report* prompted by public concern over the lack of investor protection following the collapse of major *investment* firms in the 1960s and 1970s. This has now been replaced by the *Financial Services and Markets Act 2000*. See also: *General Principles, Investment Services Directive*.

**Financial Services and Markets Act 2000 (FSMA)** FSMA replaced the *Financial Services Act 1986*, the Banking Act 1987, the Insurance Companies Act 1982, the *Building Societies Act 1986* and the Friendly Societies Act 1992 and introduced a single Statutory Regulator for the *UK* Financial Services Industry – namely the *Financial Services Authority (FSA)*. FSMA determines the governance, structure and scope of the FSA, which is responsible to the *Treasury*, which confirms the appointment or dismissal of the *FSA* Chairman. The Act attempts to determine regulatory objectives and procedures as well as the licensing of *member firms* and individuals, the promotion of products and services and categories of authorised persons and their clients. It also attempts to cover investigations, disciplinary procedures and penalties. It deals with arbitrators, the *Ombudsman* and complaints generally. It covers the promotion and provision of all financial services in the *UK* from *insurance* underwriting to *options* trading; and brings banking and related industries within the scope of the FSA, rather than the *Bank of England,* for the first time. To quote the *Treasury* summary: 'The Act provides the framework within which a single regulator for the financial services industry, the *Financial Services Authority*, will operate. It equips the Authority with a full range of statutory powers and creates the Financial Services and Markets Tribunal. The Act also establishes the framework for single ombudsman and compensation schemes to provide further protection for consumers.' Businesses authorised and regulated under the Act include: *banks, building societies, insurance companies, friendly societies,* credit unions, *Lloyd's, investment* and *pensions* advisors, *stockbrokers,* professional firms offering certain types of *investment* services, *fund managers, derivatives* traders and since the Act received Royal Assent *insurance brokers* and *mortgage* advisors have been added to this list. Credit *brokers* still (2009) operate outside the Act but are likely to be included eventually. The OFT monitors the commercial and competitive aspects of the impact of the Act and reports to the *Treasury* in this respect.

**Financial Services Authority (FSA)** The Financial Services Authority is an independent, non-governmental body, given statutory powers by the *Financial Services and Markets Act 2000*. Its role is to regulate the financial services market in the *UK*. Initially, the *FSA* took on the duties of the old *Securities and Investments Board*. It has become the sole regulatory watchdog of the *UK* financial world. To this end, two Acts of Parliament – the Bank of England Act 1998 and the *Financial Services and Markets Act 2000* – were passed by Parliament. The Bank of England Act 1998 transferred all *bank* supervisory powers to the *FSA*. The *Financial Services and Markets Act 2000* brought all other financial regulation under the *FSA*. This includes *building societies, friendly societies* and the *Securities and Futures Authority*.

**Financial Times Share Indices** Since 1984 the *London Stock Exchange* in cooperation with the Financial Times and the Institute and Faculty of Actuaries has developed the *FTSE* Actuaries Share Indices. In 1995 the *London Stock Exchange* and the Financial Times set up a jointly owned *company* called *FTSE* International to report the *FTSE* and FT-A Indices. *FTSE* International aims to develop and extend the use of its *indices*. All existing *London Stock Exchange* and FT Indices are operated by *FTSE* International, including the *FTSE* 100, *FTSE* 250, *FTSE* Actuaries All-Share and FT-A Fixed Interest and Gilt *indices*. *FTSE* International also runs a large number of international indices. The *London Stock Exchange* also calculates the ISE/Nikkei 50. Constituent *companies* of the real-time *indices* are reviewed quarterly. The *UK* series: *FTSE* 100. Often referred to as the '*Footsie*'. Calculated as an arithmetic *average* of the top 100 UK-listed *companies*, with an approximate *market capitalisation* of above £1.2 *billion*. Weighted by *market capitalisation*. Account for 81% of market by *value*. Calculated in real-time. It is the basis for *futures* and *traded options listed* on LIFFE. Base: 3 January 1984 = 100. *FTSE* 250. A *benchmark index* of medium-sized *companies* (after band of *companies* in the *FTSE* 100) in the *UK*. Their approximate *market capitalisation* is £150 million to £1.2 *billion*. Account for 15% of market by *value*. Calculated in real-time. The *index* was backdated to 31 December 1985 with a base *value* of 1,412.6 (which is the same *value* as the *FTSE* 100 at that date). Calculated with and without *investment trusts*. *FTSE* Actuaries 350. Provides a *benchmark* for investors focusing on more actively traded large and medium-sized *companies*. It is a combination of the *FTSE* 100 and *FTSE* 250 *indices*. Real-time *indices* are calculated for each of the industry sectors (corresponding roughly to other international *stock market* definitions) within the *FTSE* Actuaries 350, known as 'industry baskets'. There are 38 sectorial *indices*. The *FTSE* Actuaries 350 *shares* account for ca. 88% of *market* by *value*. The *index* was back-dated to 31 December 1985 with a base *value* of 682.9 (same as *value* of *FTSE* Actuaries All-Share Index at that date). *FTSE* SmallCap. Performance of approximately 360 smaller *companies* (approx. *market capitalisation* of £30 million to £150 million) is indexed. Calculated at end of business day. Launched January 1993. *FTSE* Actuaries All-Share. The main *benchmark* for *UK portfolio* performance. The *composite index* of nearly all *UK shares* on the *London Stock Exchange*. Covers all three segments of the market (small, medium and large). Accounts for around 99% of market by *value*. It is a weighted arithmetic *index* calculated at the end of each trading day. *FTSE* Actuaries Fledgling. Comprises those *shares* that are too small to be included in the *FTSE* Actuaries All-Share Index. Calculated at the end of each business day, including and excluding *investment trusts*. Launched January 1995. *FTSE* Actuaries 350 Higher Yield. Consists of *stocks* that have an annual *dividend yield* above the average *yield* of the *FTSE* Actuaries 350 Index. Calculated daily. *FTSE* Actuaries 350 Lower Yield. Consists of above-average *dividend yield stocks* on the *FTSE* Actuaries 350. Calculated daily. The FTSE indices also cover many international markets, with specialist indices for areas such as commercial property, global infrastructure and socially responsible investment (FTSE4GOOD). The FTSE All-World Index service covers 2,700 stocks representing 90%–95% of investable market capitalisation.

**financial year** For individuals the financial year is the *fiscal year*. For corporations it is a selected 12-month period (each year) covered by their *accounts*.

**fine paper** A cheque, *bill of exchange* or the like, drawn on or guaranteed by a reputable *bank* or similar institution.

**fineness** The measure of purity in a precious metal. See: *assay*.

**Finland** Helsinki Stock Exchange (HSE) was established in 1912. Its main *index* is: HEX Index. Base: 28 December 1990 = 1,000. Standard *currency*: euro. 1 *euro* = 100 *cents*. Its *currency* was the *markka*, until the introduction of the *euro* on 1 January 2002.

**firewall** A computer network protection term used to mean *Chinese wall*. See: *Chinese wall*.

**first in first out (FIFO)** A method of accounting for *stock* (*inventory*) whereby, quite literally, the *stock* is assumed to be sold in the chronological order in which it was purchased. The cost of goods sold (COGS) is taken to be the *stock* at the beginning of the *accounting period* plus purchases of *stock* during the period, less the *stock* left at the end of the *accounting period*. The *FIFO* method contrasts with the *LIFO* (*last in first out* method). In an inflationary period, the *FIFO* method produces a higher ending *stock*, a lower cost of goods sold figure and a higher *gross profit* and is the approved method of *stock* accounting in the *UK*.

**fiscal drag** The benefit received by the government from not increasing tax allowances and bands in line with overall economic growth. The result is that more people are dragged into the tax net and more taxpayers pay higher rates of tax. The UK government has relied heavily on fiscal drag as a means of stealth taxation. The number of higher rate taxpayers is a good example of the effect: in 2008/09 this was estimated by HMRC to be 3.64m, a 55% increase from ten years previously.

**fiscal policy** A demand-side policy *instrument* employed by government authorities. Fiscal policy is the use of government spending and taxation (and transfer payments, such as *unemployment* benefit, child support etc.) to achieve macroeconomic goals. Its use generally follows *Keynesian economics* through the use of the *multiplier* (sense 1). For example, an expansionary fiscal policy means that government expenditure is increased, which causes a corresponding increase in aggregate demand. If the supply side of the economy allows it, the *national income* (= national output) will increase, curbing *unemployment*. But the increased public expenditure must be financed by taxation and/or *bond* sales. The *bond* sales will increase *interest rates* which will crowd-out *investment* and thus partially reduce the expansion in the aggregate demand. Taxation effects are similar: increased taxation will partially offset the aggregate demand increase. The overall effect of the expansionary fiscal policy on the *balance of payments* is indeterminate; the overall increase in output will cause a deterioration of the *current account*, but the rise in *interest rates* will cause an increased inflow of funds into the economy from abroad, thus causing an improvement of the *capital account*. Note that, as distinct from *monetary policy*, the *money supply* in the hands of the *private sector* is left unchanged, since the *money* derived from selling *bonds* is spent on government expenditure. See also: *crowding-out*, *balanced budget multiplier*, *internal balance*, *Central Government Net Cash Requirement*.

**fiscal year** Also called: *tax year*. The *UK* fiscal year runs from 6 April to midnight on 5 April in the following year. In the *US*, the fiscal year starts on 1 July and ends on 30 June in the following year.

**Fisher Effect** Longer-term *exchange rates* are, in theory, determined by *purchasing power parity* and the *inflation* differential between two *currencies*. The Fisher Effect is a theorem that combines these concepts in order to demonstrate the link between *interest rates*, *inflation* and *foreign exchange rates*. The equation is:

$$\frac{1+r^*}{1+r.} = \frac{1+i^*}{1+i}$$

where r and r* are the domestic and foreign *interest rates* and i and i* are the domestic and foreign *inflation* rates. It is hence possible to calculate the forward *exchange rate* using the *spot exchange rate*. See: *covered interest parity*. Compare: *uncovered interest parity*.

**Fitch** Fitch is the third largest ratings agency behind *Standard & Poors* and *Moody's*. It uses the same lettering approach as *Standard & Poors*.

**fix** A price determined at a set point in time by negotiation between interested parties. Normally, the establishment of a specific *benchmark* for the price of a *commodity* for information purposes only.

**fixed assets** Those *assets*, such as land, property and equipment, which have a determinable and potentially realisable *value* (thus *intangibles* such as *goodwill* can be included), and are utilised within a business rather than being held to trade in. Fixed assets plus *current assets* comprise a business's total *assets*. See: *balance sheet*.

**fixed asset turnover** A performance *ratio* that is calculated by dividing the *turnover* figure in a *company's accounts* by the *fixed assets*. The *fixed asset* figure should exclude *intangibles* and *investments*. It thus shows how much *turnover* is generated per *pound Sterling* of tangible *fixed asset*.

**fixed charge** A deed or debenture allowing creditors to take charge of a specific asset in the event of a failure to meet certain debts. See: *floating charge*.

**fixed deposit** A *deposit* which is entered into for a fixed period of time in order to obtain a preferential rate of *interest*.

**fixed exchange rate** An *exchange rate* that is determined and set by the *central bank* and does not fluctuate other than by formal re- and de-valuation. Normally operated by countries with non-convertible *currencies* who do not trade actively internationally. Particularly common in the USSR before the fall of communism.

**fixed interest security** A *security* (or *stock*) which carries a fixed rate of *interest* (*coupon*), normally payable for a predetermined period. Issuers of such *investments* can be governments, local authorities and corporations. Such *stock* has many different forms but is generally known as *gilts* for *UK* government issues and *loan stock* for corporate issues, both of which normally have set *redemption dates* on which the *par value* is repaid. The *stocks* can however be bought and sold daily in the fixed-interest markets. The *value* of the *stock* is invariably related to the *value* of the fixed rate of *interest* it provides (*nominal yield*) in relation to the general level of prevailing *interest rates*. When the general level of *interest rates* is high the price of fixed-interest *stock* tends to be low as high rates are available elsewhere. When *interest rates* fall, the *value* of such *stock* tends to go up as the fixed *yield* becomes more attractive. Fixed-interest *stock* bought in times of high rates and sold when *interest rates* are lower will usually show a *capital profit* as well as providing the fixed *yield*. The reverse obviously occurs when the general level of *interest rates* rises. Such *stock* is also normally issued at a price below *par value* so that an automatic gain will occur if the *stock* is held until its *redemption date*, when it is repaid (redeemed) by its issuer; indeed some fixed-interest *stock* gives no *income* and returns are reflected purely by this gain (see: *zero*). Fixed-interest *stock* issued in the *UK* by public *companies*, local authorities, utilities and the Treasury is normally free of *capital gains tax* for private investors. See: *bond*.

**fixing** See: *fix*.

**FJD** *currency code* for: *Fiji* Dollar.

**FKP** *currency code* for: *Falkland Islands* Pound.

**flag** A *chart* formation used in *technical analysis*. It is a *continuation pattern* of short *duration* (less than four weeks). The envelope lines of the flag *pattern* are parallel, though they may both slant up, down or sideways (see diagram). Either side of the flag there are sharp, near vertical, price movements called '*masts*'. Volume tends to decrease during the formation, with an increase on *breakout*. The minimum expected move after *breakout* (c to d) is the height of the previous *mast* (a to b). See: *pennant*.

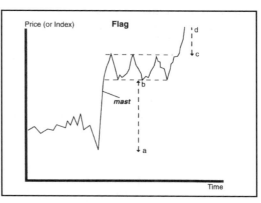

**flat yield** See: *yield*.

**flight to quality** When nervous investors sell higher *risk investments* and buy into potentially lower *risk* investments such as government *bonds* or *gold*.

**flipper** See under: *flipping*.

**flipping** Americanism for a *stag*. Buying *shares* in an *initial public offering* and selling them immediately for a *profit*. Brokerage firms underwriting new *stock* issues tend to discourage flipping, and will often try to allocate *shares* for a minimum set period. Still, the temptation to flip a new issue and turn a quick *profit* is irresistible for many investors. An investor who flips *stocks* is called a '*flipper*'. The term is also used for a speculator who buys a property off-plan, hoping to sell out quickly before full payment has to be made.

**float** 1. An account is normally credited with a cheque when it is presented (counter credit) without the funds actually having been received – the *cash* created is known as a float. 2. A *US* term denoting those *shares* available for trading by the public as opposed to *shares* held by a *controlling interest* or privately by long-term *interests* or the corporation itself. A small float will make the *shares* more volatile than a large one, since large orders to buy or sell the *shares* will have a significant impact on market liquidity.

**float capitalisation weighted index** Refers to an *index* weighted by *companies' float* (the available amount of *equity capital*) as opposed to their total *market capitalisation*. Provides a better comparison for investors under certain circumstances.

**floater** Another name for a *floating rate note* (*FRN*).

**floating charge** An *instrument* (*lien*) allowing *creditors* to take charge of any of a corporation's *assets* in the event of its failure to pay specific debts. A *fixed charge* is secured on a specific *asset* normally by a *deed* or *debenture* and a fixed and floating charge secures a specific *asset* or *assets* and any other *assets* if the *fixed charge* is insufficient.

**floating currency** A *currency* whose *value* is determined purely by the laws of *supply and demand* without any artificial restraints or persistent *intervention*.

**floating exchange rate** The *exchange rate* of a *floating currency*, ie one that is not fixed or actively managed by a government authority. Compare: *fixed exchange rate*, managed *exchange rate*.

**floating rate note (FRN)** A *eurobond*, issued usually in the form of a *bearer security*, that has a maturity of between 7 and 15 years, and has an *interest rate* that is linked to a *base rate* (usually the *LIBOR*). Perpetual *FRNs* have no *redemption date*.

**floor** An *interest rate option* to protect investors from a rate of *interest* falling against them.

**florin** 1. Standard *currency* of *Aruba*. 1 florin = 100 *cents*. 2. A Sterling unit equivalent to 10 pence in post-*decimalisation currency*.

**flotation** The issuing of *stock* (*shares*) in a *company* to the public for the first time on a *stock market* by means of an offer document known as a *prospectus*. For *shares* in *companies* to be traded freely by members of the public, a *market value* has to be established and a price determined that will create an orderly market. The FSA has specific parameters that must be met by such *companies* dictating size, track record, reporting standards, set out in its listing rules. Shares are allocated by *tender* or *ballot*. Known in the *US*, and increasingly in Britain, as an *initial public offering* (*IPO*).

**FOB** See: *free on board*.

**FOMC** See: *Federal Open Market Committee*.

**Footsie** Colloquial name for the *FTSE* 100. See under: *Financial Times Share Indices*.

**force majeure** French for 'superior force'. An event outside the control of either party to a *contract* (such as a strike, riot, war, act of God) that may release either party from contractual obligations.

**foreclosure** The legal right of a lender of *money*, if the borrower fails to meet any of their obligations, to demand immediate repayment and take appropriate steps to recover any *security*. Such steps may require a court order, which, if granted, will set a new date for payment in an order called a 'foreclosure nisi'. In the case of property *mortgages* this is known as *repossession*.

**foreign bond** A *bond* issued by a foreign investor into another country's *capital market* denominated in that country's *currency*. For example, a German investor's dollar-denominated *bond* issued in the US is a 'yankee *bond*', a French investor's *Sterling bond* issued in the UK is a '*bulldog bond*', and an Italian investor's yen-denominated *bond* issued in *Japan* is a '*samurai bond*'. Compare: *domestic bond*.

**Foreign Credit Insurance Association** An American association of some 60 *insurance companies* underwriting export credits for *US* firms. See: ECGD.

**foreign exchange (FX)** The *currencies* of different countries bought and sold in *foreign exchange markets*. Firms or organisations require foreign exchange to purchase goods from abroad or for purposes of *investment* or *speculation*. *Currencies* of all major countries are listed in the Glossary under the country name. See: *exchange rate*.

**foreign exchange dealer** A market professional who buys and sells *foreign exchange* on the *spot* and forward *foreign exchange markets*, usually as an employee of a commercial *bank*.

**foreign exchange market** International markets in which convertible foreign *currencies* are traded, consisting primarily of *foreign exchange dealers* employed by commercial *banks* (acting as principals) and *foreign exchange brokers* (acting as intermediaries). International *currency speculation* can generate very substantial trading *volumes* and can overwhelm the *intervention* efforts of all but the largest *central banks*. *Currency* dealing has a *spot currency market* for delivery of *foreign exchange* within two days and a forward exchange market for foreign *currencies* to be delivered at agreed dates in the future, as in *futures* markets. *Options* and *futures* on forward *exchange rates* can also be traded on various world markets, including *LIFFE*, the *Deutsche Terminbörse* in Frankfurt and the *International Monetary Market* in Chicago.

**forex** See: *foreign exchange*.

**forfaiting** Without recourse financing via the *discounting* of *bills of exchange* or other negotiable *instruments*. Essentially the *factoring* of international trade debts. Where goods are exported to a foreign country on the basis of a *bill of exchange*, a forfaiter will provide immediate *cash* by accepting the *bill of exchange* and receiving payment when it falls due. The transaction does not involve the issuer of the *bill* and any *discount* in its *value* will be reflected by the issuer's ability to pay and/or the time due to elapse before payment becomes due.

**forint** Standard *currency* of *Hungary*. 1 forint = 100 *fillér*.

**Fortune 500** Listing by Fortune Magazine of the top 500 *US* manufacturing corporations ranked by sales. The *companies* are also ranked by 12 *indices*, among them sales, *profits*, *assets*, stockholder *equity*, *earnings per share growth* over a 10-year span, *total return* to investors in the year, and the 10-year annual rate of *total return* to investors. The publication also produces a Fortune Service 500 for non-manufacturing *companies*.

**forward contract** Purchase or sale of a specific quantity of a *commodity*, government *security*, foreign *currency*, or other financial *instrument* at an agreed price for delivery and settlement at a specified future date. Because it is a completed *contract* – as opposed to an *options contract*, where the owner has the choice of completing or not – a forward contract can be a *cover* for the sale of a *futures contract*. A forward contract differs from a *futures contract*. Forward contracts are so-called *over-the-counter* products, whereas *futures contracts* are exchange-traded products with set *expiry dates* (on *LIFFE* these are in December, March, June and September). In addition, forward contracts cannot be closed out by a matching transaction, whereas a *futures contract* can. See: *futures*.

**forward dealing** See: *forward market*.

**forward discount** A *forward contract* is said to be at a *discount* if the forward price is lower than the *spot price*. The *discount* is often expressed as a (negative) percentage of the *spot price*. Compare: *forward premium*. See also: *backwardation, covered interest parity*.

**forward market** Dealing in a *currency* or *commodity* for settlement at some date in the future. Concerned with dealing in the actual *commodity* or *currency*, this differs from *futures*, which represent paper *contracts* used for *speculation* or hedging. See: *forward contract*.

**forward premium** A *forward contract* is said to be at a *premium* if the forward price is higher than the *spot price*. The *premium* is often expressed as a (positive) percentage of the *spot price*. Compare: *forward discount*. See also: *contango, covered interest parity*.

**forward pricing** The price of *unit trusts* and OEICs relates to the *value* of the underlying *investment*, and when the units are priced on a forward basis this *value* will change throughout the day in accordance with the performance of the *portfolio*. When an investor purchases units, the price will not be determined until the managers calculate the *value* of the *portfolio* at that time, and this normally takes place several hours later or the following day. Most unit trusts and OEICs now use forward pricing. See: *historic pricing*.

**FOS** See: *Financial Ombudsman Service*.

**FOTRA** Free Of Tax to Residents Abroad. Certain *gilts* were sold to overseas residents free of *tax*. All gilts are now tax-free to non-residents.

**founder's shares** Shares issued to the founders of a *company*. These *shares* often have partial *dividend* rights (deferred ordinary) and are designed to allow the founders of the *company* potential additional benefits from the business's success.

**FOX** See: *Futures and Options Exchange*.

**F.P.** See: *fully paid.*

**FPC** See: *Financial Planning Certificate.*

**franc** Standard *currency* of: *Burundi, Djibouti, Guadeloupe, Guinea, Liechtenstein, Madagascar, Martinique, Mayotte, Réunion, Rwanda, St Pierre and Miquelon, Switzerland, Wallis and Futuna Islands:* 1 franc = 100 *centimes; Benin, Burkina Faso, Cameroon, Central African Republic,* Chad, *Congo, Equatorial Guinea, Gabon, Ivory Coast, Mali, Niger, Senegal, Togo:* 1 African franc = 100 *centimes; French Polynesia, New Caledonia:* 1 Pacific franc = 100 *centimes.* The franc was the *currency* of *France, Belgium,* and *Luxembourg* until the introduction of the single European Currency (*euro*) in 1999.

**France** The Paris Stock Exchange (Bourse de Paris) receives official recognition from the *UK* Treasury as an Overseas Investment Exchange. Its main *indices* are:

- *CAC-40* Index – The *CAC-40*, in operation since 1988, consists of 40 of the most representative of French *stocks* and is weighted (arithmetically) by component *stocks' market values. CAC-40* serves as a base for *derivatives* traded on the *MATIF* and the *MONEP.* Base: 31 December 1987 = 1,000. SBF 250 Index – Wider *index* used for a general view of the French economy.

- Base: 31 Dec 1990 = 1,000.

Standard *currency: euro.* 1 *euro* = 100 *cents.* The *currency* was the *franc,* until the introduction of the *euro* on 1 January 2002.

**franchise** The right to sell a manufacturer's goods or services in a given area. The manufacturer will provide discounted lines of supply as well as the use of its name and the benefits of brand awareness. The franchisee will benefit from the *profits,* although normally it has to pay the manufacturer a percentage of the business's *turnover.* A government franchise confers the right on a *company* or individual to perform some economic functions, such as the provision of military equipment.

**franked income** *Investment income* paid from corporate *profits* which is deemed to have already borne *corporation tax.* Dividends received from *UK companies* are paid with a 10% tax credit and are not liable to the further deduction of *basic rate income tax.* This can be passed on by *unit trusts, OEICs* and *investment trusts* without any further taxation. See: *unfranked income.*

**Frankfurt Stock Exchange** FWB® Frankfurter represents more than 90% of German *stock exchange* business. Deutsche Börse AG operates the Frankfurt Stock Exchange with advanced electronic trading, settlement and information systems including Xetra®.

**fraudulent conveyance** Also known as fraudulent conversion this involves the transfer of *assets* to another person for the purposes of putting it beyond the reach of *creditors.* For example, if a man transfers his property into the name of his wife because he expects to become *bankrupt* the transaction may be set aside by the court under the provisions of the *Insolvency Act 1986.*

**fraudulent preference** Settling the debts of one *creditor* in preference to another while a *company* is insolvent (see: *insolvency*) and within six months of *winding up* (or two years if the preference is given to a person connected with the *company*). Such an act can be cancelled by a court, which may make any order that it thinks fit but which must not prejudice the rights of a third party who has acquired *assets* without notice of the preference.

**fraudulent trading** Any fraudulent corporate activity, but normally applied to the accepting of *money* from customers when the *company* is insolvent and knows it cannot meet its obligations. The liquidator of a *company* may apply to a court for an order against any person who has been a party to fraudulent trading to make such contributions to the *assets* of the *company* as the court thinks fit. Thus an executive, normally a *director*, of the *company* may be made personally liable for some of its debts. See: *wrongful trading*.

**FRC**  See: *Financial Reporting Council*.

**Freddie Mac**  *The Federal Home Loan Mortgage Corporation* (FHLMC) commonly known as Freddie Mac is a government-sponsored enterprise (GSE) of the *United States* federal government. It was created in 1970 to expand the *secondary market* for *mortgages* in the US. Along with other GSEs, Freddie Mac buys *mortgages* on the secondary *market*, pools them, and sells them as mortgage-backed *securities* to investors on the open market. This secondary *mortgage* market increases the supply of money available for *mortgages* lending and increases the money available for new home purchases. The name, 'Freddie Mac', was a creative acronym of the company's full name that has been adopted officially for ease of identification. Together with *Fannie Mae* this was nationalised by the federal government during the *Credit Crunch* of 2008.

**free asset ratio**  Often applied to *life assurance companies*, this describes the ratio of *assets* less total potential liabilities to total assets and expresses this figure as a percentage.

**free cash flow**  Cash remaining after a *company* has made the required cash outlays needed to continue operating, including wages, rent, *tax*, etc. It is the *cash flow* available for discretionary spending which might be for expansion or early repayment of debt. It is calculated as operating *cash flow* less *capital expenditure* and can be computed before or after *dividends*, depending on whether *dividends* are seen as a commitment or discretionary spending. Free cash flow to firm is before *interest* payments, whereas free cash flow to *equity* is after *interest* payments.

**free issue**  Same as: *scrip issue*.

**free on board (FOB)**  A trade term denoting that the invoice price includes *delivery* at the seller's expense to a specified point and no further. The title normally passes from seller to buyer at the *FOB* point by way of a *bill of lading*.

**free trade area/zone**  An area where there is or will be complete trade freedom with an absence of *tariffs* and simplified bureaucracy. See: *North American Free Trade Agreement*.

**free-standing additional voluntary contribution**  A *pension* plan separate from a *company pension* scheme taken out by an active *member* of that *company* scheme. Benefits are based solely on contributions paid in by the *member*. New plans ceased to be marketed after April 2006 when the simplified regime was introduced. See: *additional voluntary contribution*.

**freehold**  The absolute ownership of property and land rights, as opposed to a leasehold which would be granted by the freeholder to a tenant for a certain set period of time.

**freeze out**  Pressure on remaining minority *shareholders* to relinquish their *stock* once control has been passed to a new owner.

**French Guiana**  Dependency of *France*. Standard *currency*: euro.

**French Polynesia**  Dependency of *France*. Standard *currency*: Pacific *franc*.

**frictional unemployment**  *Unemployment* associated with the normal turnover of labour only, because of the time it takes for people to find jobs that are already available. For example, it takes time for individuals entering employment, and for the first time to find employment; people changing jobs usually do not find positions immediately, even if suitable jobs already exist. See also: *full employment, structural unemployment*.

**friendly society** Societies originally registered under the Friendly Society Acts of 1896 to 1955, which exist for the provision of certain mutual benefits including *life assurance*. The tax-free *investment* plans offered by some friendly societies have a maximum premium of £25 a month. The advent of PEPs and ISAs largely killed off interest in such plans.

**friendly takeover** A *merger* or *takeover* supported by the *management* and *board* of *directors* of the *target*.

**fringe benefit** Where *investment* is concerned the term is used where *shareholders* of certain *companies* receive an additional benefit over and above the *dividends* received. Some of the better known *companies* and corresponding benefits are: British Airways, with a 10% discount on fare, and Wimbledon *debentures*, with free Centre-Court seats, use of private lounge and car park etc. Shareholder perks are gradually disappearing, not least because of the growth of nominee accounts.

**FRN** See: *floating rate note*.

**front end load** A term used to describe the *investment* allocation or charging structures on a *unit-linked* or collective *investment*. (see: *collective investment scheme*). In order for a *life assurance company* or fund manager to pay for their internal administration costs, together with rewarding the introducing agent, an initial or front-end charge is made. The 'front end load' means that a reduced percentage of an investor's *money* is actually invested when initial *investment* is made. These are the *initial charges* and are usually in addition to ongoing charges for *management* and administration. See: *bid-offer spread*, *initial units*.

**front end loaded tender offer** See: *two-tier tender offer*.

**frozen benefit** See: *frozen pension*.

**frozen pension** A preserved *pension* entitlement not subject to any *revaluation* and not benefiting from *growth*, *interest* etc. Now extremely rare.

**FRRP** See: *Financial Reporting Review Panel*.

**FRS** See: *Financial Reporting Standard*.

**FSA** See: *Financial Services Authority*.

**FSA Principles** The FSA has set down in its handbook a set of 11 core principles which, with limited exceptions, apply to all firms which it regulates:

**The Principles**

| | |
|---|---|
| **1** **Integrity** | A firm must conduct its business with integrity. |
| **2** **Skill, care and diligence** | A firm must conduct its business with due skill, care and diligence. |
| **3** **Management and control** | A firm must take reasonable care to organise and control its affairs responsibly and effectively, with adequate risk management systems. |
| **4** **Financial prudence** | A firm must maintain adequate financial resources. |
| **5** **Market conduct** | A firm must observe proper standards of market conduct. |
| **6** **Customers' interests** | A firm must pay due regard to the interests of its customers and treat them fairly. |

| **7** Communications with clients | A firm must pay due regard to the information needs of its clients, and communicate information to them in a way which is clear, fair and not misleading. |
|---|---|
| **8** Conflicts of interest | A firm must manage conflicts of interest fairly, both between itself and its customers and between a customer and another client. |
| **9** Customers: relationships of trust | A firm must take reasonable care to ensure the suitability of its advice and discretionary decisions for any customer who is entitled to rely upon its judgement. |
| **10** Clients' assets | A firm must arrange adequate protection for clients' assets when it is responsible for them. |
| **11** Relations with regulators | A firm must deal with its regulators in an open and co-operative way, and must disclose to the FSA appropriately anything relating to the firm of which the FSA would reasonably expect notice. |

**FSMA**  See: *Financial Services and Markets Act 2000.*

**FTSE**  See under: *Financial Times Share Indices.*

**full employment**  Confusingly, full employment does not mean the complete absence of *unemployment*. For this reason, the term 'full employment' is often substituted by 'high employment' in North *America*. Full employment (or *'equilibrium* employment' as economists call it) exists in an economy when the only *unemployment* present is *frictional unemployment* and *structural unemployment.*

**full listing**  A description of a *company* whose *shares* appear on the *Official List* of the *main market* of the *London Stock Exchange* and generally a *share listed* on any *Recognised Stock Exchange*. See: *listing rules.*

**fully diluted earnings**  A figure showing *earnings per share* after assuming the exercise of all *warrants* and *options* and the conversion of all *convertible* and preference *stock.*

**fully insured scheme**  A *pension* scheme where the benefits are guaranteed for each *member* by an *insurance contract* effected by the *trustees.*

**fully paid (F.P.)**  Shares on which the full *value* has been paid, ie the *shareholders* have paid the issuing *company* the full amount on each *share*. See: *partly paid.*

**fund manager**  An individual employed by an institution to manage an *investment fund* to meet predetermined objectives (eg maximum *income* or maximum *growth*), in predetermined areas or sectors, for instance *USA* Technology, Gold, *UK* Blue Chip etc.

**fund of funds**  A *unit trust* or OEIC which invests in a selection of other *trusts* and collective funds and is managed to take strategic advantage of changing market conditions. Has tax benefits of a managed portfolio of individual funds. See: *managed funds.*

**fundamental analysis**  The search for *'value'* via the *balance sheet* and *profit & loss account* of the *company* concerned, together with the investigation of the overall economic situation and *projections* made from this data. Current *trends* are extrapolated, as are *supply and demand* situations. More generally, the application of macroeconomic factors in determining the future direction of markets and *securities* prices and the practical influence of matters directly affecting them as opposed to *quantitative analysis* or *technical analysis*. See: *analysis.*

**113**

**funded unapproved retirement benefits scheme (FURBS)** The term used until A-Day for an unapproved *pension* scheme established by a *company* on behalf of one or a number of executives to provide benefits on retirement especially to counteract HMRC restrictions. Does not benefit from the *tax* exemptions granted to other pension *schemes*.

**funding** This is a process whereby the *appreciation* and *income* derived from the *investment* of a lump sum is used to contribute to a regular *investment* (see: *capital conversion plan*). Also the *capitalisation* or *recapitalisation* of a new or existing business by investors. See: *venture capital, Enterprise Investment Scheme*.

**fungibles** Items that allow one to be replaced by another without loss of *value* such as *futures contracts* offset through a *clearing house*, bearer *bonds* and banknotes. Also applied to soft *commodities*. See also: *softs*.

**FURBS** See: *funded unapproved retirement benefits scheme*.

**Furniss v Dawson** This case helped to refine the *Ramsay* principle where the courts defined the approach in dealing with an artificial scheme designed to avoid a *tax* obligation clearly due under the spirit if not the letter of the law. As a result of the *Dawson* case, intermediate steps in a prearranged series of transactions can, in appropriate circumstances, be disregarded and the 'overall approach' adopted in viewing the schemes as a whole. Such schemes must however include: 1. a series of preordained transactions (or a single composite transaction), and 2. steps inserted which have no commercial purpose apart from the avoidance of *tax*. Contrast: *arm's length*.

**future value** The future value of a certain sum of *money* today (the *present value*) is simply calculated by compounding *interest* on it until the future date. The sum of *money* plus the *compound interest* is the future value.

**futures** An *investment instrument* that involves a *contract* to buy or sell a fixed quantity of a particular *commodity, currency* or *security* for delivery at a fixed date in the future at a fixed price. Unlike an *option*, a *contract* involves an obligation (not an option) to purchase or sell and can generate indeterminate losses; especially where futures are traded on *margin*, losses can significantly exceed the cost of the initial *investment*. A *futures contract*, as an obligation, can only be closed (disposed of) by cancelling out its effect by buying or selling a *futures contract* with the opposite effect. The *clearing house* dealing with the exchange will then *net* off (*contra*) both *contracts* to ensure a nil balance on the investor's account. Futures provide a vehicle for hedging (see: *hedge*)and for speculators who provide markets with liquidity. In London, futures are traded in a variety of markets. Financial futures are traded on the *London International Financial Futures and Options Exchange* (*LIFFE*), the *Baltic Exchange* deals with shipping, the *London Metal Exchange* with base metals and the *International Petroleum Exchange* with oil. Dealing in naked futures is a *zero-sum game*. See: *derivative, forward contract*.

**futures contract** See: *futures*.

**FX** See: *foreign exchange*.

# G

**G3**  See: *Group of Three.*

**G5**  See: *Group of Five.*

**G7**  See: *Group of Seven.*

**G8**  See: *Group of Eight.*

**G10**  See: *Group of Ten.*

**G20**  See: *Group of Twenty.*

**G24**  See: *Group of Twenty Four.*

**GAAP**  Generally Accepted Accounting Principles (GAAP) is the term used to refer to the standard framework of guidelines for financial accounting includes the standards and conventions used in recording and summarising transactions and in the preparation of financial statements. Covers areas likely to include: regularity, consistency, sincerity, permanence, compensation, prudence, continuity, disclosure and *materiality*, etc.

**Gabon**  Standard *currency*: African *franc.*

**Gambia**  Standard *currency*: *dalasi.* 1 *dalasi* = 100 *butut.*

**game theory**  A mathematical theory concerned with predicting the outcome of games of strategy (rather than games of chance) in which the participants have incomplete information about others' intentions, developed by J. von Neumann and O. Morgenstern in 1944. Generally it suggests that a game played by two can never be won with certainty but a game for three is always won by an alliance of two, a game for four is never won because an alliance is countered by an opposing alliance and a game of five is won by a two party alliance the remaining three being unable to form a coherent alliance and so on; can be applied in corporate theory.

**gamma**  The rate at which a *delta* changes over time.

**gamma shares**  Formerly used to classify the smallest and least-actively traded of the *shares* on the *London Stock Exchange.* The classification has been superseded by *Normal Market Size.*

**Gann theory**  A controversial and complex *chart* theory used in *technical analysis* in order to predict future price movements. It was invented by William G. Gann who was a market trader who studied market cycles ('waves') and looked for recurring relationships between them. The rules are based on esoteric mathematical relationships between the characteristics of the waves. A 'Gann *chart*' consists of a series of horizontal lines and a number of *trendlines* fanning out at different angles from the start of the *trend*, used for plotting *chart* movements and predicting *support levels* and price targets. See also: *Elliott wave theory.*

**Gantt chart**  A linear organisational graph representing planned activity as a series of horizontal bars against time (x axis), used in project management to ensure schedules are maintained and monitored. Henry A. Gantt, 1917.

**gap**  Occurs when the traded price range of a *security* on one day does not overlap the price range on the preceding day, causing a gap in the traded price range. This gap is shown as a discontinuity in the otherwise smooth price movement on a *chart*. This usually takes place as a result of some extraordinary external event affecting the market, *company* or *commodity* and chartists believe that the prices or the *index* will eventually return to a level which will 'fill the gap'. See: *chartism.*

**garnishee** The seizing of an account on the basis of a court order to pay a *creditor* or third party. If a *bank account* is garnisheed, all the *money* in it and any further payments are directed to this *creditor*.

**gatekeeper** A controller of information. Either a news or statistical information source or a manager in a business who allows the dissemination of accounting, sales or *management* information throughout the business. The information freely available on the internet has diminished the importance of information gatekeepers generally.

**GATT** See: *General Agreement on Tariffs and Trade*.

**gazumping** Prior to the *exchange of contracts* for the purchase of a property, the *vendor* is entitled to take any *offer* regardless of any arrangements made with prospective purchasers. Tacit verbal or written agreements have no standing prior to the *exchange of contracts*.

**gazunder** Opposite to *gazumping*, involving lowering your *offer* at the last moment – sharp practice common in a falling property market and often used by bankers to take advantage of distressed situations.

**GBP** *currency code* for: Pound *Sterling*.

**GDP** See: *gross domestic product*.

**GDP/GNP deflator** A means of arriving at *real gross domestic product/gross national product* figures from (nominal) *GDP/GNP*. The *deflator* may be arrived at through a *price index*, such as *RPI*. *Real GDP/GNP* is then calculated as *money* (nominal) *GDP/GNP* (as recorded in the *UK National Accounts*) divided by the *deflator*. See: *implicit deflator*.

**gearing** 1. Investors can gear their potential *profits* or losses by borrowing the *capital* they use for *investment* and using the *stocks* they buy as *security*. American *brokerage* firms provide such a service, though it is less common in the *UK*. In *futures* trading investors normally pay a *deposit* (a *margin* payment which is a small proportion of the full *value* of an *investment*) to secure notional ownership of the whole thus gearing their returns. Such a *margin* may represent 10% of the whole *value* of the interest, and accordingly if the underlying *investment* rises by 10% the investors have doubled their *money*, or they might lose it all if the *investment* falls by 10%. See: *leverage*. 2. A term used to describe the *ratio* of a *company*'s borrowings in relation to its *capitalisation* and includes fixed *capital* and *net bank* borrowings.

**GEL** *currency code* for: Georgian Lari.

**GEMM** See: *gilt-edged market maker*.

**General Agreement on Tariffs and Trade (GATT)** An international treaty established in 1947 with the aim of improving international trade and assisting economic development by the reduction of *tariffs* and other barriers to trade. Now superseded by the World Trade Organisation (WTO). Over 100 countries were party to the treaty with other nations also applying the principles – over 90% of world trade was affected by the *GATT* provisions. *GATT* operated primarily in two ways: (i) arranging two-way *tariff* cuts between nations ('*reciprocity*') and (ii) requiring nations to apply the lowest existing *tariff* on a particular import product to all importing nations ('*most favoured nation* rule'). *GATT* supervised numerous multilateral negotiation rounds, including the Kennedy Round (1962–67), Tokyo Round (1973–79) and the *Uruguay* Round (1986–94). See also: *European Union, Organisation for Economic Cooperation and Development, World Trade Organisation*.

**General Commissioners** A tribunal appointed by the Lord Chancellor to hear appeals and arbitrate disputes over *assessments* by the *Inland Revenue* on *income*, corporation and *capital gains tax*. See: *Special Commissioners*.

**general undertaking**   The undertaking adopted by the *board* of a *company* seeking entry to a *stock market* (see: *flotation*) that the *company* will comply with the rules and regulations. See: *Yellow Book*.

**gensaki**   Japanese *secondary market* for domestic medium to long-term *government securities*.

**geometric mean**   See under: *mean*.

**Georgia**   Standard *currency*: lari.

**Germany**   The main *stock market* in Germany is the German Stock Exchange (Deutsche Börse AG) which is the supporting entity of the Frankfurt Stock Exchange. Its main *indices* are:

- *DAX* Index (*Deutscher Aktienindex*) – Comprises 30 German *blue chips* selected according to *turnover* and *market capitalisation*. The *DAX* is calculated using the *Laspeyres formula*, (see: *composite index, weighting factor*) adjusted for *capital* changes and ex-dividend markdowns. It is based at 31 Dec 1987 = 1,000.

- *DAX* 100 Index – Contains the 100 most liquid *shares*. Base: 30 December 1987 = 500.

- CDAX. The German Composite Index – Comprises all German *stocks* at the Frankfurt Stock Exchange, adjusted for *capital* changes, subscription rights and *dividends*.

- *Commerzbank Index* – Arithmetically *weighted index* of 60 *stocks* representing ca. 75% of the market, divided into 12 sections. Base: 1 December 1953 = 100.

- FAZ Aktien Index – Based on 100 industrial *stocks*. Base 31 December 1958 = 100.

Other *stock exchanges* are the Bavarian Stock Exchange (in Munich), Berlin Stock Exchange, Bremen Stock Exchange, Düsseldorf Stock Exchange, Hamburg Stock Exchange, Hanover Stock Exchange, Stuttgart Stock Exchange. The main *futures* and *options* exchange is located in Frankfurt: the *DTB* (*Deutsche Terminbörse*). The German *central bank* is the *Bundesbank*, which operates independently of the German government, but monetary control is in the hands of the European Central Bank. Standard *currency* is the *euro*. 1 euro = 100 *cents*. Prior to the introduction of the *euro* on 1 January 2002, the *currency* was the *Deutschmark*.

**Ghana**   The *stock market* was established in 1989 in Accra: the Ghana Stock Exchange (GSE). In 2009 it had a total of 35 *listed shares*. The main *index* is: GSE All-Share Index. Standard *currency*: cedi. 1 *cedi* = 100 *pesewas*.

**Gharar**   Islamic term. The root GhRR denotes deception. Bay' al-gharar is an exchange in which there is an element of deception either through ignorance of the goods or the price, or through faulty description of the goods. According to Ibn Guzayy, there are several types of gharar exchange, all of which are illegal. The following are examples:

- Selling goods that the seller is not in a position to deliver, such as a runaway horse in the desert, or an unborn calf sold separately from the mother.

- Selling unknown goods or known goods against an unknown price, such as selling the contents of a sealed box.

- Selling goods without proper description, such as a trader selling an unspecified suit of clothing in his shop.

- Selling goods without specifying the actual price, such as selling at 'the going price'.

- Making a *contract* conditional on an unknown event, such as 'when my friend arrives', if the arrival time is not specified.

- Selling a hopelessly sick animal or the goods in a sinking ship.

- Selling goods on the basis of false description.
- Selling goods without proper examination.

In short, Bay' al-gharar is an exchange in which one or both parties stand to be deceived through ignorance of an essential element of the exchange. Gambling is a form of gharar, because the gambler is ignorant of the result of his gamble.

**GHC** *currency code* for: Ghanaian Cedi.

**Gibraltar** Dependency of *UK*. Standard *currency* is the Gibraltar *pound*.

**Gift Aid** A scheme whereby an individual can make a donation to charity and deduct *basic rate tax* at the time of payment and higher rate *tax* on the self *assessment tax return*.

**gift with reservation** A qualified 'gift', where the *donor* still has some benefit from the *asset*. The reservation must be removed for the gift to leave the donor's estate for inheritance tax purposes.

**Gilt Strip Market** The gilt strip market began in the *UK* on 8 December 1997. STRIPS is the acronym for Separately Traded and Registered Interest and Principal Securities. 'Stripping' a gilt refers to breaking it down into its individual *cash flows* which can be traded separately as zero-coupon *gilts*. A three-year gilt will have seven individual *cash flows*: six (semi-annual) *coupon* payments and a principal payment. *Gilts* can also be reconstituted from all of the individual *strips*. Not all *gilts* are strippable. Official *strip* facilities have been available in the *United States* since 1985, and *France* since 1991. Official *strip* markets also now exist in *Germany*, *Italy*, *Spain*, the *Netherlands*, *Belgium* and *Canada*.

**gilt switches** These take place due to two major reasons: 1. Policy switches, taking advantage of a change in *interest rates*. If rates are rising, long-dated *stocks* are sold and short-dated *stocks* purchased (less vulnerable). 2. Jobbing or anomaly switches, taking advantage of the relative cheapness or dearness of comparative *securities*.

**gilt-edged market maker (GEMM)** A *market maker* in the *secondary market* for *gilts* separately capitalised and monitored by the Debt Management Office with whom they have direct computer links and are obliged to make markets (ie provide two-way *quotations*) in all *gilts* at a size deemed appropriate by the Debt Management Office.

**gilt-edged security** Another term for: *gilt*.

**gilts** The familiar name given to British *government securities*. The name 'gilt' comes from the original *certificates* issued, which had gilded edges. At no time has a British government failed to meet any of its funded debt obligations, whether in the nature of *capital* or *income* (with the possible exception of War Loans which should have been redeemed at the end of the Second World War but are now *undated stock*.) They are issued to fund government borrowing (see: *Central Government Net Cash Requirement*) in units of £100 and redeemed at that *value* on a specified date. They have names such as Treasury and Exchequer, denoting which government department is raising the *capital* and in the name is the *redemption date* and the *coupon* – thus Treasury 5½% 2012. They are issued for *short term*, *medium term*, *long term* and undated *term durations* at various initial prices, normally at a *discount* to their *par* (£100) *value* to provide some *growth* as well as the *coupon*. The government has also issued *index-linked gilts*. They are all traded daily for *value* on the gilt market and behave as *fixed interest securities*, being subject to prevailing and anticipated levels of *interest rates*. They can be bought through a *stockbroker* or financial intermediary or the Debt Management Office's purchase and sale service.

**Ginnie Mae** American nickname for the *US* Government National Mortgage Association and the *certificates* issued by them.

**GIP** *currency code* for: *Gibraltar* Pound.

**giro** The system operated in most European countries and in *Japan* for transferring *money* from one *bank* to another or to people with no *bank account.*

**GmbH** Short for the German: Gesellschaft mit beschränkter Haftung. Equivalent to the British: *Ltd.* Contrast: *AG.*

**GMD** *currency code* for: Gambian Dalasi.

**GMP** See: *guaranteed minimum pension.*

**GNF** *currency code* for: *Guinea* Franc.

**Gnomes of Zurich** A term coined by Labour ministers during the *Sterling* crisis of 1964 and used to describe the financiers and bankers of Zurich in *Switzerland* who were engaged in *foreign exchange speculation.*

**GNP** See: *gross national product.*

**godfather offer** A *takeover bid* or *tender offer* so generous that the *target*'s *management* is not in a position to refuse it.

**going concern** A *solvent* and active business that can be sold as a viable entity.

**going public** See: *flotation.*

**gold** The historical basis for *currency*, being a rare and precious metal and a symbol of *wealth.* The traditional way of investing directly in gold is in *bullion, eagles, Maple Leaf, sovereigns* or *krugerrands.* An alternative to this is an *investment* in gold *shares* or gold *share* funds or *trusts* or gold *futures.* Here the *investment* is more flexible, less bulky and easier to buy and provides an additional *income.* Gold *shares* are subject to extraneous factors, however, and can trade independently of the price of gold on occasion. In recent years gold-based exchange traded funds and exchange traded commodities have taken a growing share of the gold buyers' market. The largest gold ETF, SPDR Gold Trust, had holdings of over 1,000 tonnes by February 2009. See: *assay.*

**gold standard** A now little-used arrangement where the *value* of a *currency* is expressed by specific relation to the *value* of *gold.* This *gold* would be held in the vaults of the relevant country and accordingly the amount of *money* in circulation would depend on the *gold reserves* of that country.

**golden cross** A term used in *technical analysis*: a 'golden cross' is said to have occurred when the 200-day *moving average* line crosses the 21-day *moving average* line and both are heading up. If these *moving averages* cross on the way down, the intersection is called a '*dead cross*'. They are both taken to confirm a change in *trend.* If they cross when moving in different directions, this is not considered significant.

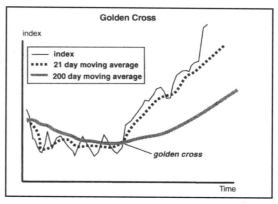

**golden handcuffs** Financial inducements used to retain key staff.

**golden handshake** Non-contractual payments, which may be taxable depending on the circumstances, subject to an exemption of the first £30,000 of the payment if it qualifies under the 'Golden Handshake' provisions.

**golden hello**  Inducement offered to prospective employees to change jobs.

**golden parachutes**  Employment contract provisions that may pre-empt a *takeover* and guarantee substantial severance payments to top *management* if they lose their jobs after a change of ownership. Golden parachutes may also operate simply if the employee concerned is fired – a controversial point in the case of large payments to former bank executives. Sometimes also referred to as '*silver wheelchairs*'.

**golden scenario**  Sustained low inflationary long-term *growth* and no more boom bust cycles. See: *Goldilocks economy*.

**golden share**  A *share* interest, normally controlled by the government after the *privatisation* of a key industry, with the power of veto or a *controlling interest* in the case of certain specific events. Generally to ensure that the *company* does not fall into unwelcome (foreign) hands.

**Goldilocks economy**  Coined at the end of President Clinton's first term to describe the combination of low inflationary *growth* in the US as a result of the *Federal Reserve Board* Chairman Alan Greenspan's successful control of a *soft landing* and the subsequent lack of *overheating*. Describes an economy that 'is neither too hot nor too cold'.

**good-til-cancelled**  An order given which will remain in force for execution at any time in the future until such time as the order is cancelled. Also known as a *resting order*.

**goodwill**  The *value* of a business reflecting its *value* as a *going concern* and its ability to generate *profits*, over and above any intrinsic or *asset value*. It is regarded as an intangible *asset*.

**gopik**  *Currency* sub-unit of *Azerbaijan*. 100 gopik = 1 *manat*.

**Gordon's Growth Model**  Gordon's growth model is a simple way to value a share based on discounted cash flow. The model says that a share's value is determined as:

$$P = \frac{D}{(k\text{-}g)}$$

Where P is the value, D is the dividend per share expected in the next year, k is the required rate of return and g is the growth rate of the dividend in perpetuity.

**gourde**  Standard *currency* of *Haiti*. 1 gourde = 100 *centimes*.

**government actuary**  A professional employed by the government to calculate anticipated *income* and expenditure over the longer term and based on the likely *trends* in areas such as employment, commerce, demographics, *inflation* and the *balance of payments*. His calculations are particularly pertinent when determining social security and *pension* provision as well as the funding of social programmes and the financing of health and education. The government *actuary* also provides a consulting service to government and Commonwealth departments.

**government broker**  The *Bank of England* division engaged in dealing and issuing *gilts* on the *London Stock Exchange* and also the *broker* to the National Debt Commissioners. Until October 1986, the government broker was traditionally the senior partner of Mullins & Co., since which time the *Bank of England* and the Debt Management Office have established their own gilt-edged dealing and *repo* division which delegates some of its responsibilities to *dealers* in *primary markets*.

**government loan scheme**  An arrangement to help small businesses where the government will guarantee 70% of the loan to the business up to a certain *value*. Additional *interest* is charged, however. See: *SFLGS*.

**government securities**  See: *gilts*.

**GPPP** Short for: group *personal pension* plan.

**Graham and Dodd method of investing** *Investment* approach outlined in Benjamin Graham and David Dodd's landmark book 'Security Analysis', published in the 1930s. Graham and Dodd founded the modern discipline of *security analysis* with their work on the purchase of *stocks* with *undervalued assets*, specifically *companies* where *current assets* exceed *current liabilities* and all long-term debt, and where the *stock* has a low *price earnings ratio*. They suggested that the *stocks* be sold after a *profit* objective of between 50% and 100% was reached, which they assumed would be three years or less from the time of purchase. Analysts today who call themselves Graham and Dodd investors look for *stocks* selling below their *liquidation value*.

**Gramm-Rudman Hollings Act** An Act passed by the *US* Congress in December 1985, this sets out predetermined and specific reductions in the *US* Federal *budget deficit*. It specifies individual categories of spending which are to be reduced if the *deficit* exceeds its target, although it permits an above-target *deficit* if there is a *recession*.

**grand** Slang for £1,000.

**grant of probate** An order authorising *probate* and thus allowing the *executors* of a will to distribute the *estate* of a deceased person. If the person died intestate or did not appoint *executors*, the *administrator* of the *estate* has to obtain *letters of administration* so that they can distribute the *estate* in accordance with the will or under the rules of *intestacy*.

**Greece** The *Athens Stock Exchange* was established in 1876. In 1994 it had a total of around 160 *listed securities*. The main *index* is: *Athens Stock Exchange* Share Price Index – Started in October 1994 and consists of 65 *stocks* selected by *market capitalisation*. Standard *currency*: *euro*. 1 *euro* = 100 *cents*. Currency used to be the *drachma*, until the *euro* was introduced on 1 January 2002.

**Greeks** These refer to the sensitivity of an *option* price to the variables in the *Black–Scholes pricing model*. They are used to measure the *risk* of an *option*. The five Greeks are *delta* (sensitivity of *option value* to a change in stock price), *gamma* (rate of change of *delta*), *vega* (sensitivity to *volatility*), *theta* (sensitivity to time to expiry) and rho (sensitivity to *risk free rate*).

**green** In *investment* terms this is used to describe *ethical investments*.

**green currencies** The *currencies* used for the purposes of the Common Agricultural Policy (CAP) in the *EC*, set at artificial rates to protect farm produce prices in the member countries from adverse fluctuations in the real rates of exchange and provide appropriate subsidies. Green currencies are based on the *euro*. See: *green pound*.

**green field** See: *green grass*.

**green grass** A project started completely from scratch. Also called: *green field*.

**green pound** Under the *EU*'s agricultural arrangements, farm produce *exports* and subsidy payments between *EU* member countries are made at a special '*green*' *exchange rate*, to overcome price and *currency* anomalies. The *green pound* therefore reflects the *Sterling* unit of exchange in this respect, which bears no relation to normal market *exchange rates*. See: *green currencies*.

**greenback** Colloquialism for a *US* one *dollar* banknote.

**Greenland** Dependency of *Denmark*. Standard *currency* is the Danish *krone*.

**greenmail** A payment received from a *target* by a *raider* who has amassed a block of *shares* and threatens a *hostile takeover*. The *company* buys out the *raider* at a *premium* over market price, ie buying off one shareholder at a price not available to others.

**Grenada** Standard *currency*: *dollar*. 1 *dollar* = 100 *cents*.

**grey knight** A counterbidder whose intentions are ambiguous and not welcome either to the *target* or to the original *bidder*. A *white knight* comes to the rescue of the *target* with a higher *offer* and is welcomed by the *target*. A *black knight* is a predatory *bidder*, unwelcome to the *target*.

**grey market** It is possible to deal in *shares* which have not yet been issued, prior to their *flotation*. Market makers can fix prices and strike *bargains* in anticipation of *allotments* which may be granted to the applicants for a new issue. The grey market therefore provides a good *indicator* of the likely trading level for these *shares*. Any shortfall for deals struck by investors who are disappointed in their applications can be made up by purchasing further *shares* in the market once they are issued.

**grey wave** In *investment* terms, this is a *company* or a sector which may show considerable potential but where such potential is so far off that it may not be fulfilled until those involved have significant quantities of grey hair!

**gross** A figure, normally *income*, before the deduction of *tax* and/or expenses and other charges. Contrast: *net*.

**gross domestic product (GDP)** The total *money value* of all final goods and services produced in an economy in one year. In other words, the *value* of output produced domestically by *UK* residents. See: *national income*. See also: *gross national product, net domestic product, real GDP, standard of living, UK National Accounts*.

**gross margin** See: *cost of sales*.

**gross profit** (*Gross margin*) *profit* before fixed costs, i.e. sales *revenue* less the *cost of sales*. Cost of sales always includes product costs (materials, manufacture, assembly, etc.), often warehousing and storage, and sometimes specific promotional, advertising and public relations costs. It excludes all other costs such as *overheads*, salaries, finance, distribution, etc.

**gross national product (GNP)** The total *money value* of all final goods and services produced in an economy in one year (*gross domestic product*) plus *net investment income* from abroad (ie *interest, dividends*, rent and *profit*). In other words, the *value* of output produced by *UK* residents from their ownership of resources in the *UK* and abroad. See also: *national income*.

**gross yield** See under: *yield*.

**grossing up** The calculation which converts a *net* return into what it would have been before taxation. Income *tax assessments* are made more on *gross income* and, since *investment rates* differ, *yield* comparisons are mainly made on the *gross* figures.

**groszy** *Currency* sub-unit of *Poland*. 100 groszy = 1 *zloty*.

**Group of Eight (G8)** Established in 1976 as the *Group of Seven (G7)* the Group's purpose is to facilitate economic cooperation among the eight major industrial powers. These are *Canada, France, Germany, Italy, Japan, UK,* the *USA* and more recently *Russia*. *Russia* has been in attendance since 1994, was made a full member in 2002, and hosted the talks in 2006.

**Group of Five (G5)** Established on 22 September 1985, the Group of Five (*G5*)'s purpose is to coordinate the economic policies of five major non-communist economic powers. These are *France, Germany, Japan, UK,* and the *USA*.

**Group of Seven (G7)** Established in 1976, the Group of Seven (*G7*)'s purpose is to facilitate economic cooperation among the seven major industrial powers. These are *Canada, France, Germany, Italy, Japan, UK* and the *USA*. *Russia* has been in attendance since 1994, though not a full member. This has led to the group being called *G8*.

**Group of Ten (G10)** Established in October 1962, the Group of Ten (*G10*) is set up on conclusion of the General Arrangements to Borrow (GAB) with the *IMF*. Its purpose is to coordinate credit policy. The title, 'Group of Ten', remained unchanged even after *Switzerland* was admitted as the eleventh member. The group is: *Belgium, Canada, France, Italy, Japan*, the *Netherlands, Sweden, Germany, Switzerland, UK*, and *USA*.

**Group of Three (G3)** The three strongest economic groups in the world: *USA, China, Europe*.

**Group of Twenty (G20)** The Group of Twenty (G20) was established in 1999 to bring together systemically important industrialised and developing economies to discuss key issues in the global economy. It is made up of the finance ministers and central bank governors of 19 countries: Argentina, Australia, Brazil, Canada, China, France, Germany, India, Indonesia, Italy, Japan, Mexico, Russia, Saudi Arabia, South Africa, South Korea, Turkey, the United Kingdom and the United States of America, and The European Union which is represented by the rotating Council presidency and the European Central Bank. The Managing Director of the *International Monetary Fund* (IMF) and the President of the *World Bank*, plus the chairs of the International Monetary and Financial Committee and Development Committee of the IMF and World Bank, also participate in G20 meetings on an ex-officio basis. The G20 has no permanent staff of its own. The G20 chair rotates between members, and is selected from a different regional grouping of countries each year. In 2009 the G20 chair is the United Kingdom, and in 2010 it will be South Korea.

**Group of Twenty Four (G24)** Established in January 1972 the Group of Twenty Four (*G24*)'s purpose is to deal with international monetary questions and promote the interests of developing countries in Africa, Asia, and Latin America within the *IMF*. The group consists of eight representatives from each of the three continents of Africa, *America* and Asia. The representatives from Africa are: *Algeria, Ivory Coast*, the Democratic Republic of *Congo, Egypt, Ethiopia, Gabon, Ghana* and *Nigeria*. The representatives from Asia are: *India, Iran, Pakistan, Philippines, Sri Lanka, Syria, Serbia* and *Montenegro*, and *Lebanon*. The representatives from *America* are: *Argentina, Brazil, Colombia, Guatemala, Mexico, Peru, Trinidad & Tobago*, and *Venezuela*.

**Group Relief** An arrangement whereby *companies* that are in a qualifying group can surrender *capital allowances* and losses between them to reduce the overall group corporation taxation liability.

**growth** 1. A *net* increase in the *intrinsic value* of any *assets*, ie the realisable *value* (less any reinvested *income* and expenses). In *investment* terms, realised growth is often referred to as a *capital gain*. Differentiated from *income* derived from *investments* (for instance in the form of *interest* or *dividend earnings*). 2. Economic growth refers to sustained increases in *national income*. See: *business cycle*.

**Growth Pact** See: *Stability and Growth Pact*.

**growth stocks** The main characteristics of *growth stocks* are: 1. continuing *growth* of sales leading to *earnings growth* and a higher return on *assets*; 2. high level of *capital expenditure* not necessarily from *retentions*; 3. *earnings growth* in part attributable to product development research and forward-looking *management*.

**Guadeloupe** Dependency of *France*. Standard *currency* is the *euro*.

**Guam** Dependency of the *US*. Standard *currency* is the *US dollar*.

**guarani** *Paraguay*'s standard *currency*. 1 guarani = 100 *centimos*.

**guaranteed income bond** Issued generally by *life assurance companies,* these provide the investors with a fixed guaranteed *income* as well as the guaranteed return of *capital* at the end of a specified *term.* Normally derived from an *annuity* and/or *pure endowment assurance.*

**guaranteed minimum pension (GMP)** In a *pension* scheme that is contracted out (see: *contracting out*) of the state scheme, the *GMP* corresponds to the state earnings-related pension scheme component of the *state pension* which the *member* would have earned while in the employer's scheme had the *member* not been contracted out.

**Guatemala** Standard *currency:* quetzal. 1 *quetzal* = 100 *centavos.*

**Guernsey** The Channel Island of Guernsey's standard *currency* is the *pound Sterling.*

**guide price** The price fixed by the *European Community* under its agricultural policy as a fair price for certain farm products. See: *green currencies.*

**guinea** A British coin first issued in the 17th century made from *gold* obtained from *Guinea.* It was taken out of circulation in 1812 but continued to be used as a unit worth 21 *shillings* (105p) for charging for professional services, goods bought at *auction* and some luxury goods.

**Guinea** Standard *currency* is the Guinea *franc.* 1 Guinea *franc* = 100 *centimes.*

**Guinea-Bissau** Standard *currency* is the Guinea-Bissau *peso.* 1 Guinea-Bissau *peso* = 100 *centavos.*

**Guyana** Standard *currency:* Guyana *dollar.* 1 Guyana *dollar* = 100 *cents.*

**GWP** *currency code* for: *Guinea-Bissau* Peso.

**GYD** *currency code* for: *Guyana* Dollar.

# H

**haircut** An American term for the *discount* in the *value* of *securities* held by a *broker-dealer* as principal. The riskier the *security* the bigger its haircut when calculating its contribution to the *value* of the *broker*'s total *assets*. Now also widely used to describe the margin between the market value of an asset and its assessed value as loan collateral.

**Haiti** Standard *currency: gourde*. 1 *gourde* = 100 *centimes*.

**halala** *Currency* unit of *Saudi Arabia*. 100 halala = 1 *riyal*.

**haler** *Currency* unit of the *Czech Republic*. Plural is 'haleru'. 100 haleru = 1 *koruna*.

**half-commission man** A *stockbroker* who is remunerated solely on the basis of 50% of *commission* that he or she generates from his/her or the stockbroking *company*'s clients.

**hammered** A *stockbroker* is hammered when he or she is unable to meet his or her obligations. The term is derived from the hammer used to bring the old *Stock Exchange* floor to silence. In modern times the expression is used when a *stockbroker* is prevented from conducting further *investment* business by the *Financial Services Authority*.

**Hancock annuity** An *annuity* effected by a *company* on behalf of a retired former employee to provide him with an *income* in retirement. The *capital* is deductible as a *company* expense against *corporation tax,* although relief might be spread over several years. The nickname 'Hancock' arose from the individual who took his case to the House of Lords to gain approval.

**hands on/off** Hands-on investors will be involved in the running of a *company* and probably have at least a *non-executive* seat on the *board*. Hands-off investors will have a passive and non-interventionist role.

**Hang Seng** See under: *Hong Kong*.

**hao** *Currency* unit of *Vietnam*. 10 hao = 1 *dong*.

**hard commission** Established and recognised fee paid to *investment brokers* and *dealers* for research *analysis*, advice or implementing a transaction. Contrast: *soft commission*.

**hard commodity** Normally a *contract* for some type of metal on a *commodity market*. See: *softs*.

**hard costs** Specific business costs requiring monetary payment and capable of budgetary assessment – *cost of sales*, raw materials, taxes etc. as opposed to indirect or intangible *soft costs* such as opportunity costs, *management* stress and distraction, health implications, lost alternatives, loss of *goodwill*, bad public image, bad brand exposure, poor morale, location etc.

**hard currency** *Currency* in which there is widespread confidence and thus readily convertible; normally that of an economically and politically stable country such as the *US* or *Switzerland*. Compare: *soft currency*.

**hard landing** Where steps to counteract *overheating* in an economy cause a *recession*. Compare: *business cycle, soft landing*.

**hard protection** A form of capital protection found in some retail *structured products*. Hard protection provides a minimum return (usually 100% of the original capital) regardless of the performance of the underlying asset (often the FTSE 100 in UK products). Contrast: *soft protection*.

**Harmonised Index of Consumer Prices (HICP)** For international comparisons, particularly with European countries, a measure of *inflation* is used called the Harmonised Index of Consumer Prices, or *HICP*. In the UK HICP is called the Consumer Price Index (CPI). This *index* uses the same basic price data as the *RPI* but is calculated according to rules specified in a series of European Regulations. It differs from the *RPI* in a number of ways including the treatment of housing costs, some of which, most notably mortgage interest, are not in the *HICP*. The CPI is the inflation measure used to set the target for the Bank of England's Monetary Policy Committee (at +/- 1%). Weightings for 2008 are: Food and Non-alcoholic Beverages 10.3%, Alcohol and Tobacco 4.3%, Clothing & Footwear 6.3%, Housing and Household Services 11.5%, Furniture & Household goods 6.8%, Health 2.4%, Transport 15.2%, Communication 2.4% Recreation and Culture 15.3%, Education 1.8%, Restaurants & Hotels 13.8%, Miscellaneous Goods and Services 10.0%. See: *Retail Price Index*.

**Hawaii** Slang for a £50 note (after the television series Hawaii Five-O).

**head and shoulders** *Chart pattern* used in *technical analysis*. It is considered one of the more common and more reliable *reversal patterns*. It marks the end of an uptrend. The first 'shoulder' is created when a few investors *cash* the *profits* made on the way up; the 'head' follows as a *rally* created by buyers gains the upper hand, but as *volume* runs out the price drops below

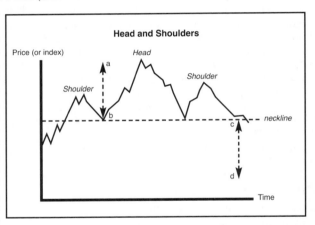

the left shoulder's high on a lower *volume* than the previous two advances. The right 'shoulder' is formed by a short *rally*, followed by a collapse in the price. The '*neckline*' is drawn across the preceding two *reaction* lows. The *breakout* is confirmed as a reversal when it goes beyond the price that is 3% below the *neckline* at the *breakout* point. It is then expected to move downwards a distance (c to d) equal to the distance between the top of the head and the *neckline* (a to b). Occasionally an inverted head and shoulders (which is upside-down) occurs in an uptrend, and is thus technically called a 'consolidated head and shoulders'. The opposite goes for downtrends: a head-and-shoulders *pattern* is a *continuation* ('consolidation') *pattern* and an inverted (or 'reverse') head and shoulders marks a reversal of a downtrend.

**headline inflation** Unofficial term denoting the *inflation* in an economy measured by changes in the *Retail Price Index* (*RPI*). Compare: *underlying inflation*.

**Heard & Mcdonald Islands** Standard *currency*: Australian *dollar*.

**heavy share** A *share* that has a high price relative to the *average* price of *shares* in the market. As investors irrationally feel that they may be getting better *value* from a lower priced *share* because they get a larger number of *shares*, heavy *shares* are split. See: *share split*.

**Heckscher-Ohlin theory** Propounded by two Swedish economists, Heckscher and Ohlin, this is a simple *trade theory* that shows the *pattern* of trade between two nations producing two *commodities* only (and having only two *factors of production*, along with some other simplifying assumptions). The theory states that a nation will have a *comparative advantage* (see: *absolute advantage*) and should therefore export that *commodity* whose production requires the intensive use of the nation's relatively abundant and cheap factor. Thus the nation should also specialise in its production. Subsequently, the nation will have a comparative disadvantage and should therefore import the other *commodity*, whose production requires the intensive use of the nation's relatively scarce and expensive factor. The direct corollary to the theory is the 'factor-price *equalisation* theorem' which states that international trade will bring about *equalisation* in the relative and absolute prices of homogeneous factors across nations.

**hedge** 1. A term applied primarily to the *commodity, stock* and *currency* markets where a physical position is 'hedged' by the use of *derivatives* such as *futures* and *options*. Here investors who hold physical *stock, currency deposits* or *commodities* will protect their positions by buying *puts* in the same *stock, currency* or *commodity* or at least in an equivalent market. Alternatively, protection against price changes can be achieved by taking a sale in *futures* to match a *physical* purchase in the *forward market* and vice versa. Thus the loss in one market is offset by a *profit* in the other. It is most commonly used when such *investments* are held in the longer term but may be subject to near-term *volatility* – the cost of selling the *physical* and the loss of any *dividends* may make hedging a viable alternative if any deterioration in prices is expected to be short lived. *Interest rates* can also be hedged by the purchase of certain *futures contracts* and, of course, all these various *derivatives* can be traded in their own right for speculative purposes as well as hedging. See also: *cap, collar, forward dealing*. 2. Refers to taking measures against some undesired effect. Eg property, *gold* and *shares* are often used as a hedge against *inflation*.

**hedge fund** Private *investment partnership* (for *US* investors) or an offshore *investment* corporation (for non-US or tax-exempt investors), often where those managing the fund have substantial personal *stakes*, whose offering memorandum allows the fund to take both *long* and *short positions*, use *leverage* and *derivatives*, and invest in many markets. Hedge funds often take very large *risks* for their clients on speculative strategies, including programme trading, *selling short, swaps* and *arbitrage*.

**Her Majesties Inland Revenue and Customs** See also: *Inland Revenue, Customs and Excise*.

**heritable bond** A Scottish term for a *debenture* or loan backed by land.

**HICA** Short for: high *interest* cheque account.

**HICP** See: *Harmonised Index of Consumer Prices*.

**hidden reserve** In certain financial institutions, the hidden reserve refers to funds held in reserve that are not disclosed in the *balance sheet. Limited companies* are not at liberty to hide funds in this way. *Life assurance companies* and smaller *banks* have found all sorts of clever ways of concealing *reserves* through provisions, but increasingly regulators are demanding transparency. See: *embedded value*.

**high water mark** Often applied to *hedge funds*, the manger can only charge performance or incentive fees when the *value* of the fund has exceeded the previous highest *net asset value*, which is called the high water mark.

**higher rate taxpayer** One whose highest marginal rate of *income tax* is above the current prevailing *basic rate*. Roughly 3.6 million people in the *UK* pay *tax* at higher rate, 12% of all income taxpayers.

**hire purchase** A loan offered by a *finance house* (often at quite high rates of *interest*) for the purchase of a product repayable over a set period – sometimes known as 'deferred purchase'. The product is owned by the *finance house* and hired to the user until the debt is repaid.

**historic cost accounting** The traditional method of accounting which makes no allowances for *inflation*. Compare: *inflation accounting* and *current cost accounting*. See: *accounting concepts*.

**historic pricing** *Unit trusts* and OEICs are usually dealt on a *forward pricing* basis, where no price can be given when the deal is struck as it depends on the current *value* of holdings in the relevant market. Some funds can, however, be priced on a historic basis, where investors can obtain a firm *quotation* at the time of dealing and this often means that the price of the units reflects the *value* of the *portfolio* on the previous day.

**HKD** *currency code* for: *Hong Kong* Dollar.

**HKFE** Short for: *Hong Kong* Futures Exchange.

**HMRC** See: *Her Majesties Inland Revenue and Customs*.

**HNL** *currency code* for: Honduran Lempira.

**hog cycles** Cycles switching between overproduction and underproduction due to time lags in the production process. The effect takes place because changes in *supply and demand* are not met quickly enough by production. See: *business cycle*.

**holding company** A *company* normally forming part of a *conglomerate* where the *shares* of all the *subsidiary companies* are held by the holding company itself. The holding company is in turn owned by the *beneficial owners* of the group itself.

**Holland** See: the *Netherlands*.

**home income plan** A scheme for older people where a loan is taken against their property and the proceeds used to purchase a lifetime *annuity* which will provide *income* over and above the cost of interest on the loan – this surplus is used to supplement spendable *income*. The property itself is used as *security* for this loan and the sale proceeds on death repay the debt. This allows people to generate *income* from their property while retaining occupation. Home income plans using *investments* other than a *purchased life annuity* are generally regarded as inappropriate.

**home reversion plan** A method of raising *capital* on a property where a full or partial reversionary interest in the property is sold. This interest allows the plan holder to occupy the property for his or her life and/or that of their spouse, although the property will be technically at least partially owned by the provider of the *capital*, and of course the appropriate share of any *capital* increase in its *value* will go to the new owner. This allows home owners to release *capital* from their property without moving.

**Honduras** In 1994, the number of *listed companies* on the Honduran Stock Exchange was 75. Standard *currency*: *lempira*. 1 *lempira* = 100 *centavos*.

**Hong Kong** The Stock Exchange of Hong Kong (SEHK) commenced trading in 1986 with the unification of the four previous exchanges: Hong Kong Stock Exchange, Far East Exchange, Kam Ngam Stock Exchange and Kowloon Stock Exchange. Its main *index* is the *Hang Seng* Index which comprises 42 *stocks*. Each constituent *stock* is weighted so that it will influence the *index* in proportion to its respective *market value*. In 2000 the Stock Exchange of Hong Kong Limited, Hong Kong Futures Exchange Limited demutualised, and together with Hong Kong Securities Clearing Company Limited, merged under a single *holding company*, HKEx. Standard *currency*: Hong Kong *dollar*.

**honorarium** A payment in gratitude for professional services in the absence of a pre-arranged fixed fee.

**horizon analysis** A method used in *investment appraisal*, where a time (the 'horizon date') other than the *investment*'s *maturity date* is used in *discounted cash flow* calculations. For instance, the horizon date could be taken as the end of a particular *business cycle* or at some suitable reference point within the investor's *portfolio*. Useful when the *maturity date* of the *investment* is not suitable for calculating comparative rates of return. See: *analysis*.

**horizontal integration** 1. This refers to a *company* specialising in a particular stage of production or *distribution* of a product instead of being involved in progressive stages in the production chain (see: *vertical integration*). Also called 'lateral integration'. 2. The joining by *merger* or *acquisition* of two (or more) firms involved in producing the same product or type of product. This is carried out mainly to exploit *economies of scale* in production (see: *increasing returns*).

**horizontal spread** An *options* strategy that involves buying and selling the same number of *options contracts* with the same *exercise price* but with different *maturity dates*.

**hostile takeover** An *acquisition* attempt resisted by the *target*.

**hot money** Money that is moved about frequently among financial centres by speculators and *arbitrageurs* seeking high short-term returns.

**HRK** *currency code* for: Croatian Kuna.

**HTG** *currency code* for: Haitian Gourde.

**HUF** *currency code* for: Hungarian Forint.

**human capital** Refers to the skills, experience, education or health of a worker, or any aspect of that worker that will be an *asset* to a *company* due to higher *productivity*. See also: *capital*.

**Hungary** The Budapest Stock Exchange was established in 1990. The market capitalisation at the end of 2008 was €13.33bn. The main *index* is: BUX Index. The *index* comprises 14 *shares*. Base: 2 January 1991 = 1,000. Standard *currency*: forint. 1 forint = 100 fillér.

**hurdle rate** Generally the minimum *rate of return* needed to make a project or *investment* attractive. In the fund management industry managers often specify a hurdle rate, such as *LIBOR*, and they will not charge a performance fee until the hurdle *rate of return* has been exceeded.

**hushmail** This is where a *company* will buy, normally from a *director*, a substantial number of *shares* at a *premium* price in return for his or her silence on sensitive internal corporate information.

**hybrid fund** An *investment fund* or *portfolio* that comprises both indexed funds (*tracker funds*) as a core holding and more actively managed *investments* biased (or tilted) towards particular sectors.

**hybrid investment** A type of *investment* that combines two different kinds of underlying *investment*. They are also called: *derivatives*, synthetics.

**hyperinflation** An unmanageably high rate of *inflation*. In recent times it was experienced during *Germany*'s reparation period, where people carried *money* around in sacks and had to pay for meals in restaurants in advance as the price would have risen by the time they had finished eating. It was caused by the uncontrolled printing of *money*; ie runaway *money supply*. Zimbabwe is the best example of current hyperinflation. Often, the term 'hyperinflation' is applied to annual *inflation* above 50%.

**hypothecation** 1. The *pledge* of property in order to secure a loan, usually by way of a *'letter of hypothecation'*. Ownership is not transferred, but the lender can sell the hypothecated property in the event of *default*. 2. *Pledge* of *securities* to a *broker* as *security* in order to purchase other *securities*. The *broker* can, in turn, *pledge* this *security* to a *bank* in order to obtain a loan; this is termed 'rehypothecation'. 3. *Mortgage* of a ship and/or its cargo, whereby the lender obtains a *lien*. When the ship (with or without cargo) is hypothecated, it is called *bottomry*; whereas when only the cargo is given as *security*, one refers to *respondentia*.

**hysteresis** 1. Describes the lagging of effects behind their causes. 2. It is also used in a similar sense to describe the continuation or irreversibility of certain circumstances in an economy. 3. In economics, this also has the implication of the path dependency of an economy en route to *equilibrium*, implying that the *equilibrium* is not unique. See: *lagging indicators*.

# I

**IAS**  See: *International Accounting Standard.*

**IASB**  See: *International Accounting Standards Board.*

**IASC**  See: *International Accounting Standards Committee.*

**IBA**  See: *industrial buildings allowance.*

**IBBR**  Short for: Inter-Bank Bid Rate. See: *London Inter-Bank Bid Rate.*

**IBEL**  See: *interest bearing eligible liabilities.*

**IBMBR**  Short for: Inter-Bank Market Bid Rate. See: *London Inter-Bank Bid Rate.*

**IBRD**  See: *International Bank for Reconstruction and Development.* See under: *World Bank.*

**ICAEW**  See: *Institute of Chartered Accountants in England and Wales.* See: *accountant.*

**ICC**  See: *International Chamber of Commerce.*

**ICCH**  See: *International Commodities Clearing House.* See: *London Clearing House.*

**ICE Futures Europe**  ICE Futures Europe is the London-based energy futures market, a subsidiary of IntercontinentalExchange. It trades nearly half of the world's global crude futures.

**Iceland**  The Iceland Stock Exchange was established in 1985 and is now part of NASDQ OMX Nordic. Standard *currency*: *krona.* 1 *krona* = 100 aurar.

**ICFC**  Short for: Industrial and Commercial Finance Corporation Limited. An independent organisation founded by the *Bank of England* and English and Scottish *clearing banks* to help small and medium-sized businesses in Great Britain by providing finance for expansion and development. It has now become 3i, a listed company focussing on venture capital investments.

**ICI**  See: *Investment Company Institute.*

**ICTA**  Short for: Income and Corporation Taxes Act 1988.

**IDA**  See: *International Development Association.*

**IDB**  See: *inter-dealer broker.*

**idiosyncratic risk**  Another term for: *unsystematic risk.*

**IDR**  *currency code* for: Indonesian Rupiah.

**IFA**  See: *Independent Financial Advisor.*

**IFC**  See: *International Finance Corporation.* See under: *World Bank.*

**IFOX**  See: *Irish Futures and Options Exchange.*

**IFRS**  Short for: International *Financial Reporting Standards.* See also: *International Accounting Standards Board.*

**IHA**  Short for: Issuing Houses Association. See: *issuing house.*

**Ijara**  Islamic term for a *contract* in which a *bank* buys, and *leases* out for a rental fee, equipment required by its client. The duration of *lease* and rental fee are agreed in advance. Ownership of the equipment remains in the hands of the *bank.* The *contract* is a classical Islamic financial one, now in increasing use worldwide.

**Ijara wa-iqtina**  Islamic term for *lease/hire purchase,* very similar to *Ijara,* except that there is a commitment from the client to buy the equipment at the end of the rental period. It is pre-agreed that at the end of the *lease* period the client will buy the equipment at an agreed price from the *bank*, with rental fees previously paid constituting part of the price.

**illiquid** 1. A firm that has a deficient *cash flow* and cannot meet its immediate obligations, though not necessarily insolvent (see: *insolvency*). 2. Not readily convertible into *cash*, such as a *stock*, *bond* or *commodity* that is not traded actively and would be difficult to sell in any quantity or *assets* for which there is not a ready market, such as tangibles.

**ILS** *currency code* for: *Israel* New Shekel.

**IMC** See: *Investment Management Certificate*.

**IMF** See: *International Monetary Fund*.

**IMM** See: *International Monetary Market*. See: *Chicago Mercantile Exchange*.

**impact day** The first date on which terms of a new issue (*flotation*) are known to the public, normally the date of the *sub-underwriting* or *placing*, and which may be determined by the *company*'s place in the *queue*.

**implicit deflator** Also called 'implicit *price index*'. A *deflator* allows one to arrive at *real national income* figures (such as *gross domestic product* or *gross national product*) by taking the nominal *national income* figures quoted in national accounts and dividing by the *deflator value*. If *real* and nominal *national income* are determined by taking *base period* and current period prices respectively then an *index* can be calculated, called the implicit deflator:

$$\text{implicit deflator} = \frac{\text{national income at current prices (ie nominal national income)}}{\text{national income at base period prices (ie real national income)}} \times \text{base index value}$$

The *index* is called 'implicit deflator' because no *price index* was used in calculating it (see: *GDP deflator*). It is considered the most comprehensive *index* of the price level since it covers all production of goods and services of a nation recorded in national accounts. It is a variable-weight *index* due to the fact that different 'bundles' of production are calculated in base and current periods. Other price *indices* are fixed-weight *indices*, such as the *Retail Price Index*.

**implied volatility** The *volatility* or *standard deviation* of a stock that is derived from the price of the *stock's option*. Using an *option* pricing model, such as the *Black–Scholes* pricing model, with a known *market price* of an *option* the unknown variable will be the *volatility*; this is called the implied volatility.

**import duty** See: *tariff*.

**imports** Goods and services produced abroad and consumed domestically. See: *balance of payments*.

**imprest account** An imprest (or *float*) account is a method of balancing petty-cash in a business. Money drawn as petty-cash must be accounted for in the form of vouchers so that the sum (*float*) remains constant.

**imputation system of taxation** A system where a proportion of *corporation tax* is treated as a *tax credit* on account of the *income tax* payable by *shareholders* on *dividends*. Such a system was introduced into the *UK* in 1972 in the form of *advance corporation tax* and abolished on 5 April 1999 (see: *ACT*).

**in-the-money option** A *call option* whose *exercise price* is below the current market price of the *underlying security*, or a *put option* whose *exercise price* is above the current market price of the *underlying security*.

**inchoate instrument**  A negotiable *instrument* (see: *negotiable security*) on which not all the relevant information has been completed.

**income**  1. All *emoluments* received by an individual or *company*, whether as a result of trading, for services rendered or from the *investment* of *capital* from whatever source, both at home and abroad. See also: *disposable income, tax schedules*. 2. See: *national income*.

**income & expenditure account**  Non *profit* making organisations' version of the *profit & loss account*. However, the *accounting concept* of *accrual* is not used. See: *accounting concepts*.

**income bond**  See: *guaranteed income bond*.

**income distribution**  The term used in the *unit trust* or collective *investment* field (see: *collective investment scheme*) where the *income* is distributed, usually half-yearly or on fixed dates, to unit holders in strict proportion to the number of units held. Virtually all the *income* of a *unit trust* or OEIC is distributed in this way after deducting *management* charges. Distributions are paid *net* of *tax*, but for *income tax* purposes they need to be grossed up at the 10% *basic rate* (20% for cash and fixed interest funds).

**income drawdown**  A means of providing pension income by making regular withdrawals from a pension plan rather than purchasing an annuity. The upper limit of the amount withdrawn each year is based on an HMRC table which takes account of age, sex and long term gilt yields. Sometimes also called income withdrawals.

**income tax**  Tax payable on all forms of *income* received by citizens in the UK declared in a *tax return* and self-assessed according to current *tax rates* less *allowances*. See: *tax schedules*.

**income withdrawals**  See: *income drawdown*

**incomes policy**  A government policy designed to control *inflation* and maintain *full employment* by holding down increases in wages and prices. Such interventionist economic policy is currently considered inappropriate and most governments restrict themselves to *monetarist* controls. See: *business cycle*.

**increasing returns**  When a firm experiences that increases in the inputs of production cause a more than proportional increase in output, one says it is experiencing increasing returns (to scale). If the input factor prices are fixed, then the firm decreases its unit costs. Also called: *economies of scale*. Compare: *decreasing returns*.

**indebtedness**  The borrowings of a *company* as at a date (the indebtedness date) which is within 28 days of the date of a *prospectus*, and which are required to be disclosed in a *prospectus*.

**indemnity**  1. In the case of damages or losses suffered by a party, an indemnity is the assurance that the situation will be rectified by another party by way of repair or monetary payments. That other party is mostly an *insurance company* in which the policyholder who has suffered damages has *indemnity insurance*. 2. A guarantee by a client to their *bank* (usually in the form of a 'letter of indemnity') that the *bank* will not be held liable for continuing to serve the interests of that client as a result of the client's loss of documents.

**indemnity insurance**  A common type of *insurance*, in which the *insurance company* agrees to compensate the policyholder by way of monetary payment, or sometimes repair, in the event of damages to the policyholder's property (which can be valued). The compensation is to be at such a level as to completely restore the status quo of the property before damages occurred, no more and no less. Contrast with *personal accident insurance*, which cannot be valued in the same way. See also: *professional indemnity*.

**indenture** *US* term for the formal details on a *bond* containing such things as amount of the issue, property pledged as guarantee, redemption, *call* privileges etc. Also called: *deed of trust, trust deed.*

**Independent Financial Adviser (IFA)** Independent Financial Advisers are authorised directly by the *FSA*. These firms provide independent advice on *investments* and financial products. They are obliged to make recommendations to clients in the light of all the various financial products available and must be impartial in their recommendations. See: *authorisation.*

**independent taxation** A system of personal taxation introduced in the *UK* in 1990–91 where a husband and wife are treated as completely separate and independent taxpayers for both *income tax* and *capital gains tax* as though each was single. Now also applies to members of civil partnerships. See: *tax.*

**index** Plural: *indices.* For details of world-wide *indices* and *stock markets* refer to individual countries. An index is a number that gives the *value* of something (eg prices of goods in a *price index*, or *shares* in a *stock market*) relative to its *value* at some other time. When an index starts (at its *base period*) it is normally ascribed a *value*, say, 100 (the base index *value*). The *base period* is commonly a specific year (since annual comparisons are the most usual) and is thus called the *base year.* If that year, is, say, 1990, then one writes: '1990 = 100' to show the *base year* and the base index *value* 100. An example of an unweighted index is if the periods in question are numbered 0, 1, 2, 3,..., n (where 0 refers to the *base period* and n is for the current period) and the *values* of the variable respectively are $V_0$, $V_1$, $V_2$, $V_3$,...,$V_n$,:

$$\text{unweighted index} = \frac{V_n}{V_0} \times \text{base index value}$$

A simple example is:

| Period | Variable value | Index | Percentage change on previous year (rounded) |
|--------|----------------|-------|----------------------------------------------|
| 0 | $V_0 = 10.0$ | 100 | n/a |
| 1 | $V_1 = 15.0$ | 150 | 50 |
| 2 | $V_2 = 18.0$ | 180 | 20 |
| 3 | $V_3 = 20.0$ | 200 | 11 |
| 4 | $V_4 = 26.0$ | 260 | 30 |

The index column shows the *points* movement of the index: from period 0 to 1 the movement is 50 *points* on the index and from 1 to 2 it is 30 *points*. But note that the percentage change from 0 to 1 is 50% whereas the percentage change between periods 1 to 2 is 20% but 30 *points*. Accordingly, an index *point* will only represent a percentage point when it refers to the *base year* at 100. Index movement may prove useful to analysts in indicating general *trends.* Indices are useful in indicating market *trends* and as *benchmarks* for comparison purposes. They are also used in *technical analysis* to anticipate future *trends.* See also: *composite index.*

**index fund** A mutual *investment,* such as a *unit trust, OEIC* or *unit-linked* life fund which invests directly or indirectly in the constituent elements of, and is designed to perform in line with, a *stock exchange index.* Preferred by investors who do not wish to rely on a *fund manager*'s ability to outperform market *indices* or those who believe in the *efficient market theory.* Also known as: *tracker fund.*

**index futures** A *futures contract* on a *financial futures* market based on movement in a *market index.*

**index option** A *call* or *put option* on an *index* of *stock.* Broad-based *indices* cover a wide range of *companies* and industries, whereas narrow-based *indices* consist of *stocks* in one industry or sector of the economy. Index options allow investors to trade in a particular market or industry group without having to buy all the *stocks* individually. For instance, someone who thought oil *stocks* were about to fall could buy a *put* on the oil *index* instead of *selling short shares* in half a dozen oil *companies.*

**index-linked gilts** Created originally in the 1981 *Budget* for the exclusive use of the *pension* fund industry, were first made available to the general public in 1982 in order to fund an increased percentage of government borrowing. There is currently over £167 *billion* of index-linked *stocks* which represents approximately 23.6% of total gilt issues. The *index* link relates to the *capital* invested. To this end, the *nominal value* of the gilt at issue (£100) is indexed by the change in the *Retail Price Index* over the *stock*'s life with reference to a base *RPI,* which is the *value* prevailing three or eight months prior to issue. All these *stocks* have a fixed *coupon* (0% – 4⅛%) which is applied to the current *capital value* of the *stock* to determine the *yield* and so in itself is indexed. A ten-year *stock,* therefore, with a *coupon* of 1% and assuming 2.5% p.a. *inflation* throughout its life would initially cost £100. Upon redemption it would have increased to £128, and its six-monthly interest payment would have increased from £0.50 to £0.64 (from £1 p.a. to £1.28 p.a.).

**index tracking** A method of passive *investment* management where the objective is that the performance of a *portfolio* or fund matches the performance of an *index.*

**indexation** The adjustment of payments or *allowances* in line with such *indices* as the *Retail Price Index (RPI).* Used for adjustments in *pensions, tax allowances, investments* etc.

**indexation allowance** For companies certain expenditure items can be indexed with respect to the *Retail Price Index* in order to mitigate inflationary effects on *capital gains.* Indexation allowance was withdrawn for individual investors from April 1998 and replaced by taper relief.

**India** has nearly two dozen *stock exchanges.* The main *stock exchange* is the *Bombay Stock Exchange* (BSE), established in 1875. In 2008, it traded in over 4,700 *securities.* Its main *indices* are:

- BSE Sensex Index, which contains 30 leading *stocks.* Base: 1978 = 100.
- BSE 100 Index (formerly BSE National Index), comprising 100 leading *stocks* on the exchanges of Bombay, Calcutta, Delhi, Madras and Ahmedabad. The *average* price of commonly traded *stocks,* weighted by free float capitalisation is used for calculating the *index.*
- BSE 200-Share Index, whose construction is similar to the 100 Index.
- DOLLEX. This is the US$ equivalent of the BSE Share India. Base: 27 May 1994 = 273.63.

Standard *currency: rupee.* 1 *rupee* = 100 *paisa.*

**indicator** Generic term referring to price investigation whose purpose is to confirm, or otherwise, the importance of a price move, into new high ground for instance. Also an economic indicator, namely a statistic gauging the performance of an economy. See: *lagging indicators, leading indicators.*

**indices** Plural of: *index*. For details of world-wide indices and *stock markets* refer to individual countries.

**indirect taxation** Tax on consumption, supply, trade etc., as opposed to personal or *direct taxation* such as *income tax*. The main UK indirect tax is VAT.

**Individual Retirement Account (IRA)** The American *pension* plan covered by the Tax Reform Act 1986 allowing tax-deferred contributions of $6,000 per year (2009) to a qualified plan or *trust* for anyone and for those contributions to be wholly or partially deductible against *income tax*. The amount is treated as a non-taxable return of *capital* any time after age 59½. See also: *Employee Retirement Income Security Act 1974 (ERISA)*, *401(k) Plan*.

**Individual Savings Account (ISA)** ISAs were introduced on 6 April 1999 as a replacement for Tax Exempt Special Savings Accounts (TESSAs) and Personal Equity Plans (PEPs). An ISA can consist of one or two components:

- *The stocks and shares component*, which can include collective funds and certain life assurance policies as well as listed securities. Cash can be held, but only on a temporary basis, pending investment.

- *The cash component*, which can be invested in cash deposits at variable or fixed rates. Proceeds from matured TESSAs could be transferred into this component.

Income from fixed interest securities and dividends from equities are free of UK income tax, although UK dividend tax credits cannot be reclaimed. Interest on cash is tax-free within the cash component, but is subject to a flat 20% charge in the stocks and shares component. ISAs are free of capital gains tax. In practice, for basic rate taxpayers the tax benefits of ISAs are small, particularly at a time when deposit interest rates are extremely low. The maximum annual investment in an ISA is currently (2008/09) £7,200 per tax year, of which up to £3,600 may be invested in the cash component with the balance invested in the stocks and shares component.

**individual voluntary arrangement (IVA)** An *arrangement* made by private individuals due to *insolvency*, with their *creditors* organised and formalised by an *accountant*. Creditors agree to take a smaller amount over an extended period rather than have individuals declared *bankrupt*, when they would probably receive less (or nothing). See also: *scheme of arrangement*.

**Indonesia** The main *stock market* is the Indonesia Stock Exchange. The number of *listed companies* in 2008 was 398. Its main *index* is: Composite Share Price Index, which comprises all *stocks* on the Jakarta Stock Exchange. Base: 10 August 1982 = 100. An *OTC market* (Indonesian Parallel Stock Exchange merged with the Jakarta Stock Exchange). The Surabaya Stock Exchange merged with the Jakarta Stock Exchange in 2007 to form the Indonesia Stock Exchange. Standard *currency*: *rupiah*. 1 *rupiah* = 100 *sen*.

**industrial buildings allowance (IBA)** Tax relief allowed on the purchase monies used to acquire a qualifying industrial building. Such buildings qualify for *corporation tax* or *income tax* relief in a scheme which has been introduced to encourage industrial development. IBAs are being phased out and will disappear from 2011/12.

**industrial life assurance** An old form of *life assurance*, designed to cover funeral expenses, where *premiums* were collected weekly or monthly in *cash* by an *insurance* inspector.

**inflation** An increase in the general level of prices in a particular economy that persists over a period of time. It reduces the *purchasing power* of *money*. Inflation is a major cause of concern for government authorities, and many policies are aimed at reducing it. It is also an important concern for investors. The rise in the general level of prices can be measured through an *index*, such as the *implicit deflator* or more commonly the *Retail Price Index* or Harmonised Index of Consumer Prices. The inflation rate is usually given as an annual figure for the economy. If the annual increase in prices is small and gradual, one refers to 'creeping inflation'. If inflation is large and sometimes even accelerating, the term '*hyperinflation*' is used. The two main explanations for inflation are *cost-push inflation* and *demand-pull inflation*. Inflationary effects are separated from the so-called 'real effects' of changes of economic variables, such as wages and output. See also: *deflation, disinflation, real interest rate, stagflation, Tax and Price Index*.

**inflation accounting** Modern accounting system which takes into account the cost of replacing *stock* and *fixed assets* at current *values*, thereby attempting to show *capital* requirements at current costs. All accounting standards on this subject have been withdrawn. See also: *current cost accounting*.

**inflationary gap** A situation in which the desired aggregate demand of an economy is in excess of the full employment level of output (supply). Thus all resources in the economy are fully used and prices must rise in order to eliminate the surplus demand. See also: *output gap*.

**inflationary spiral** Also called: price-wage spiral. A situation where the interaction of general increases in the prices of goods and services with increases in input costs (such as wages) brings about a self-sustained *inflation* in the economy.

**infrastructure** Collectively, all the systems and structures that are useful for the economy of a country, accumulated from *capital investment*, usually by government agencies, in previous periods. A nation's infrastructure includes roads, transportation, telephone networks, sewage systems, railway lines, airports, electricity plants and wiring, bridges etc., and sometimes intangible elements such as *human capital* (eg education of the workforce). Essential for the development and sustenance of an economy, especially for the *standard of living*, through economic *growth*.

**ingot** Bar of precious metal. For instance, the *US Federal Reserve System*'s *gold reserves* are kept in ingots.

**inheritance tax** The tax on gifts in lifetime or at death which replaced *capital transfer tax* in the 1986 Finance Act. Similar to *estate duty* in that a sliding scale of *tax* is payable should the death of the *donor* of a lifetime gift occur within seven years of the transfer. If it occurs within 1–3 years of death the *tax* is at 100% of the death rate, 3–4 years 80%, 4–5 years 60%, 5–6 years 40% and 6–7 years 20%. The estate on death is chargeable subject to a nil-rate band and certain exemptions.

**inheritance trusts** Schemes for mitigating *inheritance tax* marketed by *life assurance companies*. The schemes rely on interest-free loans and the *investment* medium is normally *investment bonds*.

**initial charges** Normally associated with *collective investment schemes*, these initial charges are usually represented by the difference between the *bid* and *offer price*. They cover marketing and administration costs and *commissions*, which are paid by investors. These costs are included in the price when the customer makes an *investment*. See also: *bid-offer spread, initial units*.

**initial public offering (IPO)** The American equivalent of a public *flotation*.

**initial units** Units allocated to a *unit-linked* policy where a proportion of the *income* or *growth* from the units is deducted each year to collect charges. Also called: *capital units*. Now rarely found in new policies.

**initial yield** The *income* from an *investment* expressed as a percentage of its *value* at the time of purchase. An *investment* with an initial *yield* of 10% may have a *current yield* of only 5% because it has doubled in *value*. See: *yield*.

**injection** See: *circular flow of national income*.

**injunction** An equitable remedy in which a court orders a party to do something (mandatory injunction) or orders a party to refrain from doing something (prohibitory injunction). Failure to comply is contempt of court and the penalty is a fine and/or imprisonment.

**Inland Revenue** Merged with the Customs and Excise Board in April 2005 to form HM Revenue and Customs, formerly called the *Board of Inland Revenue* and run by the Commissioners of Inland Revenue, this is the body that calculates and collects all forms of *income* and *capital* taxes in the *UK* (but not excise duty). The Commissioners appoint inspectors and collectors under the Taxes Management Act 1970 and appeals are heard by *Special Commissioners* and *General Commissioners*, which are both being replaced by tax tribunals.

**input tax** The *value added tax* included in the price paid for inputs by a firm within the chain of production of a good or service. It can be reclaimed after *output tax* has been remitted to HMRC.

**INR** *currency code* for: Indian Rupee.

**insider dealing** Also called: *insider trading*. An illegal process whereby individuals use, or encourage others to use, price-sensitive information regarding a *company*, not generally available and/or previously received through inside knowledge, to invest or divest in a position for their own financial advantage, other than in the proper performance of their employment. Originally made an offence in 1980 and covered by the Companies Securities (Insider Dealing) Act 1985. Now covered as 'market abuse' under the Financial Services and Management Act 2000. See also: *Chinese wall*.

**insider trading** Another term for: *insider dealing*.

**insolvency** Where a person or a *company* has insufficient *cash* and *assets* to cover their outstanding debts. It is an offence for a *company* to continue trading without a genuine expectation of future revenues to cover this position. See also: *administration, bankrupt, fraudulent conveyance, fraudulent preference, individual voluntary arrangement, liquidation, wrongful trading*.

**Insolvency Act 1986** The Act dealing primarily with *insolvency*, bankruptcy and *voluntary arrangements*. It consolidates previous legislation and introduces the concept of *administration* and *wrongful trading*. The 1986 Act was extensively amended by the Insolvency Act 2000. See: *bankrupt*.

**insolvent liquidation** The *liquidation* of a *company* that will yield an amount insufficient to repay all the *creditors*. See: *wrongful trading*.

**Institute of Chartered Accountants in England and Wales (ICAEW)** The Institute of Chartered Accountants in England and Wales was incorporated by Royal Charter in May 1880 following the coming together of six local societies of *accountants* in London, Liverpool, Manchester and Sheffield. The Institute received a Supplemental Charter in 1948. As a Chartered body, the Institute operates primarily in the public interest. In summary, the powers conferred on the Institute by the Charter relate to the protection of the public interest through: superior education and training, the maintenance of high professional standards and technical excellence in the field of accounting in all its forms.

**Institute of Directors (IoD)** The Institute of Directors (*IoD*) was incorporated by Royal Charter in 1903 as an association and representative for UK *company directors,* with a head office at 116 Pall Mall, London. It has 53,000 members, and has premises open for the use of those members in London, Reading, Belfast, Birmingham, Bristol, Edinburgh, Manchester, Nottingham and Paris.

**instrument** An economic variable over which government policymakers have direct control. For example, the *money supply* is an instrument of the government for a number of policies. See also: *Tinbergen's instruments–targets rule.*

**insurable interest** Someone may insure the life of another if they have an insurable interest. This is relevant in the case of husband and wife and in other cases where genuine hardship will result from the death of the insured such as a business partner, *debtor* etc.

**insurance** The provision by payment of a *premium* to an insurance *underwriter* or *company* against the costs of damage resulting from possible events such as accident, fire, theft etc., as opposed to the provision for events that will certainly happen, such as death, which is termed *assurance.*

**insured scheme** *Pension* scheme where the only mode of *investment* is an *insurance* policy (but not a *unit-linked* policy).

**intangible asset** Name, brand, *intellectual property, goodwill.* See: *intangibles.*

**intangibles** Normally refers to *assets* that have no physical form such as *patents, royalties* or *intellectual property* generally.

**intellectual property** Intangible *assets* such as *patents* and *copyrights.*

**inter-bank** The market in *currencies* and *options* made by the leading *banks* and the only international market for *spot currencies.* See also: *London Inter-Bank Offered Rate.*

**inter-bank rate** See: *London Inter-Bank Offered Rate.*

**inter-broker** Another term for: *inter-dealer broker.*

**inter-dealer broker (IDB)** An intermediary who provides a dealing service to *market makers* and will confidentially match *bargains* between them.

**interdict** The name of an *injunction* in the Law of Scotland.

**interest** In borrowing *money,* interest is the payment of *money* separate from the amount borrowed (the principal) at certain time intervals. It represents the cost of using *money* belonging to another party. Interest is usually paid at regular time intervals (for instance, annually) and is generally expressed as a percentage of the principal borrowed, called the interest rate (or: rate of interest). If the interest is allowed to accumulate on top of the principal borrowed (ie not paid to back to the lender as it accrues), one speaks of *compound interest.* On the other hand, if the interest is not summed together with the principal one refers to *simple interest.* Thus in *simple interest,* if the interest rate per time period is r and constant, the principal borrowed is P and n is the number of time periods, then the total interest I payable is given by:

$$I = Prn$$

In the case of *compound interest,* the interest rate applies to the principal plus *accrued interest.* After the first period, the interest is calculated on the principal only, after the second period interest is calculated on the principal plus interest accrued in the first period, after the third period interest is calculated on the principal plus *accrued interest* in the first and second periods, and so on. Thus the interest payments (with a constant interest rate) increase in size, exponentially. If there is a constant interest rate r per time period, P is the principal borrowed and n is the number of time periods, then the total interest I payable after n time periods is given by:

$$I = P[(1 + r)^n - 1]$$

From this formula one can see that the more frequently the interest *compounds* (ie the shorter the time period in which interest is calculated), the higher the total interest payment. Thus an interest rate of say 4% per month is not at all the same as 48% per year (ie 12 times 4%). Legislation dictates that an equivalent *annual percentage rate (APR)* is shown on all forms of borrowing. This is calculated as follows, where *APR* is the annualised interest rate equivalent, n is the number of (equal-sized) time periods per year and r is the non-annual interest rate calculated on each of the n time periods:

$$APR = (1 + r)^n - 1$$

Hence, in the above example, 4% interest compounded monthly would give an *APR* of $[(1+0.04)^{12} - 1] = 60\%$.

**interest bearing eligible liabilities (IBEL)** Bank liabilities (such as customer *deposits*), a specific percentage of which may have to be deposited in the *Bank of England* on demand, for instance in the case of restricting *money supply* in the economy as part of government *monetary policy*. See: *corset*.

**interest cover** A *company*'s *ratio* of financial status that expresses how many times a *company*'s *earnings* (ie *profit* before *interest* and *tax*) can pay for the *interest* due on its *loan capital*. It is an indication of the *solvency* of a *company*, in that it shows how safe loan payments will be. Thus:

$$\text{interest cover} = \frac{\text{profit before interest payable and tax}}{\text{interest due on loan capital}}$$

**interest only mortgage** A *balloon mortgage* where only *interest* is paid and the principal repaid at the end of the *term* by a *sinking fund* accumulated by savings, normally an individual savings account, *endowment* or *pension*.

**interest rate future** An *investment* that allows protection or *speculation* against future movements in *interest rates*. In the UK, *interest rate futures* are dealt in on the *LIFFE*, using *contracts* for three-month *Sterling*, *eurobonds* and *euros* in the short term and *long gilts*, *US Treasury bonds* and *ECU bonds* in the *long term*.

**interest rate option** *Option contract* based on an underlying debt *security* (*bond*). *Options*, unlike *futures*, give their buyers the right, but not the obligation, to buy the underlying *bond* at a fixed price before a specific date in the future. *Option* sellers (*writers*) promise to *offer* the *bonds* at a set price at any time until the *contract* expires. In return for granting this right, the *option* buyer pays a *premium* to the *option* seller. Yield-based *calls* become more valuable as *yields* rise, and *puts* become more valuable as *yields* decline.

**interest rate risk** The *risk* that a *security's value* will fall if *interest rates* move. Usually fixed rate *bonds* will fall in *value* as rates rise. Interest rate risk is measured by *duration*.

**interest rate swap** A transaction where a *debt instrument* with a fixed *interest rate* is exchanged for a *debt instrument* with a floating *interest rate* and vice versa, normally occurring between *banks*, *companies* and *security* houses, where institutions want to position their debt *portfolios* in the light of their anticipation of the short-term movement in *interest rates*. If the *swap* is in the same *currency* it is a *currency interest rate swap*, if it is in different *currencies* it is referred to as a *cross currency interest rate swap*. See also: *rate anticipation swap*.

**interest rates**  Market *interest rates* depend on a range of *supply and demand* factors, which are determined by *money supply*, government restrictions, length and security of loan, availability of loans elsewhere, *foreign exchange rates, inflation* figures etc. See: *bank rate, base rate, Federal funds rate, fiscal policy, interest, London Inter-Bank Bid Rate, London Inter-Bank Offered Rate, monetary policy, prime rate.*

**interim**  In the case of *dividends* payable half-yearly, they are termed interim and final *dividends*. Quarterly *dividends* are referred to as first, second, third or fourth quarter. Generally speaking, *dividends* paid other than at the *company*'s year end.

**interim report**  See: *interim statement.*

**interim statement**  Financial report covering only a portion of the *fiscal year*. *Public companies* supplement their *annual report* with more frequent statements (normally at six-monthly intervals) informing *shareholders* of changes in the *balance sheet* and *profit & loss account*, as well as other newsworthy developments. Companies now also issue interim management statements for the first and third quarters. These may contain little or no accounting information.

**interim trust deed**  Used to establish a *pension* scheme using general or broadly stated terms, leaving detailed rules and provisions to be provided later by a *definitive trust deed*.

**internal balance**  A balanced domestic *budget*. See: *external balance.*

**internal rate of return (IRR)**  A *discounted cash flow* method used in *investment appraisal*. The *IRR* of an *investment* is the rate of *interest* that *discounts* the future flows to a *net present value* (*NPV*) of zero. In other words, it is the breakeven *cost of capital*. It is calculated in order to find the margin of safety on top of the investor's estimated *cost of capital*. In order to calculate the *IRR*, one must perform a number of different *NPV* calculations using different *interest rates* to find the *break even point* (the *IRR*) by trial and error – this is an iterative process best left to computers if a high degree of accuracy is required. Most spreadsheets contain an inbuilt function to calculate the IRR.

**Internal Revenue Service (IRS)**  Federal *US* agency whose responsibility is the collection of nearly all federal taxes, including *income* taxes (personal and corporate), social security taxes and excise and gift taxes. The *tax* rates are set by the *US* Department of the Treasury. The *IRS* pursues tax-law infringements in the *US* Tax Court. Equivalent to the former *UK Inland Revenue.*

**International Accounting Standard (IAS)**  One of a number of published standards of accounting practice with the intent of harmonising standard practice internationally, developed by the *International Accounting Standards Committee* (*IASC*). Founder members of the Committee are: *United States, United Kingdom, Japan, France, Germany* and the *Netherlands*. The International Accounting and Standards Board (*IASB*) was set up on 1 April 2001, and this body assumed accounting standard setting responsibilities from the *IASC*. *IASB* publishes its Standards in a series of pronouncements called International *Financial Reporting Standards* (*IFRS*). Those pronouncements are designated 'International Accounting Standards' (*IAS*).

**International Accounting Standards Board (IASB)**  The International Accounting Standards Board (*IASB*) is an independent, privately-funded accounting standard-setter based in London, *UK*. Board members come from nine countries and have a variety of functional backgrounds. Effective from 1 April 2001, the *IASB* assumed accounting standard setting responsibilities from its predecessor body, the *International Accounting*

*Standards Committee (IASC). IASB* publishes its Standards in a series of pronouncements called International *Financial Reporting Standards (IFRS)*. It has also adopted the body of Standards issued by the Board of the *International Accounting Standards Committee*. Those pronouncements continue to be designated '*International Accounting Standards*' (*IAS*).

**International Accounting Standards Committee (IASC)** The International Accounting Standards Committee (1973–2001) was the predecessor body of the *IASB*. *IASC* was founded in June 1973 as a result of an agreement by accountancy bodies in *Australia, Canada, France, Germany, Japan, Mexico,* the *Netherlands,* the *United Kingdom* and Ireland and the *United States* of *America,* and these countries constituted the board of *IASC* at that time. Prior to 1 April 2001, the *IASC* had the role of setting accounting standards. This role has now been adopted by the *International Accounting Standards Board (IASB)*.

**International Bank for Reconstruction and Development (IBRD)** Established in 1945, the International Bank for Reconstruction and Development (*IBRD*) aims to reduce poverty in middle-income and creditworthy poorer countries by promoting sustainable development, through loans, guarantees, and non-lending, including analytical and advisory services. *IBRD* does not maximise *profit* but has earned a *net income* each year since 1948. Its *profits* fund several developmental activities and ensure financial strength, which enables low-cost borrowings in *capital markets*, and good terms for borrowing clients. Owned by member countries, *IBRD* links voting power to members' *capital* subscriptions, in turn based on a country's relative economic strength. See also: *World Bank.*

**International Chamber of Commerce (ICC)** A Paris-based organisation that represents business people in international corporate affairs.

**International Commodities Clearing House (ICCH)** The *London Clearing House* formed in 1888 to provide clearing services initially for coffee and sugar trades and changed into an international *clearing house* in 1973. Serves as a *clearing house* for most *futures* markets in London, *Bermuda, Singapore, Australia,* and *New Zealand.* See also: *London Clearing House.*

**International Development Association (IDA)** See under: *World Bank.*

**International Finance Corporation (IFC)** See under: *World Bank.*

**International Fisher Effect** See: *Fisher Effect.*

**International Monetary Fund (IMF)** Formed as a result of the *Bretton Woods* Agreement of 1944, the *IMF* came into operation in March 1947. Its objective is to stabilise rates of exchange, remove *exchange controls*, promote *balance of payments equilibrium*, remove restrictions on international monetary movements and facilitate multilateral clearing systems. It shifted power from London to *America* and established the *US dollar* as the world's preeminent *trading currency*. Each member country was required to subscribe to the *IMF* a *quota* (25% *gold*, 75% member's *currency*), each member's *quota* being determined by an estimate of its means. After 1976 the requirement for subscription of *gold* was dropped in favour of international reserve *assets*. The *IMF* sold its *gold* holding to finance aid to developing countries. Up to 1971, the members of the *IMF* operated an *adjustable peg exchange rate* system. In 1970, the *IMF* created an artificial international reserve *asset* called *Special Drawing Rights* (*SDRs*). It assists all members that find themselves in temporary *balance of payments* difficulties by providing short- to medium-term (usually 3 to 5 years) loans, to stabilise their *exchange rates*. In order to join the *World Bank*, countries must first join the *IMF*, which imposes certain standards of economic and financial behaviour (see: *three-D*). To a considerable extent, the *IMF* has taken over the role of the *Bank for International Settlements* (*BIS*). Located at 700 19th Street, NW, Washington DC 20431, *USA*.

**International Monetary Market (IMM)**  See: *Chicago Mercantile Exchange*.

**International Petroleum Exchange (IPE)**  Established in 1980, a London-based petroleum energy *futures* and *options* exchange. Located in St Katherine Dock, it trades Monday to Friday from 9.15 am to 8.15 pm.

**intervention**  Normally when *central banks* become involved in the wholesale *currency* markets to influence movements in the *value* of a *currency* by buying or selling in these markets. Also external involvement in *commodity markets* to protect producer prices.

**intervention price**  The price at which the European Common Agricultural Policy supports certain farm products to maintain the price for the producer. See also: *buffer stock*.

**intestacy**  If a person in England or Wales dies without leaving a will (ie dies intestate), the *estate* will be divided up according to a set scheme. The deceased's *estate* vests in the Probate Judge until *letters of administration* have been granted, whereupon the *estate* is held on *trust* for sale and is then distributed according to the scheme set out in Section 46 of the Administration of Estates Act 1925 as amended, principally by the Estates Act 1952. In the following, note that 'issue' refers to all children of the deceased, regardless of whether legitimate, illegitimate or adopted:

- spouse only (ie no issue, parent, brother or sister, nephew or niece) surviving 28 days:
  - spouse takes everything absolutely.

- spouse and issue surviving 28 days:
  - spouse takes personal chattels (car, furniture, pictures, clothing, jewellery etc.) plus the first £250,000 absolutely plus life interest (*income* only) in half of residue (ie balance), and;
  - issue takes remainder (on reaching age 18 or marrying below that age).

- spouse, no issue but parent(s) or brother(s) or sister(s), or nephew(s) or niece(s) surviving 28 days:
  - spouse takes personal chattels plus £400,000 absolutely plus half residue absolutely, and;
  - parent(s), failing a parent, then brothers and sisters (nephews and nieces step into their parents' shoes if the latter are dead), take the remainder.

- no spouse. Everything is taken by the following if they survive 28 days:
  - issue, but if none;
  - parents, but if none;
  - brothers and sisters (nephews and nieces step into their parents' shoes), but if none;
  - grandparents, but if none;
  - uncles and aunts (cousins step into their parents' shoes), but if none;
  - the Crown.

Different rules apply in Scotland and Northern Ireland.

**intrinsic value**  The build-up in *value* of an *investment* not necessarily reflected by its price. For instance, a *call option* has intrinsic value if the *exercise price* of the *option* is lower than the price of the *underlying security*. The intrinsic value is the difference between the *exercise price* and the price of the *underlying security*. The *value* of an *asset* in a *balance sheet* may be quite different from its intrinsic value.

**introduction** When *shares* in a private *company* are already in issue, but not quoted, they may be introduced to a *stock exchange listing*, without the expense of marketing and advertising, where it can be established that the *shares* are freely marketable. This is effectively a *flotation* without all the costs of advertising and issuing a *prospectus* to potential private investors. However, it should be noted that an introduction may not be permitted if there has been a marketing of the *securities* within the six months prior to *listing*. See: *placing*.

**inventory** 1. The American word for: *stock* or *stock in trade*. 2. A general term used for the *stock* of finished goods, work-in-progress and raw materials held by businesses, ie the goods of a business, in some stage of production, not yet sold.

**inverted yield curve** See under: *yield curve*.

**investment** 1. Generally, 'investment' is *cash* expenditure on financial *securities* or other *assets* with the expectation of obtaining *income* (in the form of *dividends* or *interest* and the like) and/or *capital growth*. 2. (i) Economists use the term 'investment' to mean '*real capital* formation', which means *cash* expenditure for the creation of *real capital*, such as plant, machinery and equipment ('fixed investment') and *stocks* ('*inventory* investment'). The difference between this sense ('physical investment' or '*real* investment') and the general sense (sense 1: called 'financial investment') is that the former refers to creating new *assets*, which thus add to the economy's productive capacity, whereas the latter refers to transferring the ownership of existing *assets* from one person or institution to another, which economists do not regard as investment since it is only savings that change from one form to another. (ii) In national accounts, investment is the sum of *gross* fixed *capital* formation plus the physical change in inventories by the *private sector*.

**investment analyst** Specialist in the appraisal of *investments*. Analysts usually use a combination of *fundamental analysis* and *technical analysis* to evaluate the *quality* and predict the future price movement of *investments*. See also: *investment appraisal*.

**investment appraisal** A process of examining a prospective *investment* or a *portfolio* of *investments* in order to see whether they are viable. This is a type of cost-benefit or *quantitative analysis*. Investment appraisal seeks to find the expected return on an *investment*, which must be weighed according to the anticipated *risk* involved. Simple return-evaluating techniques include *payback period* (PP) and *accounting rate of return* (ARR) which are easy to calculate but do not take into account the time *value* of *money* (ie reinvesting funds at a certain *interest rate*). More advanced methods include mainly *discounted cash flow* techniques such as the *net present value* (NPV) and *internal rate of return* (IRR) calculations. Another way of calculating the expected return involves taking a statistical *mean* of past price movements, where a measure of *risk* using the *standard deviation* of price movements can be made. Thus a risk-return profile can be established and may be compared with the *risk* acceptable to the investor. Compare: *performance appraisal*. See also: *analysis, capital asset pricing model, investment analyst*.

**investment bank** A US *bank* similar to a *UK bank* dealing with *mergers* and *acquisitions* and *corporate finance* as well as dealing in *securities* for their clients. Arose primarily because commercial *banks* in *America* were prevented from selling *securities* until the late 1980s. In the *UK* an *investment* banker is a financial intermediary who provides similar services, including selection of target firms, formulation of strategy and tactics, arranging finance and making direct *investments* themselves.

**investment bond** Single-premium *unit-linked life assurance* policy that is expressed by a unit allocation in an *asset backed life assurance* fund. These funds can be invested in a specific managed *portfolio* of *investments* or *securities* such as property, *gilts*, *UK* or overseas *equities, cash* or even with-profit funds. Investors can vary their unit allocations by switching between these funds at minimal cost without creating a *tax* charge. Internally, *tax* is charged on realised gains with no exemptions and *income* is taxed at the equivalent of *basic rate tax*, although *franked income* already reflects this charge. Growth and *income* from such *bonds* issued by UK life companies creates no *tax* charge in the hands of *basic rate* taxpayers and 5% of the initial *investment* may be withdrawn each year cumulatively to 100% on a tax-deferred basis. Any excess of this amount will be liable to higher rate *income tax*. Upon final surrender, the gain within the *investment bond* is 'top sliced' to determine the *tax* charge. If the investor is a basic-rate taxpayer at this stage there will be no taxation on the *profits*. Offshore life company *investment bonds* are taxed differently. See: *top slicing*.

**Investment Company Institute (ICI)** The USA equivalent of the *Investment Management Association*. The ICI universe in January 2009 included 8,045 mutual funds with a value of $9,411 bn.

**investment club** Group of individuals who pool their resources and decide where best to invest their *capital*. The advantages of such action are that it increases the *spread* of *risk* and reduces *broker* charges. This form of *investment* has become less popular due to the prominence of *unit trusts* and *investment bonds* where specialist *management* can be obtained.

**investment company** *Company* whose main source of *income* and *profits* is derived via the buying, selling or letting of *'investments'*, eg property. The majority of corporate *tax* advantages are denied to such *companies*. Many listed investment companies are based offshore.

**investment fund** See: *fund manager*.

**investment grade** This refers to the quality of an issuer's credit. A *bond* is investment grade if its credit is rated BBB- or higher by *Standard and Poor's*, BAA3 or higher by *Moody's* or BBB- or higher by Fitch. *Bonds* that are below investment grade are referred to as high *yield bonds*.

**Investment Management Association (IMA)** The association set up to promote the interests of collective *investments* in the *UK*; formerly the responsibility of the UTA (Unit Trust Association) and Association of Unit Trusts and Investment Funds (AUTIF).

**Investment Management Certificate (IMC)** The basic qualification recognised by the *Financial Services Authority* for those involved in *investment* management. The exam covers a broad range of investment-related topics, particularly *quantitative analysis*, statistics, markets, *accounts* and the regulatory environment. Courses are run by Hyperion and exams by the Institute of Investment Management and Research.

**Investment Management Regulatory Organisation (IMRO)** The former regulator for wholesale and retail *investment* management firms. All regulatory functions now controlled by the *FSA*, as a result of the *Financial Services and Markets Act 2000*.

**Investment Services Directive (ISD)** The ISD, first implemented on 1 January 1996. The ISD brought the single market into effect throughout Europe. It allowed regulated investment management firms falling within its scope to do business in the *EU* other than in their home member state. Such firms also have to comply with the *Capital Adequacy Directive*. The ISD was replaced by the *Market in Financial Investments Directive (MiFID)* from 1 November 2007.

**investment trust** A common name for a *company* quoted on the *London Stock Exchange* which has a fixed number of *shares*. The *value* of these *shares*, like any other *company*, is determined by *supply and demand*. The *shares* do not therefore normally reflect the *value* of its *underlying assets* and are sometimes at a *discount* on *net asset value*. Basically a trading *investment company*, it can borrow to provide *gearing*, can invest in a very wide range of *securities*, both *listed* and unlisted, and can *hedge* any *currency risks*. Investment trusts are now generally called investment companies. The Association of Investment Trust Companies changed its name to the Association of Investment Companies in October 2006.

**invisibles** Items included in a country's *balance of payments* not taken into account in its *balance of trade,* eg *insurance,* banking, tourism.

**invitation to treat** A term used in the law of *contract* to distinguish between a firm *offer* (which can on acceptance constitute a *contract*) and an invitation to treat, which merely posts a price or encourages an *offer,* and in the absence of a specific *offer* is not enforceable.

**invoice discounting** Where a *company* sells its debts at a *discount* to a third party. See: *factoring.*

**IoD** See: *Institute of Directors.*

**IOU** Legally binding document of debt. Not to be confused with a *promissory note.*

**IPE** See: *International Petroleum Exchange.*

**IPO** See: *initial public offering.* Americanism for *flotation.*

**IQD** *currency code* for: Iraqi Dinar.

**IRA** See: *Individual Retirement Account.*

**Iran** The Tehran Stock Exchange (TSE) was established in 1966. In 2009 the number of *listed companies* was 120. Its main *index* is:

• Tehran Stock Exchange Composite Index (TEPIX).

Standard *currency*: *rial.* 1 *rial* = 100 *dinars.*

**Iraq** The Iraq Stock Exchange (ISX – formerly the Baghdad Stock Exchange) but revived in 2004. It now has over 100 listed companies. The main index is the Iraq Stock Exchange Index (ISX). Standard *currency*: *dinar.* 1 *dinar* = 1,000 *fils.*

**Irish Futures and Options Exchange (IFOX)** An exchange established in 1989 in Dublin, Ireland. Mainly involved in Irish gilt *futures.*

**IRR** 1. See: *internal rate of return.* 2. *currency code* for: Iranian Rial.

**irredeemable security** A *security* which has no *redemption date.* Some *debentures* and *Consols* are irredeemable securities. Irredeemable securities are also called: irredeemables.

**IRS** See: *Internal Revenue Service.* The *US* equivalent of the former *Inland Revenue* in the *UK.*

**IS curve** A curve used in demand-side macroeconomic *analysis* that shows the combinations of *interest rates* and levels of *real national income* for which the desired aggregate expenditure equals the actual *national income.* It is called the 'IS curve' because, in the simple case of a closed economy (ie no international trade) and no government, it shows the combinations for which *investment* equals saving. For the more general model, it shows the combinations for which *injections* equal *withdrawals* in an economy. See: *circular flow of national income.* See also: *LM curve, Mundell–Fleming model.*

**ISA** See: *Individual Savings Account.*

**ISD** See: *Investment Services Directive.*

**ISK** *currency code* for: *Iceland* Krona.

**Islamic finance** The strict rules of Islam normally prevent making *profits* from or with non-Islamic parties and receiving *interest* on *capital*. However, internal *profits* within the Islamic community may be made.

**Islamic financial terms** Under Islam there are certain doctrinal restrictions relating to the payment of *interest* on loans and other related financial matters. Commerce has therefore developed its own contractual terms and disciplines which apparently conform to Islamic practice and these include: *Al-ajr, Bai al-dayn, Bai al salam, Bai bithaman ajil, Gharar, Ijara, Ijara wa-iqtina, Istisna, Murubaha, Mudaraba, Musharaka, Qard ul basan, Al-rahn, Riba*, Shariah, *Zakat*.

**isoquant** In microeconomic *analysis*, an isoquant is a curve (when only two factors of production are considered) or a surface (for the complex case of three factors) indicating all the technologically efficient combinations of the *factors of production* under consideration in producing a specified amount of output.

**Israel** The Tel-Aviv Stock Exchange (TASE) was established in 1953. In 2008, over 600 *companies* were *listed*. The main *index* is:

• TA-25. It contains the 25 most liquid and heavily capitalised *shares*, and is weighted according to *market capitalisation*. Base: 1 January 1992 = 100.

Standard *currency*: *sheqel*. 1 *sheqel* = 100 *agora*.

**issue by tender** Also called: sale by *tender*. The *offer* of new *shares* or *loan stock* based on the price that potential purchasers are willing to *bid*. A minimum price is normally set and the highest *bidders* will receive *stock* in proportion to the size of their *bid* at the *strike price*. See: *tender*.

**issued capital** The *capital* which is actually held and paid for by *shareholders*, as distinct from *authorised capital* which is authorised by the *company's Memorandum of Association*.

**Istisna** An Islamic term for a *contract* of acquisition of goods by specification or order, where the price is paid progressively in accordance with the progress of a job completion. This is practised, for example, for purchases of houses to be constructed where the payments made to the developer or builder are according to the stage of work completed. In Islamic financing, the applications of *Bai al salam* and Istisna are as purchasing mechanisms, whereas *Murubaha* and *Bai bithaman ajil* are for financing sales.

**Italy** The Italian Stock Exchange in Milan was established in 1808 by decree of Viceroy Eugène Napoléon. In 1993, all Italian *stock markets* were united into the one national Italian Stock Exchange. Its main *indices* are:

• MIBTEL General Index – which is the principal *index*. It comprises all *shares* on the computerised trading system. It is an open *index*, which means that it will include any new *shares* entering the system. Base: 16 July 1993 = 10,000.

• MIB 30 – This basket *index* includes the 30 leading *shares*, weighted by *market capitalisation*. Base: 31 December 1992 = 10,000.

Standard *currency*: *euro*. 1 *euro* = 100 *cents*. Italy used to have the *lira* as its *currency*, until the adoption of the *euro* on 1 January 2002.

**itayose** A term denoting that all orders arriving at a Japanese *broker's* office before domestic markets open for trading are deemed to have arrived at the same time and are dealt when the exchange opens.

**ITL** *currency code* for: Italian Lira.

**IVA** See: *individual voluntary arrangement*.

**Ivory Coast**  The Abidjan Stock Exchange (*BVA*) was established in 1974 and closed in 1997. It was replaced by a regional exchange (BRUM) covering Ivory Coast and six of it's neighbours, the first regional stock exchagne in the world. The number of *companies listed* in 2009 was 38. The main *index* is: BVRM 10. Base: 15 September 1998 = 100. Standard *currency*: African *franc*.

# J

**J curve** Shape of the curve showing the effect of *currency depreciation* or a *devaluation* on the *current account*. The J curve effect occurs when the prices of *exports* become cheaper as measured in terms of foreign *currency* and *imports* become more expensive measured in domestic *currency* immediately after the domestic *currency* weakens, and this leads to a worsening of the *current account*. After a while, however, the effect of more expensive *imports* and more competitively priced *exports* improves the *current account*. In the diagram

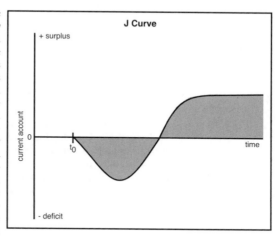

an effective *devaluation* occurs at time $t_0$ (before that time the *current account* is assumed to be at *equilibrium*). The J curve effect manifests itself by a short-run worsening of the *current account* followed by a gradual improvement as *market forces* come into play. Empirical studies suggest the short-run is about six months. The overall effect of this *devaluation* on the *current account* is represented by the shaded area. The *devaluation* is said to be effective if the area above the curve is less than the area subsequently under it, ie there is an overall improvement in the *current account*. Empirical studies estimate this to take about two years. See also: *Marshall–Lerner condition*.

**Jamaica** The Jamaican Stock Exchange was established in Kingston in 1968. In 2008, the number of *listed companies* was 43. Standard *currency*: Jamaican *dollar*. 1 Jamaican *dollar* = 100 *cents*.

**January effect** US term referring to the observation that *stocks* tend to rise appreciably between the *last trading day* in December and the fourth trading day in January. Attributed to the year-end sale of *stocks* for *tax* purposes, holiday *money* or for window-dressing a client's *portfolio*, followed by traders capitalising on the *undervalued stocks* which subsequently causes the market to rise.

**Japan** The largest of Japan's *stock exchanges* is the Tokyo Stock Exchange, established in 1878. The main *indices* pertaining to the TSE are:

- Tokyo Stock Price Index (TOPIX). An *index* of all *common stocks* on the 'First Section' of the exchange (all domestic). Weighted by *market value*. Base: 4 January 1968 = 100.

- TSE Second Section Index. The 'Second Section' (smaller *companies*) comprises those *stocks* that do not meet the requirements of the 'First Section' used in TOPIX. Newly *listed* domestic *stocks* are usually assigned to this category. Base: 4 January 1968 = 100.

- Nikkei Stock Index 225 (see: *Nikkei 225*). Comprises 225 *stocks* from the First Section of the TSE. It is an unweighted arithmetic *index*. Suitable for monitoring the level of the market and its changes.

- Nikkei Stock Index 300. Comprises 301 *stocks* from the First Section of the TSE. It is a weighted arithmetic *index*. It is suitable for tracking the *value* of the market.

Osaka Securities Exchange (OSE) is one of Japan's oldest and most respected *securities* exchanges. Main *index*:

- OSE 300 Common Stock Index. Reflects changes in aggregate *market value* of component issues. Base: 4 January 1968 = 100.

Nagoya Stock Exchange. Main *index*:

- Option 25 Index. It is structured in such a way as to be highly representative of the Japanese *stock market* as a whole.

On 1 April 1998, Japan pushed through a series of '*Big Bang*' financial reforms, designed to boost the *value* of the Japanese *stock market* and 'Internationalise' trading practices. Faced with a rapidly ageing population, the Japanese government feared there would not be enough *money* in the economy to support future pensioners. Its solution was to push through a series of radical reforms designed to change the way *money* flows around the economy and encourage *capital* flows into its *equity* markets. Other *stock markets* are: Fukuoka Stock Exchange, Hiroshima Stock Exchange, Kyoto Stock Exchange, Niigata Stock Exchange and the Sapporo Securities Exchange. Standard *currency*: yen. See: *Big Four*.

**Japanese method (yield)**  See under: *yield*.

**Jensen measure**  See: *performance appraisal*.

**JGB**  A Japanese government *bond*. JGB *futures* are traded on the *London International Financial Futures and Options Exchange* (LIFFE).

**jiao**  *Currency* sub-unit of *China*. 10 jiao = 1 *yuan*.

**JMD**  *currency code* for: Jamaican Dollar.

**JOD**  *currency code* for: Jordanian Dinar.

**joint and several liability**  Where such an undertaking or guarantee is made by a number of parties, the entire responsibility for the undertaking or guarantee applies wholly to each individual. Accordingly, each party to the agreement is individually responsible for the entire undertaking.

**joint investments**  Where an *investment* is purchased by more than one individual, the *certificate* will bear the names of all the holders, in which case only the first named receives notices. On disposal it is necessary for all holders to renounce the holding.

**joint-life annuities**  *Annuities* that involve two people (usually husband and wife). A joint-life annuity begins payment on a specified date and continues until both persons have died.

**joint-life assurance**  Life assurance on a married couple (or two parties with a demonstrable *insurable interest*) which pays either on the first (first death) or second (last survivor) of their respective deaths.

**joint-stock bank**  Banking and money-lending services were originally provided by private individuals and *partnerships*, but after some notable collapses in the 17th century some *banks* were supported by external stockholders. These *banks* found it easier to raise *capital*, as a stockholder's liability was limited only to the *value* of their *investment*, and they became public *banks*, as opposed to private *banks* who dealt only in operations approved by the partners. Public *banks* are now know as *clearing banks* and are *listed companies*. Private *banks* now tend to be limited, though many still use the *partnership* logo and '& Co.' in their title.

**joint-stock company** 1. In the *UK*, joint-stock companies are normally referred to as *limited companies,* ie the liability of the *shareholders* is limited to the *nominal value* of the *shares* they have taken up. 2. Also refers more specifically to a type of *company* originating from the 17th century where partners pooled their *stock* with that of outside investors. 3. In the *US*, a joint-stock company is a corporation with *unlimited liability* for its stockholders on a joint and several basis. Some advantages are that the *tax* burden is lighter, there is less regulation, the *company* is easily established and there is more security for *creditors*. On the other hand, it usually cannot hold the title to property (*real estate*) and the investor's individual liability is unacceptable to most investors.

**joint venture** A contractual agreement where two or more parties undertake a business activity under joint control.

**Jonestown defence** Americanism for *bid* defence tactics so extreme as to appear suicidal. The term first appeared during the Bendix/Martin Marietta/Allied/United Technologies battle in 1982/83. See: *poison pill*.

**Jordan** The Amman *stock exchange* was established in 1976. In 2009 the number of *listed shares* was 263. Standard *currency*: *dinar*. 1 *dinar* = 1,000 *fils*.

**JPY** *currency code* for: Japanese Yen.

**junior capital** See: *junior issue*.

**junior issue** *Stocks* or *shares* that are subsidiary when it comes to receiving *dividends, rights issues* or repayment of *capital* in the event of *liquidation*.

**junior security** See: *junior issue*.

**junk bond** *Loan stock* below *Standard & Poor's BBB-rating Moody's* treble-B *rating*, often where the *underlying security* is based on something that is more imagined than real. Often used to finance a *leveraged buyout* and based on the security of the *assets* of the *target*. Originally junk bonds tended to be underwritten by benign institutions aiding a *takeover* where the *bidder* is less substantial than the *target*. These days many junk bonds are *fallen angels*, bonds which initially had investment grade rating but were subsequently downgraded. The more common – and polite – term for junk bonds is now high yield bonds. See: *credit rating*.

**just in time** A method of *stock* control pioneered by the Japanese where minimal *stock* is held on site to save space and costs and where parts etc. are delivered just prior to use or 'just in time'.

# K

**kaffirs** Slang for South African *shares* quoted on the *London Stock Exchange*, especially in gold-mining *companies*.

**kaizen** Japanese word of continuous daily personal and *productivity* improvement.

**kangaroos** Slang for Australian *shares* quoted on the *London Stock Exchange*, especially when those *shares* are in tobacco, mining and land *companies*.

**Kazakhstan** Standard *currency*: tenge. 1 tenge = 100 teins.

**Kenya** The Nairobi Stock Exchange (NSE) was established in 1954. The number of *companies listed* in 2009 was 55. The main *index* is:

- Nairobi Stock Exchange – 20 Index (NSE 20). Base: 1966 = 100.

Standard *currency*: shilling. 1 *shilling* = 100 *cents*.

**Keogh plan** A *pension* scheme in the *US* established in 1962 for employees, unincorporated businesses and self-employed persons which allows contributions to a certain limit ($46,000 in 2008). Investment returns are not taxed until withdrawal of *capital*, similar to the *Individual Retirement Account* (*IRA*).

**kerb** The word 'kerb' has a special significance for the *London Metal Exchange*: during the official trading on the *LME* each metal is traded in turn for two five-minute periods in the morning and afternoon; these sessions are called *rings*. Once the *rings* are over, a period of trading occurs during which all metals are traded simultaneously and this is called the kerb. See: *kerb trading*. Compare: *curb*.

**kerb trading** 1. The name of this form of trading is derived directly from the original method of trading on the London markets. Once official trading was finished, *dealers* would leave the exchange and gather in the street (or at the 'kerb') to conclude any further business. 2. Sometimes after-hours trading over the telephone is called the 'late-kerb'.

**KES** *currency code* for: Kenyan Shilling.

**key person insurance** *Life assurance* policy effected on the life of an individual whose death would create a loss of *earnings* for his or her *company*. Key person *insurance* is appropriate in the case of *companies* where the death of a key executive would cause a disproportionate financial loss.

**key reversal** Chart term describing a price movement after a new peak or trough which is not sustained. Generally an indication of a pause but continuation in a general *trend*. See: *technical analysis*.

**Keynesian economics** School of economic thought based on the writings of John Maynard Keynes (1883–1946) and specifically his work: 'The General Theory of Employment, Interest and Money', which was published in 1935. A believer in active government intervention as the only genuine method of ensuring economic *growth* and stability, he suggested that government expenditure and taxation were the only way of ensuring a balance between *unemployment* and *inflation*. He held that market economies would only provide a balance in the long run, with wild boom and bust cycles in the interim. He also suggested that in the long run we were all dead (in response to a criticism that his theories focused only on the short run).

**KGS** *currency code* for: *Kyrgyzstan* Som.

**khoum** A *currency* unit of *Mauritania*. 5 khoums = 1 *ouguiya*.

**KHR** *currency code* for: Kampuchean Riel.

**kicker** Feature added to a *security* or other debt facility to make it more attractive to investors. Thus, in addition to *interest* payments, the investor may be able to obtain *equity* linked to the debt facility. An example of an *equity* kicker is a *warrant*. Also called: *sweetener*.

**killer bees** Usually *investment* bankers who devise strategies to help *companies* fend off *takeover bids* by making them less attractive or more difficult to acquire.

**kina** *Papua New Guinea*'s standard *currency* unit. 1 kina = 100 *toea*.

**kip** The standard *currency* unit of *Laos*. 1 kip = 100 *att*.

**Kiribati** Standard *currency*: Kiribati *dollar*. 1 Kiribati *dollar* = 100 *cents*.

**kite** Slang for a cheque drawn on an account where there are, or are likely to be, insufficient funds to meet it. Kiting is depositing and drawing cheques between accounts at two or more *banks* and thereby taking advantage of the *float*, ie the time it takes for the *bank* to deposit and collect from the paying *bank*. Kiting can also be used as slang for the act of issuing or presenting a dud cheque.

**kiting** See: *kite*.

**KMF** *currency code* for: *Comoros* Franc.

**know your customer** In the *US*, as stated in the National Association of Securities Dealers (*NASD*) 'Rules of Fair Practice', the *broker* must satisfy him or herself of the requirements of the client in order to properly recommend *investments*. Similar regulations apply in the *UK*, where customers complete a comprehensive fact finding questionnaire supplied by their financial advisor.

**kobo** *Currency* unit of *Nigeria*. 100 kobo = 1 *naira*.

**Kondratieff wave** The theory that capitalist economies are prone to major economic cycles lasting 50 to 60 years. Proposed by the Soviet economist Nikolai Kondratieff in the 1920s, who claimed to have predicted the economic *crash* of 1929–1930 based on the *crash* in 1869, sixty years earlier. Severe market *volatility* in 1987 gave the theory renewed credibility. See: *business cycle*.

**koruna** Standard *currency* unit of both the *Czech Republic* and *Slovakia*. 1 koruna = 100 *haleru*.

**KPW** *currency code* for: North Korean Won.

**krona** Standard *currency* of *Sweden*. 1 krona = 100 *öre*.

**króna** Standard *currency* unit of *Iceland*. 1 króna = 100 *aurar*.

**krone** Standard *currency* unit of *Denmark*, the *Faeroe Islands*, *Greenland* and *Norway*. 1 krone = 100 *øre*.

**kroon** *Estonia*'s standard *currency*. 1 kroon = 100 *senti*.

**kruggerand** Gold *bullion* coin minted by the Republic of *South Africa*. The coin comes in four sizes (measured in *troy weights*): one-tenth ounce, one-quarter ounce, one-half ounce and one ounce.

**KRW** *currency code* for: South Korean Won.

**Kuna** Croatia's standard currency 1 kuna = 100 lipa

**kuru** A *currency* unit of *Turkey*. 100 kuru = 1 *lira*. Not effectively used anymore, due to *hyperinflation* in *Turkey*. The smallest legal *tender* is currently the 25,000 *lira* coin. At the current *exchange rate*, this coin is worth $0.0175 (current *exchange rate* $1 = 1.5m *lira*).

**Kuwait** The Kuwait Stock Exchange, located in Safat, was established in 1984. Trading operations were suspended in August 1990 after the Iraqi invasion, and recommenced in September 1992. The number of *listed companies* in 2009 was 224. The main *index* is:

- Kuwait Stock Exchange Index, comprising all *listed companies*. Base: 31 December 1993 = 100.

Standard *currency*: *dinar*. 1 *dinar* = 1,000 *fils*.

**kwacha** Standard *currency* of the following countries: *Malawi*: 1 kwacha = 100 *tambala*; *Zambia*: 1 kwacha = 100 *ngwee*.

**kwanza** *Angola*'s standard *currency*. 1 kwanza = 100 *lwei*.

**KWD** *currency code* for: Kuwaiti Dinar.

**kyat** *Myanmar*'s standard *currency*. 1 kyat = 100 *pyas*.

**KYD** *currency code* for: *Cayman Islands* Dollar.

**Kyrgyzstan** Standard *currency*: *som*. 1 *som* = 100 tiyin.

**KZT** *currency code* for: *Kazakhstan* Tenge.

# L

**laari** *Currency* sub-unit of the *Maldives*. 100 laari = 1 *rufiyaa*.

**labour force** The population between the age of 16 and 65 available for work. Statistically this is normally taken to mean those in work plus those registered as unemployed. See: *frictional unemployment*.

**Lady Macbeth strategy** *Bid* situation where a third party appears to be a *white knight* but then changes allegiance and joins the *bidder*.

**Laffer curve** A curve showing the relationship between total *tax* revenue and the *tax* rate. *Tax* revenues are not directly proportional to *tax* rates. Higher *tax* rates act as a disincentive and encourage efforts to avoid *tax* or take advantage of deductions; furthermore, businesses and taxpayers will move to lower *tax* locations in extreme cases (for example, the 'brain drain' in the *UK* in the 1970s when the highest marginal rate of *income tax* reached 98%). As the diagram shows, as the *tax* rate as

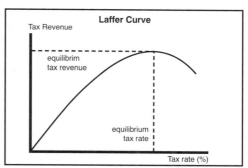

a proportion of *gross income* is raised, the revenue received initially goes up. However, if the *tax* rate is raised above a certain level (depicted as r* in the diagram), there is a significant disincentive effect on the *labour force*, and some workers will decide to leave employment (see: *poverty trap*). The American economist Arthur Laffer suggests that *productivity* and *investment* are actually encouraged by lower *tax* rates and this leads to increased economic output and ultimately higher *tax* revenues.

**LAFTA** See: *Latin America Free Trade Association*.

**lagging indicators** Economic *indicators* that lag behind the overall pace of the economy. The six main lagging indicators are the *unemployment* rate, business spending, unit labour costs, *bank* lending, the *inflation* rate and the *book value* of manufacturing *stock in trade* (*inventory*). Changes in an economy tend to occur before there is any significant change in the overall *value* or rate of such *indicators* and to detect more immediate and relevant indications of change one needs to refer to monthly or weekly changes in *leading indicators*.

**LAK** *currency code* for: Lao Kip.

**Land Bank** Another term for: *Agricultural Bank*.

**Landesbank** A German regional bank, often with large shareholdings owned by the local savings bank and state government. There are seven Landesbanks, which used to rely heavily on state guarantees for cheap funding until the EU banned the practice under state aid rules.

**Land Registry** Government department responsible for keeping records concerning the ownership of all property in England and Wales. All *freehold* property transfers need to be registered.

**Lands Tribunal** Court set up to establish the *value* of land acquired by compulsory purchase.

**Laos** Standard *currency*: *kip*. 1 *kip* = 100 atts.

**LAPR**  See: *Life Assurance Premium Relief.*

**large company**  A company that meets at least two of the following criteria (in its first financial year, or in the case of a subsequent year, in that year and the preceding year): 251 or more employees, a balance sheet of more than £11.4 million, *turnover* of more than £22.8 million. See: *blue chip, Normal Market Size, SME.*

**Lari**  Georgia's standard currency. 1 lari = 100 tetri

**Laspeyres formula**  See under: *composite index, weighting factor.*

**Laspeyres index**  See under: *composite index, weighting factor.*

**last in first out (LIFO)**  A method of charging *stock* (*inventory*) to the *profit & loss account* which treats the most recently purchased items as those used in production. This method is not acceptable to *HMRC* in the *UK*. For costing and *stock valuation* purposes the *values* of the last items taken into *stock* are those used. The cost of goods sold is calculated by adding the *value* of the beginning *inventory* to purchases and subtracting the final *inventory*. In contrast to the *first in first out* (*FIFO*) method, *LIFO* produces a higher cost of goods sold and thus a lower *gross profit* and hence less taxable *income*.

**last trading day**  The day on which *futures* trading ceases for a particular delivery month.

**lasting power of attorney**  Created by the Mental Capacity Act 2005, which came into effect on 1 October 2007 to replace the enduring *power of attorney* (EPA). Any individual is able to choose an attorney to take decisions on his/her behalf if capacity is later lost. An LPA can cover personal welfare matters as well as financial decisions. An EPA created before 1 October 2007 continues to have effect.

**Lat**  Latvia's standard currency 1 lat = 100 santimi.

**Latin America Free Trade Association (LAFTA)**  A free-trade area, formed in 1960, originally having seven members: *Argentina, Brazil, Peru, Chile, Mexico, Paraguay* and *Uruguay*; three other members joined later: *Colombia, Ecuador* and *Venezuela*. Due to differences in the level of economic development between member nations and sovereignty issues for policies, a number of the economically weaker members formed the Andean Group in 1966.

**Latvia**  The Riga Stock Exchange (RSE) was established in 1993. Standard *currency*: lat. 1 lat = 100 santims.

**laundering**  See: *money laundering.*

**LBMA**  See: *London Bullion Market Association.*

**LBO**  See: *leveraged buyout.*

**LBP**  *currency code* for: Lebanese Pound.

**LCH**  See: *London Clearing House.*

**LCH.Clearnet**  A *clearing house* formed from the merger of the London Clearing House (LCH) and Clearnet SA in 2003. LCH itself had roots going back to 1888. LCH.Clearnet is one of the leading independent central counterparty groups in Europe, serving major international exchanges and platforms and a range of over-the-counter markets. In the UK LCH.Clearnet is the clearing house for the London Stock Exchange, PLUS markets, LIFFE, and the London Metal Exchange. LCH.Clearnet is owned 73.3% by users, 10.9% by exchanges and 15.8% by Euroclear.

**LDC**  Short for: less-developed country.

**LDI**  See: *liability driven investment.*

**lead investor/bank/insurer/underwriter**  When a group of people interested in supporting an enterprise get together they will normally appoint, or expect there to be, a lead supporter of the project to co-ordinate all the relevant enquiries or *due diligence.*

This is normally someone with an understanding of the business or the *management* and who is respected by the other participants enough to encourage them to participate.

**leading indicators** To determine any changes in an economy it is important to remember that major economic statistics are historic and will lag behind events (see: *lagging indicators*). To better determine near-term changes in the future, analysts will consider business surveys of confidence and order books and consumer spending as well as borrowing activity, short-term *money supply* statistics, raw material prices etc. In *America* there is an *index* of leading indicators compiled by the *US* Commerce Department. The *index* comprises 11 components: the *average* work week of production workers, *average* weekly claims for state *unemployment insurance*, manufacturers' new orders for consumer goods and materials, vendor performance (*companies* receiving slower deliveries from suppliers), *contracts* and orders for plant and equipment, building permits, changes in manufacturers' unfilled orders for durable goods, changes in sensitive materials prices, *stock* prices, *money supply* and an *index* of consumer expectations. In the *UK* the *CBI* carries out a number of such surveys primarily gauged at determining business confidence. See also: *Tankan survey*.

**lean back** Technique in *currency intervention* where a *central bank* will wait until the *momentum* of a recent price *trend* abates before intervening.

**LEAPS** Short for: long-term *equity* anticipation *securities*. LEAPS are long-term *equity options* traded on *US* exchanges and in *over-the-counter markets*, which expire in two or three years (rather than the conventional two to six months), giving buyers a longer time for their strategy to become effective. LEAPS are traded on many individual *stocks listed* on the *NYSE*, *AMEX* and *NASDAQ*.

**lease** See: *leasing*.

**lease purchase** Often used to describe a way of generating *cash* from an *asset* you already own by selling it and then buying it back, by leasing it over a period of years from the purchaser.

**leaseback** An operation whereby an *asset* is purchased from and leased back to its original holder. Businesses often use sale and leaseback of property as a means of raising finance. See: *leasing*.

**leasing** Leasing of an *asset* is based on the concept that it is not necessary to own an *asset* in order to have the use of it. By leasing a piece of equipment a *company* can avoid the heavy *capital* outlay of purchasing it. Leased *assets* remain the property of the leasing *company* and leasing payments are fully deductible as they do not represent the *capital* purchase of an *asset*. A *balloon* payment at the end of the *lease* may secure ownership.

**Lebanon** Standard *currency*: Lebanese *pound*. 1 Lebanese *pound* = 100 *piastres*.

**Legacy Securities/Loan Programme** See: *Private Partnership Investment Programme*.

**lei** See: *leu*.

**lek** Standard *currency* unit of *Albania*. 1 lek = 100 *qindar*.

**lemon** An American expression for a dud product. A car that continually needs repair is a lemon and consumers are guaranteed a full refund in several American states under so-called 'lemon laws'. A promising *share* that fails to live up to expectations is also called a lemon.

**lempira** Standard *currency* of *Honduras*. 1 lempira = 100 *centavos*.

**lender of last resort** A *central bank* with responsibility for controlling a country's banking system, subsidiary *banks* and *money supply*. In the *UK*, the *Bank of England* fulfils this role, lending on paper *assets* or granting loans directly and setting the *base rate*. The *BoE* also acts to ensure the stability of the banking system by bailing out *banks* if necessary as a last resort.

**leone** Standard *currency* of *Sierra Leone*. 1 leone = 100 *cents*.

**Lesotho** Standard *currency*: *loti*. 1 *loti* = 100 *lisente*.

**letter of allotment** See: *allotment*.

**letter of comfort** See: *comfort letter*.

**letter of credit** Confirmation of the credit available from a *bank* or other financial institutions up to a certain limit.

**letter of hypothecation** See: *hypothecation*.

**letters of administration** Issued by the Probate Court appointing an *administrator* to an *estate*.

**leu** Standard *currency* of *Romania*. Plural of 'leu' is: *lei*. 1 leu = 100 *bani*.

**lev** Standard *currency* of *Bulgaria*. Plural of 'lev' is: *leva*. 1 lev = 100 *stotinki*.

**leva** See: *lev*.

**level playing field** A term applied to the basis on which *companies* should compete and most particularly the revision of legislation and *tax* rules governing financial products, which changed in the 1980s to allow *banks* and *building societies*, among others, to compete on equal terms.

**leverage** An Americanism for *gearing* where *companies* will use a limited *asset* base to generate substantial borrowings for speculative or business purposes.

**leveraged buyout (LBO)** Where a group of individuals or a *company* will use limited *assets* to generate substantial borrowings from a benign source to acquire a larger *target company*. These borrowings are often translated into *stock* payable from the *profits*, *assets* or *cash flow* of the combined group. This *loan stock* is usually classed as a *junk bond*. See: *leverage*.

**Lex** Influential market comment section on the back page of the first section of the *Financial Times*. Former authors include Nigel (now Lord) Lawson and Ed Balls.

**LGS** See: *Loan Guarantee Scheme*. See also: *SFLGS*.

**liability** A firm's obligation to pay cash, goods, or provide a service to another party in the future. Liabilities include *creditors, bank* borrowing, taxes owed.

**Liability driven investment (LDI)** An investment strategy, gaining popularity amongst pension funds, in which the choice of assets is at least in part driven by the nature of the liabilities. LDI will often involve swaps and derivatives to provide protection against movements in inflation, interest rates and, in a few instances, longevity.

**Liberia** Standard *currency*: Liberian *dollar*. 1 Liberian *dollar* = 100 *cents*.

**LIBID** See: *London Inter-Bank Bid Rate*.

**LIBOR** See: *London Inter-Bank Offered Rate*.

**Libya** Standard *currency*: dinar. 1 *dinar* = 1000 *dirhams*.

**Liechtenstein** Standard *currency*: Swiss *franc*. 1 *franc* = 100 *centimes*.

**lien** Legal term denoting the right to obtain possession of another's property or *asset* pending discharge of a debt.

**life assurance** With popular origins from the provision of funeral expenses by the prepayment of regular amounts, life assurance historically received favourable *tax* treatment and grew into a very sophisticated and multi-faceted industry concerned as much with the mitigation of *tax* and the provision of savings as with straightforward protection. However, since the mid-1980s the relative tax benefits have been eroded, both as a result of the anti-avoidance measures and the introduction of alternative investment options, such as personal equity plans and individual savings accounts. The statistically low chance of premature death or accident make pooled *premiums* cost-effective for a *company* covering numerous policyholders. Products were further diversified into investment-related products where the *value* of a policy can be related to a particular *unit-linked* or *asset backed investment fund*. Until 13 March 1984, new qualifying policies attracted *tax* relief at around half the *basic rate* of *tax* on *premiums*. This relief is still available to policies taken out before 13 March 1984. Regulated by the *Financial Services Authority*. See: *LAPR*. See also: *actuary, bonus, endowment, investment bond, Ombudsman, whole of life policy*.

**Life Assurance and Unit Trust Regulatory Organisation (LAUTRO)** A *Self-Regulating Organisation* which concentrated on the regulation of institutions and direct salespeople offering *life assurance* and *unit trust* services as principals. Superseded by the *Personal Investment Authority* (in 1994) and then the Financial Services Authority. LAUTRO's original maximum commission sales remain widely used as the commission basis for some products.

**Life Assurance Premium Relief (LAPR)** A 'qualifying' *life assurance* policy effected prior to 13 March 1984 and kept in force still receives the benefit of 12.5% tax relief on the *premiums* paid. Policies effected after this date no longer qualify for this relief. See: *qualifying policy*.

**life of contract** The duration of the period for which trading in a specific month on a particular *futures* market is possible, ie the day a new month is quoted until its expiration.

**lifestyle business** Normally a small business with a non-scalable *business model* that provides its *management* with a decent living but is unlikely to grow much larger. Often a niche business exploiting a small *sector* of the market overlooked by larger *companies* and often requiring a personal touch.

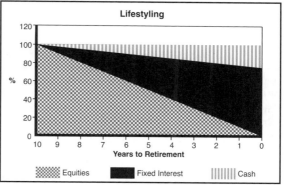

**lifestyling** An investment approach, often used for *money purchase* occupational pension schemes and *personal pensions,* under which asset allocation is systematically switched from equities to fixed interest securities and cash in the five/ten years before retirement age. The aim is to limit the impact of a downturn in equity values close to retirement.

**lifetime allowance** The lifetime allowance sets the maximum tax-efficient value of benefits under a registered pension scheme. Subject to *transitional reliefs*, the lifetime allowance is £1.75m in 2009/10 and £1.8m from 2010/11-2015/16 inclusive. If benefits have a value above the lifetime allowance, the *lifetime allowance charge* will normally apply to the excess.

**lifetime allowance charge** The tax charge levied on benefits in excess of the lifetime allowance, after adjustment for any *transitional protection*. A 55% flat rate applies to excess benefits drawn as a lump sum, while a 25% charge is levied on any excess fund used to provide pension income.

**lifetime transfers** A tapering relief is granted under *inheritance tax* rules for lifetime transfers (gifts) made within the seven years prior to the *donor*'s death, which become *tax* free thereafter.

**LIFFE** See: *London International Financial Futures and Options Exchange*.

**LIFO** See: *last in first out.*

**like-for-like** Many companies, particularly retailers, produce like-for-like sales figures which ignore any acquisitions (eg extra retail space) during the period under review. This is meant to give a better picture of the performance of the underlying business.

**likuta** *Currency* sub-unit of *Zaire.* Plural of 'likuta' is: makuta. 100 makuta = 1 zaire.

**lilangeni** Standard *currency* of *Swaziland.* Plural of 'lilangeni' is: emalangeni. 1 lilangeni = 100 *cents.*

**LIMEAN** Short for: London Inter-Bank Mean Rate.

**limit** 1. An order to a *broker* which is restricted so far as the price level at which it may be transacted is concerned. 2. The *maximum fluctuation* that can occur in a predetermined period (usually one day's trading), laid down by the various markets. Particularly common in American *futures* markets (6.5% movement pre/post market), where the price can move limit up or limit down and also common on the Tokyo Stock Exchange. See: *trading curb.*

**limited by guarantee** A *limited company* without *shareholders* or *equity capital,* normally a society, club or association where any deficiency on *winding up* is made up by the membership contributing an amount determined under terms laid out in the *company*'s *Memorandum of Association.*

**limited company** A corporate body which contracts as a corporate entity, which is capitalised by *share capital* and where the *directors,* staff and *shareholders* are protected from personal liability for the *company*'s trading debts in the event of *insolvent liquidation.* In the *UK* limited companies must be registered with the *Registrar of Companies* and must produce annual *accounts* and issue them to *shareholders.* Directors do have a certain personal liability for unpaid *PAYE* and *VAT* and in the case of insolvent trading and fraud, but *shareholders'* liability is limited to the cost of their *investment.* Private *companies* are normally limited (*Ltd*) and *listed companies* are *public limited companies* (*plc*). This is contrasted with a *partnership* where partners have a *joint and several liability* for the *partnership*'s debts as well as the products and services it provides.

**limited liability** Company *shareholders'* liability is limited to the sum originally subscribed for the *shares,* only if *fully paid.* For this privilege a *company* accepts obligations like publishing *audited accounts.* See also: *unlimited liability, unlimited losses.*

**limited liability partnership (LLP)** A legal structure which is half way between a company and a partnership. In an LLP, one partner is neither responsible nor liable for the misconduct or negligence of another partner. This is not the case in the traditional partnership, where each partner has unlimited liability. UK LLP partners are taxed in the same way as ordinary partners, although the LLP has the status of a corporate body in law.

**limited price index** An *index* used in the calculation of *pension* benefits where *pension income* can be increased and is set at the *Retail Price Index* or 5%, whichever is less.

**limited price indexation (LPI)** Defined benefit (final salary) pensions accrued between 6 April 1997 and 5 April 2005 are required by the Pensions Act 1995 to increase in payment each year at least in line with LPI, which is defined as the lesser of 5% and the increase in the *retail prices index.* For accruals after 5 April 2006, the Pensions Act 2004 reduced the upper ceiling for LPI from 5% to 2.5%.

**linkers** A slang expression for *index-linked gilts.*

**lipa** Croatian sub unit. 100 lipa = 1 kuna.

**liquid assets** Cash or *assets* easily converted to *cash,* such as marketable *securities.*

**liquidation** Occurs when a *limited company,* its bankers or its *shareholders* appoint a liquidator, normally as a result of the *company* being unable to meet its short- or long-term financial obligations or because of *insolvency.* In the case of a *member* voluntary *winding up, shareholders* of the *company* initiate the liquidation. The *company* usually ceases trading from the date of the liquidator's appointment and all its *assets* are eventually distributed to *shareholders* and *creditors* with the following preference: 1. the *Liquidator's* fees; 2. fixed *charge* holders; 3. *preferential creditors*; 4. *floating charge* holders; 5. unsecured (trade) *creditors*; 6. subordinated *creditors*; 7. preference *shareholders*; 8. ordinary *shareholders*. *Warrant* and *option* holders get nothing. Each category is paid in full before moving on to the next. See: *administration, voluntary arrangement, voluntary liquidation.*

**liquidator** A person appointed by a court to supervise a *liquidation* and governed by the *Insolvency Act 1986*. In a compulsory *liquidation*, a court appoints a 'provisional liquidator' when a winding-up petition is presented; when this is granted the court appoints the '*official receiver*' as liquidator until or unless another officer is appointed by the *creditors*. The liquidator is an officer of the court under a statutory obligation. A liquidator must be a qualified *insolvency* practitioner with membership of an approved professional body (such as the Insolvency Practitioners' Association or the Institute of Chartered Accountants). On appointment, the liquidator assumes control of the *company*, liquidates the *assets*, pays the debts, and distributes any surplus to *company members* according to their rights. Preference for payment is as follows: 1. the Liquidator's fees; 2. *fixed charge* holders; 3. *preferential creditors*; 4. *floating charge* holders; 5. unsecured (trade) *creditors*; 6. subordinated *creditors*; 7. preference *shareholders*; 8. Ordinary *shareholders*. *Warrant* and *option* holders get nothing. Each category is paid in full before moving on to the next.

**liquidity** The degree to which an *asset* or *security* can be bought or sold in a market without affecting the *asset's* price. Liquidity is characterised by a high level of trading activity and larger *capitalisation shares*. Smaller *companies* with fewer issued *shares*, that are not actively traded, can be difficult to buy or sell at a quoted price in any *volume* and are described as *illiquid*. Also, the ability to convert an *asset* to *cash* quickly.

**liquidity constraint** Limitation on the amount an economic agent can borrow. The term is usually used within the context of economic theory.

**liquidity preference** Term sometimes used in economics to mean the public's demand for *money*. See: *LM curve.*

**liquidity ratio** Cash or *near cash* as a proportion of a *company*'s current borrowings. See: *gearing.*

**lira** Standard *currency* of the following nations: *San Marino*: 1 lira = 100 centesimi; *Turkey*: 1 lira = 100 *kurus*. Formerly the standard *currency* of *Italy*, until the introduction of the *euro* on 1 January 2002, and *Malta* until it joined the eurozone on 1 January 2008.

**lisente** *Currency* sub-unit of *Lesotho*. 100 lisente = 1 *loti.*

**listed** A *limited company*'s *shares* quoted on a recognised *stock exchange.*

**listing** Admission of a *security* to the *Official List* of *securities* which are dealt on the *London Stock Exchange* or *listed* on a *Recognised Stock Exchange.*

**listing agreement** The agreement adopted by the *board* of a *company* to observe the rules and regulations of the *Financial Services Authority* on *listing.*

**listing rules** In order to gain entry to the *main market* of the *London Stock Exchange*, a number of conditions must be fulfilled by the *company*, which are known as the Purple Book of the *UK Listing Authority*, which is part of the *Financial Services Authority*:

- The expected *market value* of the *shares* issued must be at least £700,000.
- If debt is issued, its *value* must be at least £200,000.
- All *securities* issued must be freely transferable. The *company* must have traded for at least three years prior to application to the *main market.*

- At least 25% of the *capital* must be available to the public (the *float*).
- *Warrants* and *options* on the *company stock* cannot exceed 20% of the *capital* base.
- Generally, no one shareholder should have a *stake* of 30% or more.
- *Shareholders* may only give permission to waive *pre-emption rights* through a period of 15 months.
- The *company* must notify a regulated information service (RIS) of any price-sensitive information.
- The *company* must publish information about important transactions.
- The *company* must inform an RIS of any changes in the important registers of *share* ownership.
- The *company* must give notification to an RIS of *dividends* and *board* meetings involving discussion of *dividends*.
- The *company* must issue annual *accounts* within six months of the year end and publish half-yearly reports within four months of the half-year end.

**litas** Standard *currency* of *Lithuania*. 1 litas = 100 centas.

**Lithuania** Standard *currency*: *litas*. 1 *litas* = 100 centas.

**Little Dragons** Nickname for Asian nations such as *Singapore, Thailand, South Korea* and *Taiwan* that posed a threat to *Japan* (the Big Dragon) because of their lower labour costs, cheaper *currencies* and high *productivity*. In practice many Japanese companies have now outsourced production to these countries. Also known as the 'tigers'.

**Liverpool Cotton Association** An important world market in cotton, established in 1841. Trades in *actuals* and *futures*.

**LKR** *currency code* for: *Sri Lanka* Rupee.

**Lloyd's** The corporation of Lloyd's started in a coffee house established by Edward Lloyd in London's Tavern Street (1689), and after moving to Lombard Street, Popes Head Alley and the Royal Exchange (1774), it subsequently moved to its own building in Lime Street. Members are *brokers* or *underwriters* who operate in *syndicates*, and to be accepted must deposit substantial sums as *collateral*. Underlying *capital* was also provided by *'Names'* who deposit *capital* and pledge their *assets* to Lloyd's *syndicates* and who receive *income* but do not have any executive responsibility. In the early 1990s Lloyd's was hit by a financial crisis – the LMX spiral – which saw many Names lose much of their wealth. As a result most of the capital supplied to Lloyd's is now rated via special purpose companies with limited liability. The corporation has no 'corporate' responsibilities but provides standardised documents, a daily newspaper, Lloyd's List, Shipping Gazette, Shipping Intelligence, an international network of agents and a claims bureau as well as regulating the activities of members. One of the largest *insurance* markets. Lloyd's protects *risks* of almost any nature.

**LLP** See: *limited liability partnership*.

**LM curve** The curve showing the combinations of the *interest rate* and *real national income* for which the *money market* is in *equilibrium* (ie *money* demand equals *money supply*). In other words, the curve showing points for which *'liquidity preference'* equals *'money supply'*. Used in macroeconomic *analysis*. See: *BP curve, IS curve, Mundell–Fleming model*.

**LME** See: *London Metal Exchange*.

**LMIL** See: *London Market Information Link*.

**loan back** Certain occupational pension schemes, mostly small self-administered schemes, are able to lend up to 50% of their net asset value to the sponsoring employer. The HMRC rules governing such loans have been tightened regularly over the years and now require that the loan is secured for a period of less than five years, carries interest of at least 1% above base rate and is repaid in equal instalments.

**loan capital** See: *loan stock*.

**Loan Guarantee Scheme (LGS)** A government scheme whereby 70% of a *company's* *overdraft* will be guaranteed in exchange for a 2% or 3% *premium* over a bank's normal lending rate. A form of finance that is useful to *companies* who have insufficient *assets* to support normal *bank* borrowings.

**loan note** Similar to *loan stock* but often used where investors take a 'note' rather than *cash* as the result of a *share offer* to defer their liability to *tax*. Under these circumstances, the note is not normally marketable and can be redeemed for *cash* from the issuer. The *yield* is often variable and linked to *London Inter-Bank Offered Rate*.

**loan stock** In order to raise extra *working capital*, *companies* can offer such *stock* to private investors whereby they are guaranteed to receive a fixed *income* from their *investment* for the duration of the loan. The most common form of loan stock is the '*debenture*', but the *stocks* offering the highest *interest* returns are *unsecured loan stocks* (see: *unsecured debenture*) whereby the holder has no prior *call* upon the *assets* of the *company* should it cease to trade.

- *Mortgage debentures* – these are loans secured upon a specific part of the *assets* of the *company*, normally land and buildings, and sometimes in addition by *floating charge* on other *assets*.
- Debenture *stocks* – these are loans normally secured by a fixed and *floating charge* on all the *assets* of a *company* remaining after meeting any prior claims.
- Unsecured loan stocks or notes – these are loans without any specific *security*, other than the recognised financial strength of the *company*.
- Subordinated *unsecured loan stocks* – these are loans issued by financial institutions, such as *banks*, whereby the rights of the stockholders are subordinated to the interests of the depositors.
- Convertible *stocks* – this term covers all the above types of loan, with the additional right conferred upon the shareholder that he may elect to exchange the *stock* into another *class* of *security*, usually *ordinary shares*, at certain specified dates and at a predetermined conversion rate. See: *fixed interest security*.

**local** A member of a *futures* exchange who makes transactions on his or her own account.

**local authority bond** A *fixed interest security* issued by a council to raise funds to supplement revenues from *rates*, to help with *cash flow* or finance a specific project. Normally *yearling bonds*.

**lock-up** An agreement between a *target company* and a *bidder* to discourage new *bidders* once an agreement has been reached. Lock-ups may include an *option* to buy *crown jewels* or a watertight *merger* agreement. The term can also refer to a refusal of a fund – typically a hedge fund – to allow investors to liquidate holdings immediately. Instead a lock-up period applies during which the fund sells sufficient assets to meet the redemption demands.

**Lomé Convention** Established the European Development Fund in 1976 to aid developing countries outside the *European Community*.

**London acceptance credit** On shipment of goods a *UK* exporter can draw a *bill of exchange* on the foreign buyer and *pledge* it to a *merchant bank* in London, who in turn accepts an *accommodation bill* drawn by the exporter. To provide the exporter with immediate finance, the acceptance can be discounted on the *bank's* reputation rather than the foreign buyer's acceptance which would be difficult to *discount* in London.

**London Bullion Market Association (LBMA)** The *LBMA* is the London-based trade association that represents the *wholesale over-the-counter market* for *gold* and silver in London.

**163**

**London Inter-Bank Bid Rate (LIBID)** The rate of *interest* bid by *banks* for funds borrowed in the *short term wholesale market*. See: *London Inter-Bank Offered Rate*.

**London Inter-Bank Offered Rate (LIBOR)** The rate of *interest* offered by *banks* for funds lent in the short-term *wholesale market* for periods from overnight to five years. The market allows individual *banks* to adjust their liquidity positions covering shortages by borrowing from *banks* with surpluses and vice versa. This reduces the need for each *bank* to hold large quantities of *liquid assets* releasing funds for more profitable lending. *LIBOR* is quoted daily and is the most significant *benchmark* for wholesale commercial domestic and international lending. See also: *London Inter-Bank Bid Rate*.

**London International Financial Futures and Options Exchange (LIFFE)** Pronounced 'life'. Created by a *merger* between the London Financial Futures Options Market and the London Traded Options Market in 1992. *LIFFE* merged with the *London Commodities Exchange* (*LCE*) in September 1996 to form '*LIFFE Commodity Products*'. *LIFFE* is the largest *derivatives* exchange in Europe and the third largest in the world devoted to *financial futures* and *options*. *LIFFE* is authorised as a *Recognised Investment Exchange* by the *Financial Services Authority* (*FSA*). *LIFFE* switched from floor trading to its new electronic system, *LIFFE* CONNECT in November 1998. Located at: Cannon Bridge, 1 Cousin Lane, London EC4R 3XX. Tel: 020 7379 2009.

**London Market Information Link (LMIL)** Applied pricing data and *company* information system providing vendor data systems with details of *Stock Exchange Automated Quotations System* (*SEAQ*) trades on the *London Stock Exchange*.

**London Metal Exchange (LME)** The centre of the world's trading (*physicals, options* and *futures*) in the main industrially used non-ferrous base metals, established in London in 1877. Trading takes place on three platforms: open outcry trading in the ring, through inter-office telephone offers and through LME Select, an electronic trading platform. The *LME* trades copper, primary aluminium, aluminium alloy, lead, nickel, tin, zinc and two types of plastic. Trade *turnover* is around US$35-40 *billion* per day. Transactions are underwritten by LCH. Clearnet and the exchange is regulated by the *Financial Services Authority* as a *Recognised Investment Exchange*. As with any *commodity market*, its main function is to establish prices, provide liquidity for suppliers and consumers as well as hedging facilities for market participants. The *LME* established the three-months standard forward trading date over a hundred years ago which was the approximate sailing time from Santiago or *Singapore* to the *UK*. Located at: The London Metal Exchange Limited, 56 Leadenhall Street, London EC3A 2DX. Tel: 020 7264 5555.

**London Securities and Derivatives Exchange** See: *OMLX*.

**London Stock Exchange (LSE)** Dealings in *stocks* and *shares* began with the merchant venturers in the 17th century and gradually an informal market developed around the coffee houses in the City of London. In 1773 New Jonathan's Coffee House became the London Stock Exchange, although it was not formally constituted until 1802, with some 550 subscribers and 100 clerks. Although London was overwhelmingly the largest exchange (until the First World War it was the world's largest), the *growth* of the Industrial Revolution prompted the establishment of *local share* markets in other parts of the country, more than 30 at the peak. These markets first began moving towards amalgamation in 1890 when the Council of Associated Stock Exchanges was formed. By 1967, the 'country' exchanges had grouped themselves into six regional exchanges and in 1973 all the British exchanges amalgamated with the Dublin Stock Exchange to form the 'International *Stock Exchange* of the *United Kingdom* and the *Republic of Ireland*'. As a result of *Big Bang* the *Stock Exchange* floor became redundant in 1987, with the introduction of electronic dealing and the abandonment of *single capacity*. It provides a free market in the trading of quoted *shares* and *fixed interest securities* and also allows new *companies* to make their *shares* available to the general public (see: *flotation*) if they can comply with the *listing rules*. The *value* of *securities* traded is dependent purely on *supply and demand* with a price always available for both buyers and sellers. The *Stock Exchange* was deregulated on 27 October 1986 when *single capacity* was replaced by *dual capacity* and fixed *commissions* abandoned in an effort to bring the Exchange into line with international practice. As a result of European legislation, the Dublin and London Stock Exchanges separated in 1995. The London Stock Exchange is now a listed company and is regulated by the *Financial Services Authority* (*FSA*). Located at: London Stock Exchange, Old Broad Street, London EC2N 1HP. Tel: 020 7797 1000. See: *Alternative Investment Market, Big Bang, CREST, Official List, Stock Exchange Automated Quotations System, Talisman, T+5, Yellow Book*. For *indices*, see: *Financial Times Share Indices*.

**long**  See: *long position*.

**long liquidation**  The *liquidation* or *closing* out of '*long*' or 'bought' *contracts* to dispose of a holding or terminate a *long position*.

**long position**  1. The purchase of an *investment* with the expectation of an increase in its price. 2. Term also applied to a bought position on a *futures* market.

**long term**  See under: *short term*.

**Long Term Capital Management (LTCM)**  A hedge fund which included two Nobel Prize winners among its principals, but which nevertheless managed to crash in 1998, nearly bringing down the entire financial system. A $3.625 billion bail-out was hastily arranged by the *Federal Reserve*, drawing on the resources of all the major banks operating in the USA (except Bear Sterns, which refused to join in). The cause of LTCM's demise was its extreme gearing – $1.25 trillion of notional derivative exposure based on under $5 million of equity capital – and the Russian default of 1998, which wrecked LTCM's arbitrage bets.

**long term care (LTC)**  The care of the elderly is a major issue in the UK and elsewhere, as the population ages. Medical and lifestyle advances have lengthened life expectancy, but the additional years of life can often give rise to the need for care. The four different constituent countries of the UK each have subtly different approaches to dealing with the issue, but the main thrust is that outside Scotland anyone with assets much above £23,000 has to finance their own personal care and accommodation, although there is some assistance with nursing care. In Scotland a similar capital limit applies, but there is also a personal care payment (£149 a week in 2008/09). Various insurance companies have offered policies to provide long term care cover, but the market is now largely restricted to a small number of immediate care plans, such as special annuities. These are purchased at the time long term care is required or some time later. There is virtually no interest in buying future needs protection.

**long term debt**  Refers to obligations that are due in more than one year's time.

**long ton**  A measurement of weight being 2,240 lbs (= 1,016.05 kg). See: *metric tonne, short ton*.

**long-dated gilt**  A government *security* with a time to redemption of more than 15 years from now. See: *gilts*.

**long-form report**  A report prepared by the *reporting accountants* which provides detailed information on a *company* to its *issuing house* prior to a *flotation*.

**long-term incentive plan (LTIP)**  Share-based long-term incentive plans are designed to give executives the opportunity to earn *shares* in their *company*. The number of *shares* is not fixed; rather, a range is established and the number earned will depend on the *company*'s performance over a set period. Performance is determined by shareholder returns and the *company*'s results compared with its peers.

**loophole**  An opportunity that allows one to circumvent the law's intent without violating it.

**Lorenz curve**  A graphical representation of a cumulative frequency curve.

**loss adjuster** Someone engaged by an insurer to establish, often at first hand, the costs, extent and/or validity of an *insurance* claim.

**lot** Standard weight of a *contract*. See: *CAR*.

**loti** Standard *currency* of *Lesotho*. Plural of 'loti' is: maloti. 1 loti = 100 *lisente*.

**lottery** Apart from government lotteries (Lotto) a lottery is a way of allocating *shares* in an oversubscribed *share* issue on a totally random basis.

**Louvre Accord** A meeting between international finance ministers in Paris to agree an *exchange rate stabilisation* policy and concerted support for the *US dollar*. The meeting took place in February 1987, but was somewhat overtaken by the events of the following October, which saw dramatic falls in both the *dollar* and the world *equity* markets.

**low-cost endowment** A type of *life assurance* policy once commonly used to repay a *mortgage* which combines a *with-profits endowment* policy (see: *with-profits policy*) with a reducing-term *insurance* policy. The principle was that the *insurance* cover provided by the term policy would decrease at the same or slower rate as the reversionary bonuses are added to the *with-profits policy*. In practice falling bonus rates have meant that many of these policies have failed to reach their projected maturity values, leaving a mortgage shortfall.

**low-cost mortgage** A *mortgage* starting with low *interest rates* where the *interest rate* is reduced initially, with this balance being deferred to a later date. The general principle is that *inflation* will make the payments seem lower later and that the borrower will have a greater ability to pay in the future. Sometimes referred to as: *low-start mortgages*. These loans were popular in the 1980s when mortgage rates were in the teens, but have since disappeared. The accumulation of interest increases the risk of negative equity.

**low-start mortgage** Another term for: *low-cost mortgage*.

**lower earnings limit** The amount of *earnings* above which the *state second pension scheme* starts to accrue rebates are payable for those who contract out.

**LPI** See: *limited price index action*.

**LRD** *currency code* for: Liberian Dollar.

**LSD** Pounds *shillings* and pence (£sd.). Pre-decimal *currency* in the *UK*. 20 *shillings* per *pound*, twelve pence per *shilling*. See: *decimalisation*.

**LSE** See: *London Stock Exchange*

**LSL** *currency code* for: *Lesotho* Loti.

**LTC** See: *long-term care*.

**Ltd** Short for: limited. Added to the end of the name of a *private limited company*. Compare: *plc*.

**LTIP** See: *long-term incentive plan*.

**LTL** *currency code* for: Lithuanian Litas.

**luma** *Currency* sub-unit of *Armenia*. 100 luma = 1 *dram*.

**Lutine Bell** A bell rung at *Lloyd's insurance* market signalling the loss of a ship. The bell is from the SS Lutine which sank in 1799 with the loss of a cargo of *gold bullion* insured at *Lloyd's*.

**Luxembourg** The Luxembourg Stock Exchange was established in 1928. It has two main *indices*; both comprise the same 13 *securities* of Luxembourg industrial and commercial *companies*. Both are weighted by the number of *securities* outstanding in constituent *companies*. Base: 2 January 1985 = 1,000.

- Luxembourg Shares Index.

- The Luxembourg Shares Return Index takes into account *dividends* paid. Standard *currency*: euro. 1 *euro* = 100 *cents*. Used to use the *franc* as *currency*, before the adoption of the *euro* on 1 January 2002.

**LVL** *currency code* for: Latvian Lats.

**lwei** *Currency* sub-unit of *Angola*. 100 lwei = 1 *kwanza*.

**LYD** *currency code* for: Libyan Dinar.

# M

**M0** From the *Bank of England* old definition: M0 comprised of notes and coins in circulation outside the *Bank of England* (including those held in *banks'* and *building societies'* tills), plus *banks'* operational deposits with the *Bank of England*. The *Bank of England* stopped compiling M0 data in May 2006, when it was replaced by regular publication of Notes & Coin and Reserve Balances held at the *Bank of England*. See also: *money supply*.

**M2** The definition of M2 was altered in December 1992 by the *Bank of England*: Thereafter M2 (or retail *M4*) comprises the *UK* non-bank non-building society *private sector* (ie the '*M4 private sector*') holdings of notes and coin together with its *Sterling*-denominated 'retail' deposits with *UK banks* and *building societies*. M2 becomes a subset of *M4* (as *M4*'s 'retail' component). The definition of *M4* is unaffected.

**M3** From the *Bank of England* definition: The M3 aggregate (estimate of EMU aggregate for the UK) comprises monetary liabilities of Monetary and Financial Institutions (MFIs) in the UK vis-à-vis non-MFI UK residents excluding central government. The M3 measure was introduced in 1999 to replace M3H as a 'harmonised' measure of broad money. It includes currency in circulation (M1), overnight deposits (M1), deposits with agreed maturity up to 2 years (M2), deposits redeemable at notice up to 3 months (M2), repurchase agreements, money market fund shares/units and money market paper and debt securities up to 2 years in all currencies for UK MFIs.

**M4** From the *Bank of England* definition: This aggregate comprises the M4 *private sector*'s holdings of *Sterling* notes and coin and all *Sterling* deposits (including *certificates of deposit*, *commercial paper*, *bonds*, *FRNs* and other *instruments* of up to and including five years' original maturity) at *UK banks* and *building societies*. M4 is also referred to as '*broad money*'. See also: *money supply*.

**M&A (Mergers and Acquisitions)** Generally the province of corporate lawyers, *accountants*, bankers and venture capitalists, the M&A business is involved in buying, selling and merging *companies*.

**Maastricht convergence criteria** Criteria that must be met by prospective new members joining the *European Monetary Union* (*EMU*):

- *inflation* rate no more than 1.5 percentage points above the *average* of the three states with the lowest *inflation* rate;
- long-term *interest rate* within 2 percentage points of the lowest three rates;
- *budget deficit* less than 3% of *GDP*;
- *national debt* which does not exceed 60% of *GDP*;
- domestic *currency* has been within the narrow *band* of the *ERM* for two years without *realignment*. All the then 15 *EU* members met the convergence criteria when originally set in 1991, and subsequently 12 adopted the European single *currency* at the start of 1999. Only *Sweden*, *Denmark* and the *UK* chose not to enter monetary union. Monetary union was completed on 1 January 2002, with the introduction of *euro* notes and coins. Since this time many participants have stepped outside the *convergence* terms as a result of *recession* and poor economic performance. Over the same period four new members have joined.

**Maastricht Treaty** In December 1991 the leaders of the 12 *EC* countries met at Maastricht in the *Netherlands* to negotiate a treaty on the *European Union*. The treaty was agreed in December 1991 and finally signed in February 1992. The treaty moved significantly towards economic, political and social union and set out the detailed timetable for economic and monetary union (*EMU*). It also set out the *convergence* criteria for economies who wanted to join in *EMU*. It was the first major step towards the introduction of the European single *currency*. See: *Maastricht convergence criteria*.

**Macau** Portuguese dependency. Standard *currency*: *pataca*. 1 *pataca* = 100 *avos*.

**Macaulay's duration** A method of measuring the *duration* of a *bond*. Duration is the *weighted average* length of time to when the benefits of a *bond* (*coupons* and redemption *value*) are received. The weights are calculated as the *present values* of the benefits. Thus the formula is:

$$Duration = \frac{\sum_{t=1}^{t=n} t\,PV_t}{\sum_{t=1}^{t=n} PV_t}$$

where $PV_t$ is the *present value* of the *cash flow* in period t, discounted by *gross redemption yield*, and n is the number of periods until redemption. See: *convexity, net present value*.

**Macedonia** Standard *currency*: denar.

**macro** A prefix denoting a reference to macroeconomic concepts.

**macroeconomics** The fundamental aspects of an economy as influenced by *unemployment*, total output, *inflation*, *balance of trade*, *money supply*, industrial production and economic activity, as distinct from *microeconomics*. See: *top-down*.

**MAD** *currency code* for: Moroccan Dirham.

**Madagascar** Standard *currency*: *franc* malgache. 1 *franc* malgache = 100 *centimes*.

**magenta** The *basis price* of a holding quoted in a minimum of a thousand *shares*. Certain *market makers* are obliged to provide two way *quotations* in most *shares* but if they do not wish to trade small *illiquid companies* in any *volume*, they simply show a magenta price which often bears no relationship to the price at which *shares* would actually trade in any quantity.

**main market** The main market ('full list') of the *London Stock Exchange* is the market for *companies* having fulfilled the stringent *listing rules*. It is distinguished from the *Alternative Investment Market* for *companies* that meet less onerous requirements.

**main residence** A term used to describe an individual's main or principal private *residence* in the *UK*. Important because *profits* made from sale or transfer are free from *CGT* (*capital gains tax*). Where an individual has more than one property an election can be made. A married couple may only have one main residence.

**mainstream corporation tax (MCT)** The *corporation tax* which applies to large companies. Currently (2009) set at a rate of 28%.

**majority shareholder** See under: *controlling director*.

**Malawi** Standard *currency*: kwacha. 1 *kwacha* = 100 *tambala*.

**Malaysia** Malaysia's *stock exchange* is the Bursa Malaysia (MYX). Its predecessor, the Stock Exchange of Malaysia, was later named the Stock Exchange of Malaysia and *Singapore*; then after the split with *Singapore* (1973) it was called Kuala Lumpur Stock Exchange Berhad. In 2004 the exchange changed its name to Bursa Malaysia Berhad, following demutualisation. The number of companies listed in 2009 was 631. Its main *index* is:

- Kuala Lumpur Composite Index (KLCI). Comprises 102 *stocks*. Base: 4 April 1986 = 100.

The *commodity* exchange, Kuala Lumpur Commodity Exchange (KLCE), was established in 1980.

Standard *currency*: ringgit. 1 ringgit = 100 *sen*.

**Maldives**  Standard *currency*: *rufiyaa*. 1 *rufiyaa* = 100 laari.

**Mali**  Standard *currency*: African *franc*.

**Malta**  Trading began on the Malta Stock Exchange (Borza ta' Malta) in 1992. In 2009 there were two *listed shares*. Trading also exists in *government securities*. Standard *currency*: euro. 1 *euro* = 100 *cents*. The euro replaced the lira from 1 January 2008.

**Malthusianism**  The theory propounded by Thomas Malthus at the end of the 18th century that the world would run out of resources if the population were not controlled. Sometimes a more general term used to describe a depressing outlook.

**managed float**  A policy used by government authorities in order to influence an otherwise *floating exchange rate* by intervening in the *foreign exchange* without publicly announcing the *intervention* beforehand. Unexpected *intervention* has a stronger effect on the *exchange rate* than a widely anticipated one. It is a form of managing the *exchange rate*. Also called: *dirty float*.

**managed fund**  A fund linked to a variety of *assets*, normally offered by *life assurance companies* via *investment bonds* and *unit-linked* saving plans and by collective fund managers. The fund manager will give greater or less emphasis to a particular category of *asset* as a matter of *investment* policy. These funds offer varying degrees of risk from cautious to aggressive and provide actively managed *asset backed investment* facilities for the smaller investor. See: *fund of funds*.

**management**  Team of people in charge of the organisation and running of a business. Decision making and team leading are main responsibilities, and business performance is a measure of their success. Investment management can be described from a technical or fundamental viewpoint and, more recently from the perspective of *value* management. See: *analysis*.

**management agreement**  Professional *investment* advisors and *stock brokers* offer their clients formal management agreements which define the terms, objectives and costs involved in the management of a client's *portfolio*. See: *customer agreement*.

**management bid**  A *management buyout* of a publicly *quoted company*.

**management buyout (MBO)**  An arrangement where an unquoted *company* or a subsidiary of a *public company* is purchased by the people running it. This often occurs as an alternative to a *flotation*, an unwelcome *offer* for the *company* from an outside source or even closure. Its great attraction is that it provides greater incentive and direct involvement for those with the best understanding of the workings of the *company*.

**management buy-in**  A *management buyout* (*MBO*) is the purchase of a business by its existing *management*. When a business is for sale the current *management* are often best placed to develop the *company* and likely to be best motivated to make it succeed – especially with a financial interest in the business. They are in a good position to value it and subsequently run it and are often well supported by *banks* and *venture capital* firms as a result.

**manat**  Standard *currency* of *Azerbaijan*. 1 manat = 100 *gopik*.

**mandate** A written instruction giving a third party powers to act on certain specific matters, such as the transfer of *dividends* to a specific *bank account.*

**mandatory bid** The Mandatory Bid Rule (MBR) requires that any *shareholder* who either: (i) establishes new control of a firm; or (ii) takes over control by transfer of an old block position, also extends an offer for the remaining *shares* at a fair price.

**Maple Leaf** *Bullion* coin minted by the government of *Canada* in *gold* (99.99% pure), silver (99.99% pure) and platinum (99.95% pure). The *gold* and platinum coins are available in 1, ½, ¼, ⅒, ⅕ and ⅟₂₀ ounce sizes. The silver coin is available only in the one-ounce size. The Maple Leaf usually sells at a slight *premium* to the *bullion value* of the coin.

**Marché à Terme des Instruments Financiers (MATIF)** The French international *financial futures* exchange opened in 1986. Now part of the NYSE Euronext.

**Marché des Options Négotiables de Paris (MONEP)** The French *traded options* market opened in 1987. Now part of NYSE Euronext.

**Mareva injunction** A court order preventing a party dealing with specified *assets* granted in cases, particularly bankruptcy (see: *bankrupt*) where there is a substantial *risk* that the party will dispose of the *assets* to avoid a judgment. Often granted to prevent *assets* leaving the jurisdiction of English courts, but can extend to *assets* abroad. Named after the precedent in Mareva Compañía Naviera *SA* v International Bulkcarriers *SA* (1975).

**margin** The minimum amount that a client must deposit in *cash* or *securities* when borrowing to buy *securities* or trade in *futures* or *options*. In *futures* markets a deposit normally equivalent to 10% of the *contract value* is required. See also: *profit margin*.

**margin account** American *brokers* offer an account allowing customers to buy *securities* with *money* borrowed from the *broker*. Margin requirements can be met with *cash* or with eligible *securities*. In the *UK* it is normally a *cash* account used by a client to trade *futures*.

**margin call** A request for additional funds on a *margin account*, necessary to maintain original deposits as the result of the adverse movement of a specific *open position*.

**marginal cost** The extra cost of producing an additional unit of output. Used in microeconomic *analysis*, it is technically defined as the *derivative* of cost with respect to output. If the marginal cost of the last unit of output produced is less than its *marginal revenue*, it is profitable to produce more output until the marginal cost and the *marginal revenue* are equal, called the profit-maximising point.

**marginal efficiency of capital** Annualised percentage return gained by investing the last additional unit of *capital*. If the marginal efficiency of *capital* of an *investment* is less than the normal market return, it would not be profitable to invest in the *investment*. See: *quantitative analysis*.

**marginal revenue** Extra revenue earned by the sale of one additional unit of output. Used in microeconomic *analysis*, it is technically defined as the *derivative* of revenue with respect to output. See: *marginal cost*.

**marginal tax rate** The *tax* rate that would apply to an additional £1 of *income*. In countries where progressive rates of *tax* apply, this is normally the highest rate of *tax* paid by an individual. See also: *principles of taxation*.

**mark to market** Current *market value,* the *value* of a *futures contract* or *derivative* or any *investment* at the time of *valuation*. In the case of complex financial *instruments* it is sometimes difficult to obtain a current *value* and the price might be calculated on a mark to model basis (theoretical *valuation*), which is open to abuse or confusion. *Bank assets* are mostly valued on a mark to market basis and this can, in depressed market conditions or at times prior to the exercise date of an *option* or maturity of a *fixed interest* *security*, understate the intrinsic *value* of the *asset* thus affecting the *asset* ratio of the *bank* and making it look *illiquid*. In reality there is no realistic determinant of *value* other than the *market value* (what someone will pay today) and it is likely that mark to market will remain a *benchmark* valuation method.

**mark up**  A practice adopted by *stock exchange market makers* if they anticipate increased demand for a particular *stock* as a result of, say, weekend press comment.

**market capitalisation**  The *value* of a *company* represented by the total *value* of its issued *shares* (see: *issued capital*). Simply calculated by multiplying the number of *shares* in issue by the *shares'* market price.

**market economy**  An economic system where economic decisions and the pricing of goods and services are guided solely by the aggregate interactions of a country's citizens and businesses (*supply and demand*) without government intervention or central planning (capitalist). The opposite of a centrally planned economy (communist), in which government decisions determine most aspects of a country's economic activity.

**market forces**  The forces of *supply and demand*, which together determine the price in a market free from external regulatory influences. See: *equilibrium*.

**market index**  See: *indices*.

**market maker**  An institution involved in trading *securities* as a principal, making and maintaining two-way prices in *shares* or *securities* of a prescribed minimum *bargain* size (*Normal Market Size*). Replaced *jobbers* in the UK after October 1986. Market makers are required to forward details of any transaction that takes place to the *London Stock Exchange Automated Quotations System* (*SEAQ*). See: *Big Bang, dual capacity, Normal Market Size, single capacity*.

**market order**  An order for immediate execution at prevailing market prices.

**market price**  Market price, or *market value*, refers to the most recent price at which a *security* transaction took place. As an economic concept, market price is the price at which a good or service is offered at in the marketplace and at a price where market supply and market demand meet.

**market reciprocal**  A measure of the present market activity (price movement) of a *security*. It is calculated by dividing the *average range* of the price movement of a *security* over an extended time (a few years, say) by the current *average range* (over a week, say). The result is the reciprocal of the *security*'s market movement for the period. A presently active *security* would thus have a market reciprocal of less than unity; the more active the *stock*, the smaller the market reciprocal.

**market risk**  Another term for: *systematic risk*.

**market value**  The term used to reflect the amount for which an *asset* could be realised if actually sold in a free market. This could be greater or less than the initial cost of the *asset* and in the case of normal *investments* is dependent upon *supply and demand* for that holding.

**market value reduction (MVR)**  A market value reduction is a factor which reduces the face value of a unitised *with-profits* policy to reflect investment market conditions. MVRs will often depend upon the start date of the policy involved. Originally called a market value adjustment (MVA), although it never *increased* values.

**marketability**  The speed and ease with which a *share* may be bought and sold in size. Smaller *companies* with restricted shareholdings tend to be difficult to trade in large quantities, whereas larger *blue chip companies* have a higher marketability. See: *Normal Market Size*.

**Markets in Financial Instruments Directive (MiFID)** EU Directive (Nov 2007) giving a harmonised regulatory regime for *investment* services across the 30 Member States of the European Economic Area (the 27 Member States of the European Union plus *Iceland, Norway* and *Liechtenstein*). It replaced the *Investment Services Directive*. Introduced under the 'Lamfalussy' procedure designed to accelerate the adopting of legislation based on a four-level approach recommended by the Committee of Wise Men chaired by Baron Alexandre Lamfalussy. There are three other Lamfalussy Directives – the Prospectus Directive, the Market Abuse Directive and the Transparency Directive. *MiFID* retained the principles of the *EU* passport introduced by the *Investment Services Directive (ISD)* but introduced the concept of maximum harmonisation which places more emphasis on home state supervision whilst ensuring a *level playing field*. The MiFID Level 1 Directive 2004/39/EC, implemented through the standard co-decision procedure of the Council of the *European Union* and the European Parliament, sets out a detailed framework for the legislation. Twenty Articles of this Directive specified technical implementation measures (Level 2). These measures were adopted by the *European Commission* and primarily relate to the governance of markets and the management of *investments*. See: *Investment Services Directive*.

**markka** Formerly the standard *currency* of *Finland*, until the introduction of the *euro* on 1 January 2002. 1 markka = 100 *pennia*.

**Markowitz model** A *portfolio* management tool using market *portfolios* and *capital market* lines for different *risk profiles*. Devised by H. M. Markowitz. *Capital market* lines are drawn up on a similar basis to the *capital asset pricing model* and applied to the market as a whole to determine the optimum balance of *risk* and reward.

**Married Women's Property Acts** Enacted in 1870 and 1882 (Scotland 1880 and N. Ireland 1964) and allowing women to effect policies on themselves and their husbands. Policies written in *trust* under the Acts provide benefits outside the deceased's *estate* (for husband and wife) and accordingly the payment of proceeds is immediate, avoiding any delay caused by *probate*.

**Marshall Islands** Standard *currency*: *US dollar*.

**Marshall Plan** Formally called: European Recovery Program. A US-sponsored scheme set up after the Second World War by Secretary of State George C. Marshall and passed by the *US* Congress in 1948. It provided financial aid and other initiatives for the benefit of the economies of western European countries.

**Marshall–Lerner condition/criterion** A somewhat complex relationship between the *supply and demand* elasticities of *imports* and *exports* of a nation which must be satisfied for a *devaluation* of the home *currency* to have a favourable effect on a nation's *current account*. A simpler relationship can be derived, which is frequently used, if one assumes the supply elasticities to be infinite. In this case the simple Marshall–Lerner condition for a *devaluation* to improve the *current account* is that the sum of the demand *elasticity* for *imports* and the demand *elasticity* for *exports* is greater than unity. See: *J curve*.

**Martinique** Dependency of *France*. Standard *currency*: *euro*.

**Marxism** The basis for communism as developed by Karl Marx and Friedrich Engels. Marxism as interpreted by Lenin ('Marxism-Leninism') was implemented in the former Soviet Union and later in *China*. Basically allows for the state to control the means of supply, production and *distribution* rather than *market forces*.

**marzipan men** Reportedly hard-working middle management responsible for the running of City institutions during and after *directors'* luncheons.

**mast** See under: *flag*.

**matched bargain** Practice adopted by *dealers* where they will make transactions in *securities* by simply matching *share* dealings for clients who want to sell a particular holding with clients who wish to purchase these particular *shares*, where the *dealers* are not holding any of the *stock* on their *books* and market activity is limited.

**matched sale-purchase agreement** A device used by the *Federal Reserve Bank* to control *reserves* in the *US* banking system involving the simultaneous sale of *money market instruments* for immediate sale and forward *repurchase*.

**material adverse change (MAC)** Many merger and acquisition contracts are subject to MAC clauses. These allow the acquirer to terminate the deal if there are major changes during the transaction process which make the target company a less appealing purchase. For example, a change in government legislation or unexpected legal action against the target could be a MAC.

**material interests** The *Companies Acts* 1985 and 1989 oblige a shareholder of a *company* and *connected parties* to declare their *stakes* in a *company* when: 1. holdings of the shareholder and *connected parties* reach 3%; 2. the *stake* rises through one full percentage point and goes through the 4% band; 3. the *stake* falls through one full percentage point or through the 3% threshold; 4. there is a non-beneficial (*nominee*) holding of over 10%. See: *dawn raid, Section 212, Substantial Acquisition Rules*.

**materiality** An American concept regarding corporate information that may affect decisions by investors. Materiality is the term used to describe the significance of a financial statement or other information issued to decision-makers. An item of information, or an aggregate of items, is material if it is probable that its omission or misstatement would influence or change a decision.

**MATIF** See: *Marché à Terme des Instruments Financiers*.

**maturity date** The date on which a *life assurance* policy vests or matures and the *redemption date* of a *fixed interest security*.

**Mauritania** Standard *currency*: ouguiya. 1 *ouguiya* = 5 *khoums*.

**Mauritius** The Stock Exchange of Mauritius (SEM) was established in 1987 in Port Louis. The number of *listed shares* in 2009 was 40. The main *index* is:

- Stock Exchange of Mauritius Index (SEMDEX). It reflects the movement of prices on the official list. It is calculated by dividing the *market capitalisation* by the *capitalisation* at base, ie the *market capitalisation* of all the *shares* at the time of *listing*.

Standard *currency*: rupee. 1 *rupee* = 100 *cents*.

**maximum drawdown** 1. Maximum drawdown is the measure of the maximum fall in the value of an investment fund from peak to trough. It is widely used in *hedge fund* assessment. 2. The maximum amount which can be taken under *income drawdown*.

**maximum fluctuation** The maximum fluctuation that can occur in a predetermined period (usually one day's trading), laid down by the various markets. See: *limit, trading curbs*.

**Maximum Investment Plan (MIP)** A *unit-linked* regular *premium endowment*, or whole-life policy with the premium-paying term normally limited to ten years with *continuation* options. These policies normally allow investors to accumulate a fund that is tax-free in their hands after ten years, and accordingly the arrangement is most suitable for those who are or who will become higher-rate *tax* payers. The regular-*premium* facility allows advantage to be taken of *pound cost averaging* and usually the plans can be linked to a number of different *asset backed investments* with the facility to *switch* between them as conditions dictate. The plans were popular in the 1970s and early 1980s, but the abolition of the assurance premium relief and introduction of personal equality plans and individual savings accounts reduced sales dramatically. See: *qualifying policy.*

**maximum slippage** In the case of a start-up *company* which uses its *equity* finance to cover fixed overheads, there will be a point at which the maximum amount of *equity capital* can be eroded before the *company* becomes insolvent or unsalvageable. Maximum slippage is a *venture capital* term describing the anticipated period between the forecast arrival of revenue and the last moment at which the *company* can show improved *earnings*, after which the situation will become so serious that it would be virtually impossible to obtain further *funding*. See: *death valley curve.*

**Mayotte** Dependency of *France*. Standard *currency*: euro.

**MBO** See: *management buyout.*

**MCT** See: *mainstream corporation tax.*

**MDL** *currency code* for: Moldovan Leu.

**mean** A type of *average*, measured by the *arithmetic mean* or the *geometric mean* used in *quantitative analysis*:

- Arithmetic mean. This is the measure most commonly used to calculate the '*average*'. Technically, *averages* are called 'measures of central locality' to distinguish them from 'measures of dispersion', such as *mean deviation*. The *arithmetic mean* of a set of numerical items is simply their sum total divided by the number of items in the set. The formula makes this explicit:

$$\text{arithmetic mean } \bar{x} = \frac{1}{n} \sum_{i=1}^{i=n} x_i$$

where $x_i$ is an item, n is the total number of items in the set.

- Geometric mean. A measure of '*average*' less commonly calculated than the *arithmetic mean*. It cannot be used if any of the items are equal to zero. The result it yields is lower than that obtained by the *arithmetic mean* and it is less sensitive to the effects of 'outliers' (ie extreme *values*). It is usually used as an *average* of *growth* rates. The *geometric mean* of a set of numerical items (number of items is n) is calculated by taking the nth root of the product of the items. The formula thus is:

$$\text{geometric mean} = \sqrt[n]{x_1 \times x_2 \times x_3 \times \ldots \times x_n}$$

**mean deviation** A statistical measure of dispersion used in *quantitative analysis* and calculated by taking the *arithmetic mean* of the deviations (all taken to be positive) of the items from their (arithmetic) *mean value*. Thus this measure gives a simple indication of the variability (ie dispersion) of the *values* of the items. The formula is:

$$\text{mean deviation} = \frac{1}{n} \sum_{i=1}^{i=n} |x_i - \bar{x}|$$

The *mean* deviation is not as useful for *analysis* as the *standard deviation* and the *variance.*

**mean price** Another term for: *middle price*.

**median** A type of *average*. When a set of numerical items is arranged in ascending order, the median is the middle number. If there are two middle numbers (which occurs when the set has an even number of items), the *arithmetic mean* of the two numbers is taken as the median *value*. It is not affected by 'outliers'. See also: *mean, mode*.

**medium dated gilt** A government *security* with redemption due in 7 to 15 years (according to the *Bank of England*) or 5 to 15 years (according to the FT). See: *gilts*.

**medium sized company** Section 382 of the Companies Act 2006 states that in order to qualify as a medium-sized company a company must meet two of the three following criteria (in its first financial year, or in the case of a subsequent year, in that year and the preceding year): it must have a turnover of not more than £22.8 million, a balance sheet total of not more than £11.4 million, and not more than 250 employees. Compare: small company. See: *large company, Normal Market Size, SME*.

**medium term note** An unsecured note issued in a *eurocurrency* with a maturity of three to six years.

**mediums** *Fixed interest securities* (normally *gilts*) whose *maturity dates* are between 7 and 15 years from now (by *Bank of England* definition).

**MEFF Renta Fija (MEFF RF)** A *financial futures* and *options* exchange in Barcelona. Deals in *interest rate* and *currency futures* and *options*. See: *MEFF Renta Variable*.

**MEFF Renta Variable (MEFF RV)** A *financial futures* and *options* exchange in Madrid. Deals in *equity* and *stock index futures* and *options*. See: *MEFF Renta Fija*.

**MEFF RF** See: *MEFF Renta Fija*.

**MEFF RV** See: *MEFF Renta Variable*.

**megaphone** Another term for: *broadening top*.

**meltdown** Used to describe the market *crash* of October 1987. The expression was derived from the nuclear disaster at Chernobyl where overheating caused a meltdown of the nuclear containment unit.

**member** 1. A voting shareholder in a *limited company*. 2. A *beneficiary* or contributor to a *pension* scheme.

**member firm** A stockbroking firm that has at least one membership of a major *stock exchange*. All *stockbrokers* in the UK need to be members of the *Securities and Futures Authority* and/or the *London Stock Exchange*.

**members voluntary winding up** Where the *shareholders* and *directors* agree that a *company* should go into *voluntary liquidation* but with the expectation that all *creditors* can be repaid in full. The *company* will normally be wound down by *management* before a liquidator is appointed.

**Memorandum & Articles of Association** The charter or corporate bylaw for each *limited company* in the UK incorporating the *Memorandum of Association* and the *Articles of Association* and outlining the *company*'s trade, its scope and internal rules and regulations regarding shareholdings and *shareholders* rights etc. Now known as the Articles (Memorandum abandoned from October 2008). Can only be altered by a *special resolution*.

**Memorandum of Association** Since October 2008 the Memorandum is only a simple statement about the *company*. Any description of activities or restrictions on capacity will be contained in the company's *Articles of Association*. In *Australia*, the memorandum of association and *Articles of Association* have been combined since 2000 into a single document called the Constitution of the company. See: *Memorandum & Articles of Association, resolution.*

**merchant bank** Financial institution whose prime form of business was the raising of *capital* for the needs of industry. More recently, the role has been taken over by *investment banks, venture capital* firms and private equity *companies*. See also: *accepting house, bank, issuing house.*

**Mercosur (or Mercosul)** A South American Common Market or Regional Trade Agreement (RTA) among *Argentina, Brazil, Paraguay* and *Uruguay* founded in 1991 by the Treaty of Asunción, which was later amended and updated by the 1994 Treaty of Ouro Preto. Its purpose is to promote free trade and the fluid movement of goods, people, and *currency.*

**merger** Where two or more *companies* agree to combine their interests thus gaining certain *economies of scale.* The benefits can also include a better crossflow of information, a stronger *asset* base and greater strategic influence. Normally the *companies* are of a similar size and their *shares* are replaced by *shares* in the new group. Not to be confused with a *takeover*, where the *shares* of the *target company* are bought by the *bidder*, who is normally larger and/or richer. See also: *horizontal integration, vertical integration.*

**merger accounting** A means of accounting for the *assets* of a merged *company* in the *accounts* of the *parent company* using the *historic cost accounting* principle and based on the *value* of *assets* at the time of *acquisition.*

**merit goods** Also called 'social products' or 'public goods'. Goods and services provided by the government for the general benefit of the populace, eg education, health. These are paid for out of general taxation.

**metical** Standard *currency* of *Mozambique.* Plural of 'metical' is: meticais. 1 metical = 100 *centavos.*

**metric tonne** Measurement of weight equal to 2,204.6 lbs (= 1,000 kg exactly). See: *short ton.*

**Mexico** The Mexican Stock Exchange (Bolsa Mexicana de Valores – BMV) was founded in 1894 in Mexico City. The main *indices* are:

- Price and Quotations Index. Used for *shares.*
- Mexico Index. Used for *derivatives* products.

Standard *currency*: peso. 1 *peso* = 100 *centavos.*

**mezzanine finance** 1. An intermediate type of *funding* in *venture capital* terms, half-way between debt and *equity.* 2. Also the last round of *funding* before a *company* goes for a *flotation.*

**MGF** *currency code* for: Malagasy Franc.

**Mibtel** Milano Indice Borsa Telematica is the *benchmark* all-share *index* of the Italian *stock market*, the Milano Italia Borsa. The MIB 30 is the *index* of the 30 leading *shares.*

**micro** See: *micro-credit, microeconomics.*

**micro-credit** Micro-credit programmes are those that extend small loans to very poor people for self-employment projects that generate *income*, allowing them to care for themselves and their families. It is hoped that *micro-loans* will help alleviate poverty in some of the world's poorest countries. They are used for looms, sewing machines, potters wheels etc., to help establish *incomes* for the poor in Third World countries and where a sufficient number of loans are granted to ensure that bad debt is sustained at a reasonable percentage of the total.

**micro-finance**  See: *micro-credit.*

**micro-loans**  See: *micro-credit.*

**microeconomics**  The study of the behaviour of basic economic units, such as *companies*, industries or households. Research on motor manufacturers or house builders would be deemed microeconomics. Compare: *macroeconomics.*

**Micronesia**  See: *Federated States of Micronesia.*

**mid-price**  See: *middle price.*

**middle price**  The *average* of the *bid* and *offer price* relating to a particular *stock,* used in the computation of *stock* price movements over a given period. It is the middle price of a *stock* or *share* that is quoted in the financial press. See: *bid-offer spread.*

**MiFID**  See: *Markets in Financial Instruments Directive.*

**milch cow**  A term used to describe businesses or sources of revenue that provide consistent and reliable returns and good *cash flow* with little management.

**mill**  *US* term meaning one-tenth of a *cent,* the unit most often used in expressing property *tax* rates.

**millième**  *Currency* sub-unit of *Egypt.* 1,000 millième = 1 Egyptian *pound.*

**millime**  *Currency* sub-unit of *Tunisia.* 1,000 millime = 1 *dinar.*

**minimum contributions**  Contributions payable to a *personal pension* consisting of a partial rebate of *National Insurance* contributions and the incentive where applicable.

**minimum efficient scale**  The lowest level of output required in a production or *distribution* process to achieve *economies of scale.*

**minimum fluctuation**  The minimum amount that the price of a particular *futures contract* can fluctuate; varies from market to market. See: *tick.*

**Minimum Lending Rate (MLR)**  The minimum rate quoted by the *Bank of England* during the period 1971 to 1981 for lending *money* to the *money market,* used when the *Bank of England* wished to control *interest rates* other than by manipulating the market. Sometimes used as the prime *indicator* of prevailing *interest rates* in this country – now known as *official bank rate.* See: *base rate, repo rate, official bank rate.*

**minimum offering period**  The shortest time a *tender offer* or *bid* may remain open. See: *City Code.*

**minimum retirement age**  The youngest a *member* is allowed to retire from a *pension* scheme as defined by the rules, other than due to incapacity. Normally not before age 50 (55 after 5 April 2010).

**minority interest**  A holding of *shares* other than a *controlling interest.* See: *controlling director, pre-emption rights.*

**MIP**  See: *Maximum Investment Plan.*

**MIRAS**  Short for: Mortgage Interest Relief At Source (withdrawn from 6 April 2000). Was applicable to *mortgages* on owner-occupied property, the lender (*bank* or *building society*) deducted *basic rate tax* from the *mortgage interest* payments, automatically taking account of *tax* relief.

**mission statement**  Corporate objectives as part of a corporate plan, business description or logo. The most famous mission statement is from Star Trek: 'To boldly go where no man has gone before...' It is designed to describe the aspirations of a business or enterprise and is normally a succinct paragraph or even just one line.

**MIT** Short for: market if touched. An order to buy or sell *at best* if a certain price is traded, usually to initiate a position.

**mixed economy** An economy where there is both private and public (state-owned) industry.

**MKD** *currency code* for: Macedonian Denar.

**MLR** See: *Minimum Lending Rate.*

**MMC** See: *Monopolies and Mergers Commission.*

**MMK** *currency code* for: *Myanmar* Kyat.

**MNT** *currency code* for: Mongolian Tugrik.

**mode** A type of *average*. It is the item that occurs most often in a set of items. Sometimes it is not unique, in which case the mode as an *average* is not useful. Its advantage is that it is very easy to find – when observing a graph of a frequency *distribution*, the mode is simply the point at which the maximum distribution occurs (in other words the most commonly observed *value*). Compare: *mean, median.*

**Model Code** A code prepared by the *London Stock Exchange* setting out the rules with which *directors* of a *company* must comply in their dealings in the *company*'s *securities*.

**modern portfolio theory** See: *portfolio theory.*

**Moldova** Standard *currency*: *leu*. 1 *leu* = 100 *bani*.

**momentum** A tool used in *technical analysis* to measure the *speed* of price increase or decrease within a *trend*. Also called: *speed.*

**Monaco** Standard *currency*: *euro*. 1 *euro* = 100 *cents*.

**MONEP** See: *Marché des Options Négociables de Paris.*

**monetarism** Theory that *money supply* is the key to regulating an economy. Monetarists view *money* as a *commodity*, suggesting that over-supply causes a fall in its *real value* (ie causes *inflation*) and that under-supply reduces economic activity and causes *recessions*. Money supply is normally regulated by manipulating *interest rates* and credit. Contrast: *Keynesian economics*. See: *monetary policy.*

**monetarist** See: *monetarism.*

**monetary base** The *currency* held by individuals and firms and *bank reserves* kept within a *bank* or on *deposit* at the *central bank*.

**monetary policy** A demand-side measure whereby government authorities attempt to control macroeconomic variables such as total output and price levels (ie *inflation*), by controlling the *money supply* (see: '*equation of exchange*' under *quantity theory of money*). This is done by employing one of the following measures: 1. *open market operations* (*OMOs*); 2. direct controls on *money* held by the public (see: *multiplier* (sense 2); 3. simply printing more *money* (rarely used as a method because of the longer-term adverse inflationary effect on the economy but likely to be used widely in 2009). Compare: *fiscal policy*. See: *monetarism.*

**Monetary Policy Committee (MPC)** On 6 May 1997, the then Chancellor of the Exchequer, Gordon Brown, announced that the government was giving the *Bank of England* operational responsibility for setting *interest rates*; the Bank of England Act 1998, which gave the Bank that responsibility, came into force on 1 June 1998. The mechanism chosen to determine *interest rates* was to set up the Monetary Policy Committee which consists of nine members including the Governor and two Deputy Governors of the *BoE* and two other Executive Directors of the Bank plus four members chosen by the

Chancellor of the Exchequer to represent the economic intelligentsia (the four wise men). The Treasury has the right to be represented in a non-voting capacity. The *MPC* meets on a monthly basis across two days, Wednesday and Thursday. Decisions are made by a vote of the Committee on a one-person one-vote basis, with the Governor having the casting vote if there is no majority. Decisions on *interest rates* are announced immediately. The minutes of the meetings, including a record of any vote, are normally published on the second Wednesday after the meeting.

**monetisation** The sale of *gilts* by the *UK* government to finance a *budget deficit.*

**money** The word 'money' is derived from 'Moneta', one of the surnames of the Roman Goddess Juno, in whose temple Roman coins were minted. The word 'Moneta' itself is derived from the Greek 'mnemosyne', meaning an act of memory. Money is an accepted 'medium of exchange', which makes the double coincidence of wants required by *barter* unnecessary. It also has the function of 'store of *value*', ie individuals can defer making purchases until they are needed by holding money whose *purchasing power* is accepted. Other uses of money are its function as '*unit of account*' and as a 'standard of deferred payment' for debts and the like. Nowadays, nearly all money is *fiat money.*

**money laundering** Money laundering is a criminal process by which *money* from an illegal source is made to appear legally derived by 1. *placement*, where the proceeds of criminal activity are invested; 2. layering, the co-mingling of illegal and legitimate monies; 3. integration, the withdrawal and use of previously laundered illegitimate funds. The *EC* directive on money laundering determines that financial institutions in Member States implement procedures and controls to establish the provenance of funds under their control. In the *UK* money laundering is regulated by the Drug Trafficking Act 1994 until covered by the Proceeds of Crime Act 2002.

**money market** This market, dominated by *banks*, deals with the credit and finance of the City of London and other major financial centres. Larger sums of deposit *capital* can be placed on the money market by private investors to obtain a higher rate of deposit *interest* over specified periods. Primarily a *wholesale market* for short-term debt in which *money brokers* arrange transactions between *banks* and the government. The main media of exchange are *bills of exchange, Treasury bills* and *trade bills.*

**money market yield** The *yield* of a *discount instrument* (ie a short-term *security* that does not pay *interest*) that has n days to maturity is given in the following formula:

$$\text{price} = \frac{\text{maturity value}}{(1 + \text{money market yield})^{n/365}}$$

Compare: *discount rate, discount yield.*

**money purchase** This is the name given to *pension* plans where the level of benefit is solely dependent on the accumulated *value* of contributions made as opposed to a final salary scheme. See: *final salary pension.*

**money shop** High-street retail outlets set up by *finance houses* to provide loans and banking services and *foreign exchange* facilities to walk-in customers, many of whom may not have *bank accounts.*

**money stock** The old-fashioned term used to describe *money supply*, referring to circulating notes and coins, together with the *volume* of deposits in the banking system.

**money supply** The amount of *money* or the speed at which this amount of *money* circulates within an economy at a given time (which is technically known as: *velocity of* *circulation*). While the essence of *money* is that it is generally acceptable as a means of payment, this characteristic does not permit a unique definition of the actual money supply. Money can come in the form of notes and coin, credits on a *current account*, cheques, credit cards, *bills of exchange*, deposit accounts etc. The definition is important in the regulation of an economy specifically with regard to establishing appropriate rates of *interest* which, in turn, will regulate the *growth* of an economy, its *inflation* rate, the relative *value* of its *currency* and the relative competitiveness of its industry. Certain definitions of the money supply are made by the *Bank of England*, which now only uses *M2*, *M3* and *M4*. In the *UK*, the *Bank of England* controls the money supply. See: *monetary policy, multiplier, quantity theory of money*.

**möngö**  *Currency* sub-unit of *Mongolia*. 100 möngös = 1 *tugrik*.

**Mongolia**  Standard *currency*: *tugrik*. 1 *tugrik* = 100 *möngös*.

**monkey**  Slang for £500.

**Monopolies and Mergers Commission (MMC)**  See: *Competition Commission*.

**monopoly**  A market situation which is characterised by the existence of many buyers and only one selling firm (or a group of firms acting in *concert*). As such the firm has control over the market in the goods and services it produces. Associated with the market structure are the related conditions of the lack of substitute goods and services and substantial barriers to entry for other firms. Arguments for monopolies are that they can invest more funds for the advancement of research and development in order to create technological innovations, which could not be made if competition forced prices down, and also the wide uniformly affordable goods and services of certain public monopolies, such as the Post Office. Arguments against monopolies are mainly that the absence of competition leads to high prices and the lack of recognition and responsiveness to the developing needs of consumers. In the *UK*, monopoly activity is regulated by the *Competition Commission*, and in the *US* by the 'antitrust laws'. See: *cartel*. Compare: *monopsony, oligopoly, perfect competition*.

**monopsony**  Market situation where there are many sellers but only one buyer. Less prevalent than the market form of *monopoly*.

**Monserrat**  *UK* dependency. Standard *currency*: East Caribbean *dollar*.

**Montenegro**  Standard *currency*: *dinar*. 1 *dinar* = 100 *paras*.

**Moody's**  One of the two best-known *bond rating* agencies in *America*, the other being *Standard & Poor's*. It publishes manuals and *ratings* on *commercial paper*, preferred and *common stocks* and municipal short-term issues. The *company* also publishes the quarterly 'Moody's Handbook of Common Stocks' which charts more than 500 *companies*, showing industry group *trends* and *company stock* price performance. The long term *ratings* of *bonds* are as follows:

Investment grade (prime):

- Aaa. Best *quality*, smallest degree of *investment risk*.
- Aa. High *quality* by all standards. Together with the Aaa group they are known as 'high-grade' *bonds*.
- A. Security of principal and *interest* may be described as adequate.
- Baa. Considered 'medium-grade' *bonds*. Security of principal and *interest* may be described as adequate for the present but lack long-term protective elements.

Non-investment grade (non-prime). Also called *junk bonds*:

- Ba. Only moderate protection for principal and *interest*. Has speculative elements.
- B. Generally lack the characteristics of the desirable *investment*. Low assurance of security of principal and *interest*.
- Caa. Bonds of poor standing. Danger of *default* of payment of principal/interest. May already be in arrears.
- Ca. Highly speculative. Often in *default*.
- C. Lowest *bond class*.

Note that the *ratings* Aa through B can be modified by addition of the numbers 1, 2, 3 (in order of ranking). Thus the lowest investment grade is Baa 3, equivalent to BBB – from Standard and Poor's. See also: *credit rating*.

**moonlighting** Irregular jobs in addition to full-time employment, often for *cash* which is not declared to the *tax* authorities.

**MOP** *currency code* for: *Macau* Pataca.

**moratorium** An agreement extending the repayment period for a loan.

**Morgan Stanley Capital International Indices** See: *MSCI Indices*.

**Morocco** Standard *currency*: *dirham*. 1 *dirham* = 100 santimat.

**mortgage** A *debt instrument* where the borrower (*mortgagor*) gives the lender (*mortgagee*) a *lien* on property as security for the repayment of the loan. The *mortgagor* has the use of the property and the *lien* is removed when the debt is settled in full. Private mortgages can be undertaken on a repayment basis where both *capital* and *interest* are repaid over a period. Alternative arrangements rely on the *interest* only being repaid over the period and an additional form of savings or *investment* undertaken to redeem the *capital* at the end of this period. The security used can be an *endowment* policy, a *unit trust*, *OEIC* or *ISA* savings plan or a *pension*. This route can be of advantage if the parallel *investment* produces a return greater than the interest charged on the debt. However, in times of poor *investment* performance the sum accumulated may be less than required, a problem many endowment policyholders face. Mortgage repayments combining capital and interest can be calculated as follows:

$$pmt = pv \times i \ / \ (\ 1 - (\ 1 + i\ )\ \wedge -n\ )$$

where: pmt is the payment, pv is the *present value*, i is the *interest rate*, n is the time length. Time must be consistent throughout for it to work eg pmt per month, *interest rate* per month, and n in months. Most lenders do not require a repayment vehicle to be in place for an interest only loan and rely on the loan being repaid from the increased *value* of the property realised by its sale at some future date.

**mortgage backed security** See: *CMO, CDO*.

**mortgage debentures** See under: *loan stock*.

**mortgagee** The lender in a *mortgage* agreement.

**mortgagor** The borrower in a *mortgage* agreement.

**most favoured nation** An agreement between two nations in which each nation grants the other *tariff* rates that are the same as or lower than the lowest *tariff* rates previously applied to any other nation.

**mountain** A *buffer stock* created by price maintenance. It used to be common in Europe as a result of the Common Agricultural Policy (CAP) which guaranteed farmers a minimum price for their produce by buying it and storing it in the hope of selling it later. This caused severe overproduction and much of the accumulated produce (beef, butter, grain mountains etc.) could only be given away to Third World nations or charities, as the cost of storing it became prohibitive. The CAP was reformed in 2003 to break the link between aid and production. The Simple Payment Scheme now pays farmers for maintaining environmental and welfare conditions. See: *green currencies.*

**moving average** The moving average is a statistical technique of using *averages* on data for consecutive time periods to 'smooth out' the data. For instance, a 3-day moving (price) *average* is calculated by taking the prices of the 3 days up to and including a specific date, *averaging* the prices for these 3 days (ie adding the three prices and dividing by three) and using the *average* price thus obtained for that specific date. Take the following data, for example:

| Date in July | 18 | 19 | 20 | 21 | 22 | 23 | 24 | 25 |
|---|---|---|---|---|---|---|---|---|
| Price (£) | 12 | 21 | 6 | 30 | 15 | 3 | 27 | 9 |
| 3-day moving average | n/a | n/a | 13 | 19 | 17 | 16 | 15 | 13 |

The 3-day moving averages for 18th and the 19th July are not available (n/a). The moving average for 20th July is obtained by adding the 3 prices up to and including that date and dividing by 3, ie (12+21+6)/3 = 13. Similarly for 21st July: (21+6+30)/3 = 19; 22nd July: (6+30+15)/3 = 17; and so on. It can be seen that the moving average has smoothed out the data quite considerably: the range of the prices for the period is

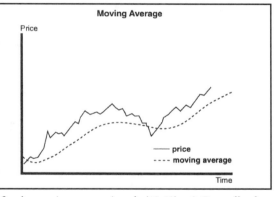

(30-3) = 27, whereas the range for the moving average is only (19-13) = 6. Generally, the longer the moving average, the smoother the data. Moving averages for *securities'* prices are calculated by taking the *average* of the *closing prices* for the relevant number of past trading days. See the diagram. Moving averages can also be weighted, as normal *averages* can, to assign more emphasis to certain items. Moving averages are often used by technical analysts to confirm price movements. See: *golden cross.*

**Mozambique** Standard *currency: metical.* 1 *metical* = 100 *centavos.*

**MPC** See: *Monetary Policy Committee.*

**MRO** *currency code* for: Mauritanian Ouguiya.

**MSCI Indices** The MSCI indices were originally produced by Morgan Stanley Capital International. In 2004 MSCI acquired Barra and in 2007 MSCI Barra was floated as an independent company. MSCI Barra provides an extensive range of global equity indices, which have become widely used international equity benchmarks throughout the investment industry, as well as bases for many *exchange traded funds* and other *tracker funds.* MSCI applies a consistent approach to its index construction across all types of market – developed, emerging and frontier markets – making it possible to aggregate individual country and industry indices to create composite, regional, sector and industry benchmarks.

MSCI index products include:

- Global, Regional and Country Equity Indices.
- Sector, Industry Group and Industry Indices.
- Global Value and Growth Indices.
- Global Small Cap Indices.
- Thematic and Strategy Indices.
- Hedged and GDP-weighted Indices.
- Custom Equity Indices.
- Real Time Equity Indices.

MSCI's international equity indices span 74 markets (23 developed, 24 emerging and 27 frontier) and are available in local currency and US dollars, and with or without dividends reinvested.

Developed markets:

- North America: Canada, United States.
- Europe: Austria, Belgium, Denmark, Finland, France, Germany, Greece, Ireland, Italy, Netherlands, Norway, Portugal, Spain, Sweden, Switzerland, United Kingdom.
- Pacific: Australia, Hong Kong, Japan, New Zealand, Singapore.

Emerging markets:

- Americas: Brazil, Chile, Colombia, Mexico, Peru.
- Europe, Middle East and Africa: Czech Republic, Egypt, Hungary, Israel, Morocco, Poland, Russia, South Africa, Turkey.
- Asia: China, India, Indonesia, Korea, Malaysia, Philippines, Taiwan, Thailand.

Frontier markets:

- Americas: Argentina, Jamaica**, Trinidad & Tobago.
- Central and Eastern Europe and CIS: Bulgaria, Croatia, Estonia, Lithuania, Kazakhstan, Romania, Serbia, Slovenia, Ukraine.
- Africa: Botswana**, Ghana**, Kenya, Mauritius, Nigeria, Tunisia.
- Middle East: Bahrain, Jordan, Kuwait, Lebanon, Oman, Qatar, Saudi Arabia*, United Arab Emirates.
- Asia: Pakistan, Sri Lanka, Vietnam.

* The MSCI Saudi Arabia Index is currently not included in the MSCI Frontier Markets Index but is part of the MSCI Gulf Cooperation Council (GCC) Countries Index.

** The MSCI Botswana Index, the MSCI Ghana Index, and the MSCI Jamaica Index are currently stand-alone country indices and are not included in the MSCI Frontier Markets Index. The addition of these countries to the MSCI Frontier Markets Index is under consideration.

**MSP**   See: *matched sale-purchase agreement.*

**MTF**   See: *multilateral trading facility.*

**MTN**   See: *medium term note.*

**Mudaraba**   Islamic term describing *trust* financing. This is an agreement made between two parties: one provides 100% of the *capital* for the project and another party, known as a mudarib, who manages the project using his entrepreneurial skills. *Profits* arising from the project are distributed according to a predetermined ratio. Any losses accruing are borne by the provider of *capital*. The provider of *capital* has no control over the management of the project.

**multilateral trading facility (MTF)** A securities trading operation which operates across a range of European markets, challenging single country stock exchanges. The appearance of MTFs is a direct result of the implementation of *MiFID*.

**multiple** The *earnings* multiple of a *company*, ie its *price earnings ratio*.

**multiplier** 1. A Keynesian notion which calculates the effects of *investment* spending by relating it to total *income*. An *investment* in a small factory, for example, increases the *incomes* of the workers who built it, the merchants who provide the suppliers, the distributors who supply the merchants, the manufacturers who supply the distributors and so on. Each recipient spends a portion of the *income* and saves the rest. By making an assumption as to the percentage each recipient saves, it is possible to calculate the total *income* produced by the *investment*. It is also possible to use the theory to determine the effect that any *capital expenditure* will have on consumer spending if, say, the government wishes to stimulate the economy by a major project. 2. In the '*deposit* multiplier' or 'credit multiplier' as it is variously known, *banks* can create *deposits* (*deposit* liabilities) which are many *multiples* of the *cash reserves* held ('fractional banking'). This impinges upon the total *money supply* available to the public.

**multiplier accelerator theory** Theory that the interaction of the *multiplier* (sense 1) and the *accelerator* causes *business cycles*.

**Mundell–Fleming model** A theory developed by James Fleming and Robert Mundell in the early 1960s. It was an advance on Keynesian *analysis* (see: *Keynesian economics*) by introducing international *capital* movements into the model. Thus the *BP curve* was added to the *IS curve* and *LM curve* already used in Keynesian theory. A wide range of conclusions can be drawn from this model which are especially relevant in *trade theory*

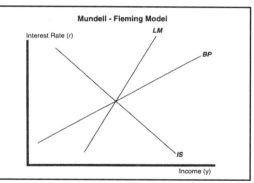

and the implications have a strong influence on policymakers. See the diagram for an illustration of the Mundell–Fleming model using IS-LM-BP *analysis*.

**Mundell's principle of effective market classification** The principle that government policies should be paired with the objectives on which they have the most influence. Mundell predicted that if this principle is not adopted then the economy may suffer from cyclical instability. See also: *Tinbergen's instruments – targets rule*.

**MUR** *currency code* for: *Mauritius* Rupee.

**Murubaha** Islamic term describing cost-plus financing. This is a *contract* sale between a *bank* and its client for the sale of goods at a price which includes a *profit margin* agreed by both parties. As a financing technique it involves the purchase of goods by the *bank* as directed by its client. The goods are then sold to the client with a mark-up.

**Musharaka** Islamic term describing *partnership* financing. This Islamic financing technique involves a *partnership* between two parties who both provide *capital* for a project. Both parties share *profits* on a pre-agreed ratio, but losses are shared on the basis of *equity* participation. Management of the project may be carried out by both the parties or by just one party. This is a very flexible *partnership* arrangement where the sharing of the *profits* and management can be negotiated and pre-agreed by all parties.

**mutual company** A *company* without *shareholders* whose ownership and *profits* are distributed among staff and/or clients of the *company*. Some *building societies, life assurance companies* and clubs are run as mutual companies where the executives, investors, employees, policy holders and clients participate in the *profits* and *income* from the *company*.

**mutual fund** The American equivalent to *UK* authorised *unit trusts* and OEICs where effectively investors pool their *money* and invest using the expertise of a professional *fund manager*.

**mutual life assurance company** These *companies* developed from *friendly societies* and have no *shareholders*. All *net profits* are therefore distributed to policyholders.

**mutual savings bank** A *US* institution run by a Board of Trustees that takes *deposits* and makes loans and is owned primarily by the depositors. See also: *thrift institutions*.

**MVA** Market value adjustment. See: *market value reduction*.

**MVR** *currency code for:* Maldive Rufiyaa. See also: *market value reduction*.

**MWK** *currency code* for: *Malawi* Kwacha.

**MWPA** Short for: Married Women's Property Act.

**MXN** *currency code* for: Mexican Nuevo Peso.

**Myanmar** Formerly: *Burma*. Standard *currency*: *kyat*. 1 *kyat* = 100 *pyas*.

**MYR** *currency code* for: Malaysian Ringgit.

**MZM** *currency code* for: *Mozambique* Metical.

# N

**NAD** *currency code* for: Namibian Dollar.

**NAFTA** See: *North American Free Trade Agreement.*

**naira** The standard *currency* of *Nigeria*. 1 naira = 100 *kobo.*

**NAIRU** Short for: non-accelerating inflationary rate of *unemployment*. The amount of *unemployment* (comprised only of *frictional unemployment* and *structural unemployment*) in an economy with *national income* at its potential level, which if maintained will result in a stable (or zero) rate of *inflation*. Compare: *natural rate of unemployment.*

**Nakasone bond** A non *yen* denominated *bond* named after the prime minister in office when it was introduced and issued by the Japanese government in overseas markets.

**naked option** An *option* where the buyer or seller owns none of the *underlying securities* or an *investment* in *securities* that is not hedged and therefore at *risk.*

**naked position** See: *naked option.*

**Name** See under: *Lloyd's.*

**Namibia** The Namibian Stock Exchange (NSE) began trading in Windhoek in 1992. The number of *listed shares* in 2007 was 24. Standard *currency: rand.* 1 *rand* = 100 *cents.*

**narrow money** See: *M0.*

**NASD** Short for the National Association of Securities Dealers. In July 2007 NASD merged with the member regulation, enforcement and arbitration functions of the New York Stock Exchange to form the *Financial Industry Regulatory Authority* (FINRA).

**NASDAQ** See: *National Association of Securities Dealers Automated Quotation System.* A computerised screen-based system used across the *US* that provides *brokers* and *dealers* with *quotations* for *securities* in the American *over-the-counter* (*OTC*) market as well as a number for *securities listed* on the *New York Stock Exchange* (*NYSE*). NASDAQ International began operations in January 1992 and provides quotes for most *US* and Canadian *stocks* internationally. NASDAQ is the second largest *stock market* in the world, exceeded in *volume* only by the *NYSE*. It is authorised by the *Financial Services Authority* in the *UK* as a *Recognised Investment Exchange*. In 1986, it established a link with the *Stock Exchange Automated Quotations System* (of the *London Stock Exchange*) and SESDAQ (the Stock Exchange of *Singapore* Dealing and Automated Quotation system). Its main *indices* are:

- NASDAQ Composite Index. It is composed of all NASDAQ National Market issues (the top tier comprising the vast majority of *securities*), with the exception of *warrants*. It is weighted by *market capitalisation.*
- NASDAQ-100. Base: 1 February 1985 = 250.
- NASDAQ Financial. Base: 1 February 1985 = 250.

See: *United States.*

**Nash equilibrium** A term used in microeconomic *analysis* of firms' behaviour. The Nash equilibrium is the *equilibrium* that comes about when firms operate at their maximum efficiency based on the existing behaviour of the other firms in the industry.

**National Association of Securities Dealers Automated Quotation System** See: *NASDAQ.*

**national debt** Accumulated as a result of a shortfall of revenues in the form of taxes against government expenditure. It represents the total amount of *money* borrowed by a government on which it has to pay *interest*. See: *Central Government Net Cash Requirement*.

**national income** The total *money value* of all goods and services produced in a country over a period of time (usually one year). Serves as a measure of economic activity and is used to calculate *standard of living* and economic *growth*. There are three methods of statistically measuring the national income, all of which should yield the same figure, save for some statistical error (discrepancy):

- Output method. Measures the *'value added'* at each stage in the production process to output, in order to avoid double-counting.

- Income method. Total *income* of residents obtained as a result of current production of goods and services.

- Expenditure method. Total domestic expenditure by residents on final consumption goods and services and *capital* goods (*investment*).

Thus national income = national output = national expenditure. National income at 'market prices' means that no adjustments have been made for indirect taxes and subsidies. National income at 'factor cost' is minus the part of expenditure paid in taxes plus subsidies obtained from the government. See: *gross domestic product, gross national product, national product.*

**nationalisation** Nationalisation in the UK was an election commitment of Clement Attlee, the Labour leader, in the build up to the July 1945 election. Nationalisation was where the state took over control of the main industries in Britain (coal, steel, electricity, rail, etc.) and where any *profit* made by these industries went to the country and not to *shareholders*. The first organisation to be nationalised was the *Bank of England* in 1946. This had been owned by private individuals since 1694. The next organisation to be nationalised was Cable and Wireless Ltd, which was the dominant force in long distance communications in Britain. The coal industry was nationalised in 1947, railways in 1948, and iron and steel in 1949. These industries were returned to the public via stock market flotation in a process known as privatisation, which began with British Telecom in 1984, followed by the privatisation of British Gas in 1986, and of Rolls-Royce, British Airways and the British Airports Authority in 1987. Utilities, steel and car makers and railways followed until 2008 when the process reversed with the nationalisation of Northern Rock and other *banks*.

**National Insurance** A scheme originally set up to provide protection against sickness and *unemployment*. Contributions help fund the National Health Service (NHS) and a wide range of other state benefits. National Insurance contributions are compulsory and charged on earnings above a certain minimum amount (£5,715 per year in 2009/10).

**National Market System (NMS)** The *securities* on *NASDAQ* which are subject to real-time trade reporting. It encompasses more than half of all *NASDAQ securities* and more than two-thirds of *NASDAQ share volume*.

**national product** Generic term for the total output produced by a country in a year. See: *gross national product* (GNP), *gross domestic product* (GDP), *national income*.

**National Savings and Investments (NS&I)** The Department of National Savings was established on 1 October 1969 and was previously known as the Post Office Savings Department. In February 2002 it was rebranded as National Savings and Investments. It is able to offer tax-free *investments* and its services currently include: the National Savings Bank (NSB), *premium bonds*, National Savings Certificates (NSCs) and Children's Bonus Bonds.

**natural rate of unemployment** When a competitive economy is operating at potential *national income*, the level of *unemployment* that results is called the natural rate of unemployment, and is associated with stable (or zero) *inflation*. For most purposes it is equivalent to the *NAIRU*, but the latter is used with respect to imperfectly competitive economies as well.

**Nauru** Standard *currency*: Australian *dollar*.

**NAV** See: *net asset value*.

**NB** New *bargain* (see: *new time*).

**NBV** See: *net book value*.

**NDP** See: *net domestic product*.

**near cash** See: *near money*.

**near money** *Investments* which are not *cash* but are considered near liquid, such as *money* invested *at call* or at short notice.

**neckline** The crucial *support level* defining a classic *chart* top or bottom formation used in *technical analysis*. The chartist believes that if the appropriate level is breached a significant move will occur. See: *head and shoulders*.

**negative cash flow** When outflow exceeds inflow of *cash* for a certain time period. See: *cash flow*.

**negative equity** When the *value* of an *asset* is exceeded by the loans secured against it.

**negative net worth/value** Shares in *companies* can have a negative *value* where loans and liabilities exceed *assets* by an amount greater than the *share capital*. Such *companies* are insolvent (see: *insolvency*) but can be so large that they are allowed to continue trading by their bankers in the hope of some resolution of their problems.

**negotiable security** The right to ownership or payment transferred from one person to another simply by the possession of such a *security*. Bank notes and bearer *bonds* (see: *bearer securities*) are prime examples. The term can include *share certificates* and *bills of exchange*, although these may need to be endorsed or accompanied by a *stock transfer form* (see: *transfer deed*) before they become negotiable.

**negotiated commissions** *Commissions* agreed by the parties to a *contract* or standard *commissions* applicable to smaller trades laid down by an exchange. *Commissions* are freely negotiated on the *London Stock Exchange*.

**Nepal** Standard *currency*: rupee. 1 *rupee* = 100 *paisa*.

**net** In general terms, this means after the deduction of *tax*, costs or charges. Contrast: *gross*.

**net asset turnover** A performance *ratio* calculated for a *company*. It is calculated as follows:

It indicates how well the *company* employs its productive capacity. Must be used with care if there have been capacity changes.

$$\text{net asset turnover} = \frac{\text{turnover}}{\text{net assets}}$$

**net asset value (NAV)** 1. The *valuation* of a collective *investment* based on the market price of *securities* held in its *portfolio*. *Unit trusts* and OEICs are valued on this basis, whereas *investment companies* have a *market value*. 2. Total *assets* less all liabilities, all potential dilution (see: *dilution of equity*) and all the prior *capital* charges (including *debentures, loan stocks* and *preference shares*). Net asset value per *share* is calculated by dividing this figure by the number of *ordinary shares* in issue.

**net assets**  The total *assets* less *current liabilities*. The amount in a *balance sheet* representing *shareholders'* funds or *capital*. See also: *net current assets*.

**net book value (NBV)**  The *value* at which an *asset* appears in a *company*'s *balance sheet*. ie less *depreciation* applied since its purchase or its last *revaluation*.

**net current assets**  Current *assets* less *current liabilities*. A conservative estimate of the *company*'s *net* worth, it rarely exceeds the *company*'s *capitalisation*. Sometimes referred to as operating or *working capital*, it effectively represents the *company*'s trading liquidity.

**net domestic product (NDP)**  The *gross domestic product* (*GDP*) of a nation less *capital consumption*.

**net exports**  *Exports* minus *imports*.

**net investment**  The addition to the stock of *capital* goods in an economy (*gross investment*), less a figure estimating *capital consumption*.

**net national product (NNP)**  The *gross national product* (*GNP*) of a nation less *capital consumption*.

**net present value (NPV)**  A *discounted cash flow* (*DCF*) method of *investment appraisal*. It entails finding the *present value* of a series of future *cash flows* due to an *investment*. The *present value* of a future receipt ('*cash flow*') is found by *discounting* it using a certain rate of *interest* (usually taken to be the *cost of capital* to the investor), and taking into account the *risk* of the *investment* providing the future receipts. The sum of the *present values* of the receipts is then calculated to give the net present value (*NPV*). At a given *cost of capital* (risk-adjusted), if an *investment* yields a positive *NPV* it should be accepted; a negative *NPV* should be rejected. The investor should be indifferent to an *investment* with zero *NPV* since it is just as profitable as the *investment* used for calculating the *benchmark cost of capital*. In this case the *benchmark* is called the break-even *cost of capital*. See: *internal rate of return*.

**net profit**  1. The *total return* on an *investment* less *tax* and all expenses. 2. The *profit* of a *company* after taking into account all expenses such as *depreciation, interest* and taxation, cost of sales and administration costs, but prior to *dividends*. See also: *profit & loss account*.

**net realisable value (NRV)**  The *net* sale *value* of an *asset*, ie the *cash* sum received less all costs associated with the sale.

**Netherlands**  The *Amsterdam Stock Exchange* (AEX) is the oldest *stock market* in the world. Records point to its origins in the early 17th century. In September 2000 it merged with the Brussels and Paris stock exchanges to form Euronext. The Dutch market is now officially Euronext Amsterdam. Its main *indices* are:

- AEX Index – A *market capitalisation weighted index* of the 25 most actively traded Dutch *stocks*, revised annually. The annual weighting of each *stock* is restricted to 10% of the *index*.

- AEX All-Share Index – Tracks movement of all *listed* Dutch *ordinary shares* (including *certificates*) and excludes *investment funds*, property funds, *holding companies*. It reflects long-term price changes. It is a weighted arithmetic *average*. Base: 31 December 1983 = 100.

- AEX Total Return Index – Uses the same *stocks* as the All-Share Index. Adjustments are made for *dividends* reinvested.

The *European Options Exchange* (*EOE*) opened in 1978 and merged with the Amsterdam Stock Exchange in 1997.

Standard *currency*: *euro*. 1 *euro* = 100 *cents*. The *guilder* was the standard *currency* of the Netherlands, until the introduction of the *euro* on 1 January 2002.

**Netherlands Antilles**  Dependency of the *Netherlands*. Standard *currency*: *guilder*.

**neutrality of money**  The hypothesis that the quantity of *money* influences only the level of prices but has no effect on the *real* level of *income* or the allocation of resources and thus relative prices. See: *quantity theory of money*.

**NEWCO**  A generic term used to refer to corporate start-ups and *spin-offs* before they are assigned a final name.

**New Caledonia**  Dependency of *France*. Standard *currency*: Pacific *franc*.

**new issues**  Shares being issued on a *stock exchange* for the first time. See: *flotation*.

**New York Cotton Exchange (NYCE)**  The oldest *commodity* exchange in New York (founded in 1870). In December 1993, it acquired the New York Futures Exchange (NYFE). The FINEX (Financial Exchange) division began operations in 1985, dealing in *financial futures* and *options*. In 1998 the New York Board of Trade (now ICE Futures) became the parent company of the NYCE. The NYCE is the world's centre for cotton *futures* and *options* trading. It also trades frozen concentrated orange juice *futures* and *options*.

**New York Mercantile Exchange (NYMEX)**  World's largest physical *commodity futures* exchange. Established 1872 as the Butter and Cheese Exchange of New York. Merged with the Commodity Exchange (*COMEX*) in August 1994. Has operated as two divisions since then, NYMEX and *COMEX* divisions. The NYMEX division trades in crude oil, coal, electricity, heating oil, gasoline, natural gas, uranium, propane, platinum and palladium *futures* and *options*. *COMEX* deals in copper, *gold*, silver and aluminium. In 2008 NYMEX was taken over by CME group, which owns the Chicago Mercantile Exchange and the Chicago Board of Trade.

**New York Stock Exchange (NYSE)**  Founded in 1792, this is the oldest and largest *stock exchange* in the *United States*. Located at 11 *Wall Street* in New York City it is also known as the *Big Board*, the Exchange, the Street and *Wall Street*. It is operated as an unincorporated association with a governing *board* of *directors* and a full-time chairman. More than 6,500 securities are *listed*, representing one third of the total *shares* traded globally. In 2007 the NYSE merged with Euronext, bringing together US and European markets. The *NYSE* quotes an *index*: *NYSE* Composite Index. Established 1956. Comprises all *common stocks listed*. Base: 31 December 1965 = 50. There exist four subgroups: Industrial, Transportation, Utility, Finance. See also: *Dow Jones Stock Averages*, *Standard & Poor's 500 Index*, *United States*.

**New Zealand**  Predecessor of present New Zealand Stock Exchange (NZX, based in Wellington) was the Stock Exchange Association of New Zealand, established 1915. The NZ operates a national screen-based trading system. The main *index* is:

- NZX 50 Capital Index. Covers 50 of the largest and most liquid *stocks* quoted on the Exchange, weighted by total free float *market capitalisation*.

Standard *currency*: New Zealand *dollar*. 1 New Zealand *dollar* = 100 *cents*.

**Newly industrialised country (NIC)**  These are countries that go through a process of industrialisation. Largescale *growth* is seen in the secondary sector and the tertiary sector, and a decline in primary industry. It represents the movement from a simple agricultural economy, to a more developed manufacturing and service economy. Countries such as *Malaysia* and *Brazil* are considered *NICs*.

**Newstrack**  See: *PLUS Market.*

**NGN**  *currency code* for: Nigerian Naira.

**ngultrum**  Standard *currency* of *Bhutan.* 1 ngultrum = 100 *chetrum.*

**ngwee**  *Currency* sub-unit of *Zambia.* 100 ngwee = 1 *kwacha.*

**NIC**  See: *Newly industrialised country.*

**NICs**  National Insurance Contributions. See: *National Insurance.*

**Nicaragua**  Standard *currency*: cordoba. 1 *cordoba* = 100 *centavos.*

**Niger**  Standard *currency*: African *franc.*

**Nigeria**  Formerly the Lagos Stock Exchange (until 1977), the Nigerian Stock Exchange was incorporated in 1960, and presently has branches and trading floors in six cities in Nigeria. In 2007 there were 283 listed companies. Its main *index* is:

* Nigerian Stock Exchange All-Share Index. Base: 3 January 1984 = 100.

Standard *currency*: *naira.* 1 *naira* = 100 *kobo.*

**Nikkei 225**  An *index* of prices on the Tokyo Stock Exchange. First calculated on 16 May 1949, based at 176.21. The Nikkei 225 is an unweighted *price index* of 225 Japanese *companies.* It was restructured for the first time in its history in late 1991 by its administrator, the Nikon Keizai Shimbun (thus 'Nikkei') the financial newspaper group, to try to reduce the impact of futures-related trading on the *index.* Membership of the *index* is now reviewed annually, when up to six members can be replaced if their *shares* become *illiquid* or unrepresentative. Previous changes only occurred when *companies* were taken over or liquidated. The index famously hit an all time high of 38,915.87. By February 2009 it was around 7,500. See also: Nikkei Stock Index 300 under *Japan.*

**Nikkei Dow**  Nikkei *Dow Jones* Index. Former name of the: *Nikkei 225.*

**nil paid shares**  A type of *share* that does not have to be paid for until some date in the future. They can be traded as nil paid against their *future value* as in the case of new *shares* made available by a *rights issue.* See: *partly paid.*

**NINJA**  Colloquial for someone with: No Income, No Job and no *Assets.* After the collapse of US property prices, *mortgages* that they were sold were classified as toxic or troubled and triggered the *Credit Crunch* in 2008. See: TARP, *toxic asset.*

**NIO**  *currency code* for: Nicaraguan Oro Cordoba.

**Niue**  Dependency of *New Zealand.* Standard *currency*: *New Zealand dollar.*

**NL**  Abbreviation appearing after Australian *company* names meaning: no liability. Equivalent to the British *plc.*

**NMS**  See: *National Market System, Normal Market Size.*

**NNP**  See: *net national product.*

**no par value**  *Securities* issued without a *par value*, common in *America* where the entire proceeds of the initial sale of the *stock* are credited to the *capital* surplus account (equivalent to the *share premium account* for *UK* firms).

**no-load fund**  A *collective investment scheme* where there is no initial charge. Here units are purchased and sold using the one price, though sometimes additional *commission* is added as a separate item in the case of each transaction. In the case of some no-load funds certain surrender penalties apply in the case of early encashment. No load funds may carry higher than average annual charges to balance the loss of the initial charge.

**noble** A platinum coin that is legal tender in the Isle of Man although mainly sold for the purpose of *investment*. The name 'noble' is also used as the generic term for the platinum group of metals.

**NOK** *currency code* for: Norwegian Krone.

**nomad** See: *nominated advisor*. See also: *AIM*.

**nominal capital** See: *par value*.

**nominal exchange rate** The *spot exchange rate* most often quoted, without any adjustments made for relative price levels between the countries. See: *effective exchange rate, real exchange rate*.

**nominal interest rate** Actual *interest rate* without taking into account *inflation*. Compare: *real interest rate*.

**nominal price** Used to indicate a price when no trade price is readily available and/or buyers' and sellers' *quotations* are wide apart. See: *magenta*.

**nominal value** Another term for: *par value*.

**nominal yield** See under: *yield*.

**nominated advisor** Called a '*nomad*' for short. Professionals who sponsor and police the new and existing *companies* on the *Alternative Investment Market* (*AIM*) on the *London Stock Exchange*. Carefully vetted and selected by the *London Stock Exchange* not least because they *underwrite* the good conduct of the *listed company*. *Companies* cannot be quoted without a *nomad* and *nomads* may lose their status if one of their *companies* breaches regulations.

**nomination** A *member* of a *pension* scheme may nominate his *beneficiaries* in case of death. This is normally done by an *expression of wish* on which the *trustees* will usually act, though they are not obliged to do so. Certain exemptions from *inheritance tax* can result.

**nominee** Shares or *investments* need not be registered in the name of their *beneficial owner*, since they may alternatively be registered under the name of a nominee, a practice often used by *stockbrokers* to ease the administration of buying and selling holdings on behalf of their clients. Although initially this may conceal the true identity of the purchaser, the *Department for Business, Innovation and Skills* and *public companies* have appropriate powers to investigate true ownership where necessary. See: *insider dealing*, *Section 212*.

**non resident** A term used to describe an individual who is not resident in the *UK* which, depending on the circumstances, has a significant effect on their *UK tax* liabilities.

**non-assented stock** See: *assented stock*.

**non-contributory pension** A *pension* where the employee makes no contribution and all contributions are made by the employer.

**non-domiciled** A term used to describe individuals who have retained the *domicile* of a country other than their country of *residence*. To obtain non-domiciled status a *UK* resident must satisfy a number of *HMRC* conditions.

**non-executive** See under: *non-executive director*.

**non-executive director** A *director* appointed to the *board* of a *company* to represent external interests, such as those of outside or minority *shareholders*, but not involved in the day-to-day running of the business. See: *arm's length, conflict of interest*.

**non-profits** Normally used to refer to a *life assurance* policy that provides a *sum assured* on maturity or death that is guaranteed but not increased by the addition of *bonuses*. A non-profit-making *company* is also a term used to refer to a *mutual company*. Contrast: *with-profits policy*, *with-profits bond*.

**non-qualifying policy** A *UK life assurance* policy that does not satisfy the qualification rules contained in Schedule 15 of the Income and Corporation Taxes Act 1988. Compare: *qualifying policy*.

**non-recourse loan** A loan where the lender is only entitled to repayment from assets or the project the loan is *funding* and not from other resources of the borrower.

**non-resident** To become a non-resident for *UK tax* purposes an individual must be resident overseas for at least a full *tax year*. During the period abroad temporary visits to the *UK* must not exceed 90 days in total per tax year on average.

**non-voting shares** See: *'A' shares*.

**Norfolk Island** Dependency of *Australia*. Standard *currency*: Australian *dollar*.

**Normal Market Size (NMS)** Shares quoted on the *London Stock Exchange* are traded in different *volumes* and *bargain* sizes depending on demand. In an effort to determine a measure of the *quality* of the market in a particular *share* the exchange has developed a normal market size calculation to give an indication of the size of an average institutional *bargain*. There are twelve *bands* that equate to the number of *shares* in such a *bargain*, ranging from 500 to 200,000. *Market makers* are obliged to quote in *NMS* sizes; trades in 'liquid' *stocks* below three times *NMS* have to be published on the *Stock Exchange Automated Quotations System* (*SEAQ*) immediately, publication of larger trades can be delayed by up to 90 minutes. The *London Market Information Link* is available for *bargains* up to 10% of *NMS*. The rules came into effect on 14 January 1991 replacing the old *SEAQ* categories of alpha, beta and *gamma* with *FTSE* 100, liquid and less liquid. All *stocks* with an *NMS* of 2,000 or more are 'liquid' and those with less than 2,000 are 'less liquid'.

**normal retirement age** A predetermined retirement date normally between 60 and 70 years. However, tax rules allow benefit to be taken from 50 onwards (55 from April 2010).

**normal retirement date** A predetermined date on which *pension* benefits may be taken and incorporated in the *pension* scheme rules, typically between age 60 and 65. See: *Barber Judgment*.

**North American Free Trade Agreement (NAFTA)** This agreement came into effect in January 1994 with the aim of completely removing barriers to trade between the *US*, *Canada* and *Mexico* over a ten-year period.

**North Korea** Standard *currency*: *won*. 1 *won* = 100 chon.

**Northern Mariana Islands** Dependency of the *USA*. Standard *currency*: *US dollar*.

**Norway** The Oslo Stock Exchange was established in 1881. In 1991, the *stock exchanges* in Oslo, Bergen and Trondheim merged into one *stock exchange* named the Oslo Børs. Its main *indices* are:

- Oslo Børs Benchmark Index. Base: 1 January 1983 = 100.
- OBX Stock Index. A capital-weighted *index* based on the 25 most actively traded *stocks* on the Exchange.

Standard *currency*: *krone*. 1 Norwegian *krone* = 100 öre.

**nostro account** A bank *account* held in a foreign country in a foreign *currency* organised through a *UK bank*. See: *vostro account*.

**notary** A professional, normally a lawyer, authorised to witness documents and swear affidavits. Sometimes called a 'notary public'.

**Nouveau Marche** An *equity* market unit of the *Paris Bourse* that deals solely in smaller, innovative, high-growth *companies*. It is the French equivalent of the *Alternative Investment Market (AIM)* in the UK.

**novation** The replacement of one legal agreement by another with the agreement of all the parties. *Clearing houses* will *net opening* and *closing contracts* in *futures* and *options* as well as balancing *writers* and buyers of *options* by novation.

**NPR** *currency code* for: Nepalese Rupee.

**NPV** 1. See: *no par value*. 2. See: *net present value*.

**NRA** See: *normal retirement age*.

**NRD** See: *normal retirement date*.

**NRV** Short for: *net realisable value*.

**numismatic coin** Coins which are collectible and have a scarcity or historical interest which exceeds the *value* of the metal from which they were minted. Originally coins were based solely on their weight of rare or precious metal, but they are now mostly tokens. Some *bullion* coins are still minted and reflect only the *value* of their metal content. See: *kruggerand, noble, Maple Leaf*.

**NV** Short for: Naamloze Vennootschap. A Dutch or Dutch Antilles *public limited company* (*plc*). Compare: *BV*.

**NYCE** See: *New York Cotton Exchange*.

**NYMEX** See: *New York Mercantile Exchange*.

**NYSE** See: *New York Stock Exchange*.

**NZD** *currency code* for: *New Zealand* Dollar.

# O

**OAT** Obligation à trésorerie. A French *Treasury bill*.

**OCAS** See: *Organisation of Central American States*.

**occupational pension scheme** The general name for a *pension* gained as a result of salaried employment. Governed by HMRC and DWP rules, it needs to comply with legislation in the Finance Act 2004 to benefit from *tax* incentives. Many occupational pension schemes are calculated as a fraction of final salary per year of service up to certain limits, mostly 2/3 (40/60). See: *capping*.

**Occupational Pensions Board (OPB)** A statutory body established under the Social Security Act 1973 (and *SSPA* 75), that was responsible for vetting appropriate schemes and issuing *contracting-out certificates* for *pension* schemes that meet statutory requirements and for supervising those schemes. The Board was replaced by the Occupational Pension Regulator in 1997, which itself has since been replaced by the Pensions Regulator.

**Occupational Pensions Regulatory Authority (OPRA)** Established by the *Pensions Act 1995* and supervised a range of legal requirements to protect people's occupational *pensions*. OPRA was replaced by the Pensions Regulator in April 2005.

**OECD** See: *Organisation for Economic Cooperation and Development*.

**OEEC** See: *Organisation for European Economic Cooperation*.

**OEIC** See: *open-ended investment company*.

**OEM** See: *Original Equipment Manufacturer*.

**OEX** *Wall Street* shorthand for the *Standard & Poor's* 100 *stock index*, which comprises *stocks* for which *options* are traded on the *Chicago Board Options Exchange*. OEX *index options* are traded on the *Chicago Board of Trade*, and *futures* are traded on the *Chicago Mercantile Exchange*.

**OFEX** Now called *PLUS*, this was an unregulated trading facility provided by J.P. Jenkins Ltd (JPJ) allowing *share* dealing in smaller unquoted *companies* and *securities* off-exchange and launched 2 October 1995. The *London Stock Exchange* had previously allowed *shares* to be traded on a *matched bargain* basis under *Rule 4.2*, and OFEX was set up to make markets in these *companies*; such dealings were classified as off-exchange (colloquially – ofex). PLUS Markets plc ('*PLUS*') is a *Recognised Investment Exchange* in the *UK* and a Market Operator under the Markets in Financial Instruments Directive ('MiFID'), authorised to operate both secondary (trading) and primary (listing/quotation) markets. See: *PLUS*.

**off balance sheet finance** The purchase of *goodwill* from *cash assets* can deplete *balance sheet assets* as *goodwill* has to be written off. Accordingly *companies* will arrange to borrow *money* through an *associate company* for such purposes and keep the transaction off the *balance sheet*. Leasing equipment rather than purchasing it has a similar effect although the *profit & loss account* will show the rental payments or the cost of supporting the borrowings of an *associate*.

**offer** A term used in the law of *contract*. The offer is the first step and an acceptance of the offer can bind the two parties. An offer should not be confused with an invitation to make an offer (called an '*invitation to treat*'). A trader who marks goods with a price tag is not offering to sell at that price, but is inviting an offer to purchase the goods. See: *offer price*.

**offer for sale** An *offer* to the public of a *company*'s *shares*, made by the *sponsor* to the issue via a *prospectus*. The *offer* may be at a fixed price, which may require a *ballot*, or by *tender* at different prices, subject to a minimum. Known also as a *public offering* it is an invitation to the general public to purchase newly available *shares* in a *company* through an *issuing house* or *merchant bank* and is the normal route for a *flotation*. Called a *tender offer* in *America*.

**offer price** The price at which a *security* is offered for sale and thus the price at which a buyer will strike a deal. Also the price at which *unit trusts* and *unit-linked life assurance* funds are offered reflecting *brokers' commission* and management charges. Compare: *bid price*.

**Office for National Statistics (ONS)** Formed in April 1996 by the *merger* of the *Central Statistical Office* with the Office for Population Census & Surveys (OPCS), it is the central government agency that collates all the economic, demographic, trade and price data used to determine the statistical state of the nation.

**Office of Fair Trading (OFT)** The organisation set up to police the Fair Trading Act 1973, designed primarily to protect the rights of consumers. It is also involved in *company mergers* and *acquisitions* where there is some possibility that competition may be restricted. Should this be the case it advises on referring the transaction to the *Competition Commission*.

**official bank rate** Also called the *Bank of England base rate*, this is the *benchmark interest rate* in the UK. The rate is determined by a vote during monthly meetings of the *Monetary Policy Committee*. The description changed in 2006 and replaced the previous '*repo rate*' (*repo* is short for repurchase agreement) in 1997. Previously (between 1981 and 1997) the title was Minimum Band 1 Dealing Rate and prior to that the *Minimum Lending Rate*. It is the rate at which the reserve bank lends *money* to the banks and the yardstick for *interest rates* in the UK.

**Official List** Prepared daily by the UK Listing Authority (UKLA), this is a record of all *bargains* effected for all the *securities listed* on the exchange. It provides details of *dividend* dates, *rights issues*, prices and other pertinent information. Also called: *Daily Official List*.

**official receiver** A government representative appointed to supervise the financial affairs of a *company* in *liquidation*. An ordinary *receiver* may be appointed by *creditors*, but in cases of public interest and/or fraud an official receiver is normally appointed.

**offshore financial centre** Low *tax* areas providing financial benefits for *non-residents*, low or nil *withholding tax* and low reserve requirements for *banks*. Some countries have dramatically improved their *balance of payments* by providing such services, particularly the *Cayman Islands*, which has become one of the world's largest offshore financial centres, as have the Channel Islands and the Isle of Man, *Andorra* and *Bermuda* – even the *Turks and Caicos Islands* have made a name for themselves in this respect. However offshore financial centres are now under pressure because of concerns from their larger onshore counterparts about tax evasion and money laundering. See: *tax haven*.

**offshore fund** Funds which operate from one of the many *offshore financial centres* outside the *UK* to obtain a *tax* advantage. These funds are administered in a similar fashion to *OEICs* but are not directly governed by the *FSA*, though some funds in the EU territories fall within the *Undertaking for Collective Investments in Transferable Securities*.

**OFT** See: *Office of Fair Trading*.

**old age pension** See: *state pension*.

**Old Lady of Threadneedle Street** Nickname for the *Bank of England*, coined by the politician/dramatist R.B. Sheridan, dating back to the Victorian era when the *Bank of England* was commonly portrayed as an elderly lady.

**oligopoly** Where a small number of *companies* control the market supply of particular goods or services and can between them manipulate market prices. Market structure between the two extremes of *monopoly* and a perfectly competitive market. Compare: *bilateral oligopoly, oligopsony*.

**oligopsony** A market situation in which there are just a few large buyers and many small suppliers. The large buyers can use their power to play off one supplier against another and to secure bulk *discounts* on purchases. Compare: *bilateral oligopoly, monopsony, oligopoly*.

**Oman** Standard *currency*: Omani *rial*. 1 *rial* = 1,000 *baiza*.

**Ombudsman** Named after an independent arbitrator sponsored by the state in Scandinavian countries. In the *UK* the term is used to describe a parliamentary commissioner appointed to impartially arbitrate complaints by the public against major industries or institutions. The service is free to the public and is funded either by government or industry associations. Prior to the *Financial Services and Markets Act 2000* individual ombudsmen operated in the fields of: *investment, building societies*, banking and *insurance*. These functions are now provided by the *Financial Ombudsman Service* which was created by the Financial Services and Markets Act 2000. The *Pensions Ombudsman* investigates and decides complaints and disputes about the way that *pension* schemes are run whilst complaints about the sales and marketing of *pension* schemes are dealt with by the *Financial Ombudsman Service*. Other ombudsman services are: Energywatch, Estate Agents Ombudsman, Financial Services Ombudsman Scheme for the Isle of Man, Health Service Ombudsman, Housing Ombudsman Service, Legal Services Ombudsman, Local Government Ombudsman, Northern Ireland Ombudsman, Police Ombudsman for Northern Ireland, Parliamentary Ombudsman, *Pensions Ombudsman*, Prisons and Probation Ombudsman, Public Services Ombudsman for Wales, Removals Industry Ombudsman Scheme, Scottish Legal Services Ombudsman, Scottish Public Services Ombudsman, Otelo (Telecommunications Ombudsman).

**omega** The change in an *option's value* as a percentage of the price change in the underlying *security*. Omega is the *derivative of gamma*, and allows the investor to see the relationship between an *option's* price and the underlying security's price. For example, a *stock option* with an omega of 2 indicates that the price of the *option* will increase 2% for every 1% increase in the price of the stock; also called *speed*.

**OMO** See: *open market operation*.

**OMR** *currency code* for: Omani Rial.

**ONS** See: *Office for National Statistics*.

**OPB** See: *Occupational Pensions Board*.

**OPEC** See: *Organisation of Petroleum Exporting Countries*.

**open economy** See: *openness*.

**open interest** The total number of purchases and/or sales in a particular month or months, relating to the entire market, which at some stage will have to be liquidated or covered; normally applied to *derivatives* markets.

**open market operation (OMO)** Activities in primary and *secondary markets* by a government dealing in its own *government securities* in order to alter prevailing rates of *interest* by manipulating *market forces*. Compare: *foreign exchange* operation (FXO).

**open market option** Introduced in the Finance Act 1978, the open market option enabled the transfer of an accumulated *pension* fund from one *life assurance company* to another to achieve a higher *annuity* rate. The requirement was subsequently legislated for in a similar form in the Financial Act 2004. This *option* must be exercised before any benefits are taken from the original *life assurance company*, be it by way of a *pension* or tax-free lump sum. See: *compulsory purchase annuities.*

**open outcry** Most trading in *futures* occurs by word of mouth (thus: 'open outcry') in a *pit* or *ring.* Traders, normally identified by badges or distinctive coloured jackets, trade by shouting or signalling to each other whereupon the prices are recorded and displayed electronically. Can be particularly frantic when markets are volatile. Other markets may also use this method of trading. Open outcry has become increasingly uncommon as electronic trading has taken over.

**open position** Where a *futures* or *options* position is running and has not been closed (see: *close,* sense 2), sold or covered (see: *cover*) and which will need to be if it is not to lapse (expire) or require *delivery.*

**open-end credit** US term for: *revolving credit.*

**open-end fund** A collective *investment* such as a *unit trust* or *OEIC* which creates and redeems units subject to demand, as opposed to an *investment trust*, which has a set number of *shares.* Another term for a *US mutual fund.* See: *open-ended investment company.*

**open-ended investment company (OEIC)** A form of retail *investment fund*, similar to a *unit trust*, governed by the Authorised Investment Funds (Tax) Regulations 2006.

**opening** 1. Term used when opening a fresh commitment as opposed to *closing* or liquidating an existing commitment. 2. The reference to the official *call-over* at the start of a trading session.

**opening purchase** A transaction in which the buyer becomes the holder of an *option.*

**opening sale** A transaction in which the seller assumes liability for the performance of an *option contract*, therefore becoming the *writer* of that *contract.*

**openness** A measure of the extent to which a nation engages in international trade. An *open economy* is one in which *imports* and *exports* comprise a relatively large proportion of *national income.*

**operating profit/loss** The *profit* or loss made by a company's normal business activities. It is *revenue* after *cost of sales* and selling, general and administrative expenses but before *interest* and before *tax.* Also called EBIT (*earnings* before *interest* and *tax*).

**opportunity cost** The cost of an alternative *investment* compared with a chosen course of action. For example, the opportunity cost of buying a house as opposed to building it yourself or even building your house as opposed to working for the *money* to buy one. Opportunity cost considers not just the monetary advantage of one strategy or another but the comparative circumstances, *risk,* time and effort necessary for one against the other.

**OPRA** See: *Occupational Pensions Regulatory Authority.*

**option** In *investment* terms an option is the right, but not the obligation, to buy (*call option*) or sell (*put option*) an *investment* holding at a predetermined price (called the *exercise price* or *strike price*) at some particular date in the future. The option price simply represents the cost (*premium*) of the right to purchase or sell an *underlying security* and its *time value* and will depend on the prospects of changes in the price of the *underlying security* to which it relates. If a *traded option* is unsuccessful the purchaser simply allows the option to lapse losing only the initial purchase price of the option (the option *money* or *premium*). In London, options in *commodity futures* are bought and sold on *LIFFE*, and options on most larger *shares, share indices*, foreign *currencies, gilts* and *interest rates* are dealt with through *LIFFE*. *Naked options* are bought by speculators (see: *speculation*), although options can be useful in protecting (see: *hedge*) or enhancing an existing position (see: *cover*). Options do not carry rights to *dividends* and are synthetic *investments* which can be traded for *value* at any time they are current, as opposed to *traditional options*. In a 'European' option the buyer only has the right to exercise the option on the *expiry date*, whereas an 'American' option may be exercised at any time up to the *expiry date*. In both cases, however, they can be traded rather than exercised at any time. *Writers* of options have an *open position* which, if uncovered, can result in 'unlimited' losses. See: *zero-sum game*.

**ordinary shares** Sometimes specified as voting or non-voting, these *shares* entitle the holder to the *company*'s *earnings* and its *assets* after all prior charges and claims have been met. They normally account for the bulk of the *company*'s *capital*. See: *equity*.

**öre** *Currency* sub-unit of *Sweden*. 100 öre = 1 *krona*.

**øre** *Currency* sub-unit of *Denmark*, the *Faeroe Islands, Greenland* and *Norway*. 100 øre = 1 *krone*.

**organic growth** The development of a *company* by its own means and resources as opposed to *growth* by acquiring other established competing or compatible businesses. *Companies* are expected by their *shareholders* to grow naturally (organically) by improving their products and services through research and development, by increasing their efficiency, by training and recruiting staff, and by expanding their markets or their market share.

**Organisation for Economic Cooperation and Development (OECD)** Replaced the *Organisation for European Economic Cooperation* (*OEEC*) in 1961. It variously assists member states in formulating government policies in order to achieve sustainable *growth* and stability; promotes cooperation in economic and social policymaking and participation in world trade; and provides economic aid to less-developed countries. It is headquartered in Paris and the 30 member states are: *Australia, Austria, Belgium, Canada, Czech Republic, Denmark, Finland, France, Germany, Greece, Iceland, Republic of Ireland, Italy, Japan, Luxembourg,* the *Netherlands, New Zealand, Norway,* Poland, *Portugal, Spain, Slovakia, South Korea, Sweden, Switzerland, Turkey, UK, USA.* It is a very important source for international economic data and compiles standardised statistics on a regular basis.

**Organisation for European Economic Cooperation (OEEC)** Following the *Marshall Plan*, the *OEEC* was set up to aid the rebuilding of post-war Europe. In 1961 it was replaced by the *Organisation for Economic Cooperation and Development* (*OECD*).

**Organisation of Petroleum Exporting Countries (OPEC)** Set up in 1960, *OPEC* is a *cartel* of the main petroleum-producing nations whose purpose is to further and protect their interests. Responsible for the more than four-fold oil price increases in 1973, causing a protracted world *recession*. Their influence has decreased in the recent past due to the use of new oil fields (eg North Sea) and alternative forms of fuel and energy. Presently, there are 12 member nations, as follows, with their joining dates: *Algeria* 1969, *Angola* 2007, *Ecuador* rejoined 2007, *Iran* 1960, *Iraq* 1960, *Kuwait* 1960, *Libya* 1962, *Nigeria* 1971, *Qatar* 1961, *Saudi Arabia* 1960, *United Arab Emirates* 1967, *Venezuela* 1960. Founder members joined in 1960. The organisation has its headquarters in Vienna.

**origin** Country where a product was made. In order to prevent circumventing *tariffs* and trade restrictions, some nations use 'rules of origin' in assessing products for *import* purposes.

**Original Equipment Manufacturer (OEM)** An *OEM* specification applies to goods made only by a specific branded manufacturer and where normally only *OEM* replacement spares and parts can be specified. This is different from goods produced under licence or franchised goods which can be made to specification by a different manufacturer.

**orphan stock** *Stock* that has been neglected by professional research analysts. Since the *company*'s *stock* is rarely followed and the *stock* infrequently recommended it is considered an orphan by investors. Orphan stocks may not attract attention because they are too small or because they have disappointed investors in the past but a change of fortune or a special situation can bring a dramatic return to favour with appropriate rewards for investors. Also called a 'wallflower'.

**OTC** See: *over-the-counter*.

**OTC market** See: *over-the-counter market*.

**ouguiya** Standard *currency* of *Mauritania*. 1 ouguiya = 5 *khoums*.

**out-of-the-money option** A *call option* whose *exercise price* is above the current price of the *underlying security* or a *put option* where the *exercise price* is below the current price of the *underlying security*.

**outcry** See: *open outcry*.

**output gap** The output gap is defined by taking the difference: potential *national income* (output) minus actual *national income* in an economy. If the output gap is positive, it is called a '*recessionary gap*'; if it is negative, it is termed an '*inflationary gap*'.

**output tax** The *value added tax* added to goods supplied.

**over-the-counter (OTC)** 1. A *security* that is not *listed* on a recognised exchange but which can be made available to the public. 2. See: *over-the-counter market*.

**over-the-counter market (OTC market)** Now one of the most popular forms of private *investment* in the *United States*, the *OTC market* in the *UK* became defunct, in 1987 (when the LSE introduced the third market – now the *Alternative Investment Market*) after failing to generate sufficient *turnover* and having had regulatory difficulties. It was abolished completely in the *UK* in 1990. In the *US*, mostly smaller *companies* that fail to meet the *listing* requirements of the *NYSE* or the *AMEX* sell their *stocks* on *OTC markets*. The rules for *OTC markets* in the *US* are made and administered by the self-regulatory *NASD*. The largest *OTC market* is the *NASDAQ*.

**overbought** A technical term suggesting that profit-taking is overdue, frequently based on an analyst's expectations that a major deviation from the *trend* will be reversed. Basically *shares* or markets that are too expensive.

**overdraft** Borrowing through an allowance agreed for a *current account* where sums exceeding *cash* held in the account can be paid. Basically an agreement by a *bank* to sustain an overdrawn *current account*.

**overheating** In a buoyant cycle an economy can, on occasion, grow too fast. This overheating can cause *imports* to be sucked in and affect both *inflation* and the *balance of payments. Interest rates* increases are most commonly used to cool down economic activity. See: *business cycle, hard landing, soft landing*.

**overhead** The ongoing costs of a business not attributed to any specific business activity but necessary for the business to function. Examples include rent, *rates, insurance,* leasing costs, subscriptions – all the costs associated with a business suddenly without employees, customers or products.

**overnight money**  *Deposits* in the *money market* due for redemption at the beginning of the day following deposit.

**overnight rate** Normally *LIBOR*.

**overnight repo**  A method of overcoming a temporary shortage of liquidity in the *money market* using *repurchase* agreements (*repos*) on an overnight basis.

**overshooting**  Term used to describe the movement of the domestic *exchange rate* beyond that predicted by purchasing price *parity* (thus 'overshooting') when the *money supply* changes. The overcompensation is due to 'sticky' (ie inflexible) price levels and speculators' expectations. In the long run, the *exchange rate* moves toward *P.P.* The theory behind this was provided by R. Dornbusch (in 1976), in the first *exchange rate* model that adequately explained large and prolonged departures of the *exchange rate* from *P.P.*

**oversold**  A technical situation where a market may have declined too rapidly, due to excessive selling pressure. Generally *shares* or markets that are cheap. Compare: *overbought.*

**oversubscription**  Shares are said to be oversubscribed when more applications for a *flotation* are received than there are *shares* for offer. In this event, applications are usually scaled down *pro rata*, although sometimes small applications are met in full and the larger ones scaled down. There can also sometimes be a *ballot*. See: *allotment.*

**overvalued**  Market prices that overstate the worth or *value* of the *company* or market given its historical performance.

**overwriting**  Speculative practice by an *option writer* who believes a *security* to be overpriced or underpriced and sells *call options* or *put options* on the *security* in quantity on the assumption that they will not be exercised.

# P

**P11d** A form recording taxable and non-taxable benefits received by employees and *directors* on *PAYE*.

**P&L** See: *profit & loss account.*

**PA** 1. See: *personal account.* 2. See: *power of attorney.*

**pa'anga** Standard *currency* of *Tonga.* 1 pa'anga = 100 *seniti.*

**Paasche formula** See under: *composite index, weighting factor.*

**Paasche index** See under: *composite index, weighting factor.*

**PAB** *currency code* for: Panamanian Balboa.

**pac-man defence** An *offer* made by a *target* for the *shares* of a *bidder,* after the *bidder* has made a *hostile takeover* attempt.

**Pacific Stock Exchange (PSE)** See under: *United States.*

**PADA** See: *Personal Accounts Delivery Authority.*

**paid-up** The term is used when *premiums* to a *life assurance* policy or *pension* plan cease before the *maturity date* and the policy is not encashed. There are usually penalties imposed if this occurs in the early years, and with life policies these are equivalent to those imposed on surrender; the remaining amount is then allowed to appreciate to the end of the chosen term, in accordance with the performance of the selected *unit-linked* fund or a relevant *bonus* allocation. In *pension* plans this can be referred to as *preserved benefits.*

**paid-up capital** The amount *shareholders* have paid the *company* for the *shares* issued, the *shares* having been fully subscribed. The *shares* can be *fully paid* or *partly paid.* Also called: *fully paid capital* (where the prefix 'fully' refers to subscription, not to payment).

**paid-up share** A *fully paid* (*F.P.*) *share.*

**paisa** *Currency* sub-unit used in the following countries: *India, Nepal, Pakistan*: 100 paisa = 1 *rupee*; *Bangladesh*: 100 paisa = 1 *taka.*

**Pakistan** The main exchange is the Karachi Stock Exchange (KSE), established 1947. The main indices are:

* KSE 100
* KSE 30
* KSE All Share

The other *stock exchange* is the Lahore Stock Exchange (LSE), first incorporated in 1936, but closed during post-war *depression.* Restarted operations in the early 1970s. Its main *index* is:

* LSE-25 Index.

Foreign *investment* is now permitted on these exchanges; *profits* and principals invested can be repatriated to the investor's home country.

Standard *currency*: the Pakistani *rupee.* 1 Pakistani *rupee* = 100 *paisa.*

**Palau** Standard *currency*: *US dollar.*

**Panama**  The Panama Stock Exchange (Bolsa de Valores de Panama) started operations in 1990. At the end of 1993, the number of *listed securities* was 125.

Standard *currency*: *balboa*. 1 *balboa* = 100 *centésimos*.

**Panel on Takeovers and Mergers (POTAM)**  A panel comprising many important financial organisations in the City of London. Its statutory functions are set out in Chapter 1 of Part 28 of the Companies Act 2006. It includes representatives of the Association of British Insurers, Investment Management Association and the Association of Investment Companies. Their function is to ensure that the general principles in the *City Code on Takeovers and Mergers* are adhered to. If it is found that an organisation is in breach of these regulations, *POTAM* has at its disposal the power to impose remedial and compensatory action. Under the Companies Act 2006 it has the ability, in certain circumstances, to seek court enforcement of its rulings. See: *dawn raid*, *Substantial Acquisition Rules*.

**Papua New Guinea**  Standard *currency*: *kina*. 1 *kina* = 100 *toea*.

**par**  See: *par value*.

**par bond**  A *fixed interest security* bought and sold at its *face value* without a *discount* or *premium* and normally with a variable *coupon*. See: *certificate of deposit*.

**par value**  Sometimes known as *nominal value*, this is the *face value* of a *security* as opposed to its *market value*. Par values for *shares* represent their original *value* when the *company* was constituted and often represent only the nominal *capital* by a nominal amount per *share*, say, 25p. Par values often have no *investment* significance other than the amount at which the *company* was capitalised on incorporation or *flotation*. *Shares* issued in the *United States* of America have *no par value*. *Gilts* will always be redeemed *at par*, ie £100 and the *nominal yield* (say Treasury 9% 2008) on most *fixed interest securities* refers to the *par* or redemption *value*.

**para**  *Currency* sub-unit of the countries *Serbia* and *Montenegro* (formerly: Yugoslavia). 100 paras = 1 *dinar*.

**paradox of thrift**  The apparent inconsistency that if households start saving more, this can lower *national income* and cause a general fall in the *standard of living*. Thriftiness or saving is considered beneficial to the economy (at least in the longer-term) because it finances *investment*. However, if businesses plan to invest less than households intend to save, then in the *circular flow of national income* model, '*withdrawals*' exceed '*injections*' and this will cause a decrease in the *equilibrium* level of *national income*, which is associated with a drop in living standards.

**paradox of value**  The apparent inconsistency that certain items that are very important to mankind, such as water, are very cheap to buy, whereas other non-essential items, such as *gold*, are so expensive. It is a striking economic illustration of the law of *supply and demand*. The prices of water and *gold* are established to a greater extent by their relative abundance (ie supply) rather than their importance (ie demand).

**Paraguay**  Asunción Stock Exchange was established in 1977, and was inactive for many years, reopening in October 1993. Legislation allows the free flow of foreign *capital*.

Standard *currency*: *guarani*. 1 *guarani* = 100 *centimos*.

**parent company**  Another term for: *holding company*.

**Pareto's Rule**  In 1906, Italian economist Vilfredo Pareto created a mathematical formula to describe the unequal distribution of *wealth*, observing that 20% of the people owned 80% of the *wealth*.

**pari passu** Latin for: 'with equal step'. A term used when a new issue of *stock* or *shares* is made which has the same status as existing *capital*. Pari passu basically means equal in its position or like for like.

**Paris Bourse** See under: *France*.

**Paris Club** See: *Group of Ten*.

**Paris Inter-Bank Offered Rate (PIBOR)** The Paris equivalent of the *London Inter-Bank Offered Rate (LIBOR)*.

**parity** *Equilibrium* in *commodities* and *securities* in different markets and the equivalence of one *currency* to another using the *spot exchange rate*.

**Parliamentary Commissioner for Administration** The *Ombudsman* responsible for investigating complaints, referred through an MP, by members of the public against public bodies and government departments. See: *Ombudsman*.

**participating certificates** See: *American Depository Receipt*.

**participating interest** The *UK* Companies Act 2006 determines that a holding of 20% or more of the *shares* or *options* for *shares* in an organisation constitutes a participating interest in the absence of specific indications to the contrary. See: *controlling director*.

**partly paid (P.P.)** Refers to *shares* whose full *nominal value* has not been paid up and where there is a further *call* due on the balance. Large new *share* issues, such as *privatisation* issues, are sometimes floated in this way, with one or more *calls* (ie further payments) at specified dates.

**partnership** An unincorporated association of two or more people formed for the purpose of carrying on a business and governed by the Partnership Act 1890. A partnership has no corporate substance of its own and purely represents a collection of individuals who are jointly and severally responsible for the partnership's debts and liabilities (see: *joint and several liability*). Any partner may end the partnership, provided that notice of the intention to do so is given to all the other partners, and can demand a cessation or *winding up*, though the partners' liability prior to this date extends in perpetuity. Partnerships are governed by a partnership agreement (partnership *deed*) that determines the *distribution* of *profits* as well as other matters, including the terms for allocation and withdrawal of *capital* (from each partner's *capital account*) and the procedure to be adopted on death, retirement or bankruptcy. Partners receive *income* based on the surplus revenue of the partnership which is liable for their *tax*. In the UK limited liability partnerships became possible from 6 April 2001. In the *US* general partners are fully liable for partnership obligations; limited partners are liable only to the extent of their *investment*.

**passing off** Illegal practice of pretending to be someone else or another *company* by using a similar name or logo in order to vicariously gain status, business or customers, etc.

**pataca** Standard *currency* of *Macau*. 1 pataca = 100 *avos*.

**patent** An exclusive right to exploit an invention. In the *UK* patents are granted through the *Patent Office* which is part of the *Department for Business, Innovation and Skills (BIS)*. An applicant for a patent (usually the inventor or the inventor's employer) or his agent (a patent agent – a specialist who prepares a detailed application) must prove that the invention is new and is capable of industrial application. If the *Patent Office* grants the patent it gives exclusive rights in the *UK* and publishes the details. A patent remains valid for 20 years from the date of application provided that the patent holder (patentee) continues to pay the necessary fees. During this time, the patentee may assign the patent or grant licenses for the manufacture of the product, which must be registered in a public register at the *Patent Office*. To protect the product overseas the inventor must obtain patents in foreign countries, although the Patent Office in Munich covers the whole of Europe. See also: *intellectual property*.

**Patent Office** A *UK* government office that administers the Patent Acts, the Registered Design Act and the Trade Marks Act, and provides an information service about *patent* specifications. See: *patent*.

**pathfinder prospectus** A document issued prior to the full *prospectus*, outlining the circumstances and aims of the *company* prior to *flotation*. In general terms this is no more than advertising material. It is helpful to the *company* in determining potential interest for the *shares*.

**patrimony** Inherited *wealth* passed through the male line of a family, normally the eldest son.

**pattern** A *chart* formation made by price movements on a *chart* representing an important argument in determining the future *trend* in the price of a *share* or movement of a *market index*. Certain such formations are easily recognisable, such as *head and shoulders, double bottom, triangle*, etc; others less so. But most give an experienced analyst the ability to gauge the likely extent of the next major move once the pattern has been confirmed. See: *technical analysis*.

**Pay in Lieu of Notice (PILON)** Statutory or non-statutory payments made by an employer to an employee in lieu of notice being given. Normally taxable in the *UK*.

**pay-as-you-earn (PAYE)** The essence of the *UK unified tax* system is that each employee is issued with a code number relating to his or her employed *earnings*. This *tax* code number reflects the employee's personal and other *allowances*, and other items to be taken into account in calculating the employee's *tax* liability. Income *tax*, including higher-rate *tax*, is then deducted at source by the employer and settled with *HMRC* direct.

**pay-as-you-go** A *pension* scheme where *pensions* are paid to retired *members* out of *money* paid by contributing *members*, with no provision for future liabilities.

**payback period (PP)** A simple method used widely in *investment appraisal*. It is the length of time an *investment* takes to cover its cost. For example, an *investment* with a *capital* outlay of £50,000 yielding an annual *income* flow of £10,000 has a payback period of five years. The major drawback of this method of appraising *investments* as opposed to *discounted cash flow* (*DCF*) methods is that it does not take *cash flows* after the payback period into account, nor does it regard the *time value* of *money*. Also known as 'recoupment'.

**PAYE** See: *pay-as-you-earn*.

**payee** The name of a person or organisation that benefits from a transferable financial instrument. In the case of a cheque the payee is the person or organisation to whom the cheque is made payable.

**payment in kind** Where goods or services rather than *cash* are used to fulfil transactions. Trade with Third World countries often involves the exchange of say, mangos for tractors. See: *barter, counter trade*. A term also applied to bonds or loan notes where the borrower has the option to pay interest or issue further bonds/loan notes. Payment in kind (PIK) bonds are often associated with highly leveraged buyouts.

**payroll tax** A *tax* based on the total of an organisation's payroll apparently designed to discourage employment but more likely used due to ease of collection. In the *UK*, employers' Class 1 *National Insurance* contributions are a payroll tax.

**PBT** Short for: *profits* before *tax*.

**P/BV** Price per *book value*. Obtained by dividing the current *share* price by the current *book value* per *share*. The current *book value* per *share* is calculated by using the most recent annual *book value* (as opposed to *interim book value*) as given on the latest *balance sheet* divided by the total number of *shares* outstanding (all classes) at that *balance sheet* date, making adjustments for *capital* changes if necessary.

**P/CE** Price per *cash earnings*. Obtained by dividing the current *share* price by the trailing 12 months' *cash earnings per share*. The *cash earnings per share* is the sum of the past 12 months' *net earnings* plus the most recently available *depreciation* figure, divided by the total number of *shares* outstanding (all classes) at the *earnings* date, making adjustments for *capital* changes if necessary.

**P/E** See: *price earnings ratio*.

**P/Sales** See: *price/sales*.

**PCLS** See: *pension commencement lump sum*.

**pe** See: *price earnings ratio*.

**peg** 1. The fixing of the *value* of a country's *currency* on *foreign exchange markets*. See: *crawling peg, fixed exchange rate*. 2. The fixing of wages at existing levels by government order to control wage *inflation*.

**PEG** Price-earnings growth factor, calculated as the price earnings rates divided by estimated year ahead earnings growth. In theory the lower the PEG, the more attractive the share.

**PEN** *currency code* for: Peruvian Nuevo Sol.

**pennant** A pennant is a *chart* formation, of short duration (less than four weeks), similar to a *flag* and with the same implications, the difference being only that the envelope lines are converging. See diagram.

**penny** *Currency* sub-unit used in England: 100 pence = 1 *pound Sterling*.

**penny shares** *Shares* with a market price of less than £1, although there is no commonly agreed threshold. For perhaps illogical rea-

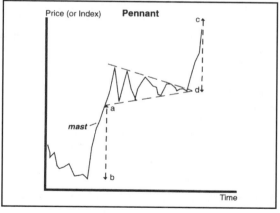

sons investors feel that they get better *value* by owning a greater number of low priced *shares* than a few *heavy shares*. It is also the case that a *penny* movement in a *penny share* can represent a large percentage *profit*. Perhaps the only real attraction is that some of the *shares* may represent potential recovery situations in *companies* whose *shares* were once traded at a much higher price or *shares* that have been neglected by analysts. See: *orphan stock*.

**pension** An *income* paid to an individual having reached retirement age or date; by the state or a pension provider or their former employer(s). The subject of pension provision is a complex one dealing with individuals in various vocations. An employee or *director* and/or their *company* can make contributions towards a scheme. Similarly, individuals may fund their own schemes. The state provides a basic *state pension* which is funded from *National Insurance* and *tax* payments, but as people are living longer it will become increasingly difficult to finance. Accordingly, individuals will need to make personal provision, especially if they want a pension that relates to their *earnings*. Traditionally pensions were employee accumulated from regular contributions to an occupational scheme provided by an employer through a combination of payments deducted from the individual's salary and a contribution from the employer. The employee could take out an additional scheme if they wanted to top this up or, if there is no work scheme or they work for themselves, they can take out a *personal pension*. In the majority of cases their contributions accumulate to build up a fund which is used to buy an *annuity* which provides their pension *income* when they retire, though some of this fund can be taken as a *cash* lump sum. Other schemes guarantee to provide a pension equivalent to a proportion of retirement salary based on length of service. The occupational scheme is still common, but very few new schemes are being established. Many employers now opt for group stakeholder pensions or group personal pensions. The rules for tax treatment of pensions were radically changed with the introduction of the simplified regime in April 2006. Contributions normally qualify for *tax* relief, and *investments* within a pension scheme are *tax* exempt. A pension in payment is subject to *income tax* as though it were earned *income*. Pensions can be set up to escalate and pay a reduced *income* to a surviving spouse, though they cease on death with no residual benefit to the deceased's *estate*. See: *annuity, commutation, compulsory purchase annuity, contracted-out money purchase scheme, contracting out, deferred annuity, funded unapproved retirement benefits scheme, Hancock annuity, money purchase, normal retirement age, open market option, pensioneer trustee, pension fraction, personal pension, protected rights, Section 32, self-administered pension, self-employed pension, state earnings-related pension scheme, top hat.*

**pension commencement lump sum (PCLS)** The lump sum that may be taken when pension benefits are drawn from a registered pension scheme. Normally the maximum PCLS is 25% of the total value of benefits being drawn, although it may be higher if *transitional protection* applies. The PCLS is often referred to as tax-free cash or pension lump sum.

**pension fraction** The fraction of *pensionable earnings* for each year of *pensionable service* used to calculate the proportion of final salary to be paid as *pension*. If the fraction is one-sixtieth, then forty years' service will give a *pension* of two-thirds final salary, the maximum under the pre-April 2006 pension rules.

**pension loan back** See: *loan back.*

**pension lump sum** See: *pension commencement lump sum.*

**pension mortgage** A portion of the benefits available from a *pension* plan can (at retirement) be withdrawn as a tax-free *cash* sum and used as a means of repaying a *mortgage* which is offered on an interest-only basis. *Tax* relief is normally allowed on the *pension* contributions, which in turn can grow free of *tax*.

**pension Protection Fund (PPF)** A government-created fund, maintained by a levy on all *pension* funds, designed to protect the *beneficiaries* of a defined benefit *pension* scheme affected by the bankruptcy of the sponsoring *company*. Set up in April 2005, the levy is based on the size and potential *risk* of individual funds. Benefits are capped for non-pensioners.

**pensionable age** The age at which a person is entitled to receive the *state pension*. In a private or *company* scheme the retirement date can be different. See: *Barber Judgment.*

**pensionable earnings** The definition of remuneration for the purposes of calculating *pension* and can include (or exclude) *income* other, or in addition to, salary such as bonuses or overtime.

**pensionable service** The period during which *pension* benefits are deemed to accrue, normally as defined by the scheme rules.

**Pensions Act 1995** The 1995 Pensions Act introduced wide-ranging reforms designed to improve standards and *security* in the operation of *occupational pension schemes*. The act equalised the retirement age for men and women at 65, it gave the courts power over *pensions* in divorce cases, and most significantly created the *Occupational Pensions Regulatory Authority*, to regulate occupational *pensions*.

**Pensions Act 2004** The Act which introduced a new regulatory framework for occupational pensions, replacing *OPRA* with *The Pensions Regulator,* and created the *Pension Protection Fund*.

**Pensions Act 2007** The Act which made a variety of amendments to the *basic state pension* and *second state pension*, increased state pension ages from 2024 onwards and established the *Personal Accounts Delivery Authority*.

**Pensions Act 2008** The Act which detailed the framework of the *Personal Accounts* regime.

**Pensions Ombudsman** See under: *Ombudsman*.

**PEP** See: *personal equity plan*.

**peppercorn** Nominal or very small. Peppercorn rent is commonly used to describe a rental well below the prevailing market rate – perhaps as a result of grace and favour or as repayment for a debt or kindness.

**per capita income** The *gross domestic product* (GDP) per head of the population. Used to compare international standards of living.

**per diem** From Latin meaning: 'per day'. Denoting a daily rate for fees charged by a professional person.

**per mille** Cost per mille (CPM), also called cost ‰ and cost per thousand (CPT) (in Latin mille means thousand), is a commonly used term in *insurance*.

**per pro (p.p.)** Short for the Latin 'per procurationem' meaning: 'by procuration'. Denoting an act by an agent, acting on the authority of a principal. The abbreviation is often used when someone signs letters or documents on behalf of a *company* or *partnership* which, if they are formally authorised, accepts responsibility for documents so signed.

**per proc** See: *per pro*.

**perestroika** The introduction of market-orientated economic reforms aimed at improving industrial efficiency, introduced by President Gorbachev in the former Soviet Union. See: *Marxism*.

**perfect competition** Market situation in which there are many (infinite) buyers and sellers. Compare: *bilateral oligopoly, monopoly, monopsony, oligopoly, oligopsony*.

**performance appraisal** A method used in *quantitative analysis* for assessing the performance of a managed *portfolio* of *investments* against a predetermined *benchmark*. Includes a number of risk-adjusted measures such as Sharpe (using *standard deviation*), Treynor (using *systematic risk*) and *Jensen measures* (using the *capital asset pricing model*). Compare: *investment appraisal*.

**performance bond** A surety bond issued by an insurance company or a bank to guarantee satisfactory completion of a project by a contractor.

**performance fee** When referring to funds this is a fee based on the increase in value of a fund as opposed to a flat percentage fee that is charged regardless of performance, common to *hedge funds*. Also called an incentive fee.

**perk** Incentives for employees or customers which can include a company car, expenses, tickets to shows, special outings. Also benefits offered to *shareholders* in the form of *discounts* for the products offered by the *company* whose *shares* are held. From 'perquisite' meaning an *emolument* in addition to salary or wages. See: *fringe benefit*.

**permanent health insurance (PHI)** Now commonly called income protection. This provides a replacement *income* up to *pension* age or possibly a fixed term to substitute *income* lost through prolonged sickness or disability normally defined as 'unable to perform any part of normal duties'. Payments start after a deferred period of a minimum of four weeks but it is more likely to be thirteen weeks plus. *Premiums* depend on age at entry and occupation and are either fixed once the *contract* is in force or reviewable, typically every five years. Benefits are tax-free for individual policies, but taxable where the policy is set up on a group basis by an employer. This should not be confused with 'sickness and accident *insurance*' where the benefits are paid out after a few days, are also *tax* free and only last for a limited period, where *premiums* may be increased each year and renewal can be refused if disability has occurred.

**permanent interest-bearing shares (PIBS)** *PIBS* are *fixed interest securities* with no *redemption date*, issued by *building societies*. The *yield* on *PIBS* is relatively high, partly because a *building society* is theoretically not obliged to pay out if doing so would drive it into a loss. Also, the market is relatively small, and the '*shares*' may not always be easy to buy and sell. Many PIBS became perpetual subordinated bonds (PSBs) when building societies demutualised.

**perpetual FRN** An irredeemable or undated *floating rate note (FRN)*.

**perpetual inventory** Useful for *just in time stock* control where a double entry account is kept for each *stock* item covering deliveries and usage providing a continuous record of the number of items in *stock*. This method is used in large organisations anxious to limit the amount of *capital* tied up in *stock* and associated costs such as *warehousing*.

**perpetual subordinated bonds (PSBs)** The limited company equivalent of *permanent interest-bearing securities (PIBS)*. Many PIBS became PSBs when their building society issuers demutualised. See: *permanent interest-bearing schemes*.

**Perpetuities and Accumulations Act 1964** Originally transactions and gifts were not valid unless they occurred within a lifetime (ie the lifetime of a person living at the date of the gift) plus 21 years. The 1964 Act reformed the law by allowing a specific period of up to 80 years but still restricting bequests that rely on a series of events to establish ownership.

**personal accident insurance** *Insurance* against the possibility of injury or disability arising from an accident.

**personal account (PA)** 1. Colloquial term for transactions professional *investment* advisors make using their personal *capital* for their personal benefit. 2. A new form of money purchase occupational scheme to be introduced from 2012. For employees aged over 22 and under state pension age, membership will be automatic unless they are already members of a pension arrangement which gives at least equivalent benefits. However, employees can opt out. Contributions will eventually be a minimum of 8% of earnings between £5,035 and £33,540 (in 2006/07 terms), with the minimum employer element of this being 3%. The scheme is being established by the *Personal Accounts Delivery Authority*, but will be run at arms' length from the government.

**Personal Accounts Delivery Authority (PADA)**  The body established by the Pensions Act 2007 to develop and launch *personal accounts*.

**personal allowance**  See: *allowance*.

**personal equity plan (PEP)**  Introduced in 1987 under the 1986 Finance Act, with no contributions possible after 5 April 1999. Merged into ISAs from 6 April 2008. They were designed to broaden scope for direct *investment* in *UK shares* for investors of 18 years and over. An arrangement allowing private investors to purchase *UK shares* and *unit trusts* and OEICs, the *profits* and *income* from which were *tax* exempt if the *investment* was made via an approved *PEP* manager. *PEPs* came in various different guises. Originally, they allowed only *investment* in quoted *UK shares*, but they were gradually modified to allow a portion of the *investment* to go into collective *investments* and overseas *unit trusts* as well as *fixed interest securities*. PEPs could be managed or 'self select' where the client chose the underlying *shares* and if held for more than a year allowed *tax* exemption on both *growth* and *income*. Single *company PEPs* were introduced to allow *quoted companies* to market their own plans, mostly to employees. A limited amount was allowed each *tax year* and they became so popular that the inflows of new *capital* before 5 April each year had a noticeable effect on the *UK* market.

**personal financial planning (PFP)**  The provision of financial advice regarding matters such as investing, *insurance*, borrowing, saving and retirement planning. Professionally, the advice is given only after the financial situation of the client is unveiled through a thorough fact-finding and *analysis* exercise. Many PFP advisers provide a general financial advisory service which incorporates the principle of understanding the client's situation before advice are given. This is known as the 'know your customer' rule. Once the client's actual financial situation is known, a set of prescriptions is provided by the *financial adviser* to optimise the client's finances. *Financial advisers* may or may not hold distribution contracts with financial institutions as part of their business. Those who do not are often referred to as *Independent Financial Advisors* (*IFAs*) as they are not influenced by the commissions they get for recommending financial products, and hence are considered less biased when advising their clients. All need to be licensed by the *FSA*.

**Personal Investment Authority (PIA)**  The PIA was a *Self-Regulating Organisation* formed in 1994, taking over from *LAUTRO* and *FIMBRA*. The *PIA* regulated nearly all types of *investment* business conducted with or marketed to the private investor, and its *member firms* were normally *life assurance* and *pension companies* or collective *investment* providers (though these latter tended mainly to be regulated by *IMRO*). The *PIA* stopped its role as a regulator after the *Financial Services* and *Markets Act 2000* was introduced, and the *Financial Services Authority* was created. Since the *Financial Services Authority* assumed its full responsibilities in 2001, the *PIA*'s role has been subsumed within the *FSA*.

**personal pension**  The personal pension plan replaced *deferred annuities* and *Section 226 pension contracts* from 1 July 1988. A personal pension may be taken up by individuals whether or not they have an occupational scheme and can use a personal pension to provide *pension* benefits as a replacement for *second state pension*. It is also currently possible to retire from age 50 with a personal pension (55 from 6 April 2010). A PPP is a portable *money purchase pension* available to anyone who has *pensionable earnings*, whether employed or self-employed. The relevant legislation (ie the simplified regime) is contained in the Finance Act 2004.

**PERT** Short for: Programme Evaluation and Review Technique. This is a continual review of the procedures developed by critical path *analysis*, with a view to maximising efficiency and making necessary adjustments or improvements without delay.

**Peru** The Lima Stock Exchange (BVL) was established in 1860. Its main indices *are*:

• IBBVL Selective Index. Comprises 15 *securities*. Base: 30 December 1991 = 100.

• IGBVL General Index. Comprises 38 most commonly traded companies.

Standard *currency*: nuevo *sol*. 1 nuevo *sol* = 100 *cents*.

**peseta** Formerly the standard *currency* of *Spain*, until the introduction of the *euro* on 1 January 2002. 1 peseta = 100 *céntimos*.

**pesewa** *Currency* sub-unit of *Ghana*. 100 pesewas = 1 *cedi*.

**peso** Standard *currency* of the following countries: *Argentina, Chile, Colombia, Cuba*, the *Dominican Republic, Guinea-Bissau, Mexico*, the *Philippines*: 1 peso = 100 *centavos*; *Uruguay*: 1 peso = 100 *centésimos*.

**PET** 1. See: *potentially exempt transfer*. 2. See: *property enterprise trust*.

**petrodollars** The substantial *dollar* deposits in *banks* accumulated by oil exporting countries.

**Petroleum Revenue Tax (PRT)** This *tax* was the primary means used by the UK government in gaining a *share* in the *profits* made from oil in the North Sea and is a *tax* on the *profits* from oil exploration and mining under the authority of licences granted by the Petroleum (Production) Act 1934 or the Petroleum (Production) Act (Northern Ireland) 1964.

**Pfennig** Formerly *currency* sub-unit of *Germany*. 100 Pfennigs = 1 *Deutschmark*. Now replaced by the *euro*.

**PFI** See: *Private Finance Initiative*.

**PFP** See: *personal financial planning*.

**PGK** *currency code* for: *Papua New Guinea* Kina.

**phased retirement** Phased retirement is a means of drawing a retirement income from a pension arrangement by systematically crystallising part of the benefits and treating both the pension commencement lump sum and the annuity as income. For example, to obtain a benefit of £20,000 in the first year, £70,000 of pension fund could be crystallised creating a pension commencement lump sum of £17,500 and purchasing an annuity to provide £2,500 a year net. In the following year the annuity would be in place and only an additional £17,500 would need to be produced, which could mean a £61,000 fund supply, £15,250 tax-free cash and another annuity, this time of £2,450 a year net.

**PHI** See: *permanent health insurance*.

**Philippines** The Philippine Stock Exchange (PSE) was established in 1992 in Manila. It superseded the former two *stock exchanges*: the Manila Stock Exchange (MSE, est. 1927) and the Makati Stock Exchange (MKSE, est. 1963). Its main *index* is:

• PSE (Manila) Composite Index. Comprises 30 *stocks*. Base: 2 January 1985 = 100.

• PSE All Share Index, which includes all traded stocks (244 listed companies as at 31 December 2007).

The Manila International Futures Exchange was established in 1984.

Standard *currency*: Filipino *peso*. 1 Filipino *peso* = 100 *centavos*.

**Phillips curve** A curve that shows the frequently observed relationship between the level of *unemployment* and the rate of change of the monetary *value* of wages (*money* wages). The curve is called the 'Phillips curve' due to the work on this subject by the economist A.W. Phillips. *Inflation* rates can be inferred from the rate of change of *money* wages; thus indirectly the curve depicts the relationship between *unemployment* and *inflation* and is explained as follows: the lower the *unemployment* rate, the greater the aggregate demand in the economy and the greater the willingness of firms to grant their workers higher wage increases, as demand for their goods or services increases. At high levels of *unemployment*, and thus lower demand, firms are not willing to pay workers high increases in wages – with very high *unemployment* wages can often decrease. The *unemployment* level at which wages do not change (marked U* in the diagram) is called the *NAIRU*. However, in recent years, high *unemployment* and accelerating *inflation* (*stagflation*) have been observed to coexist, leading many economists to abandon the Phillips curve or reformulate it (for instance, the 'expectations-adjusted Phillips curve').

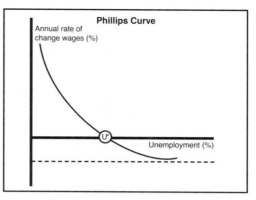

**PHP** *currency code* for: Philippine Peso.

**physicals** The actual *investment: shares* themselves as opposed to *options*; the *gold* itself as opposed to a *gold futures contract*. The opposite of a *derivative*. See: *actuals*.

**PI** See: *professional indemnity*.

**PIA** See: *Personal Investment Authority*.

**piastre** *Currency* sub-unit of *Egypt*, *Lebanon*, *Sudan* and *Syria*. 100 piastres = 1 *pound*.

**PIBOR** See: *Paris Inter-Bank Offered Rate*.

**pibs** See: *permanent interest-bearing shares*.

**piggybacking** See: *tailgating*.

**PILON** See: *Pay in Lieu of Notice*.

**PINC** See: *property income certificate*.

**Pink Book** An annual volume entitled '*UK Balance of Payments*' providing comprehensive *balance of payments* data on the previous year issued by the *Office for National Statistics* (*ONS*).

**pink form** A preferential application form normally for employees or customers of a *company* whose *shares* are about to be floated. Under *stock market* regulations *companies* are allowed to set aside 10% of the *shares* exclusively for employees. See: *flotation*.

**Pink Sheet** Informal name of Pink Quote founded in 1913, now an electronic quotation system operated by Pink OTC Markets that displays quotes for many *over-the-counter securities*. Originally printed on pink paper by the National Quotation Bureau prior to the introduction of electronic quotes in 2000. *Market makers* and other *brokers* can also use Pink Quote to publish their *bid* and ask *quotation* prices. The term Pink Sheets is also used to refer to a market tier within the current Pink Quote system and regarded as the riskiest due to being small, new, thinly traded, not subject to full disclosure or poorly researched, etc.

**pip** 1/100th of 1% of the *market value* of a *security* used to express price differentials. See: *basis point*.

**pit** An area of a *financial futures*, *options* or *commodity* exchange in which dealings take place by *open outcry* (see: *LIFFE, call-over, London Metal Exchange*). *Dealers* in these markets are called pit traders or *brokers*. See: *rings*.

**pitbull economics** Coined by President Reagan in 1987, this term refers to recessionist and protectionist economic programmes, which he suggested would tear the heart out of *America*'s industrial prosperity. See also: *Reaganomics*.

**Pitcairn Island** Standard *currency*: *New Zealand dollar*.

**PKR** *currency code* for: *Pakistan* Rupee.

**placement** *US* term for: *placing*.

**placing** An issue of new *shares* or a *tranche* of existing *shares* placed with buyers in advance. The buyers are normally existing clients of the *underwriter*. This is an inexpensive way of issuing new *capital* or bringing a *company* to the market and is often used in start-up *companies* or as a means of introducing new *capital* to existing *companies* where the *capital* is raised privately (see: *private placing*). As a method of *flotation* it is normally used for *companies* with a smaller *capitalisation*. The regulations are less stringent than for a public *flotation* and the marketing expenses are greatly reduced. In the UK placements are more common than public flotations.

**plain vanilla** See: *vanilla*.

**Plaza Agreement/Accord** The hotel in which the *Group of Five* met to apply concerted pressure to reduce the *value* of the *dollar*.

**plc** See: *public limited company*.

**pledge** A pledge arises when title or goods are delivered to one person (pledgor) or by another person (pledgee) to be held as *security* for the payment of a debt or the discharge of an obligation upon the understanding that the goods or title will be returned once the obligation is discharged. The delivery of these goods or title is sufficient confirmation of the transaction, although when a *bank* accepts a pledge it usually requires its customers to sign a memorandum setting out the terms of the transaction. This is often referred to as a *letter of hypothecation*, a letter of pledge or a letter of *lien*.

**PLUS** See: *SEATS PLUS*.

**PLUS Market** Formerly *OFEX*, a quote and order driven market replacing the *matched bargain* service offered by JPJ through *OFEX*. PLUS claims to offer trading services in over 7,000 *securities* admitted to trading on *EU Regulated* Markets including approx. 900 *securities* that are classified as 'liquid *shares*'. This is in addition to the *securities* of PLUS-quoted and AIM *companies* which are available to be traded on the PLUS market.

**PLZ** *currency code* for: Polish Zloty.

**PMI** Short for: the Pensions Management Institute.

**point** See: *basis point*.

**point and figure chart** A special *chart*, believed to have been created by Charles Dow, which is used in *technical analysis* to see the up or down *momentum* in the price movements of a *security*. There is no time scale on the *chart*; instead, only price changes are recorded. Squared paper is used and the vertical axis shows the price of the *security*. When the price moves upward, an X is put on the graph above the previous *point*. As long as the price does not change direction by a specified amount (the reversal), the *trend* is considered to carry on and no new column is made. When a reversal occurs a new column is started and an O is placed one square down. Further declines are marked as Os in that column until another reversal occurs and a new column of Xs must be started. The *chart* thus obtained will show the *momentum* of *trends* of the *security*.

**poison pill** Tactics employed by a *company* resisting an unwanted *takeover*, usually involving an issue of *securities* designed to make the *takeover* candidate considerably less attractive to the *bidder* should the *bid* succeed. The *securities* issued normally have a conversion *option* triggered if the *bid* succeeds, allow-

**Point and Figure Chart**

ing *shares* to be purchased at a reduced rate or at a *value* including the *acquisition premium*. The ultimate effect of a poison pill is designed to turn the *target company* from an *asset* to a liability in the unwelcome *bidder*'s hands and thus forestall the *takeover*.

**Poland** The Warsaw Stock Exchange (est. 1817) closed in 1939 and reopened in 1991. The number of *listed shares* in 2009 was 372. Its main *indices* are:

• Warsaw Stock Exchange Index (Warszawski Indeks Gieldowy) – WIG. It is a *total return index* weighted by *market capitalisation* of all *shares* in the *main market*. Base: 16 April 1990 = 1,000.

• WIG 20. Comprises the 20 *companies* with highest *turnover* and *market value*; its composition is revised every quarter.

Standard *currency*: *zloty*. 1 *zloty* = 100 *groszy*.

**polarisation** The *FSA* system which differentiated between *tied agents* or salesmen and independent intermediaries (*Independent Financial Advisers*). Polarisation existed until the end of 2004, when the FSA changed the regulatory regime to permit multi-tied advisors, who effectively fitted between the tied adviser and the independent adviser. Potential clients need to be fully aware of whether their adviser works exclusively for one or a limited number of financial institutions or whether the advice that he or she gives is independent and unbiased. *Unit trust/OEIC* and *life assurance companies* and their employees would generally be regarded as tied, whereas independently owned financial consultancy firms providing a broad range of financial products would tend to be independent.

**Policyholders Protection Act** Enacted following the collapse of Nation Life in 1974 to protect *life assurance* policyholders. It provided that in the event of a *UK life assurance company* collapsing, their policyholders were assured of receiving no less than 90% of the *value* of their policy. They were reimbursed from a 'lifeboat' fund made up of contributions levied on *UK* life *companies*. It also had the provision of enabling another *life assurance company* to take over the *assets* and liabilities of that *company*. The role of the Act has now been taken over by the Financial Services Compensation Scheme.

**pony** Slang for £25.

**ponzi** A fraudulent investment scheme where fictitious *profit* distributions are financed by new subscribers. American term for pyramid fraud and described by Charles Dickens in 'Martin Chuzzlewitt' and in 'Little Dorrit' at Merdle's bank; the term was coined in connection with a very successful scheme perpetrated by the Italian immigrant Charles Ponzi in *America* in 1903. In 2008 the former chairman of *NASDAQ*, Bernard Madoff, was charged with perpetrating the biggest individual fraud in history when Bernard L Madoff Investment Securities turned out to have been 'one giant ponzi scheme' and, on information from his sons Andrew and Mark, Madoff was arrested and charged with an estimated $50bn shortfall.

**porcupine provisions** Americanism for corporate charter or bylaw provisions designed to deter *takeover* attempts. Examples include *fair price provisions*, *poison pills* and *staggered directorships*.

**portable pension** *Pension* plans that can be transferred from one employer to another without the loss of *value*, as are all *personal pensions*. Virtually all *pension* benefits now have a transfer *value* which can be moved in/out of different schemes.

**PORTAL market** A market in the *USA* established in June 1990 and operated by the National Association of Securities Dealers (*NASD*) for qualified investors to trade privately in *unquoted securities*.

**portfolio** A collection of *investments* held by or to the account of an individual, corporation, fund or *trust*. Normally the portfolio will have predetermined objectives, such as a *growth* portfolio or *income* portfolio. It may also be managed in a certain way such as a discretionary portfolio, or even contain certain types of *investment*, such as an *equity* portfolio or *unit trust* portfolio. See: *performance appraisal*.

**portfolio theory** The management of a *portfolio* based on *quantitative analysis*, where the selection of *securities* in a *portfolio* is made as a result of a mathematical assessment of the *risk* and return against the market as a whole and/or by reference to the *risks* or returns determined by the client for the *portfolio*. Portfolio theory will assess risk-free returns and the likelihood of returns made by market timing, determining the benefits of *investments* by their *volatility* (*beta coefficient*) or dispersion (*risk*) and the *capital asset pricing model*. Also called: *modern portfolio theory*.

**Portugal** The main *stock exchange* is the Euronext Lisbon Stock Exchange (Bolsa de Valores de Lisboa – BVL). The exchange is now part of NYSE Euronext. Its main *indices* are:

- BVL General Index – Calculated daily. Comprises all officially *quoted companies*, with adjustments for new admissions, removals and changes in number of *shares*, *capital* increases with subscription rights, issue of bonus *shares*, change in the *nominal value* and payments of *dividends*. It is weighted by *market capitalisation* and is *chain-linked*. Base: 2 January 1988 = 1,000.

- BVL 30 Index – Similarly constructed. Comprises 30 *shares* considered most representative in terms of liquidity and *market capitalisation*. Selected quarterly.

Portugal's other *stock exchange* is the Oporto Stock Exchange.

Standard *currency*: euro. 1 *euro* = 100 *cents*. The *escudo* was previously used, before the introduction of the *euro* on 1 January 2002.

**POTAM** See: *Panel on Takeovers and Mergers*.

**potentially exempt transfer (PET)** Under *inheritance tax* regulations, an outright lifetime gift other than to a trust will be free of *tax* provided it occurs more than seven years before the death of the *donor*. Accordingly, a gift is potentially exempt from *inheritance tax* should the *donor* survive beyond this period.

**pound** Standard *currency* of the UK. Also called *Sterling*, in order to differentiate it from pound weight (lbs) in avoirdupois and pounds used in other nations' *currencies*. In the *Republic of Ireland*, the *euro* is used. The pound underwent *decimalisation* in 1971, when it was divided into 100 new pence having formerly comprised 20 *shillings* each of twelve pennies. Other countries and territories using their own pound include: *Falkland Islands*, *Gibraltar*: 1 pound = 100 pence; *Egypt, Lebanon, Sudan, Syria*: 1 pound = 100 *piastres*.

**pound cost averaging** The practice of allocating a fixed sum for the purchase of a particular *investment* on a monthly or other periodic basis. When prices fall, the fixed amount will buy more *shares* or units, and conversely, when prices rise, fewer *shares* or units are bought. The overall effect is that the *average* purchase price over a period is lower than the arithmetical *average* of the respective market prices.

**poverty trap** Where social security benefits are reduced by an amount equivalent to *earnings* from employment. In some cases individuals can actually be worse off in work than they would be unemployed and receiving *unemployment* and social security benefits due to anomalies in the benefit system. Generally considered to be most undesirable but difficult to eradicate in a multi-layered benefit society.

**power of attorney (PA)** Signed and notorised document that authorises a particular person to perform specific or general acts on behalf of another.

**PP** See: *payback period*.

**p.p.** Short for: 1. per procurationem. See: *per pro*. 2. See also: *partly paid*.

**PPI** See: *producer price index*.

**PPIP** See: *Private Partnership Investment Programme*.

**PPP** See: *purchasing power parity*.

**PPP** *Public private partnership*. See: *Private Finance Initiative*.

**pre-emption** First *call*: the right of a person to be the first to be offered something when it becomes available for sale. Sometimes referred to as first refusal, it is often an informal agreement to make something available for a private sale before it is offered on the open market.

**pre-emption rights** A statutory principle to protect minority *shareholders*, determining that any new *ordinary shares* issued by a *company* must first be offered to the existing *shareholders*. Accordingly a new issue is offered to all *shareholders* as a *rights issue*.

**pre-tax profit** *Net profit* before taxation.

**preference share** While *loan capital* represents borrowings repayable before any *distribution* of surplus *assets* to *shareholders*, preference capital is part of the *share capital* of the *company*, ranking after *creditors* but before ordinary *shareholders* in the event of *liquidation* while bearing no additional *risk*. Preference *capital* can consist principally of two types: 1. Preference shares: the holders of these have certain preferential rights, as defined by the *Articles of Association*, as to the rate of entitlement to a *dividend*, *distribution* of surplus *assets* and to voting. The *dividend* is payable at a fixed rate and may be *cumulative*, ie a *dividend* unpaid one year will be payable out of *profits* for the *company*'s succeeding years, or non-cumulative. *Shares* may be redeemable, although public issues of *redeemable preference shares* are now uncommon; such *shares* can only be redeemed from accumulated *reserves*. 2. Participating preference shares: these confer, in addition to the normal rights of preference shares, a further participation in *profits*, often relating to the *dividends* payable on the ordinary *capital*.

**preferential creditor** A *creditor* in a *liquidation* who will be paid before unsecured trade *creditors* and *shareholders*, salaries and *premiums* to *occupational pension schemes*. *Creditors* are paid in the following order: 1. the liquidator's fees; 2. *fixed charge* holders; 3. preferential *creditors*; 4. *floating charge* holders; 5. *unsecured creditors*; 6. subordinated *creditors*; 7. preference *shareholders*; 8. ordinary *shareholders*.

**preferred stock** *US* term for: *preference share*.

**premium** 1. A sum paid in addition to the *market value* of an *asset*. Opposite to a *discount*. 2. A contribution due to a *life assurance*, *investment* or *pension* policy be it monthly, quarterly, annually or a single payment. 3. The price that a *put* or *call* buyer must pay to a *put* or *call* seller for an *option contract* over and above its *intrinsic value*. See: *time value*. 4. The amount by which the market price of a *bond* exceeds its *par value*.

**premium bonds** Administered by *National Savings and Investments,* a premium bond is a returnable £1 deposit entered for monthly draws for tax-free prizes of between £25 and £1,000,000. There is a maximum holding of 30,000 premium bonds per person. The prize fund is distributed to winners drawn at random by *ERNIE* (Electronic Random Number Indicator Equipment). Premium bonds are eligible for prize draws once they have been held for a complete calendar month, following the month in which they were bought. Each *bond* is then eligible for every subsequent draw.

**present value** The present *value* of an amount of *money* in the future is calculated by *discounting* (sense 2) that amount using a certain *interest rate*. Used in *discounted cash flow* (*DCF*) techniques.

**preserved benefits** The Pensions Act 2004 provides that *occupational pension schemes* preserve retirement benefits for those leaving the scheme with at least two years' service. For employees with at least three months' service, a transfer value must be offered as an alternative to a refund of contributions.

**price earnings ratio (P/E)** A term used in *investment analysis* for the relationship between the *market value* of *share capital* and the *profit* for the year. The *net profit* is divided by the number of *ordinary shares*, giving *earnings per share*. This is then divided into the market price giving the price earnings ratio. The lower the *P/E ratio* the 'better *value*' the holding. The higher the *P/E*, the greater is the expectation in terms of increased future profitability. The price earnings ratio is also called the '*multiple*' of the *company*.

**price index** See: *composite index, index, Retail Price Index*.

**price/sales** Current *share* price divided by the trailing 12 months' sales per *share*. Sales per *share* is obtained by dividing the most recent trailing 12 months' sales by the total number of *shares* outstanding (all classes) as of the sales date, making adjustments for *capital* changes if necessary. Frequently used for *emerging markets indices*.

**price-to-book** A *company*'s *share* price divided by its *net asset value*.

**primary market** Market on which *securities* are sold for the first time and where they are dealt by principal stockholders. Most primary markets deal in *bonds* and *gilts*, providing facilities for principals and institutions rather than members of the public. Different from a *secondary market*, on which existing (ie 'second-hand') *securities* are traded. Many markets, for instance the *London Stock Exchange*, fulfil the role of both primary and *secondary markets*.

**primary protection** A form of *transitional protection* only available to those whose pension benefits were valued at over £1.5m on 5 April 2006 and who made the appropriate election to HMRC by 6 April 2009. Primary protection protected from the *lifetime allowance charge* the value of benefits at 5 April 2006, increased in line with the rise in the lifetime allowance. Contributions can continue to be paid, although this may be inadvisable. Contrast: *Enhanced protection*.

**prime costs** The direct costs involved in producing a product (rather than administering the *company* that produces it) up to the point it leaves 'the factory gates'. The production costs for the product consist of the direct costs plus the indirect costs (usually an allocation of the overhead costs).

**prime rate** The American equivalent of *bank base rate*, this is the *interest* charged on loans to *blue chip* clients by *US* commercial *banks* and is approximately equal to three-month *LIBOR* plus 1%. See: *Federal funds rate*.

**principle of effective market classification** See: *Mundell's principle of effective market classification*.

**principles of taxation** There are three main ideas underlying taxation (which are the subject of some controversy): 1. Ability to pay: the principle that taxation should take into account the financial standing of the individual, ie those with higher *income* can pay larger amounts of *tax* than those on low *incomes*. This has led to the *progressive tax* system used in most countries. 2. Benefits received: the principle that those individuals who benefit most from public goods and services should pay the *taxes* from which they are financed. 3. Income redistribution: the taxation system should be used to distribute *income* from the richer individuals to poorer individuals in society through transfer payments (eg *income* support, *unemployment* benefit and other welfare measures). See also: *canons of taxation, Laffer curve*.

**prior year adjustment** An adjustment to the *accounts* of a *company* to correct matters relating to the previous year, such as material adjustments arising from either changes in accounting policies or the correction of fundamental errors; made by adjusting the opening balances of *reserves*.

**Private Equity Fund** A fund controlled by corporate venturers who buy *controlling interests* in large, often quoted, *companies* with a view to maximising *shareholder* return. Have been variously described as *asset* strippers and *scalpers*, or benign and creative entrepreneurs depending on the commentator's perspective.

**private finance initiative (PFI)** *PFI* provides a way of funding major capital *investments* without immediate recourse to taxpayers. Private consortia, usually involving large construction firms, are contracted to design, build, and in some cases manage new projects. *Contracts* typically last for up to 30 years during which time the building is leased by a public authority.

**private limited company (Ltd)** See: *close company, limited company*.

**private market value** The underlying *value* of *assets* sold individually and not as part of a *going concern*.

**private medical insurance** Insurance taken out to provide for the cost of private health treatment.

**Private Partnership Investment Programme** An initiative by the Obama administration to remove up to $1 trillion of toxic assets from US bank balance sheets via two schemes easing problems caused by the Credit Crunch. The US government would inject $100bn of TARP funds in the hope of encouraging private capital with assisted leverage (guaranteed by the FDIC at up to six times) to buy toxic and secondary mortgage assets in the hope of making a profit in the longer term. The prices of these 'assets' being established at auction and the two schemes called Legacy Loan Programme and the Legacy Securities Programme; the latter for mortgage backed securities and backed by the Federal Reserve's Term Asset-Backed Securities Loan Fund (TALF).

**private placing** A *placing* of new or existing *shares* in a limited or *public limited company* (but not normally a *quoted company*) with a pre-selected individual or institution or group of individuals and not available generally either to the public or other institutions. Normally the arrangement has been formulated with the involvement of all parties to the *placing* and is not underwritten. Called a 'private *placement*' in *America*.

**private resident's relief** See: *main residence*.

**private sector** Industry not owned by the government or state-owned corporations and institutions. Compare: *public sector*.

**privatisation** The return of a nationalised industry to private investors via a *stock market flotation*. The economic justifications for a privatisation are the improved efficiencies that commercial management and market competition bring, as well as the ability to raise *development capital* on the open market, as opposed to the bureaucratic and commercial inefficiency of the state.

**pro forma** Literally: 'as a matter of form'. Figures or statistics based on potential rather than actual circumstances. A pro forma invoice requires payment before delivery and although required by the seller is not binding on the buyer. A pro forma schedule is normally a draft for discussion yet to be formally agreed.

**pro rata** Usually used in connection with a payment, 'pro rata' means in proportion to; each equally. From the Latin, it means literally 'according to the rate'. See also: *pari passu*.

**probate** The official approval of a will enabling the *executors* to distribute the *estate*. See: *intestacy*.

**probate value** The *value* of a *portfolio* of *investments* on the date of its owner's death. This is the *value* from which *capital gains tax* starts to apply to the new owners (there being no *capital gains tax* charge on death). The probate valuation should technically be based on the quarter-up principle, which is the lowest price quoted in the official *stock exchange* list (see: *Official List*) plus a quarter of the difference between the buying and selling prices. It is now common practice however to produce a *valuation* based on the *middle price*.

**procuration fee** Payment of *commission* to someone who has arranged or negotiated a loan or external *equity injection*.

**producer price index (PPI)** Replaced the 'wholesale *price index*', as was also the case in *America*. A wide *price index* of some 10,000 goods and *commodities* (but not services) that are manufactured or used by the industrial sector of the *UK*. Can be an accurate precursor to changes in the *RPI*, as increases tend to be passed through to the consumer eventually. See also: *Retail Price Index*.

**product liability insurance** An *insurance* policy covering the manufacturer or distributor against claims for loss or damage caused as a result of a product in normal use or from faulty or defective manufacture, materials or parts. As a result of ferocious awards in the *US* it is almost impossible to obtain in *America* and has led manufacturers worldwide to use disclaimers and warning notices on their products to prevent misuse.

**productivity** A measure of the efficiency of production. Productivity is defined as the amount of output resulting from a unit of input (of a *factor of production*) per unit of time period. Usually labour productivity is meant, ie the amount of output produced per employee hour.

**professional indemnity** An *insurance* policy covering a professional firm against claims from clients for losses as a result of negligence. See: *fidelity insurance*.

**professional investor** Someone such as a solicitor or *accountant* who is expected to have a certain basic understanding of *investment* and who accordingly does not require a written *client agreement* (or requires a short form agreement) when dealing with an *investment broker*.

**profit** 1. As distinct from *capital gain*, profit is the excess of the price of the article or service being sold over the costs of providing it, ie the *value* of output less the cost of input. 2. For a trading period it generally represents the surplus of *net assets* at the end of a period over the *net assets* at the beginning of the period, adjusted where relevant for amounts of *capital* injected or withdrawn, expressed either pre- or post-tax. As profit is notoriously hard to define, it is not always possible to derive one single figure of profit for an organisation from an accepted set of data (see: *profit & loss account*), and accordingly the *value* of a business needs to be determined by a number of different methods encompassing both fundamental and *quantitative analysis*. 3. In *microeconomics*, economists use the term 'profit' in a different way from the 'accounting' definition (sense 2). They consider the opportunity *cost of capital* provided by entrepreneurs (also termed: normal profits) as a cost of production, whereas *accountants* count the opportunity *cost of capital* as a part of profits. When microeconomists use the term 'profit', they are usually referring to what is technically known as: pure profit, supernormal profit, above-normal profit or economic profit. In other words, the accounting is split into normal profit (which is counted as an economic cost) and supernormal (ie economic profit) by economists. So it is possible for a firm to be making an accounting profit while operating at an economic loss. 4. In *macroeconomics*, the term 'profit' excludes *interest* on borrowed *capital* but not the return on the owner's *capital*.

**profit & loss account** 1. Colloquially known as: the *P&L*. The profit & loss account is drawn up to show the *net profit* of a business for a specific *accounting period*. *Limited companies* are required by the Companies Act to publish a profit & loss account which must be filed annually with the *Registrar of Companies*. There are four permitted formats for the profit & loss account. The formats inherently contain, but do not show, three distinct parts which form a sequence: i. The *trading account* in which *turnover* less cost of sales yields the '*gross profit*', which, less *distribution* and administrative costs, gives a figure for 'operating *profit*', also known as '*profit* before *interest* and *tax*'. ii. The *net profit account* starts with the figure arrived at for operating *profit* and subtracts *interest* payable, yielding '*profit* before *tax*', which, less taxation on *profit*, gives a figure for '*profit* after *tax*', ie the *net profit*. iii. The *appropriation* account starts with the *profit* after *tax* figure and subtracts the *dividends*, giving a final figure for 'retained *profit*', transferred to *reserves*', ie the figure that is put in the *balance sheet* under 'profit & loss account' (see sense 2) which is within the '*capital* and *reserves* account'. 2. The sub-account within the '*capital* and *reserves* account' on the *balance sheet*, providing the link between the *balance sheet* and the general profit & loss account (sense 1).

**profit forecast** A forecast made by the *directors* of a *company* of the *profits* for a particular period in the future. Required to be reported on (as to the calculations, consistency of accounting bases and care exercised in its preparation) by the *reporting accountants* and the *sponsor* when connected with a *share* issue. There is no formal requirement for a *company* to provide a *profit* forecast; if it is provided it must, however, be reported on by *auditors*.

**profit margin** A performance *ratio* of a *company*. It is calculated as:

$$\text{profit margin} = \frac{\text{profit before tax and interest payable}}{\text{turnover}}$$

A good indication of the *risk* involved in a business can be obtained by investigating the fluctuations in the profit margin over an extended period.

**program trading** Professional investors and institutions often use computer-generated buying and selling programs as part of their trading activities. These normally buy or sell *shares, options* or *futures*, on the basis of market movements and operate automatically. Can cause considerable market *volatility*. See: *trading curbs, triple witching hour.*

**progressive tax** A *tax* in which the rate of taxation increases as *income* increases. The *UK* operates a *tax* on personal *income* (and other *income* such as *company profits*). This means that as the *income* increases past certain limits, the *marginal tax rate* for that *income band* increases.

For the tax year 2009/10, the UK tax bands are:

| Tax rate | Taxable income after allowances |
|---|---|
| Starting savings rate 10%* | £0 - £2,440 |
| Basic rate 20% (10% for dividends) | £0 - £37,400 |
| Higher rate 40% (32.5% for dividends) | Over £37,400 |

*\* The 10p starting rate is for savings only. If an individual's non savings taxable income exceeds the starting rate limit, the 10p starting rate for savings will not be available for savings income.*

There is a personal allowance in 2009/10 of £6,475, which is deducted before any income is taxable. See also: *canon of taxation, principles of taxation, regressive tax.*

**projection** Estimate of future performance made by economists, corporate planners, and credit and *securities* analysts. Economists use econometric models to project *GDP*, *inflation, unemployment* and many other economic factors. Corporate financial planners project a *company*'s operating results and *cash flow*, using historical *trends* and making assumptions where necessary, in order to make *budget* decisions and to plan financing. Credit analysts use projections to forecast debt service ability. *Securities* analysts tend to focus their projections on *earnings trends* and *cash flow* per *share* in order to predict *market values* and *dividend growth.*

**promissory note** Certification of an unconditional promise to pay a specified sum of *money* to a named person or the bearer of the note.

**property enterprise trust (PET)** A collective *investment* which purchased commercial property in certain *enterprise zones* offering special *tax* concessions. See: *enterprise zones.*

**property income certificate (PINC)** A *certificate* giving the bearer a *share* in the *value* and rental *income* of a particular property. *PINCs* can be bought and sold.

**property valuation** See: *valuation.*

**prospective earnings** Refers to the anticipated returns of the next reporting period or the end of the next full *accounting period*, as opposed to historic data which are based on what actually happened. Also called: *prospective multiple, prospective yield.* See also: *price earnings ratio, yield.*

**prospective multiple** Another term for: *prospective earnings.*

**prospective yield** Another term for: *prospective earnings.*

**prospectus** A document which describes and advertises a new *share* issue to the public generally or investors specifically, the contents of which are laid down by *company* law, the *Department for Business, Enterprise and Regulatory Reform* and the *UK Listing Authority* and which provides all the information deemed necessary for a prospective shareholder to consider investing in the *shares* covered by the prospectus. *Company* law imposes extensive legal responsibilities on the *directors* of the *company* issuing a prospectus. See: *flotation.*

**protected position** Normally an open *physical* position that has been matched by a defensive opposite position in the *futures* or *options* market. See: *hedge*.

**protected rights** In a personal pension arrangement used for contracting out of the state second pension (S2P) or its state earnings-related pensions scheme (SERPS) predecessor, any National Insurance Contributions rebates are allocated to protected rights. Similarly any transfer of guaranteed minimum pension (GMP) benefits from a defined benefit occupational scheme is also allocated as protected rights. Protected rights must be identified separately from other pension benefits and are subject to special rules on the pension annuity which may be provided. The government's current plans are that protected rights will be scrapped from April 2012. See: *guaranteed minimum pension, contracting out.*

**protected rights annuity** The *pension income* provided by the *protected rights* within an *appropriate personal pension scheme* or a *contracted-out money purchase scheme.*

**protectionism** Policies instituted by a country to shelter certain industries from international competition and usually identified by specific import *tariffs* or bans on certain goods. For example, the Italian motorcycle industry survived the onslaught from the Japanese simply because no foreign motorcycles were permitted in *Italy*.

**provision** An amount allowed for in a set of *accounts* against anticipated losses or claims against the *company*. When the *accountants* and/or *directors* of a *company* are unsure of their liabilities in certain respects, they will agree upon a figure that represents an appropriate provision for this expense in their *accounts*. This is set against their *pre-tax profits*.

**provisional allotment letter** A notification sent to *shareholders* showing them how much of a *rights issue* they may take up. They will either take up the *shares* they are allotted, which will be in proportion to their existing shareholding, sell the rights *allotment* in the market (which will have a *value* if the *rights issue* is at a price significantly below the current *share* price) or refuse to take up the *shares* at all (normally when the *share* price has subsequently fallen to below the rights price).

**proxy** A person acting in place of another at a *company* meeting when voting takes place. Proxy forms are sent to *shareholders* who may then choose to give the *company*'s *directors* the discretion to vote on their behalf at an *annual general meeting* or *extraordinary general meeting*.

**PRT** See: *Petroleum Revenue Tax.*

**prudence concept** See under: *accounting concepts.*

**PSDR** See: *Public Sector Debt Repayment.*

**PSE** See: *Pacific Stock Exchange.*

**PSFD** See: *Public Sector Financial Deficit.*

**Pty** Short for: proprietary *company*. An abbreviation used in *Australia* and the Republic of *South Africa*. It is the equivalent of the *UK* abbreviation 'Ltd' for *private limited companies*.

**public company** Generally a *company* whose *shares* are available to the public and *listed* on a *stock exchange*, as opposed to a private *company*, whose *shares* are not for sale to the public. See: *plc*. Contrast: *public corporation*.

**public corporation** A state-owned or council-owned *company* providing infrastructural services to the community.

**public finance** The payment of goods and services provided by national and local government and financed by *tax* and duties.

**public finance accountant** A person who prepares the financial *accounts* for or acts as a management *accountant* for government agencies, local authorities and nationalised industries. As many of these bodies are non-profit making and governed by special statutes, the professional skills required of public finance accountants differ from those in the *private sector*. A member of the *Chartered Institute of Public Finance and Accountancy*.

**public limited company (plc)** A *limited company* registered under the Companies Act 1980 whose *shares* are available to the public, although not necessarily quoted on a *stock exchange*. Issued *share capital* must not be less than £50,000, 25% of which must be paid up. Similar in constitution to a *limited company* (but with a *Memorandum of Association* complying with table F of the Companies Regulations 1985). Records must be kept for longer (six years instead of three), *annual returns* must be submitted earlier (within seven months) and the *annual report* needs to be more comprehensive. If a *plc* is quoted on a *stock exchange* it must conform to the rules of that exchange (the *London Stock Exchange*, *AIM* or *PLUS markets*) with regard to its reporting, *share* dealings and actions in *takeovers* and *mergers*. See: *nominated advisors, UKLA*.

**public offering** The *US* term for: *offer for sale*.

**public private partnership (PPP)** See: *Private Finance Initiative*.

**public sector** The part of an economy that covers the activities of the government and local authorities. This includes education, the National Health Service, the social services, public transport, the police and local public services, as well as state-owned industries and *public corporations*. Contrast: *private sector*.

**Public Sector Debt Repayment (PSDR)** The amount by which the *tax* and revenue raised by the government exceeds its expenditure, the surplus being used to repay accumulated *public sector* borrowing (ie the *national debt*). It is the *public sector surplus* for the period.

**public sector deficit** See: *Central Government Net Cash Requirement*.

**public sector surplus** See: *Public Sector Debt Repayment (PSDR)*.

**public sector transfer** Arrangements within the *transfer club* to which mainly *public sector pension* schemes belong.

**public service pension** A *public sector pension* scheme covering, for instance, the civil service, police and local authorities, where the scheme's rules and particulars are defined by statute.

**public trustee** A government department that can be entrusted with the administration of a will, the guardianship of children or as a *trustee* or general administrator. This is usually done in cases where people are either financially or intellectually ill-equipped to look after these matters.

**Puerto Rico** Standard *currency*: *US dollar*.

**pul** *Currency* sub-unit of *Afghanistan*. 100 puls = 1 *afghani*.

**pula** Standard *currency* of *Botswana*. 1 pula = 100 *thebe*.

**pullback** When a price returns to the *chart pattern* after it has broken out temporarily on the downside. Compare: *breakout, throwback*.

**pump priming** A government policy aiming to encourage *investment* and raise business confidence, thus leading to a *multiplier* effect on the economy by repeatedly injecting small amounts of government spending into an economy. It was widely viewed as being ineffective and inflationary and was largely abandoned when *Keynesian economics* was adopted by policymakers, but is still now used in times of *recession*.

**punt** Formerly the standard *currency* of the *Republic of Ireland*, until the introduction of the *euro* on 1 January 2002. 1 punt = 100 pence.

**punter** Slang for a speculator on a *stock exchange, financial futures* market or *commodity market*, especially one who hopes to make quick *profits* for personal gain.

**PUP** See: *paid-up pension.*

**purchased life annuity** An *annuity* purchased by a private individual and ceasing on death in accordance with Chapter 7 of Part 4 of ITTOIA 2005 where part of the *income* is free of *tax.*

**purchasing power** The extent to which a unit of *money*, say £1, can buy goods and services. The more goods and services that can be bought with £1, the greater is the purchasing power of the *pound*. Purchasing power is inversely related to the rate of *inflation*: the higher *inflation* is, the lower is the purchasing power of the *pound*. In other words, *inflation* erodes *money*'s purchasing power.

**purchasing power parity (PPP)** Purchasing power parity between two *currencies* exists when their *exchange rates* are in *equilibrium* with each other, ie their domestic *purchasing powers* at that *exchange rate* are equivalent ('at *parity*'). For instance, the *exchange rate* of £1 = $1.60 would be in *equilibrium* if £1 could buy the same amount of goods and services in the *UK* as $1.60 would buy in the *US*. If indeed they are equivalent in terms of *purchasing power* at that *exchange rate*, one says that *PPP* holds. Otherwise one *currency* is *overvalued* with respect to the other. *PPP* theory is important in international economics and finance. The basic underlying idea is that *arbitrage* forces will come into play if one *currency* is *overvalued* relative to the other, and these will eventually lead to the *equalisation* of goods and services prices internationally (taking into account the *exchange rate*). As such, *PPP* theory is a 'law of one price'. In reality, *PPP* theory seems to hold relatively well in the long-run, but is quite unreliable in the short-run. It is especially deficient as a theory in that it cannot explain the high *volatility* in *exchange rates* and prolonged divergences from PPP. Other theories that build on *PPP* have been introduced which are slightly more satisfactory – *overshooting* for example. Probably a major reason for the unsatisfactory performance of *PPP* theory is that international comparisons and estimates of the price of equivalent baskets of goods and services are extremely difficult to make accurately.

**pure endowment assurance** *Life assurance* designed purely to provide *growth* without any additional death cover.

**put** The right to sell an *asset* at an agreed price by a specific date. See also: *short.*

**put option** The right, but not the obligation, to sell specific *securities* at a pre-agreed price at or by a certain specific date in the future. See: *option.*

**put-call** A commercial arrangement for equal partners or equal *shareholders* designed to break a deadlock over the *acquisition* of each other's *assets*. They can agree using a put-call agreement (by *deed*) that if one makes an *offer* for the other's *stake* and it is refused, the refusing party is obliged to purchase the other's *stake* at the same price within a predetermined period.

**put-through** A simultaneous deal effected by a market-making institution (see: *market maker*) for two clients where one is selling a holding and the other is buying. Normally for very large transactions where an arbitrated price is required.

**pya** *Currency* sub-unit of *Myanmar* (formerly: *Burma*). 100 pyas = 1 *kyat.*

**PYG** *currency code* for: *Paraguay* Guarani.

# Q

**Q ratio** Often referred to as Tobin's Q after its inventor, James Tobin. It is a measure of the worth of a company calculated as a ratio between market value and asset value:

$$Q = \frac{\text{(Equity Market Value + Liabilities Book Value)}}{\text{(Equity Book Value + Liabilities Book Value)}}$$

If Q is less than 1.0, then the market value is less than book value, suggesting that the company may be undervalued and taking it over is cheaper than acquiring new assets. The opposite is also true. The yardstick is sometimes also used at total market level.

**q theory** A theory developed by Professor James Tobin which suggests that a firm should continue to invest in *capital* goods as long as the *value* of their *shares* exceeds the replacement cost of the physical *assets* of the firm. The q refers to a *ratio* of two numbers: the first is the total *value* of the firm to its *shareholders* as calculated by the *net present value* of the expected future *profits* of the firm; the second number is the replacement cost of the physical *assets*. If the *ratio* (q) exceeds unity, then the firm should expand by investing in more *assets*, since the expected *profits* from the existing *assets* are greater than their cost. If q is less than 1, the firm should engage in *divestment*, ie selling the *assets* is more profitable than using them. The firm should invest or divest until q equals one. See: *Q ratio.*

**QAR** *currency code* for: Qatari Rial.

**Qard ul basan** Islamic term describing a benevolent or good loan. Generally an *interest* free loan given either for welfare purposes or for bridging short-term funding requirements. The borrower is required to pay back only the amount borrowed.

**Qatar** Standard *currency*: Qatari *riyal.* 1 Qatari *riyal* = 100 *dirhams.*

**QE** See: *quantitative easing.*

**qindar** *Currency* sub-unit of *Albania.* Plural of 'qindar' is: qindarka. 100 qindarka = 1 *lek.*

**QROP** Qualifying Overseas Pension Scheme. A scheme based overseas that has been approved by HMRC to receive *pension assets* and rights accumulated in a *UK* authorised *pension* scheme. This is primarily for those pensioners who move abroad but may have the added advantage of not requiring the purchase of a lifetime *annuity* and thus allowing the transfer of *assets* to succeeding generations.

**QTQ** *currency code* for: Guatemalan Quetzal.

**qualified accounts** Where a *company's auditors* cannot obtain sufficient information from books and records and rely on the statements made by the *directors* of a *company.* If a *company's accounts* are qualified, it is considered to be a less than satisfactory state of affairs.

**qualified director** Some *companies* insist on *directors* holding a certain number of the *company's shares* in order to be eligible for an appointment to the *board.*

**qualifying policy** A qualifying *life assurance* policy is one on which regular *premiums* are paid, whether annually or more frequently, for a period of ten years or more. The *premiums* must be fairly evenly spread over the life of the policy. The policy will cease to qualify if the *premiums* payable in any one year are more than twice the *premiums* paid in any other year. In the first ten years, the *premiums* paid in any one year must not exceed one-eighth of the total *premiums* paid in the ten years. *Single premium* policies and certain variations of *single premium* policies are not 'qualifying' policies. In the case of policies taken out after 1 April 1976, the sum assured on a whole life policy must be not less than 75% of the total *premiums* paid during the term of the policy. There is an exception to this in the case of policies taken out by a person aged 55 or more, the stipulated proportion of 75% being reduced by 2% for each year by which the proposer's age exceeds 55. Qualifying policies include most forms of life policy, eg whole life, *mortgage* protection, *endowment assurance* and family income policies. No *basic rate income tax* or *capital gains tax* is payable on the maturity proceeds of a life policy, whether it be a qualifying or *non-qualifying policy*. In the case of qualifying policies taken out after 13 March 1984, no *tax* relief is available (see: *Life Assurance Premium Relief*).

**qualifying service**  The expression, defined by the *Pension Schemes Act 1993*, determining the requisite service for a member to qualify for short service benefit. Currently two years' qualifying service is required for a preserved pension. See: *preserved benefits*.

**qualitative analysis**  An *analysis* that is not or cannot be made in terms of numerical figures and normally based on impressions. The factors involved may not be expressible on a numeric scale, for instance, experience or the aesthetics of a product. Thus, a qualitative analysis has the drawback of being imprecise and emotive, but advantages may be ease and *speed*. Compare: *quantitative analysis*.

**quality**  1. In general terms, the quality of a *fixed interest security* is a measure of the reliability of the issuer in terms of whether *interest* and principal will be paid on time. See: *credit rating* agency. 2. The quality of a *share* is a measure of the stability of the market price, ie a high-quality *share* will not fluctuate widely. However, individual investors may have other subjective preferences associated with their opinions of quality. See: *analysis*.

**quality of earnings**  Term used to distinguish 'real' from 'artificial' *earnings* that a *company* makes. A high quality of earnings means that the *earnings* of a *company* are derived mainly from real factors, such as higher *volume* of sales and lower *real* costs in production, as opposed to those that are deemed 'artificial' or inflation-affected, such as *stock value* increases and other *asset appreciation* due to *inflation*. Investors often pay more for *companies* with higher quality of earnings. See: *dividend cover*.

**quality of life**  See under: *standard of living*.

**quango**  See: *quasi-autonomous non-government organisation*.

**quantitative analysis**  An *analysis* of factors that are purely measurable on a numerical scale (eg financial data, *investment yields*, price history, *volatility*). Involves the use of mathematical, logical and/or statistical techniques to compare *risk* and return. Usually yields a numeric solution that can be directly compared to alternatives.

**quantitative easing (QE)**  Euphemism for increasing the money supply beyond normal levels in order to stimulate an economy. Normally combined with very low interest rates, it is often a last ditch effort to avoid stagflation. A central bank can do this by buying government bonds in the open market, or by lending money to deposit-taking institutions, or by buying assets from banks in exchange for currency, or any combination of these actions. Quantitative easing was used by the Bank of Japan to fight domestic deflation in the early 2000s. More recently, QE policies have been announced by the US Federal Reserve under Ben Bernanke and in the UK by the Bank of England under Mervyn King to counter the effects of the credit crunch and forestall a severe recession.

**quantity theory of money**  A monetarist theory (see: *monetarism*) revolving about the values of the variables in the *'equation of exchange'*:

$$Mv = Py$$

M stands for the *money supply*, v for the *velocity of circulation*, P for the price level and y for the *real income* (hence Py is the *money*, or nominal, *income*) in an economy, in any particular time period. Note that the *equation of exchange* is a platitude (ie true due to the definitions of the variables, and holds regardless of the theory). The quantity theory of *money* asserts that the velocity v is more or less constant for a particular *real income* y. Thus, regarding v and y as fixed in the *equation of exchange*, the theory comes to the simple conclusion that the economy's *money supply* M varies in line with the general price level P. In other words, the effect of an expansionary *monetary policy* will tend to be purely inflationary.

**quantum meruit** An amount paid for goods, services or for an unfulfilled *contract* with the absence of a prior agreement as to price. The justifiable amount.

**quarter days** The legal definition of the four days in each year when quarterly payments may take place, especially with regard to property rents and rent reviews. In England and Wales the quarter days are Lady Day (25 March), Midsummer (24 June), Michaelmas (29 September) and Christmas (25 December). In Scotland they are Candlemas (2 February), Whitsun (15 May), Lamas (1 August) and Martinmas (11 November).

**quartiles** Rankings for comparison purposes divided into four hierarchical sections. Accordingly the first two quartiles will be the top half and the second two the bottom half. In *investment* terms, quartile performance is used as a measure with the long-term target being the maintenance of upper quartile performance in comparison with similar *portfolios*.

**quasi-autonomous non-government organisation (QUANGO)** An organisation, some of whose members are civil servants, appointed by a minister in order to carry out a state-financed function. Even though they are not government agencies they must report to a government minister. QUANGOs are also commonly known as non-departmental public bodies. They are often much criticised as they are non-elected bodies spending public *money*, and so are not democratically accountable for their decisions. Attempts have been made to counter this by improving transparency, accountability and by cutting their numbers. According to the Economic Research Council, in 2006 there were 524 quangos in the UK. The largest quangos in terms of funding are Primary Care Trusts.

**QUEST** Short for: Qualifying Employee Share *Trust*. A trust empowered to hold *shares* for the host *company* for the purposes of fulfilling *options* or *share* savings schemes for employees.

**quetzal** *Guatemala*'s standard *currency*. 1 quetzal = 100 *centavos*.

**queue** *Companies* waiting in line for a *listing* on the *London Stock Exchange*.

**quick assets** Another term for highly *liquid assets*.

**quick ratio** A *ratio* that measures a *company*'s liquidity. It is calculated by adding the figures for *cash*, marketable *securities* and *debtors*, all divided by *current liabilities*. Note that the calculation omits *stock*, which is considered less liquid than the others. The quick ratio indicates whether the *company* has enough readily *convertible assets* to pay the *current liabilities* if sales were discontinued suddenly. Thus a quick ratio of about one or more should prove satisfactory. It is also called: *acid test ratio*, quick-asset *ratio*.

**quid pro quo** Latin term for 'something for something'. Something in return for something received, for instance not a gift nor a unilateral transfer. *Contracts* must be quid pro quo, ie there must be *consideration* involved for there to be a contractual agreement.

**quorum** A minimum number of individuals required to carry out an official meeting. For a *limited company* the quorum is defined in the *Articles of Association*.

**quota** The maximum amount allowed by an authority, eg a trade quota is the maximum amount of products that may be imported into (or exported from) a country as laid down by the government authorities. A milk quota is the maximum volume a herd can produce, etc.

**quotation** 1. The price (consisting of two figures) given in a market indicating the *range* of buying and selling prices. 2. A *security* that has been admitted to a recognised *investment* exchange thus receives a *listing*. 3. Legally, a product's price quotation does not necessarily imply an *offer* by the seller, merely an *invitation to treat*.

**quoted company** A *company* whose *shares* appear on the official list of any worldwide *Recognised Investment Exchange* (*RIE*). A *quoted investment* will be either a quoted company or a collective *investment* whose unit price is quoted in a recognised journal such as the Financial Times.

**Quoted Comapnies Alliance** Originally established as **City Group for Smaller Companies (CISCO)** An association or pressure group set up in December 1992 by 17 firms including venture capitalists (see: *venture capital*) and *brokers* to represent the interests of smaller *companies* on the *London Stock Exchange,* to further their interests to analysts, institutions, regulators and the investing public, ensure adequate market representation and promote the benefits of their *shares* as a *class*. See also: *Alternative Investment Market*, PlusMarkets, *small company, Venture Capital Trust*.

**quoted investment** See under: *quoted company*.

# R

**rack rent** The highest rental obtainable for a property, whose tenants are then considered to be on the rack!

**raider** A person, group or *company* triggering a *hostile takeover*. Often a specialist in exploiting *undervalued asset* situations and in *takeover bids*.

**rainmaker** Individual who brings significant amounts of new business to a *brokerage* firm. The rainmaker may bring in wealthy *brokerage* customers who generate large *commissions*, or he or she may be an *investment* banker who attracts corporate or municipal finance, underwriting, or *merger* and *acquisition* business.

**rally** A rise in price which follows a previous price fall. Compare: *reaction*.

**ramping** The price of a specific *share* can be ramped by circulating rumours, encouraging press comment, heavy institutional promotion and some strategic buying. This serves to enhance the *share* price and can occur where a *takeover* is envisaged that involves the exchange of these *shares*. Ramping can also allow large sellers to release a substantial proportion of their *shares* at worthwhile levels. This is regarded as market abuse by the Financial Services Authority.

**Ramsay** W.T. Ramsay Ltd. v Inland Revenue Commissioners (1982). A case brought before the House of Lords to ascertain whether a series of 'artificial' steps constituted one *contract* and could benefit the individual by the avoidance of *tax*. In summary, if an individual (or *company*) enters into a pre-ordained series of transactions (or a single composite transaction) where steps have been inserted which have no commercial purpose other than to avoid the payment of *tax*, the inserted steps will be disregarded for fiscal purposes and *tax* levied accordingly. See: *Furniss v Dawson*.

**rand** Standard *currency* of *Namibia* and *South Africa*. 1 rand = 100 *cents*.

**random walk theory** The theory that *share* prices move as though they have no memory and that they do not follow prescribed *patterns*, thus suggesting that past price performance is a less than effective way of anticipating future price movements, especially in the shorter term, a theory first espoused by Louis Bachelier at the turn of the century and disputed by advocates of *technical analysis*, who say that *charts* of past price movements enable them to predict future price movements.

**range** Simply the difference between the high and low in the price of a *security* for a certain time period.

**RAT** Retirement Annuity Trust. A *discretionary trust* which acts as a self-administered private *pension* scheme for individuals resident overseas. RATs are very flexible *pension* vehicles and are approved by both the *UK* and some overseas *tax* authorities which do not require the purchase of a lifetime *annuity* and thus allow the transfer of *assets* to succeeding generations, as well as *capital* drawings indefinitely.

**rate anticipation swap** An *interest rate swap* related to a predicted *interest rate* change.

**rate of exchange** The rate at which one *currency* is converted into another. As with other *investments*, two prices are always quoted, ie, buying and selling. The difference between these prices reflects the '*commission*' charged by the individual or corporation carrying out the exchange.

**rate of return** Normally used to compare *investments* with a fixed *capital value* or to compare *income* from *investments* ignoring any *capital* fluctuations (see: *yield*) as opposed to *total return* which includes *growth*. The annual amount of *income* from an *investment*, expressed as a percentage of the original where it is important to note whether a quoted rate is before or after *tax*. In order to make true comparisons, because some rates are payable more frequently than annually, it is necessary to consider the *annual equivalent rate* (*AER*) which most *investment* institutions are obliged to declare.

**rates** A local authority *tax* applied to the owner or occupier of commercial property and calculated on the rateable *value* of residential or commercial property. The non-domestic rate is set at a national level by the government (48.1p in the pound for small businesses and 48.5p in the pound for large businesses in 2009/10). Domestic rates were replaced in the *UK* by the community charge, which in turn was replaced by the current Council Tax.

**rating** See: *credit rating*.

**rating agency** See: *credit rating*.

**ratio** Ratios are used in the *analysis* of *company accounts*. They can be used for cross-sectional comparisons (ie comparisons among *companies* of the same industry) and/or time *trends* (ie comparing a *company* at various times in its history). Commonly, *company* ratios are divided into three groups: 1. Performance ratios – these indicate how well the *directors* conduct a *company*'s business. The main performance ratios are the *return on investment* (*ROI*) measures and the *profit margin*. Others include: *tax ratio, net asset turnover, fixed asset turnover, stock turnover, debtor turnover,* and *creditor turnover*. 2. Financial status ratios – these show a *company*'s liquidity (ie ability to deal with shorter term liabilities) and *solvency* (ie ability to deal with longer term liabilities). The *solvency ratios* are: *debt ratio* and the *interest* cover. The *liquidity ratios* are: *current ratio* and *quick ratio*. 3. Stock market ratios – these relate to *quoted company profits* and *dividends* to *share* prices and to the number of *shares* in issue. Examples are: *earnings per share* (*eps*), *price earnings ratio* (*P/E*), *dividend yield* (see: *yield*), *dividend cover,* and *dividend payout ratio*.

**ratio analysis** Analysis of *company ratios* derived from financial statement figures. Investment analysts use ratio analysis as a tool in evaluating *companies*.

**RCH** See: *Recognised Clearing House*.

**reaction** A decline in price which follows a previous price advance. Compare: *rally*.

**Reaganomics** Economic program instituted by the administration of President Ronald Reagan beginning in 1980. Reaganomics stressed lower taxes, higher defence spending and curtailed spending for social services. Reduced *growth* in the *money supply*, applied by the *Federal Reserve Board*, combined with Reaganomics to produce a severe *recession* in 1981–1982, and the following Reagan years were characterised by huge *budget deficits*, low *interest* and *inflation* rates and high economic *growth*. In theory Reaganomics was meant to be about smaller government and spending restraint, but the combination was never achieved.

**real** *Net* of *inflation*.

**real estate** An American expression used to describe a piece of land and all physical property related to it, including houses, fences, landscaping and all rights to the air above (with a few exceptions) and earth below the property.

**real exchange rate** The *nominal exchange rate* adjusted for relative price levels between the two countries under consideration, in order to eliminate *inflation* effects. Usually expressed as an *index*. See: *effective exchange rate*.

**real GDP** Adjusted *GDP* figure to take into account the effects of *inflation*. See: *GDP/GNP deflator*.

**real growth** 1. See: *real value*. 2. Economic *growth* after adjusting for *inflation*. See also: *real national income*.

**real interest rate** The real interest rate is obtained from the prevailing (nominal) *interest rate* by making adjustments for the effects of *inflation*. The formula relating the *real interest rate* j, the *nominal interest rate* i and the rate of *inflation* f (where all rates are annualised) is:

$$\text{real interest rate } j = \frac{i - f}{1 + f}$$

This is sometimes also written as $(1+j)(1+f) = (1+i)$.

From the formula, if the *inflation* rate is relatively small (less than 10%, say) then the equation can be approximated by:

$$\text{real interest } j = i - f$$

This is the formula most often used to estimate real interest rates. The anticipated (expected) *inflation* rate must be used in the formulas for calculating future expected real interest rates.

**real national income** *National income* (national output) with adjustments made for *inflation*.

**real national output** See: *real national income*.

**real property** Land or buildings (*realty*) as distinct from personal property (*personalty*).

**real rate of return** *Profit* (normally *income* but can include *growth* in the case of *real total return*) less a selected measure of *inflation* over the same period. See: *real interest rate*.

**real terms** The presentation of a scenario where all relevant factors have been adjusted for the effects of *inflation*.

**real value** The effectiveness of an *investment* after taking account of *inflation*. In determining *value* the opportunity *cost of capital* employed both in terms of *inflation* and *interest rates* can sometimes be taken into account.

**realignment** The process that occured in the *European Monetary System* before the launch of the euro when one or more *currencies* fell outside its designated *band*. It normally entailed a *currency* being devalued. See: *devaluation*.

**realisation account** An account used to determine the *profit* or loss of *assets* on disposal. Realisation accounts are debited with the *book value* of the *asset* and credited with the sale price of the *asset*, the balance being applied to the *profit & loss account*.

**realised loss** See: *realised profit*.

**realised profit** The gain or loss on an *asset* that has been disposed of and the proceeds received as opposed to the notional *profits* or losses on *assets* still owned.

**realtor** The *US* name for an estate agent or chartered surveyor.

**realty** See: *real property*.

**rebasing an index** Sometimes *indices* are rebased when a different period's *index value* is assigned the base *index value* and all the other periods' *values* have to be recalculated.

This is sometimes done when the *index* number becomes cumbersome or its constituents change significantly. The formula used for rebasing is:

$$\text{new index value} = \text{old index value} \times \frac{\text{new index for rebased period}}{\text{old index for rebased period}}$$

Thus for the example used under the Glossary entry for *index*, if period 2 is rebased to 100:

| Period | Variable value | Old index | New index | Year-to-year percentage changes for the new index (rounded) |
|--------|---------------|-----------|-----------|-------------------------------------------------------------|
| 0 | 10 | 100 | 55.6 | n/a |
| 1 | 15 | 150 | 83.3 | 50 |
| 2 | 18 | 180 | 100 | 20 |
| 3 | 20 | 200 | 111.1 | 11 |
| 4 | 26 | 260 | 144.4 | 30 |

Notice that the year-to-year percentage changes remain the same for the new *indices*, even though the *point* movements are different. See also: *chain-linked*.

**recapitalisation** Alteration of a corporation's *capital* structure, such as an exchange of *bonds* for *stock*. *Administration* is a common reason for recapitalisation; *debentures* might be exchanged for reorganisation *bonds* that pay *interest* only when earned. A healthy *company* might seek to save taxes by replacing *preferred stock* with *bonds*, or a smaller *company* might alter its *capital* structure in order to prepare for *flotation* or in anticipation of development finance. The *Credit Crunch* has meant many banks have had to seek recapitalisation, often with government being the only supplier of capital.

**receivables** American term for *debtors*. Money due to a business from customers.

**receiver** Appointed by a *company* or sometimes the government (see: *official receiver*) to administer the affairs of a *company* that is unable to continue trading for some reason (that is in *receivership*). A receiver and his or her staff are automatically considered as executive officers of the *company* and will endeavour to maintain the *company*'s business and *goodwill* with a view to selling off parts of the *company* and salvaging it as a *going concern*. A receiver acts on behalf of *creditors* and *debenture* holders and is normally appointed where there is a danger of *insolvency*. See: *administration, bankrupt, liquidation*.

**receivership** A situation where a *receiver* is appointed to recover specific debts from a *company* that has defaulted or where there has been fraud by the *directors* or where a potentially viable *company* needs to be reorganised or sold to pre-empt its *liquidation*.

**recession** A downturn in economic activity generally represented by a decline in the *gross national product* of an economy in at least two consecutive quarters. In the USA, the National Bureau of Economic Research has assumed a role of announcing the recessionary dates in an economic cycle, but it usually reaches its decisions some while after the event. The NBER says the current US recession started in December 2007, a decision it announced on 1 December 2008.

**recessionary gap** See under: *output gap*.

**reciprocity** Most commonly used in international trade negotiations where *tariffs* or *quotas* are raised or lowered on a reciprocal basis. In cases, for example, where foreign cars were being imported from a country that did not permit *imports* there would be no reciprocity and a trade *embargo* of the country might well prompt them to lift restrictions. Free trade is considered the ideal environment for industrial economies and most free trade nations expect reciprocity from their trading partners. Where this is not the case or agreed *quotas* are exceeded, *tariffs* may be temporarily applied to specific goods. See: *protectionism*.

**Recognised Clearing House (RCH)** *London Clearing House* recognised by the *Securities and Investments Board*.

**Recognised Investment Exchange (RIE)** An *investment* exchange authorised under the *Financial Services and Markets Act 2000* directly by the *Financial Services Authority*. Can also be applied to overseas *investment* exchanges where the local rules are considered to be compatible with *UK* legislation and regulations. The exchanges authorised to conduct *investment* business in the UK are: *London Stock Exchange, LIFFE* (incorporating *London Commodities Exchange*), *London Metal Exchange, EDX London, ICE Futures Europe, PLUS Markets and SWX Europe,* and the Recognised Overseas Investment Exchanges include: *NASDAQ, Chicago Board of Trade, Chicago Mercantile Exchange, Sydney Futures Exchange, ICE Futures US* and *New York Mercantile Exchange* (*NYMEX*). Virtually all of the major – and not so major – world investment markets that do not carry on regulated activities in the UK are FSA Designated Investment Exchanges. Designation allows FSA regulated firms to treat *transactions* with designated exchanges in the same way as transactions with RIEs.

**Recognised Professional Body (RPB)** Until 30 November 2001 a professional organisation was permitted by the *Financial Services Authority* to authorise its members to carry out *investment* business where it did not form part of their main activity. Solicitors and *accountants* came under this heading. The *RPBs* were: The Law Society (of England and Wales), The Law Society of Scotland, The Law Society of Northern Ireland, The *Institute of Chartered Accountants in England and Wales,* The Institute of Chartered Accountants of Scotland, The Institute of Chartered Accountants in Ireland, The *Chartered Association of Certified Accountants,* The *Insurance Brokers Registration Council* and The Institute of Actuaries. Firms which used the RPB approach would only continue to give individual investment advice after 30 November 2001 if they registered directly with the FSA. The RPB system continues in a restricted form based on Designated Professional Bodies (DPB). See: *Designated Professional Bodies, authorisation*.

**Recognised Stock Exchange (RSE)** UK tax legislation uses the term 'recognised stock exchange' widely, eg only securities officially traded on a recognised stock exchange can be held within an ISA. The definition of recognised stock exchange is now to be found in section 1005 of Income Tax Act 2007, which says:

'In the Income Tax Acts "recognised stock exchange" means—

(a) the Stock Exchange, and

(b) any stock exchange outside the United Kingdom which is for the time being designated as a recognised stock exchange for the purposes of this section by an order made by the Commissioners for Her Majesty's Revenue and Customs.'

A list of overseas recognised stock exchanges is given on the HMRC website (www.hmrc.gov.uk/fid/table2-rse.pdf). As at May 2009 there were 60 such exchanges.

**recommended takeover** A *takeover* recommended to the *shareholders* by the *board*.

**recoupment** Recovery of the *capital* in an *investment*, a term often used in media projects to describe the point from which the investor or *angel* starts to make a *profit* (ie after recoupment). See: *payback period*.

**recourse agreement** An agreement between a *finance company* and a retailer, in which the retailer undertakes to repossess the goods if the buyer fails to maintain their *hire purchase* payments.

**recovery stock** A *share* which, having fallen in price and popularity, is assessed to have the potential to reinstate its former *value*.

**rectangle** A *chart pattern* used in *technical analysis* in which the envelope of a price movement consists of horizontal (or near horizontal) parallel lines. These formations can be of very long *duration*. A rectangle can be either a reversal or a *continuation pattern*. If the *breakout* is in the opposite direction to the preceding *trend*, then the rectangle could equally well be called a 'multiple top' (for a preceding uptrend) or a 'multiple bottom' (for a preceding downtrend). The price movement after *breakout* is expected to be at least the (horizontal) width of the rectangle.

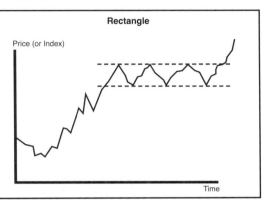

**Red Book** Informal name for the detailed government spending and revenue forecasts which accompany each *Budget* speech. Formally known as the Financial Statement.

**red chip company** A term now applied to a company board in mainland China but incorporated elsewhere and listed on the Hong Kong stock exchange. The business is nevertheless usually controlled by Chinese shareholders. Red chip originally referred to a *Hong Kong listed holding company* connected with or run by the Chinese Communist Party (CCP).

**redeemable preference share** *Preference shares* which the *company* reserves the right to redeem. These can be redeemed either out of *distributable profits* or the proceeds from a further issue of *shares*.

**redemption date** The repayment date for *gilts*, *debentures* and other *fixed interest securities at par* or other specified amount by the issuer. The *maturity date*.

**redemption yield** See under: *yield*.

**reduced balance depreciation** Another term for: *diminishing balance depreciation*.

**reduction in yield (RIY)** The amount by which the returns from a financial product are reduced by charges and measured as an annual amount. This is calculated by comparing a charge free *annual return* with equivalent underlying *growth* from the financial product. For example, a notional investment of £100 grows at 10% per year and is worth £161 after five years. At 10% per year underlying *growth* a financial product (such as a collective investment or *endowment*) is valued at £147. This represents a compound *growth* of 8%. The *RIY* is therefore 2% – reflecting product costs of 2% per year. This can be very useful when comparing different products.

**refinancing** The repayment of an existing loan or loans by borrowing new *money* at better terms or at different rates over different periods. See: *rescheduling*.

**reflation** An economic policy aimed at increasing the level of activity in an economy by reducing *taxes* and *interest rates*, increasing government spending, increasing *money supply* or a combination of these. Normally applied in times of *recession*.

**register of charges** 1. A register of certain *charges* (such as *debentures*) on *assets* of *limited companies* kept by the *Registrar of Companies*. The types of *charge* that must be registered in this way are set out in the Companies Act 2006. Failure to register the *charge* within 21 days renders it unenforceable in the case of a *liquidation* although the underlying debt remains valid only as an *unsecured debt*. 2. A list of *charges* that a *company* must itself maintain at its *registered office* together with its books of account.

**register of companies** All *companies* must file certain documents with the *Registrar of Companies* at *Companies House* before they can obtain a *certificate of incorporation*.

**register of debentures** This is not a register of *debenture* stockholders but a register of all *mortgages* and *charges* affecting a registered *company*'s property. These must be filed with the *Registrar of Companies*.

**register of directors** Every *company* must keep a register of *directors* giving names, addresses, nationalities, business occupation, dates of birth and other directorships held. A copy of this register must be sent to the *Registrar of Companies*, who should also be notified of any alterations by the *company secretary*.

**register of directors shareholdings** Every *company* must keep a register showing the number, description and amount of *shares* and *debentures* of the *company* held by its *directors* and provide these in its *annual return*. The *directors* are obliged to notify the *company* in writing of any *acquisitions* or disposals made in these *shares*. Interests of an *associate*, wives or infant children are considered to be interests of the *director*.

**register of members** A list of all the *shareholders* of a *limited company*, normally kept by a private *registrar* for a *quoted company* and by the *company secretary* for a private *company*, containing the names and addresses of the *shareholders*, the dates on which their *shares* were registered and the number, *class*, price and sale date if appropriate. The register must be available for inspection by *members* free of charge for at least two normal office hours per working day and for others on payment of an appropriate fee.

**registered office** The address of the registered office of a *UK limited company* as notified to the *Registrar of Companies*, to which correspondence can be sent. Any change must be notified to the *Registrar of Companies* within 14 days and published in the 'London Gazette'. All the *company*'s legal documentation and *accounts* must be available from this address which in turn must be disclosed on stationery and in the *company*'s *annual return* (a statutory obligation).

**registered number** Each *company* registered at *Companies House* is given a unique number for reference purposes.

**registered pension scheme** A pension scheme registered with HMRC under the provisions of the Finance Act 2004. This places the scheme within the *simplified regime*.

**registrar** The person (now normally a specialist organisation) responsible for keeping a register of *shareholders* (*members*) and issuing *certificates* for individual *quoted companies*. They also deal with all other shareholder administration including *dividend distribution*, rights and *scrip issues* etc. For a smaller private *company* this work is done by the *company secretary*.

**Registrar of Companies** Based in *Companies House*, the Registrar is officially responsible for holding details of all *UK limited companies* as well as a wide variety of administrative functions, including maintaining the *register* of *companies* and the *register of charges*, issuing *certificates of incorporation* and receiving *annual returns*. All the information held is deemed to be in the public domain and is available for inspection by anyone.

**regression analysis** A statistical technique used in the *analysis* of *securities* markets and in the risk-return *analysis* of *portfolio theory*. Generally speaking, it shows to what extent one quantity varies as another quantity changes. It thus shows the correlation between the two varying quantities. This correlation can be illustrated graphically: one variable quantity is plotted on the horizontal (or 'x') axis and the other is shown on the vertical (or 'y') axis. The strength of the correlation

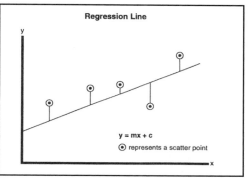

can be calculated using the *correlation coefficient*. The resulting scatter diagram visually indicates the type and roughly the extent of the correlation. The most frequently used tool for regression analysis is the method of 'least squares'. This method involves finding the straight line which minimises the sum of the squares of the (vertical) distances between the line and all the individual scatterpoints. It is thus often called the 'line of best fit'. This line can be found by the following formula:

$$y = mx + c \quad \text{where} \quad m = \frac{\text{cov}(x, y)}{\text{var}(x)} \quad \text{and} \quad c = \bar{y} - m\bar{x}$$

**regressive tax** *Tax* that decreases in proportion to the revenue or *income* to which it is applied. Normally flat fees or indirect *taxes* are considered regressive. Purchase *tax* or *VAT*, for instance, are marginally regressive, as a higher proportion of lower *incomes* is spent on consumer goods. See: *principles of taxation*.

**reinsurance** Where a substantial *risk* is too great a burden for one *insurance company* or *syndicate* it will offer the *risk* to other insurers for part of the *premium*, thereby spreading the potential liability and reducing its exposure.

**relative strength** A measurement of the price performance of an individual *security* against the performance of its *market index* normally in the form of a *ratio*. See: *relative strength chart*.

**relative strength chart** A *chart* used in *technical analysis* that plots the relative price movement of the *security* in question with respect to the movement of the market as a whole. If a *security* rises by 15%, then this rise is not very impressive within the context of an overall rise of the market by 20%. A change in the *relative strength trend* of a *security* can be the prelude to a change in the price of the underlying price of that *security*.

**REMIC** Acronym for the *US*: *'real estate mortgage investment* conduit'. A REMIC is a vehicle created under the *US* Tax Reform Act 1986 to issue multiclass mortgage-backed *securities*. REMICs may be organised as corporations, *partnerships* or *trusts*, and participation may be in the form of senior or junior, regular (*debt instruments*) or residual (*equity* interests). The practical meaning of REMICs has been that issuers have more flexibility than is afforded by the *collateralised mortgage obligation* (*CMO*) vehicles. Issuers can thus separate *mortgage* pools not only into different maturity classes but into different *risk* classes. Whereas *CMOs* normally have *AAA bond ratings*, REMICs represent a range of *risk* levels.

**remortgage** Replacing an existing *mortgage* or *mortgages* with a new *mortgage*.

**renewable term insurance** A life *insurance* policy with a limited term that can be converted into a new life *insurance* or *assurance* policy without further medical evidence. See: *term insurance*.

**renminbi** Name of *China*'s *currency* (literally: People's *currency*). However, the unit of *currency* is called: *yuan*. 1 *yuan* = 10 *jiao* = 100 *fen*.

**rente** Annual perpetual *interest* on *rentes*.

**rentes** An undated government *bond* issued by several European governments particularly *France*. The *interest* is called: *rente*.

**renunciation** When a *security* is issued for the first time, it will initially be effected by an *allotment letter* (see: *allotment*) with a renunciation form included. During the renunciation period, the rights to these *shares* may be sold by completing this section. Similarly, when disposing of a *unit trust* holding the investor(s) need merely complete the renunciation form on the reverse of the *certificate* and forward it to the *trust* managers.

**reorganisation relief** Under certain circumstances capital gains can be carried forward through change of ownership. Relevant in cases where investors receive new shares or loan notes by way of an exchange in a company takeover – often referred to as a paper-for-paper transaction.

**repayment mortgage** A *mortgage* where the *capital* as well as *interest* is repaid over the period by regular level payments (in the early stages most of this payment is *interest*, but as small amounts of *capital* are repaid the *interest* content reduces, so that by the end of the period the payment is mostly *capital*) as opposed to other types of *mortgage* (interest-only or *balloon*) where *capital* repayment is dealt with by way of a *sinking fund* created by a *pension* or *endowment* policy. Also called an *amortising mortgage*.

**repo** A repo is a 'sale and *repurchase* agreement' which allows the holder of a *bond* to sell his or her holding in order to raise *cash*, simultaneously entering into an agreement to *repurchase* the *bond* holding at a certain date in the future at the same price plus *interest* (as opposed to selling it for *value* in the market). The *interest* is calculated on a simple basis according to the *repo rate* and the duration in days. The 'reverse repo' is the opposite side of the repo agreement, where the investor buys *bonds* now for *cash* and simultaneously enters into an agreement to sell the *bond* back at the specified date in the future. This allows participants in the market to go *short* of *bonds*, ie 'borrow' *bonds* now in order to settle *short* trades. Most repos are of short-term duration, many even just overnight. Repos that are longer than overnight are referred to as 'term repos'. Some repos are allowed to run on without a fixed *maturity date* until one side of the *contract* decides to terminate the deal – these are the 'open repos'. See: *official bank rate*.

**repo market** In January 1996 the *Bank of England* gave the green light to the development of an open repo market in *gilts*, which brought it more in line with other government debt markets.

**repo rate** The rate at which the *Bank of England* will *repurchase short term money market instruments* and thus the minimum lending rate. See also: *repo*. The repo market is now the main way in which the Bank of England controls short term rates.

**report and accounts** The annual or *interim statement* issued by all *public limited companies* and *private limited companies* to their *shareholders* or *members* which by law must include a *directors report* and at least the annual *accounts* of the *company*. For larger *companies* and all publicly *quoted companies* the *accounts* must be audited. There are additional rules on reporting for *listed companies* dictated by the rules of the exchange on which they are quoted, and for the *London Stock Exchange* the UKLA rules apply. Many larger *companies* provide additional information at their discretion, and copies of the *report and accounts* can be substantial and comprehensive documents designed to inform and encourage *shareholders*. See: *annual report*.

**reporting accountants** The firm of *accountants* who report on the financial information contained in a *prospectus* and who deal with other accounting matters connected with a new issue. The reporting accountants are often the *company*'s own *auditors*, although this depends primarily on their experience of new issue and *stock exchange* work.

**repossession** Exercising rights of occupation or ownership. Where an *asset* is charged (see: *charge*) or where a *lien* is granted on it, ownership vests in the party holding the *charge* or *lien*. In the event of the obligations so determined (such as the repayment of a loan by regular payments) not being met, the holder of the *charge* or *lien* may take possession of their property and sell it to recover their outstanding liabilities, any surplus being returned to the party granting the *charge* or *lien* such as the occupier or user. See: *foreclosure*.

**Republic of Ireland** The Irish Stock Exchange (ISE) was established in 1973 in Dublin. In 1973, the Irish Stock Exchange amalgamated with the *London Stock Exchange* and other regional exchanges, becoming known in 1986 as the International Stock Exchange of the *United Kingdom* and the Republic of Ireland. As a result of European legislation, the Irish Stock Exchange separated from the *London Stock Exchange* in 1996. In 2009, around 70 *companies* were listed. The main *indices* are:

- Irish Stock Exchange Equity (ISEQ) Index – Comprises all *stocks* on the *Official List* and the IEX. Base: 4 January 1980 = 1,000.

- ISEQ Total Return Index – Similar to the ISEQ but also includes dividends.

Standard *currency*: euro. 1 *euro* = 100 *cents*. Currency was the *punt*, until the introduction of the *euro* on 1 January 2002.

**repurchase** The purchase of a *security* by the issuer. Normally associated with *unit trust* holdings where the units are repurchased by the managers from the holder or *gilts* at maturity (see: *redemption date*). See: *repo*.

**rescheduling** Loans can be restructured for borrowers who are unable to redeem a loan by a set date. The term is most commonly used in the international debt markets, where Third World countries cannot meet their debt burden, and in some cases it can involve the writing off of certain parts of a debt or converting debt to *equity*.

**Reserve Bank** See: *Federal Reserve Bank*.

**reserve capital** See: *reserves*.

**reserve currency** The main trading *currencies* considered suitable for governments to hold as their official *reserves* (sense 3). These may normally include the *US dollar*, the *euro*, *yen* and *Sterling*.

**reserve tranche** The proportion of its total *quota*, to which an *International Monetary Fund* member has unconditional access, pays no charges and for which there is no repayment obligation, for the purposes of *balance of payments stabilisation*. The reserve tranche corresponds to the 25% of *quota* that was paid in *Special Drawing Rights* (*SDRs*) or *currencies* of other *IMF* members and counts as part of the member's foreign *reserves*. Before 1978 it was paid in *gold* and known as the '*gold tranche*'. See: *conditionality*.

**reserves** 1. In accountancy terms, reserves represent the balance of *net assets* for *shareholders* in addition to the *nominal value* of the *share capital*. It is a reflection of all the *real assets* of the *company* minus the liabilities. 2. *Profits* accruing to the owners of a business but not distributed for reasons of policy. 3. A *central bank*'s holdings of foreign *currency*, used for *foreign exchange* operations.

**residence** *UK tax* is payable by all those resident in the *UK* unless they can prove they are *non-resident* for each relevant *fiscal year*. An individual is resident in the UK if they are present in the UK for six months or more in total in a tax year. If they are not resident in the UK for any day of the tax year, the individual is non-resident. In between the two extremes there is a large grey area. An individual employed overseas for at least one complete tax year will be regarded as non-resident provided that on average they do not spend more than 90 days per tax year in the UK. The *UK* also has the concept of 'ordinary residence', which denotes a habitual residence and requires scrutiny of a person's movements and intentions over a number of years. See: *domicile*.

**resistance level** A *chart* line used in *technical analysis* to show the upper level of a rising *trend* beyond which it is not expected to move. This is caused mainly by a sufficient supply at that level (possibly a large seller at that price) to cause a drop in prices. If, however, the price line breaks through the resistance level, the consequent outlook is bullish. Compare: *support level*.

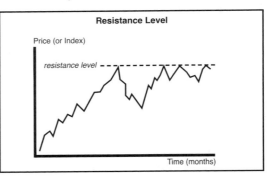

**resolution** Often referred to as a *shareholders'* 'ordinary resolution', this is a binding decision made by the majority of the voting *shareholders* of a *limited company* at a *shareholders* meeting (either an *annual general meeting* or *extraordinary general meeting*). The Companies Act prescribes this type of resolution which is required for matters such as the appointment of *auditors* or the removal of a *director*. If a resolution is called by the *shareholders* then 28 days' notice must be given followed by the *company* giving 21 days' notice to all the *shareholders*. An '*extraordinary resolution*' required, for instance, to wind up a *company* voluntarily is one for which 14 days' notice is required. The notice should state that it is an extraordinary meeting. A '*special resolution*' required to change the *company*'s constitution (*Memorandum & Articles of Association*) requires 21 days' notice to the *shareholders*. Both special and *extraordinary resolutions* require a 75% majority. The type of resolution required may be prescribed by the *Companies Acts* or by the *company*'s articles.

**respondentia** See: *hypothecation* (sense 3).

**resting order** See: *good-til-cancelled*.

**retail banking** Banking services provided by *clearing banks* to the general public.

**Retail Price Index (RPI)** The *RPI* is calculated by the *Office for National Statistics* and is widely used as the *benchmark* for *inflation*. It is an arithmetically calculated expenditure-weighted *price index*. It was started in the *UK* in 1914 but, at that time, only the basic things were priced – bread, potatoes, lamp oil and candles were covered – biscuits, cakes, fresh fruit and electricity were not. It was also called the 'cost of living *index*'. It is constructed by defining a basket of goods and services of the 'typical household', and monitoring expenditure on each item within the basket. The weights are obtained from a number of sources but mainly from the Family Expenditure Survey. Each year a sample of about 7,000 households throughout the country keep records of what they spend over a fortnight and also give details of their major purchases over a longer period. To keep the sample representative, the households with the top 4% of *incomes* and low-income pensioners, who are mainly dependent on state benefits, are excluded. The basket of goods and services is fixed for a year at a time, but it is reviewed every year. The weights for the *index* are changed each year and the *index* is *chain-linked* in order to avoid distortions due to changes in the constituents of the *index*. The *RPI* includes virtually all types of household spending, with some notable exceptions such as savings and *investment* and charges for credit. The weights are (for 2008): Food (10.5%), Catering (4.7%), Alcohol (6.8%), Tobacco (2.9%), Housing (23.8%), Fuel & Light (3.9%), Household Goods (6.6%), Household Services (6.5%), Clothes (4.4%), Personal Goods (3.9%), Motoring (13.3%), Fares (2.0%), Leisure Goods & Services (10.9%). The most recent *base date* is January 1987 with a base *value* of 100. The *index* always refers to a Tuesday near the middle of each month and is usually published on a Thursday one month after the Tuesday *index* date. In the 50 years to 2009 £1 became worth 5.8p due to the effects of *inflation*. See also: *headline inflation, implicit deflator, producer price index, RPI-X, RPI-Y, Tax and Price Index, underlying inflation, HICP.*

**retained benefits** *Pension* or death benefits from prior employment.

**retained earnings** *Net profit* of a *company* which has not been distributed to *shareholders* and is kept back by the *company*, it is part of *shareholders'* funds.

**retentions** Sometimes referred to as retained *profits*, this is the amount of a *company's* annual *profit* after all deductions including *dividends* to *shareholders*. Retentions are generally the only item from annual trading which adds to the *company's* net assets (*balance sheet*) in the form of *retained earnings*.

**retirement annuity** A *pension* policy started before 1 July 1988 providing *income* in retirement. Sometimes used to describe a *personal pension* or a *self-employed pension*. See: *deferred annuity*.

**return on capital employed (ROCE)** A *company* performance *ratio*. It is a *return on investment* (*ROI*) measure. Also called: *return on net assets, return on capital invested, return on imputed capital*. The *ratio* is expressed as:

$$\text{ROCE} = \frac{\text{profit before interest payable and tax}}{\text{capital employed (= net assets)}}$$

This *ratio* does not take into account the *tax* impact or financing method (ie whether the *capital* is debt or *equity*), as for instance the *return on equity* (*ROE*) *ratio* does.

**return on capital invested** Another term for: *return on capital employed*.

**return on equity (ROE)** A key *company* performance *ratio*. It is a *return on investment* (*ROI*) measure. It takes the *tax* impact into account and the financing method, which is *equity capital*. It is calculated as follows:

$$ROE = \frac{\text{profit after tax}}{\text{equity (= ordinary shareholders' funds)}}$$

*Tax* and, if applicable, preference *dividends* and *minority interests* are subtracted from *tax* in this calculation. See also: *return on capital employed (ROCE)*.

**return on imputed capital** Another term for: *return on capital employed*.

**return on investment (ROI)** Both the *return on capital employed* (ROCE) and the *return on equity* (ROE) *ratios* are return on investment (ROI) measures.

**return on net assets** Another term for: *return on capital employed*.

**return on shareholders' funds** Pre-tax *profit* divided by the ordinary *capital*, *reserves* and preference *stock*.

**Réunion** Dependency of *France*. Standard *currency*: euro.

**Reuters** A worldwide agency dealing in news, financial information and trading services. Founded in 1851 as a worldwide network news service for newspapers. Merged with Thomson Corporation in 2007 to form Thomson Reuters. It provides a wide range of financial information and prices.

**revalorisation** Changing or renaming a national *currency* unit when, normally due to *inflation*, the basic *currency* unit has become too small or worthless. Many South American countries experienced this, and there were cases where the paper cost more to buy and print than the *value* of the *currency* it represented. Compare: *revaluation*.

**revaluation** 1. *Pensions* can be revalued by applying *indexation*, *escalation*, *dynamisation* or by discretionary increases. 2. Corporate *assets* can be revalued due to an intrinsic increase in their *value* and/or *inflation*. The Companies Act 2006 makes it obligatory for the *directors report* to state whether the *value* of land differs materially from the *value* in the *balance sheet*. The Companies Act 2006 lays down the procedures to adopt when *fixed assets* are revalued, and the difference between the *value* of a *company*'s *assets* before and after revaluation is shown on a 'revaluation reserve account' or, in the *US*, an 'appraisal surplus account'. 3. *Currencies* may be fixed or pegged at certain *values* that do not represent their current true *value* especially where there is a recurrent *balance of payments* surplus, and under these circumstances a revaluation may occur. Compare: *devaluation*, *revalorisation*.

**revenue** *Income* from any source. Can be specific such as sales revenue, *investment* revenue, property revenue, etc.

**Revenue and Customs** See: *Her Majesties Inland Revenue and Customs (HMRC)*.

**reversal pattern** A *chart pattern* which breaks out in the opposite direction to the preceding *trend*. Compare: *continuance pattern*.

**reverse takeover** To obtain a public *listing*, a private *company* can take control of an existing *public company*, which may often be larger than itself. The *public company*'s name is then changed to that of the acquirer, who takes over the *listing*. Certain *stock exchange* regulations stipulate that the nature of the acquiror's business be compatible with that of the *target company*. The arrangement has two advantages, firstly that the *assets* of the *company* with the *listing* can sometimes be purchased at a *discount* and secondly, that the overall costs involved can be less than a new offering on the *stock exchange*.

**reverse yield gap** An occasion where the *yield* on *equities* or property would be higher than the *yield* on *long-dated gilts* or *deposits* because of the higher perceived *risk*, *volatility* or illiquidity of the former. The *Credit Crunch* has seen a prolonged return of the reverse yield gap in the UK for the first time since 1959. See: *yield gap*.

**reversion** The right to regain or obtain the ownership of land, property, *assets* or *money* at some time in the future as a result of some specific event, such as the expiry of a *lease*, the maturing of a policy or the terms of a *trust* being fulfilled. See: *foreclosure, repossession.*

**reversionary bonus** Applies to *with-profits life assurance contracts* (see: *with-profits policy*) and represents an amount added to the *value* of the policy based on a factor of the *sum assured. Bonuses* are added on a regular basis, normally annually or tri-annually, and depend on the profitability of the *life assurance company* and/or the results it has achieved from its *investments*. Once a reversionary bonus is allocated it cannot be withdrawn provided the policy runs to maturity or a death claim arises. If the policy is encashed early a reduction in the *bonuses* allocated is made, dependent on how long the policy has been in force. See: *terminal bonus.*

**revert to donor** See: *revert to settlor.*

**revert to settlor trust** A form of trust under which the *settlor* of the trust could regain the benefit of their gift, either because of the discretionary action of the trustees, or because of the happening of a contingency over which the settlor had no control, eg death of a beneficiary. These trusts have been the subject of a variety of inheritance tax anti-avoidance measures over the years and for that reason are now little used.

**revolving credit** An agreement between a *bank* and its customers, where the *bank* makes a loan for fixed periods (usually a year) and where the amount repaid over the period can be borrowed again under the terms of the agreement.

**rho** Used to determine the potential exposure to variables in a *derivatives portfolio*, and a measure of the *portfolio's* linear exposure to changes in the risk-free *interest rate*. See: *Greeks.*

**rial** Standard *currency* of the following countries: *Iran*: 1 rial = 100 *dinars*; *Oman*: 1 rial = 1,000 *baizas.*

**Riba** Islamic term. Literally, an increase or an addition. Technically, in a loan transaction, it describes the advantage obtained by the lender as a condition of the loan. In a *commodity* exchange it denotes the quantity or time of delivery.

**RIE** See: *Recognised Investment Exchange.*

**riel** Standard *currency* of *Cambodia*. 1 riel = 100 *sen.*

**rights issue** An invitation to existing *shareholders* to acquire additional *shares* in a fixed proportion to their holding. These *shares* are usually offered at a price below the current *offer price* of existing *shares* and are free of *stamp duty* and *broker commission*. Where a *company* wishes to raise additional *capital* to fund an *acquisition* or for development by issuing new *shares* it must ensure that the shareholdings of existing *members* are not diluted. The *shareholders* have statutory rights in this respect in the UK, known as *pre-emption rights*, and accordingly they must first be offered the opportunity to subscribe for sufficient of these new *shares* to maintain their percentage share in the *company*; if they decline, the *shares* can then be placed elsewhere.

**ring trading** A term associated with dealing in *futures* whereby *dealers* congregate and deal between themselves by *open outcry*. See: *London Metal Exchange, rings, call-over.*

**ring-fenced** When a particular element of a business, financial entity or even an *investment portfolio* is isolated for examination or protection it is said to be ring-fenced. Most commonly used to describe the profitable or valuable parts of otherwise unsuccessful businesses that are financially isolated from the business as a whole for special treatment or separate sale.

**rings** In the *UK* the name applies particularly to the *London Metal Exchange* (*LME*) and refers to the method of trading. The *LME* is an old market (over 100 years old) and by convention and practically, the traders sit in a circle (a 'ring') and trading is done by *open outcry* across this ring. The *LME* has a ring of seats around a copper bowl; each seat is purchased by a ring dealing member who has been properly vetted by the committee. During certain official trading hours the *dealers* take their seats and communicate by shouting and signing across the ring. Clerks circulate behind the *dealers*, confirming the deals done. At the end of each trading period a bell is rung and trading ceases. Now applied to *futures* markets where trading is done verbally.

**risk** All *investments* contain some element of risk. The following are sources of risk:

- *income* of the *investment* (*dividends* or *interest*)
- *interest rates* (affecting the price of *bonds*)
- *inflation* risk (erodes the *real* return of the *investment*)
- *default risk* (of *dividend* payments, *bond coupon* payments and principal repayment)
- *marketability* factors (ie risk of not being able to sell the *investment*)
- issue-specific factors (eg risk of *call*, reinvestment risk)
- fiscal risk (eg *tax* increases on *investments*, foreign *capital* controls locking in the *investment*)
- *exchange rates* (can devalue overseas *investment* in domestic terms)
- economic risk (overall *business cycle* phase)
- political risk (eg nationalisation of *company* in which one has invested)

*Quantitative analysis* uses historic price movements of an *investment* to establish a measure of risk using the statistical *standard deviation* ($\sigma$). Rational investors will demand a *return on investment* commensurate with the risk that they face. Diversifying the *portfolio* of *investments* held will reduce the risk. For *analysis*, total risk ($\sigma_T$) is decomposed into *systematic risk* ($\sigma_S$) and *unsystematic risk* of the *investment* ($\sigma_U$). Unsystematic risk (also called 'specific' or 'idiosyncratic' risk) is the variability in the returns of an *investment* as a result of factors specific to that *investment* only, whereas *systematic risk* (also called 'market' risk) is due to general market influences causing *volatility* in the *investment* (and all other market *investments*). *Unsystematic risk* can be eliminated through diversification but *systematic risk* cannot. The effectiveness of diversification will depend on the degree of correlation between the returns on the *investments*, as measured by the *correlation coefficient*. Thus the undiversified investor faces the full risk ($\sigma_T$) of the *investment* and will expect a return higher than the diversified investor who only faces the *systematic risk* ($\sigma_S$). The relationship between the total risk and its components, the systematic and *unsystematic risk* is:

$$\sigma_T^2 = \sigma_S^2 + \sigma_U^2$$

This shows that risks are combined by adding *variances* (square of *standard deviation*). See: *analysis, capital asset pricing model, investment appraisal*.

**risk arbitrage** *Arbitrage* involving *risk*, as in the simultaneous purchase of *stock* in a *company* being acquired and the sale of *stock* in its proposed acquirer. Also called '*takeover arbitrage*'. Traders called *arbitrageurs* attempt to *profit* from *takeovers* by cashing in on the expected rise in the price of the *target company*'s *shares* and drop in the price of the acquirer's *shares*. The *risk* is that if the *takeover* fails the traders may be left with substantial losses. Risk arbitrage differs from riskless *arbitrage*, which entails profiting from the differences in the prices of two *securities* or *commodities* trading on different exchanges by simultaneous trades undertaken without *risk* and taking advantage of anomalies.

**risk capital** See: *venture capital*.

**risk free rate/return** See: *capital asset pricing model*.

**risk management** Originally a description of *insurance* where risks were assessed and *insurance* cover provided against such *risks* (fire, theft, flood, accident, etc.) for a fee (*premium*). Risk management has been extended over the years to cover finance and corporate issues, again primarily through *insurance*; *credit insurance* is a factor and debt *insurance* caused the downfall of AIG in 2008, and also spawned the *Credit Default Swap* market. Enterprise Risk Management is now an acknowledged corporate *management* tool that includes the assessment of all *business risks* and their amelioration through marketing, *acquisition* and strategic *management* as well as *insurance*.

**risk premium** The difference between the expected *rate of return* on an *investment* and the risk-free return (on *deposit* account or *gilt* held to redemption) over the same period. See: *risk*.

**risk profile** An assessment of the degree to which an investor is prepared to accept losses as the price for potential gain. See: *risk*.

**risk/reward ratio** Generally means the amount which one stands to lose in an *investment*, which is closely correlated with the amount one stands to gain. See: *risk*.

**RIY** See: *reduction in yield*.

**riyal** The standard *currency* of the following countries: *Qatar*: 1 riyal = 100 *dirhams*; *Saudi Arabia*: 1 riyal = 100 *halala*; *Yemen*: 1 riyal = 100 *fils*.

**ROCE** See: *return on capital employed*.

**ROCI** *Return on capital invested*. See: *return on capital employed*.

**ROE** See: *return on equity*.

**ROI** See: *return on investment*.

**ROIC** *Return on invested capital*. See: *return on capital employed*.

**ROL** *currency code* for: Romanian Leu.

**roll over credit** A medium or *long term bank loan* where the rate of *interest* varies with short-term *money market* rates (such as *LIBOR*) because the *bank* has itself had to borrow the *money* on the primary or secondary *money market* and is lending it on at a *premium* to what it has to pay.

**roll over relief** A capital gains tax relief available when certain classes of business assets are replaced by fresh assets. The capital gain on the disposal of the old asset is deducted from the cost of the new asset for tax purposes and no tax is levied at the time of the transaction.

**roll up funds** A fund, normally offshore, where the *income* is rolled up with the *value* of the *investment*, ie where the *profits* are not distributed. This can occasionally be used where investors find it useful to defer their *tax* liability, but the *profits* are all charged to *income tax* in the end event. See: *distributor funds*.

**rolling settlement** The system now most commonly employed on *stock exchanges* of settling a transaction a fixed number of days after the deal is struck. The *London Stock Exchange* currently operates the *T+3* system, ie a three-day rolling settlement, which means that the investor must pay for the *shares* bought or deliver the *shares* sold three days after the transaction was made. See also: *account, CREST*.

**Romania** The Romanian Stock Exchange was established in 1992 in Bucharest. Standard *currency*: *leu*. 1 *leu* = 100 *bani*.

**rouble** Standard *currency* of *Russia* and *Tajikistan*. 1 rouble = 100 copecks.

**rounding charge** An adjustment to *unit trust* prices to avoid inconvenient fractions of a *penny*.

**Royal Mint** The *UK* organisation controlled by the Chancellor of the Exchequer that has had an exclusive Royal Charter to manufacture British coins since the 16th century. Originally situated in the City of London it was moved to Llantrisant in Wales in 1968. It also prints banknotes and mints *UK* medals, memorial coins and coins for overseas countries.

**royalty** *Income* paid under licence for the use of someone else's property. Most common are licences for *intellectual property*, such as music or novels, but can include the license of a commercial product covered by *patent* or a branded product.

**RPB** See: *Recognised Professional Body*.

**RPI** See: *Retail Price Index*.

**RPI-X** The *Retail Price Index* (*RPI*) calculated using all items excluding *mortgage interest* payments. RPI-X was used to set the Bank of England's inflation target (at 2.5%+- 0.5%) until it was replaced by the Consumer Price Index in 2003. See: *underlying inflation*.

**RPI-Y** The *Retail Price Index* (*RPI*) calculated using all items excluding *mortgage interest* payments and indirect taxes (defined as including: Council T*ax*, *VAT*, duties, car purchase *tax* and vehicle excise duty, *insurance tax* and airport *tax*).

**RSE** See: *Recognised Stock Exchange*.

**rufiyaa** Standard *currency* of the *Maldives*. 1 rufiyaa = 100 *laari*.

**rule of 20** The rule of 20 is a useful tool in measuring whether a market is over- or *undervalued*. The *price earnings ratio*, minus the annual rate of *inflation*, plus the annual percentage change in *productivity*, will provide a figure that can be compared to 20. If the figure obtained is above 20, then the market is *overvalued*. Conversely, if the figure is less than 20, the market is *undervalued*.

**rule of 72** Formula for approximating the time it will take for a given amount of *money* to double at a given *compound interest rate*. The formula is simply 72 divided by the *interest rate* in per cent. In six years £100 will double at a *compound* annual rate of 12%, thus: 72 divided by 12 equals 6. Sometimes also reduced to the rule of 70.

**run** When everyone wants to sell or divest. With *banks* people want their money out and will form queues outside to get it, with *currencies* everybody is *bearish* and dramatic falls can follow. Generally a run is symptomatic of panic.

**running yield** See under: *yield*.

**rupee** Standard *currency* of: *India*, *Nepal*: 1 rupee = 100 *paisa*; *Pakistan*: 1 rupee = 100 pice; *Mauritius*, *Seychelles*, *Sri Lanka*: 1 rupee = 100 *cents*.

**rupiah** Standard *currency* of *Indonesia*. 1 rupiah = 100 *sen*.

**RUR** *currency code* for: Russian Ruble.

**Russell Indices** Frank Russell Company (*USA*) publishes the following *market capitalisation* weighted *indices* (among others):

- Russell 3,000 Index – comprises the 3,000 largest *US share companies* in terms of *market capitalisation*.

- Russell 1,000 Index – is highly correlated to the *S&P 500* Index, consisting of the 1,000 largest *company shares*.

- Russell 2,000 Index – consists of the remaining 2,000 *shares*, ie the 1,001st to the 3,000th largest *US share companies*; its *capitalisation* is about 11% of that of the Russell 3,000 Index; it is a popular measure of the *share* prices of smaller *companies*.

- Russell Top 200 Index – called the '*blue chip*' *index*; the 200 largest *US share companies*.

- Russell 1,000 Value Index – contains those *companies* in the Russell 1,000 Index with a smaller than *average growth* rate; *companies* generally have a lower *P/E ratio* and a higher *dividend yield* and lower forecast *growth rates*.

- Russell 1,000 Growth Index – consists of those *companies* in the Russell 1,000 Index with a greater than *average growth* rate; *companies* generally have a higher *P/E ratio* and greater forecast *growth rates*.

**Russian Stock Exchange**  The Russian Trading System (RTS) was established in 1995 as the first regulated stock market in Russia. It now trades the full range of financial instruments from cash equities to commodity futures. The RTS Classic Market is the sole trading platform in Russia that permits settlement in roubles and foreign currency.

The main index is:

- RTS Index. Comprises of the Exchange's 50 most liquid and highly capitalised shares. Base: 1 September 1995 = 100.

Standard currency: rouble: 1 rouble = 100 copecks.

**Rwanda**  Standard *currency*: *franc*. 1 *franc* = 100 *centimes*.

**RWF**  *currency code* for: *Rwanda* Franc.

# S

**S2P** See: *State second pension.*

**S&P 500** See: *Standard & Poor's 500 Index.*

**SA** 1. Short for: société anonyme. The equivalent of a *public limited company* (*plc*) in French. 2. Short for: sociedad anónima. A Spanish *plc*. 3. Short for: sociedade anónima. A Portuguese *plc*. Compare: *Sarl.*

**safety net** Providing a *buy-back* price lower than the current market price. One of the best examples is the *Bank of England*'s offer to *repurchase partly paid* BT *shares* after the unsuccessful *flotation* in 1987.

**saitori** Intermediaries between *brokers* on the Tokyo Stock Exchange who cannot deal directly with non-members of the exchange.

**salary sacrifice** Where an employee agrees to forgo a proportion of salary for an equivalent contribution to a *pension* scheme run by their employer for his or her benefit.

**sale and leaseback** See: *leaseback.*

**saleage** In the production of certain *commodities* there is waste. Saleage is that proportion which is of merchantable *quality* as opposed to useless waste.

**Sallie Mae** Colloquialism for the *US Student Loan Marketing Association.*

**Samoa** Standard *currency*: tala.

**samurai bond** *Loan stock* issued by foreigners and the *World Bank* in Tokyo. Denominated in *yen* and not subject to *withholding tax.* Compare: *shogun bond.*

**San Marino** Standard *currency*: euro.

**sandbag** A stalling tactic whereby a *target company* agrees to talk, but draws out negotiations in the hope that a *white knight* will come riding to the rescue.

**sanmekai** A committee of Japanese city *banks* that determines short-term *interest rates.*

**sans frais** The French expression used to describe the position where the issuer of a financial *instrument* is not responsible for the costs of obtaining payment.

**São Tomé e Príncipe** Standard *currency*: dobra. 1 *dobra* = 100 *centavos.*

**SAR** *currency code* for: Saudi Riyal.

**Sarl** 1. Short for: société à responsabilité limitée. French equivalent of a *private limited company* (*Ltd*). Compare: *SA.*2. Short for: società a responsabilità limitata. An Italian *private limited company.* Compare: *SpA.*

**SARs** See: *Substantial Acquisition Rules.*

**satang** Currency sub-unit of *Thailand.* 100 satang = 1 *baht.*

**Saturday Night Special** A sudden attempt by a *company* to take over a *target* by making a public *tender offer.* The term was coined in the *US* in the 1960s when a large number of such *takeover bids* were undertaken, usually announced over weekends. This type of *takeover* is now regulated by the *UK* by the *City Code on Takeovers and Mergers* and the *Competition Commission* and the *Williams Act* 1968 in the *US.*

**saucer** *Chart pattern.* Name depicts the shape of the *pattern.* It is taken to indicate that the bottom has been reached and that the movement is consequently upwards. An 'inverse saucer' is the opposite. See: *technical analysis.*

**Saudi Arabia** Standard *currency*: Saudi *riyal*. 1 *riyal* = 20 qursh = 100 halala.

**save-as-you-earn (SAYE)** Savings in *building societies* and banks linked employees purchasing *shares* in the *companies* they work for, if undertaken regularly, may qualify for certain *tax* privileges. Maximum investment £250 a month.

**saving rate** See: *savings ratio*.

**Savings and Loan Companies** The American equivalent of *UK building societies*. They have greater flexibility in the choice of underlying *investments* and more commonly lend at fixed rates of *interest*, often known as 'thrifts'.

**savings certificate** See under: *National Savings and Investments*.

**savings ratio** 1. An individual's personal savings divided by his or her personal *disposable income*. 2. An important macroeconomic variable represented by the *ratio* of aggregate saving over total *disposable income* in an economy over a certain time period, usually one year. Saving plus consumption equals *disposable income*. *Disposable income* is total *gross income* less any *direct taxation* and other obligatory direct payments to government authorities. Saving represents deferred expenditure, whereas consumption is present expenditure. Consumption is often regarded as beneficial to the economy, since it represents, in simple macro-analyses, an *'injection'* into the economy, whereas saving is seen as a 'leakage' from the economy. In the long run, since savings finance *investment*, they are ultimately beneficial to the economy. See: *circular flow of national income*.

**SAYE** See: *save-as-you-earn*.

**SBD** *currency code* for: *Solomon Islands* Dollar.

**SBLI** See: *Stock Borrowing and Lending Intermediary*.

**scalpers** Market operators actively trading in relatively small transactions to make a quick *profit*.

**SCARP** See: *structured capital-at-risk product*.

**scheme of arrangement** A formal *arrangement* by a *debtor* to avoid being made *bankrupt* or discharged from bankruptcy under which a plan is drawn up to settle the debt or part of the debt to the *creditors'* satisfaction and that of the bankruptcy court. See also: *individual voluntary arrangement*.

**Schilling** Formerly the standard *currency* of *Austria*, until the introduction of the *euro* on 1 January 2002. 1 Schilling = 100 *Groschen*.

**SCON** Short for: scheme contracted-out number. See: *contracting out*.

**scorched earth defence** The practice of spoiling a *company*'s *balance sheet* or profitability by a reversible process such as borrowing *money* on exorbitant terms in order to make it unpalatable to an unwelcome *bidder* or extreme defence tactics that threaten to leave the *target* depleted and therefore unattractive. An example would be selling off the '*crown jewels'*, ie the most valuable *assets* of the *company*. See also: *poison pill*.

**SCR** *currency code* for: *Seychelles* Rupee.

**scrip** See: *scrip issue*.

**scrip dividend** A *dividend* that is automatically paid as an issue of new *shares* instead of *cash*. The *company* benefits, as it receives the *dividend* back as *capital*, but the investor still has to pay *tax* on the *income*. This makes some sense for investors who do not require the *income* but makes their *capital gains tax* computations complicated. Scrip dividends were beneficial for corporate cash flow when advance corporation tax existed. Now most companies offer a dividend reinvestment plan (DRIP) instead.

**scrip issue** Also called: *bonus issue, free issue*. Sometimes the original *capital subscribed* to a *company* bears little relationship to the *capital employed* in an expanding *company*, due to a large increase in *reserves*. A scrip issue is an issue of free *shares* to the existing *shareholders* of a *company* by capitalising the *company's reserves*. Normally the reserve accounts affected are the *share premium account* and the *profit & loss account*, which are sub-accounts in the *company's capital* and reserve account. The free *shares* are issued in proportion to existing issues, eg a '2 for 3 scrip issue' means that 2 free *shares* are issued for every 3 *shares* in the holding of each *shareholder*. Subsequently, the market price of the *shares* adjusts to the point at which the total *value* of the shareholdings is the same as it was immediately prior to the scrip issue, so that each *shareholder's* holdings retain the same total *value*. The number of issued *shares* increases by two-thirds but the *par value* of each *share* remains the same. For example, a *company's issued capital* is £3 million (3 million *shares at par* of £1 each) and the *market value* per *share* is 240p (which gives a *market capitalisation* of £7.2 million). If the *company* then decides to carry out a scrip issue of 2 for 3, the *company's issued capital* increases to £5 million (5 million *shares at par* £1), the additional £2 million coming from the *capitalisation* of the *share premium* and *profit & loss account*. As a result of the increased shareholdings, the market price of each *share* should drop to 144p (ensuring that the post-scrip issue *market capitalisation* remains the same at £7.2 million). The reasons for the scrip issue are mainly 'cosmetic' and to tidy up the reserve account. Compare: *capitalisation issue*. See also: *share split*.

**SDD** *currency code* for: Sudanese Dinar.

**SDR** See: *Special Drawing Rights*.

**seal** Historically a small pool of soft wax impressed with the sealer's mark to validate a document. Today the document is simply impressed with the mark. The most common use of *company seals* today is to certify legal documents although most *companies* now have a clause in their *Memorandum & Articles of Association* that confirms their ability to execute documents without using a *company seal*.

**SEAQ** SEAQ is the London Stock Exchange's trading service for the Fixed Interest market and AIM securities that are not traded on either SETS or SETSqx. As at January 2009 SEAQ covered approximately 1,300 securities, nearly all of which were AIM shares.

**seasonality** Fluctuations in commercial, economic or market activity that result from seasonal fluctuations, such as car sales in August, toys and greetings cards at Christmas, travel in summer and increased consumption of electricity in winter.

**SEC** See: *Securities and Exchange Commission*.

**Second state pension (S2P)** See: *state second pension*.

**secondary bank** A smaller *bank*, often a *finance house* specialising in certain areas of finance but not providing clearing facilities.

**secondary market** A market where previously issued *securities* are traded, as distinct from the *primary market*, where *securities* are originally issued (ie sold for the first time). The proceeds from the secondary market go to *dealers* and investors, as opposed to issuing *companies* in the *primary market*. The secondary market's main functions are to provide liquidity for the *primary market* and to allow participants to diversify their *investments* and spread their *risk*.

**Section 13(d)** Relevant to *takeovers*, the section of the *US* Securities Exchange Act of 1934 as amended by the *Williams Act* 1968, which requires that notice of beneficial ownership be filed within 10 days with the *Securities and Exchange Commission*, the *target company* and with each exchange on which the *target's stock* is *listed*. Notification of beneficial ownership needs to be filed when 5% or more of the *stock* is held by one party. The disclosure form includes source of funds and plans as to control.

**Section 13(d) window**  In *America* this is the 10 days between the *acquisition* of 5% or more of a firm's *stock* and the required public disclosure (see: *Section 13(d)*). During this period the acquiror may continue to buy the *target* firm's *stock*, and thus may own considerably more than 5% when disclosure is finally made. See also: *creeping takeover*.

**Section 21 orders**  The predecessor to section 148 orders, originally found in the Social Securities Pensions Act 1975.

**Section 32**  This is a *contract* into which *paid-up pension* rights and entitlements from previous employment can be transferred. The benefits are not available until retirement, though the arrangement can be used to improve existing benefits by transferring them to a *life assurance company* offering more beneficial rates. The relevant legislation has long since been superseded, but the term section 32 has stuck as a description. See also: *buyout policy*.

**Section 148 orders**  Instructions issued annually in accordance with Section 148 of the Social Security Administration Act 1992 specifying the rate of increase to be applied to the *earnings* factors on which the *additional component* and *guaranteed minimum pensions* are based and relates to the increase in *average* national *earnings*.

**Section 212**  Under Section 212 of the Companies Act 1985 (now replaced by section 793 Companies Act 2006), a *public company* has the right to: ask existing *shareholders* to reveal the beneficial ownership of *shares* held in their names (see: *nominee*) or ask any particular individual whether he or she has been an owner of its *shares* in the last three years. Generally, it is the duty of the *company secretary* to deal with Section 212 investigations.

**sector**  A term used to differentiate *investments* from each other by way of country, market or prime source of business.

**secular**  Refers to long-term time frames (approximately 10 years and over) in business and economic *trends*, as distinct from seasonal (see: *seasonality*) and cyclical (see: *business cycles*) time frames.

**secured creditor**  Someone who is owed *money* but is covered by *security* or *collateral*. See: *debenture, liquidation*.

**secured debt**  Debt that is guaranteed by *assets* or *collateral* pledged by the *debtor*. It may be in the form of a *fixed charge* or a *floating charge* on the *assets* of the *debtor*.

**secured loan**  See: *secured debt*.

**Securities and Exchange Commission (SEC)**  The *US* government agency set up in 1934 following the *stock exchange crash* in the late 1920s. Effectively a statutory body closely governing the activities of the *securities* industry in *America*. Its function is to promote public disclosure and protect investors against investment-related malpractice. It also oversees *takeovers*. It regulates virtually all aspects of the *investment* industry in the US; for instance, all organised *securities, futures* and *options* markets and *over-the-counter brokers* and *dealers, investment companies* and *investment* advisors fall under the auspices of the *SEC*. It issues a number of guidelines, including the 'Securities and Exchange Commission Rules' for the *investment* industry, and has virtually unlimited powers of enforcement.

**Securities and Futures Authority (SFA)**  Formed following the *merger* in April 1991 between the *AFBD* (*Association of Futures Brokers and Dealers*) and the *TSA* (*The Securities Association*). It was the *Self-Regulating Organisation* (*SRO*) which enforced the provisions of the *Financial Services Act 1986* (which became effective in April 1988). The *SFA* regulated firms involved in the *securities* and *futures* sectors of the financial services industry. The regulated sector thus included *shares, bonds, traded options, corporate finance, financial futures* and *commodities futures*. The *SFA* ceased to exist after the implementation of the *Financial Services and Markets Act 2000*.

**Securities and Investments Board (SIB)** The *SIB* was the designated agency to monitor the prescriptions of the *Financial Services Act 1986* (effective on *'A' day* in 1988). Following the *Financial Services and Markets Act 2000*, the *SIB* and other financial services regulators, such as the *PIA*, were combined to form the *Financial Services Authority* (*FSA*). The *FSA* then assumed the role and responsibility of all financial service regulators, including the *SIB*.

**Securities Industry Automation Corporation (SIAC)** The American organisation established in 1972 to provide communications and computer systems for the *New York Stock Exchange (NYSE)* and the *American Stock Exchange (AMEX)* which owned two-thirds and one-third respectively. In 2006 the NYSE bought AMEX's stake.

**securitisation** A procedure allowing debt, loans, *goodwill, debentures* and other borrowings and interests in a business or project to be converted to *equity* represented by *shares* in the business or project. See: *rescheduling, sliced and diced, CMO*.

**securitised mortgage** See: *CMO, CDO*.

**security** 1. As originally defined by the Prevention of Fraud Investments Act 1958, *securities* include *shares, debentures, government securities*, rights to *money* lent or disposed with an industrial and provident society or *building society*, but not any type of *insurance* policy. Includes *unit trusts* and *collective investment schemes*. 2. An assurance given or guaranteed by the borrower as a safeguard for a loan. See: *collateral*.

**security market line** See under: *capital asset pricing model*.

**seed capital** Initial *capital* to fund the development and research necessary to determine the potential and effectiveness of a project *company* prior to its establishment.

**SEK** *currency code* for: Swedish Krona.

**self-administered pension** A *pension* arrangement where the contributing *company* controls the management and *distribution* of the *pension* fund itself without subcontracting to an *insurance company* or other institution. A *small self-administered pension scheme* can be set up for as few as just one *member*. These can be particularly useful where the *company* itself wishes to retain some access to the *pension* fund monies, eg via loan back. The *directors* of the contributing *company,* and indeed the *members* themselves, can act as *trustees* to the *pension* fund. See also: *pension, small self-administered pension scheme*.

**self-employed pension** Earlier self-employed *pension contracts* have been replaced by the more flexible *personal pension* plan where contributions are generally eligible for the highest rate(s) of *tax* relief. See also: *personal pension, Section 226*.

**Self-Employment Individuals Retirement Act** See: *Keogh plan*.

**self-invested personal pension (SIPP)** A *personal pension* plan where the *beneficiary* controls the *investment* of the *underlying assets*. The structure is widely used for plans which invest only in unit trusts and OEICs.

**self-investment** The *investment* of a *pension* scheme's *assets* in the business or *shares* of the employer including loans made to the employer or associated *companies*. The rules for this are governed by the Finance Act 2004.

**Self-Regulating Organisation (SRO)** Following the statutory regulation of the *UK investment* industry with the *Financial Services Act 1986*, the *Securities and Investments Board* (*SIB*) created two groups of organisations, the *Self-Regulating Organisations* (*SROs*) and the *Recognised Professional Bodies* (*RPBs*) to deal with the day-to-day practicalities of *authorisation* and running the regulatory structure. These *SROs* were:

- *SFA* (see: *Securities and Futures Authority*).
- *IMRO* (see: *Investment Management Regulatory Organisation*).

- *PIA* (see: *Personal Investment Authority*) which took over from *LAUTRO* (*Life Assurance and Unit Trust Regulatory Organisation*) and *FIMBRA* (*Financial Intermediaries Managers and Brokers Regulatory Association*).

The structure was replaced by the Financial Services and Markets Act 2000.

**self-tender** *Companies* are entitled to buy their own *shares* and will do so when they wish to concentrate *earnings per share* or when they feel their *stock* is under-represented in the market.

**selling short** See: *short* (sense 1).

**semilogarithmic scale** The vertical axis of a *chart* has a semilogarithmic (semilog) scale if equal distances represent equal percentage changes. This differs from a linear scale, where equal distances along the axis represent equal absolute changes. For example, take a semilog scale on which the price increases by, say, 100% (ie it doubles) every centimetre up the scale. So if it starts at 10, the next interval would show 20, the next equal interval 40, then 80 etc. The equivalent linear scale would show 10, then 20, 30, 40 etc.

**sen** 1. *Currency* sub-unit of *Cambodia*: 100 sen = 1 *riel*; *Malaysia*: 100 sen = 1 ringgit. 2. Formerly a *currency* sub-unit (one-hundredth of a *yen*) in *Japan*. It is, however, still used as a *unit of account*.

**sene** *Currency* sub-unit of *Western Samoa*. 100 sene = 1 *tala*.

**senior capital** Normally an *investment* characterised as *equity, loan stoc*k or debt that ranks above other similar *capital* or debt and has priority treatment on repayment.

**Senegal** Standard *currency*: African *franc*.

**senior debt** In the event of *liquidation* of a *company*, senior debts are those loans or *debt instruments* that have a claim to the *company*'s *assets* before junior or other subordinated debts and *shareholders* are paid. Senior debt usually includes funds borrowed from *banks, insurance companies* or other financial institutions, *debentures* and other fixed and *floating charges*.

**seniti** *Currency* sub-unit of *Tonga*. 100 seniti = 1 *pa'anga*.

**sensitivity** The degree to which the price of *fixed interest securities* is affected by a change in *interest rates* (as measured by *gross yield, redemption yield*) and is dependent on the term to maturity and *coupon* of the *security*.

**separate taxation** Since 6 April 1990 *investments* held by either spouse have been taxed separately (prior to this date a woman's *investments* were taxed as though they belonged to her husband). The *tax* regime generally treats both husband and wife equally as separate individuals. *Capital gains* on *joint investments* are divided 50/50 as is the *income* for *tax* purposes unless a declaration of ownership to the contrary is supplied to HMRC.

**sequestration** Appropriation of a property or *assets* by a third party in the case of bankruptcy (see: *bankrupt*) or disputes regarding ownership.

**Serbia** Standard *currency*: dinar. 1 *dinar* = 100 *paras*.

**Serious Fraud Office (SFO)** Established by the Attorney General in the *UK* in 1987 as a specialist unit to prosecute larger, more serious and complex frauds. Due to the increasingly sophisticated nature of modern fraud it was considered appropriate to consolidate the resources available within a statutory body separate from the police force that could focus exclusively on serious fraud. Prosecutions have nevertheless been hard to sustain.

**SETS** See: *Stock Exchange's Electronic Trading Service*.

**SETSqx** See: *Stock Exchange's Electronic Trading Service – quotes and crosses*.

**settlement date** Before the introduction of *rolling settlement* on the *London Stock Exchange*, settlement date was the date on which a *contract* had to be settled (paid). See also: *account*.

**settlor** A term much used with regard to *inheritance tax* which refers to the *donor* or the person in a transaction whose *estate* is made less by a *transfer of value*.

**Seychelles** Standard *currency*: the Seychelles *rupee*. 1 *rupee* = 100 *cents*.

**SFE** See: *Sydney Futures Exchange*.

**SFLGS** Small firms loan guarantee scheme; a variant of the *loan guarantee scheme* offered by the UK government via high street *banks* where a loan is partly underwritten by the *Treasury*. Such loans are designed to stimulate small business and help when *banks* might otherwise be reluctant to lend. Generally hidebound by narrow criteria and conflicting requirements of *bank* managers and head office control. Also normally an additional *interest rate* is levied over and above the *banks*' usual interest charge.

**SFO** See: *Serious Fraud Office*.

**SGD** *currency code* for: *Singapore* Dollar.

**shadow director** Somebody who controls a *company* and the other *directors* but is not a *director*.

**shake-out** A change in *investment* market conditions normally resulting in losses in more marginal and more highly-rated *shares*.

**Shanghai Stock Exchange** The main *stock market* in *China*. See: *China*.

**share** The ownership of a *limited company* is divided amongst its *shareholders*, who are people who have subscribed a sum of *money* to the *company*'s *capital* in return for a proportion of the *profits* (in the form of *dividends*). Shares in *public companies* are freely transferable on a *stock exchange*. Shares on the UK *stock market* come in three categories: *FTSE* 100, liquid and less liquid, as classified by *Normal Market Size*. See: *share capital*. See also: '*A*' *shares*, *equities*, *ordinary shares*, *preference shares*, *redeemable preference shares*.

**share capital** The share capital of a *company* represents ownership, as distinct from debt. Share capital is also called *equity*. Debt plus *equity* represents the total *capital employed* in a *company*. The *Memorandum of Association* of the *company* specifies the maximum amount of share capital it is authorised to raise, called the '*authorised capital*' (or 'nominal *capital*', 'registered *capital*'). The *company* can decide to issue any amount up to that maximum, called the 'issued share capital'. The issued share capital has to be completely accounted for (subscribed): for example, if in a *flotation* the issued share capital is not fully subscribed, the underwriter/sponsor must pay for the unsubscribed portion. The issued share capital may be paid in separate 'instalments' termed *calls* – until the last *call*, the share capital is only *partly paid* (P.P.) and called '*partly paid* share capital' (or 'called-up share capital'). The investor who subscribes to *shares* issued in this way is legally obliged to pay for subsequent *calls*; the investor can also sell the *partly paid shares* on the market to avoid this obligation. After the last *call*, the issued *share capital* is *fully paid* (F.P.) and is called '*fully paid* share capital'.

**share certificate** Certificate issued by the *registrar* that documents ownership of *shares* in a *company*. It includes the *class* of *shares* (eg ordinary or preference or '*A*' ordinary), number of *shares* and serial numbers of *shares* held by the investor. It may have the *company seal* stamped on it. It cannot be sold on to anyone else unless accompanied by a *transfer deed*, ie it is not negotiable. Most transactions are now dematerialised (paperless). This is accomplished electronically by the *CREST* system in the *UK*, though some private investors still choose the option of a paper *certificate*. When parties to a transaction execute a deal each electronically confirms the transaction by file transfer. Both parties are required to submit confirmation details to *CREST* to register and verify the transaction. Compare: *bearer security*. See: *nominal value, Talisman, CREST*.

**share exchange** Where *shares* are exchanged for another form of *investment*, certain *companies* offering collective *investments* will give preferential terms to people who exchange their *shares* for a *unit trust, OEIC* or *investment bond*. Terms will vary from product *company* to product *company*, but the event is still chargeable for *capital gains tax* purposes.

**share option** 1. See under: *option*. 2. The privilege sometimes offered to encourage *company* executives or employees to purchase *shares* in the *company*. Incentives can include *tax* savings or the *shares* can be issued at a *discount* to market price or at a preferential fixed price. See: *employee share ownership plan, employee share ownership trust*.

**share premium** The amount above *par value* that a *company* issues *shares* at. If, for instance, the *par value* per *share* is 25p and the *company* issues them on the market at 33p, the share premium per *share* is 8p. The *value* of the share premium times the number of *shares* issued is the total share premium of the issue and is recorded in the *company*'s *share premium account*.

**share premium account** Sub-account of the *capital* and reserve account in a *company*'s *balance sheet*. It represents the amount above nominal *share value* received (see: *share premium*) following an issue. It cannot be used to pay *dividends* to *shareholders*, but is used in capitalising *reserves* in a *scrip issue*.

**share register** A list kept by the *registrar* or *company secretary* of all the *shareholders* in any one *limited company*. For publicly *quoted companies* such lists are public information and can be obtained on request at nominal cost.

**share split** Where the *share* price of a *company*'s *shares* has become large, due to the *growth* of its *value*, it is often considered appropriate to issue additional *shares* for a lower *value* so that they become a more palatable size. Take, for example, a *company* that has 4 million *shares* in issue (*par value* £1; thus the nominal *share capital* is £4 million) at a market price of 2,000p each. The *market capitalisation* is thus £80 million. The *company*'s *directors* may consider that the *share* price is too high for 'cosmetic' reasons (investors seem to dislike *heavy shares*) and wish to lower it to make them more marketable. Thus a *share split* is undertaken and each existing *share* is *split* into ten. The result is that there are now 40 million *shares* of *par value* 10p in issue (the nominal *share capital* remains at £4 million) and since there is no 'real' difference in the *value* of the *shares*, the market price will be adjusted to 200p per *share* (as reflected by the fact that the *market capitalisation* stays the same at £80 million). Share splitting is similar to a *scrip issue*, the difference lying in the fact that in a share split the *par value* of the *shares* changes and the reserve account is not capitalised. Compare: *capitalisation issue*. Called a *stock split* in the *USA*.

**share transfer** On the *London Stock Exchange*, a *stock transfer form* must normally be completed by the seller of a registered *security* instructing the *company* to remove his or her name from the register and substitute the name of the buyer. See: *CREST, share certificate*.

**Shared currency option under tender (Scout)** This is a *currency option* designed for instances where several *companies* are tendering for the same *contracts* in a foreign *currency*. To save them each having to *hedge* themselves against unfavourable *currency* movements the scout enables them to *share* the cost of a single transaction.

**shareholders** Sometimes known as *members*, they are all those who own *equity* in a *company*.

**shareholders equity** Another term for: *shareholders'* funds.

**shareholders funds** The *called-up capital* plus the *reserves* of a *company*. Constitutes a *company*'s *equity capital*.

**shark repellent** Provisions in *corporate by-laws* or a *company*'s *Memorandum & Articles of Association* designed to prevent *hostile takeover bids*. See also: *porcupine provisions*.

**shark watchers** Consultants who observe *trading patterns* to help corporations identify buyers of their *stock*, in order to provide early warning of *stock* accumulators and potential *raiders*.

**Sharpe measure** See: *performance appraisal*.

**Sharpe Ratio** In 1966 W F Sharpe introduced a measure for the performance of *mutual funds* (collective investments) which has been variously modified and interpreted since. It is effectively a measure of *risk*/reward or the market price of *risk*. Also known as *Sharpe measure* – see also: *Treynor measure*.

A broad definition of the Sharpe Ratio (S) is:

$$S(I) = ( RI - RF ) / StdDev(I)$$

where:

I is the *investment*,

RI is its average annual *rate of return*,

RF is the *rate of return* of a risk-free *investment* (ie *cash*), and

StdDev(I) is the *standard deviation* of RI.

**shell company** A *company* not actively engaged in business, or a non-trading *company* with or without a public *quotation* used either as a vehicle for corporate transactions or kept as a dormant *company* for future use.

**sheqel** Standard *currency* of *Israel*. 1 sheqel = 100 *agorot*.

**shibosai bond** A *samurai bond* issued to investors by means of a *private placing*.

**shilling** Standard *currency* of *Kenya*, *Somalia*, *Tanzania* and *Uganda*. 1 shilling = 100 *cents*. See: *decimalisation*.

**shogun bond** A non-*yen* denominated *bond* issued on the Japanese market by a foreign institution. Compare: *samurai bond*.

**short** 1. To deal or sell short is to sell a *security* which one does not hold in the hope of buying it back at a lower price to make a *profit*. 2. To be short is to expect prices to fall or to be a *bear*.

**short covering** When a *bear* sells *stock* to make a *profit* in a falling market by buying it back at a later date (hopefully at a lower price; see: *short*); the trader will need ultimately to *cover* his or her position by making this purchase. Prices can be inflated by a number of *bears covering* their *short positions*. Such a rise in the market is best not confused with a genuine *rally*. See: *bear trap, dead cat bounce, spike*.

**short position** A trader in *securities* is said to have established a short position when the sales made by the trader exceed holdings, ie the trader is selling *securities* that he or she does not possess. This is done in anticipation that the market will fall so that those *securities* sold *short* can be covered (ie bought) at a lower price, thus creating *profit* for the trader. Compare: *long position*.

**short selling** Sales made by a trader who thus establishes a *short position*. See: *short covering*.

**short term** Generally speaking, a time period that is less than the medium and *long term*. How long exactly depends on the context. 1. In accounting, the short term is equated with the term 'current', usually meaning to be within the normal operating cycle of a business, which in turn is normally taken to mean one year. 2. In *investments*, short term usually means in one or two years. 3. For the purposes of taxation, short-term holdings are those for less than one year.

**short ton** A measurement of weight in *America* equal to 2,000 lbs (= 907.19 kg), as opposed to a *metric tonne* of 2,204.6 lbs (= 1,000 kg exactly) and a *long ton* being 2,240 lbs (= 1,016.05 kg). The 'lbs' referred to here are avoirdupois pounds (1 avoirdupois pound = 16 ounces) as distinct from troy pounds (1 troy pound = 12 ounces).

**short-dated security** *Fixed interest securities* including *gilts* that are repayable in less than seven years (according to the *Bank of England*) and five years (according to the *FT*).

**short-form report** A report included in a *prospectus* and prepared by the *reporting accountants*, which deals with the trading record of the *company*, the *source and application of funds* and the latest *balance sheets*.

**shorts** 1. *Securities* sold *short* by a trader, ie *securities* sold by a trader that are not in his or her possession at the time of the trade. See: *short position*. 2. A short-dated *gilt* repayable in less than seven years by *Bank of England* definition, five years according to the Financial Times.

**show stopper** A lawsuit by a *target company* that seeks a permanent *injunction* against a *hostile takeover bid*, based on a legal defect in the acquiror's (*raider's*) offer.

**SHP** *currency code* for: *St Helena* Pound.

**SIAC** See: *Securities Industry Automation Corporation*.

**SIB** See: *Securities and Investments Board*.

**SICAV** Short for the French: Societies d'Investissement a Capital Variable. A French *UCIT*.

**side pocket** When a *hedge fund* separates *liquid investments* from *illiquid investments*, the illiquid investments may be held in a side pocket. Once the *investments* are in a side pocket new *investors* will not gain exposure to these investments and existing investors who redeem their holdings will not get paid the *value* of the *investments* in the side pocket until they are finally liquidated.

**side letters** Side letters are agreements between a fund and selected investors that give them terms which are not available to all investors, such as preferential redemption terms. These are found in some *hedge funds*; ideally they should be disclosed to all investors.

**Sierra Leone** Standard *currency*: *leone*. 1 *leone* = 100 *cents*.

**silver wheelchairs** See: *golden parachutes*.

**SIMEX** See: *Singapore International Monetary Exchange*. See under: *Singapore*.

**simple interest** See under: *interest*.

**simplified regime** The current tax regime for UK pensions, introduced on 6 April 2006 (*A-Day*) by legislation in the Finance Act 2004, is known as the simplified regime. The new regime was applied to all existing pension arrangements, unlike earlier attempts at reform which left old regimes largely untouched. The simplified regime removed many of the detailed limits imposed by the previous regimes, but has itself now become rather complex. See *lifetime allowance, annual allowance, transitional protection*.

**sine die** Latin for 'without a day'. Means that the matter in question is adjourned indefinitely, without a specific date for resumption.

**Singapore** The Stock Exchange of Singapore (SES) was established in 1973 after the break-up of the joint Stock Exchange of *Malaysia* and Singapore. Its main index is:

• SGX Straits Times Industrial Share Price Index.

The *Singapore International Monetary Exchange* (*SIMEX*) was the first *financial futures* exchange in Asia (est. 1984). It merged with the Singapore Stock Exchange to form the Singapore Exchange (SGX) in December 1999.

Standard *currency*: Singapore *dollar*. 1 *dollar* = 100 *cents*.

**Singapore International Monetary Exchange (SIMEX)** See under: *Singapore*.

**single capacity** Prior to October 1986 *stockbrokers* acted as agents for private clients and institutions buying *shares* through a *jobber* as principal. Each acted independently and *London Stock Exchange* transactions could only be made through a *jobber* via a *stockbroker* each in their single capacity. An institution can now act in the capacity of both *jobber* and *stockbroker* as *market maker*. The client is protected from a *conflict of interest* by established arrangements preventing any cross-flow of information from *market maker* to salesperson. See also: *Chinese wall, dual capacity*.

**single premium** A term associated with *endowment* and *unit-linked life assurance investment* vehicles where the investor invests a once-only *capital* sum as opposed to paying regular *premiums*. See also: *investment bond*.

**single tax system** A single *tax* system is one in which a single type of *tax* is responsible for most of the *tax* burden on individuals. It would usually be a *tax* on the *income* of an individual, where '*income*' is defined more widely to include *capital gains*, inheritances and the like. The *UK*, along with most other countries, operates on a multiple *tax* system (which includes *income tax, inheritance tax, capital gains tax*, etc.) which is considered more flexible and equitable but is by its very nature more avoidable and more costly to administer. See: *canons of taxation*.

**sinker** *Loan stock* on which *interest* payments and repayment of the principal is made from a *sinking fund*.

**sinking fund** 1. *Capital* accumulated on a regular basis in a separate *trustee* account in order to redeem outstanding *loan stock*. 2. A specific method of repaying a long-term debt. It involves paying the *interest* as it falls due and creating a fund (called the sinking fund) to accumulate the principal by the end of the *term* of the loan. The sinking fund is created by a specific schedule of equal-sized *deposits* at regular intervals (calculation of which involves the *discounting* of an *annuity*). This same sinking-fund schedule calculation can be used to ascertain the size of *deposits* an individual or *company* needs to make at regular intervals in order to accumulate a specific amount. For example, if a *company* requires £100,000 (= S, say) to purchase some equipment (or alternatively to pay back the principal on a loan) in five years' time (n=5), the *interest rate* i being 16%, the annual *deposits* R into the sinking fund can be calculated using an ordinary simple *annuity* formula:

$$R = \frac{S}{s_{n;i}} = \frac{£100,000}{s_{5;16\%}} = £14,540.94$$

Thus annual *deposits* of £14,541 must be made annually over five years into the sinking fund to produce £100,000 at an *interest rate* of 16%.

**SIPP** See: *self-invested personal pension*.

**Six Sigma** A business *management* strategy, originally developed by Motorola, with widespread applications primarily in manufacturing quality control. Six Sigma seeks to highlight and mitigate the causes of defects and errors in manufacturing and business procedures. It uses a set of quality *management* methods, mostly statistical, and creates a special infrastructure of expert people within the organisation, known as 'Black Belts', who follow a defined sequence of steps, quantified financial targets and quality improvements to achieve cost reductions or *profit* increases.

**skip-day** Payment for a *security* on a *US money market* must be made within the skip-day, which is the two-day period after purchase.

**sleeping beauty** A potential *takeover target* that has not yet been approached by a *bidder*. Such a *company* usually has particularly attractive features, such as a large amount of *cash* or *undervalued assets*.

**sliced and diced** A general term for *securitised mortgages* (*CMOs* or *CDOs*) where underlying *mortgages* of varying *quality* have been mixed together and sold on. This 'mince' is difficult to grade from a quality perspective and became part of the TARP bail out of *bank assets* in the *Credit Crunch* of 2008. See: *toxic asset*.

**sliding peg** Another term for: *crawling peg*. See: *intervention*, *peg*.

**slippage** A *venture capital* term used to describe below-anticipated performance from a start-up *company* which could lead to additional *funding* being required.

**SLL** *currency code* for: *Sierra Leone* Leone.

**SLMA** See: *Student Loan Marketing Association*.

**Slovakia** The Bratislava Stock Exchange (BSSE), established 1991, commenced trading in 1993. Its main *index* is:

- Slovak Stock Index (SAX). Comprises those *securities* which have largest *capitalisation* and are most frequently traded. Calculated daily. Employs the *Paasche formula* (see: *composite index, weighting factor*). Base: 14 September 1993 = 100.

Standard *currency*: euro (from 1 January 2009). 1 euro = 100 cents.

**Slovenia** The Ljubljana Stock Exchange, established 1924, closed in 1941 and reopened in 1989. The number of *listed securities* at the end of 2008 was 84. Its main *index* is:

- Slovenian Stock Exchange Index (SB120). Comprises 15 *listed shares*. Uses an unweighted arithmetic *average*. Base *value* = 1,000.

Standard *currency*: *euro*.

**slump** 1. The point in a *trade cycle* when economic activity is at its lowest. 2. Used to describe a temporary period of low *stock* or market performance. See: *business cycle, crash, depression, recession*.

**slush fund** A fund set up by a *company* or organisation for payment of services that are deemed confidential in one way or another. This may include payment for sensitive information, the discreet buying of gifts or other services for influential individuals that in return can benefit the organisation, etc.

**small companies rate** A lower rate of *corporation tax* that applies to *small companies* with *profits* of £300,000 or less (for *tax year* 2009/10). In 2009/10 it stands at 21%, and the full rate of *corporation tax* is at 28%. The small companies rate will rise to 22% in 2010/11. There is marginal relief for *profits* between £300,000 and £1,500,000.

**small company** Section 382 of the Companies Act 2006 states that in order to qualify as a small company at least two of the three following criteria must be met (in its first financial year, or in the case of a subsequent year, in that year and the preceding year): it must have a turnover of not more than £5.6 million, a balance sheet total of not more than £2.8 million, and not more than 50 employees. Compare: medium-sized company. See: *Normal Market Size, SME.*

**small self-administered pension scheme** A *pension* scheme with generally less than 12 *members,* typically controlling directors. See also: *self-administered pension.*

**SME** The recognised abbreviation for Small and Medium-Sized Enterprises. The majority of the workforce is employed by SMEs. Approximately 99% of the 4.7 million businesses in the UK are small firms with not more than 50 employees and 0.6% are medium firms with 51–250 employees.

In the UK, sections 382 and 465 of the Companies Act 2006 define a SME. To qualify as a small company a company must meet two of the three following criteria (in its first financial year, or in the case of a subsequent year, in that year and the preceding year): it must have a turnover of not more than £5.6 million, a balance sheet total of not more than £2.8 million, and not more than 50 employees. To qualify as a medium-sized company a company must meet two of the three following criteria (in its first financial year, or in the case of a subsequent year, in that year and the preceding year): it must have a turnover of not more than £22.8 million, a balance sheet total of not more than £11.4 million, and not more than 250 employees. The British Bankers Association has its own definition where small business customers are defined as sole traders, partnerships, limited liability partnerships and limited companies with an annual turnover of under £1 million, as well as associations, charities and clubs with an annual income of under £1 million. The European Commission has added a third category called micro enterprises. A micro enterprise must have a headcount of less than 10. If it has a headcount of less than 10, it must then either have a turnover or a balance sheet total of not more than €2 million.

In the USA, the definition of small business is set by a government department called the Small Business Administration (SBA) Size Standards Office.

**smokestack industries** Traditional manufacturing industries in the *UK.* Normally long-established heavy-engineering *companies.*

**smurfing** Dividing a large amount of *money* into smaller sums to *make money laundering* easier and ensure it falls under reporting thresholds for *cash deposits* (US is $10,000 and Europe €10,000); after the small cartoon characters.

**snake** A monetary system adopted among some nations in Europe in 1972. The *exchange rates* between participating countries were limited to fluctuations of up to 2.25%, ie the *currency exchange rates* were allowed to 'snake' about between the limits. The nations involved were *Belgium, Denmark, France,* Ireland, *Germany, Italy* and the *Netherlands.* Britain did not take part. In 1979 the system was replaced by the *European Monetary System (EMS).*

**SOD** *currency code* for: Somali Shilling.

**SOFFEX** See: *Swiss Options and Financial Futures Exchange.* Now part of Eurex. See under: *Switzerland.*

**soft commission** Favours or benefits granted by *brokers* and *dealers* to conceal or inflate declared levels of *commission* or additional incentives. Compare: *hard commission.*

**soft costs** See: *hard costs.*

**soft currency** The *currency* of a country that is fixed at an unrealistic *exchange rate* and not backed by *gold.* Generally not freely convertible to major *currencies.*

**soft landing** Gradual reduction in the activity within an economy that is *overheating,* without causing a *recession.* Contrast: *hard landing.* See: *business cycle.*

**soft loan** A loan with a very low rate of *interest.* Such loans are sometimes made to less-developed countries for political reasons.

**soft protection** A form of capital protection found in some retail *structured products.* Soft protection will provide a minimum return (usually 100% of the original capital) only if the underlying asset (often the FTSE 100 in UK products) does not breach a barrier level. If the level is breached, all protection is lost. Contrast: *hard protection.*

**softs** A general term to describe those *commodity futures* that are not metals, such as coffee, sugar, wheat, soya beans, cocoa etc.

**sol** Standard *currency* of Peru. 1 sol = 100 *centavos.*

**sole agency** An arrangement where an agent is the exclusive distributor of a product or service in a country or region. With estate agents a *discount* is offered if they are the only agent selling a property.

**sole trader** A self-employed person who trades on his or her own account. See: *tax schedules.*

**Solomon Islands** Standard *currency*: Solomon Islands *dollar.*

**solvency** The ability to settle all debts and monies owing in full when they become due. A *solvent company* has a surplus of realisable *assets* over its liabilities. Similar to *liquidity* (see: *liquid assets*) but has the connotation of a longer-term ability to settle debts. See also: *free asset ratio, insolvency, wrongful trading.*

**solvency margin** The difference between an *insurance company*'s *assets* and its liabilities. This margin is regulated by the *Personal Investment Authority.* See also: *solvency ratio.*

**solvency ratio** 1. For *banks,* the *ratio* of *assets* to liabilities regulated by the *Bank of England.* 2. A *ratio* used to evaluate the financial status of a *company,* more specifically the ability of a *company* to meet its longer-term liabilities. Among the solvency ratios are: *debt-equity ratio, debt ratio, interest cover.*

**solvent** Generally to have more *assets* than liabilities or, for a *company,* to have a positive *balance sheet.* Specifically, not being insolvent. (See: *insolvency, solvency*).

**Somalia** Standard *currency*: Somali *shilling.* 1 Somali *shilling* = 100 *cents.*

**SORP** Statements of recommended practice (SORPs) are issued by the Accounting Standards Board to provide specific accounting guidance in particular industries or sectors.

**source and application of funds** A section in a set of *accounts* now more commonly called: *cash flow statement.*

**source of official funds** See under: *balance of payments.*

**South Africa** South Africa has only one *equity* exchange, the Johannesburg Stock Exchange (JSE, est. 1887). Its main *indices* are:

• FTSE JSE-Actuaries Equity Indices:

   (i) All-Share Index; (ii) SA Resources Index (iii) Industrial Index.

Previous All-Share Index was revised when a joint venture with the FTSE started on 24 June 2002.

Standard *currency*: *rand*. 1 *rand* = 100 *cents*.

**South Korea** The Korea Stock Exchange (KRX) is located in Seoul. Its main *indices* are:

• Korea Composite Stock Price Index (KOSPI). Base: 4 January 1980 = 100.

• KOSPI 200. Underlying *index* for *stock* price *index futures* trading. Weighted by aggregate *market capitalisation*. Comprises 200 *blue chips* selected on a variety of criteria. Base: 3 January 1990 = 100.

Standard *currency*: *won*. 1 *won* = 100 jeon.

**South Sea Bubble** A classic example of an investment bubble which eventually burst with calamitous results. One of the most referred-to crashes. It revolves around *speculation* in the South Sea Company, which failed disastrously in 1720. The *company* was formed in 1711 by Robert Harley, who needed allies to carry through the peace negotiations to end the war of Spanish Succession. Holders of £10m worth of government *bonds* were convinced to exchange their *bonds* for *stock* (with 6% *interest*) in the new *company*, which was given a *monopoly* of British trade with the islands of the South Seas and South America. The *monopoly* was based on the expectation of securing extensive trading concessions from *Spain* in the peace treaty. These concessions barely materialised, however, so the *company* had a very shaky commercial basis. Nonetheless, it was financially active, and in 1719 it proposed that it should assume responsibility for the entire *national debt*, again offering its own *stock* in exchange for government *bonds*, a transaction on which it expected to make a considerable *profit*. The government accepted this proposal, and the result was an incredible wave of *speculation*, which drove the price of the Company's *stock* from £128 in January 1720 to £1,000 in early August. Many dishonest and imprudent speculative ventures sprang up in imitation. In September 1720, the bubble burst. By the end of the month the stock was priced at £150. Banks failed when they could not collect loans on inflated *stock*, prices of *stock* fell, thousands were ruined (including many members of the government), and fraud in the South Sea Company was exposed. Robert Walpole became First Lord of the Treasury and Chancellor of the Exchequer, and started a series of measures to restore the credit of the Company, and to reorganise it. The bursting of the bubble, which coincided with the similar collapse of the Mississippi Scheme in *France*, ended for some time the prevalent belief that prosperity could be achieved through unlimited expansion of credit. As a result legislation was enacted that forbade unincorporated joint *stock* enterprises. However, as recent events have shown, the notion that prosperity could be achieved through unlimited expansion of credit was not completely expunged.

**sovereign** *UK gold* coin first minted in the reign of Henry VII and fixed at a *value* of £1.00 in 1817. As a *gold* coin it has a *value* for its *bullion* price, though it is not now legal tender.

**sovereign loan** A loan provided by a *bank* to the government of a foreign nation, especially when the foreign nation is a less-developed country. See: *soft loan*.

**SpA** Societa per azioni – An Italian *public limited company* (*plc*). Compare: *Sarl*.

**SPA** Short for: state *pensionable age*.

**Spain** The four Spanish Stock Exchanges, Madrid (est. 1831), Barcelona (est. 1915), Valencia (est. 1970), Bilbao (est. 1890), are now all part of the Bolsas y Mercados Españoles (BME), the Spanish Stock Exchange. The main *indices* are:

- IBEX 35 – Weighted by *market capitalisation*. Calculated in real-time. Includes 35 of the most liquid Spanish *stocks*. Base: 29 December 1989 = 3,000.
- Madrid Stock Exchange Index. Base: 30 December 1985 = 100.

Standard *currency*: euro. 1 *euro* = 100 *cents*. The *peseta* was the standard *currency* of Spain, until the introduction of the *euro* on 1 January 2002.

**SPDR** Acronym (pronounced '*spider*') for: *Standard & Poor's* Depository Receipt. A SPDR is a *US exchange traded fund*. SDPR has a portfolio of common stocks designed to track the Standard & Poor's 500 Index. The fund, launched in 1993, is now valued at $62bn. It is now part of a large family of similar funds, trading a wide variety of indices, both in the US and overseas. The SPDR pays quarterly distributions from the dividends of the portfolio less trust expenses. See: *tracker fund, exchange traded fund*.

**special clearance** The normal clearing period for a cheque is three days. A recipient of a cheque who wants to know as soon as possible whether it will be paid can ask their bank to specially present that cheque. Their bank then sends the cheque by first-class post directly to the paying bank, on the following working day contacting them by phone to confirm whether it will be paid. The payee may not receive the funds any sooner, but has the knowledge that there are sufficient funds to pay the cheque.

**Special Commissioners** A body of specialised *tax* lawyers appointed by the Lord Chancellor that used to hear appeals against *assessments* to *income tax*, *corporation tax* and *capital gains tax*. A taxpayer could appeal to the Special Commissioners, rather than the *General Commissioners*, in cases where legal rather than factual matters are at issue. Both sets of commissioners were replaced by new tax tribunals from 1 April 2009.

**special deposits** When the *Bank of England* wishes to restrict credit in the economy (as a result of government policy, for instance), it instructs *clearing banks* to make special deposits with it. As a result the *banks* have less *deposits capital* at their disposal and hence less to lend out, restricting credit. See: *corset*.

**Special Drawing Rights (SDR)** Colloquially known as 'paper *gold*' these are a measure of a nation's *reserves* in the international monetary system. They were first issued by the *International Monetary Fund* (IMF) to member nations in 1970. Their main function is to supplement the *reserves* of *gold* and convertible *currencies*, and can thus be used to maintain stability in the *foreign exchange market*. SDRs can also be used to settle international *trade balances* and to repay debts owing to the IMF. Accordingly, SDRs function as a neutral *unit of account*. The IMF allocates SDRs to member countries in proportion to their predetermined *quota* in the fund, which is calculated as a factor of their *gross national product* (GNP). Since the introduction of SDRs, *gold* has declined in importance as a reserve *asset*. On 1 January 1970, the *value* of one SDR was set at US$1.00 and the *dollar* equivalent of other key *currencies*. Since the introduction of *floating exchange rates*, the SDR's *value* has fluctuated relative to a basket of major *currencies* and is used to denominate *securities* on the *eurobond* market. As at February 2009, one SDR was worth $0.67.

**special Lombard rate** If for some reason the normal *Lombard rate* has been suspended, the German *Bundesbank* establishes the special Lombard rate for lending to commercial *banks*.

**special resolution** See under: *resolution*.

**special situations** A general *investment* term used to describe an *investment* with above-average *growth* prospects brought about by, say, a possible *bid*, a new discovery, the *revaluation* of *assets*, the successful sale of a loss-making subsidiary or some other anticipated benefit. Some collective *investment funds* specialise in this type of *investment*.

**specie**  *Money* in the form of coins, as opposed to banknotes or *bullion*.

**specific risk**  Another term for: *unsystematic risk*.

**specific tax**  A *tax* exclusive to one product or one business, such as *Petroleum Revenue Tax* or a windfall *tax* on utilities.

**speculation**  An activity that is characterised by taking above-average *risks* in order to realise above-average *profits*. The primary purpose of speculation is to achieve short-term *capital gains* (as opposed to conventional investors who have longer term aspirations and also invest for *income*) and speculative methods tend to rely on more sophisticated vehicles such as *futures*, *options* and other *derivatives*. A speculator is an individual participating in *investment* markets with a view to *profit* without the need to *hedge* a physical commitment. In the *stock market* the phrase tends to be used to describe the participant who holds a short-term perspective on his position though speculators are an important part of any market as they provide liquidity and iron out anomalies. See: *arbitrage*, *hedge fund*.

**speed**  Another name for *momentum*, a technical *indicator* measuring the rate of increase or decrease of a price *trend*.

**spider**  See: *SPDR*.

**spike**  In a rapidly falling market there tends to be a technical *reaction*. This can be due either to *short covering* or to a premature surge of genuine buying at lower levels. The spike proves particularly painful in this latter context as it represents only a temporary upturn on the way to still lower levels. See: *bear trap*, *crash*, *dead cat bounce*.

**spin-off**  Occurs when a *subsidiary company* or division of a *company* becomes an independent *company*. Usually the *shares* of the new *company* are distributed to the *parent company*'s *shareholders* on a *pro rata* basis, but the spin-off *company* can be floated (see: *flotation*) separately by a *placing* or *public offering*.

**split**  See: *share split*.

**split trust**  Also called split capital trust. An investment trust or investment company which in its simplest form is divided into a *growth* holding and an *income* holding so that all the *income* arising on the combined *investment* is allocated towards one *trust* and all the *growth* of the combination allocated to the other. Accordingly, one is designed to provide *growth* and the other *income*, and each receives twice the allocation of either *growth* or *income* but none of the other. This is useful for investors with an exclusive preference for *income* or *growth* and who, for instance, want a higher *income* and are prepared to forgo any *growth* (and vice versa). Some split trusts have more complex structures which include zero dividend preference shares which have first claim on assets after any borrowings repaid. In the 2000-2003 bear market some highly geared UK split capital trusts were forced into liquidation and many investors lost all or most of their investment. New split trusts are now rare. See: *zero dividend preference share*.

**sponsor**  The *issuing house* responsible for all matters connected with a new issue, with responsibility for the fairness of the impression given by the *prospectus* and for ensuring that the *company* is aware of and capable of complying with its obligations as a *quoted company*. See: *nominated advisors*.

**sponsored spin out**  A new *company* formed by a *management* team, their previous *parent company* and venture capitalists to exploit new technological developments or untried market opportunities. See: *spin-off*.

**spot**  1. This refers to a *commodity* or *currency contract* due for immediate delivery or immediate fulfilment. 2. A spot *exchange rate* is the current *exchange rate*, as opposed to at a future date. See: *cable*.

**spot currency market** A market where *currencies* are traded on their *spot* (see sense 2) *quotations* for delivery within two days, as opposed to the *forward market* where deliveries and rates are quoted for some period in the future.

**spot price** The current *cash* price for a physical *commodity* or *currency* or any *security* traded on a *futures* market. For instance when a *commodity* has been purchased for *cash* the title passes together with the holding costs to the buyer until such time as it is sold at the prevailing spot price. See: *cable, spot*.

**spread** In *investment* terms this is used to describe the difference between the buying and selling price, ie the *bid-offer spread*. This can vary depending on the demand for the *investment* and the *volumes* in which it is normally traded. Collective *investments* normally have a set spread.

**spread betting** Originally a bet with a bookmaker on a result between two figures – a lead of 2–4 goals or a win by between 50–100 runs or a finish of between 5th and 7th place, etc. Spread betting is now available as an alternative to *CFDs* for *shares* and *indices* due to the *tax* free nature of the proceeds of gambling, and works in very much the same way as *CFD* trading where an up or down bet can be placed on most financial market *assets*.

**Square Mile** The popular name for *the City* of London now more normally used to describe London's financial centre (which occupies approximately that area in *the City* of London bounded by Waterloo and Tower Bridges).

**squeeze** 1. Restrictive policy implemented by a government with the view to reduce *inflation*: (i) an *income* or pay squeeze is a policy that limits increases in salaries and wages of the *labour force*; (ii) a credit squeeze is a limit on how much lending institutions such as *banks* can lend, or restrictions on borrowing by raising *interest rates*; the *credit squeeze* is also called a 'credit crunch'; (iii) a *dividend* or *profits* squeeze is one which limits the *dividend* payments of *companies*. 2. Any situation where the increased costs incurred by a *company* cannot be passed on in the form of higher prices to consumers, so the *profits* of the *company* are 'squeezed'. 3. A market situation where prices start to rise, thus forcing *bear* traders to *cover* their *short positions* to avoid further losses, which in turn forces prices up further.

**SRG** *currency code* for: Surinam Guilder.

**Sri Lanka** The Colombo Stock Exchange (CSE) was established in 1896. The number of listed companies in March 2008 was 235. The main *indices* are:

- All-Share Price Index (ASPI).
- Milanka Price Index (MPI). Comprises 25 selected *companies*.

Standard *currency*: Sri Lankan *rupee*. 1 *rupee* = 100 *cents*.

**SSAP** See: *Statement of Standard Accounting Practice*.

**SSP** 1. Short for: state scheme *premium*. 2. Short for: statutory sick pay.

**St Helena** Dependency of the *UK*. Standard *currency*: St Helena *pound*.

**St Kitts and Nevis** Standard *currency*: East Caribbean *dollar*.

**St Lucia** Standard *currency*: East Caribbean *dollar*.

**St Pierre and Miquelon** Dependency of *France*. Standard *currency*: euro.

**St Vincent and the Grenadines** Standard *currency*: East Caribbean *dollar*.

**stabilisation** 1. Stabilisation of an *exchange rate* by the government authorities of a country is achieved by foreign market operations in which the domestic *currency* is bought or sold on the *foreign exchange market*. Also called 'pegging'. See: *intervention, peg*. 2. Achieving stability of major economic factors by way of government policies. *Business cycles, unemployment, inflation, balance of payments* etc. can be influenced by monetary and fiscal policies and other government measures.

**Stability and Growth Pact**   The Stability and Growth Pact of the *European Union* was agreed on 7 July 1997 and principally consists of two European Council regulations covering:

1) the implementation of the excessive *deficit* procedure and

2) the strengthening of the surveillance of budgetary positions and the surveillance and coordination of economic policies.

The *EU* Stability and Growth Pact principally determines that countries in the *eurozone* (that use the *euro*) must not run a *deficit* in their public budgets of more than 3% of their *gross domestic product* (*GDP*); breach of which risks escalating fines. The Pact also demands that public debt cannot climb higher than 60% of the *GNP* in *euro* Member States. In the difficult economic conditions of 2001/02 both France and Germany exceeded the 3% limit without being penalised. Other countries used some creative accounting to comply with the letter, if not the spirit, of the rules. At the behest of France and Germany the Pact was watered down in 2005. Although the 3% and 6% ceilings remained, greater leeway was granted for states to exceed the limits in a variety of circumstances. Some critics now regard the Pact as meaningless. See: *Maastricht convergence criteria*.

**stag**   One who applies for a new issue in the expectation of realising a *profit* as soon as dealing in *shares* begin. A short-term investor only interested in *speculation*. See also: *STAGS*.

**stagflation**   The combination of slow or zero economic *growth* and high *unemployment* (*stagnation*), and rising prices (*inflation*). The characteristic of stagflation is that economic and monetary policies designed to stimulate the economy and reduce *unemployment* serve only to stimulate the inflationary influences that caused them in the first place.

**staggered directorship**   A defensive tactic against *hostile takeover* attempts that ensures that *directors* terms are staggered and their removal is prevented except for due cause so that the hostile acquiror cannot control the *board* even if it controls the *stock*.

**staggered terms**   The practice of varying the terms and conditions under which *directors* are elected by rotation so that all *directors* do not come up for election by *shareholders* each year. Thus if an outsider gains control of a proportion of the *shares* it can take some time to unseat the entire *board* without an *extraordinary general meeting*. See: *staggered directorship*.

**stagnation**   The combination of slow or zero economic *growth* and high *unemployment*. See: *stagflation*.

**stake**   An *equity* holding in a *limited company* that participates in its *growth* and *profits*.

**stakeholder pension**   A form of *money purchase personal pension*, introduced in April 2001, with low charges and minimum standards. It was designed to appeal to people on low and middle *incomes* who wanted to save for retirement but for whom existing *pension* arrangements were too expensive or unsuitable. Stakeholder pensions were not a great success and will be effectively replaced by personal accounts from 2012. In the meantime they continue to offer a low cost alternative to the personal pension.

**stamp duty**   Stamp duty on the purchase of UK company shares is 0.5% of the consideration, with no charge applying at £5 or under. Fixed interests securities and overseas shares are exempt.

**stamp duty land tax (SDLT)**  Stamp duty land tax was introduced on 1 December 2003 as a tax on land transactions in replacement of stamp duty, which was strictly a tax on documents. SDLT was designed to close many of the tax avoidance loopholes in the old tax regime. The current rates of tax are based on consideration as follows:

| Residential | Commercial | Rate |
| --- | --- | --- |
| £175,000*or less | £150,000 or less | Nil |
| Over £175,000* up to £250,000 | Over £150,000 up to £250,000 | 1% |
| Over £250,000 up to £500,000 | Over £250,000 up to £500,000 | 3% |
| Over £500,000 | Over £500,000 | 4% |

*From 3/9/09: £125,000 or £150,000 for property in disadvantaged areas*

The structure of the tax is such that it encourages clumping of values at the thresholds: an extra £1 of consideration can add £5,000 to the SDLT bill at the £500,000 level.

**stamp duty reserve tax (SDRT)**  Stamp duty reserve tax is the substitute stamp duty levied on paperless share purchases.

**Standard & Poor's**  An American corporation providing *investment* services including *rating* and *index* services, many of which are used as *benchmarks* for *stocks* and markets. The *rating* system is analogous to that provided by *Moody's*. They provide a *rating* system for *bonds* according to *risk* which is as follows:

Investment grade (prime):

- *AAA*. Highest *rating*. Capacity to pay *interest* and repay principal on time is very strong.
- AA. Capacity to pay *interest* and repay principal on time is strong.
- A. Somewhat more susceptible to possible adverse economic conditions than the higher two *ratings*.
- BBB. Adequate capacity to pay *interest* and repay principal.

Non-investment grade (non-prime), also called *junk bonds*:

- BB, B, CCC, CC. Predominantly speculative with regard to *interest* payment and principal repayment. BB indicates the lowest degree of *speculation* and CC the highest degree.
- C. Bond on which no *income* is being paid.
- D. Signifies that the *bond* is in *default*, ie the payment of *interest* and/or principal is in arrears and/or unlikely.

Note that the ratings AA through B may be modified by the addition of + or –.

See also: *credit rating, Standard & Poor's 500 Index*.

**Standard & Poor's 500 Index (S&P 500)**  Most frequently used of the family of S&P *indices*. The *index* comprises 500 *stocks* of the industrial, transportation, financial and *utility sectors* in the US. Only *companies* of large *float* are selected. The composition of constituent *stocks* is updated quarterly.

**standard deviation**  Used to evaluate *risk*. Technically a measure of statistical dispersion of a *distribution* of *values* or prices. It is the square root of the *variance* and is usually assigned the symbol: . Described as the 'root-mean-square of the deviations from the *mean*', which follows from the definition of *variance* as '*mean* of the square of the deviations from the *mean*'. Is used more often than the *variance* since, as distinct from the *variance*, the standard deviation is measured in the same units as the variable being described.

**standard of living**  The level of well-being experienced on average by a society. Sometimes 'standard of living' is used in the narrower sense to include only monetary elements, as measured by *GDP* per head (ie *per capita income*), and is then differentiated from '*quality of life*' which also includes non-monetary *considerations*. Taking 'standard of living' in the wider sense, it is measured by a number of factors, for instance *real GDP growth*, number of mobile telephones per 100, cars per 1,000, infant mortality per 1,000 births, TVs per 1,000, life expectancy at birth, doctors per 100,000 and so on. The most important factor in raising standards of living is *real GDP growth*. International comparisons are usually made by comparing *per capita income* on the basis of *purchasing power parity exchange rate*, which is the *exchange rate* that equates the prices of a representative bundle of goods in the countries concerned.

**standby agreement**  An in case of need agreement between the *International Monetary Fund* (*IMF*) and a member state, enabling the member to arrange for immediate *drawing rights* in the case of an unforeseen requirement, such as a temporary *balance of payments* imbalance.

**standby credit**  A *letter of credit* that guarantees a loan will be repaid by a third party if the borrower *defaults* on payment. Normally issued by a *bank,* it requires the applicant to obtain a *certificate* of *default* and is often used where the borrower is insufficiently creditworthy.

**standing order**  An instruction by a client to their *bank* (*bankers order*) or *building society* to pay a specific fixed sum at specific intervals to a certain third party. Now largely replaced by the *direct debit*.

**standstill agreement**  An agreement whereby the *bidder* agrees to buy no more of the *target*'s *stock* for a specific period of time.

**state pension**  The basic state *pension* payable to anyone who has fulfilled the minimum *National Insurance* contribution requirements which from 6 April 2010 will broadly be a contribution record (or appropriate credits) for at least 30 years. The current (2009/10) weekly rate is £95.25 for a single person and £152.30 for a married couple. It is a set amount determined by the Treasury in the Budget and is payable currently to single people over 60 for women and 65 for men or retired couples. State pension age for women will start to rise from April 2010, reaching 65 by April 2020. Thereafter the equalised age will increase to 66 between 2024 and 2026, 67 between 2034 and 2036 and 68 between 2044 and 2046. This *basic component* can be enhanced by the second state pension for employees, but not the self-employed.

**state second pension (S2P)**  The state second pension was introduced by the Welfare Reform and Pensions Act 1999 as a replacement for the state earnings-related pension scheme (SERPS) from April 2002 for employees. In practice S2P was a modest reworking of SERPS which weighted the *additional pension* to those on modest earnings (up to £13,500 in 2008/09 terms). It left nobody worse off than under the former SERPS regime. The *Pensions Act 2007* made further changes to S2P, which started to take effect from April 2009. In the long term (estimated to be 2031/32 by the *DWP*) the Act's reforms will result in S2P being a flat rate pension worth, in 2008/09 earnings terms, a maximum of about £68 a week.

**statement of adjustment**  A public statement prepared by the *reporting accountants*, which reconciles figures published in a *short-form report* in a *prospectus* with those shown in the *audited accounts*. Such adjustments may be required, for example, to ensure consistency of accounting treatment over the period reported on.

**statement of affairs**  *Balance sheet* of *assets* and liabilities during bankruptcy (see: *bankrupt*) or during *liquidation*.

**statement of source and application of funds**  Now more commonly called: *cash flow statement*.

**Statement of Standard Accounting Practice (SSAP)** One of a number of statements issued by the Accounting Standards Committee on *UK company* accounting practice, covering: disclosure, group accounting, taxation and various specific topics. In September 1991, the Accounting Standards Committee was replaced by the *Accounting Standards Board* (*ASB*), which issued the first of its *Financial Reporting Standards* (*FRSs*) that will eventually supersede the *SSAPs*. Unless there is any disparity between the old *SSAPs* and the new *FRSs*, the *SSAPs* remain valid. For instance, *FRS* 1 requires all *medium companies* and *large companies* to publish *cash flow statements*, and replaces *SSAP* 10, which required a somewhat similar statement *listing* sources and applications of funds. See also: *International Accounting Standard* (*IAS*), *Urgent Issues Task Force* (*UITF*).

**statutory accounts** See: *accounts, abbreviated accounts.*

**STD** *currency code* for: São Tomé e Príncipe Dobra.

**sterilisation** Activity in the *money market* by government authorities to offset the effect on the monetary base of *foreign exchange intervention*. Conversely, a policy of non-sterilised *intervention* means that the authorities allow the reserve changes resulting from their *interventions* to affect the monetary base. For instance, if the government has a *fixed exchange rate* policy and wishes to expand the *money supply* by *open market operations*, the increased *money supply* will cause a fall in *interest rates* and probably an increase in *income*. This will cause a *balance of payments deficit*, implying an excess supply of domestic *currency* in the *foreign exchange market*. The *currency* will depreciate unless the authorities intervene in the *foreign exchange market* by purchasing domestic *currency* with their *reserves* (*foreign exchange* operations).

**Sterling** The *UK currency* is the *pound* Sterling, as distinct from *pounds* in other countries' *currencies*. The name probably comes via the Old English word 'steorra', which means star, since some early Norman silver coins bore a small star. The term is used to avoid confusion with avoirdupois pounds (lbs).

**STI** See: *Straits Times Index*. See under: *Singapore*.

**stochastic** Statistical term for 'random'. Eg a stochastic outcome is one that is determined by chance only; a random outcome.

**stock** 1. *UK* term for *fixed interest securities*, normally with a *nominal value* of £100. 2. *US* term for an ordinary *share* or *common stock*. 3. The unsold or unfinished products of a *company*. Also referred to as (especially in the *US*) *inventory*. See: *stock in trade*.

**stock exchange** Also called: *stock market*. For details of world-wide *indices* and *stock markets* refer to individual countries. A market that deals in *securities*. *Market forces* determine the price of the *securities* traded. The very first stock exchange dates back to 1602, in Amsterdam. The first British stock exchange came about in London, 1698. A necessary institution for capitalism, *stock markets* fulfil the function of raising *capital* for organisations and for providing *liquidity* for investors. They were banned after the Second World War by communist countries, to be reintroduced in many after communism was abandoned. The three biggest stock exchanges (in terms of *market capitalisation*) are New York, Tokyo and London. See under country name for more details on the *stock market*(s) of that country.

**Stock Exchange** See: *London Stock Exchange.*

**Stock Exchange Daily Official List** See: *Official List.*

**Stock Exchange Electronic Trading Service (SETS)** SETS is the London Stock Exchange's main platform for the trading. It now offers market making in all stocks including those deemed to be "liquid" under the Markets in Financial Instruments Directive (MiFID).

**Stock Exchange Electronic Trading Service – quotes and crosses (SETSqx)** The London Stock Exchange's SETSqx (Stock Exchange Electronic Trading Service – quotes and crosses) supports four electronic auctions a day along with continuous stand alone quote driven market. Since 8 October 2007, all Main Market and EURM AIM equity securities not traded on a full order book are traded on SETSqx. They joined the Main Market and AIM securities with less than 2 market makers which were added on 18 June 2007 following the replacement of SEATS Plus.

**Stock Exchange Mutual Reference Library** A list of *stockbrokers'* clients and their status. Used by *brokers* to check on new clients and ensure that they have no history of *defaults* etc.

**stock in trade** Work in progress plus raw materials plus finished *stock* constitute stock in trade or, in the *US, inventory.*

**stock indices** Various *indices* of markets or *sectors* within markets which represent *average* performance and are used as a guide for general *trends*. See: *index.*

**stock jobber** See: *jobber.*

**stock market** Another term for: *stock exchange.*

**stock option** See: *share option.*

**stock split** American term for: *share split.*

**stock transfer form** See: *transfer deed.*

**stock turnover** A performance *ratio* calculated for a *company*. It is the *turnover* figure in the *accounts* divided by the *stock* figure. It gives an indication of how rapidly *stock* moves through the business.

**stockbroker** Prior to the *Big Bang*, stockbrokers acted as intermediaries between the public and the *jobber*. Acting as an agent for clients they derived a *commission* on the amount invested or realised and often also provided additional facilities, such as research and *analysis*. Stockbrokers now provide a broad range of services. An agency stockbroker will deal exclusively through external *market makers* on behalf of both institutional and private clients. Stockbroking firms that have their own market-making facilities can promote the *shares* of *companies* in which they make markets as well as others and all firms can be involved in *flotations, placings* and advising *companies* on *rights issues* etc. *Quoted companies* all have an appointed *broker* or sometimes more than one.

**stockmarket ratio** See: *ratio.*

**stockpile** Where *commodities* are accumulated either to provide for future shortages or maintain producer prices. See: *buffer stock, mountain.*

**stop-loss order** An order placed in a *securities* or *commodities* market to *close* the position once a certain price level is reached, thus limiting the loss. Such *investment* techniques are more commonly used in markets where price *volatility* is high and where trading is done on a *margin* basis in order to ensure that losses do not exceed the *margin* itself.

**stotinka** *Currency* sub-unit used in *Bulgaria*. 100 stotinki = 1 *lev.*

**STOXX** European *stock index* – The *Dow Jones* STOXX 600 Index is derived from the *Dow Jones* STOXX Total Market Index (TMI) and a subset of the *Dow Jones* STOXX Global 1800 Index. With a fixed number of 600 components, the Dow Jones STOXX 600 Index represents large, mid and small capitalisation companies across 18 countries of the European region: *Austria, Belgium, Denmark, Finland, France, Germany, Greece, Iceland,* Ireland, *Italy, Luxembourg,* the *Netherlands, Norway, Portugal, Spain, Sweden, Switzerland* and the *United Kingdom.*

**straddle** Where *option* or *futures contracts* for the same *stock, bond, currency* or *commodity* are simultaneously bought forward and sold forward for the same period. This can enable a transfer of *assets* to be effected once the *contracts* are closed or can be used to protect a position against significant fluctuation in price. See: *butterfly, double option*.

**straight line depreciation** See under: *depreciation*.

**straights** *Fixed interest securities* with a fixed payment rate and a fixed *maturity date*.

**Straits Times Index** See under: *Singapore*.

**strap** An *option contract* combining one *put option* and two *call options* in the same series. These can be bought at a lower cost than three *options* individually. Also called: triple *option*. See also: *strip*.

**strike price** 1. Another word for: *exercise price*. 2. Following a *tender offer* (eg in a new issue of *shares*), the issuers who have received *bids* fix a price (*striking price*). Normally, *bids* below the *striking price* receive none of the new *shares* issued, whereas *bids* above the *striking price* receive the amount *bid* for or at least a proportion *bid* for. All *shares* are allocated at the strike price regardless of the price tendered. 3. Initial index level used in setting the terms of a structured product.

**striking price** See: *strike price*.

**strip** An *option contract* comprising two *put options* and one *call option* in the same series. These can be bought at a lower cost than the individual *options*. See also: *strap*.

**strips** Strips are 'stripped *securities*', where the registered *interest* and principal can be negotiated separately as 'interest only' (I.O.) and 'principal only' (P.O.) *securities*.

**STRIPS** Acronym for Separately Traded and Registered Interest and Principal Securities. See: *Gilt Strip Market*.

**structural unemployment** *Unemployment* occurring as a result of a mismatch between the available jobs and the *labour force*, even when the total demand for labour equals the total supply. This may come about because workers are not in the part of the country where labour is required or do not have the skills necessary for the jobs available. See: *frictional unemployment, full employment, NAIRU*.

**structured capital-at-risk product** A term used by the *Financial Services Authority* to describe a retail *structured product* which could result in the investor losing part or all of their original capital at maturity. See: *soft protection*.

**structured product** A structured product is an investment product based on derivatives. They may be traded on a stock exchange, dealt *over-the-counter* or be purely a packaged retail investment.

**Student Loan Marketing Association (SLMA)** Colloquially known in the *US* as *Sallie Mae*, this is a corporation that guarantees *US* student loans traded in the *secondary market*. It was set up by federal decree in 1972 in order to increase the availability of education loans to college and university students.

**sub-prime mortgage** A *mortgage* sold to someone with limited ability to repay (NINJA) in the hope of sustained rises in property prices. Such *mortgages* were then securitised and mixed (*sliced and diced*) with better quality loans and sold on. The collapse of property prices worldwide highlighted the deficiencies in these *CMOs* and triggered the *Credit Crunch* in 2008. See: *NINJA, Credit Crunch, toxic asset*.

**sub-underwriting** The *sponsor* to a new issue (who will normally *underwrite* its terms) may *spread* its financial *risk* by sub-underwriting a proportion of its total commitment with other financial institutions.

**subfund** An *investment* in a *collective investment scheme* where the units can be linked to a subfund or range of subfunds normally in different geographical areas. These are usually part of *umbrella funds*.

**subordinated debt** See: *junior debt*.

**subordinated loans** A loan where the *interest* of depositors takes precedence over the *shareholders* and stockholders, but which cannot be repaid other than from surplus *assets*. Such loans can also be subordinated to an event such as the maintenance of a *liquidity* margin determined by a regulatory body.

**subordinated unsecured loan stock** See under: *loan stock*.

**subrogation** The substitution of the rights of one *creditor* to another. For instance, an *insurance* policyholder who has been subjected to damages by a third party may be able to claim from the *insurance company*. Due to subrogation, the *insurance company* may be able to sue the third party to obtain compensation for the damages claimed by the policyholder.

**subsidiary company** A *company* is a subsidiary of another *company* (termed the parent or *holding company*) if the *holding company* holds (controls) more than 50% of the *voting shares* of the subsidiary. *Companies* may be otherwise linked and here they are referred to as *associate companies*. A *holding company* together with all its subsidiaries together form a group of *companies*, which are required to file group (consolidated) *accounts* in accord with the Companies Act 2006.

**Substantial Acquisition Rules (SARs)** Rules regarding large purchases of *company shares* in the *UK*, designed to limit the practice of *dawn raids* bringing potential predators to just below the level of a 30% *stake* requiring a 'mandatory *bid*' under the *City Code on Takeovers and Mergers*. The *SARs* are administered by the *Panel on Takeovers and Mergers*. The *SARs* relate to *stakes* of between 15% and 30%. The following four provisions must all be adhered to for a substantial *acquisition* to be allowed (and not deemed as a *bid* or disallowed): 1. the *stake* is acquired from more than one person; 2. it is made within seven calendar days; 3. it is 10% or greater; 4. the acquiring *shareholder* thus achieves a holding of 15% or more. If an *acquisition* is allowed under these rules but takes a *shareholder* to a *stake* of between 15% to 30%, then this must be disclosed to the *company* by noon the next business day, who will then inform the *UKLA*.

**sucre** Standard *currency* unit of *Ecuador*. 1 sucre = 100 *centavos*.

**Sudan** Standard *currency*: *dinar*. 1 *dinar* = 10 *pounds*.

**sum** Standard *currency* of *Uzbekistan*.

**sum assured** A guaranteed amount payable under a *life assurance* policy as a result of a claim by way of death or maturity. This amount is fixed on outset and *bonuses*, if any, are added to this.

**sumptuary law** Restrictions on personal spending which can be applied at times of economic difficulty, such as rationing.

**superannuation** Income in retirement paid by a previous employer, ie a *pension*.

**Superannuation Funds Office (SFO)** A department within the old *Inland Revenue* that dealt specifically with *pension* funds and the benefits therefrom. Now HMRC Audit and Pension Schemes Services (APSS).

**supermajority provisions** *Corporate by-law* provisions in *America*, whereby certain decisions (such as approval of a *merger*) can be passed only by a vote of a 'supermajority' (usually 69% to 90%) of *shareholders*, as opposed to the simple majority required for most votes.

**supply and demand** The basic determining factor in the *value* or price of any *investment*. The price of virtually anything reflects popularity and availability and these two factors are prime determinants in establishing a price, in the absence of external controls (for instance, government controls). Supply and demand operating freely are termed *market forces*.

**supply-side economics** 1. The factors that are involved with the supply side of the economy, such as labour. 2. A theory of economics contending that significant reductions in *tax* rates will stimulate productive *investment* by *companies* and wealthy individuals to the benefit of the economy (*trickle-down effect*). Championed in the late 1970s by Professor Arthur Laffer (see: *Laffer curve*), supporters of supply-side theory included Ronald Reagan (see: *Reaganomics*) and Margaret Thatcher ('Thatcherism') in recent years, though they were opposed by those who followed Keynesian theory (see: *Keynesian economics*), who believed in the effectiveness of demand-side policies.

**support area** The price range in which considerable demand is anticipated.

**support level** A *chart* line used in *technical analysis* to show the lower level to a downward *trend*. The price movement is expected not to go below the support level. The reason for this is that at the support level prices are low enough (or perceived *value* is high enough) to generate sufficient demand and thus avert further price drops. If, however, the price line does break through the

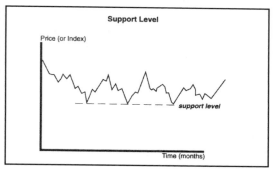

support level, then this is taken to signify further downward movements in price and is considered *bearish*. Compare: *resistance level*.

**supranational** *Securities* that transcend national boundaries, ie that are traded freely in markets outside the domestic or issuing market.

**surety** 1. *US* term for an individual or a corporation (usually an *insurance company*) that guarantees a third party. 2. Short for: surety *bond*. *US* term for a *bond* that guarantees the performance of a person (eg a contractor), or that pays an employer should a guaranteed employee commit theft. See: *fidelity insurance*.

**Suriname** Standard *currency*: Suriname *guilder*. 1 *guilder* = 100 *cents*.

**surrender value** Normally associated with *life assurance* policies, the surrender value is the current *value* of the *investment* less any penalties chargeable for early surrender. Often the surrender value offered by the *life assurance company* for a with-profits policy is less than the *value* of the policy if sold on to another party, and firms exist for trading and auctioning such policies. The surrender value will depend on the performance of the underlying *investments* or the *bonuses* allocated to the policy and the term that it has run and the expenses incurred by the life company. In the case of longer-term *life assurance* policies surrender penalties are usually high for early encashment. See: *Life Assurance Premium Relief, paid-up*.

**sushi bond** A *bond* issued by a Japanese institution, not denominated in *yen* but still officially classified as a *domestic bond*. These *bonds* are advantageous for Japanese *trust banks*, whose holdings in *foreign bonds* are limited. See also: *samurai bond*.

**suspension** Trading in *shares* of a particular *company* can be suspended in advance of a major announcement or to correct an imbalance of buy and sell orders. The relevant *stock exchange* will call a halt to all dealings in the *shares* and the price will remain at the level just prior to suspension until trading resumes.

**Svalbard and Jan Mayen Islands** Dependencies of *Norway*. Standard *currency*: Norwegian *krone*.

**SVC** *currency code* for: *El Salvador* Colon.

**swap** 1. Generally, an exchange of payments between two parties (sometimes called: *counterparties*), directly or through an intermediary: (i) *currency swap*: an agreement between two parties to exchange future payments in one *currency* for payments in another *currency*, in order to eliminate *currency risk*. At maturity of the swap *contract*, the principal must be exchanged; (ii) *interest rate swap*: an agreement between two parties such that one party pays the other a fixed *interest rate* in exchange for a floating *interest rate* at predetermined intervals. The *interest rate* is calculated on an agreed amount, the 'notional principal amount'. In contrast to the *currency swap*, this principal is not exchanged on maturity of the *contract*. The benefit of such swaps is that each party perceives an advantage in managing their asset-liability structure; (iii) the exchange between two parties of one *security* for another of equal *value*. Each party anticipates an improvement of *quality* of the *security* or its *yield*. See also: *rate anticipation swap, currency interest rate swap, swap jockey*. 2. On the *foreign exchange market*, the purchase/sale of a *currency* in the *spot* market made against the concurrent purchase/sale of the same amount of the same *currency* on the *forward market*. 3. Also called: *swap line*. A bilateral credit agreement between two *central banks*, in which one *central bank* repays on a *forward contract*.

**swap jockey** A *swap* specialist/broker/dealer.

**swap line** See: *swap* (sense 3).

**swaption** An *option* to enter into a *swap contract*.

**Swaziland** Standard *currency*: *lilangeni*. 1 *lilangeni* = 100 *cents*.

**sweat equity** *Shares* for work; often in new or start-up *companies* participants provide executive or non-executive services in exchange for *shares* rather than deplete newly raised *cash* resources. These *shares* are issued by capitalising a notional invoice from the executive providing the services.

**Sweden** Sweden's only *stock market*, the Stockholm Stock Exchange (established 1863) is the largest Nordic exchange. It was acquired by OMX in 1998 and in 2003 was merged with the Helsinki Stock Exchange. Its main *indices* are:

- OMX Stockholm All-Share Index – Comprises all *listed stocks* on the A-list *chain-linked* for issues and *stock splits*, but not adjusted for reinvested *dividends*. Base: 31 December 1979 = 100.

- OMX Stockholm 30 Index – *Index* of 30 market value weighted most traded stocks.

Standard *currency*: Swedish *krona*. 1 *krona* = 100 *öre*.

**sweep facility** An automatic facility provided by some *bank accounts* that will transfer account funds that are above a certain level into an account that earns a higher rate of *interest*.

**sweetener** *Equity* provided as part of a larger transaction to provide additional benefits if the venture goes well.

**SWIFT** Short for: 'Society for Worldwide Interbank Financial Telecommunications'. A global information system set up in 1977 to inform member *banks* of transfers between each other. It is not a clearing system for payments. Compare: *CHIPS*.

**swing line** A short-term credit arrangement to reconcile different *settlement dates* and times in different *commercial paper* markets.

**Swiss Options and Financial Futures Exchange (SOFFEX)** See under: *Switzerland*.

**switch** 1. The term used for encashing one *investment* and investing the total proceeds into another. In the case of *shares,* OEICs and *unit trusts*, this could give rise to a *capital gains tax* liability. Switching *investments* in *unit-linked life assurance* plans does not give rise to any such charge and can normally be effected for little or no cost. See: *gilt switches*. 2. The *closing* of an open period on a *commodity market* in favour of *opening* a similar position in the same *commodity* for a different *delivery* period.

**Switzerland** In Zurich, the Swiss Exchange (SIX) is the main exchange, the other being the Berne Exchange. The exchanges of Basle, Geneva and Zurich merged to form what is now SIX, which commenced operations in 1995 as SWX. The main indices are:

- The Swiss Index Family, comprising the Swiss Performance Index (SPI) the Swiss Market Index (SMI), the SWX Special Industry Index (SXI), the Swiss Leader Index (SLI) and the Swiss Bond Index (SBI). They are all weighted by *market capitalisation.*

The *Swiss Options and Financial Futures Exchange (SOFFEX)* was set up in 1988, and in 1998 merged with the German derivatives market (DTB) to form Eurex.

Standard currency: *Swiss franc. 1 franc = 100 centimes*

**SWOT** Strengths, weaknesses, opportunities and threats. An *analysis* often contained in a *business plan.*

**SWX Europe** SWX Europe is an established *Recognised Investment Exchange (RIE)* based in London and was launched in 2001 as virt-x Exchange, the first cross-border trading platform for pan-European blue chips. SWX Europe is a wholly-owned subsidiary of the SIX Swiss Exchange.

**Sydney Futures Exchange (SFE)** See under: *Australia.*

**syndicate** A group of investors or *companies* pooling their resources for projects such as *commodity investment, venture capital* projects or the provision of *insurance.*

**syndicated loan** An extremely large loan made to a borrower by a *bank* that syndicates most of the loan to other *banks* and financial institutions in order to *spread* the *risk.* Such loans are usually made on a small *margin.* If the borrower wishes to know the names of all the members of the *syndicate*, one refers to a 'club deal'.

**synergy** The joining of separate parts that yield a *value* greater than the sum total of the *values* of the parts when separate. This ideal is sought in *mergers*, where it is hoped that the combined enterprise will display performance superior to the separate businesses, and hence produce higher *earnings per share.*

**synthetics** Similar to *exotics*, a synthetic is a *derivative* combining two or more financial *instruments* to create an artificial *asset* in order to produce a *profit, arbitrage* or provide a *hedge* or, in some cases, purely to generate *commissions* for the *broker.*

**synthetic asset** An intangible *investment* comprising one or a number of *derivatives* as opposed to a *physical*. Synthetics are generally *investments* that determine notional *value* from events in the economy or movements in *shares* or markets, as opposed to *real* or *intrinsic value* provided by *asset backed investments*. A synthetic *equity* can be created by buying and selling *options* to create exactly the same *capital* performance as the underlying *equity* but without owning the *share.*

**systemic risk** Systemic *risk* is risk that is posed to the financial system or the economy, as opposed to *risk* that is faced by an investor or a *portfolio*. Systemic *risk* is most commonly considered in relation to the *risks* posed by *banks* and financial institutions. The failure of a major financial institution can have serious consequences, for example if a *bank* fails, not only will its depositors lose *money* but it is also likely to renege on obligations to other financial institutions. Both the depositors and the other institutions are then likely to be under financial pressure, which can lead to further failures of both *banks* and other businesses. See: *Credit Crunch*.

**SYP** *currency code* for: Syrian Pound.

**Syria** Standard *currency*: Syrian *pound*. 1 Syrian *pound* = 100 *piastres*.

**systematic risk** See under: *risk*.

**SZL** *currency code* for: *Swaziland* Lilangeni.

# T

**T+3** The period in days that elapses before *share* settlement is due or paid. It stands for transaction plus five (or one, three or ten) days. T+5 used to be the system used in the *equity* and corporate debt market, however, in February 2001, the *London Stock Exchange* changed it to a T+3 system. The long-term aim is to reduce to a T+1 system. Private transactions undertaken in *shares* via a *stockbroker* can operate on a longer timescale such as on T+14, ie settlement is required on a longer timescale such as within 14 days following the date of the transaction. See: *rolling settlement*.

**T+10** See: *T+3*.

**T Bond** See: *Treasury bond*.

**Taft-Hartley Act** Another name for the *US* federal law which restored some of the labour unions' bargaining power after the Second World War in the Labor Management Relations Act 1947.

**tailgating** An unethical practice of a *broker* who, after a customer has placed an order to buy or sell a certain *security*, places an order for the same *security* for his or her own account. The *broker* hopes to *profit* on the presumption that the customer has particular knowledge of the holding or is trading in sufficient size to move the price.

**Taiwan** The Taiwan Stock Exchange was established in 1961 in Taipei. In 2007, the number of *listed companies* was 698. Its main *index* is:

• Taiwan Stock Exchange Weighted Stock Index (TWSE). Calculated using the *Paasche formula*. (see: *composite index, weighting factor*) Base: 30 June 1966 = 100.

Standard *currency*: New Taiwan *dollar*. 1 *dollar* = 100 *cents*.

**Tajikistan** Standard *currency*: Somoni.

**taka** Standard *currency* of *Bangladesh*. 1 taka = 100 *paisa*.

**takeover** An offer made to the *shareholders* of a *company* by an individual or organisation intending to gain control of that *company*. If the *company* is quoted on a *stock exchange*, the *bidder* is expected to observe certain *stock exchange* regulations and those laid down by the *Panel on Takeovers and Mergers*. In *America* this is generally known as a *tender offer*. See: *bid, City Code on Takeovers and Mergers*.

**Takeover Panel** See: *City Code on Takeovers and Mergers*.

**tala** Standard *currency* of *Western Samoa*. 1 tala = 100 *sene*.

**TALF** The Federal Reserve Board created in March 2009 the Term Asset-Backed Securities Loan Facility (TALF), a facility to help market participants meet the credit needs of households and small businesses by supporting the issuance of asset-backed securities (ABS) collateralized by student loans, auto loans, credit card loans, and loans guaranteed by the Small Business Administration (SBA) in America. Under the TALF, the Federal Reserve Bank of New York (FRBNY) lends up to $200 billion on a non-recourse basis to holders of certain AAA-rated ABS backed by newly and recently originated consumer and small business loans. The FRBNY lends an amount equal to the market value of the ABS less a haircut and will be secured at all times by the ABS. The US Treasury Department, under the Troubled Assets Relief Program (TARP) of the Emergency Economic Stabilization Act of 2008, provides $20 billion of credit protection to the FRBNY in connection with the TALF. See also: *Private Partnership Investment Programme, TARP.*

**Talisman** Short for: Transfer Accounting, Lodgement for Investors and Stock Management. The *London Stock Exchange*'s old computerised transfer system covering most *UK shares*. It was superseded by a paperless settlements system, *CREST*, in April 1997.

**talon** If bearer *bonds* have *dividend coupons* and these have been used up, a detachable slip called a talon will be used to claim further *coupons*.

**tambala** *Currency* unit of *Malawi*. 100 tambala = 1 *kwacha*.

**tangible assets** 1. See under: *asset*. 2. An *investment* where physical ownership and possession of the actual *asset* is required rather than just certified ownership. Applies to *investments* such as diamonds, silverware, works of art, antiques, *gold bars* or *kruggerands*, Persian carpets, port and wine.

**Tankan survey** A quarterly survey of managers in the manufacturing sector in *Japan*, conducted by the *Bank of Japan*, in order to determine an outlook or general sentiment on the Japanese economy. The survey asks questions on specifics such as the numbers of orders received by firms in the previous month, which are given a score and from which a 'diffusion *index*' is created. It is similar to the *UK*'s 'Purchasing Managers Index' and carries significant credibility as an active *indicator*. See: *leading indicators.*

**tanshi company** Japanese *company* that trades on the *money markets.*

**Tanzania** Standard *currency*: Tanzanian *shilling*. 1 *shilling* = 100 *cents*.

**tap stocks** Some fund raising issues in the primary government bond market may not be fully subscribed or some *stock* may be kept in reserve. The balance is therefore retained and released on to the market slowly as market conditions and demand allow; hence the expression tap stocks. A tap may naturally depress prices when 'on', offering an opportunity for *switches*.

**tape** The service reporting prices and *volume* of transactions in major exchanges. Named after the ticker tape that produced printed tape before the process was computerised.

**taper relief** See: *Entrepreneurs relief.*

**target** The object of a *takeover bid.*

**tariff** A *tax* on *imports* or *exports* designed to raise revenue and protect domestic industry from competition and economics from a *trade deficit*. See: *protectionism.*

**TARP** The Troubled Assets Relief Programme was part of the Emergency Economic Stabilization Act 2008, which created the framework for up to a $700bn bail out of financial institutions and the purchase of *shares* and *assets* of major *banks* and other financial *companies*. Enacted during the *Credit Crunch* to stabilise the American financial system and followed by similar action in other countries including the *nationalisation* of several *banks* in the *UK* and elsewhere. See: *Credit Crunch, toxic asset.*

**TAURUS** Short for: Transfer and Automated Registration of Uncertificated Stock. Was a major IT project at the *London Stock Exchange* for the 'dematerialisation' of *share certificates* to create paperless trading and computerised shareholdings. It failed to ever take shape, and the TAURUS project was abandoned in March 1993. *CREST* was born from the ashes of TAURUS and eventually went fully live in April 1997.

**tax** See: *canons of taxation, principles of taxation.* See: *Westminster doctrine.*

**Tax and Prices Index (TPI)** Launched by the Treasury in 1979, the *TPI* is an *index* measuring the rise in *gross* wages needed to maintain *purchasing power* after taking into account changes in the amount of *tax* and *National Insurance* deducted from wages as well as changes in prices. It was designed to give a more representative indication of the *real purchasing power* of *UK incomes* than the *Retail Price Index* (*RPI*) which does not include *tax* and *National Insurance* payments. While the TPI is still published, very little attention is paid to what was essentially a political creation.

**tax avoidance**  The legal practice of minimising *tax* payment to the government *tax* agencies. Also called: *tax* planning. Contrast: *tax evasion*.

**tax clearances**  Clearances obtained from HMRC, in relation to past or proposed transactions with possible *tax* consequences (for example in relation to a *share capital* reorganisation), that *assessments* to *tax* will not be made as a result of the transactions.

**tax credit**  A *dividend* slip or voucher confirming that *tax* has already been paid on a *dividend*. In the case of *franked income* this cannot be reclaimed for non-taxpayers.

**tax deposit certificate**  *Tax* can be paid in advance by the use of such a *certificate* (minimum £500 – paid to the Shipley collection office) which pays a higher rate of *interest* if the *certificate* is ultimately used to settle a *tax* liability (rather than redeemed).

**tax evasion**  The illegal practice of reducing taxation by omitting disclosure and/or giving false information to government *tax* authorities. Contrast: *tax avoidance*. See: *black economy, money laundering*.

**Tax Exempt Special Savings Account (TESSA)**  A *deposit* account formerly available with *banks, building societies* and other financial institutions where the amount invested was exempt from *tax* provided the *capital* was not withdrawn during a five-year period. Introduced in the 1990 Finance Act, such accounts were designed to provide a low-cost method of encouraging tax-exempt savings. TESSAs were replaced by ISAs in 1999, although the last TESSA did not mature until April 2004. Any money left in a TESSA became a cash component ISA beyond maturity, often still wrongly referred to as TESSA-only ISAs.

**tax-free cash**  See: *pension commencement lump sum*.

**tax haven**  A term used loosely to describe low-tax or nil-rate territories outside the jurisdiction of the *UK* and therefore not subject to *UK tax* laws. See also: *offshore financial centre, offshore fund*.

**tax ratio**  The tax ratio of a *company* is calculated by dividing the *tax* provided by the *profit* before *tax*.

**tax return**  The form used each year by private individuals to declare and self-assess *earnings* and gains to HMRC.

**tax schedules**  The old *Inland Revenue* differentiated different types of *earnings* by separate tax schedules, namely A, B, C, D, E and F, each of which had its own *allowances* and expenses. The schedules have been replaced by a number of different Tax Acts, such as the Income Tax (Earnings and Pensions) Act 2003.  See: *canons of taxation, principles of taxation*.

**tax shelter**  A form of *investment* like an *Enterprise Investment Scheme* or *personal equity plan* which is legitimately sheltered from *tax*.

**tax tribunal**  From 1 April 2009, the tax appeal mechanism based on *General Commissioners* and *Special Commissioners* was replaced with a system of tax tribunals. The First-Tier Tribunal (Tax Chamber) meets at various locations throughout the country and hears taxpayer appeals against HMRC decisions. The Upper Tribunal is a Court of Record with jurisdiction throughout the UK and is based in London. It deals with appeals from, and enforcement of, First-Tier Tribunals.

**tax year** For individuals this ends at midnight on 5 April each year, and for *companies*, *partnerships* and the self-employed this is a regular twelve-month period of their choosing. See: *financial year, fiscal year*.

**technical analysis** Also called: *chartism*. The study of price movements of an *investment* (using *charts*) in order to make predictions about future price movements. The basic underlying tenet of this approach is that a relatively small number of *chart* movements have displayed historically repetitive *patterns* which thus have a high probability of repeating themselves in the future. A vast array of techniques have been devised, some of them only capable with the use of computers, to identify these *patterns* and thus to predict future price movements. This research has become very popular, especially in the *US*, with the interesting result that the very action of trading in accordance to chartists' predictions can have a 'sympathetic' effect on the *security*'s price movement; thus to a certain point the chartists are not only identifying price movements but also influencing them. Often, technical analysis is supplemented by *fundamental analysis*, whose approach is non-price specific. The Glossary contains a wide range of *chart patterns*; see under the required *chart pattern* name.

**technical rally** A temporary rise in a *security*'s price within a general falling *trend*. Usually arises as a result of *speculation*. See: *rally*.

**telegraphic transfer (TT)** See: *bank transfer*.

**temporary annuity** An *annuity* payable for a limited period.

**tenancy in common** A situation where land is to belong to a number of persons in common. It is vested in the first four persons mentioned in the *deed* and these hold it in *trust* for all persons concerned. These four persons are legally 'tenants in common'. Each tenant in common's share is a part of their estate and does not pass automatically to the surviving tenant on death.

**tender** A method of issuing *securities* (or offering a *contract*) where investors (*bidders*) may bid at prices above a minimum price. The subsequent allocation of these *securities* is made according to the prices bid. This form of issue can ensure that the *best price* is received for an issue but discourages *stags*, thus reducing the potential number of subscribers. When all the tenders are received the issuers fix a price (*strike price*). Normally, *bids* below the *strike price* receive none of the new *shares* issued, whereas *bids* above the *striking price* receive the amount *bid* for or at least a proportion *bid* for in relation to the price *bid* – the highest *bidder* will usually receive all the *shares* required, but at the *strike price*, and so on. All *shares* are allocated at the *strike price* regardless of the price tendered. Each tenant in common's a part of their estate and does not pass automatically to the surviving tenant on death.

**tender issue** See: *tender*.

**tender offer** The American name for a public *offer* (*bid*) to buy some or all of the existing *stock* of a *company* within a specified period. Notice of the *offer* must be filed disclosing, among other things, certain financial information concerning the *bidder*. The price offered is generally well above the current market price of the *stock*, to induce stockholders to *tender* their *shares* to the *bidder*. Not to be confused with an *issue by tender*.

**TEPs** See: *Traded Endowment Policies*.

**Tequila Slammer** The crisis in *Mexico* caused by a collapse of the *peso* in 1994 that impacted on most world *emerging markets*. Many *emerging markets*, especially those in Latin America, were too reliant on short-term external *capital* and lacked domestic savings to fund dramatic new *investment* resulting from exposing the economy to *market* *forces*. This destabilised both the market and the *currency* and caused a temporary collapse – similar to the potential effects of the drink after which it was named!

**TER**  See: *Total Expense Ratio*.

**term**  A fixed period of time. For instance, the term of a *gilt* is the time period from issue to redemption.

**term certificate**  A *certificate of deposit* (CD) with a longer-term *maturity date* (ie one to ten years).

**term insurance**  An *insurance* policy taken out for a fixed period on an individual's life. If death occurs within that period the full *sum assured* is payable to the deceased's *estate* or *nominees*. If, however, the deceased survives the period, nothing is paid by the insurers. This form of *insurance* is normally used to cover loans or to provide for an individual's family during the course of the person's working life. It is one of the cheapest forms of life cover.

**term loan**  An Americanism for a medium- to long-term *secured loan* (ca. 2–10 years) provided to a *company* usually to finance *capital* equipment or for *working capital*.

**term shares**  A *building society* account whereby the investor invests his or her *capital* for a fixed term and in return receives a preferential but variable rate of *interest*.

**terminal bonus**  An additional *bonus* added to a *with-profits life assurance* policy when it matures (ie when it has run for the period specified at outset). Terminal bonuses are not guaranteed and any change from year to year depends on the *profits* achieved by the life office and/or its *investment funds*. In a particularly good year a reserve is made to ensure that a terminal bonus can be paid in less profitable years by some life offices. In assessing the future benefits of a *with-profits policy* it may be sensible to *discount* the terminal bonus in future *projections*.

**terminal funding**  A *pension* scheme that is only funded on the retirement of the *member*.

**terminal value**  In accounting terms this refers to the salvage *value* of an *asset* at the end of its useful life. When the term is used regarding the *valuation* of a *company* it refers to the *value* of the company at a future date based on the present value of the subsequent *cash flows* the *company* will generate.

**TESSA**  See: *Tax Exempt Special Savings Account*.

**testament**  See: *will*.

**testator**  Person who was the subject of the *will* and *testament*. 'Testator' is the masculine form, '*testatrix*' is the feminine form.

**testatrix**  See: *testator*.

**Thailand**  The Stock Exchange of Thailand (SET) was established in 1974 in Bangkok. The number of companies *listed* in 2009 was 474. The main *index* is:

- SET Index. Comprises all *listed shares*. Base: 30 April 1975 = 100.

Standard *currency*: baht. 1 *baht* = 100 *satangs*.

**THB**  *currency code* for: Thai Baht.

**the City**  The financial centre in London represented by the *Square Mile* bounded by Waterloo and Tower Bridges. An international port and trading centre since medieval times, it houses the head offices or trading centres for *insurance, foreign exchange*, banking, clearing and *investment* houses, exchanges and financial institutions. See: *Bank of England, Lloyds, London International Financial Futures and Options Exchange, London Metal Exchange, Securities and Investments Board*.

**The Pensions Advisory Service (TPAS)** Originally the Occupational Pension Advisory Service (OPAS), a division of the Occupational Pensions Board established to provide advice and help to members of pension schemes and now an independent body, part funded by the DWP.

**The Pensions Regulator (TPR)** The regulator set up by the Pensions Act 2004 to replace the *Occupational Pensions Regulatory Authority*.

**thebe** *Currency* unit of *Botswana*. 100 thebe = 1 *pula*.

**theta** See: *time decay*.

**three-D (3D)** Term applied to *International Monetary Fund* policy recommendations to certain developing nations to improve their economies and sometimes as a condition for loans. It stands for: 1. Devaluation of *currency*. 2. Deflation. Attempt to achieve *deflation* through tight *fiscal policy* (ie less government spending, higher taxation) and tight monetary policies (ie high *interest rates*). 3. Deregulation.

**thrift institution** Also called: thrift. *US* organisations that hold *deposits* of personal savings (thus most of them are called 'savings *banks*') and make most of their loans in the form of residential *mortgages*. Recent effects of the Credit Crunch have seen the emergence of local 'thrifts' in the UK where depositors from local communities are used to provide local borrowers and mortgagees with loans, proving increasingly popular as major clearing banks lose credibility.

**throwback** When a price returns to the *chart pattern* after it has temporarily broken out from the top side of the *pattern*. Compare: *breakout, pullback*.

**tick** Also: tick point. The smallest unit of price movement. The size of the tick (tick size) will depend on the particular market. It is often expressed as a percentage, a *point* or fraction of a *point* of an *index* or monetary amount of the *nominal value* of the trading unit. The 'tick *value*' is the tick size times the *nominal value* of the trading unit times the length of the *contract* expressed in years. On *LIFFE*, for instance, a tick *value* is £12.50 and represents half a *basis point* in a *financial futures contract*.

**tied agent** An agent of a *life assurance company* authorised to sell only their products. Under the Financial Services Act such agents must declare the fact that they can only offer the products of the one *company* to which they are tied. A tied agency is different from somebody who is employed directly by the *insurance company* and normally works for a *broker* although it remains the case that that *broker* can only offer the products of the *company* to which it is tied. See: *authorisation, polarisation*.

**tigers** See: *TIGR*.

**TIGR** Short for: Treasury Investment Growth Receipt. Created by Merrill Lynch in 1982, these are *zero-coupon bonds* linked to *United States Treasury bonds* with a semi-annual compounding *yield*. Denominated in *dollars*, the *growth* is taxed as *income* in the year of encashment or redemption for *UK* taxpayers. See also: *cats, deep discount bonds, STAGS, zebras*.

**time decay** Any fixed term *option* or *warrant* to buy or sell something in the future is likely to become less valuable the nearer it comes to its date of expiry; either because it has to be exercised (see: *exercise price*) before this time or because it becomes valueless after this date. The *ratio* of the change in an *option* or *warrant's* price to the decrease in its time to expiration, it normally reflects the reduction in potential opportunities the nearer the expiry of the *contract*. Also called *time value* decay or *theta*. See also: *time value*.

**time draft** See: *draft*.

**time value** The *value* of an *option* not represented by its *intrinsic value*. Effectively the *option premium*, this is an amount paid for the privilege of having a period of time over which the *underlying asset* price may move sufficiently to make the *option* profitable – as this time elapses the chances of this happening reduce, as does the time value of the *option*.

**timeshare** The purchase of a property by a group of people who are each entitled to use it for a certain period during the year. Timeshares can be exchanged and bought and sold depending on the demand for the property and its location.

**Tinbergen's instruments–targets rule** The principle that a government needs to employ as many government policies (*instruments*) as there are targets for the economy (eg *external balance, internal balance*). This idea was propounded by the Nobel Prize-winning Dutch economist Jan Tinbergen. The principle was further refined by *Mundell's principle of effective market classification*.

**tithe** A fixed amount drawn from *income* for a charity, church or institution devoted to good works. It was originally one-tenth of an individual's *income* deducted for the upkeep of a local church or shared facility, like a barn.

**TJS** *currency code* for: Tajikstani Somoni.

**TMM** *currency code* for: *Turkmenistan* Manat.

**TND** *currency code* for: Tunisian Dinar.

**Tobin-q** See: *q theory*.

**toea** *Currency* unit of *Papua New Guinea*. 100 toea = 1 *kina*.

**Togo** Standard *currency*: African *franc*.

**Tokelau** Standard *currency*: *New Zealand dollar*.

**Tokkin** Japanese *interest rates* have been regular for many years, with the result that large corporations have tended to invest surplus *capital* in the *stock market*. Such *portfolios* are actively traded, with *investments* entered at cost or realised *value* in the *balance sheet*. Encouraged by major Japanese *banks*, large *profits* were generated actually or artificially from these Tokkin funds when investment conditions were favourable. See: *zaitech*.

**tombstone** Brief announcement of an important financial transaction, such as an *acquisition* or *merger*, made in the newspaper press.

**ton** 1. *Bond* trader's jargon for £100 million. 2. For weight, see: *short ton*.

**Tonga** Standard *currency*: pa'anga. 1 pa'anga = 100 *seniti*.

**TOP** *currency code* for: Tongan Pa'anga.

**top hat** A now largely unused expression used to describe an *executive pension plan*.

**top slicing** The treatment of assessing the *tax* payable on a chargeable gain occurring within a *life assurance* policy. The gain on the policy, ie the proceeds plus all *capital* withdrawals that fall within the cumulative 5% annual tax-free *allowance* less the amount of *premiums* paid, is divided by the number of full years for which the policy has been in force. This amount is then added to the taxpayer's other *income* for the year in which the *chargeable event* occurred. If this places him or her in the higher rate *tax* band then the gain falling within the higher rate band is charged at the appropriate marginal rate, ie 20% for UK policies and 40% for offshore policies. If the sum does not exceed the band for basic rate tax then no further tax is payable on a UK policy. In practice top slicing is now of little relevance, given that until 2011/12 there is only one higher rate tax band. For now top slicing only helps those basic rate taxpayers who become higher rate taxpayers as a result of the addition of the policy gain to their income.

**top up**   To increase the benefits of an existing arrangements. Normally associated with *pension* provision where salary increases make it possible to increase contributions or where benefits can be improved by a lump sum contribution.

**top-down**   The assessment of an *investment* based on macroeconomic and political circumstances and *trends*. The top-down assessment of an oil *company* would be based on the prospects for the price and supply of oil, the political stability of oil-producing nations and the prospects for consumption in the medium term. The top-down approach ignores the particular circumstances of the individual *companies* such as the strength of its *management*, its *balance sheet*, order book and *cash flow*. See: *bottom-up*.

**Total Expense Ratio (TER)**   A method of calculating the costs of fund management, expressed as the Fitzrovia Total Expense Ratio (*TER*), the formula measures the diminution of fund performance generated by all annual operating costs including administration, *trustee* and accounting fees in addition to the basic annual management charge. The *TER* is the annual percentage reduction in fund performance resulting from all operating costs. Calculated on an identical basis to the management charge *TER* effectively represents an accurate *reduction in yield* (see: *RIY*) over any given period, ignoring the effect of initial expenses.

**total return**   The total benefit from an *investment*, the aggregate total of *capital appreciation*, *dividend* and *interest* payments. All *income* and *growth* added together.

**tourist rate**   See: *exchange rate*.

**toxic asset**   An *investment* that has become significantly less valuable since its creation and whilst not becoming a *liability* has certainly become an embarrassment. Can be a non-*investment grade* bond, speculative grade *bond* or *junk bond*; but has most recently become a *CMO* or *CDO* which contains an element of *sub-prime mortgage* collateralisation which triggered the *Credit Crunch* and was targeted by TARP and other bail-out measures. See: *Credit Crunch, TARP, sub-prime mortgage*.

**TPAS**   See: *The Pensions Advisory Service.*

**TPE**   *currency code* for: Timor Escudo.

**TPI**   See: *Tax and Prices Index.*

**TPR**   See: *The Pensions Regulator.*

**tracker fund**   Synonymous with: *index fund.*

**trade balance**   See: *balance of trade.*

**trade barrier**   See: *protectionism, tariff.*

**trade bill**   A *bill of exchange* used to pay for goods normally forming part of international trade and normally underwritten by a *bank*. These are usually held to maturity or exchanged for other *bills*.

**trade bloc**   Group of countries that have established special trading arrangements.

**trade cycle**   More commonly referred to as: *business cycle.*

**trade deficit**   An excess of visible *imports* over visible *exports* in a country's *balance of trade*. Tends to worsen the nation's *balance of payments*. See also: *trade surplus.*

**trade gap**   The difference in local *currency* between the goods and services imported and those exported. *Imports* and *exports* are normally divided between trade goods and *invisibles* (tourism, *insurance*, etc.) the latter being more difficult to measure.

**trade mark** A distinctive logo, name, phrase or symbol that is identified with a *company* or its product. It is classified as an intangible *asset* in a *company*'s *balance sheet*. 1. Trade marks in the *UK* must be registered with the Registrar of Trade Marks at the *Patent Office*. Exclusivity lasts for an initial period of seven years, and is renewable after that period. Parties that violate the trade mark may be sued in civil court. Remedy can be obtained through *injunction* and/or damages. 2. Trade marks in the *US* must be registered with the *US* Patent and Trademark Office. Exclusivity lasts for twenty years and is renewable.

**trade surplus** An excess of visible *exports* over visible *imports* in a country's *balance of trade*. Tends to improve the nation's *balance of payments*. See also: *trade deficit*.

**trade tariffs** See: *tariff*.

**trade theory** Any economic theory that attempts to explain the *pattern* and composition of trade existing between countries using a set of simplified assumptions and assertions. The theory of *absolute advantage* was superseded by the theory of *comparative advantage*, then in turn progress was made with the *Heckscher-Ohlin theory* and its corollaries though no completely satisfying theory has yet been established.

**Trade Union Congress (TUC)** In the *UK*, the *TUC* represents member trade unions when negotiating with government and employers' organisations.

**trade war** A situation in which a group of countries that trade with each other engage in policies that attempt to reduce competing *imports* and increase *exports*. The effect of these policies usually backfires on the participating nations, as reduced trade has negative effects on the whole group. See: *beggar my neighbour policy*, *protectionism*.

**trade-weighted index** An *index* of the (effective) *exchange rate* of a certain country's *currency* in terms of its (nominal) *exchange rate* with a 'basket' of other countries it trades with, the other countries' rates being weighted in terms of the share of total trade they have with the country in question. See: *effective exchange rate*.

**Traded Endowment Policies** *Endowment* or *with-profits life assurance* policies that, instead of being surrendered, are sold by intermediary traders or at *auction* to investors who will take on the *premiums* and reap the full benefits of the policy on maturity. Policies surrendered early are subject to occasionally severe penalties, and policyholders may be able to get more by selling them through a firm specialising in the sale of secondhand policies by *assignment*.

**traded option** An *option* which itself has an *intrinsic value* and is quoted in the traded *options* market. Compare: *traditional option*.

**trading account** See: *financial year*.

**trading curb** See: *curb*.

**trading currency** A freely convertible *currency* accepted as a medium of exchange for international trade. See also: *convertibility*, *hard currency*, *reserve currency*.

**trading pattern** See: *channel trend*.

**trading pit** See: *pit*.

**trading profits** The *profit* of a *company* after the deduction of financial items such as *interest*, *director*'s remuneration and *auditors*' fees.

**traditional option** An *option* taken in a *share* on the *stock exchange* which, unlike a 'traded option', relates to a specific number of underlying *shares* on which *brokerage* and *stamp duty* must be payable. The *option* itself cannot be traded, and for any *profit* to arise it needs to be exercised. See also: *exercise notice*, *exercise price*, *expiry date*.

**tranche**  Derived from the French word meaning: 'slice'. 1. One round of a succession of issues of a *fixed interest security*, as prearranged by the issuing institution. A '*tranchette*' is a small issue of *gilts* sold by the government. 2. An instalment in the payment or allocation of a large loan, or other sum of *money* for a particular purpose. 3. In the *US*, a category into which a *collateralised mortgage obligation* (*CMO*) or a *REMIC* is divided. For instance, a 'C tranche' *CMO* represents a slow pay *bond*.

**tranche CD**  A *certificate of deposit* (*CD*) which is a sub-unit of a much larger *CD*. Apart from their smaller size, they are identical to the larger *CD* (ie the same *interest rate*, issue date, maturity etc.).

**tranche funding**  Successive rounds of finance available on a prearranged basis and dependent on the *company* reaching certain predetermined business targets.

**tranchette**  See under: *tranche*.

**transfer club**  A group of *pension* scheme providers (employers and institutions) which has agreed to a common basis for transfer payments. In the UK, most transfer clubs are found in the public sector.

**transfer deed**  Also known as: *stock transfer form*. This document must be signed by the seller of a registered *stock* to legalise the transfer of *shares*. See also: *CREST*.

**transfer of value**  The accumulated *cash value* of a *pension* that can be transferred from previous employment to a new *pension* fund. The *value* is calculated by an *actuary* and is normally transferred to the new employer's scheme, a *Section 32 bond* or a *personal pension* transfer plan.

**transfer pricing**  In theory a multi-national company can minimise its tax liability by routing sales through low cost countries and transferring goods from high tax countries to low tax countries at cost. In practice many governments, including the UK's, have detailed anti-avoidance rules aimed at countering this tax avoidance-inspired process, which is known as transfer pricing.

**transfer value payment**  An amount paid from one *pension* scheme to another (or to an *insurance company*) into a *buyout policy* in lieu of contributions already accrued.

**transitional relief**  The introduction of the *simplified regime* in April 2006 could have meant some pension arrangements suddenly attracted tax penalties. Special transitional arrangements were introduced to prevent a *lifetime allowance charge* being triggered or maximum *tax-free cash* reduced. See: *Enhanced protection, primary protection*.

**Treasury**  The Treasury (HM Treasury) is the *United Kingdom's* economics and finance ministry. It is responsible for formulating and implementing the government's financial and economic policy. Its stated aim is 'to raise the rate of sustainable growth, and achieve rising prosperity and a better quality of life with economic and employment opportunities for all'.

**Treasury bill**  A *bill of exchange* issued in the primary *money market* by the government (through the *Bank of England*) and repayable in three months. They are issued by *tender* every week in very large amounts to the *discount houses*.

**Treasury bond**  Negotiable *debt instruments* (*fixed interest securities*) issued by the *US* government and free of state and local, but not federal, taxes. Normally with initial maturities of ten years or longer that are issued in minimum denominations of $1,000 or more. American equivalent to *UK gilts*. See: *Dutch auction*.

**Treasury model**  Econometric equations were used by HM *Treasury* from the late 1950s, and in the 1970s these equations were combined to form a macroeconomic model with 200 variables. With improvements in computing power and the need to provide more detail, the model was expanded until it became unwieldy and in 1989 the number of variables was reduced from 1,275 to 530. It was subsequently further reduced. The module is also used by the Ernst and Young ITEM club (Independent Treasury Economic Model).

**Treasury stock** See: *gilts, government securities.*

**trend** The overall direction of a price move, measured over the short, medium or *long term.* See: *trendline.*

**trendline** Line used in *technical analysis* showing the general movement of the price over a certain time period. It is sometimes quite difficult to draw a trendline because any long-term price movement will have several different *trends* for various periods. A rising *trend* ('uptrend') is usually drawn underneath the *chart pattern*, whereas a falling *trend* ('downtrend') is normally drawn above the *chart pattern.* A sidewise is drawn under-

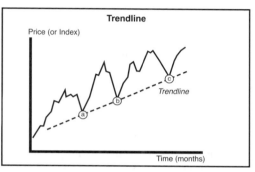

neath the *trend.* There should be at least three points of contact with the line (shown by a, b, and c on the diagram). Close attention should be paid when a price breaks through the trendline, as there should be a reversal (ie a move in a different direction). A reversal from a downtrend is substantiated when the price passes the level of the previous peak; a reversal from an uptrend is indicated when the price moves beyond the level of the previous trough.

**Treynor measure** See: *performance appraisal.*

**trial balance** A method of checking the accuracy of accounting totals by adding up all the debit items on one side and all the credit items on the other. In double-entry bookkeeping these totals must be equal, otherwise an error has been made.

**triangle** A triangle is a *chart* formation used in *technical analysis.* They are so-called because of the appearance of the envelope on the *chart pattern.* They usually occur as two envelope lines converging (to the right). Occasionally, however, they consist of two lines joined at the left and diverging – these are called inverted (or 'broadening') triangles. The triangles are classified as either right-angled (where one side is practically horizontal) or symmetrical triangles.

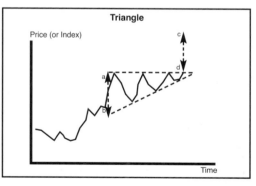

- Ascending triangle – Belongs to the class of right-angled triangles. Here the top line is horizontal and the other line slants upwards towards a vertex at the right (see diagram). The ascending triangle can occur in both uptrends and downtrends. In either case, the resulting outlook after the ascending triangle formation is bullish, with the expected *breakout* through the horizontal line. The resulting *chart* movement is expected to carry on at least as far as the distance of the broadest part of the triangle (ab = cd).

- Descending triangle – Belongs to the class of right-angled triangles. Can occur within an uptrend or a downtrend. A descending triangle is characterised by a horizontal bottom line with the upper side slanting downward towards an intersection point to the right. The prospective outlook is *bearish*, with the expected *breakout* through the horizontal side. The movement is expected to carry on at least the same distance as the broadest side of the triangle.

- Symmetrical triangle – Also called: 'coil'. The boundary lines must slant in different directions to meet at a point to the right, ie one upward and the other downward, otherwise the formation would be called a *wedge*. Trade *volume* tends to fall during the formation. The formation could be a reversal or a *continuance pattern*. When the *pattern* breaks out, it is expected to continue at least the same distance as the widest part of the triangle.

- Inverted right-angled triangle – Also called: 'right-angled broadening triangle'. These usually have *bearish* implications regardless of which side is horizontal, ie whether they are inverted ascending or descending triangles. The *chart* movement after *breakout* (once affirmed by a 3% move beyond *breakout*) is at least as big as the distance between the sides of the triangle. See: *broadening top*.

- Inverted symmetrical triangle – Lines are diverging, otherwise this formation carries the same implications as the symmetrical triangle. See: *broadening top*.

**trickle-down effect** See: *supply-side economics*.

**trillion** 1,000 *billion* or a million million (this used to be a *billion* before American usage was adopted – see: *billion*).

**trin** A measure of the strength of a *stock market*. It is equal to the *advance decline ratio* (ie the number of issues *companies* that went up in price divided by the number of issues *companies* that went down in price) over the advance volume-decline *volume ratio* (ie the total number of *shares* that went up in price divided by the total number of *shares* that went down in price).

$$\text{trin} = \frac{\text{advance} + \text{decline}}{\text{advance volume} + \text{decline volume}}$$

A trin of below unity is considered bullish, whereas a trin of above unity is regarded as an *indicator* of a *bearish* market.

**trinh** *Currency* sub-unit of *Vietnam*. 1000 trinh = 1 *dong*.

**Trinidad & Tobago** The Trinidad & Tobago Stock Exchange was established in 1981. The number of *listed shares* in 2009 was 32. The main *index* is:

- Trinidad & Tobago Stock Exchange Composite Index. Base: Jan 1983 = 100.

Standard *currency*: Trinidad & Tobago *dollar*. 1 *dollar* = 100 *cents*.

**triple witching hour** An event on *Wall Street* normally occurring on the third Friday of the final month of each quarter when considerable market *volatility* can occur. Caused by complicated *arbitrage* strategies involving contrary purchase of *actuals* and *futures*. The phenomenon is the result of the simultaneous expiry of the S&P futures contract, the S&P 100 index option and option contracts on individual stocks. A similar situation arises in the UK where the FTSE expiry is an intra-day event (between 10.10 and 10.30 am). There is now also a quadruple witching hour, thanks to the introduction of the individual stock futures.

**TRL** *currency code* for: Turkish Lira.

**troy weight**  The measure of weight used for precious metals and gems. A troy ounce is equal to 31.1035 metric grammes.

**trust**  1. An arrangement set up under a *trust deed* to look after the property or *investments* of other persons. The *trustees* are the legal owners of the *assets*, but are obliged to use the *assets* for the benefit of the other persons, called the *'beneficiaries'*. This may not necessarily entail the management of the *assets* but the trust will be responsible for such management. See: *discretionary trust, client account, unit trust*. 2. In the *US*, a form of corporate *monopoly* in which a small *board* of *trustees* were given the *voting rights* of a number of *companies* by their owners to further their interests. They were common until the creation of antitrust laws in the late 19th and early 20th century.

**trust bank**  A type of Japanese *bank* ('shintaka ginko') that carries out banking and *trust* activities and acts as a savings institution.

**trust corporation**  A *company* empowered under the Public Trustee Act 1906 to act as *custodian trustee* and which is expected to provide professional expertise in managing *trusts*.

**trust deed**  The *trust deed* is a document under *seal* which lays down the terms of a *trust*. It deals with the *investment* aims, the areas allowed for *investment*, the minimum *liquidity* level required, the ways in which *income* and *capital* can be distributed, the *beneficiaries* and other relevant applications for the monies contained in the *trust*. See: *trustee investment*.

**trustee**  An individual, group of people or independent institution responsible for the management of the *trust* as defined by the *trust deed*. The trustees have the power to veto any *investment* which they feel does not adhere to the *trust deed*.

**trustee in bankruptcy**  The *administrator* of the *estate* of a *bankrupt* party, in order that the proceeds of the *estate* be divided among the *creditors*.

**trustee investment**  Unless otherwise specified, *trustees* must follow *investment* policies laid down by the Trustee Act 2000 (in England and Wales). The Act removed the restrictions on trustee investment imposed by the Trustee Investments Act 1961 and allowed trustees to choose any suitable investments, subject to taking appropriate advice where necessary.

**TT**  See: *telegraphic transfer*. See also: *bank transfer*.

**TTD**  *currency code* for: Trinidad and Tobago Dollar.

**TUC**  See: *Trade Union Congress*.

**tugrik**  *Mongolia*'s standard *currency*. 1 tugrik = 100 *möngös*.

**Tunisia**  The Tunis Stock Exchange (Bourse des Valeurs Mobilières de Tunis – BVMT) was established in 1969. The number of *listed shares* in 2009 was 51. Its main *index* is:

- TUNIDEX. Comprises 44 *stocks*. Capitalisation weighted absolute return index. Base: 1 April 1998 = 1,000.

Standard *currency*: dinar. 1 *dinar* = 1,000 milliemes.

**Turkey**  The Istanbul Stock Exchange (ISE, established 1986) has its roots in the first *securities* market of the Ottoman Empire (Dersaadet Securities Exchange) which was established after the Crimean War in 1866. Its main *indices* are:

- ISE National 100 Index. Comprises 100 *companies*, reviewed quarterly. Adjusted for *capital* increases through *rights issue*. Float-capitalisation weighted. Base: 1986 = 100.

Standard *currency*: Turkish lira. 1 *lira* = 100 *kurus*.

**Turkmenistan**  Standard *currency*: manat. 1 *manat* = 100 tenge.

**Turks and Caicos Islands** Dependency of the *UK*. Standard *currency* is the *US dollar*.

**turn** Also called: *margin*. This is the difference between the price at which a *market maker* will buy a *share* (*bid* price) and sell it (*offer price*); thus the *market maker*'s *profit*.

**turnkey contract** Where the contractor has complete responsibility for the entire *contract*, payment for which will only become due when the project is completely finished – when all you need to do is 'turn the key'.

**turnover** 1. The total sales (ie revenue) of a *company net* of *discounts* and *taxes* on the revenue in a certain period, usually one year. 2. The total *value* (ie number of transactions times their price) in a market in a certain period, usually one trading day, though some markets specify that turnover relates to number of *shares* or the number of *bargains*. See also: *Normal Market Size, volume*.

**Turquoise** A *Multilateral Trading Facility* based in London and owned by nine investment banks: BNP Paribas, Citigroup, Credit Suisse, Deutsche Bank, Goldman Sachs, Merrill Lynch, Morgan Stanley, Société Générale Corporate & Investment Banking and UBS.

**Tuvalu** Standard *currency*: *dollar*. 1 *dollar* = 100 *cents*.

**TWD** *currency code* for: *Taiwan* Dollar.

**two-tier tender offer** An American *takeover* strategy comprising of an initial *offer* for a *controlling interest*, usually in *cash*, followed by an *offer* to acquire the remainder of the *stock* at a lower price. This would usually be in some form of paper or a combination of *shares* and *cash*. *Bidders* use this technique in the hope that *shareholders* will stampede to sell at the initial, higher *cash* price. Restricted in the *US* by *fair price provisions*. In the *UK* regulations ensure that the same price was available to all *shareholders* once the initial *offer* secured control and the *offer* became unconditional. See: *bootstrap*.

**two-timing** Where a banker acting on behalf of a client in a conventional capacity has a merchant banking arm acting for an unwelcome *bidder*. An awkward situation for a *bank* who is paid by both parties to the *takeover*, normally resulting in the *target company* finding new bankers

**TZS** *currency code* for: Tanzanian Shilling.

# U

**UAE**  See: *United Arab Emirates*.

**UAG**  *currency code* for: *Ukraine* Hryvnia.

**uberrimae fidei**  'Utmost good faith', applies mainly in insurance where a contract is made on the basis that the proposal (details provided by the insured) is accurate and that all relevant information has been disclosed. If it subsequently turns out that pertinent information has been deliberately and knowingly withheld the contract is likely to be invalidated.

**UCITS**  See: *Undertaking for Collective Investments in Transferable Securities*.

**Uganda**  Standard *currency*: shilling. 1 *shilling* = 100 *cents*.

**UGS**  *currency code* for: *Uganda* Shilling.

**UIP**  See: *uncovered interest parity*.

**UITF**  See: *Urgent Issues Task Force*.

**UK**  See: *United Kingdom*.

**UK Balance of Payments**  An *Office for National Statistics* (*ONS*) publication, containing detailed *balance of payments accounts*. Published yearly. Also known as the '*Pink Book*'.

**UK National Accounts**  An *Office for National Statistics* (*ONS*) publication, containing a breakdown of *gross domestic product* estimates. Appears monthly. Also called the '*Blue Book*'.

**Ukraine**  Standard *currency*: hryvnia.

**ULS**  See: *unsecured loan stock*.

**ultra vires**  'Beyond the powers'. Means that a certain act of an official or organisation is outside the scope of his power. *Companies* acting ultra vires (that is, outside the scope of their *Memorandum of Association*) can be sued in court.

**umbrella funds**  Unitised collective *investment funds* (see: *collective investment scheme*), issuing *shares* of various *classes* to allow investors participation in various *investment sectors*. Originally found offshore but structure is now common for UK OEICs. See also: *subfund*.

**unamortised cost**  The original or revalued cost of an *asset* less total *depreciation* to date and therefore equivalent to the current *value* of *assets* in the *balance sheet* or their present *book value*.

**unbundling**  A term referring to selling off the peripheral business of a *conglomerate* to pay (in part) for its *takeover* or a *break-up bid*. Also refers to any exercise where charging is broken down into constituent components.

**uncalled capital**  Also called: *reserve capital*.

**uncertificated units**  Very few collective fund groups now issue unit certificates or share certificates. The result is that holdings are uncertificated. The investor's proof of purchase is their contract note.

**unconditional bid**  In a *takeover* attempt, an unconditional bid is an *offer* made by the bidding *company* that indicates it will pay the offered price irrespective of the number of *shares* that will be thus acquired, ie whether or not a *controlling interest* in the *target company* is thus gained. Contrast: *conditional bid*. A *bid* also becomes unconditional once the majority of *shareholders* have accepted whereupon the *bidder* is obliged to accept *shares* at the price offered in the *bid*. See: *City Code on Takeovers and Mergers*.

**unconscionable bargain** See: *catching bargain.*

**uncovered interest parity (UIP)** A condition that holds between the *interest rates* of two countries and their mutual *exchange rate*. Assuming that (i) *capital* is 'perfectly mobile' between the two countries (A and B), ie investors can invest instantly in either country without difficulties, and (ii) *bonds* are considered to be equally risky in both countries, this condition must hold. The *UIP* condition merely reflects the fact that under these circumstances the expected rates of return on the *bonds* should be the same. Thus if the *interest rate* in say country A ($r_A$) is higher than the *interest rate* of country B ($r_B$), then the difference in *interest rates* ($r_A - r_B$) must be matched by an equivalent expected percentage *depreciation* of country A's *currency* (with respect to B's *currency*). Thus the equation is: expected *depreciation* of A's *currency* = $r_A - r_B$. Obviously, if B's *interest rate* is higher than A's, the negative difference implies an expected *appreciation* of A's *currency* (measured in terms of B's *currency*). For example, if the *UK*'s *interest rates* are 5% and those of *Germany* are 3%, the *exchange rate* being €1.10 = £1, then *Sterling* will be expected to depreciate by 5% – 3% = 2% during the year, to an expected *exchange rate* of €1.078 = £1. Compare: *covered interest parity, Fisher Effect.*

**undated stock** A *fixed interest security* which has no *redemption date.*

**underlying asset** See: *underlying security.*

**underlying inflation** Unofficial term that was given to the *inflation* rate in an economy as measured by changes in the *RPI-X*, ie the *Retail Price Index* figures excluding *mortgage interest* payments. The Consumer Prices Index has now taken its place as the measure of underlying inflation, although RPI-X is still calculated. Compare: *headline inflation.*

**underlying security** The *asset* that the holder of an *option*, *futures contract* or *warrant* is entitled to trade.

**Undertaking for Collective Investments in Transferable Securities (UCITS)** A series of EU Directives which enable an open-ended collective (see: *collective investment scheme*) fund to be marketed in any *EU* country. See: *MiFID.*

**undervalued** An *investment* which *fundamental analysis* estimates to be worth more than its current *market value*. Contrast: *overvalued.*

**underwrite** An *issuing house* will underwrite a *flotation*, *rights issue*, *placing* or new issue, for a *commission*, as a guarantee that the *shares* will be taken up even if the issue is not fully subscribed by existing *shareholders* or the public. Underwriters are obliged to buy all such *shares* not taken up by the public. See also: *flotation, sponsor*. Also someone who covers a *risk* in an *insurance* market to assess risk and premium for insurance. See also: *writer.*

**underwriter** See: *underwrite.*

**underwriting agreement** The agreement between the *underwriter* (see: *underwrite*), the *directors*, the *vendors* of *shares* and the *company* which deals with the underwriting of a *flotation, rights issue, placing* or new issue. This agreement normally contains *warranties* by the *company*, its *directors* and the *vendors* as to information on the *company* disclosed in the *prospectus*. More generally, it covers indemnities to the *company* and the *sponsor* by the *directors* and the *vendors* in relation to the *company*'s *tax* position and other matters. Also called a *placing* agreement.

**underwriting commission** *Commission* paid to the *underwriter* (see: *underwrite*) for entering into the *underwriting agreement*, normally at the rate of 2% for an *offer for sale* (0.75% in the case of a *placing*) out of which the *underwriter* will pay *commission* to the *stockbrokers* of 0.25% and *commission* of 1.25% to any sub-underwriters.

**undischarged bankrupt** A person whose bankruptcy (see: *bankrupt*) has not been discharged or who still has outstanding obligations.

**undistributable reserves** These are known under the Companies Act 2006 as *reserves* not distributed to *shareholders* as *dividends*. They include *profits* from the *revaluation* of *assets* in the *revaluation* reserve account and *profits* made on the issue of *shares* above *par value* recorded in the *share premium account*. See: *reserves*.

**undue influence** A court can decide to deem a *contract* invalid if completed as a result of excessive pressure or coercion.

**unearned income** *Income* that does not arise from employment and includes *dividends*, *bank* and *building society interest*, *income* from *trusts* and rents from property *investments*.

**unemployment rate** The *Office for National Statistics* (*ONS*) produces official estimates of unemployment using the International Labour Organisation (ILO) definition. Under this definition people aged 16 and over are unemployed if they are:

- out of work, want a job, have actively sought work in the last four weeks and are available to start work in the next two weeks.

- out of work, have found a job and are waiting to start it in the next two weeks.

The unemployment rate is calculated by dividing this number by the total number of employed and unemployed in the population. The ONS also measures claimant count, ie the number of people claiming unemployment-related benefits, which is normally a lower number than the ILO unemployment figure.

**unencumbered** 1. Property and *assets* free and clear of all *liens*. When a homeowner pays off his or her *mortgage*, for example, the house becomes unencumbered property. 2. *Securities* bought with *cash* instead of on *margin* are unencumbered.

**unfettered** Relating to the discretionary powers of an *investment* manager where he or she has both the ability and the capacity to invest in an unrestricted range of *investments* of certain types. See: *authorisation*.

**unfettered fund** A fund of funds in which any fund may be chosen, not just those belonging to the investment management group offering the fund.

**unfranked income** All types of *investment income* other than *franked income*. Franked income is *investment income* paid by UK companies. *Dividends* received from *UK companies* are paid with an accompanying 10% tax credit and are not liable to the further tax for *basic rate income taxpayers*. This net income can be passed on by *unit trusts*, OEICs and *investment trusts* without any further taxation.

**unfunded pension scheme** A *pension* scheme where benefits are met by the employer as they arise, eg *terminal funding*, or where the *pensions* are provided on a *pay-as-you-go* basis.

**unified tax** A *tax* regime that applies equally to all types of *income* or gains. In the UK *income tax* for instance is a unified tax as it applies at the same rate to each level of *income* regardless of its source.

**unilateral relief** *Tax* that need not be paid in the *UK* after it has already been paid in another country, even though the *UK* has no double-taxation agreement with that country. See: *double taxation relief*.

**unissued share capital** The difference between the amount of *share capital* issued (see: *issued capital*) and the authorised *share capital* (see: *authorised capital* ) of a *company*.

**unit of account** Established *currency* unit or sub-unit accepted as legal tender.

**unit trust**  A *trust* formed to manage *securities* on behalf of a number of small investors giving the combined benefits of diversification, security and a sufficient weight of *assets* to ensure cost-effectiveness and merit the attention of leading *fund managers*. The *trustee*, normally a major *bank*, is the legal holder and *custodian* of the *securities* involved and ensures that the *investment* managers adhere to the *trust deed*. UK-based unit trusts are normally authorised and regulated by the *Financial Services Authority*. The FSA rules set various limits on the range and spread of investments that can be held. For example, a fund cannot hold more than 20% of its value in any one other collective fund. Over 700 unit trusts are available in the *UK* designed to invest in different *sectors* throughout the world and provide varying combinations of *growth* and/or *income*. Prices are quoted daily on a bid/offer basis (see: *bid-offer spread*). This *spread* takes into account any *commission* to the intermediary, the manager's charges and the cost of buying and selling the *underlying securities*. The *dividends* payable from *UK* authorised unit trusts are paid with a 10% dividend tax credit or, in the case of fixed interest funds, after the deduction of *basic rate tax*. *Capital gains tax* is chargeable on the realised gains in the hands of the investor. See also: *cancellation price, creation price, forward pricing, historic pricing, initial charges*. The number of unit trusts has shrunk over the years as many existing trusts have converted to OIECs, which now outnumber unit trusts by more than 2:1. In *America*, unit trusts are called: open-ended *mutual funds*.

**unit-linked**  Prior to the 1970s, *profits* on *life assurance* policies were dictated by the addition of *bonuses*. These *bonuses* were to all intents and purposes at the discretion of the *life assurance company* and were based on the combination of their *investment* success or, in the case of *mutual companies*, the profitability of the *company* itself. As a result of the fact that *life assurance* policies were at the time generally highly tax-efficient, a system was introduced where investors could link the *profits* on their policies to individual (*asset backed*) *investment* markets by being allocated a number of units related to a *portfolio* invested in these markets. The *portfolio* was unitised, certain units being granted per policy and the unit price itself being published on a daily basis. Unit-linking gained in popularity in the 1980s and 1990s. It now dominates the investment–oriented life assurance and pensions industry. The choice of funds is now huge, with most major players offering funds which are 'wrappers' for unit trusts and OEICs from a range of management groups. See also: *asset backed, bid-offer spread, capital units*.

**United Arab Emirates (UAE)**  Standard *currency*: *dirham*. 1 *dirham* = 100 *fils*.

**United Kingdom (UK)**  The framework for the regulation of the *UK*'s *securities* markets is provided by the *Financial Services and Markets Act 2000*. A designated agency, called the *Financial Services Authority* (*FSA*), was specifically set up within the Act. The *FSA* is responsible for the whole financial services market. The *FSA* is accountable to Parliament through the Treasury. The *FSA* also regulates the activities of the so-called *Recognised Investment Exchanges* (*RIEs*), the *Designated Professional Bodies* (*DPBs*) and the *Recognised Clearing Houses* (*RCHs*). The main *RIEs* are the *London Stock Exchange, LIFFE Commodity Products, International Petroleum Exchange* of London and *London Metal Exchange*. For relevant *indices*, see *Financial Times Share Indices*.

Standard *currency*: *pound Sterling*. 1 *pound Sterling* = 100 pence. See: *decimalisation*.

**United Kingdom Listing Authority (UKLA)**  The FSA, acting as the competent authority for listing, is referred to as the UK Listing Authority (UKLA), and maintains the *Official List*. The UKLA took over responsibilities for the *Official List* in November 2001 from the *London Stock Exchange*.

**United Nations Common Fund for Commodities (CFC)** Set up in 1989, the *CFC*'s function is to help international *commodity markets* obtain finance and to research the development of *commodity markets*. Currently the Common Fund has 107 member countries plus the *European Union (EU)*, the African Union (AU) and the Common Market for Eastern and Southern Africa (COMESA). The Common Fund is an intergovernmental financial institution. The rationale of the Common Fund's mandate is to enhance the socio-economic development of *commodity* producers and contribute to the development of society as a whole. In line with its market-oriented approach, the Fund concentrates on *commodity* development projects financed from its resources (voluntary contributions, *interest* earned, part of *capital* subscription). Through co-operation with other development institutions, the *private sector* and civil society, the Fund endeavours to achieve overall efficiency and impact in *commodity* development.

**United States (US)** All *investment* activity is regulated by the *Securities and Exchange Commission*. The main *stock exchanges* in the *US* are: *New York Stock Exchange (NYSE)*, *NASDAQ* Stock Market and the *American Stock Exchange (AMEX)* which was acquired by the NYSE in 2008. Other *stock markets* are: Chicago Stock Exchange, and the Philadelphia Stock Exchange (now part of NASDAQ).

Other major markets are: *Chicago Board Options Exchange (CBOE)*, *Chicago Board of Trade (CBoT)*, *Chicago Mercantile Exchange (CME)*, *New York Cotton Exchange (NYCE)* and the *New York Mercantile Exchange (NYMEX)*. Important *indices* are: *Dow Jones Stock Averages, Standard & Poor's 500 Index*, and the main *stock market indices* (see under the *stock exchange* name).

Standard *currency*: US dollar. 1 *US dollar* = 100 *cents*.

**unitisation** Where a *collective investment scheme* divides its *assets* into a number of units which are then allocated to investors in proportion to their original *investment*. This can also apply to an *investment trust* or investment company which can reduce its *discount* to *net asset value (NAV)* by turning itself into a *unit trust*, thus ensuring that its *assets* are valued on a *NAV* basis rather than by the market.

**unlimited company** Incorporated bodies, normally *partnerships*, where the ultimate liability for the body and its debts rests with the principals personally without limitation.

**unlimited liability** A *sole trader* or a *partnership* is liable for all the debts and liabilities incurred in the business. *Option writers* also have no limit to their liability when writing a *naked option*.

**unlimited losses** In some *investment* forms, the amount one can lose as a result of investing may be larger than the initial amount invested. For example, this can happen when writing *options* or trading *futures* on *margin*.

**unlisted investment** An *investment* in a *share* or a collective *investment* which is not recognised either by the *Securities and Investments Board* or quoted on a *Recognised Investment Exchange*.

**Unlisted Securities Market (USM)** Introduced in 1980 and dissolved at the end of 1996, the *USM* was a market for *shares* in *companies* who could not or did not wish to fulfil the requirements of or go to the expense of a full *London Stock Exchange quotation*. Replaced by the *Alternative Investment Market (AIM)*.

**unmatched book** A *portfolio* in which the *maturity dates* of *investment assets* differ from the *maturity dates* of liabilities.

**unquoted securities** See: *unlisted investment, over-the-counter*.

**unsecured creditor** An unpaid supplier or contractor owed *money* by a *company* in the event of a *liquidation*.

**unsecured debenture** A *debenture* or *loan stock* which is not secured on a particular *asset* or *sinking fund* or *general undertaking* other than a promise to pay and which ranks with *unsecured creditors* in the event of non-payment.

**unsecured debt** Debt that is not backed up by any *assets* as guarantee for payment.

**unsecured income** The HMRC term for any method of drawing retirement income from a pension arrangement that does not involve an annuity or a scheme pension. The most common example is *income drawdown*.

**unsecured loan stock** See: *unsecured debenture*.

**unsystematic risk** See under: *risk*.

**up tick** A transaction in a *security* made at a higher price than the preceding one in the same *security*. See: *tick*. Contrast: *down tick*.

**upper band earnings** *Pensionable earnings* between the lower and the upper accrual point (fixed at £770 per week) *earnings* limit on which the *state second pension scheme* is based.

**upside potential** Resulting from the *analysis* of an *investment* form (eg *shares*, *commodities*), the upside potential refers to the expected rise in price of that *investment*.

**Urgent Issues Task Force (UITF)** Subsidiary of the *Accounting Standards Board* (*ASB*), whose function is to assist the *ASB* in accounting issues where there are accounting standards (*Statements of Standard Accounting Practice* or *Financial Reporting Standards*) or Companies Act provisions, but where these give rise to or are likely to give rise to unsatisfactory or conflicting interpretations. In addition the *ASB* may use the *UITF* in areas of significant developments where no accounting standards or statutory provisions exist. The *UITF* issues 'Abstracts' which must be adhered to by *companies* in such cases in order for their *accounts* to give a 'true and fair view'. See: *accounting concepts, audit*.

**Uruguay** Standard *currency*: *peso*. 1 *peso* = 100 *centésimos*.

**US** See: *United States*.

**US Treasury bill** This is a discounted *money market instrument* issued by the *United States* Federal Reserve with a maturity of up to 1 year (usually 3, 6, or 12 months).

**US Treasury Bond** A *US* government *bond* issue of over 10 years original maturity (up to 30 years).

**US Treasury note** A *US* government *bond* issue of from 1 to 10 years original maturity (usually a 2, 3, 5, or 10-year issue)

**USA** See: *United States*.

**usance** The period which it takes to honour a foreign *bill of exchange*. See: *forfaiting*.

**USD** *currency code* for: *US* Dollar.

**USM** See: *Unlisted Securities Market*.

**usury** The lending of *money* at extortionate rates of *interest*.

**utility** A theoretical economic concept for the amount of pleasure or satisfaction a consumer derives from the consumption of a particular good or service, the unit of which is called 'util'.

**UYP** *currency code* for: Uruguayan Peso.

**Uzbekistan** Standard *currency*: sum.

**UZS** *currency code* for: *Uzbekistan* sum.

# V

**vacancy rate** The *ratio* of the number of available jobs which remain unfilled to the total available *labour force*. Since not all available jobs are notified to the authorities (ie local employment centres or job centres), the actual vacancy rate is greater than the official rate. See: *unemployment*.

**validation** 1. Used to describe the action of government authorities sustaining ongoing *inflation* by increasing the *money supply*. 2. Confirming a transaction or checking *certificated stock*.

**valorisation** The artificial but legitimate manipulation or *fixing* of a price or *value* of a *commodity* or *currency* at a certain level, usually undertaken by a government authority. See: *buffer stock*, *intervention*.

**valuation** 1. A summary of an *investment portfolio* showing the *values* and costs as at a given date. 2. In *property valuation*, there are five conventional methods of valuation (of which the comparative and *investment* methods are most frequently used):

- Comparative method – This method entails making valuations based on comparison with similar properties recently sold. Various considerations must be borne in mind as to the differences in the properties in comparison, and these differences must be measured in monetary terms. It is probably the most widely used method and even if the valuer uses one of the other four methods, he or she will most often apply this method as a check.

- Contractor's cost method – This method is used only to *value* the types of properties that are not bought and sold on the market. This method of valuation is based on the assumption that cost and *value* are related. Basically the method involves calculating the cost of the site plus the cost of rebuilding to give the *value* of the land and buildings as one unit. Deductions for *depreciation*, dilapidation and obsolescence are made. This method is used mostly on public buildings such as libraries, schools and hospitals.

- Development residual method – This method is used when a property has development or redevelopment potential. Often used when residential properties to be valued are considered to have latent *value* which could be realised if *money* were spent on improvement and modernisation. The basic approach is to estimate the *value* of the completed development ('*gross* realisation') and then subtract one's estimate of total expenditure on improvements and developments to give the *value* of the site or property in its present condition (the 'residual *value*').

- Accounts profits method – This method is based on the assumption that the *value* of some trading properties (other than normal shops) is related to the *profits* which can be made from their use. Not normally used if there is recourse to the comparison method, and is generally used only where there is some degree of *monopoly* attached to a property. The basic approach involves calculating *gross earnings* less purchases (= *gross profit*) less working expenses (except rent) giving the *net profit*. This *net profit* is then split into an amount due to the tenant's enterprise and the amount available for rent. Normally used in the valuation of hotels and pubs, and sometimes for cinemas and theatres. It is regularly used in rating valuation (see: *rates*).

- Investment method – This method is based on the principle that annual *values* (*income*) and *capital values* are related to each other by a factor called the '*yield*' (also called: *Years Purchase*), ie:

**capital value × yield = income**

The *yield* can be mathematically calculated from expected future *income* flows via *discounted cash flow* techniques or similar methods. If the *income* flows from rents are not known, the rental *value* can be predicted by comparison with similar properties that have been let.

**value** Economic concept of what a good, service, *asset* or the like is worth in monetary terms. Some early economists (eg Adam Smith, David Ricardo) emphasised the importance of 'supply' considerations, that is the value of a good depends on the amount of labour (and other *factors of production*) consumed in its production. Later economists (such as William Jevons) emphasised 'demand' factors, ie subjective considerations of the value of a good as in how much *utility* one can gain from it. In general, economists today widely accept that both demand and supply factors interact to produce a market price of a good and that price represents its value. Value in *investment* terms is often relative and usually determined by *analysis*.

**value added** The difference between the *value* of the 'output' and the cost of the related 'inputs' in the production of a good or service. For example, a product such as a car goes through a number of steps from raw material stage to finished product in which *value* is added at each stage.

**value added tax (VAT)** An indirect *tax* levied on the *value added* in the production of a good or service, from primary production to final consumption. The method of payment of *VAT* is best explained with a simple example: say a good goes through three different stages at three different firms (A, B and C) until it can be sold to the final consumer. Let *VAT* be 10%. Firm A starts the production chain, and from initial resources, adds £500 of *value* to the good. The output *value* of the good is thus £500, which firm A sells to firm B for £550, which is £500 + £50 *VAT*. The £50 *VAT* that firm A collects is remitted to the government. Firm B, in turn, adds £300 of *value* to the good, whose output *value* is then £800 (= £500 + £300). Firm B sells the good on to firm C for £880 (= £800 + £80 *VAT*). Firm B can offset the £50 *input tax* paid against the £80 *output tax* collected, and remits the difference of £30 to the government (which equals the *tax* on the *value added* at that stage). Similarly, firm C adds £200 of *value* to the good, whose output *value* is then £1,000 (= £800 + £200). The good is sold on to the final consumer, who is at the end of the chain, for £1,100 (= £1,000 + £100 *VAT*). Firm C offsets the £100 *output tax* received from the consumer against the £80 *input tax* paid to firm B, and remits the difference of £20 (the £20 being 10% of the *value added* at that stage). Thus in total the government receives payment from each stage at which *value* is added: £50 + £30 + £20= £100 total *VAT* for the good. This amount is borne in full by the consumer. In practice, the firms do not offset *output tax* received against *input tax* paid, but remit the full amount of output *VAT* to HMRC, and subsequently reclaim the *input tax* paid. In the *UK*, housing, books, education, health services, basic foods, *exports* and some financial services are excluded from the *tax*. From April 1991 until 30 November 2008 the main rate of *VAT* was 17.5% in the *UK*. From 1 December the rate was cut to 15% as part of an economic stimulus package. It will revert to 17.5% from 1 January 2010. A lower (5%) rate applies to a limited range of goods, eg domestic fuel.

**value date** 1. The date when an *investment* becomes liquid. 2. The date until which *accrued interest* is added; usually coincides with the *settlement date*, except when the latter is not a business day (in which case the next business day is the settlement day). 3. In the forward exchange market, the next business day after the *maturity date* of the *contract*. See: *redemption date*.

**value driver** An activity or organisational focus which enhances the perceived *value* of a product or service in the perception of the consumer and which therefore creates *value* for the producer. Advanced technology, reliability, or reputation for customer relations can all be value drivers.

**value for money audit** An *audit* of an non-profit-making organisation to establish whether it is efficient and viable.

**value management** An organised effort directed at analysing the functions of goods, processes, and services to achieve those necessary functions and essential characteristics in the most profitable manner. This involves a number of aspects, including a deliberate effort to identify what is being furnished and what the market needs, as opposed to perceived wants. It is used, for example, in engineering production and marketing to define the priority requirements from the point of view of the customer or stakeholder, and includes the product's target selling price. The cost is determined by generating and evaluating a range of alternatives including new concepts, reconfiguration, eliminating or combining items, and modifying process and procedures. This also considers environment, safety, operations and maintenance of the product or process over its normal life expectancy — the cost of ownership. In commerce the end results must satisfy the intended business purpose such as timeliness of development, compatibility with other product lines, resources, market share, *growth*, and after-market. It essentially describes attributes as seen from the customers' sense of *value* and has recently been applied to Value Investing where *share* prices are assessed in terms purely of the potential return to investors rather than from a technical or fundamental basis.

**value of money** See: *purchasing power*.

**value transferred** When determining the *value* of the transfer of an *asset* for inheritance tax purposes one has to look at the loss to the *donor* rather than the *value* to the recipient. When a gratuitous transfer (ie a gift ) has been made by an individual, the *value* of the gift is deemed to be the amount by which the *donor*'s (giver's) *estate* is made less.

**vanilla** Plain, uncoloured, with no extras or unusual features, used to describe financial *instruments* when they are essentially at their most basic, without bells or whistles – the opposite of *exotics*.

**Vanuatu** Standard *currency: vatu*.

**variable costs** Costs, such as raw material costs, that change depending on the volume of a company's production. Variable costs plus fixed costs make up total costs.

**variable rate mortgage** A type of *mortgage* agreement in which, according to variations in the market rates, the *interest rate* of the *mortgage* is varied by the lender.

**variable rate security** A type of *security* whose *interest rate* varies in line with market rates. See also *eurobonds, floating rate notes*.

**variance** 1. In statistics, when speaking of a certain variable, variance is a measure of *spread* (or *volatility*) of its *values*. The *values* form a distribution and the variance indicates how far the *values* generally are from the *mean* position. If the variable is say, x, the variance of the variable x is the '*mean* of the square of the deviations from the *mean*'. Explaining this definition part by part:

- Deviations from the *mean* are ($x_i$ – X), where X is the *mean* of the x-values, and $x_i$ is one of the *values*.
- Squares of the deviations ($x_i$ – X)$^2$ are taken so that *values* further from the *mean* count for more in the calculation and to eliminate negative *values*.
- Then the *mean value* of these squares of deviations is taken to find the *average* 'dispersion'; this is the variance.

So the formula is (for n *values*):

$$\text{var}(x) = \text{mean of } (x_i - X)^2 = \frac{1}{n} \sum_{i=1}^{i=n} (x_i - X)^2$$

Furthermore, the variance is the square of the *standard deviation*, which is an alternative measure of *volatility* or dispersion. Variances are used in *quantitative analysis* to calculate *risk*. 2. In accounting, the difference: standard cost (as in the *budget*) minus actual cost. 3. The difference between the anticipated, budgeted, projected amount and the actual amount.

**variance analysis** An accounting term for the *analysis* of the actual costs, *income* or *profits* in relation to what they were budgeted to be. See: *variance* (sense 2).

**variation margin** Refers to *margin* payments for *derivative* transactions. If an investor has a position that is losing *money* they may be asked to deposit a variation margin to cover potential losses and bring their position back to the *margin* requirement.

**VAT** See: *value added tax*.

**Vatican City** Standard *currency*: euro.

**vatu** The standard *currency* of *Vanuatu*.

**VCT** See: *Venture Capital Trust*.

**vega** Used to determine the potential exposure to variables in a *derivatives portfolio* and defined in much the same way as *delta*, as a linear approximation for the *sensitivity* of the *market value* of a *portfolio*. The difference is that *delta* measures *sensitivity* to a specific *underlying asset*; whereas vega measures *sensitivity* to the *volatility* of the *underlying asset*. See: *Greeks*.

**velocity of circulation** The *average* number of times each *money* unit (ie each *pound* in the *UK*) is used to purchase the total output (*GDP*) of the economy in one year. For instance, if *GDP* is £1,500 *billion* and there is a total of £3,100 *billion* in circulation (that is, the total *money supply*), then the velocity is 5. In other words, each £1 unit has 'changed hands' five times on *average* in that year. It is a variable used in macroeconomic theory. See also: *quantity theory of money*.

**vendor** A seller of his or her own property or *shares* as opposed to the agent, who may act on the vendor's behalf.

**vendor placing** A *company* that wishes to acquire another *company*'s business may do so by issuing new *shares* to the latter as a form of payment and/or where these *shares* are pre-sold to a *market maker* to raise the *cash*. In the latter case this can be quicker and/or cheaper than raising *cash* by a *rights issue* or issuing new *capital*. See also: *bought deal*, *placing*.

**Venezuela** The Caracas Stock Exchange (BVC)was established in 1947. The number of *companies listed* in 2007 was 60. The main *index* is:

- Indice Bursatil Caracas (General). It comprises the 17 most actively traded *companies*. Base: January 1971 = 100.

Standard *currency*: bolivar. 1 *bolivar* = 100 centimos.

**venture capital** *Risk capital* offered by individuals or institutions for *investments* in new or developing businesses where the *capital* is provided at least partially in exchange for *shares* (*equity*) in the business rather than as a loan. See: *Venture Capital Trust*.

**Venture Capital Trust (VCT)** A collective *investment* comprising holdings in *shares* of *small companies* and which attracts 30% income tax relief on the purchase of newly issued shares. Dividends are free of tax and gains are free of capital gains tax.

**verification** The procedures which are adopted to confirm the accuracy of statements made in a *prospectus* and to ensure that the view it presents of a *company* is fair and not misleading. Such procedures are designed to ensure that the *directors* of a *company* have discharged their responsibilities in issuing a *prospectus* (and ultimately to protect them), and are normally evidenced by the solicitors to the issue requiring detailed notes or evidence to support all material statements.

**vertical integration** The extent to which a *company* controls the successive stages in production and *distribution*. *Companies* can move 'forward' to integrate retailing and *distribution* (forward integration) or 'backward' to integrate with sources of raw materials (*backward integration*). This may be advantageous for a *company*, since it can eliminate intermediaries' *profit margins* and secure reliable supply of inputs and *distribution* markets for outputs. Compare: *horizontal integration*.

**vertical line charting** A detailed *chart* of the traded prices of a *security* used in *technical analysis*. For each trading day, the *chart* shows the high and low of traded prices (represented by a vertical line), plus the *closing* price (depicted as a short horizontal mark). Technical analysts determine from these *charts* whether a *stock* or a market is continually *closing* at the high or low end of its trading *range* during a day. This is useful in understanding whether the

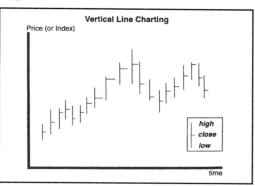

market's action is strong or weak and therefore whether prices will advance or decline in the near future.

**vertical merger** *Merger* between two (or more) *companies* in order to increase their *vertical integration*.

**vertical spread** *Option* strategy that involves purchasing an *option* at one *exercise price* while simultaneously selling another *option* of the same *class* at the next higher or lower *exercise price*. Both *options* have the same expiration date.

**vested benefit** A specific benefit to which a *member* of a *pension* scheme is entitled.

**vested interest** 1. Generally, an involvement in a business or scheme from which an individual expects personal benefit. 2. A legal term referring to the interest of an individual in something (for example, property) subject to the occurrence of an event that is certain to happen, not something that may or may not occur (see: *contingent interest*).

**vested rights** *Pension* rights for active *members* to which they would be entitled unconditionally on leaving service; *preserved benefits* for deferred pensioners and for pensioners the benefits to which they and their dependents are entitled.

**vesting** The accumulated rights acquired by an employee as a result of length of service. This may refer to *pension*, profit-sharing or *share option* benefits.

**vesting date** The date from when an *assurance* policy matures and pays or when an incentive *option* scheme can be exercised or when a *pension* plan can pay out.

**Vietnam** Standard *currency*: *dong*. 1 *dong* = 10 *hao* = 100 *xu*.

**Virgin Islands** Dependency of *US*. Standard *currency*: *US dollar*.

**Virt-X** See: *SWX Europe*.

**visibles** Term used especially with reference to trade, referring to goods that are tangible (ie can be seen), as distinct from *invisibles*, such as services, *investment income* and transfers. In *balance of payments* statistics, the visible account (also called: trade account, merchandise account) measures visible *exports* minus visible *imports* (which equals the *balance of trade*).

**VIX** See: *Chicago Board Options Exchange Volatility Index*.

**VND** *currency code* for: Vietnamese Dong.

**volatility** 1. The *speed* and magnitude of price changes measured over a certain period of time. A price that frequently moves dramatically will be considered to have a high degree of volatility. See: *variance*. 2. Within *bond* markets, 'volatility' refers to interest-rate *risk*.

**volume** Generally this is a term used to denote the quantity of business done; the word *turnover* is used in a similar manner. More specifically, volume is the number of transactions and *turnover* is the *value* (ie price times volume) of transactions, although *turnover* can be specified as the number of *shares* traded or number of *bargains* in some markets. In the *commodity markets* the terms are intermingled, but volume refers to the number of *lots* of soft *commodities* traded and *turnover* to the tonnage of metals on any day.

**voluntary arrangement** An *arrangement* a *company* in financial difficulties enters into with its *creditors* in order to delay or mitigate repayment to avoid *liquidation*. Under the 1986 Insolvency Act, a qualified *insolvency* practitioner must ensure that the parties to the *arrangement* agree and that it is binding. See: *administration, individual voluntary arrangement, members voluntary winding up, voluntary liquidation*.

**voluntary liquidation** Where a *company*'s executives and *shareholders* decide to appoint a liquidator when a *company* can no longer trade profitably, has been the victim of fraud or simply runs out of *cash*. This is perhaps less common than the *company*'s bankers appointing a liquidator and normally occurs when the *company* is still just *solvent*, though a voluntary liquidation does not necessarily mean that the *creditors* and *shareholders* will receive any more *value* than if the *liquidation* was compulsory. The *Insolvency Act 1986* deems it a criminal offence to trade while insolvent and with no genuine expectation of being able to pay *creditors*. See: *insolvency, liquidation, members voluntary winding up*.

**vostro account** A *UK* bank *account* held by a foreign *bank*. The opposite scenario: a foreign *bank account* held by a *UK bank*, is called a *nostro account*.

**voting rights** See: *voting shares*.

**voting shares** Certain *classes* of *share* carry the right for the holder to vote either in person or by *proxy* at *company* meetings. These are normally *ordinary shares* as opposed to 'A' *shares, debentures* or a *fixed interest security*, which are non-voting.

**VUB** *currency code* for: Venezuelan Bolivar.

**VUV** *currency code* for: *Vanuatu* Vatu.

# W

**W formation** Another term for: *double bottom*.

**wage-push inflation** A type of *cost-push inflation* caused by an increase in wages.

**waiter** The name given to messengers at the *London Stock Exchange* and at *Lloyd's* derived from the coffee house origins of these markets.

**Wall Street** 1. Common name for the *New York Stock Exchange* (*NYSE*), which is actually located at the corner of Wall Street and Broad Street. 2. More generally, the term given to the financial district at the lower end of Manhattan in New York City, home of the *New York Stock Exchange* and the *American Stock Exchange*, and numerous *brokerage* firms and other financial institutions.

**Wallis and Futuna Islands** Dependency of *France*. Standard *currency*: *euro*.

**wallpaper** American term for worthless *securities*, as a result of issuing parties going *bankrupt* and defaulting. See: *busted bond*.

**war babies** American jargon for *shares* in *companies* primarily involved in defence contracting. Also called: *war brides*.

**war brides** Another term for: *war babies*.

**war chest** American term describing a fund of *cash* whose primary purpose is to pay for or defend against *takeovers*.

**war loan** A *gilt* issued following the Second World War by the government; the 3½% War Loan has no *redemption date* , although it was supposed to be redeemed after hostilities ceased. Approximately £1.9bn remains in issue.

**warehousing** 1. Holding large amounts of *stock* on a temporary basis to prevent it from being available for sale in the market and depressing the price. 2. In a practice contrary to the *City Code on Takeovers and Mergers*, warehousing is the anonymous accumulation of small *lots* of *shares* prior to a *takeover bid* using *nominees*, in order to avoid making a statutory declaration of interest in the *target company*. See: *Section 212*.

**warrant** A *stock market security* with a quoted market price of its own that can be converted into a specific *share* at a certain predetermined price and date. The *value* of the warrant is therefore determined by the *premium* (if any) of the *share* price over the conversion price of the warrant. Warrants are equivalent to *stock options* in the *US*.

**warranty** Contractual statement made either explicitly (express warranty) or implicitly (implied warranty). If unfulfilled, the *contract* is still valid, but a court may order damages to be paid.

**wash sale** *US* term for the purchase and sale of a *security* either simultaneously or in a short time period by a party wishing to artificially create market activity in that *security* to *profit* from a resulting rise in price.

**watered stock** See: *stock watering*.

**waterfall** Refers to a project or development that is linear and sequential with each phase automatically and irreversibly following the other as water falls from a cliff until it reaches the bottom. Development moves from concept, through design, implementation, testing, installation, troubleshooting and ends up at operation and maintenance allowing easy budgeting and control but not easily capable of revision or modification.

**weak market** Market situation where there are more sellers than buyers and a general decline in prices.

**wealth** The total *value* of *assets* owned by an individual or other economic entity. 'Marketable wealth' is the total of physical and financial *assets* which are relatively liquid. Wealth is a very important variable in economic theory: more important than *income* in determining an individual's economic behaviour but harder to measure in practice; thus *income* statistics predominate in applied economics.

**wedge** A *chart* formation, similar to a symmetrical *triangle*, used in *technical analysis*. The envelope lines converge in the same direction (instead of in opposite directions, as with a symmetrical *triangle*). They either both converge upwards, in the case of 'rising wedges' or both downwards, in the case of 'falling wedges'. Normally the formation takes more than 3 weeks to complete, with *volume* decreasing through the formation. The expected *breakout* direction of a rising wedge is down, and

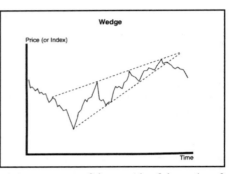

that of a falling wedge is upward. The minimum extent of the outside of the wedge after *breakout* is anticipated to be the vertical height of the wedge.

**weighted average** Also called: weighted *mean*. A statistical measure of the *average* of a set of items, some items being regarded as more important and thus given a larger weight in the calculation. This assignment of weights can be arbitrary, but it is more meaningful to base them on some related quantity. For example, if a person purchases a basket of *commodities* every week consisting of 20 eggs (at 15p per egg), 5 loaves of bread (at 100p per loaf), and 6 pints of milk (at 50p per pint), then the simple *average* price would be $(15p+100p+50p)/3 = 55p$; whereas a weighted *average*, based on the quantities of items bought, would be $[(20 \times 15p)+(5 \times 100p)+(6 \times 50p)]/(20+5+6) = 35.5p$.

$$x_{\text{WA}} = \frac{\sum_{i=1}^{n} w_i x_i}{\sum_{i=1}^{n} w_i}$$

where x is the variable in question, $w_i$ is the weight of item i, and n is the total number of items.

**weighted ballot** A *ballot* for a new issue of *shares* that is oversubscribed where the allocation is biased towards smaller or larger investors and based on the amount of *shares* applied for.

**weighted index** An *index* that is constructed along similar lines to a weighted *mean*. It gives a more realistic picture of the subject being indexed, since it takes into account one or more relevant factors such as the size of the constituents and their importance. The most commonly used factor for weighting is the quantity (number or *value* of *shares*) of the item being weighted. Thus, for example, a quantity-weighted *price index* (of a single item) is:

$$\text{index} = \frac{P_n Q_n}{P_0 Q_0} \times \text{base index value}$$

where P is the price (*share* price) of that item and Q is the quantity, 0 and n referring to the base and current periods respectively. In practice this is applied to a number of items and the *index* takes the sum of these weightings. *Investment* markets often use weighted *indices*, and these are known as weighted *composite indices*. See also: *chain-linked, composite index, rebasing an index*.

**weighting factor** A factor used for calculating arithmetic *indices* (see under: *composite index*). It uses the alternative but equivalent methodology of assigning a weight to each item (based on the proportion of the whole quantity represented by the quantity of the item) and then summing up the weighted relative price *indices* for all the items to arrive at the composite arithmetic *index*.

Using the same notation as in the explanation of *composite index*:

$$\text{index} = \sum_{i=1}^{m} W_i \left( \frac{Pi_n}{Pi_0} \right)$$

where $W_i$ are the weights assigned to the individual items. They are computed as follows:

$$W_i = \frac{Pi_0 Qi_n}{\Sigma_{i=1}^{m} Pi_0 Qi_n} \quad \text{for the Paasche index}$$

$$W_i = \frac{Pi_0 Qi_0}{\Sigma_{i=1}^{m} Pi_0 Qi_0} \quad \text{for the Laspeyres index}$$

$$W_i = \frac{Pi_0 Qi_n}{\Sigma_{i=1}^{m} Pi_0 Qi_0} \quad \text{for the date-weighted index}$$

**Western Samoa** Standard *currency*: *tala*. 1 *tala* = 100 *sene*.

**Westminster doctrine** It is entirely appropriate to take all necessary steps to pay as little *tax* as possible. A doctrine defined by Lord Tomlin in a judgment in 1935 in the case of the *Tax* Commissioners v. the Duke of Westminster when he stated: 'Every man is entitled if he can to order his affairs so that the *tax* attaching under the appropriate Acts is less than it otherwise would be. If he succeeds in ordering them so as to secure this result then, however unappreciative the Commissioners of *Inland Revenue* or his fellow *tax*-payers may be of his ingenuity, he cannot be compelled to pay an increased *tax*.' He was echoing the ruling made in 1929 by Lord Clyde: 'No man in the country is under the smallest obligation, moral or other, so to arrange his legal relations to his business or property as to enable the *Inland Revenue* to put the largest possible shovel in his stores. The *Inland Revenue* is not slow, and quite rightly, to take every advantage which is open to it under the Taxing Statutes for the purposes of depleting the taxpayer's pocket. And the taxpayer is in like manner entitled to be astute to prevent, so far as he honestly can, the depletion of his means by the *Inland Revenue*.' Ayrshire Pullman Motor Services v. *Inland Revenue* [1929].

**white knight** A preferred *takeover bidder* for a *company* who will replace an unwelcome *bidder* (a *black knight*) with improved terms. When a *company* receives a *hostile takeover* approach, it will often look for a white knight who it feels will be a more suitable owner of the business, thus rescuing it from the clutches of the *raider*. See also: *grey knight*.

**whole of life policy** A *life assurance* policy (available with or without *bonuses* or *unit-linked*) with no *maturity date* and where the *premiums* are payable for life or up to a certain age; designed to provide an *assured* benefit on death whenever it occurs. See also: *qualifying policy*.

**wholesale** The sale of goods, usually in quantity, for the purpose of resale to consumers. Wholesale is distinguished from retail, which is the direct sale of goods to the consumer. Thus wholesale banking is providing banking services to other financial institutions, rather than to individuals.

**wholesale banking** 1. Large-scale lending, as between *banks* or among other financial institutions, government agencies, *pension* funds etc. 2. Bank services offered to large corporate businesses at preferential rates.

**wholesale market** The interbank *money market*.

**wholesale money** Funds obtained from the *wholesale market*.

**widows pension** The *pension* to the surviving spouse of the *beneficiary* of a *pension* scheme, typically 50% of the deceased *member's pension*.

**will** When signed and witnessed, a legally binding document (also called: *testament*), that gives instructions on how a person (called the *testator*) wishes his or her *estate* to be divided up upon death. It is desirable that all persons owning any possessions should make a will not only for their peace of mind and the ease of administration on death, but to ensure that maximum advantage is taken of *inheritance tax* concessions and to prevent the difficulties presented by rules for *intestacy*. See: *intestacy*.

**Williams Act** The legislation in *America* covering *takeovers* and specifically *tender offers,* enacted in 1968. Such *offers* now have to be filed with the *Securities and Exchange Commission* and the *target* and outline both the terms and the credentials of the *bidder*. This same information is required when more than 5% of a *company* is acquired.

**windbills** See: *accommodation bill*.

**windfall profits** Extraordinary and unexpected one-off *profits*, (see: *extraordinary item*) or *income*, such as those experienced by oil *companies* in 1973 due to *OPEC* price increases.

**winding up** 1. Term given to a business ceasing to carry on business and going into *liquidation*. See: *members voluntary winding up, winding up order*. 2. The process of terminating a *pension* scheme and distributing its *assets*.

**winding up order** A British court order under the *Insolvency Act 1986* putting a *company* into *liquidation*.

**windmills** See: *accommodation bill*.

**window** The limited time ('window of opportunity') in which a possibility to invest or borrow should be seized; otherwise it will be lost.

**window dressing** An attempt to make a given situation look more favourable. For instance, *accountants* can use certain practices such as inclusion of intangible *assets* whose *value* is impossible to ascertain precisely to make financial statements look better, or *fund managers* may sell losing positions in order to present a *portfolio* to clients in which only successful and acceptable holdings are displayed.

**window warrant** A *warrant* that is not exercisable (ie *convertible* into *stock*) other than during a specific period, that period being called a '*window*'.

**WIP** See: *work in progress*.

**witching hour** See: *triple witching hour*.

**withdrawal** See under: *circular flow of national income*.

**withholding tax**  *Tax* deducted at source from *dividends* or *income* paid to *non-residents*. Individual investors can reclaim or offset this *tax* as long as there is a *dual taxation* agreement between the two countries.

**without prejudice**  Legal disclaimer written on a document aiming to prevent the signatory from being legally or contractually bound by the content of the document.

**without recourse**  In general, a phrase meaning that *credit risk*, or risk of nonpayment, is assumed by the buyer, rather than the seller, of a *promissory note* or the holder of a negotiable *instrument*. In negotiable *instruments* law, the endorser of a check or *draft* cannot be held accountable for payment to subsequent holders in the event the maker or drawer fails to pay, if the *endorsement* contains the words 'without recourse'. No recourse finance in a *secondary market* sale of loans, *certificates of deposit*, etc. is where the seller is under no obligation to reimburse the investor for any losses suffered. Transactions where the buyer can ask for compensation are regarded by *bank* regulators as financings and do not qualify as sales of *assets*; the loans or deposits involved must remain on the seller's *balance sheet*. A no recourse financing agreement in asset-based lending is common in *factoring* whereby the lending institution cannot charge back unpaid invoices caused by the account *debtor's* financial instability.

**with-profits**  See: *with-profits policy*, *with-profits bond*. Contrast: *non-profits*.

**with-profits bond**  A *bond* with additional *value* in the form of *bonus* payments. A unitised *single premium pure endowment assurance* policy issued by a *life assurance company*. Effectively a lump sum *endowment* policy. Contrast: *non-profits*.

**with-profits policy**  A *pension* or *life assurance* policy in which the policyholder has the right to amounts above the *sum assured* or death benefit, resulting from *profits* made on the *investment* of the fund or by the addition of *bonuses* to the *sum assured*. Contrast: *non-profits*.

**won**  Standard *currency* of *North Korea* and *South Korea*. 1 won = 100 *chon*.

**work in progress (WIP)**  Goods in a manufacturing process that have not yet reached their final form or services provided as part of a larger *contract* yet to be concluded. Usually valued at cost (of materials and labour to date, plus some estimate of overhead allocation). Work in progress plus raw materials plus finished *stock* constitute *stock in trade* or, in the *US*, *inventory*.

**working assets**  Another term for: *working capital*.

**working capital**  The *assets* (*capital*) of a *company* that are consumed within the normal operating cycle of business. Equals *current assets* less *current liabilities*. Also called: *net current assets*, *working assets*.

**World Bank**  Common name for the *International Bank for Reconstruction and Development* (*IBRD*) and the *International Development Association* (*IDA*). The International Centre for Settlement of Investment Disputes (ICSID), the *International Finance Corporation* (*IFC*) and the Multilateral Investment Guarantee Agency (MIGA) are all affiliates. Following a conference in *Bretton Woods*, New Hampshire, *USA*, in 1944, the *UK*, the *USA* and *Canada* came to an agreement to restore the world's economy following the war. Accordingly, in 1947 the *IBRD* (the original 'World Bank') and the *IMF* (*International Monetary Fund*) were established. The *IBRD* aimed to provide economic aid to member countries, especially the less-developed nations (known as the Third World). Its main source of funds come from the *capital markets* of Europe, the *US*, *Japan* and the Middle East. In comparison, only about 17% of funds (*authorised capital* US$191 *billion*) available to the World Bank and the *IMF* come from members' contributions. Of these members, the *USA* is the largest shareholder, with about 29% of capital subscriptions, followed by

*Japan* (approximately 13.8%), then *Germany*, the *UK* and *France* (each with about 8%). The loans that the *IBRD* make are not interest-free and it does not lend to governments that it considers incapable of repaying the loans. It lends at rates related to those it has to pay for borrowing on the *capital markets*, and once a loan is made it does not change the terms and *interest rates* (ie does not reschedule the agreement as commercial *banks* are inclined to do). Also, unlike most commercial *banks* the *IBRD* has made a *net profit* every year since 1948. Since then, the World Bank has expanded its activities and functions, adding three more organisations to the original *IBRD*: Firstly, the *IDA* was set up in 1960. It differs from the *IBRD* in that its loans are interest-free and it helps only the poorest countries. It now lends over US$19 *billion* per year. Secondly, the *IFC* was established in 1964. It funds *private sector* ventures. Total *investments* at the end of 2008 were US$21.1 *billion*. It also has an advisory service in many developing countries to aid corporations and *capital markets*. Thirdly, the more recent MIGA was founded in 1988. Its aim is to provide *insurance* in order to encourage foreign *investment* in the developing countries. The World Bank is based at 1818 H Street, NW, Washington DC 20433, *USA*. It is a substantial organisation with around 6,500 staff from over 100 member countries. Its total lending in 1994 was over US$639 *billion*. The World Bank and the *IMF* together support the world's financial and economic structure. In order to become a member of the World Bank countries must first join and conform to the strict standards of the *IMF*.

**World Trade Organisation (WTO)** An international organisation dealing with the global rules of trade between nations. Its main function is to ensure that trade flows as smoothly, predictably and freely as possible. At the heart of the system – known as the multilateral trading system – are the WTO's agreements, negotiated and signed by a large majority of the world's trading nations, and ratified in their parliaments. These agreements are the legal ground-rules for international commerce. Essentially, they are *contracts*, guaranteeing member countries important trade rights. They also bind governments to keep their trade policies within agreed limits to everybody's benefit.

**WPI** See: *Wholesale Price Index*.

**writ of delivery** A *writ of execution* calling for the court officer to seize either goods or their monetary *value* from the defendant and for them to be delivered to the plaintiff.

**writ of execution** Court judgment addressed to a court officer to collect damages from the defendant.

**writ of summons** A High Court order demanding the defendant (the person on whom it is served) to defend, or appear in court to answer, the civil allegations made in the writ by the plaintiff.

**write** 1. To sell (or *underwrite*) a *put* or *call option*. 2. To cover (accept liability) for an *insurance risk*.

**write off** When an *asset* is charged to expense or loss. The effect of a write off is to reduce the *value* of an *asset* (or in some cases to completely eliminate it) and thus reduce the *value* of the *balance sheet*. Causes of write offs are: (i) systematic *depreciation* of a fixed *asset*; (ii) systematic *amortisation* of an intangible *asset* such as *goodwill*; (iii) bad debts, ie debts that are deemed irretrievable. (i) and (ii) are charged to the *profit & loss account*.

**writer** 1. The person who sells (*underwrites*) *put* and *call option contracts* and collects the *premium* as *income*. The writer of a *put option* is obliged to buy and the writer of a *call option* is obliged to sell the relevant *stock* at a set price by a set date to the *option* holder if the *option* is exercised. 2. The term is also applied to an *insurance underwriter*.

**writing naked** A speculative strategy employed by *option* traders involving selling *options* without hedging (see: *hedge*) or owning the *underlying security*.

**written down value** 1. For accounting, the *value* of an *asset* less accumulated *depreciation* (or *amortisation*) *charges*. Also called: *net book value*. 2. For taxation, the *value* of an *asset* after deducting *capital allowances*.

**wrongful trading** A *company* continuing to engage in trading and incurring debts even though there is no reasonable prospect of avoiding *insolvent liquidation*. In this case, one or more *directors* of the *company* can under the Insolvency Act 1986 (which makes wrongful trading a criminal offence) be made personally liable and directed to contribute to the *company*'s *assets*. The case differs from *fraudulent trading* in that there may not have been intent to defraud by the *directors*, but in practice the result is similar. See: *insolvency, limited liability*.

**WST** *currency code* for: Samoan Tala.

**WTO** See: *World Trade Organisation*.

# X

**X inefficiency** A term from *microeconomics* describing the difference between the actual output cost of one unit of production and the minimum attainable cost of one unit of that product. This difference may be the result of *management* shortcomings, inefficient use of resources, bureaucratic rigidities, motivation of employees etc.

**x.a** Short for: *ex all* benefits – a combination of, say, rights, *dividend* and *scrip*.

**x.a.** See: *ex all*.

**x.b.** See: *ex bonus*.

**x.c.** See: *ex capitalisation*.

**x.cap.** See: *x.c., ex capitalisation*.

**x.cp.** See: *ex coupon*.

**x.d (x.dist.)** Short for: *ex distribution* (the most recent *dividend*). See: *ex dividend*.

**x.d.** See: *ex dividend*.

**x.dist.** See: *x.d.*

**x.div.** See: *ex dividend*.

**x.in.** See: *ex interest*.

**x.r** Short for: *ex rights issue*.

**x.w** See: *ex warrants*.

**XAF** *currency code* for: CFA Franc *BEAC*.

**XAG** *currency code* for: Silver ounces.

**XAU** *currency code* for: Gold ounces.

**XCD** *currency code* for: East Caribbean Dollar.

**XDR** *currency code* for: *International Monetary Fund* (*IMF*) *Special Drawing Rights*.

**XETRA DAX** The XETRA trading platform is a fully electronic trading system which aggregates buy and sell orders of licensed traders in a central computer. If the number of *securities* and their price correspond, the orders are automatically matched. 90% of all trading in German exchanges now uses the XETRA platform. XETRA was launched in 1997, and since then floor trading has diminished in importance. All trading on *DAX* now occurs electronically, with the use of computers and the internet.

**XOF** *currency code* for: CFA Franc *BCEAO*.

**XPD** *currency code* for: Palladium ounces.

**XPF** *currency code* for: CFP Franc.

**XPT** *currency code* for: Platinum ounces.

**xu** *Currency* sub-unit of *Vietnam*. 100 xu = 10 *hao* = 1 *dong*.

# Y

**Yankee bond/CD** Dollar-denominated *bonds* issued in the *US* by foreign borrowers or negotiable *dollar certificates of deposit* issued in the *US* by branches and agencies of foreign *banks*. Issued in the *US* when market conditions there are better than the borrower's domestic market (and other alternative markets).

**yard** Slang for a *billion* (one thousand million).

**yearling bond** A *bond* issued by a *UK* local authority which is redeemable (matures) one year after issue.

**Years Purchase** See '*investment* method' under: *valuation* (sense 2).

**Yellow Book** The name given to a book entitled 'Admission of Securities to Listing' issued by the Council of the *London Stock Exchange*, which set out the rules and regulations in relation to admission to the *Official List*, and subsequent obligations of fully quoted (*listed*) companies. Now replaced by the UK Listing Authority rules.

**Yemen** Standard *currency*: *riyal*. 1 *riyal* = 100 *fils*.

**yen** *Japan*'s standard *currency*.

**YER** *currency code* for: Yemeni Rial.

**yield** A general term for the rate of *income* from an *investment* expressed as an annualised percentage and based on its current *capital value*, ie the relationship between *income* generated and the *value* of the principal. Yield is normally quoted as a *gross* annual equivalent. See: *annual percentage rate, compound interest, coupon*. There are a number of different types of yield applied to various types of *investment*. Most are quoted as a *gross* figure (ie without making deductions for charges and *tax*) and some as *net* figures (showing the actual return to the investor before higher rates of *tax*). Where the *investment* fluctuates in *value* exact calculation can be quite complex and often shorter approximate formulas are used.

- Nominal yield – A *fixed interest security* pays *interest* (normally every six months) in the form of a *coupon* as a percentage of its *nominal value* (see: *face value, par value*). This percentage is the nominal of that *security*. It ignores the *market value* of the *security* and any *capital gains* or losses and is thus less useful for comparison purposes. For example 'Treasury 8% 2021' pays £8 p.a. per £100 of nominal *stock* and will pay £9 regardless of its current *value*. The formula is simply:

$$\text{nominal yield (\%)} = \frac{C}{NV} \times 100$$

where C is the *gross money value* of the *coupon* and NV is the *nominal value* of the *security*.

- Running yield – Also called: *current yield, interest* yield, *earnings yield, flat yield*. This is the conventionally calculated yield. It takes into account the current market price of the *security* and assumes the *value* of the *investment* will remain unaltered from its current level. In *gross* terms it is calculated as follows:

$$\text{running yield (\%)} = \frac{C}{MP} \times 100$$

where C is the *coupon* (the nominal annual *interest* payment or the *gross* amount of *money* paid as *income* in one full year) and MP is the current *market value*. Notice that as a *security*'s price (MP) increases its yield decreases, and vice versa. This is the most common form of yield expression and is usually used for comparison purposes. It takes no account of the compounding effects of *income* reinvestment.

- Redemption yield – Also called: *yield to redemption*, maturity yield, *yield to maturity*. This yield takes into account the current market price of the *security*, but also allows for the change in *capital value* for the definite period until redemption, ie the *total return* on the *security* expressed as an annual yield.

The full formula is based on an *internal rate of return* calculation which is complex and lengthy, especially where there is a long period to redemption. The IRR is a common spreadsheet function. A shorthand approximation of (*gross*) redemption which may be helpful is as follows:

$$\text{gross redemption yield (\%)} = \left[ \sqrt[B]{(F \div E)} - 1 \right] \times 100$$

where:

A = annual *coupon* (in *money* terms)

B = number of years to redemption

C = redemption *value* (= *nominal value*)

D = (A + C) / CE = present market price

$D = (A + C) \div C$

$E$ = present market price

$F = D^B \times C$

$F = D**B \times C$

An even simpler estimate of the *gross redemption yield* is applied especially on Japanese markets. The *redemption yield* is calculated as the *running yield* with an adjustment for *capital gains*/losses on redemption:

$$\text{gross redemption yield (Japanese method, in \%)} = \left[ \frac{C}{MP} + \frac{(NV - MP) \div n}{MP} \right] \times 100$$

where C is the annual *coupon* (in *money* terms), MP is the market price, *NV* is the *nominal value* and n is the number of years to redemption.

- Dividend yield – The *gross running yield* is the current declared annual *gross dividend* per *share* (D) against the current *share* price (MP), accordingly:

$$\text{dividend yield (\%)} = \frac{D}{MP} \times 100$$

The financial press usually quotes yields for market *securities* as a *gross* annual equivalent based on the current market price. To obtain the *net* (after *tax*) yield, *tax* needs to be deducted from the *coupon* or *dividend*. Where domestic *deposit* rates are concerned rates are usually quoted gross.

**yield advantage** The additional *income* an investor will receive on purchasing a *convertible security* instead of the ordinary *share* of the same *company* assuming that the *security* can be converted into those same *ordinary shares*. For the calculation to be meaningful, allowance must be made for the conversion costs, reflected in the differential between the conversion price and the current market price.

**yield basis** A method for expressing the *value* of a *security* by means of a *yield* or *rate of return* rather than by price. In markets that deal on this yield basis, the *dealer* states two *yields*: the *bid yield* and the offered *yield*. The *bid yield* means that the *dealer* will quote a price for the *security* which would provide that *yield* for the seller. The offered *yield* indicates the price the *dealer* will sell at, to give that *yield* for the buyer. *Certificates of deposit* are dealt on this basis. See also: *basis price*.

**yield curve** A curve on a graph showing the relationship between the *yield* of *fixed interest securities* against the length of time they have until maturity, for a set of *securities* with similar (or ideally the same) *risk*. This is also called: the term structure of *interest rates*. The *yield* curve normally slopes upwards, to compensate investors for loss of *liquidity* and the effects of *inflation* over longer periods of time. There are, however, other possible yield curve shapes: (i) Ascending (positive, normal) yield curve. Indicates that investors are averse to the uncertainty from the increased price *volatility* and *liquidity* of longer-term issues or the investor expects higher rates in the future. (ii) Descending (negative, inverted) yield curve. Probably points to expectations of a fall in short-term rates in the future. (iii) Horizontal (flat) yield curve. The investor is indifferent to maturity *risk* or *liquidity* concerns. (iv) Humped yield curve. Characterised by a bump or bumps in the yield curve with lower *yields* either side. Usually suggests an over-supply in a maturity area or that investor preference is segmented for other reasons.

## Yield curves

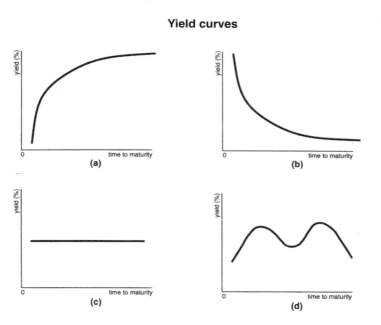

**yield differential** The *spread* between *bid* and offered *yield* in a market where quotes are expressed in terms of *yields*. See: *yield basis*.

**yield equivalence** When taxation applies to one *security* but not to another of similar *quality*, the taxable *security* must have a higher *yield* than the tax-exempt one to give an equal *net rate of return*. If their *yields* are such as to produce an equal *net yield*, they are said to show yield equivalence.

**yield gap** The difference between the *average yield* on *shares* (*dividend yields*) or property rents and the *average yield* on *long-dated gilts* or the *money market*. To compensate for the additional *risk* involved in *equity investment* one might expect *equity yields* to exceed *gilt yields*. However, *inflation* considerations provide incentives for investors to invest in areas that protect their *capital* best against *inflation*, and *shares* (and property) are seen as a better *hedge* than *gilts* and *deposits* as they have historically provided *real capital gains* in addition to *income*, and until recently this has caused *gilt* and *deposit yields* to exceed *equity yields* – the difference between the two being the yield gap. If the requirement for safety was stronger than the need for *real growth*, *gilt* and *deposit yields* might then be lower than *equity yields* and this would be a *reverse yield gap* – the current situation.

**yield spread** See: *yield differential*.

**yield to average life** The *redemption yield* calculated for a *security* when that *security* is redeemed systematically before the *maturity date* in accordance with a certain *amortisation* schedule. Thus the theoretical maturity equals the *average* life of the *security* and this *average* is used in calculating the *redemption yield*.

**yield to call** Yield calculation on a *security* assuming the *security* will be redeemed at its first *call* date at the price specified in the *indenture* agreement. The *redemption yield* is thus calculated using that *call* date as the *maturity date*.

**yield to equivalent life** Calculation of the *yield* for *securities* with an *amortisation* schedule. The future *cash flows* generated by the *security* as stated in the *amortisation* schedule can be used in an *internal rate of return* calculation to give the yield to equivalent life of the *securities*. The figure obtained is usually close to the *yield to average life*.

**yield to maturity (YTM)** See: *yield*.

**yield to redemption** Also called: *redemption yield*. See under: *yield*.

**yo-yo stock** *Stock* that displays high *volatility*, rising and falling quickly in price.

**YTM** See: *yield to maturity*.

**yuan** Unit of Chinese *currency*. 1 yuan = 10 *jiao* = 100 *fen*. See: *renminbi*.

**YUN** *currency code* for: Yugoslav New Dinar.

# Z

**Z bond** The last in a series of *bonds* forming a *collateralised mortgage obligation* (*CMO*).

**Zaire** Standard *currency*: zaire. 1 zaire = 100 makuta. (singular of 'makuta' is: *likuta*).

**zaitech** Used to describe the methods by which some Japanese industrial *companies* generate a substantial proportion of their *profits* from the *stock* and *bond* markets rather than from the goods and services they produce. See also: *Tokkin*.

**Zakat** Islamic term describing religious *tax*. There are two types of Zakat: 1. Zakat al-fitr, which is payable by every Muslim able to pay, at the end of Ramadan (the month of fasting). This is also called zakat al-nafs (poll *tax*). 2. Zakat al maal is an annual levy on the *wealth* of a Muslim (above a certain level). The rate paid differs according to the type of property owned. This *tax* is earmarked, primarily, for the poor and needy.

**Zambia** Standard *currency*: kwacha. 1 *kwacha* = 100 *ngwee*.

**ZAR** *currency code* for: South African Rand.

**zebras** A discounted *zero-coupon bond*. Similar to *cats* and *tigers* but where the accrued *income* is taxed annually rather than at the date of maturity or redemption and all returns are liable to *income tax*. See also: *deep discount bonds, zero-coupon bonds*.

**zero** Shorthand for *zero dividend preference share*.

**zero-based budgeting** A method of setting a *budget* that requires justification of all expenditure, not only that which exceeds the prior year's allocation. Accordingly, all *budget* lines are said to begin at a zero base and are funded according to outright merit rather than according to the level approved for the preceding year.

**zero-coupon bond** A *debt instrument* (*fixed interest security*) issued by governments and large *companies* which does not carry a *coupon* or *dividend*. Accordingly they are offered at a large *discount* on their eventual maturity *value*, thus providing returns by way of *capital appreciation*. For *UK* taxpayers the *growth* is normally taxed as *income* in the year of encashment. Also called: *zero*. See also: *bond, cats, deep discount bonds, tigers, zebras*.

**zero dividend preference share** A class of preference share, usually found in *split capital* investment trusts, which pays no dividend but offers a fixed return at a specified date, provided there are sufficient assets in the trust. Gains on zero dividend preference shares are subject to capital gains tax. Contrast: *deep discount bonds*.

**zero-rated** For the purposes of the *value added tax* system, a zero-rated good or service has a *tax* rate of zero but is included within the *VAT* system and must be accounted for. As opposed to an *exempt* good or service which falls outside the *VAT* system, does not need to be accounted for *VAT* and from which there is no opportunity to offset *input tax*.

**zero-sum game** A situation in which one party's gain is always equal to the other party's loss. The gains and losses in this situation always sum to zero, hence the term. A bet is a zero-sum game where, if the punter makes a *profit*, the bookmaker makes an equivalent loss (ignoring *tax*) and vice versa. This is the same for *derivatives* and *options* where the punter is the investor and the bookmaker is the *writer*, either another punter or an institution. It is, however, quite different in physical markets, where actual *stocks, bonds* or *tangible assets* are traded. If an investor buys a *share* and its *value* rises, this is not matched by a corresponding loss but made up by an increase in the *intrinsic value* of the holding and the worth of the *yield* or *dividend*, which represents *profits* earned by a trading *company – wealth* is actually created in these circumstances. There is no *net wealth* creation in a zero-sum game.

**Zimbabwe** Formerly: Rhodesia. Standard *currency* is the Zimbabwe *dollar*. 1 Zimbabwe *dollar* = 100 *cents*.

**zloty** The standard *currency* of *Poland*. 1 zloty = 100 *groszy*.

**ZMK** *currency code* for: Zambian Kwacha.

**zombies** *US* term for *companies* which continue to operate even though they are insolvent and *bankrupt*.

**Zurich Stock Exchange** See under: *Switzerland*.

**ZWR** *currency code* for: *Zimbabwe* Dollar.

**Notes**

# Notes

# Notes

**Notes**